LEN LYE

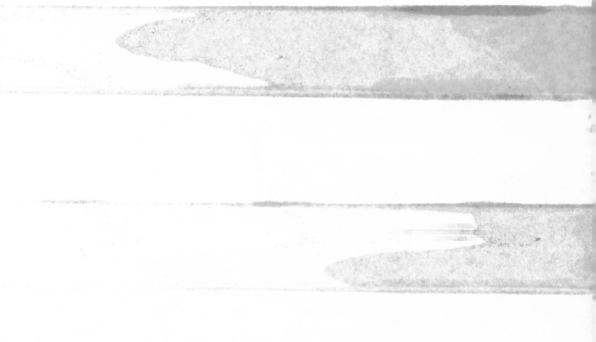

LEN LYE

a biography **Roger Horrocks**

AUCKLAND
UNIVERSITY PRESS

to Shirley
for help & inspiration

First published 2001
Reprinted 2002
Auckland University Press
University of Auckland
Private Bag 92019
Auckland
New Zealand
http://www.auckland.ac.nz/aup

© Roger Horrocks, 2001

ISBN 1 86940 247 2

Publication is assisted by

ARTS COUNCIL OF NEW ZEALAND *TOI AOTEAROA*

Cover design by Sarah Maxey
Front cover photograph: Len Lye in Sydney, c.1925,
photographed by Mary Brown. Courtesy Len Lye Foundation.
Back cover: Strips of direct film from *Colour Cry* (1953).
Courtesy Len Lye Foundation.

Printed by Spectrum Print, Christchurch

contents

part three free radical

(USA, New Zealand)

introduction

Len Lye stood out even within the colourful worlds of art and film for his singularity. In the words of painter Julian Trevelyan, 'He was like a man from Mars who saw everything from a different viewpoint, and it was this that made him original.'[1] Lye's exuberance, his unique taste in clothes, his quirky turn of phrase, and his free-wheeling life style made him a legendary figure among fellow artists and film-makers. These were outward signs of the deep and uncompromising commitment to experiment and risk-taking in the arts that sustained him for more than 60 years as he applied his innovative approach to film, sculpture, painting, photography and writing.

Lye was a member of many important art groups, starting with the Seven and Five Society in London in the 1920s and the international Surrealist movement in the 1930s. In the same decade he was part of John Grierson's GPO Film Unit, and contributed as a writer and artist to notable avant-garde magazines and publishing ventures. Moving to New York he became involved with the Abstract Expressionist painters and the underground film-makers of the 1950s. In the following decade he played an important role in the international upsurge in kinetic art. He was never tempted to slow down and just a few months before his death at the age of 78 he completed a remarkable series of paintings and one of his most radical films.

As the first account to bring together the many facets of Lye's eventful and singular life, this biography suggests that his personality was as remarkable as his art. Ann Lye (his wife) once said, 'Len's greatest creation was himself', and the poet Alastair Reid felt similarly that 'his day to day life was some of his best work', making him 'the least boring person who ever existed'. As I researched the biography I found that the mention of Lye's name almost always produced a warm welcome and a rush of anecdotes about (in the words of sculptor Kenneth Snelson) 'this crazy, excited and exciting guy'.[2] Photographer Barbara Ker-Seymer spoke for many of his friends when she warned me it was an impossible challenge to capture such a personality on paper.

I was also drawn to attempt the biography by the unusual breadth of Lye's journey through twentieth century art. He was one of the rare examples of an experimental artist able to appeal not only to artists and critics but also to a broad public. Today his films are still screened regularly on MTV Europe and at rock concerts. His kinetic sculptures have attracted record crowds in a way that is rare for abstract art, and while viewers may not feel they understand his work they are fascinated and stirred by it. Lye's art has often been surrounded by controversy — from the noisy mixture of cheering and booing that greeted his first direct films to the debates today about the setting-up of his giant sculptures in public places. Such polarised responses have at times helped to make the artist prominent in popular culture as well as high culture.

This biography differs markedly from previous accounts of his life because they have tended to rely on a few sources. Though reticent as a young man, Lye became a lively interview subject in his later years and most critics and curators were happy to use his colourful anecdotes without bothering to seek independent confirmation. It's not that the artist was trying to deceive anyone but that his mind worked in a particular, creative way — he liked dramatic stories, he disliked boring details, he turned memories into myths. His anecdotes conveyed the spirit and mood of his experiences but streamlined the facts. Many artists have indulged in personal myth-making but Lye was an extreme case, particularly in his later years. When asked to date an event or painting he would offer an answer that was as confident as it was unreliable.[3] It is sobering to observe how many essays and catalogues have continued to recycle the same answers as facts.

The present biography is the result of research spread over two decades in search of independent sources and reliable evidence. I should add that the artist gave his own blessing to my project and encouraged frankness (he was never comfortable with an 'overload of lauding').[4] As my research developed I was pleased to find that what I uncovered — the details he had forgotten or transformed — were just as interesting in their own way as his streamlined memories. In the late 1970s and through the 1980s I was fortunate to be able to interview many members of Lye's generation who have since died — including the artist himself, his brother Philip, his first wife Jane and second wife Ann, friends who had grown up with him in New Zealand, and artists and technicians who had worked with him in England. Jack Ellitt, now (in 2000) living in Australia at the age of 97, is one of the few surviving colleagues from those early years.

I would describe the method I have adopted as similar to a documentary film, in particular an 'over the shoulder' approach that sticks as close as possible to its subject. I have often used Lye's own words complemented by interviews with the people who were round him. I have tried to keep my own commentary to a minimum but have not hesitated to add contextual information where it was needed. In seeking the immediacy of an observational documentary I have allowed first-hand accounts to carry much of the narrative. Direct quotations tend to interest me more than paraphrase because of what they reveal about personalities, contexts, and contemporary discourses. Together with the oral history I gathered through interviews, I was fortunate to have at my disposal a rich archive of Lye's own writings in which he put on record the personal flavour and meaning of many of his experiences, often as a case study to illustrate his theories of the 'old brain'. It took me years to find my way round this chaotic collection of fragments and drafts but ultimately it proved a goldmine. My 'new brain' biography (with its independent sorting of facts) provided a structure that could carry the texture of the artist's 'old brain' descriptions.

I was pleased when a reader said the book felt at times more like an autobiography than a biography. Some readers may, however, be disappointed that I have not done more of the work for them by supplying more generalisations and judgements. Certainly I have formed a number of opinions but I am keeping most of that material for a later, more technical book. I decided that writing an accessible biography was the first priority because of the breadth of interest in Lye (not only among specialists) and the fact that discussions of the man and his career have almost always been fragmentary and under-researched. My task was to fill in the gaps (or as many as possible) and to present his personality in a way that was more rounded, more coherent, and more immediate.

To stress a documentary approach is of course not to pretend that the results are purely objective. Any account that has had to be assembled from thousands of small pieces of information necessarily involves numerous acts of interpretation. While pointing towards my own conclusions, I have nevertheless tried to maintain a certain openness by providing readers with enough data to allow them to make their own judgements. Such an openness seemed to me appropriate for a book premised on the belief that our traditional ways of thinking about modern art have not done justice to the complexity of the field nor been fully able to accommodate a maverick such as Lye.

Part One of the biography covers the artist's early development in New Zealand, Australia, and Samoa. Part Two looks at the blossoming of his art in England, where he made a number of important films and paintings. Part Three (which is chronologically the longest) surveys his career in the United States where he made kinetic sculptures as well as films, before re-establishing his links with New Zealand in the final years of his life. Lye's critics have tended to work within traditional frames of reference by focusing on one medium or one country at a time, thus providing us (for example) with a New Zealand Lye, a British Lye, and an American Lye. While that approach has yielded valuable insights, it is only by tracking all the phases that it becomes possible to understand the lifetime coherence of his interests and to appreciate his disregard for boundaries.

The account of Lye's early years holds a special resonance for me — and perhaps also for other New Zealanders — in documenting the emergence of one of the country's first modern artists. I hope overseas readers will also find it interesting as the story of someone from the working class in a small, colonial country who, in the course of educating himself, becomes so passionately involved with modernism that he ends up a member of the international avant-garde. I would also suggest that a knowledge of his New Zealand origins is necessary to an understanding of the sources of his art and some aspects of his personality. Not that this was a simple matter of nationalism, for Lye created his art as much in rebellion against his environment as in sympathy with it.

My search for visual evidence turned up a profusion of photographs, enabling his daily life to be observed through the eyes of friends, lovers, and fellow artists. It also seemed important to present a broad range of his art, in so far as an art of motion can be illustrated on the page. Strips of film, blurred shots of sculpture in motion, and sequential photographs can be more informative than static images.

Bringing together the many sides of Lye's career has left me in no doubt that — in addition to providing us with new insights into the history of modernism — he is still an important artist for today. He developed a distinctive physical or kinaesthetic way of understanding movement that is yet to be fully grasped by critics or fully exploited by artists. He also arrived at an original conception of the unconscious mind, its links with the body and with the process of making art. It has at last become technically possible to realise some of the plans he left behind for giant kinetic sculptures. His films continue to delight audiences and influence animators, and in a medium too often ruled by commercialism and conservatism he provides an alternative role model — that of the passionate artist and innovator. To quote a comment made in 1997 by another risk-taking director, Peter Greenaway: 'Len Lye was a perfect example of trying very, very deliberately to put the perfect characteristics of the projective image into new places. [We need] a brand new cinema which will fit the imaginations of the next century.'[5]

part one sense games

one the flash

Len Lye's first clear memories belonged to the weeks that followed his third birthday. His father Harry was sick and the family had come to stay at West Eyreton with Aunt Emma and Uncle Charles. At night the boy was jolted awake by the sound of his father coughing and the other adults bustling about, their voices urgent. When he got up to see what was happening they shooed him out of the room, but he knew some terrible change was coming over his father who lay in bed sweating and gaunt. During the day he would hear the adults lower their voices when they thought he was listening. His mother Rose would give him a cuddle, together with his baby brother, but she was evasive when he asked her why she was crying.

One day being kept from seeing his father he flew into a tantrum, shouting and kicking, giving himself over completely to his rage. The adults were horrified — the house must be kept quiet, Harry had to rest — and so his uncle bustled the boy out through the back door into the yard. It was a winter afternoon but the sun burned brightly. Left to seethe in the asphalt area under the clothes line, the boy spotted a kerosene can, large and inviting. He ran over and with every ounce of power in his wiry legs began kicking it. The effect was vastly more dramatic than he had imagined: 'I kicked that can around to make the most god-awful racket my lungs and kicks on the can could. I can still feel the impact of my kicks on that can and hear an echo of tinny clashes. But what is most clear is a great flash of quivering sunlight that came from the can. I stood stock still. I don't know what I did next. I think I went over and sat on a log and looked at the can. We're all stopped short by wonder some time, and that's when it first stopped me in my tracks.'[1]

The 'great flash' was soon followed by another mystery as the adults brought him news that his father had died. 'I couldn't figure out where he had gone. How could someone living and moving simply vanish?'[2] Destitute, Rose and her children now faced their own struggle to survive. But in later years Len Lye could never think back to the shock of his father's death without also remembering the excitement of the flash — as though the three-year-old had touched an electric current, had discovered he could summon up his own thunder and lightning. Eventually he would make a career out of shaping this energy, producing highly original films and mechanised steel sculptures that combined powerful effects of light and sound. Today, the flash and reverberation of his most dramatic kinetic sculptures, both outdoors and in galleries, continue to make a terrifying impression on the children who experience them.

His earliest memories came from 1904, a year when a few modernists in Europe were laying the foundations for the kind of art to which he would later devote his life. Eventually he would join those artists and exhibit his work alongside theirs. But in 1904 such developments were associated with the underground cultures of the largest cities of Europe, whereas Lye was born in New Zealand, a country so small and remote that it would be hard to imagine a less propitious starting-point at that time for an avant-garde artist. This tension between living in the South Pacific and tuning in to radical ideas from distant centres of art would help him to develop his own unique version of modernism.

New Zealand was in European terms a young country and a raw colony. If the country was known at all overseas it was not for its culture but for its nature, for its landscapes. It was fitting that Lye's flash — which he later interpreted as his first experience of art — should have happened outdoors in bright sunlight. Not that New Zealand had escaped civilisation — indeed, it prided itself on its close links with Britain, though this meant in practice that much of its culture had a hand-me-down awkwardness, being a little old-fashioned and not always a good fit for the new environment. To grow up in this culture was to feel as though one saw the world from the margins, from a cheap seat at the back — yet this outsider perspective also provided the potential (which our artist would one day use to the full) to see the world differently, lit by flashes of new meaning.

But not all of New Zealand's cultural life was European and off-centre, for the indigenous inhabitants, the Maori, had been living here for a thousand years. They were the tangata whenua, the people of the land, with their own language and traditions of art. At the beginning of the century their population had shrunk to 43,000 and the white settlers who had come to occupy most of their land believed mistakenly that the race was dying out and that their culture would only survive as a tourist attraction. Maori culture would become profoundly important for Lye as he struggled to extricate himself from Victorian ways of thinking. In Europe since the early 1900s the modernists had turned in their search for new directions to the study of African art. Lye's involvement with Polynesian cultures would come from a similar impulse though the results would be different.

These were a few of the contexts into which Leonard Charles Huia Lye was born on 5 July 1901. 'Huia' was a Maori name, an unusual choice in those days for a child who was Pakeha (or non-Maori). Rose, his Irish mother, said she had taken the name from a warrior chief who had 'given the colonising English army one hell of a rotten tactical time'.[3] Later Lye would speculate that his own rebel streak was inherited from his mother, who was 'not so much anti-English as fiercely pro-Irish'[4] — indeed, 'more sentimental about the old sod than many a shamrock fancier living on it'.[5] Lye felt green coursing through his veins and grew up on 'gory tales of derring-do in Ireland'.[6] Rose's parents had both emigrated to New Zealand from Ireland — Elizabeth Martin from Cork and John Cole (a baker) from Dublin — before meeting and marrying in Wellington. Rose's future husband Harry had also been born in New Zealand but he had grown up in a very different world because his family was English and Anglican, not Irish and Catholic. His father Arthur, a tailor and bootmaker, and his mother Amelia had emigrated to New Zealand from Surrey, England, in 1859. British immigrants, Protestant and Catholic, had brought their old conflicts to the new colony.[7] Protestants feared that the Catholic Church in New Zealand was conspiring to seize political power. And Catholic priests warned Rose that her proposed marriage to a boy from a Protestant family would not be recognised by the Church as legitimate.

Lye thought of his parents as a union of opposites — Rose was romantic and superstitious while Harry represented the more practical 'English side'. She was a warm-hearted, good-looking woman with a fine singing voice. He was tall and slim and a good talker with an appetite for argument. Prematurely bald, he worked as a hairdresser. The tobacco and barber shop at 196 Colombo Street, Christchurch, which he shared with Joseph Eslick, became 'a theological and political hot-bed of conversation' as Harry 'culled the locks of priests and vicars and draymen'.[8] Though the romance between Harry and Rose was vigorously opposed by both their churches, the determined couple got married on 19 July 1900 at Lyttelton. For years the priests continued (in her son's phrase) 'to give Rose hell'. Although she never lost her Catholic faith, her tribulations would fuel her son's hatred of orthodoxy.

Rose and Harry set up home at 272 Manchester Street in Christchurch. In the distance were pasture lands bounded by the snow-capped Southern Alps. With a total population of around 60,000, Christchurch was the second largest city in New Zealand.[9] It was as English as it could be, with its own river Avon, its Church of England cathedral, and its cricket fields. The main public event in 1901, the year of Lye's birth, was the death of Queen Victoria.[10] The continuity of the royal line was emphasised a few months later by the visit to New Zealand of the Duke and Duchess of Cornwall and York (the future King George V and Queen Mary), who came to acknowledge the settlers' success in conquering the wilderness and creating a prosperous agricultural outpost of the British Empire. In 1903 the Lyes had a second son, Philip John,[11] but by then Harry was suffering from an advanced case of tuberculosis of the lungs. The disease was widespread in New Zealand and there were no drugs to treat it. The best hope of recovery was to seek rest, fresh air, and good food, but tuberculosis thrived on poverty since hard-pressed families such as the Lyes could not afford such treatment. By 1904 Harry was unable to work and he and Rose could no longer afford to rent their house. They were rescued by Harry's sister Emma and her husband Charles Bourke, the headmaster of a school at West Eyreton, about 20 kilometres from the city. Emma looked after Harry and the children while Rose searched for paid work. It was this period that left their son with his two mysteriously linked memories, the flash of sunlight and his father's death. Years later Lye spoke cryptically of the sun as a 'symbol for energy, for patriarch, for light, for life over death, at the time a three-year-old's father lay haemorrhaging to death'.[12] He speculated about whether his later impulse to become an artist was his way of filling in 'the vacuum of who the hell was my father'.[13] Eventually he even came to see growing up without a father as having a positive aspect because it left him to establish his roots 'in nature rather than in a patriarch'.[14] But at the time it happened, Harry's death was a disaster for the whole family. His wife had immediately to find a job because the state gave no financial assistance to widows. The only jobs available to her were housekeeping and cleaning, and most employers did not want small children around. Forced to board out her sons, Rose placed them as often as she could with relatives. She lost touch with her husband's family, but over the next few years she sent her children to stay with three of her own sisters and one of her brothers. The boys hated being separated but sometimes had to be boarded with different families. Rose retrieved her sons whenever she could and their reunions were times of great happiness. The boys had few possessions and their childhood was full of upheavals but they never had any doubt that their mother loved them — it was the one continuity they had in a confused flux of houses, families, and guardians.

Rose Lye was a resilient woman and a devoted mother. As a so-called 'char-lady' she worked long hours, was poorly paid, and was treated with condescension. In those days society made few efforts to understand or to ease the role of the solo mother. Her younger son later said of her: 'Rose was a marvellous person. People's attitudes were very narrow and Victorian but she was broad-minded, and probably a lot of that was due to her own experience, having to battle for herself and her two kids.'[15] She set firm ground rules for her children, but her older son would later describe her affectionately as his 'self-raising flower' who had given him the best kind of unselfish love. She understood and valued the fact that he was as strong-minded and argumentative as his father had been, and he was always profoundly grateful for that tolerance: 'She let me come to my own divinings of what was what, even though she then had to accept my wildest conclusions.'[16]

two cape campbell

Four years after their father's death, when Len was 6 and Philip 3, their mother brought them to Aro Street in Wellington and introduced them to Frederick Ford Powell, a tall, good-looking man with blue eyes and jet-black hair. She and Powell were living together and they planned to marry. A year younger than Rose Lye, Powell seemed to be a man of few words but many thoughts. Some acquaintances were impressed by his scholarly seriousness, others found him moody or strange. His father, also named Frederick Ford Powell, had emigrated from England to become a house decorator in Christchurch. It was rumoured the Powell family was relieved that this eccentric young man was getting married.

Powell was generally friendly to the boys, entertaining them by playing 'Pop Goes the Weasel' and other favourites on his violin. Rose Lye with her fine voice would join in. The boys were also impressed by Powell's efforts as an inventor, which included a plan to make the family's fortune out of soot. He had a secret formula for turning soot into black bootpolish. He collected barrels of soot from the chimney sweep, mixed it up with some waxy substance and put it in little brass tins. There were stacks of tins all over the house. The boys were let in on the secret and kept busy collecting soot in shoe-boxes.[1]

Living in cramped conditions in the city and forced to realise that his inventions were not going to support a family, Powell signed up for a three-year term as assistant keeper of the Cape Campbell lighthouse. Cape Campbell, on the north-east tip of the South Island, was very isolated and the starting salary was modest, but the job seemed well suited to a person with practical interests who was certainly no extrovert. Keepers and their families made themselves self-supporting by looking after small farms and vegetable gardens. It was usual for a keeper to be married, and so Rose Lye and Ford Powell went back to Lyttelton for a wedding on 15 June 1908. Then, with the two boys, they took a boat to Cape Campbell.

At the lighthouse Len and Philip 'slept under a roof of very good tin for rain. It sloped to the waves that pounded on the flat rocky beach. . . . The sea and wind sounds were always good at night.'[2] Cook Strait was known for its wild seas and there were sudden storms even during the summer. In January 1909 when the brig *Rio Loge* sank with her crew of twelve, the boys found wreckage washed up on the beach. A month later they heard the adults discussing the HMS *Penguin* which had struck a rock in Cook Strait and gone down with the loss of 75 lives. Cape Campbell had unpredictable tides, and the children were warned of the dangers of being swept out to sea by high waves. From the top of the hill the 73-foot-high lighthouse sent its beam out into the night every minute or so like a giant movie projector. The flashing effect which distinguished lighthouses from other shore lights was created by a revolving clockwork mechanism that had to be rewound once every hour and a half. This white iron tower which rose 100 feet above the other buildings was secured to a 20-foot concrete base by iron bolts 8 feet long. It cast its shadow over the house, dominating the landscape and the lives of its inhabitants. To the 7-year-old boy, this huge kinetic contraption with its oil-burning incandescent lamp magnified by the glass lens of the dome was another magnificent 'flash', and he would lie in bed fascinated by the complex reflections of light on the window.

Powell was assistant to William Elijah Tutt, a keeper who had worked at many lighthouses. One keeper took over from the other at midnight. There was a surprising amount of work to do — winding the clockwork, making weather reports, cleaning the glass, repainting the lighthouse, farming, and gardening. Tutt lived with his wife and seven children who ranged in age from 6 to 22. The youngest, Jessie, became a close friend of Len Lye's. One of their many adventures was exploring under the house and discovering a collection of old glass negatives of the lighthouse. Lye was energetic and inquisitive and often in trouble. He and the Tutt children engaged in great friendly battles using 'nice speckled pullet-size eggs gathered for ammunition down on the flat gravel where millions of sea birds laid their eggs'.[3] Further afield the children were horrified to discover pits containing human bones and skulls. Their parents told them that Maori war parties from the North Island used to land at Cape Campbell and on their way back to the canoes these raiders would stop to kill and eat some of the prisoners they had taken. The adults did not think of such a place as tapu and casually allowed the children to collect skulls as curiosities.

The boys did not receive a great deal of schooling. An inexperienced teacher visited for three months of the year, and occasionally 16-year-old Albert Tutt gave them a lesson, but even with their other chores they still had plenty of time to roam the countryside. Lye, a wiry, independent boy who was always sneaking off outdoors, felt secure and happy in this 'marine Garden of Eden'. Its sights, sounds, and smells were intense for a city child — bare feet on dewy grass, 'the frost-crunchy-grass-blade feeling', the smell of home-baked bread, the motion of horse-riding, the touch of a cow's udder, the smells of seaweed and rock pools, the sea and wind sounds at night. The sea was a constant presence. As he later expressed the feeling: 'A wave's motion seeps into my shoulder blades and it is as if I am turning a large water wheel, turning, turning.'[4]

A later keeper's child who lived at Cape Campbell was struck by its wildness and its special air of privacy from the outside world: 'Thinking back, I can only account for this by the windswept, arid appearance of parts of the foreshore — the small pieces of sun-dried seaweed clinging to the rusty wire fence between sea and house, where they had been cast by the wind — the salt which had to be removed from the clothes-lines on washing day and the close proximity of the sea. But whatever the reason we seemed to enjoy a wild, intoxicating freedom here, not quite equalled at other places.'[5] Lye loved to go exploring on his own. The lighthouse was situated on a promontory, one side of which had a large platform of rock full of knee-deep pools when the tide went out. He spent hours peering at 'sea slugs and various prickly affairs'. He learned how to catch flounder hiding at the bottom of the pools. The wavy movements of fins stirred up just enough sand to be detected by a sharp eye, so 'you'd creep up and stand on one and put a barbed spear between your toes, and that was supper'.[6] The beach on the foreshore was a gallery of unusual shells and pieces of driftwood. On the other coast the terrain became rugged about half a mile past the lighthouse. On one expedition Lye sighted an octopus — there were a lot of tentacles oozing up from the sea as it flushed up and down in the deepest crack. After a long contest he finally got the octopus 'between rocks in the shallows and jabbed and poked and prised . . . and in an utter frenzy killed him. . . . Judging by the mess he had a lot of ink. I don't think I told anyone about it, not even my younger brother. I felt quite good about it but a little strange. Octopuses are marvellous things but they look no good to a kid. It was my first moment of utter madness.'[7]

On another occasion: 'I was netting gangs of little fish for frying. The day was crisp and the water, sky and seaweed so clean that I must have felt the prickly call of the sun because I stopped fishing. I downed both net and catch and gazed straight at the sun. I must have been crazed because I looked so long and hard at the sun it turned to a black ball in the sky and I went home empty-handed with a ball of fire in my head.'[8] There was another moment of madness at the end of a day of catching rabbits in a hill near the sea. 'You guessed which holes to block with dirt and stones and which holes to dig out with a sharp stick. I caught some baby rabbits and took one for me and one for my brother. It was late and I went back by the beach. The sun was going down and huge walls of waves kept coming in from a storm. They got twisted up on the steep beach into slopes of muddled water. Streams of spray swept back off the tops of the waves and the sun made a red tunnel through the spray. I stopped to look at the big half-circle of the sinking sun. I felt the spray on my teeth and felt how the waves moved while I stood still. The red sun made a path right to the beach. I took one rabbit out of my shirt by the ears and threw it high over the waves into the sun.'

The 7-year-old boy could not understand his impulse except as a kind of 'sacrifice to the sun'.[9] He was running wild in this landscape with which he felt a strange kinship. 'If I'd known about cave painting, and had found a great cave, I'd no doubt have painted fish and rabbits on the cave wall.'[10] But Cape Campbell would not have meant so much to him if Powell had not acted as his guide. A keeper had to be a jack of all trades, and Powell explained many skills to Lye as he worked, displaying a special rapport with natural things. In Lye's words: 'One day he was showing me how to clean fish at the sink and I was up close as he opened the fish bellies with a knife. He showed me how fish had insides like mine, with hearts and livers and they use air too. The sun came through onto their silvery insides and for a moment I knew what it felt like to live in the sea. To get that feeling properly inside your guts it has to be part of a revelation, and he knew how to do it.'[11]

Initially Powell was popular with all the children at the lighthouse and he would go to the beach with them and join in their games. He gave violin lessons to Albert Tutt. But there were days when he would fall strangely silent. The Tutt family assumed the cause of the problem was Rose who seemed to be having difficulty adjusting to the isolation and the rural life style. They were scandalised one day when she left for Wellington without warning, taking advantage of a visit by the lighthouse service steamer *Hinemoa*. In Albert Tutt's words, 'Rose waited until unloading of supplies was nearly completed and then, ready dressed for the journey, she ignored her husband and walked over to find out about a passage to Wellington'.[12] After she returned the Tutts began to feel more sympathetic towards her because they could see Powell was a difficult man to live with, a man of strange moods. One day the keepers were taking turns being hauled up by block and tackle to repaint the top of the lighthouse. When William Tutt asked to be brought down, Powell began for no apparent reason to rock the hoist. When the shaken keeper was eventually lowered, his language was terrible and he told the audience of open-mouthed children to disappear while he sorted things out with Powell.[13] After this the Tutt children were afraid to accompany Powell on any of his trips to Blenheim for supplies.

One night the Lye boys were startled from sleep by the screams of their mother who had woken to find her husband's hands around her throat. Now Rose came often to talk to Mrs Tutt or her oldest daughter Agnes. The children noticed she had black eyes. Meanwhile, though Powell continued his normal work, his need to take days off was putting a strain on the head keeper. Powell seemed happiest when playing music. On top of the lighthouse was a balcony with a railing and at night if the wind was not too strong, he would walk round and round the balcony playing his violin.

Eventually William Tutt summoned a doctor and a police constable who could sign papers for his assistant to be committed to a mental hospital. The first day these visitors were at the lighthouse Powell acted normally. Then during a meal he lost control, talking more and more wildly. The head keeper removed the carving knife surreptitiously from the table and hid it. Afterwards Powell was taken away to a hospital in Blenheim. When two members of the Tutt family paid him a visit some weeks later they were told he had gone 'completely'. For the Lye boys, Powell's disappearance was as complete and mysterious as the death of their father. The adults seemed to find the subject of mental illness too difficult to talk about, though the older Tutt children did their best to explain to the boys what had happened. A boat came to take them back to Wellington where Rose went back to work as a cleaner, eventually reverting to the surname of her previous husband, and the boys had to be boarded out once more. They never saw Powell again, but they were later told that with the help of his family he had been sent to a good hospital in Australia.[14]

three the first sketchbook

Lye was sent to Masterton with his brother to board with 'Aunt Aggie' (Agnes McEwan), her husband Alfred James, and their three sons. The most exciting thing that happened during his stay in the McEwan household was learning to draw. At first he had felt miserable and confused about leaving Cape Campbell, and though his aunt did her best to make the boys feel at home they missed their mother who was miles away in another town sorting things out. Stuck indoors one afternoon, Lye began leafing through magazines which contained pictures of 'cowboys and goddesses' from the new medium of the movies. He liked the look of these drawings so much he found a pencil and began to copy them. He began with a cowboy, one of his favourite characters. When he was taken to a western film — a rare treat in those days — he would study the way the heroes moved so he could imitate them: 'I walked with a waddle, as if I'd just got down from a duck!'[1] Now he discovered that if he worked carefully he could create a spitting image of a black-and-white poster-style cowboy. Although his picture was merely the copy of a copy, the process gave him an uncanny sense of closeness to the world he was representing.

He drew all the cowboys then turned his attention to their co-stars, 'the queens of loveliness'. Sketching faces was a way of discovering what he liked about them and it also demonstrated what could be achieved by going to a lot of trouble: 'You looked at a finished drawing and saw the magic of your best powers of self staring at you.' Lye had made pictures before but the pleasure he felt during his portrait binge was new and addictive. 'In no time at all you're an art novice, a dedicated sprout on the tree of art. You could think about it first thing in the morning and last thing at night. You could think about it at any time during the day, whenever you saw something.'[2] His new passion helped to compensate for the lost paradise of the lighthouse.[3]

Meanwhile the adults encouraged his new hobby because it kept him quiet. It was characteristic of Lye that once he liked something he was happy to devote an unlimited amount of time to it. After wearing down many pencils copying 'notable heads galore', he was allowed to graduate to pen and ink which got him closer to the look of the original. He saved up to buy his first sketch book and quill pen: 'There was Higgins Indian ink in a magic bottle with a quill-end-cork, a long nipple as a handle, and a sharpened goose quill that dipped down into the blackness of distilled lava — or was it octopus ink?'[4] He worked slowly, taking care not to smudge his work. He came to love the feeling of a quill, pen, or brush in his hand and found drawing a pleasure in itself regardless of the subject. As he later described sketching with a pad on his knee: 'I can feel its vibrations transmitted to my thigh bone. The nib makes a pleasant rubbing sound.'[5]

Soon he tired of cowboys and began to 'branch out to drawings of boats and trees and horses and whatever looks like you'll get a kick out of copying'.[6] Months later when his mother paid a visit he surprised her with his sketchbook full of pictures. She took her time turning the pages then said, 'Len, it looks as if you're going to be an artist.' This gave him a deep pleasure, reinforced when she told him that his father had also been a painter, albeit an occasional one. Examples of his oil painting included a cigar box lid decorated with flowers, a large white swan on a suede cushion, and most impressive of all, a sizeable seascape named 'Land's End'.[7]

After two years with the McEwans the boys were sent to board with the Rooney family in Nelson Street, Wellington. Michael Rooney worked as an engineer on a ferry boat. The Rooneys were welcoming but once again Lye had to adapt to a large new family. Not that he had trouble sticking up for himself. Despite his slight build he was daring, energetic, precocious, and quick-witted in bantering with the other children, sneaking apples from the greengrocer, or mixing it with boys who made fun of his name. Electric trams had recently replaced horse-drawn trams and it was one of Lye's games to jump on and off them for free rides. Another risky game he played with his brother was climbing tall pine trees that were planted close together, then trying to cross from one tree to another as they swayed in the wind.

The Rooney household had a very definite routine and it was inevitable that Lye would somehow fall foul of it. It was a family tradition for their eight children to kneel together in prayer before going to bed. The Rooneys were not ostentatiously devout — they regarded their prayer session as a normal Catholic practice — and they were baffled by Lye's absolute refusal to take part. It was not easy for him to explain his stand since it was a reaction to many things that had happened in his life, including the opposition of the Church to his parents' marriage.[8] The Rooneys could not force Lye to pray but they did require him to go to bed early. He had difficulty getting to sleep and he was not allowed to take his sketchbook to bed, so to pass the time he created his own memory game which consisted of trying to remember all the events of the day.

Bedtime began with foot-washing since Lye, like many children of the period, seldom wore shoes even to school. Once in bed he would wriggle his clean toes to feel the sheets and then proceed to re-live the day: 'I would start from which side I woke up; whether I first looked out the window at the weather or guessed it with closed eyes from the feel of the light and the feel of the air in the plain room; how I had laid the fire that morning and how it had caught; the soap in the kitchen when I washed after fixing the fire; how the porridge tasted — thick, thin, lumpy or burnt, for it always tasted different; whether I had spread sugar all over it or had dumped it in the middle to make a gradually smaller and sweeter island.'[9] And so on, through the day, until he got back to squiggling his toes in bed. If he was not asleep by the time he arrived at the end of his review he would go back to the incidents that pleased him most — 'climbing, and smiles, and any good shots with stones, and watching seagulls flying'.[10]

He felt no need to share his sense game with others — he was used to having his own intense thoughts and keeping his own counsel. Gradually his nightly sortings became more specialised. For example, he would concentrate on a single one of the senses. On a colour day: 'I'd remember the first thing about colour that had struck me when I woke up, a gilt picture frame, the floor, or shaded wall, the light at the window, the sky, the tones of the clouds, the steely colour of the street, the texture and colour of any peeling paint I had seen, horses, clothes, and so on, and which colours I liked best.'[11] There were sound days, taste days, smell days, weight days, distance days, and other variations. Sometimes he would select a sense as soon as he woke up: 'The very first image your senses pick up, such as hearing something or seeing the colour of something or feeling your bare feet on the linoleum floor — whatever it may be, then that is the day it is. For instance, if you've just heard someone clanking a nice bit of metal outside your windows, then it's a sound day'.[12] Replacing prayers by his sense game helped Lye to develop his memory and to discover the kinds of sensation he liked best: 'Now I was getting to know my own mind.'[13]

From the age of 10 he worked as a newsboy. In Wellington he delivered morning papers, then with his brother he would sell evening papers near the railway station. 'If someone on a tram whistled, one of us would tear like mad, leap on, sell him a paper for a penny and leap off again. We had to gear our leap to the speed of the tram. Soon as we hit the ground we ran to keep pace, so we wouldn't fall on our face.'[14] The morning deliveries were an equally physical business, pushing a bike loaded with newspapers up the steep streets of Wellington.[15] Lye and his friends built their boneshaker bicycles from old parts found in city dumps.[16] Eventually he was put in charge of a large team.[17] Besides

making him wiry and a good diviner of weather, these newspaper jobs helped to
stretch a tight family budget.

Between 1913 and 1917 the boys lived with their mother at 157 Aro Street,
except for several periods when she was hospitalised (once for a cancer operation).
The three were delighted to be able to live together again. When Rose did cleaning jobs in office buildings at night the boys sometimes went along to help her.
On other occasions they would sit up waiting. Philip would never forget the feel
of the old wickerwork chair in the lounge in which he used to curl up, sometimes
waking to find she had already come home and carried him off to bed. Sundays
were luxurious for the boys because they had no newspapers to deliver. 'Every
Saturday night when we were asleep my mother put something on our bedside
tables (which were painted fruit-cases). Every Sunday the table was the first thing
we'd look at. On it would be a small brown paper bag with twisted corners full of
boiled sweets, or the latest copy of *Comic Cuts*, a kids' weekly.'[18]

Although the boys revelled in the luxury of being back with their mother, it
was a difficult time for Rose. She was expert at getting 'three dinners for three of
us out of a sixpenny shin of beef. She'd make soup, and we'd have a meat meal as
well.'[19] As lean as their childhood was, the boys did not feel underprivileged since
the standard of living of the average family was meagre by today's standards. It
was normal for the boys and their friends to feel always more or less hungry and
to be tempted now and then to steal something from the shops.[20] A busy life did
not prevent Rose from having relationships with men, although as a Catholic she
felt guilty about them. As Philip later recalled, 'There were several nice blokes
including a sea captain called Hannah who smoked a Maori carved pipe. He
astonished us with tales of how he'd been round the world many times.'[21]

Out of respect for his mother Lye still attended church but often his brother
noticed that 'while he was holding up a prayer book and looking very religious,
he had paper inside it and he was drawing the people round him'.[22] His mother
felt duty-bound to see that her children received a Catholic upbringing and when
Lye finally told her he no longer believed in God it troubled her very deeply. She
persuaded her son to have a lengthy session with the parish priest. In Lye's words:
'The priest had some good arguments but when he likened the moon and night
and day to a watch, and told me that someone had to wind it up, that was enough.
I felt I knew as much about the moon and the winds and the tides as he did. My
feeling of inner conviction became so strong that my brain lit up for a moment.
He left. My mother came in and looked at me. I said, "It's no use, Mum".'[23]

For Lye, standing up to the priest was the first time he 'really knew what
thinking felt like'. While he was in most respects a typical boy of his age, more

interested in sport than books, he displayed an unusual intensity of mind. He would take nothing for granted and having worked an issue out for himself he would be very difficult to budge. His mother would sigh and accept the inevitable: 'She saw that here was a little lamb that wouldn't follow everywhere the Virgin Mary went.'[24] Lye agreed to attend Easter Mass but otherwise ceased going to church. The priests continued to pressure Rose, who sent her younger son to a Marist Brothers school where (as Philip saw it) 'Religion was mostly fear of the hereafter, damnation and burning in hell'. He became frightened that his brother would be struck dead for skipping church, but then after time passed he thought, 'Nothing has happened to Len', so he started to skip church himself. When a priest found them one Sunday morning on the waterfront and began lecturing them, Philip was proud of his brother's confident reply: 'Aw, that's the stuff you tell kids!'[25]

Lye was at Mitchelltown School during 1912 and 1913, then moved to Te Aro School in 1914. To start with he had to 'intuit exams' because he had received little schooling while shifting from place to place.[26] He was quick at picking things up but never very studious since he was more drawn to sport — rugby, hockey, swimming, tennis, and shooting. Lye was slight in build but very fast as a rugby 'runner and zig-zagger'. He became the school's unofficial boxing champion when he felled the school bully in the Mitchelltown playground, but the macho glamour of this title soon faded because he was expected to keep defending it. He would often arrive home with his face raw, and Rose would blow her top and hurry him off to the handbasin.[27] For this athletic student with a flair for sport, the only academic subject that mattered was art and he was forever attempting to talk or trick his teachers into letting him spend more classroom time on it. As Lye's school friend Joe Davis later recalled, the art teacher recognised that this was a student with exceptional talent.[28]

The First World War began in 1914, and to support the British war effort, 100,000 men — a huge part of New Zealand's total population of 1.2 million people — volunteered or were conscripted. The casualty rate was appalling — 16,700 New Zealanders were eventually killed and more than 40,000 came back wounded. Lye was too young to be conscripted but he was shocked to learn that some of the older students at his school had volunteered. When he and his brother were boarded out with a Norwegian family named Heidenstrom in Mitchelltown, a suburb with 'a remarkable mixture of races but like the Wild West at times',[29] they saw men come to blows over New Zealand's support for Britain. On one occasion they had to run for cover when an argument between members of the Heidenstrom family escalated into a knife fight. Then Rose's youngest brother Pat — one of the boys' favourite uncles — returned to New Zealand seriously wounded by splinters from a bomb. Rose offered to look after him and he came to stay permanently.

At the end of 1914 Lye left school, graduating with a Standard Six Certificate of Proficiency. Despite his relaxed attitude to study, this was a grade higher than the basic Certificate of Competency. But in the light of his family's financial circumstances, advancing to high school was not an option open to him. Though he had grown up in poverty, Lye saw so many other families engaged in similar struggles that he did not feel disadvantaged. A succession of foster homes had left him not insecure but fiercely independent with a strong desire to think for himself. While he was capable of intense anger — particularly when something struck him as unjust — such blow-ups happened rarely. This 13-year-old boy's zest for life and appetite for new sensations were exceptional. He was a natural leader, known and liked for his determination, quick wit, and good humour. His popularity with girls and his involvement in male activities such as rugby, boating, and hunting helped shield him from the stereotypes routinely applied by the conformist local culture to any boy considered intellectual or 'arty'.

Art had become a passion for Lye and he could not imagine a more interesting job, but the only employers of that kind in his vicinity were advertising agencies and newspapers, and the idea of making a career even in those areas seemed too remote an ambition. When he left school and headed out into a world full of news about war and class conflict, his first thoughts and those of his family focused not on a fulfilling career but simply on the struggle to survive.

four composing motion

On the strength of his school results it was decided that Lye should tackle a commerce course. Bookkeeping held no interest for him but he needed a meal ticket. His Certificate of Proficiency entitled him to a free place in a full-time commercial course at the Wellington Technical College so long as he continued to make satisfactory progress. The Technical College, the first of its kind in New Zealand, had been created as an alternative to secondary schools which tended to be the preserve of the middle and upper classes. The college offered practical training in four areas — commerce, engineering, homecraft, and art — to a broad range of students. Common to all options was a core curriculum that included English, arithmetic, and (surprisingly) drawing. Drawing had been championed from the beginning by Arthur Riley, prime mover of the college, who believed that 'drawing was as necessary as writing in the modern age . . . [and] should be universally taught'.[1]

At the end of his first two years at the Technical College Lye received a general report from the director, W. S. La Trobe, confirming that 'his attendance, diligence, conduct and progress have been satisfactory'. But in the middle of the following year, 1917, the director warned Rose that because of her son's poor attendance his free place in the commercial course was in danger of being cancelled. Unless she could supply a medical certificate for him, she would be called upon to pay fees.[2] In fact Lye did have medical problems, including a spinal injury suffered when he made a high dive at the Te Aro baths and struck the bottom with his head.[3] But the real problem was that he was fed up with bookkeeping and tired of his part-time jobs. Currently he was working for Sargood, Son and Ewan Ltd, a clothing warehouse, a job which his mother was proud of having arranged for him through a family for whom she did cleaning. Lye was so bored by office work that he started to exploit another of his health problems — a tendency for his face to turn alarmingly dark if he walked up stairs too fast — as a way to get lots of days off.

Despite having invested two years in his commercial course, and against everyone's advice, Lye decided that somehow he must build his life around art. He took his sketchbooks round to all the businesses he could find that employed artists, and to his great relief obtained a junior position at Chandler & Co. Ltd, an advertising agency. Posters were a very important medium for advertising in the 1910s and the Chandler agency designed posters, pasted them up, and maintained the sites. Lye's job was very prosaic but he felt that at last he was headed in the right direction. He took another decisive step by enrolling for evening courses at the Wellington Technical College in 'General Drawing' (1918–1919) and 'Art' (1920–1921). He was excited to become an art student even though materials were scarce and students had to work elbow-to-elbow in noisy and poorly lit classrooms. Hundreds of students took art because the department provided training for many areas of applied art such as architecture, cabinet-making, metalwork, jewellery, signwriting, and so on. As for the fine arts, the general approach at the college and at other New Zealand art schools of the period involved an emphasis on technical skills rather than personal expression or innovation. 'Craftsmanship' and 'draughtsmanship' were key words. As David Low summed up his art studies in Christchurch: 'I was put to drawing and shading up carefully, first, blocks of wood, then a plaster bust of Homer, then a "life" model whose "life" was apparently only when she was not posing.'[4]

The values promoted by art education mirrored those of the local art market. Buyers of paintings liked picturesque landscapes or flower vases or subjects full of sentiment such as tired old men, domestic scenes, and patient horses.[5] The only well-paid painters were those making commissioned portraits of prominent citizens. Reviewers chided artists for any details that seemed out of proportion or abnormal. Leading New Zealand painters took their bearings from the conservative mainstream of English art. Although the influence of some French art did reach New Zealand, it generally came second-hand by way of England. In theory the thinness of the New Zealand art scene should have encouraged a spirit of innovation, but to date it had tended to make artists insecure and parochial. 'The brave and bold spirits left the country.'[6] Among those who remained there was almost no awareness of the upheavals of modernist art that were taking place in many parts of Europe during the 1910s.[7]

The most lively New Zealand artists were those who at least made a determined effort to get outside the studio to draw from life, or who looked for new subject matter if not new techniques. The teacher at Wellington Technical College who made the strongest impression on Lye was Harry Linley Richardson, an artist with a great store of technical knowledge who had arrived in New Zealand from England in 1908 and was now head of the art department. Richardson encouraged detailed observation of nature and his art included scenes of everyday work.[8] He also took an interest in Maori life and mythology. His basic approach was still orthodox, being that of 'the English professional artist, with art school prizes and first-class anatomy lessons firmly built into his foundations',[9] but he gave encouragement to a wide range of students and welcomed discussion in the classroom. 'One might not agree with all the work,' he would say, 'but it is nice to see people trying to strike out on their own.'[10]

Lye was already an accomplished draughtsman by the time he started classes at the Technical College, and Richardson was very impressed.[11] Fine arts students 'were seldom the children of the poor'[12] and this one stood out by the intensity of his approach and by a certain self-educated roughness and independence. In the evening class Lye developed traditional drawing and painting skills, as he did during the day in his work as a commercial artist, but he also kept his eye out for new styles. Stylistically the most adventurous of the New Zealand painters were those coming to terms with Impressionism — artists who painted outdoors, and who were often warned by reviewers that their brushwork or use of colour was too free. Lye was so impressed by the 'pale violet hills and coasts' of the local painter Nugent Welch that he felt he could 'never match such beauty, no never'.[13] He also picked up ideas from the work of English painters influenced by Impressionism such as Philip Wilson Steer and George Clausen (his model 'for light sparking on and through leaves').[14] Since he did not have access to original paintings of this kind he spent a lot of time in Wellington's free public library exploring books and magazines on art. He was particularly interested in painters who focused on transient effects of colour and movement. He was very struck by Turner's light and Constable's oil sketches of clouds.[15] He would enthuse about Frans Hals's 'Gipsy Girl', a well-known seventeenth-century Dutch painting of a young woman with a mischievous laugh.[16] He remarked to his brother: 'What a pity that picture can't move!'

Joe Davis recalled: 'Almost every weekend or free day Len would pack up a lunch and with a sketchbook he would go to the many places around Wellington, particularly in the hilly areas, where you could get an abundance of wonderful sea views and landscapes.'[17] Years later Lye wrote a vivid description[18] of one such walk which took him over farm hills to Happy Valley: 'I was a serious artist. I was watching colours. I had the best place there was for it.'[19] He paid minute attention to the lighting changes at sunset: 'The sun hits the grass on the edge of some near cliffs which goes green-yellow. All the cliffs that line the far half of the crescent bay are in shadow transparent enough to see their fissures . . .'.[20] Then he described his walk back to Wellington: 'There's no need to stop thinking of colour just because it's night. I stop on a hill and look down at barns and milking-sheds and try to imagine how to get the velvety-blacks-and-blues and greeny-dark-browns of things in the moonlight.'[21]

As an artist Lye seemed to be heading towards Impressionism with its emphasis on the greatest possible naturalism and immediacy, in contrast to the precise line-drawing he continued to practise at the Technical College. In addition to his landscape experiments he constantly sketched people from life. Having converted the woodshed at the back of the family home into a studio, he would persuade the young men who worked as models at the college to visit so he could continue sketching them outside class hours. His brother remembered him asking 'characters off the street to come in and sit for him' so that he could draw them in charcoal and chalk under the gaslights.[22]

One evening Richardson, who was strolling round the life class looking at the students' drawings, told Lye that he was getting good light into his drawing. Naturally the student warmed to this subject and asked: 'Which way of painting light do you like, Clausen's or Steer's?' Richardson thought that over and said, 'They're both equally good, I think.' Lye persevered: 'If you only had enough money to buy one of their paintings, whose would you get?' As a good teacher Richardson tried to shift the discussion to basic principles: 'If one painter did a lot of his own thinking about art and the other one didn't, I'd buy the former. So of two equally good paintings, the one by the thinker might be a little deeper.'[23] For Lye these remarks were a revelation. Richardson could not have imagined the intensity with which they were received by his student. Often out of all a teacher says, it is a brief, off-the-cuff remark that makes the biggest impression. Lye believed he had just heard a manifesto for originality. He had been struggling to fill in gaps in his education by reading famous books about art — 'sweating over John Ruskin and Sir Joshua Reynolds and all the early guys'[24] — but so far the only result had been feelings of confusion and inadequacy. 'Richardson's remark hit me between the eyes because it seemed to mean I could have my own ideas about art.'[25]

Like most students of the period, Lye felt weighed down by the reverence constantly shown to the great artists of the past.[26] Richardson believed that artists should be thinkers but he also stressed the importance of studying old masters. The idea of originality was seldom mentioned because the first priority was to teach craft skills — but this was the idea Lye had been waiting for because it meant there was a direct route by which even an under-educated kid from the colonies could become a serious artist.

He felt Richardson had given him a licence to think for himself, but what he needed now was an original theory of art. 'I stopped stodging through tomes and instead mulled like mad on my early morn paper-rounds and got up even earlier to see the sun rise.'[27] This was a favourite time for musing, watching the changes of light as the sun came up. One morning he was at the top of a hill in the kind of windy weather for which Wellington is known. As he later described the experience: 'It had been raining all night, and there were these marvellous fast little skuddy clouds in the blue sky. As I was looking at those clouds I was thinking, wasn't it Constable who sketched clouds to try to convey their motions? Well, I thought, why clouds, why not just motion? Why pretend they are moving, why not just move something? All of a sudden it hit me — if there was such a thing as composing music, there could be such a thing as composing motion. After all, there are melodic figures, why can't there be figures of motion?'[28]

Lye felt he had just had 'the best idea of his life',[29] though he would need time to work out its implications. It linked up with the Impressionists and their interest in changing patterns of light and the uniqueness of every moment. It could also be related back to English Romantic writers and their sense of 'a motion and a spirit' (as Wordsworth expressed it in 'Tintern Abbey') that permeates nature. But Lye had a new angle. Merely to animate the image of a cloud or a laughing girl was not enough because movement was not necessarily artistic. What excited him was the idea of composing movement as cleverly as painters composed canvases or composers created melodies.[30]

Deeply grateful to Richardson for giving him that first push, he was pleased to join with 20 other students from the 'Day Art Class of 1921' when they gave their teacher a haversack (Richardson was a keen tramper) and a signed card in the shape of a palette. At least two other members of that class — Helen Stewart and Gordon Tovey — would go on to have notable careers in art. Stewart went to London in 1925 to study, and then after a brief return to New Zealand travelled to Paris in 1928. Although becoming an honoured figure in Australia where she later lived, her work would still be rejected as too modern by the Academy of Fine Arts in Wellington when she sent paintings home in 1946. Tovey, who was the same age as Lye, would eventually become a key figure in art education in New Zealand. As 'a nonconformist, a seeker, a person excited about new ideas', he had much in common with Lye, and these two unusual young people gravitated to each other.[31] As a painter Tovey was also deeply interested in Constable. Lye told him about the revelation he had had while observing clouds — the discovery that 'it was possible to create art in a moving form'. Lye was accustomed to keeping his serious thoughts to himself but he opened up to his fellow student. Tovey later said of Lye, 'What a spark he was! We used to talk for hours about movement and the clouds moving across the skies of Wellington!'[32]

Over the next year Lye struggled to develop his new conception: 'What the hell do I compose motion with? What's going to carry the motion? Well, that problem knocked me bandy.'[33] He turned first to sketching since that was the medium he knew best. Through observation of nature he experimented with a kind of Impressionism of movement. His sketches recorded 'the shapes of motion made by the lines of flight of both low and high flying gulls; squiggly lines of movement seen when ropes and masts reflect from undulating water; the direction of the currents seen on the eddies of babbling brooks; the top of a comber at various stages of its downward curlings; the surface patterns of rifflings on water ponds; the wind patterns made on a field of green oats when seen from up in a tree; and endless other things'. The seagull motion 'came out looking like a tangle of fishing lines, and the boat masts like a bunch of snakes'.[34]

Sitting on the back of a horse-drawn cart Lye sketched the changing folds made in the clothes of pedestrians: 'I stared at such things as the diagonal lines in their flapping overcoats as they swung along or criss-crossed lines formed on a skirt by the owner's walking motion.'[35] The people he drew 'would be wondering what the hell was going on'.[36] Also: 'my potty-looking notions made my work look crazy unless people were given some explanation, so I quit bothering to show it. The explanations were far more difficult to make than the sketches.'[37] It became a basic habit of Lye's to keep his experimenting to himself and simply get on with it. At the same time he was keeping up the more conventional public side of his work as art student and commercial artist.

Lye was not entirely satisfied with his 'spaghetti-looking sketches'[38] but they became part of the ritual of his evening sense exercises: 'One looks at one's notes of the day, last thing at night, and one tries to remember the motions they represent.'[39] He could tell from his sketches whether the creases and folds he had drawn were from faster or slower movements.[40] He tried varying the style of his notation which had so far concentrated on lines of motion.[41] Since cycles or rhythms of movement were more interesting to him than single lines he developed a pattern of three choreographic marks:[42] 'You select a boat mast that's dancing on the water and really watch it. You take out your sketchbook and draw the left side of the pattern of mast wiggles. You do the same for the right, but you leave an open space between these two sides. Now you look at the middle line of the mast's dance on the water and shift your eye back to the blank space on the paper and mentally transpose those middle wiggles to the paper.'[43]

Applying this method of 'repetitive movement marks'[44] to other subjects he sometimes chose not to record the middle line or backbone of the motion so that later he would be forced to remember the particular dance that had taken place between the contours.[45] All these sketches helped Lye to become more alert to figures of motion but he felt that they were not yet succeeding as art. It was now clear to him that the realism practised in art school was only one possible way to represent or notate the world but he had yet to find an adequate alternative.

five modernism

Lye was now searching books and magazines for any ideas that could be linked to his interest in motion. Fortunately Wellington's population of 80,000 had access to a free public library and Lye spent many evenings learning how to make good use of catalogues and bibliographies. His discoveries made him a passionate believer in the value of such institutions: 'Libraries are an absolute cinch for kids, you've just got to have them if you want social revolution.'[1] His success in digging out information about art that his teachers were not aware of strengthened his belief that real education is something that one does alone. He had no interest in impressing people with the specialised knowledge he was acquiring, and some of his acquaintances would have been amazed to learn that he ever went near a book.

The focus of his research shifted from England to other parts of Europe. Excited by his first encounter with the work of Gauguin, Van Gogh, and Cézanne, Len set out to collect all the information he could find, mostly limited to brief quotations or occasional black-and-white illustrations. What drew him to Cézanne was not motion but stillness: 'I'd been sketching the action quality of clothes so much that the static sculptural quality [of his paintings] got me. I was reading what Cézanne had to say about the artistic value of three dimensions, and he certainly put emphasis on the rounded quality of his apples and bottles, and in the folds of clothes, napkins and tablecloths. It was the opposite of motion, but part of it, like the opposites silence and sound.'[2]

One lunch hour Lye took his sketchbook down to the harbour and — as practice in applying Cézanne's ideas — started drawing a man seated like a rock on the end of the wharf: 'I had just mapped out some very good rock veins of clothing folds when, you wouldn't believe it, this rock began to topple. It swayed a little forward, and then a little back, hesitated, and a bit forward again. I couldn't adjust to the motion, immobility changing to an inverted pendulum swinging back and forward. And then it dawned on me that my model was sleeping, dreaming of some swing under some faraway tree. I stepped out of my open-mouthed static stance to try to stop him, but I only managed to stretch out and touch the tail of his coat as he changed from a rock into a propeller, spinning down into the sea, and a great spread-eagled splash.'[3] Lye dived in and saved this 'drunken old salt', an exploit that earned him a measure of local fame.⁴ It also cost him a number of drawings since his sketchbook had disappeared by the time he returned to the wharf.

Some items about Italian Futurism alerted him to the fact that a wave of new ideas was sweeping through European art. More highly organised than other vanguard artists, the Futurists went after publicity so vigorously that some newspapers applied the word 'Futurism' indiscriminately to all forms of modern art. The reporting was not very coherent but there was enough talk of artists interested in movement to make Lye wildly excited. He began an extensive search for more information and gradually became acquainted with many forms of modern art. In those days there was no guidebook, no academic survey of movements which explained that Impressionism had given birth to Post-Impressionism which in turn had sired Cubism, etc. Many modern artists felt like Robinson Crusoe, isolated without a map, exhilarated on those rare occasions when something useful drifted in with the tide. To quote from an American account of this period: 'If somebody had a French magazine with a picture of Picasso's in it, *that* was news. It was big stuff. The picture would be brought around and discussed. . . . There was . . . a sense of curiosity, of wonder and excitement that is lacking now. [Artists] were aware of a more mysterious world out there.'⁵ Such material seldom travelled as far as New Zealand. Lye set out to map this alternative world with the help of every piece of information he could scratch up, doing his best to read between the lines of the incredulous or sarcastic reviews published in English magazines.

Although Futurism was his first love, some of the excitement gradually faded as he came to realise it was only one of the many forms of modern art. While there were affinities between Lye's choreographic marks and Giacomo Balla's motion paintings such as 'Girl Running on a Balcony' and 'Dynamism of a Dog on a Leash', or Marcel Duchamp's controversial 'Nude Descending a Staircase',⁶ the Futurists tended to be more interested in dynamism generally than in what Lye called figures of motion (which tended to involve cyclic movement such as swinging or spinning). He focused on natural or body movements and did not share the Futurists' enthusiasm for high-speed machines such as cars, trains, and aeroplanes. As for their love of public scandals, Lye was not tempted to mount a one-man avant-garde offensive on the New Zealand art world, despite the inviting target it must have offered. Not that he ever lost his interest in Futurist art — in fact, he was never able to find enough illustrations to satisfy his curiosity.

The boldness of modern art appealed immediately to Lye's individualism and appetite for the new. It confirmed his hunch that the world of art was much broader and wilder than the provincial version in which he had been trained. The ideas of modernism — though they reached him only through second-hand, incomplete accounts — presented an exciting intellectual challenge. He was also delighted to hear about artists defying sexual censorship and other forms of Victorian propriety.

In the first years after he discovered modernism and came up with his own idea of an art of motion, there was an odd Jekyll-and-Hyde aspect to Lye's career. His traditional drawing skills enabled him to earn his living as a poster artist, and he continued to attend art classes at the Wellington Technical College's school. He still took pride in his craft skills. As late as 1922 he sent entries to the national competition for art students conducted annually by the New Zealand Academy of Fine Arts, and in that year the judges (who included Lye's former hero the painter Nugent Welch) gave him the first prize in two categories, 'Head From Life' and 'Figure From Antique', as well as commending his 'Figure From Life' (all black-and-white drawings).[7] Meanwhile he pursued his underground interests, tracking down information about modernism and making motion sketches 'in his various systems of scriggles and scraggles'.[8] These private and public aspects of Lye's art remained totally separate. If other modernist art had been exhibited in Wellington, there would have been an incentive for him to display his own experiments, but he came across nothing comparable. Even in Europe many modernists had similarly divided loyalties and split artistic personalities — an artist had to feel stifled before going over completely to the new art.

By 1921 Lye had moved from Chandler's to a more interesting job at the Charles Haines Advertising Agency in Featherston Street. He said of advertising art: 'It was so different from what I was interested in that it did me no harm in my thinking.'[9] The agency had a staff of about thirty people including A. O. Aitken who remembered that 'everyone did a bit of everything because the advertising business was not yet divided up into various specialisations'.[10] The work consisted mostly of line drawings for newspapers (whose printing methods could not handle half-tones). Sometimes Lye got into trouble because of his zeal: 'I'd sketch commercial art as if it were fine art. I'd think of Rembrandt and my favourite etchers, [Anders] Zorn of Sweden and P. Wilson Steer.'[11] He objected to being told to imitate advertisements from overseas magazines,[12] and wanted to draw everything from life. He was always happy when lunchtime arrived and he was able to leave the agency 'to its jam labels', going off to sketch men at work on scaffoldings or seagulls on the harbour while nibbling his sandwiches.[13]

In the office of his boss, Charles Haines, Lye discovered a couple of early paintings by Frances Hodgkins. Hodgkins had gone overseas in 1901, the year

Len was born. Apart from two return visits to New Zealand (in 1903 and 1912)
she had stayed in England and Europe. In Paris she had come to recognise that its
art scene was 'far more experimental and vital' than London's.[14] Lye was very
impressed by her Impressionist-style paintings and would sneak a look at them
whenever his boss was away.[15] Aitken remembers Lye as 'well groomed and
rather dapper, not like some of the other artists'.[16] In the words of his brother:
'At this stage of his life Len had a Latin look about him, a swarthy (or olive)
complexion and slightly slanty eyes.' The 'slanty eyes' were sometimes wrongly
interpreted as a sign of Chinese ancestry.[17] As he moved into his twenties he
started to go bald as his father had done. He developed a reputation for unusual
hats such as a prized green Borsalino acquired from his mother's friend Captain
Hannah. Lye's social manner was relaxed and cheerful. He was not an aesthete (a
style taken over from the English art world by some young artists in the colonies)
— he was too down-to-earth for that — but there was an air of sophistication
and self-confidence about him. From his Jewish friend Joe Davis he learned the
Yiddish phrase 'Ich gebibble', meaning 'I should worry!' or 'Who cares!', and
this became one of his favourite sayings.[18] The phrase was popularised in the
United States by stage comedians and by comic strips such as Harry Hershfield's
Abie the Agent.[19] It was meant to be spoken for real effect with a pronounced
shrug, shoulders elevated and palms up. Lye's capacity for happiness was
exceptional — he was able (in his own words) to 'just live as fucking mad about
life and work and art'.[20] He could be thoughtless and selfish at times, and
certainly he possessed a temper — his Irish temper, as Rose called it — but it
surfaced only rarely. When it did, the occasion was often an argument about art
and then all hell would break loose. But Lye's dark moods never lasted long, and
what characterised him above all was his great zest for life.

How did he come to develop such a positive attitude? In his words: 'When I
was a kid a lot of disturbing things happened round me. My old man died of TB,
then I was farmed out to relatives. But none of this really touched me, as it doesn't
touch a lot of kids. And I was pretty independent.'[21] Lye learned to improvise, to
make good use of whatever was available. But to have this confidence he needed
the support and encouragement that were provided in his childhood by Rose Lye.
In his brother's words: 'My mother and I, we thought the sun shone out of Len.'[22]
This respect was mutual, but as Lye became an increasingly restless and
opinionated teenager he sometimes leaned heavily on them both. In a later
tribute he described the gauche way he had sometimes used his mother as an
audience: 'Like most young artists I had an amazing ego and I sounded off with
it long, loud and often. "Mother, the right name for Christianity is hypocrisy" —

and she'd never flinch from my tirades but instead gave me a little smile, or a look of knowing exactly what I was meaning.'[23]

Philip's fiancée Merania found this intense, bald-headed intellectual somewhat intimidating but she was touched when he made a drawing for her. Outside of his family and closest friends Lye kept his ideas and intensity under wraps so he was known as a quiet, good-humoured companion.[24] But in private this was a very restless time in Lye's life, as his brother recalled: 'He did drawings of his friends, Joe Davis for example. Joe would say, "Let's have a look at that, Len" but Len would tear it up — he was never satisfied — "I can do better". Everything that he did seemed to lead him on to something else. Like gaining knowledge, it just kept opening up. That was Len, right through his early art. With so many things, he'd go RIIIIPPPP!'[25]

Despite his fanaticism for art Lye found time for outdoor activities such as boating. His personality was well-rounded, living as intensely through his body and senses as through his mind. Like many New Zealanders he had friends who owned boats and he would never pass up an opportunity to go sailing.[26] Boats linked up with his interest in movement. For example, he described stretching out on a yacht: 'My body seemed to spread out over the whole of the aft deck. It felt like the deck of the world from which to watch the great spanking sail belly out firm in the breeze, and feel the pull it gave the boat down its mast to the keel and along the deck to my flat back.' On this occasion he saw a yellow butterfly suddenly 'step out into the blue' from behind the sail, a visual surprise that seemed to cleave him 'down the middle like a meat-chopper, so fast'. He felt the butterfly's light movements contrast with 'the solid world of the boat and the heavy bouncy sea'.[27]

He came to realise the extent to which the body as well as the eye is involved in sensing movement. To watch an athlete is to be conscious of strain, weight, and balance, and often this makes one's own body tense. Lye was intrigued by those 'bone-deep feelings of affinity'[28] and he developed a game of assigning particular types of movement to particular areas of the body. Observing the curling top of a wave, for example, he would imagine a similar movement in his shoulder. Watching a cat stretch its back he would try to transfer the feeling to the arched instep of his foot. Or to remember the pitch and lurch of a boat's deck, he would think of tightening his stomach muscles.[29] In general: 'I tried to plait particular motion characteristics into my sinews — to attach an inner kind of echo of them to my bones.'[30] His long-term aim was to get more of this physical dimension — this 'body English', as he was to call it — into his art.

As well as providing him with ideas about movement, Lye's boat trips were lively social events. Weekends would sometimes achieve 'a nicely balanced mix-ture of sex and ozone'.[31] He had received an early sex education: 'I was 4-ish when two older girls played trying to fit my tassle into one of their quims, me mostly on top — it was fascinating manipulation.'[32] His brother remembered that as a teenager Lye had had many affairs — not merely casual flings but warm, steady relationships. He was lucky to have had such positive experiences in a society that was ruled — despite the physical emphasis its way of life inherited from pioneer times — by religious puritanism. He was well informed about methods of contraception, such as condoms which had recently become available, and had many nights of 'fantastic exhilaration'. In his words: 'those beaming moon trips were perfectly planned, such as raincoats to un-dew the grassy sward, a rubber population-control sheath plus a pessary, and candy from hard-earned pocket-money resources.'[33] He felt very much at ease with his body, and he also believed that his close friendships with girls had helped to moderate 'the sterility of the masculine strut'[34] — the narrow-minded, macho attitudes he saw in many young men.

On holiday trips Lye always took a wind-up gramophone and records which reflected his love of jazz. He had never warmed to classical music — 'I loathed the sound of either the organ or strings, they were too god-awfully sanctimonious or floridly romantic for me'[35] — and was therefore pitied as the one member of his family lacking in musical talent. Rose sang, Philip played wind instruments, and Uncle Pat had been a bandmaster in the army. Lye had a poor sense of pitch but in jazz he discovered an area of music that put great emphasis on rhythm. Artists such as Louis Armstrong, King Oliver, and Ma Rainey were riding their first wave of popularity in the United States though they were still little known in New Zealand. For Lye it was 'jazz, jazz, jazz, listening to it morning, noon and night, mostly down at a moon-drenched week-end beach cottage with [local] children doing a wild dance to the zig-lay-boom-boom of King Oliver and his cats'.[36] Lye loved jazz for its body energy, not only in its rhythms, but also in the physical resonance of its performance. A good trumpet solo had (in his words) 'the personal tonal quality of breathing, it is very distinctive of the particular player'. Above all he liked jazz because it had 'so much to do with happiness'.[37]

Lye was lean, wiry, and tough yet he had some persistent health problems.[38] He still suffered backaches from his old diving injury. He tried to ignore them but they became more and more painful and his mother insisted that he seek treatment. Suspicious of doctors, he went to a Wellington chiropractor named Ward, a tough ex-sailor whose manipulations were so painful that he feared he had put himself in the hands of a quack. But eventually his backaches subsided and he was convinced that this self-educated healer possessed special insights into the body.³⁹ Ward also passed on some self-defence methods learned in his fights as a sailor. Lye improved his punching by thinking of his fist as a cricket ball made of thick dark red leather to be thrown as fast as possible at the wicket (the nose of anyone threatening him). Other tactics involved gripping an arm and turning it like the rim of a steering wheel, or seizing a hand in the way a heron snatches fish. Lye was less interested in street fights than he was in Ward's vivid way of visualising body movements.

Lye hated his mother's fussing about his health, but she was understandably concerned in the light of her husband's early death from consumption. Being treated as an invalid added to her son's restlessness. After all he had read about world art, he was itching to travel. In Philip's words: 'His mother never said "You can't go" or "Who's going to look after me?" But she did advise him to wait until he was 21. Lye's usual reply was "Well, I might be dead by then." But he accepted what she said and stayed.'⁴⁰ Philip recalled that one day his brother had had a surge of impatience with his job: 'Whenever he had a problem he went and saw the head, never the underlings. That was Len. Anyway on this occasion he went to the manager and asked for a raise but the manager knocked him back. He reminded Len there were men who'd been working there for fifteen years. Len said, "In fifteen years I could be dead. I'm doing good work now." The manager said, "All right, we'll give you a raise but don't tell anybody." But Len refused to accept it on that condition.'⁴¹

For years Rose had worried about her son's tendency to have blackouts and the way his face sometimes turned unnaturally dark. Around 1921 these problems grew worse and she finally persuaded him to see a specialist. The doctor made a diagnosis of Bright's disease, a kidney disorder associated with the young — potentially a very serious condition. Rest was prescribed and a special diet. A friend recalls: 'For years Len ate raw vegetables for health reasons. So, during this period, he farted a lot. He was good at concealing this by getting up and walking to the door and continuing the conversation from there!'⁴² When his health showed no improvement, Lye lost patience with all the anxious attention he was receiving and decided to enjoy what time he had left.⁴³ His savings had run out but he was determined at least to have a change of scene. In Philip's words: 'He came home one day and said, "I'll be leaving on Monday, I've got a new job — hop-picking in Nelson." He'd always do a thing and *then* tell people, so there could be no bloody argument!'⁴⁴ He persuaded his mother to lend him a little money, packed his swag-bag and set off.

For half-a-crown a sailor smuggled him into the hold of a mailboat for an overnight trip to the South Island. He spent a strange night sliding round on a hilly bed of mailbags.[45] Reaching Nelson he enquired at the pub where fruit was being picked, then hitched a ride with a milk-cart and was dropped off among the hop fields. As his brother reported the rest of the story: 'The hop-pickers were earning only a halfpenny for two baskets. Len wasn't there very long but he got the hop-pickers to go out on strike for another farthing a basket. Personally he couldn't have cared two hoots in hell, but he thought it was unfair. He didn't like people being put upon.'[46] Politics remained only an occasional interest for Lye but he felt sufficiently committed at this time to write 'to a socialist paper in sympathy with the underdog (the worker) against the big wig (the capitalist boss)'.[47] The hop-pickers won their dispute but Lye moved on restlessly to Christchurch, the city in which he had spent his early years. The art scene in Christchurch was now reputed to be the liveliest in the country.[48] As for his health, Lye felt vastly better after his spell of hard work and vowed never to go near a doctor again.[49]

six hei-tiki

In Christchurch, where Lye was able to board with Frank and Maud Cole (an uncle and aunt), he enrolled at the beginning of 1922 for evening and Saturday classes at the Canterbury College School of Art.[1] He already knew its director, Archibald Frank Nicoll, who had taught an evening art class he had attended in Wellington while still a schoolboy. Nicoll took an interest in Lye. Born in Scotland in 1886, he was in many ways an artist of the same type and generation as Richardson, combining a thorough academic training with a commitment to the close observation of nature.[2] His landscape paintings were close to Impressionism in their heightened emphasis on light and colour and their lively brushwork, but like Richardson he was best known as a portrait painter. University professors, governors and their wives, chief justices, and mayors 'flowed smoothly' onto his canvases.[3] It was a measure of public taste that such portraits by Nicoll and Richardson enjoyed more recognition than their other work.

Nicoll was sufficiently impressed by Lye to give him one of his landscapes. And when the young artist found it difficult to adjust back to an orthodox art syllabus, Nicoll allowed him to spend his time making sketches of things in motion.[4] Lye continued to practice this exercise, as shown by his note: 'See the folds in those blankets pegged to the clothesline — well, when the breeze blows, so the fold goes, is gone, is back, and is always different at the bottom, sides hanging and flapping corners (make a pencil sequence in the sketchbook).'[5] But drawings of blankets, water reflections, the shoulder muscles of horses, and other objects in motion bore so little relevance to what was being discussed at the school that he left after the first term.

Nicoll generously helped Lye to obtain a bread-and-butter job as an artist for the *Christchurch Sun*. The *Sun* (later absorbed into the *Christchurch Star*) pioneered the use of illustrations at a time when other New Zealand editors avoided them because they considered visual material frivolous and beneath the dignity of a serious newspaper.[6] Lye put his craftsmanship to work, making careful line drawings though he sometimes experimented with a freer line (as in a sketch of two circus elephants which he later gave to Maud Cole). At the *Sun* he often thought about David Low the cartoonist who had worked for various Christchurch newspapers before moving on to the Sydney *Bulletin* and then to

London. Lye was not interested in cartooning — he felt he 'couldn't caricature for sour apples'[7] — but he was dying to travel.

While the official art scene in Christchurch held no surprises for him, the collection of 'ethnological' or 'primitive' art at the Canterbury Museum had a profound effect on his thinking. Opened in 1870, the museum held examples of Maori carving, Aboriginal art, tapa from the Pacific Islands, and indigenous designs from many other parts of the world, presented as anthropological exhibits rather than as works of art. Reading about modernism had alerted Lye to the new overseas interest in such art, particularly African carving, among sculptors such as Constantin Brancusi and Jacob Epstein. At the beginning of the century almost no one in European art circles had taken a serious interest in African work, but then (as Clive Bell noted in 1919) artists such as 'Picasso, Derain, Matisse, and Vlaminck began picking up such pieces as they could find in old curiosity and pawn shops'.[8] Then in England young artists started to visit 'those long dreary rooms [in the British Museum] that once were abandoned to missionaries, anthropologists, and colonial soldiers enhancing their prestige by pointing out to stay-at-home cousins the relics of a civilization they helped to destroy'.[9]

To avant-garde artists, such work offered striking proof that there were powerful styles of representation that lay completely outside the traditional aesthetics of European art. Also, artists were impressed by the frank sexuality of some of this work and its ability to stir the subconscious mind. Here were images of sex, death, natural energy, and the spirit world that made the official Victorian masterpieces seem shallow and prudish by comparison. The modernists took the conventional terms 'primitive' and 'savage' and gave them positive associations, in contrast to 'civilisation' — that favourite Victorian term — which they associated with the timidity and exhaustion of bourgeois art. This was a new reading of 'primitive art', paying serious attention to it as art, contemptuous of the attitudes of the ethnographer, who saw such objects merely as scientific exhibits in a museum, or of the coloniser, who saw them as spoils of empire, or of the collector, who saw them as exotic curiosities or souvenirs of travel. The objects the modernists valued most were those made prior to European contact; thus they cancelled out the idea of progress. There was a great feeling of relief in lifting aside the dead weight of Western civilisation to make space for other traditions and new discoveries. This is not to deny that the modernist approach created its own set of problems by imposing a cultural framework of its own and a new sense of exoticism. But we should not forget what a radical step it was in the early years of the century to be championing the work of indigenous peoples, for this activity challenged the public mystique of the British Empire and other European empires.

Lye was hugely excited by his first encounter with pictures of traditional African art: 'I knew I was not a chip off the Western art block, I knew it in my bones.'[10] He saw the carved figures as rich in implied movement, the work of artists acutely sensitive to stance and gesture. As Robert Farris Thompson has written: 'African icons remain *trésors de souplesse*, in the memorable phrase of Jean Rouch, for traditional sculptors in West Africa seem more influenced by the vital body in implied motion, by forms of flexibility, than by realism of anatomy per se.'[11] Lye found this work intriguing not only in terms of movement but more generally in its approach to physicality. The teachers he had known during his many years of life classes would have seen the 'distortions' of the body in African sculpture as a naive lack of interest in anatomy, but he developed a different interpretation: 'I thought the reason why African sculpture looked so bodily right was because the negro artist didn't carve eyes, noses, mouths in the way they looked in everyday life. He didn't caricature their appearance but emphasized their dimensional *feeling*. For instance, if you close your eyes and think of your nose and concentrate on the feeling of its shape, you can soon come to feel that it is much larger than your mirror version. . . . It can seem to go right over your forehead. Soon you can make it keep going until it makes a high ridge over your head. Or, try to feel the shape of your face with your face, and you'll find that it can seem either to be smooth and round and flat, or have undulating contours in smooth hills and dales. Still with your eyes closed, now concentrate on your cheekbones. You'll find they can be felt to protrude even beyond your nose. And the same treatment can be given to get the bodily feeling — rather than the brain's recollection — of your arms, legs and torso.'[12] Whether or not such an interpretation was valid, it provided Lye with a new approach to drawing the human body. It also gave him a new way of responding to modernist sculpture by artists such as Constantin Brancusi.[13]

Learning about tribal dance rituals gave Lye a more direct way of linking traditional African art with movement, and in a search for information he read many anthropological books. Meanwhile at the Canterbury Museum he was excited to realise that there were traditions of tribal art closer to home, including Aboriginal art from Australia, masks from Papua New Guinea, and many forms of Maori art. Now (in Lye's words) 'not only did I go to books, I went to the real things and copied them very assiduously'.[14] The museum collection fired his interest in tapa from the Pacific Islands: 'Tapa design is really just joy, it's beautifully, geometrically sorted out and coloured, and it's on this marvellous cloth, you know, off-white, creamy coloured textural stuff'.[15] The art of the Australian Aborigines had a huge impact on him with its 'clear, clean-cut, aesthetic'[16] and 'beautiful colour'.[17] Like tapa design, it was not bound by three-dimensional perspective. Besides copying the work in the museum, he read *The Northern Tribes of Central Australia* (1904) by Baldwin Spencer and F. J. Gillen, and this became a favourite book for its illustrations of sand and rock paintings and shield designs. He also read G. A. Stow's *The Native Races of South Africa* (1904), which argued that the Australian Aborigines had come originally from the same race as the African Bushmen and had carried 'into widely separated countries, similar germs of primitive art'.[18] Lye was more interested in the art than the history, but such a theory held considerable appeal for him.

What the museum offered most richly was its collection of Maori carvings, and Lye was profoundly impressed to discover that there was a major tradition of indigenous art in his own country. He was particularly interested in carved canoes and the many versions of the tiki. According to Maori tradition, the first human being created by the god Tane was 'Tiki', and the name came to be applied to any carved human figure. The kind of small tiki worn round the neck was properly described as a hei-tiki. This was usually made of pounamu (greenstone), but there were some old ones carved in bone, and in ancient times they may have been carved in wood. The hei-tiki figure had a large head, sometimes tilted to one side, and a small straight body projecting down from it with the arms forming symmetrical loops. The legs, which were also symmetrical, tucked in under the body with the feet meeting in a stylised meshing of toes. In this way the human figure was translated into a flat, rhythmic pattern of curves. The hei-tiki had been interpreted as a fertility charm depicting a foetus, but some authorities regarded it simply as a stylised human figure. To Lye it was 'a fantastic image' and he copied many examples.

Maori carving was a living tradition, but the best work was being done in remote rural areas, and Lye had grown up without coming into contact with it. In the early years of the century fewer than 3000 Maori lived in the South Island. Even in the North Island the Maori, devastated by war, illness, and loss of tribal land, had tended to retreat into rural seclusion. Eventually the decline in population was reversed and Maori culture reasserted itself vigorously. It is unfortunate that Lye did not meet someone who could have helped him gain access to a traditional Maori community. In Christchurch in 1921 his approach was to educate himself as best he could by studying the museum's collection and by reading anthropological papers.[19] However, he did make some trips to Maori meeting houses,[20] and his relationship with this kind of art and knowledge of its contexts was certainly more local and immediate than the relationship of European modernists to African art.

There were New Zealand artists who made picturesque Maori portraits or borrowed design motifs but Lye saw this work as still so Victorian in spirit it could not seriously engage with Maori or any other tradition of tribal art. The challenge was how to internalise a tribal aesthetic, how to pass from theory to practice. He tried to complement his conscious studies by immersing himself in the particular feeling of a work and then leaving intuition to do the rest. As usual he developed this into a nightly exercise: 'I would take my sketch book and put it by my bed; then, last thing, with everything else under control — pants folded, socks away, teeth done — I would glance through the pages, lingering on the feelings of the works I liked for both their aesthetic and their play of dimensional qualities (sometimes seemingly more than 3D and sometimes less). I'd come to the work I'd reproduced in a sketch earlier that day. I'd look and look at it reviving the particular aesthetic feeling the real object had given me. When I thought I had it and could hold it fast, I'd leave the book open at that page and put it face up under my pillow and then go to sleep.'[21]

Around this time he made another important discovery — Ezra Pound's 1916 book *Gaudier-Brzeska*[22] about a French sculptor killed in the First World War. Despite its small print run, this book exercised a deep influence on young artists. (It was a turning point for Henry Moore, for example.) Lye was fascinated by Gaudier-Brzeska's art, by the radicalism of his ideas, and by the eventful life he had led before dying at the age of 24, only a few years older than he was. He was fascinated by a manifesto in which Gaudier-Brzeska launched an attack on the whole of the Western tradition,[23] celebrating as an alternative various forms of the 'primitive' such as cave art and the tribal arts of 'Africa and the Ocean Islands'. Gaudier-Brzeska used vivid phrases such as: 'they [the artists] fell into contemplation before their sex: the site of their great energy'.[24] Alongside the tribal artists he acknowledged a handful of modern Western artists such as Alexander Archipenko, Constantin Brancusi, and Jacob Epstein, who worked with similar imagery.

For Lye the book was a treasure-trove of information about 'Cubism, Expressionism, everything that was going on'.[25] Particularly striking was the way Pound and Gaudier-Brzeska rejected the Impressionists as old-hat and considered the Futurists to be merely Impressionists in modern dress. The true modern artist was urged to avoid such loose styles and instead to concentrate on the precise arrangement of surfaces and planes, or 'masses in relation'.

It would take Lye a long time to come fully to terms with these ideas but he was immensely attracted by the modernism that the book communicated with such intensity. 'All this is new life,' wrote Pound, 'it gives a new aroma, a new keenness for keeping awake.'[26] But while the book confirmed the relevance of modern art and tribal art, it had little to say about kineticism. Much of Gaudier-Brzeska's work emphasised solidity, though the sculptor did depict dancers and wrestlers with a strongly implied sense of movement and energy. And Pound quoted some evocative remarks about art by Laurence Binyon: 'It is not essential that the subject-matter should represent or be like anything in nature; only it must be alive with a rhythmic vitality of its own.' And: 'You may say that the waves of Korin's famous screen are not like real waves: but they move, they have force and volume.'[27] Lye was also very impressed by a Japanese *haiku* quoted by Pound — 'The fallen blossom flies back to its branch: A butterfly'[28] — and he often returned to it when musing about his own art of motion.

Pound's introduction to modernism made Lye even more determined to go overseas. He went back to Wellington, then restlessly moved north to Auckland. He was offered an advertising job at seven pounds per week but to keep his head clear he decided to work instead as a builder's labourer, earning 'a couple of quid a week' on a council housing scheme at Western Springs where the job involved digging and concreting. His health had improved considerably since he went to Nelson. He became friendly with a tall, proud man, a Maori named Pete. One day the foreman told Pete to go faster: 'Shovel that mud, or you and I will not agree.' The workman retorted: 'To hell with your mud. And we don't agree.'[29] This line by Pete as he exited from the job became a favourite saying for Lye. To Rose's dismay her son was becoming increasingly 'bolshie'[30] with no ambitions for a middle-class career. Though he studied constantly he seemed to have no desire to benefit from all his hard work. He had the drive and innovative spirit of an entrepreneur but the world of business held no appeal for him. His rebel stance was growing stronger and more uncompromising.

His brother followed him to Auckland, got a job as a truck-driver, and became a boarder in the same house. He remembers that Lye had a period off work because of injury and used the time to make a wood carving which took the hei-tiki as its point of departure but transformed it in the manner of Gaudier-Brzeska or Brancusi.[31] The large head became a self-contained oval tilted to one side. Apart from a few curving lines for facial features, it was smooth as an egg. Whereas a hei-tiki usually had large eyes, this had narrow slits so the head created an overall feeling of dreamy repose. Rather than add a straight body with curved limbs, Lye made the whole of the trunk curve so that the usual symmetry was replaced by a series of rounded shapes which ended in a curved leg. The holes or gaps functioned as part of the overall pattern.

Because the hei-tiki was worn as a neck ornament the back was usually flat, but Lye carved an almost naturalistic back. One leg was tucked behind the other and the arms met behind the head in a relaxed pose that reinforced the peaceful look of the face. This figure was at ease, curled up in what Lye would have called a state of 'no trouble'. A person lying down with their eyes closed could imagine the body in this way.

Tiny as the carving was (about 6 cm by 6 cm), it illustrated the thorough way in which Lye was engaging with Cubism. The Cubism of Picasso and Braque involved a dialogue with African art, whereas Lye was engaging with Maori art. Though a hei-tiki is not a sacred object, Lye's carving might today be seen as misappropriation or too free a treatment of conventions. But in relation to the Pakeha tradition of art it was boldly innovative, based on a serious engagement with the formal aspects of both Maori art and European modernism. At this time (1922) it would have been difficult to find any other Pakeha artist who shared his interests.

seven sydney

Around the end of 1922 Lye sailed for Sydney, Australia.[1] He would have preferred Europe as his destination but boat travel was expensive, and any overseas trip — even the 1600 miles from Auckland to Sydney — was regarded as a huge step for a young person to take. In the words of Lye's friend Stitch Hemming, 'If anyone was leaving New Zealand, you'd look a second time and wonder what had come over him or her — what was that person going away for?'[2] But Sydney beckoned as 'that fabulous Australian city which stood for pleasure to New Zealanders as Paris does to the English'.[3] In the words of David Low it had 'the reputation of being, in contrast to our simple honest New Zealand towns, smart, tough, and rather wicked. It was known also as a nursery for poets, writers and caricaturists.'[4] Lye had long been curious about the outside world, as Dorothy Hemming recalled: 'You never knew what he was going to do. I remember him saying "I want to find out how everybody lives".'[5] In Australia he was also looking for art, including Aboriginal work in which he had recently developed a strong interest.[6]

What first impressed Lye about Australia was nature rather than culture. 'I used to do canoe trips up the Parramatta River [and then up one of its tributaries]. Four of us would paddle our big canoe with a small sail to help. Sharks could be poked with a paddle. The Australian landscape has the most unique and invidiously permeating nostalgic colour on earth and the most I get out of all my memories of colours and anything else, including one of the best outdoor breakfasts I've had, is a moment of light reflected from the eddies lapping beside the canoe tied up beneath a huge gum tree into its leaves, with appropriate gurgles and rustlings.'[7] Getting to know the Australian landscape revived his old interest in Impressionism and the first local artist who caught his attention was a painter of transient light, J. J. Hilder (who had died in 1916).

The novelist D. H. Lawrence, who arrived in Sydney at around the same time as Lye, saw the city as still at a raw, formative stage. The central character in his novel *Kangaroo* says of Sydney: 'This London of the Southern Hemisphere was all, as it were, made in five minutes, a substitute for the real thing.'[8] And: 'Look at these Australians — they're awfully nice, but they've got no inside to them. They're hollow. . . . The colonies make for outwardness . . . all the mad struggle with the material conveniences — the inside soul just withers.'⁹ This was a common British stereotype of Australia. But to a New Zealander Sydney could offer many new experiences since its population was almost three times greater than that of any city back home,¹⁰ and its culture was less British, with a stronger anti-authoritarian streak. One of the urban pleasures Lye discovered was bohemianism, a style of life in which he felt instantly at home. The first artists he hung around with in pubs were 'a great gang of fellows from *Smith's Weekly*'.¹¹ Lye disliked the magazine's right-wing politics but loved its black-and-white cartoons and comic strips. Jobs were much sought after because of the wild reputation of the art department: 'Parties were likely to break out at any time among *Smith's* artists. . . . What no one could be sure of was when they would finish, and what damage would be done before they did.'¹² Sampling other pubs and parties, Lye got to know various subcultures of artists and writers. Bohemianism, as he experienced it, was about lively people seeking one another out and finding ways to have a good time on little money. It was about intellectual independence, about radical or irreverent views on religion and politics, and about sexual freedom. It saw itself as egalitarian and classless (although Sydney's version of bohemia tended still to be male-dominated). There was much talk about the 1917 Russian Revolution, and much talk about the arts, though Lye noted that many talkers seldom turned theory into practice. Personally he preferred to listen and to save his best energies for work.

One of his favourite haunts was the Café La Bohème in Wilmot Street, a 'meeting-place of artists and writers and actors and singers and pugilists and cat-burglars'.¹³ There he became friendly with a poet named Geoffrey Cumine, one of the liveliest of the local bohemians. In Kenneth Slessor's words Cumine 'got a lot of pleasure out of wearing startling clothes, usually velvet trousers, a red shirt, a green coat and a bright blue beret. He also had brass ear-rings, and a blue butterfly tattooed on one cheek. One day, as a sarcastic allusion to the journalism by which he occasionally earned a living, he had his forehead tattooed with the words "To Let".'¹⁴ ('Obviously unfurnished,' commented a fellow writer.) Cumine, twelve years older than Lye, had served in the war and that experience had left him deeply cynical about mainstream politics. 'What bloody rot!' was a favourite expression.¹⁵ He was an athletic person who liked motorbikes and had frequent accidents because he drove too fast. His poetry reflected Georgian and aesthetic influences, and a modernist such as Ezra Pound would probably have found it old-fashioned, but there was enough sex, blasphemy, and black humour to give it a lively, rebellious spirit.¹⁶ The poet's casual attitude to getting his work published and his refusal to attach too much importance to fame or posterity seemed basic to his style of bohemianism. Lye, who was always looking for artist role models, admired Cumine's extremism and the feeling was mutual.

In the visual arts Sydney offered a much wider range of modern styles than New Zealand, though Lye was still not able to find any artists who shared his specific interests in motion and primitivism. Between 1918 and 1920 Roy de Maistre had exhibited abstract paintings and collaborated with Roland Wakelin to make a 'colour disc' machine but those artists had left for Europe around the time of Lye's arrival. Some Australian artists were hostile to primitivism on the grounds that what the country needed more urgently was European sophistication. 'Primitivism as an expression of mind has failed to get even a hearing here,' Norman Lindsay remarked triumphantly in 1922.[17] But there was a keen interest in other aspects of modernism among those associated with Dattilo Rubbo's art school and there were important individual artists such as Margaret Preston.[18] Indeed it is surprising that Lye did not get to know more of them — he seems to have been drawn more often to people from other fields. Once again he was displaying a maverick tendency to go it alone in the visual arts.

Though Lye hated doing commercial art, it enabled him to earn his living in Sydney. Drawing posters for an advertising agency, he impressed everyone with his 'terrific draughtsmanship with pen or pencil or brush'.[19] Philip Lye recalled 'a poster Len did for the Bank of New South Wales which won a competition — a full-page advertisement of a farmer working and banking his money'. And there was a poster for the Australian Labour Party 'which impressed them so much they asked Len if he was interested in standing for parliament!' Constantly making drawings, Lye still did representational work such as his sketches of Edna Dixon (one of his girlfriends in Sydney) and Geoffrey Cumine. He also made Impressionist sketches such as a couple on the beach at Bondi caught with a few quick lines.[20] He tried to free-lance as a commercial artist so he would have more time to do his own work but this involved some very lean periods. One of his most interesting commissions was a bookplate with a stylised nude for his friend Hutton Vachini, an artist who collected bookplates.

When Lye had been in Sydney for eight months, he was visited by Walter Tutt who had kept in touch with him since their childhood days at Cape Campbell. In Tutt's words: 'Len showed me drawings I couldn't understand — they were very modern. But I could see he was very good.'[21] Lye took his friend round the galleries, and they spent evenings playing poker with one of his friends, a travelling paint-salesman who kept him supplied with cheap tubes of paint. In those days there was a strong community spirit among those who free-lanced in the art business. Tutt was struck by Lye's determination to keep travelling — he said he had come to Australia 'to learn some more stuff first'.

Lye made the most of the city's bookshops, libraries, and museums. He was an avid reader of all avant-garde publications and whenever he had the money he placed an order for imported magazines such as *The Dial*.[22] But public collections continued to be his main source of information. In Sydney he explored the Mitchell Library and the general Public Library which had larger collections than any New Zealand city. He spent so much time there that he would sometimes 'dream about looking up stuff'.[23] Hungry for more information on tribal art he checked out all the ethnological studies, and one day the title *Totem and Taboo* led him to a book by Sigmund Freud, a writer whose name he had never heard before.[24] At first he was disappointed there were no illustrations, but as he read through the book he got more and more excited. It was complex and obscure but here was a thinker that took tribal culture seriously enough to seek to grasp its inner workings. In Freud's words: 'If we go behind these [conscious] structures which are like a screen concealing understanding, we realize that the psychic life and the cultural development of primitive savages have hitherto been inadequately appreciated.'[25] In his own way Lye was as eager for 'inwardness' as D. H. Lawrence, and what he gained from Freud was the concept of the unconscious mind. The book suggested to him that 'primitive' cultures were based on the same unconscious mental processes as 'civilised' cultures but the latter had tried (unsuccessfully) to disguise and repress them. Freud's insistence on the power of sexuality posed a powerful challenge to the prudish attitudes that had been carried over from the Victorian age. Censorship was a key issue for many writers and artists of the period (such as Lawrence who had both paintings and novels banned). Freud's sexual emphasis made his work modern and liberating, and that was certainly part of the attraction for Lye.

Psychoanalysis provided a possible explanation of the power that could be tapped by a maker of images. Lye had discovered two types of imagery that instantly attracted him — modern art and tribal art — both of which opened up worlds of possibility outside orthodox culture. He could now add a third type, the imagery of the unconscious — the imagery of dreams, madness, and sexual fantasies.[26] Lye was sure there was an affinity between the three areas of imagery but exactly what this might be was yet to be discovered. It was as though he was gradually locating the pieces of his own culture and weaving them together.

Lye went to W. C. Penfold's and purchased a 7-inch by 9-inch notebook with unlined pages in which he proceeded to transcribe *Totem and Taboo*. Such an activity was common in the days before photocopying machines, but in Lye's words, 'I was also hoping this humdrum chore would give me time to digest its

meanings in relation to my own'.[27] Freud's intellectual style was a real workout
for him. Sometimes he tried to bring Freud down to earth by making sentences
more colloquial. (Thus a comment about 'violating a . . . social prohibition'
became 'What will the Home folks say?') Lye wrote on every second page and
then filled the facing pages with ink drawings of tribal artefacts, some copied
from books and others sketched on the spot in the museums he visited. 'I would
never write 2 or 3 pages unless I had 2 or 3 pages of drawings on the other side.'[28]
This dialogue between words and images made the notebook a beautiful object,
illustrating the careful, loving way he was studying the ideas and forms of art
that interested him.

He worked his way to the end of *Totem and Taboo* though he condensed some
sections. Freud seemed to him ultimately too much of a rationalist, but his work
was rich in information about the workings of the unconscious, including aspects
of tribal culture such as totemism, animism, and magic. One passage described
the tendency of 'primitive man' to project his 'inner perceptions' into the 'outer
world', and this idea struck Lye as similar to his own explanation of how African
artists represented the body. In an attempt to bring modern art into the
discussion, he singled out Freud's remark that cave drawings were not simply 'to
arouse pleasure, but to conjure things' and related it to Cézanne's talk of
'conjuring form'.

Lye carried the notebook round with him everywhere, re-reading it and
occasionally adding a new item alongside an existing image which it resembled.
His visual examples were as wide-ranging as Freud's verbal descriptions of
totems and taboos. He juxtaposed tribal images from various parts of the world
and also drew comparisons between tribal and modern images. On one page for
example he brought together a Maori wooden float from a fishing net, an African
carving, and a figure by Mikhail Larionov (a Russian painter whose stylised
figures mixed peasant art with modernism). On another page he drew a 'Negro
love charm' alongside a Maori hei-tiki. His choice of modern Western artists
included Gaudier-Brzeska, Jacob Epstein ('The Rock Drill'), Fernand Léger, and
Clément Pansaers. Larionov was strongly represented with illustrations taken
from a 1920 English translation of *The Twelve*, Alexander Blok's poem about the
Russian Revolution. By juxtaposing traditions Lye hoped to discover connections
— not that he was trying to blur everything into a single kind of art, for his way
of comparing things was always intended to be open-ended and exploratory.

He still lived and worked within mainstream culture but alternative cultures
were becoming steadily more important and more real to him. But they reached
him as fragments and he wanted to build a somewhat more coherent world out

of them. His notebooks were a site in which he could assemble the fragments, pore over them, rearrange them, and gradually weave together his new culture. This was always work in progress, subject to constant revision. Initially the main ingredients were tribal art, modernism, psychoanalysis, and motion. Pound's book offered some connections, as did his favourite magazines, but there were still many gaps to puzzle over. It was a slow business but he was persistent and determined. Having to do so much work on his own forced him to absorb the material thoroughly and put his own stamp on it.

After transcribing *Totem and Taboo* into his first notebook, Lye made new links by copying many pages of *Gaudier-Brzeska*, particularly its advocacy of tribal art which was still his primary interest. Although he was passionately interested in all forms of modern art, the examples he chose to copy tended to be those that bore a strong resemblance to tribal images (such as a Léger imitation of African art or a head by Pansaers that reminded him of a carving from the Bismarck Archipelago). For tribal art Lye's favourite hunting-ground was the Australian Museum. He devoted special attention to Papuan masks, and also to Aboriginal shields such as those from north-east Queensland: 'I liked the small nibbling grooves in the wood. I thought those ten-by-four inch small oval shields were the best abstract carvings anywhere, though the African sculptors were more "all around" in the arts.'[29] He drew these objects with pencil, Indian ink, and sometimes watercolour (to record 'the beautiful colour of the Aboriginals'). Though his painstaking approach reflected his deep respect for the carvings,[30] there was a discrepancy between their non-Western aesthetics and the way Lye drew them — like an art student copying classic Greek statues, using shading and perspective to achieve a three-dimensional look. Lye's draughtsmanship at least provided him with a detailed record of the objects for later study. But as he moved through his notebooks his style loosened up; he used bolder lines and became more interested in abstract patterns.

In *Gaudier-Brzeska* Pound had quoted with approval De Quincey's remark that a miracle 'can be wrought if only one man feels a thing more keenly, knows it more intimately than anyone has known or felt it before'.[31] Lye's goal was similar: 'All I wanted to maintain was complete and utter pre-occupation with the aesthetic feeling [of] the primitive brain.'[32] As Pound had praised Gaudier-Brzeska's ability to understand Chinese ideograms by pure intuition, Lye tried to make sense of tribal objects before reading any commentaries. Though he was interested in what the ethnographers wrote, he wanted above all to develop his gut response. He was still practising his bedtime exercise which he described as 'going to sleep on the feeling of a particular work, listening to how it looked'.[33]

He wrote:

> I used to put colour sketches just copied
> from Abo. shields in Sydney museums
> under my pillow every night
> to soak up their zimmer . . .
> an early morning pillow coma
> got from all night steeping
> in Negro Bushman Ocean Island Australian Aboriginal art
> to whirl them on a boomerang
> and get their feeling back like that[34]

Wasn't Lye — who had quarrelled with advertising agencies over their lack of originality — becoming merely an imitator of tribal art? 'I got to the point where I was rather shamed by it, for myself. I was bloody well copying . . . ! But when these guys, you know, like Cézanne, and everybody, copy Old Masters, I thought, well, who the hell am I to worry about it?'[35] Lye was certain that once he had paid his dues — once he had absorbed the aesthetics of the tribal 'Old Masters' — he would at last be 'capable of inventing authentic new primitive stuff'. But sometimes, with a young artist's impatience, he was deeply frustrated by the slow speed at which he was developing. He thought of Gaudier-Brzeska producing so much important work before his death at 24. Lye could only hope his preparation would pay off in the end. Despite his personal isolation, he was not the only artist working along these lines. Young artists in Europe were also looking for unique ways to combine tribal art with modern art, and they were starting to add Freudian ideas to the mix. What gave Lye's work the potential for distinctiveness was his singular personality, his engagement with forms of indigenous art from his own region of the world, and his interest in movement — an interest that was about to surge strongly back into his art.

eight kinetic theatre

Lye was impressed enough by Freud's idea of the unconscious to write in his sketchbook at the end of the *Gaudier-Brzeska* transcription: 'Since then Psycho-Analysts have shown a new path to follow.' He now pursued other books on the subject, hoping particularly to find discussion of art. He was excited to come across *Expressionism in Art* by Dr Oskar Pfister,[1] a book recently published in London, which included the detailed case study of an unnamed French modern painter with an interest in African art. As part of the analysis the artist made automatic drawings, giving free rein to unconscious impulses. Lye copied one drawing — a vision of the artist's wife — into his sketchbook and also recorded the artist's long sequence of verbal associations. He began using Pfister's term 'expressionism' to describe any art that rejected naturalism and projected inner feelings outwards. Ultimately there was something unsatisfactory about Pfister's attitude to modern art and primitive art but the book was important for Lye in introducing him to the idea of automatic drawing and providing some striking examples (such as the picture 'Birds and Fishes', a tangle of organic forms by 'an hysterical lady'). He was also fascinated by the psychoanalytical method of free association which in this case involved a weaving of myth-like stories around abstract images.

Even more astonishing was the recently published *Psychopathology* by Edwin J. Kempf, MD, a clinical psychiatrist at St Elizabeth's Hospital in Washington, DC (the hospital to which Ezra Pound would later be committed). Kempf's book included a detailed case study of a Negro 'paranoiac' who believed that God had directed him to build 'the first church' of 'perpetual motion'. Worshipping God as the primal force that made the world move, he built a shrine about five feet high using pine boards, pieces of boxes, a broomstick, ropes, a metal container, and a number of cast-off spiral springs.[2] A sense of perpetual motion was created by the springs which allowed parts of the machine to continue rocking for a long time after receiving an initial push. The broomstick was kept spinning by a rope winding and unwinding, and there were pieces of a colourful barber's pole turned by levers. The maker of this construction sent photographs to a news-paper and attempted to have his design patented. Kempf could see that the object might be regarded as a work of art, but he preferred to see it in Freudian terms as a phallic symbol. Jerking up and down and bouncing around, this symbol of perpetual motion was the patient's compensation for his own impotence, and his religious talk was an attempt to conceal the sexuality in an atmosphere of archaic mystery.[3] Lye couldn't have cared less about Kempf's diagnosis. The excitement for him was the pulley-belt construction — 'it twonged *Totem and Taboo* out of the window!'[4] Having never lost his interest in motion he had been trying to link it more strongly with tribal art by looking for descriptions of dances and rituals. He had also studied the body language and implied activity in carved figures but they stayed at one remove from literal movement. Now here was a work that moved. The construction made perfect sense to him as a modern kinetic version of the sexual fetishes and fertility charms of tribal art.

In Lye's words: 'I did not pull the page with the reproduction out to stick under my pillow so instead I made my own pulley-belt construction.'[5] His work was very different in character. Although it has not survived, we can gain an impression of it from various descriptions. Lye took an old fruit case, turned it on its side, made holes in the back and inserted shafts. At the back of the box he attached these shafts to wheels with pulley belts then added a handle from a hand-wound phonograph. By turning the handle he could make all the shafts rotate. Finally he attached various shapes to the shafts, experimenting with a mixture of abstract patterns and forms derived from Aboriginal art — 'a new moon', 'circles or comma-shaped things or squares', 'dots and strokes', 'the letter S', a 'figure 8', boomerang shapes, and copies of some of his favourite Aboriginal shields with their coloured patterns.[6] He built this machine 'purely for motion's sake, just to see what would happen if I tried to control the relationships between form and movement'.[7] By using bigger or smaller pulley-wheels he could give different rotation speeds to the various shapes. Lye had a highly developed sense of movement but he was certainly no engineer and it took him a great deal of practice to get the hang of it.[8] Also, since it was necessary for him to stand at the back to turn the handles, he had to place a mirror in front to view the results.

Lye was frustrated by the limitations of his kinetic theatre but it gave him a taste of what it would mean to compose motion. Primitive as the mechanism was, he made it only a few years after the first examples of kinetic sculpture in Europe. In Moscow in 1920 Naum Gabo had used an electric doorbell to set a thin steel rod vibrating. (With his brother Antoine Pevsner he wrote: 'We renounce the thousand-year-old delusion . . . that held the static rhythms as the only elements of the plastic and pictorial arts. We affirm in these arts a new element, the kinetic rhythms, as the basic forms of our perception of real time.')[9] In the same year Marcel Duchamp made 'Rotary Glass' and Man Ray made 'Spiral'. There had also been a handful of experiments with colour machines of the spinning-disc type, including one in Sydney. These experiments had received little publicity and Lye was not aware of them.

Soon after this he had another big idea, inspired by *Pearls and Savages*, Frank Hurley's feature-length documentary film about the so-called 'Stone Age' Papuans. At a time when 'tribal dancing and the living conditions of primitive society had only been seen in the remoteness of the still picture', Hurley's film made a huge impression on audiences, especially in Australia.[10] The film offered exotic images of Papuan life, including masks, dances, and body painting. In the words of Frances Calvert, 'Hurley was a real showman. He would show a bit of film, then he would lecture, often about how the adventure was very dangerous, and then show lantern slides and artefacts that he had brought back. . . . He would also play wax cylinders that he had recorded in Torres Strait. It was a real multi-media type thing.'[11] After his successful first screenings in 1921 Hurley returned to Papua to shoot more footage, and Lye saw an expanded version entitled *With the Headhunters in Papua* around October 1923.[12] Although Hurley commented that 'The simple happy life of these carefree children of nature holds much that civilization has lost', his basic attitude to these Papuans was very condescending. The film claimed to be ethnology but Hurley's real interest was commercial success.[13] Lye was not impressed by Hurley's opinions about 'fuzzy-wuzzies' but he was astonished by the immediacy with which a film could represent the Papuans whose art he had been studying: 'Here were the guys that I'd really paid homage to, you know, dancing and strutting around.'[14] To many viewers the film would simply have offered an evening of exotic adventure, framed by the civilised values of its explorer-commentator, but to Lye it provided news from the front lines, information about his heroes, and a few vivid glimpses of their art.

He had often gone to the cinema for entertainment, but conventional films had so little relevance to his specialised interests that he had never taken them seriously. And he had never heard of experimental films. (German film-makers had begun making abstract animated films in 1921, screened to small audiences in Europe, but no examples had reached New Zealand or Australia.) Hurley was a fairly conventional film-maker but he had an eye for composition and an interest in movement. There were point-of-view sequences from a canoe and from an aeroplane in motion, and lively dance sequences in which the dancers had elaborately painted faces and wore feather head-dresses, some of them extraordinarily tall. Other scenes showed men spinning a stick to start a fire and playing with large spinning toys, keeping them on the move by rhythmic hand-gestures. It struck Lye that film might be just the technology he needed: 'If you could learn about film, you could control motion with more than just turning a shaft by your hand.' It was also a revelation for Lye that a film could make dramatic use of colour. There was no colour film stock on the market yet, but some details of Hurley's film had been hand-coloured by Pathé in Paris.[15]

And so Lye went looking for a film-making job. He found one at Filmads Ltd at 17 Bond Street, one of the few local companies that produced animated advert-isements. Their ads for products such as cigarettes and beeswax screened in cinemas all over Australia.[16] Filmads also produced a monthly film magazine, *Picture Show*, which ran stories about popular feature films and stars and pub-licised the company ('Let Us Prepare A Scenario For You — This Entails No Obligation Whatever'). Lye found the Filmads staff 'a great gang of people', supervised by Garnet Agnew who also drew cartoons for the *Bulletin*. There was not much connection between these banal commercials and the qualities that had attracted him to film-making, but he was familiar with the advertising world. He understood visual narrative from comic strips and he remembered being intro-duced to it as a child: 'I had this cousin who used to babysit and she got me onto sequential sketches, through telling little stories in sequential drawings.'[17] From the Filmads animators Lye learned how to apply similar methods to the film medium and in the process he discovered film editing ('I suddenly realized that films had cuts and sequences').[18]

Because he was a new member of the staff he did not have the opportunity to make finished drawings, but he experimented in his spare time by composing 'many motion sketches which simulated sequential abstract action by flipping pages of a sketch book'.[19] He also became interested in the scratches and other accidental marks that he saw on leaders (the pieces of film at the beginnings of reels). He was so impressed by the way these marks wriggled that he made some 'fiddly scratches' of his own on a strip of film and stayed behind after work to project them.[20] He said later of this experiment: 'I got my first real intensity out onto something [i.e. film images] that could reflect it back, at least to me — and that was plenty because no one had the least idea of what I was up to. . . . [You should] try sometime the exhilaration of discovering your own motion imagery. I can still feel the effect of that moment in my heart muscles somewhere.'[21]

But Lye did not follow up his discovery at this time — 'I experimented but let it go, because there were a lot of other things I wanted to do.'[22] Not long after this he left the film company — he was having another attack of restlessness, being bored with advertising art which felt increasingly trivial compared with the art he was studying in libraries and museums. Lye had many dreams but which one should he pursue? Should he try to go to Europe to meet other modern artists? Or go where there were more opportunities for film-making? Or, following Hurley's example, head for some remote corner of the world? He was determined to travel but first felt he should make a brief return visit to Auckland to see his mother and brother.

nine samoa

Lye arrived back in Auckland in time to celebrate his brother's twenty-first birthday (9 May 1924). For the next few months he shared a room with Philip at the home of the Malloy family in Norfolk Street, Ponsonby, and obtained a job on the wharves so that he could save money while making up his mind what to do next. His mother was delighted to see him again but disappointed to learn he was still restless. During the weekends he would go with her to visit old friends, the Hemplemans, in Onehunga. Dorothy Hempleman remembered Rose as a woman with 'a very nice voice, very clear, and a great sense of humour'.[1] Rose and her son thought the world of each other but there were times when she lost patience with his casual style. Dorothy remembered an afternoon when Lye, who had arrived ahead of his mother, was 'sitting by the fire, cross-legged, smoking a pipe, with a pair of old white sandshoes on'. He was exchanging stories with Dorothy's fiancé, Stitch Hemming, who had just told a joke about a dog peeing on a power line and causing a short-circuit all through the city. 'Len had a great laugh. This joke really appealed to his sense of humour and he threw his head right back and laughed.' Rose who had just arrived took a hard look at her son lounging on the floor in old clothes and snapped: 'Well, Len, either you leave or I leave.' He got up and left without an argument.

Lye still showed no signs of settling down and was less interested than ever in seeking a middle-class career. He said bluntly that he preferred labouring jobs to commercial art. Rose who had worked as a cleaner for many years 'used to get on to him about his grubby habits, such as rolling Bull Durhams and dropping tobacco on the carpet'.[2] Lye dressed as a casual labourer, though he would always add an unusual cap or pipe or some other detail that would make him stylish in the eyes of his peers. Though many people felt there was something unusual about him, they did not jump to the fact that he was an artist. He almost never talked about art but worked at it quietly in his spare time, perusing books and magazines in the public library and making countless drawings. During his stay in Auckland he also made metal casts of his wooden hei-tiki, one of which ended up as a mascot on the bonnet of his brother's Austin car.[3]

On expeditions with his sketchbook to the Auckland Museum, Lye concentrated on Maori art. He was unaware of the striking similarity between his sketchbook and that of Paul Gauguin who had spent ten days in Auckland in 1895, making drawings of Maori carvings from the same collection (drawings that later served as source material for some of the canvases he painted in Tahiti).[4] Gauguin admired many forms of tribal art and was convinced intuitively that there were strong affinities between the different traditions. Lye had never seen an original painting by this artist, but on the basis of what he had read he numbered Gauguin among his heroes. Public interest in Gauguin had been boosted after 1919 by the publication of W. Somerset Maugham's popular novel *The Moon and Sixpence*.

Lye made a trip to Wellington where he studied the Maori collection of the Dominion Museum and was impressed by a book on Maori spiritual concepts by Elsdon Best, a member of the Museum staff.[5] Lye now realised that he needed to experience a tribal way of life directly so he 'could better appreciate how their artists felt about their environments'.[6] One way to proceed would have been to make contact with a traditional Maori community (such as the Tuhoe), but Lye felt a restless desire to go overseas. He dreamed of visiting a remote area of Papua or Africa but he did not have the money. What he could afford was a ticket to the islands of the South Pacific. There were boats leaving regularly from Auckland, and in the islands it was possible he might find somewhere off the tourist track that would be 'a wonderful place to work at art'. At the least it would be an interesting place to live while he sorted out his plans.[7] So he went to the Thomas Cook travel agency and signed up for one of their Cook's Tours of the Pacific Islands. He also organised a job for himself so that he could stay in Samoa if he liked the feel of the place. Burns Philp, one of the largest traders in the islands, had its headquarters in Auckland, and Lye with his usual confidence found his way to the manager, showed him samples of his commercial art, and talked him into organising a job for him in Apia as a window-dresser and ticket-writer.

The Pacific Islands had not yet become a common tourist destination but already a great deal of romantic mythology was associated with them. There was a continuing demand for the books of Robert Louis Stevenson who had spent his final years in Samoa as Tusitala, Teller of Tales. Travel writers such as Alva Carothers spoke of the Pacific in such terms as these: 'Stevenson, searching for home, health and happiness, explored the South Seas and at last came to the Samoan islands — far flung, mystic, delectable — ringed with cocoanut palms that fringe brilliant green lagoons — lined with corals that flash colored fires strangely alive — inhabited by a charming, childlike people. There Stevenson made his abode and these islands became for him, "Isles of Paradise".'[8] Lye was contemptuous of phrases such as 'child-like people', believing that in some respects the Samoans had a more mature culture than their white colonial masters. But though he was not expecting to find anything utopian, he was not completely immune to the European mythology. He sometimes poked fun at his own mixture of motives: 'In a burst of romanticism I went off to live forever in Polynesia!'[9]

Lye's tour included Fiji, the Cook Islands, Tonga, and Samoa, with a stay of several days in each place. He wrote: 'I remember waking up and realizing the ship's in port because there's no engine noise, and bam, framed in my porthole is the epitome of everything unbelievably beautiful about South Seas islands with languid coconut palms arching out over a curving beach edging a glass clear sea.'[10] At each island: 'When the others went off in their white outfits and [pith] helmets, and took their cameras and stuff, I just put on an old T-shirt and khaki trousers and just ambled on over to the locals who were working on the wharf.'[11] 'Most of the local wharfies could speak a bit of English and I'd tell the most likely looking chap that while I was here I wanted to know how it felt to live here, and that if he knew anyone who was going fishing, fixing a garden, building or anything, and could use me, alright.'[12] Alternatively 'I would say to him, "Look, how about if I brought your family a present, you could fix it so I was invited for a meal. I want to eat some of this stuff you've got here, not all that junk they're giving me on the ship".'[13]

'We berthed at Tonga and the young wharfie I spoke to said, "Alright, meet me after four here with a bike." I went into town and hired a bike and we rode out together. He must have gone home at lunch time because his family in a Tongan village by the sea were all prepared for us. We had fancy Tongan drinks, a lot of laughing, singing, and a few dancing lessons, and I was asked to stay the night. The next day I was shown around and helped with the gardening and did a bit of fishing out in a dinghy, saw how they cut wood blocks to print tapa, and so on.'[14] Lye also went into town and asked the local traders if they had any jobs. He received a couple of offers but decided to move on to Samoa.[15]

The Samoan islands were of volcanic origin, mountainous, with unusual rock formations, rivers, waterfalls and rich vegetation. Control of the islands was divided between the United States (which administered the area known as American Samoa) and New Zealand (which administered the area that today forms the independent state of Samoa). Lye landed in Apia on the island of Upolu, capital of the New Zealand 'mandated territory'. He liked the look of the place and as he came to know the local people he was impressed by their ability to hang on to Samoan traditions. They were receptive to European culture but were not going to let themselves be pushed around by arrogant administrators who took little interest in *fa'a Samoa* (Samoan custom). This was the New Zealand government's first experiment in running a colony and in 1918 it made its first disastrous mistake when it neglected to quarantine a ship suspected of carrying influenza. The new illness wiped out one-fifth of the native population. In contrast American Samoa was successful in isolating itself from the epidemic. Nonetheless New Zealand had its mandate confirmed the following year by the Treaty of Versailles. George Spafford Richardson, the English-born military man who became Administrator in February 1923, tended in his enthusiasm for Western progress to regard the Samoans as children who needed firm parental guidance. At this time many Samoan villages remained basically unchanged despite more than a century of European contact.[16] Few among the 35,000 Samoans spoke English and few *palagi* (people of European descent) spoke Samoan.[17] The job Lye had arranged was at Chisholm's store in Apia, the trading centre where white merchants lived in white cottages with well-kept lawns.[18] But even here the European atmosphere was transformed by the lush tropical vegetation — large hibiscus bushes, banana trees, coconut trees, and flowers of many kinds. Lye was put to work selling over the counter with little chance to use his window-dressing talents. With two other young staff members he lived in 'comfortable digs above the store and had a Chinese cook and valet',[19] but this was not what he had come to Samoa for.

'As soon as the Samoan young people came into Chisholm's, their feet hit this wooden smooth floor, and immediately they started just skating on the wood with their bare feet, and I was just enjoying this sensuous business because I was a body guy.' One of the young men working in the store was a Samoan named Solavao (or Sola i le Vao) Tauai, whose father was chief of a village about 20 miles out of Apia.[20] When they became friends Lye told him of his desire 'to get the hang of Samoan life in a village'.[21] A month later, when Solavao left Apia, he invited Lye to come to join his household. He lived not with his father but in a village on the edge of Mt Vaea, the 1150-foot mountain behind Apia. While Lye was not moving far in terms of physical distance, he was making a big cultural shift, from a European to a Samoan style of life. He joined his friend and his wife and son in one of the thirteen *fale* (Samoan houses) that made up the village.[22] In Lye's words: '*Fale* consist of a wonderful oval-shaped roof supported by good-shaped upright poles. The Samoans have mats they arrange in venetian-shutter style between the roof's upright poles, that you let down all around the oval *fale* if you want lamplight, seclusion, and/or friends. You sleep on the softest closely-woven panama-weaved mats you ever slept on. They sleep firm yet feel soft with give. The floor is made of deep-set gravel and you put circles of coffee-table-sized mats around to sit and eat and drink *kava* and talk. The trouble was that you never quit dreaming when you were alone in such a lush place. You could look out and see the way the palms look clean-stark, with sugarcane and taros doing a moonlight-in-the-sunshine.'[23]

The inhabitants of the village lived a communal life with a shared plot of vegetables, pigs, and chickens. They rarely required money and only took it when there was an immediate requirement such as a shirt. When they built Lye a hut of his own, the most they would take for it was five pounds. However, he discovered that there was a complex etiquette in terms of returning gifts. 'If you wanted something you gave the person a present.'[24] In social situations such as visiting Solavao's father, Lye had to operate by intuition: 'I didn't know any of the customs . . . and there were a lot of right things to do. But without being told, you could sense it. It's like a poker game — you get great satisfaction out of just sensing the right thing, the right move.'[25] He enjoyed the village activities as an extension of many of the things he had grown up doing in New Zealand: 'We swam, danced, sang, feasted, built *fale* or repaired them after a storm, got copra, gardened, and fished galore.' He was taught how to manage an outrigger canoe and took part in night-time fishing expeditions. His only problem was his difficulty with the language. As a Maori girlfriend had pointed out to him years earlier, he was hopeless at learning a second language.

Lye was very impressed with the Samoan wrap-around garment, the *lavalava*, and it became his regular costume. He learned 'to tie it so that it wouldn't come off when running, swimming, or sleep-walking'.[26] His friends encouraged him to have a Samoan tattoo or *pe'a* which extended from the small of the back to below the knee. In his words: 'They wanted to blood-brother me further by tattooing me from arse to breakfast, to signify full Samoan citizenship, I declined, asking myself who was I kidding, that it would all be by name and dye alone.'[27] At the same time he was determined to keep his distance from the local Europeans and was angry at the way missionaries were destroying the local culture by imposing their own values.[28] The European style of life was symbolised for him by Vailima, the large mansion built by Robert Louis Stevenson in 1890, where the great man from Edinburgh had once 'garbed his princely retainers in *lavalavas* made of the Stewart Tartan'.[29] This mansion was now the home of the New Zealand governor. When Lye climbed Mt Vaea to see Stevenson's white stone memorial, he was not impressed: 'I thought how much better Australian Aboriginal coloured burial posts are.'[30]

Lye happened to be in Samoa around the same time as the American filmmaker Robert Flaherty, who was living with his family on the island of Savaii

making the feature-length documentary *Moana*, and the American anthropologist Margaret Mead, who was in American Samoa doing fieldwork for her book
Coming of Age in Samoa. Both Flaherty and Mead would be criticised in later years
for having come to Samoa with romantic preconceptions. Their approach was different from and arguably more sophisticated than previous myth-makers', and
Flaherty was to disappoint his Hollywood investors who expected him to take a
more exotic and dramatic approach; but there was still a tendency for them to use
Samoa as a screen on which to project some of the dreams and concerns of their
own culture.[31] Though Lye did not hear about Mead, he did meet Robert Flaherty
and his brother David in Chisholm's when he was working there. By not mention-
ing his interest in films or visiting their location on Savaii, he missed an opportunity to learn from a noted director and cameraman. He saw David Flaherty on
one other occasion, in conversation with a German trader Lye had come to see.
When David took out a cigarette: 'I offered him a match but he took no notice of
me, and just got out his own, and left me hanging there. I felt rather stupid and I
left after that. I thought, I can take a hint, you've got business to talk with this guy,
O.K.'[32] Lye made no further attempt to contact the Flahertys.

Lye had needed to be self-sufficient in developing his artistic interests, but
sometimes his stubborn independence and refusal to compromise were so
extreme that he passed up valuable opportunities. His almost perverse decision to
keep his distance from the Flahertys was an example. He had decided that *Moana*
was bound to be 'a lot of crap', a trivial outsider's view. That was his usual
(though not always consistent) attitude in Samoa: 'I didn't want any part of the
whites.'[33] Later when he saw the film it was better than he had expected and he
felt a twinge of regret. Self-sufficiency had become such an important value for
him that he was sometimes too quick to turn his back on potential allies.

ten deportation

The Natives are loyal, happy and contented; they are
proud to be associated with the British Empire....
Here in Samoa is a splendid but backward Native race.

Major-General George S. Richardson, 1913[1]

In his first year and a half as Administrator Richardson had alienated many people, European residents as well as Samoans. He saw himself as bringing Samoa the benefits of Western civilisation in such fields as medical care and hygiene, but his paternalistic and bureaucratic approach ignored the subtleties of the Samoan way of life. He was determined to replace communal ownership by private property and to reform the sexual behaviour of the Samoans by enforcing the Christian conception of marriage, but such policies were having complex effects he had not anticipated. On Savaii the Flahertys were amazed to observe Richardson's bizarre strategies such as sending his public works engineer ahead of him to create the impression that he was planning to build a new bridge, which ensured that the chiefs prepared a great reception for his arrival. He brought a movie projector on his visits so he could screen a war-time newsreel which showed him acting as a guide to the New Zealand Prime Minister visiting the trenches in France. The interpreter would call on the Samoans to applaud whenever Richardson appeared on screen.[2]

In Lye's village there were numerous jokes about Richardson as a wowser, for he had continued to enforce the total ban on alcohol introduced by one of his predecessors. Lye's Samoan friends found a chemist in Apia willing to sell them yeast and other ingredients for a home brew called *fa'amafu*: 'We had to bury it in cans to keep it hidden. It was the fastest fur-growing stuff for your tongue I've ever tasted, a very quick effect followed almost immediately by the most crushing of hangovers.'[3] Lye was also contemptuous of Richardson's puritanical attitude that sex had to mean marriage, but at the same time he had made a personal decision not to 'get trapped into family stuff' with any of the young women that Solavao was trying to pair him up with. Despite his intention of keeping his distance from the *palagi* he became involved with 'a romantic red head in Apia, the daughter of a physician in the Island Hospital'.[4] With her there was no risk because 'she could look after the contraceptives and stuff perfectly'.[5] However, the mere fact that Lye was living in a Samoan village was enough for other Europeans to assume that he was involved with Samoan women, and under Richardson's rules this was a serious offence.

In Lye's words: 'Richardson called me up and said, "You can't live with Samoans any more. We have an edict out. All Europeans with Samoans, out you go. Or else set up shop somewhere on your own with the whites. Too many half-castes around, and they're causing a lot of racial trouble."'[6] (The issue of 'half-castes' was an obsession with Richardson, who saw them as responsible for the political resistance to his government.) Lye replied: 'Sir, you're barking up several wrong trees. One, I'm not running round with Samoan girls, much as I'd love to. Two, I've got people to back up the statement that I am here with a definite study project: Samoan design. And I can give you the names of anthropologists.'[7] He invited Richardson to 'come round and see my sketches of Samoan art some time'.[8] The Administrator was furious and warned Lye that he was likely to be deported. Deportation and exile were the Administrator's favourite tactics, and Lye was (in the later words of Monica Flaherty) 'a type of person who would *really* have ruffled up dear old Richardson'.[9]

This encounter left Lye pondering how much time and energy he was prepared to spend fighting against deportation. He enjoyed the Samoan way of life but had stopped feeling any compulsion to make art, the activity that had previously been central to his life.[10] 'Gauguin and others have managed it but I was too young to sit around introspectively while there were so many marvellous things going on around me all the time.'[11] As the months passed he became worried about his 'gap of nothing in the way of ideas'.[12] There was, however, truth in his claim to Richardson that he was studying Samoan design. Tapa cloth (as Lye described it) was 'made from pounding the bark of the mulberry tree. It had a creamy panama-straw colour with a soft tactile quality all its own.' For everyday wear tapa cloths were usually left plain because dyes stiffened them but for other uses there was a wide range of stylised patterns, applied by rubbing the cloth against a grooved, inked board (the *upeti*) or by painting designs freehand (which were often bold and brightly coloured).[13] Lye took notes and made sketches of the best *siapo* (tapa) patterns.[14] Despite their abstract appearance, many of the motifs had 'descriptive names drawn from the natural world, such as breadfruit leaves, pandanus leaves, pandanus bloom, fishnet, trochus shell, starfish, worm, centipede, and footprints of various birds'.[15] Such motifs were repeated with slight variations across the tapa cloth, creating visual rhythms.

Tapa design encouraged the shift that had already started in Lye's style away from modelling and shading towards images that were flatter, bolder, and more linear. He was also very interested in tapa designs from Fiji, Tonga, and Hawaii: 'I think the best tapa cloths are the early Hawaiian. They're knock-outs.'[16]

He was still studying the African art he had documented in his notebooks and one night he had a particularly vivid dream about it: 'I was in a village seeing a Negro friend. We were both artists and he was showing me how to use an adze.' They were making black wood sculptures and Lye was admiring the texture of the marks left by the adze. They talked of how traditional African art was in danger of dying out. Just then a war started between their village and the neighbouring one, and despite strenuous efforts Lye could not persuade his mentor to stay and continue carving. Suddenly a spear hit Lye and he yelled and woke up, only to discover that he had been stung in his sleep by a scorpion.[17]

At times he went up 'on a kind of oil rig submerged in the middle of a coconut plantation to sit with a notebook and try to think about art and life', but nothing much came of this.[18] He missed having access to good libraries. His only source of art news was *Time* magazine which he borrowed from Father Diehl, an American priest popular with the Samoans.[19] *Time*, which had begun publication in 1923, referred occasionally to modern artists though it did so with caution. In March 1924 *Time* said of Henri Matisse that his 'crude nudes and restless still-lifes have long been flaunted before a sceptical public'.[20] One early issue reported that 'A piece of machinery is to be exhibited as a work of art at the Spring Salon',[21] and another cited the Ukrainian artist Alexander Archipenko as an artist who 'experiments with bizarre media for sculpture — glass, wood, papier-maché and paint, polished sheet-iron reflecting surrounding men and things'. *Time* felt duty bound on this occasion to end by quoting a reviewer's comment that 'Only a fundamental degeneration could have produced [this sculpture], and it is an ominous sign when any sane human being finds it of interest',[22] but such stories were always music to Lye's ears. Indeed, the longer he stayed in Samoa the more hungry he felt for modern art. He decided that if Richardson were to deport him, he would try to head for one of the centres of modernism.

As he reviewed the possibilities in his mind, the one that excited him most was Moscow. He knew nothing of the Russian language, but neither had he known Samoan. *Time* in its enthusiastic comments on the Moscow Art Theatre's visit to New York in 1923 had said: 'It is a very trifling barrier that the Moscow players use their native tongue. The reality and expressiveness of the performance make broader meanings as clear as daylight.'[23] Since the 1917 Revolution, Russia had generally been viewed by other governments with fear and hostility.

This attitude was strongly represented in the pages of *Time*, but even *Time* admitted that unusual things were happening there in the arts. Lye was not worried about Communism — indeed, he had heard some of his bohemian friends in Sydney talk about it enthusiastically, and the community he was living in at the moment had little interest in private property. But what interested him about Russia was less the revolution in politics than the revolution in art that seemed to have accompanied it. Reading avant-garde material in Sydney he had been astonished by a report on the activities of Vsevolod Meyerhold, a founding member of the Moscow Art Theatre who now had his own company. Imbued with the spirit of Constructivism, the Meyerhold group designed costumes, sets, and stage movements as though their plays were modern paintings in motion. Their work celebrated the machine as the symbol of the future, and conceived of the actor in terms of 'biomechanics' as 'a rather wonderful engine composed of many engines'. 'The new problem of the theatre [was] how to get this engine in full motion.'[24] Meyerhold's solution was a robust, physical style of performance developed from such precedents as the Commedia dell'arte.

What sent Lye's enthusiasm into orbit was Lyubov Popova's set for Meyerhold's 1922 production of *The Magnanimous Cuckold*.[25] For this outrageous sexual farce, Popova created a large, machine-like construction which combined a propeller (representing a windmill) with steps, wheels, and ramps reminiscent of a children's playground. In her words: 'The movement of the doors and window, and the rotating of the wheels were introduced into the basic score of the action; [and] by their movement and speeds they were to underline and intensify the kinetic value of each movement of the action.'[26] In the course of the play the wheels and propeller whirled round with increasing speed to mark the accelerating emotional climaxes.[27] Lye saw the set as a giant piece of kinetic sculpture even more impressive than the work from St Elizabeth's. If he could get to Moscow he would surely find kindred spirits at Meyerhold's theatre. He liked the prospect of sampling life in a big city that was seething with political and artistic experiment, and while there were terrible shortages of food and supplies he was used to living rough. Language was again going to be a problem but Meyerhold's highly visual style of production made him hopeful he could communicate as a fellow artist.

By now Lye had become sufficiently skilled in the handling of a small outrigger to take it through the reef surrounding his island, out to the open sea. He would do this whenever he saw a big ship anchored off the reef.[28] 'I would go up and ask to see the mate. Or the captain. "What for?" "Well, I want to know if you need a hand — anybody jumped ship? — because I want to work my way to

Vladivostok." "What the *hell* do you want to go to Vladivostok for?" "Well, if you must know, I aim to cross over to Moscow. By the time I get to Moscow, I'll know a bit of the language". He would say: "Well, you're out of luck".'[29] When Lye realised he was not going to find a suitable boat, he decided to bargain with Richardson for a trip that would take him part of the way.[30] The Administrator was so eager to get rid of Lye that he offered a free passage to New Zealand. But to Lye this was a backwards step, and so there were more heated negotiations and finally he was offered a trip to Sydney. According to Lye, Richardson made sure that such a situation never arose again: 'From that time on, nobody was allowed to go to Samoa unless they had the fare to get back.'[31]

When Lye left Samoa around the beginning of 1925,[32] he had not been there long enough to develop a thorough inside knowledge of the culture but he had at least got beyond tourist stereotypes and the experience had made a deep and lasting impression on him.[33] His Samoan friends with their customary generosity gave him wonderful presents such as a large bouquet of flowers made of intricately woven coloured grasses and some inlaid tortoise-shell rings. He had to talk them out of giving him their finest block-printed and hand-painted tapa cloths.[34] From Apia he took a small ferry to Pago Pago and then got a free first-class passage on an American boat to Sydney.

The image of his departure that he would remember most vividly was seeing a Samoan about the same age as himself on the deck of the ferry. In Lye's words: 'I think to myself: I am leaving Samoa and he's going to another island. Wearing a tapa *lavalava* in the ancient voluminous style he finishes his banana-leaf-wrapped cigarette, and unwrapping his bundle of tapa he lets his head rest on deck and winds the tapa around himself and self-consciously cocoons himself down.' Around him were bags of scented cargo, such as the deep chocolaty smell of cocoa beans and the slightly rancid smell of copra. Under a full moon the whole scene began to settle into a design: 'The moon behind the sleeping Samoan is getting brighter, the sea colour fades out of my mind and is replaced with the colour of the wooden deck' — an intense moonlight glow he would remember always as like 'the creamy colour of tapa'.[35]

eleven jack ellitt

Having made few drawings in Samoa, Lye's first impulse when he got back to Australia was to concentrate on his art. But first, being short of money, he needed a well-paid labouring job. Then he could send some money back to his mother, have a spell of being a full-time artist and, ideally, have enough left for a boat ticket. Manual work was easy to find and by putting in the hours he could make more money than he could by commercial art. Also, such jobs did not leave him feeling compromised. Not that he had any illusions about the work — 'it was an utter waste of time' — but he did his best to duck the monotony by playing games to develop his sense of physical movement. He would swing his shovel 'in as clean a series of motions as possible'. Attempting to describe the accompanying sensations, he wrote: 'The shovel's clean blade bites into the sand and the friction between the blade and the grains of sand can be felt running up the wooden handle with a marked degree of tactile resonance, to be felt in reverse when the sand is slung from the shovel with a faint metallic "shrring". Even sticky clay which is worse than getting shit off a shovel is something one can rationalise into feeling some aesthetic in shovelling if, for example, one decides to keep the sides of the ditches one is digging as smooth as the cut sides of a piece of store cheese.'[1]

Lye worked as a quarry and building labourer, a carpenter's mate, a packer, a miner, and a rail-layer. His best-paid job was outside Sydney on a farm — a huge, ranch-like station near Cooley which ran sheep and cows and grew wheat.[2] When he first arrived at the farm, the owner was dismayed to discover how little he knew about farming. Fortunately for Lye, 'They're stuck with you way out there.' It was a long time since he had ridden a horse and he had to relearn rapidly since horses were basic to farming in those days before tractors. Here the only ones available were 'neurotic race horses no longer fit for racing'.[3] Lye survived a wild ride on a horse that bolted — 'the greatest arrow-in-flight sensation of smooth horizontal going yet known'[4] — and on another occasion he just managed to stop a runaway team of eight horses before they wrecked an expensive harvesting machine. As the tenderfoot on the farm Lye was assigned to the cooking — 'mainly frying and inventing things like putting lots of garlic with the bacon and eggs and cooking flapjacks when the bread ran out'.[5] From time to

time he helped with farming jobs such as fencing and milking cows. Then came
the wheat harvest, and Lye was fascinated by the sight of large fields of wheat
rippling in the wind — a kinetic landscape that chimed strongly with his
'passionate interest in movement'.[6]

Working outdoors Lye was fascinated by the sun, light, and landscape: 'Australia has the most unique landscape colours of all time for sunups and sundowns.
Back in the bush as the sparsely wooded country is called, all the shadows are
purple and violet and remain blue all day, not sharp violet colours but soft rich
pastels. On a four-day trip taking our great wagon-load of wheat drawn by eight
horses over the plains to a silo by a station we passed absolutely black and
absolutely red soils. The vegetation is like warm-hearted mesa with occasional
marvellous big yellow and black pinto lizards slooking off.'[7] Lye got to know a
farmhand called George who 'had some Aboriginal in him'. This was Lye's only
close contact with someone Aboriginal during his two visits to Australia. It may
seem strange that he did not make more effort to meet indigenous people but his
stay in Australia was confined to New South Wales, and — as one of his friends
put it — 'To see Aborigines in a tribal context Lye would have had to trek into
the interior. The few that we met around Sydney tended to have lost touch with
their tribal culture.'[8]

Lye left the farm with enough money to hang around the museums and
libraries for several months.[9] Back in Sydney he made a new friend — Jack Ellitt
— who became the first person with whom he could share all his artistic
interests. Ellitt's parents were Orthodox Jews who had emigrated from
Lithuania to England, and then when their son was 2 or 3, an uncle had persuaded them to move to Sydney. Ellitt's birth name was Abraham (Avrom) Isaac
(Yitzhak). He was called Jankel, which was changed to Jack, and his surname
was anglicised from Elitski to Ellitt. Even after shedding his Jewish names he
was still often the target of anti-Semitism. Ellitt developed an early interest in
composing music and won a scholarship to the New South Wales State Conservatorium of Music. He also supported himself by playing in the pit for musical
comedy shows. By his early twenties he was strongly involved in modern music
and art, an interest not appreciated by his parents who wanted him to become a
lawyer.

Ellitt knew bohemians such as Geoffrey Cumine and drank with them at a
pub near the Rocks. It was from Cumine and his friends that he first heard of
Lye. 'When someone mentioned Lye, they always spoke with respect.'[10] One day
Ellitt saw a tall young man, 'lean, wiry and hard,' sitting on the kerb outside the
pub sketching. He had 'an unlined face, calm steady eyes, and a completely

hairless skull'.[11] 'I looked over his shoulder to see what he was doing and he appeared to be drawing geometrical designs which I recognised as designs I'd seen on Mexican pots in the Sydney Museum. As he turned over the sheets of his pad I saw he was drawing another kind of design which looked very much like forms you'd see under a microscope — again, nothing related to the human figure or what we'd expect an artist to be drawing. When I asked him what it was about he had the greatest difficulty in explaining to me. He seemed to be struggling for words and somehow getting them all mixed up. But as I got to know him, after a couple of weeks, I found that he was far and away ahead of practically all the art people I was in contact with in Sydney. He was steeped in all the artistic activity going on on the Continent.'[12]

Ellitt came to admire Lye's independence, his deep commitment to art, and his freedom from any attitudes that were pretentious or merely fashionable. Ellitt, a person of equal seriousness, judged Lye to be a major talent and the guide he needed for his own study of modernism. At first he wondered if his friend's difficulties of expression involved some kind of 'aphasia or dyslexia' as Lye 'had no subject or predicate to his sentences, the tense was always mixed up, the genders were mixed up. He knew what he wanted to say but he was beyond putting it into words at that time.' There was always a sense of space around him — he was part of the pub scene but drank sparingly and talked seldom. 'He appeared to be a real loner, although he mixed with all the people I knew and they liked him and respected him greatly. He was a good listener.'[13]

Ellitt, himself a loner, was the one person he opened up to. Their conversations were a little like the ones Lye used to have with his younger brother. Ellitt would 'try to say something sensible in reply, occasionally, so as to keep him talking. I think I may have helped Len to become more articulate by all the practice I gave him.' But often Lye would stop abruptly and say 'It's all just talk!' and go back to his silence.[14] When he did discuss artists he expressed 'great admiration particularly for the drop-out types — people like Gaudier-Brzeska, Van Gogh, Gauguin, and Brancusi — artists who had broken away and were working on their own line. He was thoroughly determined that sooner or later he would get into the middle of this. Sydney was a backwater at the time. He decided he must get out and go to London, go to France, go anywhere.'[15] A person who knew both men observed: 'When Len came to Sydney he was full of ideas but he was inarticulate. He needed interpreters. And Jack could interpret.'[16]

One interest they were not able to share was classical music. As a gifted student at the Conservatorium Ellitt became a member of its orchestra and was a soloist in its performance of Gustav Holst's *The Planets*, considered a daring modern work at the time. (Ellitt had studied the bassoon as well as the violin and piano, and in *The Planets* he played a contra-bassoon which had to be imported for the occasion.)[17] He was an admirer of Scriabin's mystic chords and colour symphonies, and worked hard at keeping in touch with contemporary music by writing away for scores and magazines. Lye on the other hand was rather tone-deaf. Ellitt would hear him whistle some music and would think how interesting and modern it sounded, but then realise it was a merely a popular melody Lye was mangling. When Ellitt played him a Bach fugue, his only comment was: 'Is that Oriental music?'[18]

Both men were good swimmers and made frequent visits to Bondi beach. Ellitt remembers that 'a lot of men would meet there and loll about, some of them naked (though it wasn't a homosexual scene), and they'd talk, really talk. People had time for it then. A lot of the talk was about politics — such as the recent Russian Revolution.'[19] Ellitt and Lye also spent many hours together in libraries where they would search for overseas art magazines. Lye gave his friend books by Engels, Freud, Jung, Adler, and Frazer (*The Golden Bough*). They visited art galleries but spent more time exploring the collections of the Australian Museum where (in Ellitt's words) 'We fossicked away among Mexican pots, African gods, cannibal totems, masks, carvings and shields.'[20]

In his own art Lye was still doing representational work, such as a 6-inch by 9-inch pencil drawing of his girlfriend Mary Brown (who took a memorable photograph of him laughing). In this example of what Lye described as his 'last draughtsmanship style',[21] Brown is evoked by a few bold lines without shading, in a style reminiscent of Matisse. More geometrical in approach is a linocut of a woman sitting on a chair. Not long after making these drawings Lye decided to abandon 'draughtsmanship' or 'white art' as he called it, and to 'quit drawing from life'. He now intended to concentrate on 'black art'.[22] The work that clinched matters for him was 'a Negro figure' which he came across in the September 1923 issue of the *Dial* — a carving in black wood from Gabon (West Central Africa) showing a standing woman naked except for some bracelets.[23] Describing the figure in 1926, Paul Guillaume and Thomas Munro spoke of its bold visual rhythms: 'The spaces between the arms and body are eloquent; they alternate rhythmically with the masses, and contribute . . . a rangy, dynamic quality in keeping with the abrupt and irregular movement of the contours'.[24] Lye tore the page out of the magazine, pasted it into his sketchbook, and talked of the carving as one of the touchstones of art.[25] Another African carving that Lye copied into his sketchbook was a four-legged structure representing a woman with a sharp mask-like face and large breasts, described as a 'Maternity

Goddess'. This was a form of head-dress used in dances of the Simo secret society of French Guinea.[26] Lye was now sketching such objects in a more vigorous style, investing the lines with a greater sense of speed and energy.

His interest in African carving gave him the desire to make three-dimensional objects of his own and he decided to pay a visit to the sculptor G. Rayner Hoff, an artist he had met at the pub, to get advice on tools. Seven years older than Lye, Hoff was the instructor in drawing and sculpture at the East Sydney Technical College. Recently returned from England, he was one of the best sculptors in Sydney. Though his approach was not particularly radical, his sculpture was still able to generate controversy.[27] Lye found him 'most kind and wise, so, instead of yarning away about art he occupied himself' by using his visitor as the model for a marble portrait head.[28] Hoff offered a piece of marble and sculpting tools in return.[29] Lye made an interesting model because of the clean lines and smooth oval shape of his head, emphasised by the scarcity of hair. (Lye sometimes shaved off the hair that still grew.) The final sculpture elongated the head's oval, balanced on box-like shapes substituting for a neck. Lye's eyes looked almost closed and his lips carried the faint suggestion of a smile. In 1927 this serene image won the Wynne Art Prize, a major Australian art award administered by the Art Gallery of New South Wales, and the gallery added it to its permanent collection.

In the backyard of the house where he rented a room Lye started carving the piece of marble he had been given, working directly on the marble in contrast to Hoff's method of starting with a clay model. In this carving a man and woman, simplified to a few geometrical shapes, grasped each other so tightly that they formed a single 'Unit' (the title of the work). The heads and shoulders of the couple formed a semi-circle. Lye's design was influenced by Brancusi's 1908 stone carving 'The Kiss' which showed a couple from the waist up with their arms round each other, their bodies pared down to a few lines. This sculpture was itself a reaction to earlier and more realistic versions of the same motif such as Auguste Rodin's 1886 carving 'The Kiss'.[30] Lye felt that he in turn was going a step beyond Brancusi because his sculpture was more abstract and more vigorous: 'Whereas I portray a tight-like-that embrace, Brancusi portrays his embrace in a utopian "babes-in-the-wood" hold-me-tight manner.'[31]

'Unit' had another point of departure — a Maori carving that Lye had once seen on the gable of a Maori pa which showed 'the female astride the male's thighs'.[32] He had no hesitation in bringing together tribal art, the modern art influenced by it (such as Brancusi's), and machine imagery (such as the 'perpetual motion machine' from St Elizabeth's which had been also based on interlocking

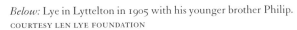

Left: Lye's mother and father, Rose Ann (Cole) and Harry Lye.
COURTESY LEN LYE FOUNDATION

Below: Lye in Lyttelton in 1905 with his younger brother Philip.
COURTESY LEN LYE FOUNDATION

Above: A portrait of the Lye brothers (Len at left) taken at the Electric Studio in Wellington in 1918.
COURTESY LEN LYE FOUNDATION

Top left: The Cape Campbell lighthouse and the houses where the keepers lived with their families.
PHOTO: RYKENBERG PHOTOGRAPHY

Bottom left: Lye in 1904 around the time of his father's death. He was staying with the Bourke family and is shown with his cousin Alice Bourke. COURTESY LEN LYE FOUNDATION

Above: Harry Linley Richardson (at left) teaching
an outdoor art class in 1915, three years before Lye became one
of his students. COURTESY ENID RICHARDSON

Above left and left: Two early drawings by Lye —
'Old Jim' and a portrait of Lye's girlfriend Edna Dixon.
COURTESY LEN LYE FOUNDATION

Below: These drawings of waves (from the 1960s)
are examples of Lye's lifetime habit of sketching and analysing
'figures of motion'. (His earliest experiments,
circa 1920, have been lost.) COURTESY LEN LYE FOUNDATION

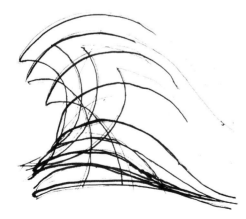

Two Maori carvings and a Maori rafter pattern (*kowhaiwhai*) sketched by Lye
at the Dominion Museum in Wellington. COURTESY LEN LYE FOUNDATION

A page from Lye's 'Totem and Taboo' notebook, circa 1924. He was making stylistic comparisons by juxtaposing the large figure (a Maori carving he sketched in the Auckland Museum) with an African carving (top left), another Maori carving (bottom left) and a drawing by the contemporary Russian artist Mikhail Larionov.

MANGAIA

HERVEY

(Gaudier-B head = ⊙)

Hervey Is.

PAPUA ?
ADMIRALTY. IS.

HERVEY ISLANDS

Pelgian Congo

Another page from the 'Totem and Taboo' notebook, comparing design motifs from different parts of the world.
Lye has added to the comparison a stylised head by Henri Gaudier-Brzeska. COURTESY LEN LYE FOUNDATION

pattern similar in diagonally opposite squares; when owing to irregularity of squares or misplaced pattern then other dark accents added so as to full white space to best advantage
Samoan Siapo pattern

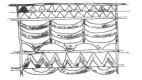

Left: Lye's Samoan friend Solavao (or Sola i le vao) and his wife.
COURTESY LEN LYE FOUNDATION

Bottom left: Lye's analysis of a Samoan *siapo* (tapa) pattern. (From a notebook.) COURTESY LEN LYE FOUNDATION

Below: Lye's best friend Jack Ellitt (right) is rehearsing with his bassoon teacher Norman Ingamells for the Australian premiere of Gustav Holst's *The Planets* in 1926. Ellitt's contra-bassoon had to be imported for the concert. COURTESY JACK & DORIS ELLITT

Lye in Sydney circa 1922. He sent this photo back to his friend Joe Davis from whom he had picked up one of his favourite sayings — the Yiddish 'Ish Ki Bibble' (or 'Ich gebibble'), meaning 'I should worry!' COURTESY JOE DAVIS

male and female symbols). He saw the traditional aesthetic of tribal art as perfectly capable of dealing with modern subject matter such as machines, which could be regarded as the totems or fetish objects of our time. The machine shapes in 'Unit' include the lovers' hands and arms represented as tools. The woman's hand is shaped differently from the man's, suggesting not only the grip of a spanner but also female genitals. Though 'Unit' is small (26 cm in length, 16 cm in height, and 10 cm in width), it is a powerful work with its unusual fusion of the human and the mechanical, and the vivid impression it conveys of sexual energy and the lovers' tight embrace. A couple making love in the dark could feel the shape of their bodies in this way.

Since developing an enthusiasm for kinetic sculpture and Russian stage sets, Lye had been thinking about mechanical forms as a new source of imagery. He made drawings for his sketchbook of a carburettor, a high tension insulator, a loudspeaker, a pump ram, drills and lathes and so on. He noted similarities of shape between machines and tribal objects — for example, he related the form of an armature coil to that of a 'New Ireland head'.[33] He speculated that the design of machines embodied 'the unconscious symbolisings as mooted by Freud to exist in all forms created by man'. Around this time many modern artists were using mechanical imagery, including the Russian Constructivists, Duchamp, and Picabia who depicted sex in terms of bizarre machinery. Pound had compared the 'enjoyment of machinery' by modern artists with the 'enjoyment of nature' by Renaissance artists.[34]

As Lye ran short of money, Jack Ellitt helped him to obtain a commission for a bookplate from Nigel Pearson (a bibliophile who had studied piano at the same time as Ellitt). On first glance the image seemed mechanical and abstract, but a closer look revealed the figure of a pianist with his hand poised over a keyboard. Curiously the bold lines and flat patterning of the bookplate were also reminiscent of Polynesian art. Pearson submitted the bookplate to a competition and it won first prize.

Now that Lye had done a spell of solid work, he was eager to move on to sample some 'world art hub'. He could not afford to travel as a passenger and jobs on ships were scarce. Then someone advised him to go down to the docks where sailors hung out to see if one of them was willing to do a deal. He took to drinking in sailors' pubs. One night he met Tom Harris, a stoker on the *Euripides*, a 22,000-ton White Star liner which was about to leave for London.[35] After a night of drinking the stoker admitted to Lye that he was about to jump ship and agreed to sell him his papers for five pounds. Lye had to leave the very next day without telling anyone. He hastily packed some examples of his art in a wooden case and on 27 September 1926 he reported to the *Euripides* under the assumed name of Tom Harris.

This was the last time he would see New Zealand or Australia for many years. He would write often to Rose and she would always be proud to hear of her son's activities but she made it a matter of pride never to pressure him to return home. For Lye, London was not as exciting a destination as Moscow, but at least it had been the home of Pound, Gaudier-Brzeska, Epstein, and other heroes. There was a certain irony in the fact that London had always been the traditional destination for New Zealanders — it seemed a destiny that even an artist as unconventional as Lye could not escape. Katherine Mansfield, Frances Hodgkins, and David Low were among the ambitious New Zealanders who had already emigrated. The next generation of New Zealand artists — such as Colin McCahon and Gordon Walters who were born eighteen years after Lye — would be the first to dig in and stay. Together with a new generation of writers such as Allen Curnow, Robin Hyde, and Frank Sargeson, they would take on the uphill task of creating a more dynamic local (Pakeha) culture. If Lye had still been living in New Zealand, he could have been part of this exciting period of culture-building, but in the preceding years he would have achieved little of what he hoped to achieve in film-making and the visual arts. The shift to Sydney had given him access to greater resources but he was still too far from the action. Though he was excited by the richness of Maori art and the other indigenous arts of Australia and the Pacific, he felt — in terms of his interest in modernism — very isolated.

When he went overseas, his personality retained the imprint of his years in New Zealand and Australia. His art continued to be influenced by the natural environment of sea and sun he had grown up with. His many outdoor activities such as sport, sailing, and labouring had helped to heighten the physical energy that is a striking feature of his work. In terms of influences the local conjunction of Maori, Pacific Island, and Aboriginal art gave a distinctive slant to his modernism. It is also relevant that life in New Zealand in the early years of the century had encouraged a 'certain republican equality of manners' (in Keith Sinclair's words) and an admiration for the resourceful person who could go it alone.[36] Lye had an anarchist streak and no fear of authority. He was used to surviving with style on little money. His tendency to distrust anything wordy or pretentious, and the down-to-earth style of his own intellectual approach, were right in line with New Zealand attitudes of the period. Most of these traits were also typical of Australian culture and some were equally at home in Samoa. They could also be related to Lye's working-class background and self-education.

Whatever their source, they gave Lye a different style from many of the artists, critics, patrons, and officials he would meet in the art world overseas.

But while Lye was clearly shaped by this antipodean context, in other respects he had created his own personality precisely in opposition to it — and that was an impressive achievement, to have transcended an insecure, needy childhood to become confident and self-sufficient — and again, to have escaped the limits of what was then a narrow, provincial culture by self-educating himself as a modernist. Overseas he would find comrades, fellow conspirators of modernism, émigrés or outsiders like himself, whose allegiance to the international art movement was stronger than any national ties.

part two individual happiness now

twelve stoker sculptor

The *Euripides* (part of a Scottish shipping line which named its boats after ancient Greek artists and intellectuals) was known as the longest ship in Australian waters and one of the heaviest. It carried nearly five hundred passengers. Below decks was a seaman known as Tom Harris trying to figure out the jargon of the stokers and what to do when bells rang. He had the job of a trimmer, which meant filling a wheelbarrow with coal and delivering it to the stokers. Lye figured out that each barrow-load of coal helped to carry the ship forward an eighth of an inch.[1] It was also the trimmer's responsibility to keep trim the pile of coal beside one of the stokers, and when the stoker had raked ashes and clinkers (the impurities in the coal which had not burned) out of the furnace, it was the trimmer's job to move them aside and hose them down. Lye was impressed by the rhythm of a stoker's movements. 'He is a romantic looking guy. With a neat side-step to keep his face from the glare of the furnace he clangs his shovel on its iron door with a leaning-to-the-bull motion to give it a shove shut.' The furnace had a 'primeval' interest but 'if you worked close you felt your face was a potato up for baking. The sting could be as fierce as having a huge cigarette-end stubbed out in your face.'[2]

As the ship headed from Australia to the Cape of Good Hope, the stokers and trimmers began cursing the poor quality of the coal, 'grey soft muck' from Germany that burned erratically — a desperate cost-cutting exercise by the Aberdeen (Thompson) Line which was going into receivership. Negotiations were now in progress with one of its shareholders, the White Star Line, whose previous ventures had included the *Titanic*. Soon the *Euripides* began falling behind schedule, and then the coal and some cargo shifted to the port side and gave the boat a dangerous list. The trimmers were ordered to speed up their work, and a long ramp was built so they could carry coal from the port side of the heap. Loaded barrows sometimes toppled off the planks and trimmers were seriously injured. Even veterans collapsed from the effects of heat and coal dust. Perhaps Harris had had a premonition of what lay ahead when he agreed to sell his ship's papers.

Although Lye had experienced a wide range of labouring jobs including mine work in Australia, he had never felt a sense of relief as powerful as when he finished a shift in the stokehold and came out into the fresh air.[3] Food for the crew on this Potemkin of a ship consisted (in Lye's words) of 'fibrous wood, pickled flannel, and various types of bilge-water'. Between shifts the trimmers and stokers spent almost all their time sleeping. Lye wrote later that the only moment of sentiment he got from the trip was an occasion when he woke early and began singing a popular song in his frog croak, unaware that anyone was listening. Then a voice said: 'Go on mate.' Lye felt that working on the *Euripides* helped him to understand what it meant to sing the blues. Most of the time all he could think about was the job, whose basic figure of motion he summed up in a gyroscope image — wobbling up and down the planks he felt like a heavy ball inside a lighter ball, with one ball trying constantly to act as a counterweight to the other. Alternatively he thought of his wheelbarrow as the balancing pole of a tightrope walker, though this balancing pole had a will of its own and could see-saw unexpectedly. One minute Lye would be pushing his barrow uphill against the force of gravity, the next he would be digging his heels into the planks to save himself from whizzing downhill and smashing into the side of the ship. Meanwhile the *Euripides* would be adding its own swivels and shudders to further confuse the footwork.[4]

Living among Cockney trimmers and stokers made Lye realise he had grown up with a stereotyped view of English people — 'even though my Irish mother had married one'. In the stokehold of the *Euripides* Lye saw that his English shipmates could work as hard as anyone he had ever met. Everyone felt enraged with the job and 'all the galley slaves helped one another'. Eventually the ship reached Durban, South Africa, where a number of the crew jumped ship. Lye stuck with the job because he was determined to get to England. On 24 November 1926, eight weeks after leaving Sydney, Tom Harris disembarked in London with a certificate of discharge describing him as 'very good' in terms of both ability and general conduct.[5] Lye had added fifty pounds to the seventy-five pounds he had set out with. He summed up the voyage with the comment that Hell must be a furnace where everyone had to shovel soft German coal.[6]

Having several small cases of sculpture in his possession, he was nervous about Customs because of a current court case in New York involving his hero Brancusi.[7] Works of art could enter the United States free of duty but Customs officials had seen 'Bird in Space' as suspiciously similar to a propeller blade or other industrial object. They refused to believe it was sculpture and imposed a commercial import tax.[8] Brancusi took the Customs Department to court and eventually won, but his case was still in progress when Lye arrived in London. Lye managed to persuade the driver of a horse and cart to smuggle him and his luggage through the wharf gates for five shillings. A policeman stopped the cart but the driver spun a plausible yarn and was allowed to continue. Beyond the gates Lye offered the driver extra money for a ride to Chelsea, which he had heard described as the suburb where artists lived. By 1926, however, Chelsea had been overrun by affluent dilettantes whose 'chief influence on art was to make the rents of studios rise so high that real artists could no longer afford them'.[9] Lye took a room there for a few days while he searched for something closer to his ideals: 'I had a crazy idea that there was a good shed somewhere that I could keep warm for somebody for the winter, and . . . by just leaning over my recumbent body [they could] pick up their shovel and go dig the garden and I would get up and help them, and they would find me a very useful kind of animal to have around.'[10] He looked up names in the telephone book, starting with the art critic Roger Fry and the sculptors Jacob Epstein and Frank Dobson. None of them was home, but Dobson's wife Cordelia suggested that he phone another sculptor, Elizabeth Muntz, who knew people with gardens.[11] Muntz referred him in turn to Eric Kennington who found Lye's personal story so intriguing that by the end of the telephone conversation he had invited him to come and work in his Hammersmith studio.[12] Kennington could not offer him accommodation, but in Eyot Gardens not far from the studio Lye was able to rent a toolshed just big enough 'to turn around and sleep in'.

Eric Kennington lived with his wife Celandine on Chiswick Mall, a street which ran along the Thames. At 38 he was thirteen years older than Lye, a talented portrait painter who had turned to sculpture in 1922 when commissioned to design a war memorial for the 24th Division with whom he had fought. His work was not avant-garde, but its departures from realism still created a stir in London. Kennington looked (according to a writer for the *Studio*) more like a farmer than an artist, with a cheerful, friendly manner and a strong suspicion of the official art world which he regarded as both pretentious and corrupt.[13] He was exceptionally helpful to Lye because the newcomer appealed to him — as he would appeal to other maverick intellectuals in London — as a natural artist, free of affectation. This 'stoker-sculptor'[14] with a working-class manner had appeared out of the blue with some extraordinary works of art — such as his sketchbooks, his hei-tiki, and his stone carving 'Unit' — in an idiom that was both primitive and avant-garde by London standards. Lye had lively anecdotes about living in New Zealand, Australia, and Samoa, countries remote from England. And he was exceptionally self-possessed, energetic, and clear about his priorities.

After their first meeting Eric Kennington 'took Len to town and gave him a grand dinner'. Then, to offer a sample of London's intellectual life, he took him to George Bernard Shaw's play *Pygmalion*.[15] As Kennington described the evening to a friend: 'Len lay back in his seat and whistled while the performance was in progress. I asked him "Don't you think this was worth coming to?" "No", said Len, "no, I don't" — so loud that all the pit could hear.'[16] Back at the studio Kennington asked Lye what he thought of the bust he had made of his friend T. E. Lawrence. Lye judged it 'serene'. But when pressed to comment further he excused himself on the grounds that personally he had given up art that bore 'any relation to life'.[17] Kennington was surprised and delighted by Lye's frankness. He at once reported his arrival to artist and writer friends in the neighbourhood: '[This man] has come from Australia with several very good ideas, worked out with great labour. And he has produced several very good things.'[18] And: 'He is completely unspoilt, a real savage. I don't think he will ever get corrupted. He will be the salvation of Chiswick!'[19]

Lye quickly became part of the local artistic community which included among others the painters John Aldridge and Nancy Nicholson and the writers Norman Cameron, A. P. Herbert, Laura Riding, and Robert Graves (who was married to Nicholson but in love with Riding). Lye formed a particularly close friendship with Riding and Graves: 'If they were going up town to get a good steak or something, or going up to Maidenhead to have a swim, or to Oxford or somewhere . . . they would make sure I came along.'[20] To some observers this stoker sculptor or cowboy from the colonies must have seemed an unlikely friend for such highly educated writers, but Riding and Graves were mavericks in their own way and admired the New Zealander for his freedom of spirit. Lye's total lack of interest in etiquette or class distinctions became legendary among his friends. When he was staying with Robert Graves and Nancy Nicholson in the country, for example, the group was invited to the local manor house to dine with its aristocratic owner. When he was shown to a chair at the dining table Lye said he felt like sitting on the floor. The butler was thrown into confusion but the lady was too well-bred to express surprise. Her eccentric guest was served his meal on the floor where he sat comfortably leaning against a wall listening to the conversation.[21] As an artist Lye's arrival in London was that of a 'vertical invader', to borrow a term John Berger has applied to artists such as Pablo Picasso who grew up in a provincial or working-class situation and then 'invaded' the large cities of Europe with ideas for radical change. An artist of this kind startled the audience like 'a primitive man, a barbarian appearing on the stage through the trapdoor'.[22] Lye, the confident invader, made a dramatic entrance and within a year was exhibiting with leading London artists.

To the painter Julian Trevelyan, Lye was 'like a man from Mars who saw everything from a very different viewpoint, and it was this that made him original'.[23] T. E. Lawrence was 'delighted by the common-clay directness and simplicity of Len Lye as an artist'.[24] To others he was — as Stan Brakhage put it — 'the wildest man in town'.[25] This is not to suggest that Lye's friends naively saw him as a noble savage, but the curiosity that greeted his arrival certainly owed something to his role as an exotic outsider. Lye even played up to this a little. The danger was that in future years people would expect him to continue playing the same part.

On the walls of his shed Lye stuck stills from the film *Moana*, which he had seen recently. Often he wore a Samoan *lavalava*. He shared one end of Kennington's nearby studio with a remarkable young woman sculptor named Kanty Cooper who had adopted the direct carving method. She had taken up sculpture after her paintings were ridiculed by a professor at the Slade who was in the habit of telling women students they should stick to sewing. She persuaded the Royal College of Art to allow her to study with the one person on its staff that interested her — Henry Moore. Influenced by African art, her sculpture was both bold and innovative. In 1927 she kept a diary which provides vivid glimpses of Lye's first year in Kennington's studio:

> He was working on a stone shape. He was introduced to me and came rushing across the studio to shake hands. Len dressed in a don't care way. His boots might have belonged to a farm labourer. He is good looking, but does not look at you when he is speaking to you. Later he said he must take his stone back to his room to consider it, and went off with it like a butcher with his tray of meat.[26]

> After Eric and his friends had gone, Len came back, asked if they had gone, and then started talking art. He spoke of the terrible academic art of Australia. Len asked me if I only did abstract sculpture. I said, 'No, not by any means, and when I do, I feel I'm working in the dark.' He said, 'Yes, so do I. It is all working in the dark.'[27]

> Len heard a woman visiting EK's studio ask 'Who did that abomination?' (looking at Len's work). He was very upset. The next day he would not speak to anyone. And then he started working like mad.[28]

> Len raged against art schools, asked why I continued to go to the Royal College. 'No one can help you because only you can know what you are doing.'[29]

Although Cooper's diary foregrounds Lye's serious side, she remembers his most typical gesture as throwing his head back and laughing exuberantly. When there was an intellectual discussion he tended to keep quiet and the talkers would forget he was there 'until at the end he would toss in a wry comment, pulling our legs!'[30]

thirteen batiks

Since Celandine Kennington operated a workshop for hand-printed fabrics, Footprints, in two boatsheds on the Thames next to her husband Eric's studio, Lye took the opportunity to produce a number of batiks. Some of his batiks were exhibited in galleries, others were sold or given to friends for use as scarves or shawls.[1] During the 1920s the batik method became fashionable in London, often using balloon-silk remaindered after the war.[2] Footprints was based on the William Morris principle of home crafts as an alternative to mass production and was located only a few hundred yards from Kelmscott House where Morris had lived and worked. Footprints had grown into a thriving business with a number of employees and two retail outlets.

Lye worked with pieces of silk or linen approximately 3 feet by 5 feet (a size that reminded him of the Samoan lavalava). His style of painting was now based on flattened forms, clear edges, and bright colours, features well suited to the batik method. Using German aniline dyes he learned to produce mouth-watering colour effects,[3] and his batiks soon developed a reputation for their distinctive colours as well as forms. Someone who knew nothing about the artist might have imagined that the images on these batiks were the work of an unfamiliar tribal culture. Such a tribe must have been in contact with a number of other South Pacific cultures since the work carried echoes of Maori, Aboriginal, Papuan, and other forms of art. This wide range of influences had been absorbed into an imagery that was highly evocative and difficult to pin down. Forms of the kind seen through a microscope appeared alongside forms seen through a telescope. Many of the forms appeared to be organic and alive, yet it was also possible to interpret them as machines — as though biological and mechanical processes were working side by side, or as though one could be understood in terms of the other. Even after many viewings the images retained their mystery. Lye wanted them to provide not so much a puzzle for the conscious mind as an ongoing stimulus for the subconscious.

The batik 'Polynesian Connection'[4] was on one level clearly about sex. What appeared at first to be a single creature was revealed as a couple locked in a tight embrace, with the lovers' bodies simplified down to a few straight lines, curves, and circles so that they looked something like a Cubist guitar or machine. This was clearly another version of the sexual embrace represented in 'Unit', which had its precedents in Brancusi's 'Kiss', in the kinetic sculpture from St Elizabeth's, and in the carving 'once seen on the gable of a Maori pa'.⁵ The earthy colours — red ochre and indigo — reinforced the Maori connection.⁶ Lye had composed the batik so that not only the two lovers but the two halves of the picture fitted together and balanced each other in shape and colour. Creating a strong sense of movement, there were creatures flying counter-clockwise around the couple, suggesting sperm, eggs, and blood.⁷ Anxiety was present as well as harmony. Did the zigzag shapes suggest *vagina dentata*? Could the lizard-like figure on the left be devouring its mate? Did the lovers represent the union of two races (for his figure was darker than hers), with results either creative or destructive? The strangeness of the details kept generating new questions and new answers. A picture so highly charged with sexual associations must have startled viewers when it was exhibited in the Beaux Arts Gallery in 1928. In the following year a London exhibition of D. H. Lawrence's paintings was closed by the police who wanted the canvases burned because they included genitals. That Lye's picture escaped the same fate was perhaps because its female genitals and erect penis were too stylised for the censors to recognise them.

In the brightly coloured picture now known as 'Land and Sea', a creature whose body consisted of concentric circles (or rather ovals), antennae, and various arms and legs was shooting a bolt of energy into the centre of a flower-like shape on the left. This flower (or 'cave' as Lye once described it) was surrounded by other circles which reinforced the idea of a target. With 'Polynesian Connection' in mind one might think of the energy as sexual making this an image of the male fertilising the female. But the picture had the power to spark off many other associations. One could imagine the flow of energy running both ways like an alternating current. Then there were the strange details of the creature on the right, floating above the surface of a lake (or an entire world) onto which it was pouring some kind of liquid. Whether such upheavals were sexual or geological, the picture buzzed with energy. Lye said he made it without any conscious symbolism except for a vague sense that he was dealing with some 'primeval stage in the earth's evolution'.⁸ The brilliant colours and bold style were well suited to the medium of batik.

A rocket motif turned up in the batik 'Abo Imp', combining the ancient with the modern and the natural with the mechanical.⁹ The subject was topical around 1926 because Robert Goddard had just demonstrated the world's first liquid fuel rocket. Lye translated this motif into a kind of tribal totem figure with the stars as eggs laid by the rocket as it flew along. There was a quirky humour in such images that led — as Freud suggested in his study of jokes — towards the unconscious. The title of the batik was evidence of how strongly Lye's work was influenced during his early years in England by Aboriginal art (with its circle and dot motifs, its 'X-ray' style, its flatness and linearity).

'Laura Riding Shawl' was made for the poet Laura Riding.[10] This whimsical image had a theatrical aspect, as though it depicted some type of stage set. But this stage was not for human actors. There was a free-standing ladder which seemed to be alive and growing, like some kind of cactus. On each side there was a build-up of circular or oval forms which might be seen as cacti or as microscopic creatures or as worlds in space. Once again the range of colours was distinctive — yellows and oranges with some blue and maroon.[11] Like the other batiks, it created the kind of shallow space characteristic of early modernist painting, where perspective was replaced by a series of planes or layers whose relationship to one another was somewhat shifty. Laura Riding forwarded a photograph of the shawl to *Transition*, a leading avant-garde magazine based in New York, and it published the image in its Fall 1928 issue. *Transition* was one of Lye's favourite magazines and he was thrilled to find himself in the company of writers such as James Joyce and Gertrude Stein and painters such as Hans Arp and Joan Miró — evidence of his rapid progress as a 'vertical invader'.

These were a few of the many batiks Lye made during his first years in London. Some images were more abstract and geometrical, though even the most abstract of his designs still contained suggestions of natural forms and processes. The completed batiks were given to friends such as Robert Graves and Laura Riding, or Eric and Celandine Kennington,[12] or sent home to his mother,[13] or offered for sale at approximately five pounds.

The income from batiks was not enough to live on but Lye also gained a job as stagehand at the Lyric Theatre, Hammersmith, for one pound a week. This was arranged for him by Alan Herbert, a friend of Eric Kennington, who lived with his wife Gwen (a painter) in Hammersmith Terrace, which backed on to the Thames near Footprints. As 'A. P. Herbert' he was a popular novelist, contributor to *Punch*, and writer of musicals. He had made a pleasant visit to New Zealand in 1925, summing it up in a way its citizens never forgot: 'New Zealand . . . is more English than the English, more loyal than the Crown.'[14] Although his political career was taking off, he remained an unpretentious man, notorious for his casual style of dress. As river guides on the Thames passed his home their megaphone voices were often heard pointing out 'the famous writer A. P. Herbert — the one without the shirt'.[15] Because his musicals were often premiered at the Lyric Theatre, he was able to persuade its director, Nigel Playfair, to offer Lye a job as a 'fly man' operating the machinery in the flies that raised or lowered the curtain and changed sets between the scenes. While Lye's set-changing at the Lyric was a far cry from the operation of his small kinetic theatre in Australia, or from what he had hoped to do at Meyerhold's theatre, the Lyric was one of the liveliest theatres in London. John Gielgud was one of many actors for whom it provided an important stepping-stone. And for Lye the job was a godsend since he was often so short of money that he would live for three days off a cod's head purchased for a few pence.

The work itself was not always lyric as he suggested in this description of a winter night in the wings: 'We're sitting around up here at the Lyric us stage-hands life of the party without pleased to meet you. You know — Mary warm the bed I'll be right over. . . . The rain on the roof makes the stage talk dudder than ever and no one knows the way to curl. Me, where's them sheets?'[16] He entitled this account 'You Know the Kind of Weather,' and he was in fact horrified by the London winter and 'all this greasy English stuff, Windsor soup, fog!'[17] It didn't help that he was living in a cramped shed. Again Herbert and Kennington came to the rescue. Herbert said to Lye: 'We've got this old barge way up on one of the canals, and it's just rotting away. . . . Why don't you go up, take a good mechanic and get the motor running, and come on down and we'll moor it alongside the wharf here.'[18] Lye could live on this barge rent-free. Herbert who was passionately interested in river boats and the history and lore of the Thames had already made several long trips in this boat, the *Avoca* (nicknamed 'Ark'). He had drawn on those experiences for his book *The Water Gypsies*, which later became a feature-film.[19] Lye, delighted with the idea of living on the Thames, set off to retrieve the boat with Kennington's chauffeur and another helper.

Seeing the English countryside for the first time Lye was amazed at how pastoral it was in comparison with the landscapes he had lived in — 'fields of buttercups spilling over into the canal' and 'cows brindling behind a row of trees copyrighted by English painters such as Alfred East'.[20] On their leisurely return journey Lye's companions taught him the Black Bottom and other popular dances: 'It must have been some sight to see me going down the canal, practising dancing with a chair on the roof of the Ark'. Each night they would moor at a pub and find partners 'for a Charleston workout'.[21] As Lye summed up the mood of these years: 'To be in one's twenties during The Twenties was to hear a continuous roar made by some sort of ozone fallout which affected everyone into feeling loose planks in their shanks.'[22]

After negotiating various canal locks they eventually tied up the barge at the

Atlanta Wharf in front of Kennington's studio, and it was refurbished for Lye's use. There was a sign disclaiming any responsibility for what might happen to visitors — 'This barge is top heavy and may capsize!' Lye lived there for two years. His view of the Thames was richly varied, with tugs, barges, rowing sculls, and police launches creating a hubbub at certain times of day, while at other times there was nothing on the river except gulls and swans. 'The water you see from your window is alive', wrote Herbert. 'The fish jump, the waterfowl cry or quack, the owl and the heron are heard at night.'[23] Lye could gather duck eggs on Chiswick Eyot, a small island near the barge. Coal could be scavenged from the river bed around the wharves where barges had unloaded their cargoes, or bought cheaply through the local black market. There was a strong sense of solidarity among those who lived on the river. 'If you needed a tarpaulin, you mentioned it to the river people, and next night one would drop onto your barge with no questions asked.'[24] Between low and high tide the river rose as much as ten feet, and twenty feet during a flood. At low tide Lye had to climb out by a ladder attached to the wharf. After one storm, the Ark 'strayed like a cow' over the wharf wall into the back yard of Footprints.

This accommodation cost only a few shillings a week to cover the wharf fee. There was a letterbox on a nearby wharf. The barge had two cabins with bunks, and there was a wood and coal fire for heating and a primus stove for cooking. But rats were a problem, and to have a bath or shower it was necessary to visit someone's house on shore. The only toilet was a hole in the side of the barge. Lye and other Londoners still swam in the Thames — there were great bathing parties — but the river was becoming dangerously polluted. Robert Graves (who lived on the *Ringrose*, a barge moored alongside Lye's) described the rubbish at high-tide as 'baskets, cabbages, chairs, fruit, hats, vegetables, bottles, tins, heaps of rushes or straw, dead things . . .'.[25] Not only dead cats and dogs floated by but occasionally the body of someone who had committed suicide. On one occasion a couple tried to drown together but, though the man had tied his hands and feet, he could not sink and he came floating past the Ark piteously shouting: 'Flora, I can't drown!'[26]

This was the dark side of the Thames that T. S. Eliot had evoked vividly in 1922 in his poem *The Waste Land*. But as a New Zealander who had always been accustomed to living by the sea, Lye found it a fruitful situation for working at art. His ark kept him in touch with 'all the associations of the primeval river and mud and tidal activity and moon'.[27] At the same time it was tied up alongside a large modern city. He saw this combination as ideal in terms of his aim of navigating the London art world according to his own artistic charts.[28]

fourteen tusalava

To join the *Euripides* under an assumed name, Lye had left Sydney in such a hurry that he had not had time to warn his friends. Jack Ellitt was mystified, being left with a dramatic image of Lye from their last trip to the beach: 'We were jogging along on the sloping mirror of cool wet sand just below high water mark. Suddenly Len stopped, stared long at the sun, and he turned, waved his hand, ran, dived under the dumpers, . . . out into the deep blue water, and out of sight. I kept on jogging until the beach grew cold and empty. Next day he was gone, he left no address.'[1] Eventually a letter arrived telling Ellitt that he should come on over. Ellitt was excited by the idea and within a year he was in London, sharing the *Ark*, working part-time at the Lyric Theatre, and free-lancing as a musician.

Ellitt found his friend well-established: 'Everyone liked Len, his work was good.' He was impressed by the batiks and paintings with their 'strange elemental forms in raw colour. They belonged to no school, no period, no modern trend or gimmick.' But now Lye was obsessed with movement and talked constantly of how he might bring those strange static forms to life.[2] Tribal art had strongly influenced painting and sculpture but it had never been introduced to the film medium, at least not in the radical manner Lye proposed. Early in 1927 he began making sketches for an animated film.

His curious starting-point was the witchetty grub, a source of food for the Aboriginal people. He had never seen such a grub but he remembered pictures of 'Aborigines daubing their bodies for a Witchetty Grub dance', standing in line 'in readiness to mime the motions of the grub'. As he later explained: 'I may have unconsciously chosen the grub for my film not only because I like Aboriginal art but, also, because it would be something that would wiggle quietly and move slowly and give me plenty of time to think out its life span as I went along.'[3] The name itself intrigued him by its 'spastic' sound quality. Lye derived some of his interest in the witchetty grub from F. J. Gillen and Baldwin Spencer's *The Native Tribes of Central Australia* (1899), a book with striking illustrations of Aboriginal art, one of which he had copied into his Sydney sketchbook. The book included a detailed account of the witchetty grub mythology of a tribe at Emily Gap near Alice Springs. It said that members of the tribe had the grub as their totem and

believed that human beings were descended from grubs. Many of the illustrations in the book included patterns of dots, a strong motif in Lye's art. As he said
of his film: 'Dots are used to convey organic life in a primary stage. All the shapes
. . . are derived from dots. (Dots are an age-old motif — ask any primitive or a
Bond Street tie shop).'[4] He did no research on the grubs themselves because he
was more interested in what his unconscious might fish up: 'I doodled to assuage
my hunger for some hypnotic image I'd never seen before.'[5]

Lye had learned some of the basics of film-making in Sydney and now he
managed to get a part-time job in a London studio, Hopkins and Weir, that
produced cartoon commercials for beer and toothpaste.[6] While working as a
'filler in' he studied the use of the rostrum camera and other aspects of animation.
Then he bought his own drawing table which had a glass top and a light box
behind it and register-pins for the holes in the cartoon drawing sheets.[7] As each
drawing was laid on top of the previous one he could estimate the change of
position needed to animate it. He set up his table in a corner of Kennington's
studio and got down to business, producing an average of eight drawings a day.[8]
This represented one second of film since projectors operated then at a speed of
approximately sixteen frames per second, and it was a common practice to
photograph each drawing twice. It took him more than two months to produce a
minute's worth of film.[9] Animation was one of the most time-consuming of all
forms of art, and he spent nearly two years creating the 4400 or so drawings for
his nine-minute film. He was kept going by the thought that at last he was
creating a major piece of work.[10]

In terms of visual style *Tusalava* was influenced by both Maori and Aboriginal
art, and as he went along Lye often considered 'how it would look if an Australian
Aboriginal was doing it'.[11] He created hard and definite two-dimensional drawings, and the most dramatic moments in the film involved the making or breaking
of those clear-cut boundaries. The film explored the whole area of the screen with
forms dancing along its edges. Because this was his first film it was a struggle for
him to shape and control the movement. Each of the grubs had about 20 parts
which had to be animated separately 'like cogs in a bicycle chain'.[12] And: 'Instead
of a spastic grub, it was a goddamned drugged grub. It was dopey. . . . I tried to
push this grub around with my drawings.'[13] He kept worrying that the film
lacked rhythm and speed, though it certainly displayed a distinctive sense of
physical movement. The split-screen layout — an idea he was using at this time in
some of his batiks — produced a lively counterpoint between movements on each
side of the screen. Creatures rose up like snakes, muscular forms pulled and
pushed, concentric circles span this way and that.

In Ellitt's words: 'When Len had done a lot of drawings the boss of the commercial studio let him photograph them on his rostrum camera. Then it was very exciting to see these figures come to life, strange and prehistoric.'[14] At this stage the project halted because of the cost of drawing materials and film processing. Though the budget of *Tusalava* was absurdly small by commercial standards it was still a struggle for Lye to pay all the bills, so he took samples of his work to the London Film Society. The society — the first of its kind in England — had been created in 1925 to champion the idea that film-making was a serious medium.[15] It broke much new ground by its adventurous programming, its high standards of presentation, and its fight against film censorship. Its screenings were gradually helping 'to transform English intellectuals' attitudes towards the "pictures" from scorn or condescension to attention and excitement'.[16] Lye sounded off to its committee: 'Look, you got a film-maker on your hands, etc., etc., and where is your film industry for this kind of art-film stuff?'[17] Though the society's budget was tight, the committee agreed to assist Lye with his project. Those who took a special interest in it included Ivor Montagu and Thorold Dickinson (film-makers and critics), and Ben Nicholson (an avant-garde painter). Three society members even made personal donations — Robert Graves, Norman Cameron, and Sidney Bernstein (a far-sighted patron of the arts who was head of the Granada chain of theatres and later head of Granada Television).

With the support of the society, the stack of drawings steadily increased. Lye always had difficulty explaining what his film was about, beyond describing it as a kind of creation myth, a story from the Dreamtime. The drawings showed simple forms such as dots evolving into more complex forms such as grubs. Finally two creatures confronted each other — the first an almost human shape described by Lye as 'a totem of individuality'[18] and the second 'a monstrous python shape'[19] that developed into 'a cross between an octopus and a spider'.[20] This ink-squirting monster attacked 'the human core shape', toyed with it and consumed it but apparently destroyed itself in the process. The film ended as it began with dots and welling circles. The title came from a Samoan phrase *tusa lava*, meaning 'just the same'.[21] For Lye it carried a rich range of associations such as 'Everything eventually goes full cycle, in other words, lives out a life span'.[22] On another occasion he translated it as 'Don't worry, everything is just the same',[23] thus connecting it with 'No trouble' and 'Ich gebibble', his other slogans for warding off anxiety. Since Lye and his art usually created an impression of extraordinary happiness, it is striking to see such a strong strain of anxiety in *Tusalava* and some of the paintings of this period. He once said of the film:

'When I was a kid, a lot of disturbing things happened round me. But . . . happiness became my whole theory of life. Not hedonism but happiness of a lasting kind, like art. Art replaced God for me very early on. I ducked anxiety, but it was still there, it had to be there somewhere. The *Tusalava* octopus-spider was a kind of death-figure.'[24]

Lye still wanted to allow each viewer to understand the anxiety in their own way. Interpretations of the film have been various: the beginnings of life on earth which means the emergence of conflict; giving birth to a child who becomes a threat to its parent; an artist creating a work of art that drains his own energies; the battle of the sexes (a mating dance which becomes a deadly struggle); and problems at a microscopic level inside the human body. Lye himself entertained all these possibilities and others.[25] Any good work of art was like a spirited horse that the conscious mind attempted to corral but which kept escaping back into the wilds. And this film was playful as well as spirited, powered as much by humour as by anxiety. When the spider-octopus was toying with the human core shape, for example, it flipped it about like a child with a yo-yo. Combining whimsy with seriousness is not unusual for an artist of the subconscious (as shown by the work of Joan Miró, say, or Paul Klee). The casual viewer could enjoy *Tusalava* simply as a cartoon, though Lye's extraordinary imagery and sense of movement made it a great deal more than that.

The film was premiered on 1 December 1929 at the New Gallery Cinema as part of the London Film Society's 33rd programme. Someone with a sense of humour scheduled *Tusalava* after a documentary called *The Frog* from 'The Secrets of Nature' series. Lye went to the screening with his current girlfriend Jane Thompson. (The audience also included two women who would become important in his life years later — Ann Hindle and Barbara Ker-Seymer — and both were very struck by the film.) Early in the making of *Tusalava* Lye had asked Jack Ellitt to compose music that could be played as a live accompaniment. Films did not yet have soundtracks though they were usually accompanied by live or recorded music. Ellitt had sometimes assisted the London Film Society by selecting music suited to particular films and playing it on a gramophone during screenings. He was excited to be composing music directly for *Tusalava* because he had many ideas about the relationship between music and film such as the fact that both art forms were based on movement. As he helped Lye with the animation, he experimented with music 'suitable for these primitive forms'. Determined to create something radically new, he experimented with highly energetic, rhythmic music produced by two pianos.[26] Over the course of two years he wrote half an hour of music, and then, as the premiere approached, he struggled to edit it to the nine-minute length of the finished film.[27] By 1929 films were using the new talkie apparatus to synchronise their music[28] but Lye could not raise the money needed to obtain a print with a soundtrack. Then budget problems forced them to reduce the two pianos in the cinema to one. Ellitt, a passionate perfectionist, was deeply troubled by these compromises. He withdrew from playing at the premiere himself and one of the Society's other pianists was left to make what he could of this avant-garde score. Doris Harrison recalled: 'The music was all rhythms — not a scrap of melody and difficult to follow. The pianist did his best but there were places where he gave up and just ran his fingers up and down the keys.'[29]

The screening was reviewed by the *Daily Sketch* which singled out Lye's film as 'the most remarkable item in the programme' even though it was 'weird'.[30] A detailed review appeared in the specialist magazine *Close Up* ('The Only Magazine Devoted To Films As An Art') where Oswell Blakeston described Lye as 'a great artist with great ideas'[31] and was particularly impressed by his search for an alternative to the usual conventions of film editing.[32] Whereas other animators imitated the rapid, abbreviated editing of live-action films, Lye concentrated in *Tusalava* on patterns of movement that unfolded slowly and continuously. Reflecting his distinctive sense of motion, this was a striking preference at a time when the rapid editing of directors such as Sergei Eisenstein was being hailed by critics as the most innovative area of contemporary film-making. Blakeston understood this aspect of Lye's originality because he was currently making his own experimental film, *Light Rhythms*, in collaboration with Francis Brugiere and Jack Ellitt, which shifted the emphasis from editing to light effects.

Tusalava appeared at a time when only a small number of films had been seriously influenced by modern art. Lye's involvement with Maori and Aboriginal art as well as modernism ensured that nothing like this film had ever been seen before. Unfortunately this also meant that *Tusalava* was doomed to remain isolated, for though viewers were intrigued by it, they were not sure how to talk about it or how to contextualise it. A copy went to the continent and made a deep impression on a few film-makers such as Hans Richter.[33] In England it had occasional screenings[34] but there were few outlets for experimental film-making, so Lye had little return for his two years of work. His best moment was receiving out of the blue a highly perceptive letter from Roger Fry, the well-known Bloomsbury art critic, who wrote: 'When I saw the announcements of your *Tusalava* I made a point of going to Sunday's performance. I want to tell you that it seemed to me most interesting and full of promise. I thought that you had seen the essential thing as no-one had hitherto — I mean you really thought not of forms in themselves but of them as movements in time. I suspect it will need a new kind of imagination to seize this idea fully but you are the first as far as I know to make a start. You managed so to time and adjust your sequences that I was absolutely held by them. It's the same thing as telling a story well — so that each moment is anticipated — only it must be incredibly difficult to conceive that in relation to visible forms. I hope you'll go on.'[35]

Before *Tusalava* could be screened outside the Film Society it needed a certificate from the British Board of Film Censors. Astonishingly the board considered banning the film. It had already refused a certificate to the French Surrealist film *The Sea-Shell and the Clergyman* on the grounds that 'the film is so cryptic as to be almost meaningless' and 'if there is a meaning it is doubtless objectionable'.[36] The board had the same reaction to *Tusalava* and demanded to know what the film was about and what its title signified. Could Lye convince them that its images were not full of sex and violence? He explained to them in detail that the film 'represented a self-shape annihilating an agonistic element'. At that point the censors threw in the towel and issued a certificate.[37]

fifteen jane thompson

Lye, who had always been popular with women, had a number of affairs during his first years in London. His most serious relationship was with Liz Johnson, a beautiful black Jamaican who lived in Hammersmith in St Peter's Square. Since her teenage years she had been a dancer in stage musicals. If some of her friend-ships with men seemed to have a commercial aspect, it was for a good cause — paying the fees of her daughter at a convent boarding school. The father, described as an Arabian seaman, had disappeared.[1] Some of Lye's associates disapproved of his relationship with Johnson because of her reputation.

In 1927 another woman arrived in the Square who became even more impor-tant to Lye. Florence Winifred Thompson had been born in London but her father (a quantity surveyor) had moved the family to Johannesburg in South Africa when she was 7. Sent to a convent school her childhood was strict and sheltered but she maintained a spirit of independence. At 19 she dismayed her family by eloping with a man called Ewart Abinger Keeling. The marriage rapidly proved a disaster, and she had an abortion and left South Africa. She settled in London where she revelled in the big city atmosphere but found it hard to survive on her wages as a typist. A writer friend who visited Winifred in Bayswater was shocked to find her 'starving slowly' and at once mounted a rescue operation. Through her contacts the friend found cheap accommodation for Winifred at 31 St Peter's Square. Here she boarded with a remarkable woman called Faith Oliver who was at the time having an affair with Havelock Ellis, the pioneer writer on the psychology of sex.[2] Meeting the writers and artists who lived in St Peter's Square, Winifred felt that this was the milieu she had always been searching for. Though she regarded herself as 'not really a creative person', she had struggled hard to escape the conservatism of the culture in which she had grown up.[3]

When she moved into the new flat Oliver said: 'Your name's a problem because I know too many Winifreds.' She replied: 'Then call me Jane!' She was in the mood for a fresh start, and 'Jane Thompson' sounded more down-to-earth for Hammersmith than 'Winifred Keeling'. Soon after this she met Lye and was struck by his flair for enjoying life: 'It was always an uplift when he came into the room.'[4] He told stories about Samoa, showed her his sketchbooks, and described his film-making. He was intrigued by a recording of Zulu work songs she had brought from South Africa. From her perspective: 'I think the thing we had most in common was movement. I've always been fascinated by anything moving — I can spend hours watching people skating or skiing. Len and I did a lot of dancing.'[5] They made a striking couple — Jane (at 23) slim, elegant, sophisticated, and extremely good-looking and Lye (at 26) relaxed and sun-tanned, with a quirky style of dress. It was a pleasure to watch her agility and his syncopation — she danced so gracefully that she later gained a job as dancing instructor, while he danced a little off the beat but made a style out of his stiffness.[6] They went often to the movies: 'There was a fleapit along Kings Road [towards Chelsea] with ninepenny seats. If there was something Len was feeling very special about we would pay 2s 6d and go up to the West End so we could see the new print before it got messed up. God, if you knew what excitement! We sometimes moved four times until we got dead centre on the screen.'[7] They also bought cheap tickets to Covent Garden where she succeeded in passing on to Lye a little of her enthusiasm for ballet. In her words: 'We were good friends for about three months and then — I don't know what lit the spark but something did — and we became lovers.'[8] Soon she had a tough choice to make because a South African friend who had moved to England was showering her with attention and hinting at marriage. He was a talented entrepreneur who later became a millionaire through the business of printing cinema tickets. But 'I decided Len was too fascinating — I couldn't give him up — so I said goodbye to the other man.'[9] Her parents had assumed that this time she would marry well, as all her school friends had done, and they were shocked to hear that now she was involved with an artist critical of the institution of marriage and unconcerned about money or other practicalities.

At the end of 1927 Thompson learned that she would have to find new accommodation because Faith Oliver was getting married (to the architect Albert Powys, A. P. Herbert's neighbour). Laura Riding, who had recently moved in with Robert Graves at 35a St Peter's Square, told Lye and Thompson it was obvious they should live together ('Laura was very apt to arrange people's lives').[10] Early in 1928 the couple moved in to 9a Black Lion Lane which was midway between his barge and St Peter's Square. They called it The Barn because it consisted of a single room, 'long, narrow and very high'. They built a platform with a stepladder for their bed. One reason The Barn was only ten shillings a week to rent was the absence of any bathroom or shower, but they made do with a tub. Nancy Nicholson, Graves's wife, who was then living on a Thames barge, gave them chairs and a silver teapot, and the painter John

Banting smuggled leather out of his father's bindery to cover the chairs. Another friend gave them a stove to keep the place warm in winter.

Some of the artists and writers who knew them had reservations about the relationship. Those who liked to think of Lye as a wild man found his partner a little too civilised. Even Laura Riding sometimes referred to her unkindly as 'the gold-digger', a curious comment since it was Thompson who kept bread on the table during periods when Lye made no money from his art.[11] She was in an awkward position since her behaviour was too bohemian by middle-class stand-ards (living with a man outside marriage was still scandalous in those days) yet too middle-class by bohemian standards (she could never wholly shed her accent and upbringing). Though she was seen as poised and sophisticated, she suffered from serious confidence problems: 'The only places I knew well were in Africa and that was far away. I didn't paint, I didn't write, I wasn't a poet — so what business had I in this circle except I was dragged in on Len's coat-tails?'[12] Some visitors such as T. E. Lawrence simply ignored her. But her relationship with Lye was strong: 'He and I sort of complemented each other. People could see that we improved each other'.[13]

When Lye arrived in London his intention had been a short stay before moving on elsewhere, but he was persuaded to settle by the congenial social scene in Hammersmith and by Kennington's and Herbert's kindness in giving him a place to live and work.[14] His experience of Sydney's bohemia had served as a warm-up for what he found in London. None of his new friends shared his interests exactly, but he was used to that. What was novel was the amount of intellectual stimulation and the fact that there were so many busy people around him producing ambitious work. In this environment he was himself becoming highly productive, making batiks, paintings, and now a film. Whenever he moved outside the Hammersmith circle he was horrified to discover just how conservative the rest of London could be, and that would start him wondering what it was like to live in the other big cities of Europe; but although he still dreamed of going to Moscow, the thought of having to learn another language was one of the few things in life that made him nervous. For this and other reasons London seemed a good place to live and work for a few years.

The area of Hammersmith down by the Thames was full of writers and artists who had fled from Chelsea and Bloomsbury when the wealthy and fashionable moved in. As in New York's Greenwich Village in the 1910s, the low rents in Hammersmith attracted a lively assortment of counter-cultures — artists, political radicals, sexual nonconformists, and those who lived by their wits or by petty crime. To add to the mixture, some wealthy art-lovers would drop in to see what was happening. Describing a poker school in St Peter's Square, Lye said of the players: 'We were a mixed crowd: poets, artists, film, crafts, ballet boys, hustlers, Calypso friends, Chelsea, Bloomsbury, and Mayfair, with the Mall people thrown in. We overlapped a lot and I felt I was in the middle of everything, although I knew it was only the periphery.'[15]

St Peter's Square has been described by James Moran as 'one of those enclaves in which London used to abound. . . . There is a pleasant garden in the centre and the houses . . . are embellished with stone eagles.'[16] Among the residents of the Square that Lye knew during the 1920s or early 1930s were John Aldridge, Norman Cameron, Richard Church, Kanty Cooper, Jack and Doris Ellitt, Robert Graves, Tommy and Ann Hindle, Nancy Nicholson, Laura Riding and Basil Taylor. Artists living nearby included John Piper, Ceri Richards and Julian Trevelyan. Aldridge and Cameron (who shared the studio at No. 27, St Peter's Square) became particularly close friends of Lye and Thompson.

Cameron, who had come down from Oxford in 1928, was 'a strange tall man with an uncombed mop of hair' and 'a kind of breezy, serious gusto'.[17] Described by Lye as 'a long-legged walking essence of poetry',[18] he made a living by working part-time as an advertising copy-writer and would then spend the afternoons writing poetry or translating the work of the French poet Arthur Rimbaud. He was an incorruptible person who got into trouble at his advertising agency because he managed his expense account with such honesty it was only half the size of anyone else's.[19] Originally Lye had assumed that poetry was 'a lot of romanticised junk'[20] but spending time with Cameron, Graves and Riding soon put an end to that stereotype. When Lye started to read modern poetry, he thought the much talked-about work of T. S. Eliot was dreary, but he was impressed by Gerard Manley Hopkins, and completely won over by Cameron's translations of Rimbaud. In Lye's words: 'Rimbaud is a visual [poet], all his images are visual. And then [Cameron's] translation was the most vivid kind — each word was as if cut out of marble or projected. . . . I woke up'.[21] He even considered making a film about Rimbaud's life.[22]

Visitors to the area who heard about the stoker sculptor turned film-maker were curious to meet him. Notable people such as the poet Siegfried Sassoon and the scientist Jacob Bronowski would call on Lye and Thompson out of the blue, usually bringing a jug of heavy cream at the suggestion of Laura Riding who knew Lye's weakness for the sort of cream he remembered from New Zealand. On Saturdays and Sundays the couple would join their friends at the Black Lion Pub which was only a few doors away from The Barn. Built in the eighteenth century, the pub included a skittles alley which A. P. Herbert helped to develop into a Hammersmith cult.[23] The game — outdoors in summer, indoors in winter — involved the throwing of a heavy elliptical 'cheese' down a 21-foot alley towards a set of ninepins. Lye socialised with a number of artists at the pub including the sculptor Henry Moore and Stanley William Hayter, who was an influential teacher of print-making. Later, remembering such contacts, Hayter remarked: 'It seems to me that a certain osmosis takes place among artists working at a given time and place even if not actually collaborating.' And: 'I always considered Len as a major painter and sculptor, apart from his most original work on films. He is one of the people who supported my thesis that humour is an essential element of thought. A very warm and charming person and very widely appreciated.'[24]

What Lye liked best about living in Hammersmith was knowing there were so many good artists at work just down the road, and that whenever he ran out of steam, that thought gave his work a new 'propulsion'.[25] Also important to Lye was the atmosphere of 'no trouble', the ability of his friends to enjoy themselves even when they had no money. The writer Naomi Mitchison, another Hammersmith resident, was struck by 'the impecunious scale' on which these artists managed to live well: 'Hammersmith was presumably thought in other circles to be very avant-garde and we had a good share of love and hate affairs, rushing in and out of one another's lives, having parties and from time to time swimming in the Thames. . . . It was thick brown water, . . . but if we kept our mouths shut, not swallowing so much as a cigarette packet or an old French Letter, nothing went wrong. . . . There was always argument, admiration, dressing up and parties. Those at St Peter's Square were like today's: beer and bangers rather than claret cup and sandwiches as they would have been at more ordinary houses.'[26] Lye and Thompson would get together with close friends for poker, jazz records, dancing, or good talk. He was well known as a peacemaker because when arguments broke out, he was (in Mitchison's phrase) 'the kind of person who tried to disentangle things'.[27] He was exceptionally relaxed and tolerant, prepared to accept anyone until he learned otherwise.[28] In general, that was the Hammersmith way — to welcome newcomers, as Lye had discovered when he arrived: 'Nobody particularly took advantage. . . . There weren't a lot of panhandlers.'[29] Nor were there many prima donnas, for as Tom Matthews said of John Aldridge: 'Like the rest of us, he held his own future in contempt.'[30] The visiting modernist László Moholy-Nagy was fascinated by the humour and 'amateurism' of British art, which he contrasted with the grim pressure within German culture to specialise.[31]

sixteen the seven and five society

A great deal of the best and most challenging art made in England during the Twenties and Thirties was to be seen in the annual exhibitions of the Seven and Five Society. Established in 1919 as an alternative to the London Group, which was dominated by Bloomsbury artists, the society took its name from the seven painters and five sculptors who were the original members. It became more explicitly a base for modernist art after Ben Nicholson joined in 1924 and succeeded in introducing tougher rules for membership. The artists who were later voted in as members included Henry Moore, Barbara Hepworth, Kanty Cooper, Cedric Morris, Christopher ('Kit') Wood, and Len Lye. Nicholson, who had admired *Tusalava*, brought Lye into the society's January 1927 exhibition as a guest (represented by 'Unit'), and then in 1929 he backed him for full membership.[1]

Introduced to Nicholson by Robert Graves (who was his brother-in-law), Lye found him impressive but austere, with 'a kind of monkish . . . attitude about everything. . . . He treated art as a religion. I did also, but I didn't get all strict on the deal.'[2] The poet Kathleen Raine once described Nicholson as 'an elf-man, untouched by human joys and sorrows' and added this anecdote: 'I remember saying to him, in what I intended as reproach, "You know Ben, you have been married to two very remarkable women". "Yes, I know," said Ben. "From Winifred I learned a great deal about colour, and from Barbara [Hepworth] about form." So much for marriages.'[3]

In 1929 and 1931 Lye was elected to the Seven and Five Society's hanging committee. After his isolation as an artist in New Zealand and Australia, this degree of involvement was a novel experience for him: 'Here was this . . . highly sensitive, strongly opinionated bunch of people. To be part of that swim was terribly important for all of us. We respected each other and although no one else may have understood what you were after, at least people in your own group, although they were entirely different, had a sense of it.'[4] Many of the artists became Lye's friends.[5] Although much of the work in the annual exhibitions was still moderate by European standards, English reviewers were left floundering — they could respond only with flippant remarks or moral disapproval. *The Studio*, for example, described the society's 1928 exhibition as 'another show in which eccentricity ran riot with rather lamentable results'.[6] The *Daily Express* spoke of 'weird puzzles in paint' and judged its members incapable of ever reaching 'a wider circle'.[7] The *Apollo* diagnosed Lye as suffering from 'a regrettable kind of vermiform [worm-shaped] complex'.[8] But there were artists outside the society who did understand the importance of what the society was doing — for example the painter Paul Nash who wrote of seeing Lye's work for the first time at a Seven and Five exhibition: 'I was at once attracted by its unusual kind of life, it had a totally different life from any of the other exhibits. Most conspicuous of any quality was the sense of rhythm, but it had expressed itself eccentrically — not in the tiresome sense, but in the way of utter independence.'[9]

Lye's contributions to the 1928 exhibition were a metal version of 'Tiki' (which Kennington had helped him cast), two batiks, and three 'constructions'. The constructions represented the climax of Lye's interest in machine imagery.[10] 'Eve' was a three-foot-high rectangular structure that translated the figure of a woman into a geometrical pattern of circles, curved tubes, rectangles and black stripes. This Eve made of painted tin and brass was perceived by reviewers both as 'ultra-modern' and as 'primitive'. The second work, described simply as 'Construction', was two feet high and consisted of black-and-white geometrical shapes like a strange set of signals, or a stage set for Meyerhold's theatre. The third sculpture, 'Flies Back to the Branch', was based on the haiku quoted by Ezra Pound. Its figure of motion had made a deep impression on Lye: 'The fallen blossom flies back to the branch: A butterfly.'[11] Lye liked to interpret the poem as a myth in which the souls of dead children changed into butterflies. His two-foot-high construction was based on a butterfly shape, although he teased uncertain viewers by explaining on one occasion that it was a musical instrument and on another that it was a penny-in-the-slot machine![12]

One sympathetic review in a London newspaper, the *Daily Chronicle*, included photographs of 'Eve' and 'Construction' with the comment: 'Most arresting are the sculptures by Len Lye, a young New Zealander who stoked his way from the Antipodes to take London by storm. . . . His originality even surpasses that of his London colleagues.'[13] This hyperbole brought him to the attention of the London correspondent of the *Evening Post* who passed on the news to readers in Wellington, New Zealand, a few days later. Under the heading 'Ultra-Modern Art: Herod Out-Heroded: New Zealander's Effort', Lye was said to have won fame in the artistic world for paintings that made critics giddy. His batiks were 'not unlike the pictures presented by psychic adepts of astral bodies in violent perturbation'.[14] Two other New Zealand newspapers published stories about this 'Futurist New Zealander' who had 'created a sensation' in London with his 'mechanised art'.[15]

In comparison, the specialised art magazine *Art in New Zealand* made only one reference to Lye's work during this period, a sarcastic comment about 'a young Australian, one Len Lye' who was the 'good joker' who contributed 'some peculiar panels' to the 1933 Seven and Five exhibition alongside the 'fourth dimensional scrap paper efforts by Ben Nicholson'.[16] One New Zealand artist who did take Lye's work seriously was Gordon Tovey, an old friend and former member of Linley Richardson's art class. Tovey contacted Lye when he visited London and they renewed their old brain-storming sessions. He was particularly struck by Lye's conception of the unconscious (which linked with his own study of Jung) and by his enthusiasm for the art of indigenous peoples. He could see that Lye's stay in Samoa had been an important experience for him.[17] After Tovey returned to New Zealand in 1930 he would become a key figure in art education in schools, promoting a new spirit of experiment and giving strong support to the energies of Maori culture. There were many affinities between the two men and Tovey's later career gives us a glimpse of what Lye's life might have been like if he had gone back to New Zealand and joined in the upsurge of local culture that began in the Thirties. But Lye had no wish to leave London where he was taking advantage of opportunities he had never had at home to realise his avant-garde ambitions in film and the visual arts.

His interest in machine imagery seems to have come temporarily to an end in 1929, and his batiks and paintings during the early Thirties concentrated on nature and evolution.[18] Lye's art was no longer an ever-changing mixture of modern and tribal influences — he had settled into a style that was consistently his own. From his many batiks and his strong representation in Seven and Five exhibitions it was clear he had struck a rich lode. Now the shapes in his pictures looked like unknown species of fish, animals, plants, or microscopic organisms. Often these creatures (or 'protagonists', as Lye called them) seemed to be undergoing a major change — an amoeba was turning into a plant, the plant was starting to fly, its roots were changing into limbs. Some creatures were fighting with claws and projectiles, others were mating with seeds and eggs. Trying to interpret Lye's batiks — or the related images of his film *Tusalava* — was like discovering new life forms in a microscope and being uncertain how to describe their behaviour. The artist avoided all questions of interpretation while he was working, but once the pictures were complete he would speculate about them in a playful way, as though trying to reconstruct the myths of a tribe that had left nothing behind but a few enigmatic images. Titles changed frequently — from

'Tree of Life' to 'Tree God' to 'Night Tree'; from 'Cagn Who Made Things' to 'God of Light' to 'The Big Bang Man'; and from 'Marks and Spencer in a Japanese Garden' to 'Fresh Water Things' to 'Pond People'. This complex imagery of processes in nature allowed Lye to draw upon many layers of memory including the marine life at Cape Campbell, the colours of the Australian landscape, and the tropical vegetation and coral reefs of Samoa.

Lye still played the sense games he had developed in New Zealand, such as focusing each day on a particular sense, but now a new exercise became central to his art — the activity of doodling which developed alongside his work on *Tusalava*.[19] To doodle, according to the dictionary, is 'to scribble aimlessly, especially when the attention is elsewhere'.[20] Like any artist Lye had done plenty of scribbling, and he had read Freudian analyses of doodles, but while making animation drawings he arrived at a new understanding of the process. Doodling was a way of subverting his years of draughtsmanship, allowing him to dive below the surface of the mind and to catch consciousness and its preconceptions napping. It was possible to develop it as a regular exercise, and provided he was very careful he could overcome the contradiction of aiming deliberately to make aimless drawings. To devote your art to aimlessness requires a great deal of faith in the unconscious. Doodling for Lye involved learning to trust the hand to think for itself. He found the results were mixed because 'doodles come from different levels of the unconscious'.[21] He gave himself a working rule: 'If ever I was doing a shape and I had seen something like it somewhere else, I'd quit.'[22] He waited for an image that was free of literary associations yet aesthetically satisfying and imbued with a strange, hypnotic quality. Whenever such an image emerged, it had the excitement of a gift. But its magic needed to be tested over a period of time, and so Lye would add it to his collection and review it later to see if it still had the same kick. Those that qualified were so precious he would hoard them, small images on notebook pages or motley scraps of paper, as a starting point for paintings and films.

Not all of these 'starter doodles' were produced by pencil or brush. Lye also came up with his own version of the photogram method being used in Paris by Man Ray. The method itself could be traced back to the early nineteenth century when Henry Fox Talbot had placed objects such as lace and leaves on pieces of sensitised paper and then exposed them to bright light.[23] Such experiments had been sidelined by the development of the camera, but in the 1920s Ray recognised their Surrealist potential. He would arrange unlikely combinations of objects in the dark on a photographic plate or strip of film and then expose it by flicking a light on and off. Lye made some photograms of this kind, such as his juxta-

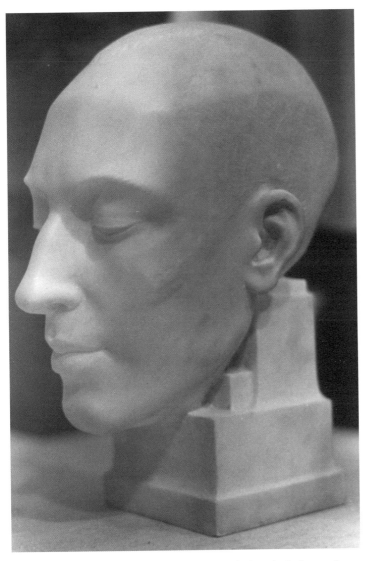

Above: The marble portrait head of Lye by Sydney sculptor
G. Rayner Hoff, which won the Wynne Art Prize in 1927.
COURTESY LEN LYE FOUNDATION

Bottom right: A photo of Lye while he was modelling for the sculpture,
taken by the sculptor's brother, Thomas Hoff (circa 1925).
COURTESY LEN LYE FOUNDATION

Top right: Lye's bookplate for the pianist Nigel Pearson, Sydney,
circa 1925. COURTESY LEN LYE FOUNDATION

LEN LYE

Three pencil drawings made by Lye in Sydney, circa 1925. The older man is the poet Geoffrey Cumine. The woman is Mary Brown, and Lye described this drawing as an example of his last representational style before his art became more 'primitive' and abstract. COURTESY LEN LYE FOUNDATION

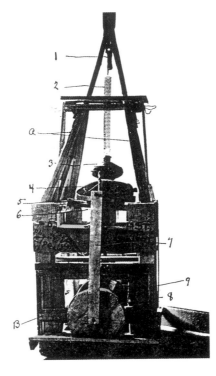

Above: Lyubov Popov's stage set for the Meyerhold Theatre production of *The Magnanimous Cuckold* in Moscow in 1922. Lye was so excited by a picture of the set that he made plans to go to Moscow.
COURTESY LEN LYE FOUNDATION

Left: It was this photograph in Edwin J. Kempf's book *Psychopathology* that inspired Lye to start making kinetic sculpture. Kempf's caption described the object as a 'Copulation fetish by [an] impotent negro paranoiac' instructed by God to build the 'first church of perpetual motion'. COURTESY LEN LYE FOUNDATION

Right: Lye's wooden carving 'Tiki' (or 'Hei-Tiki'), Auckland, 1922.
PHOTO JOHN B. TURNER

Below: 'Unit', a marble carving Lye made in Sydney circa 1925, representing a man and a woman clasped in a tight embrace.
PHOTO BRIAN DONOVAN

Sculptor Kanty Cooper, who worked alongside Lye in Eric Kennington's studio in London in the late 1920s, specialised in the direct carving of wood and stone. These examples of her sculpture include the bold ebony carving (above) of a child on a mother's shoulders. COURTESY KANTY COOPER

Top: The 'Euripides', on which Lye worked
his way to London as a stoker in 1926.
COURTESY LEN LYE FOUNDATION

Above: Eric Kennington and A. P. Herbert's
barge *Avoca* (nicknamed 'The Ark') sailing
down the Thames. Lye lived on this barge
after his arrival in London.
COURTESY LEN LYE FOUNDATION

Right: Lye, Jack Ellitt, and Celandine
Kennington by the Thames.
COURTESY LEN LYE FOUNDATION

Bottom right: Jack Ellitt and Doris Harrison.
From 1927 Ellitt had lived with Lye on the
Avoca. After Ellitt and Harrison got married
they lived on the *Ringrose*, a barge moored
alongside the *Avoca* at Hammersmith.
COURTESY JACK & DORIS ELLITT

Above: Jane (Florence Winifred)
Thompson, who later became
Jane Lye, in Hammersmith.
COURTESY JANE LYE

Left: Lye going to the Black Lion pub
for beer. PHOTO JOHN PHILLIPS.
COURTESY LEN LYE FOUNDATION

This photo and caption appeared in the Auckland newspaper *The Sun* on 19 May 1928 describing Lye's contributions to a Seven and Five Society exhibition. The edge of his batik 'Polynesian Connection' is visible at top left.

position of an eye bath, a fork, and a coiled light chain, but he came to prefer the stranger, more abstract shapes that he produced by moulding plasticine in the dark on a sheet of photographic paper. The process required him to think with his fingers rather than his eyes. Batiks and paintings which began as photograms included 'Watershed', 'Pond People', and 'Night Tree'.[24] Thompson remembered him 'spending an awful lot of time' making such images in the late 1920s — 'this was his Man Ray period, though I don't know if Len had met him or simply heard what he was doing'. The New Burlington Galleries exhibited a selection of Lye's photograms in 1930.[25]

Lye was also interested in children's art and in graffiti. One of his paintings was inspired by a graffito on the wall of a tube station in Chiswick which he copied on to the only paper he could find — a discarded cigarette packet.[26] He also derived images from cracks and peeling paint: 'If you want to get a grip on the energy and . . . structure of . . . various forms . . . such as cement or stone [or] wood, you start drawing the particular shapes made when they crack.'[27] Here was 'the possibility of hitting terrific images' such as the stress mark on which Lye based his gouache 'Earth Cools, Plants Arrive, and Fire Devil Departs'. He played with the idea that this was 'the devil of dryness and drought' that had been living in the cracks of dry wood until 'pried loose with a doodle'.[28] Cracks provided evidence of subterranean energies, as did stains, saps, and seepings.[29] In the course of the 1930s Lye became increasingly concerned with the kinetic aspects of doodles — for example, the impression of speed created by vigorous lines and swishy brushstrokes.

When the mood was right — when he felt a heightened response to those small forms — he would select a doodle and start drawing and re-drawing it to see where it might lead. In the case of 'Fire Devil': 'I struggled for about three months and I must have done about thirty drawings in different forms and gradually the shape evolved and at long last I had it.'[30] The process of turning his doodles into paintings could not be hurried because any attempt to apply the usual rules of art had the effect of bringing the artist back to the surface and scaring away the very thing he had been diving to find. Sometimes one doodle would link up with another though it was not possible to explain why. Paintings such as 'Helium' and 'Ice Age' assembled a 'gang of images' which seemed to share a family resemblance. Arrangement had to be arrived at in the same slow intuitive way as the images themselves — there could be no rules of composition. It was only after all these demands had been patiently followed, and the painting felt complete, that the artist could afford to relax and play with titles and mythical stories about the protagonists.

Lye's approach to art seemed eccentric but there were precedents. Many artists have talked about being influenced by doodles, including Leonardo da Vinci who advised artists to try staring at an old wall covered in dirt.[31] In the 1920s one of the key methods of the Surrealists was 'automatic writing', an extreme form of doodling that could be applied to either words or images, in order to liberate the mind from moral or aesthetic assumptions. Few examples of such work were available in London, but Lye was a regular reader of magazines such as *Cahiers d'Art* and *Transition*. Enthusiasts such as Herbert Read and Humphrey Jennings established links with the continental avant-garde and helped to keep London artists informed, and Lye was able to meet artists who visited Kennington's studio.[32] He was aware of Surrealism but strongly preferred 'painterly' practitioners such as Joan Miró (who ditched realism entirely and relied upon doodling) to 'literary' ones such as Salvador Dali (who rendered his dream images with an 'old masterish glamour').[33] Lye had no direct contact with Miró but watched for his work because of the strong affinities he felt, even though at first glance their images appeared very different.[34] Miró's seemingly abstract paintings were full of suggestions of natural forms,[35] and Lye always admired the risk-taking and confidence in the brushwork. Miró spoke of lines having different speeds and he could make a brushstroke swish like a whip. In the words of the painter Robert Motherwell: '"Doodling" in the hands of a Miró has no more to do with just anyone doodling on a telephone-pad than the "representations" of a Dürer or a Leonardo have to do with the "representations" in a Sears catalog.'[36]

seventeen robert graves and laura riding

Next to his lover Jane Thompson and his film-making partner Jack Ellitt, the two people Lye was closest to in London were the writers Robert Graves and Laura Riding. Graves was a brilliant poet who always tried to put his best energies into poetry, but the only way he could make a living was to write popular works of prose, such as his 1927 bestseller *Lawrence and the Arabs* (about his friend T. E. Lawrence). As Tom Driberg described him, Graves was 'tall and burly, with a heavy, gypsy-like face that looked, in repose, sulky, and a sensual mouth'.[1] His clothing was an unpredictable mixture of the 'squire' and the 'scarecrow'.[2] Born in London, he had had a conventional upbringing which had had the effect of leaving him unhappy and rebellious. The fact that he was six years older than Lye made a major difference because it meant he had gone to the First World War. Graves fought bravely in the front lines but the conduct of the war reinforced his lack of respect for the British establishment, and years of trench warfare left him a haunted man. After the war he studied psychology (including psychoanalysis) to try to gain some control over his anxieties, but he would not trust his case to an analyst because he was afraid that if he became too normal he would lose the impulse to write poetry.[3] Despite the risk of madness Graves still believed (as Lye did) that art must cultivate the unconscious mind as its primary source.

In 1918 he had married the talented artist Nancy Nicholson, who was Ben Nicholson's sister, and they now had four children whom they looked after in an unorthodox but loving way. What drew him to Lye, who knew little of literature? Alastair Reid, a fellow poet and friend of Graves, recalls: 'Robert treasured Len as someone who seemed as though he had come from a different planet. Len always left the same residual impression in everybody — whenever you mentioned Len, they always lit up, and immediately you would hear stories that had some smack of eccentricity. He created such an amazing visual environment. When he set the table it would have some little extra layout to it that no one would have thought of but him. On a winter's night when Len would light a fire it would be like a huge celebration, it would be like the first fire anybody had ever lit, and we just had to watch it. He really sparked things all the time.'[4] Lye's company could bring out the joyful side of the sometimes melancholy poet. Graves was still struggling to free himself from some aspects of his upbringing, whereas Lye showed a complete disregard for convention. Lye was one of the few people who did not express surprise or disapproval at the fact that Laura Riding had joined Graves and Nicholson in a *ménage à trois* ('the trinity' or 'the three-life' as they called it). Intellectually Lye's style was often different from that of his scholarly friend but they shared an interest in ancient art and mythology. Graves was fiercely loyal to his friends and Lye became a particularly close friend. The artist's sophisticated taste in jazz was only one of several enthusiasms he passed on to Graves and Riding.

Laura Riding was 'slight, pale and fey, as spare and taut as her verse',[5] and had a great deal of personal charisma: 'Like a brooding, sultry day, there was electricity around [her].'[6] Supremely intelligent and energised by a new way of seeing the world, she had a sureness that others found either magnetic or disturbing. She would swing from being immensely charming to being fiercely judgemental. Born as Laura Reichenthal in New York in 1901 (the same year as Lye), she received a strong political education from her father who wanted her to become an American equivalent of Rosa Luxemburg, the famous political activist,[7] but at the age of 15 she rebelled against his socialist faith. In her early twenties, after the breakdown of her brief marriage to a professor of history, she selected 'Riding' as a new surname for herself. By now her own writing was highly original in its approach to language, and her closest literary ally was Gertrude Stein in Paris. She arrived in England in 1926 (the same year as Lye) to meet Graves and Nicholson who had written to tell her they admired her poetry. At first the three of them got on well together since Riding's feminist beliefs seemed to match those of Nicholson, and (as Lye observed) her knowledge of modernism 'brought Robert a lot of points of view he would never have got otherwise'.[8] During 1927 there were some strains in the three-way relationship and Nicholson and the four children went to live on the Thames barge the *Ringrose*, moored next to the barge that had been Lye's, while Graves and Riding lived nearby in the top flat at 35a St Peter's Square. The three of them shared the children and a kind of intellectual friendship survived between Nicholson and Riding.

Riding had assessed the artistic scene in England as 'a loose assemblage of unsure positions, occupied with a varying show of modernist daring'.[9] Her own intellectual and personal sureness could attract artists like a magnet. Although poetry was what she knew best, she was astute at recognising talent in other areas of art. She and Graves were both impressed by Lye's independence — this artist had found his own way to modernism instead of following the usual models (such as Picasso). He was doing work unlike anyone else in England and was not in the least overawed by the art scene. (As Lye wrote in a letter to Eric Kennington: 'After all the fuss and when the art critics have stopped making history there's nothing left but a few designs by Aus., Af., Am., or Ocean Is[land] aboriginals, designs complete in themselves, unattached to history or sentiment; done because they were feeling good and not goofy. . . . The welterweight mass of London still means nothing.')[10] Lye's work often went unnoticed because he was operating on a different wavelength from other artists, but Riding was quick to tune in. She wanted to create a community of people working in all the arts and Lye was a suitable candidate both as a film-maker and as a painter.

One aspect of his work she particularly liked was his 'no trouble' approach to time, which she linked with her desire for art to have a timeless or 'after-time' quality: 'Making a poem is like being alive for always: this is what I mean by laziness and there being no hurry or purpose.'[11] She described Lye in a poem as 'the least time-troubled of the exact'.[12] Lye interpreted this line to mean: 'I was slow but I had confidence'.[13] His letters to Riding often described such states of 'mental well-being', for example: 'Linger longer Laura, it's not Later yet, we've done better work before we do it, we'll be there. . . . The marvel just now is to know now and yet feel good.'[14]

Lye found Graves, Riding, and their friends heady company — a strong taste of the intellectual excitement he had hoped to find in Europe. Riding influenced Lye by encouraging him to get his ideas on to paper — she was one of the best teachers of writing he could possibly have had. She had a flair not only for recognising talent but also for boosting confidence. Lye's partner Jane remembered how she and other friends would often come away from a visit to Riding with the feeling of being special. The problem was that this made some people dependent on her. As Lye later remarked: 'She made a helluva rigmarole [which was] all very interesting. . . . If I hadn't come across such a person I would have wondered what all these bloody Californian movements were about. They're all about somebody like Laura . . . dictating health and happiness . . . and hypnotising everybody.'[15] Besides Graves (who treated her as his muse), Riding's disciples came to include John Aldridge, Norman Cameron, Tom Matthews (later the editor of *Time* magazine), Jacob Bronowski (author of *The Ascent of Man*), the sculptor Dorothy Simmons, and writers Alan Hodge, James Reeves, and Honor Wyatt. Her editing of their work was both brilliant and dictatorial. Riding also felt qualified to sort out the artist's personal lives. She attempted to split up Tom Matthews and his wife Julie;[16] she helped to create relationships for John Aldridge and Norman Cameron; she urged Lye and Jane Thompson to cohabit;[17] and she also gave a nudge to Jack Ellitt and Doris Harrison (who had been nurse to the Graves children). As Harrison recalled: 'She treated us as though we were already involved, she was always leering.'[18] Although they would develop a strong, lifelong relationship, Ellitt had the uneasy feeling in the beginning that Riding was sending him on 'a mission to take Doris's virginity'.[19] Outsiders were amazed by the extent to which Graves allowed his daily life to be managed by Riding, though it would probably have passed without comment if the reverse had been the case. Riding's authority helped to relieve Graves of some of his anxieties, and he had already been persuaded by Nicholson that men needed to learn more from women. He also seemed to be writing better poems under Riding's influence. At the same time her style of feminism was different from Nicholson's in that some women found her unsupportive, even threatening.

Lye had always been drawn to artists and writers who were extremists, but he was too independent, too much a self-made artist, to become merely one of Riding's 'human paintbrushes' (as Tom Matthews described them).[20] At the same time Thompson was very conscious of a tug-of-war: 'Laura was attracted to Len and would have liked to dominate him as she dominated the others. But I was not terrified of her as other women were, because I was certain that he was not going to fall so much under her influence. . . . She might have got him in bed with her — I don't know, she's probably the only one I've got doubts about. (The others I'm quite certain of!)'[21]

At the end of 1927 Graves and Riding installed an 1872 Crown Albion printing press in their flat at St Peter's Square and gave their operation the name of 'Seizin', an old legal word for 'possession as of freehold'.[22] This name meant a great deal to them because it signified their control of the means of production.[23] Their first publications were Riding's *Love as Love, Death as Death* and Gertrude Stein's *An Acquaintance with Description*. Both of these powerful books had title-page symbols by Lye, who became Seizin's principal artist. He based the Stein symbol on the Maori *koru* motif. A brochure carrying one of his machine-like images announced that *No Trouble*, a collection of Lye's letters, would be published by Seizin in April 1929. But this turned out to be a month of disasters.

Riding had had casual affairs with other men besides Graves but now she became seriously involved with an Anglo-Irish poet named Geoffrey Phibbs so that the so-called 'three-life' became a 'four-life'.[24] Phibbs left his wife Norah, started living on the *Avoca*, then moved into 35a, but was unable to adjust to the group situation. After an unsuccessful attempt to persuade Riding to run off with him he decided to go back to his wife. Riding was sufficiently distressed to mobilise all her friends in an attempt to track him down. Lye was persuaded to go and trick Phibbs's aunt into revealing his whereabouts: 'Len told her that he had a steady job to offer Geoffrey but needed to know immediately whether or not he could take it. The aunt told him that Geoffrey had gone to Rouen with Norah.'[25] (Riding later co-authored a fictionalised account of these events which transformed Lye into Joho, a tough guy who got his hands on an important address by pretending to be a reporter.)[26]

Graves went and brought Phibbs back to London on 26 April, but Phibbs and Riding continued to argue all night, with Graves and Nancy Nicholson in the background. Next morning Thompson received a phone call: 'It was Robert saying, "Would you ask Len to come over at once?" I said, "Yes, anything urgent?" and he said, "Laura's in trouble". So Len ran over to find that Laura had thrown herself out the window. They had been arguing things out when Laura apparently took half a bottle of something, then walked to the window, got out and hung on the ledge for a while, and then just fell.'[27] Graves was so distraught that he had run down one flight (to the third floor) and then jumped himself. He escaped with a shake-up but Riding was severely injured. The surgeon at Charing Cross Hospital is said to have remarked to those in the operating theatre: 'It is rarely that one sees the spinal-cord exposed to view — especially at right-angles to itself.'[28] After Phibbs made allegations to the police, Graves was questioned on suspicion of attempted murder. He offered satisfactory answers but then realised there was a strong possibility that Riding would be charged with attempted suicide, still a criminal offence in those days. By appealing to a friend in Whitehall, Graves succeeded in averting a prosecution,[29] but the story circulated through the literary community and became one of the most talked-about literary scandals of the day. Soon he had quarrelled with, or been disowned by, most of his friends. Lye and Thompson were among the few exceptions — in fact they drew closer to Graves and Riding during this period, and they also remained friends with Nicholson. On 6 May Nicholson made a definite break with Graves and henceforth had full custody of the children. There was another piece of news — she and Geoffrey Phibbs had decided to live together.

Riding defied the medical prognosis that she would remain crippled. During one of his hospital visits she instructed Lye to make a batik incorporating her 'damson-coloured surgical scar' with its pattern of stitches which she saw as her 'new icon'.[30] The suicide attempt and recovery had given her 'an extraordinary perspective from which to address everyone still confined in ordinary life'.[31] She could now conform even more fully to her ideal of art as timeless and uncompromising. In the words of Deborah Baker: '"Out of the windowness" became the sine qua non determining who was really with Laura and who was not.'[32]

Hearing of Riding's fall and recovery, Gertrude Stein wrote the following letter of support: 'My very dear Laura and Robert, I am rather selfishly glad that the result of it all means you both more completely together, you do mean that to me the two of you with Len [Lye] firmly in the background because after all it is hysteria that is vulgar and the complete absence of hysteria is very rare . . .'[33] Stein had not yet met Lye but she had heard of his firm stance and 'had admired the "freshness" of Lye's prose since she had been shown it in 1928'.[34] Her letter went on to invite Riding to visit her in Paris. Riding and Graves were both fed up with England but they were also short of money. Then Graves came up with the idea of quickly writing a book, an autobiography, that could solve their money problems and serve as his 'bitter leave-taking of England'.[35] Under the title *Good-Bye to All That*, this sifting of memories was his own way of extricating himself from history and culture. His alienation expressed itself in a style that was not so much angry as coolly detached and this gave novelty to his unromantic account of life in the trenches during the war.

Initially Graves had great difficulty with the writing of the book. Meanwhile hospital expenses were mounting and the need for money was becoming more urgent.[36] One day Thompson said: 'Look, Robert, I can come here in the morning and you can talk to me about it. Then I can rough it out on the typewriter and you can look at it when you're going up in the train to visit Laura, and then I can retype it.'[37] So he started dictating the book to Thompson, and the process worked so well that he completed it in eleven weeks: 'He would walk up and down remembering his experiences during the war. I'd lost all the shorthand I'd ever learned but I had my own way of squiggling things down. He said afterwards that he thought the narrative flowed well because he was able to talk it out. In recognition of which he gave me the corrected galleys which I subsequently sold for ten pounds when we were broke, as we usually were.'[38]

Having insisted on the right to select a dust-jacket for the book, Graves asked Lye to design it. The result was a striking piece of avant-garde design. When the publisher, Jonathan Cape, saw what Lye had produced, he sent Graves a 'stiff letter' warning him that many thousands of sales might be lost.[39] The front cover combined a photograph of the author with a photograph of 'Tomb Cylinder', a construction made for the occasion consisting of various circular shapes with string pulley-belts and a futuristic machine or cylinder enclosing a solitary frag-ment of nature — a branch with leaves. The almost transparent materials produced complex shadows. The back cover was another kind of war memorial — a collage that included a map of France, cigarettes, a cup, a glove, and another leafy branch. Graves would not be talked out of using Lye's design, and later wrote to the publisher: 'On the several occasions on which you and I have got on the subject of . . . covers, etc., we have always been at cross-purposes. You think that my taste is much too modernistic and I think yours disgracefully on the safe side.'[40] He added: 'As the photographed head was his [that is, by Lye] and was the best photograph ever taken of me, I think you were very lucky'. When Graves's book was about to be issued in the United States the American publisher wrote to Jonathan Cape asking him to explain the covers. Cape passed the request on to the artist. Lye's reply to Cape was: 'I could spend a couple of weeks explaining it and they still wouldn't understand it — so just tell them it's a dustjacket.'[41]

The book became a subject of fierce controversy, a bestseller, and eventually a classic. Graves made far more money than he had dared to hope — and far more than he would ever make out of poetry. Meanwhile he and Riding had left for Europe in October 1929 while *Good-Bye to All That* was being printed. Dedicated to her, the book ended with a brief account of her fall and the events surrounding it (a revealing 'Epilogue' that Graves was to remove from later editions). When the premiere of *Tusalava* took place in December, Lye included a note in the Film Society programme thanking his absent friend for financial help.[42] Meanwhile Graves and Riding had followed up one of Gertrude Stein's suggestions and rented a cottage on Mallorca in the Balearic Islands. They urged Lye and Thompson to come to visit them as soon as possible.

eighteen mallorca

Soon after the *Tusalava* screening Lye headed for Mallorca, accompanied by Jane Thompson, John Aldridge, and Kanty Cooper. Their first port of call was Paris on 28 December. Lye had brought several films, including *Tusalava*, which film-makers associated with the Studio des Ursulines were eager to see. This cinema had been the venue for the stormy first screening of *The Seashell and the Clergyman*, the French Surrealist film banned in England. With his usual distrust of Customs, Lye decided not to declare the films but to give each of the group some cans to hide. Cooper recalled: 'We all looked rather a queer shape, especially me with a film in my inside hip pocket under a tight-fitting coat!' Once safely through Customs, they caught a taxi to the Studio des Ursulines. This was Lye's first visit to Paris and for once he was overawed and anxious. In Cooper's words: 'I had never seen Len serious before! He kept saying "But Montparnasse can't be as far away as this, the taxi driver must be taking us round in circles!"'[1]

The group went on to have lunch with Gertrude Stein and Alice B. Toklas at 27 rue de Fleurus. Stein in a tweed suit and bow tie showed them round her remarkable collection of paintings, and Lye handed over a batik on Japanese silk commissioned by Riding as a gift for her. That evening he and his companions met Nancy Cunard, an Englishwoman who was playing an important role in the avant-garde through her Hours Press, which published the work of writers such as Samuel Beckett and Ezra Pound. The premises of the press at 15 rue Guenegaud were decorated 'with paintings by Miró, Malkine and Tanguy as well as pieces from her growing collection of primitive art: painted shields, fetish figures and sculptures from Africa, New Guinea and the South Seas'.[2] Besides promoting art and writing, Cunard was active as a campaigner against racism. She had met Lye previously in London and commissioned him to design covers for three Hours Press poetry books — two by Riding and one by Graves. This put him in good company since other cover artists in the same series included Man Ray and Yves Tanguy. Cunard, a perceptive viewer of Lye's work, said later that his cover for *Twenty Poems Less* had helped her understand Riding's writing and its ambition to be timeless: 'I thought I [could] not comprehend [her] particular symbolism. . . . But when Len Lye's beautiful photomontages for the covers of her book came, it seemed to me that he was in perfect communion with what she was expressing. . . . Made of assembled fragments, that might be found on some exotic or dream strand, these designs suggested nature's world in a sort of petrified permanence. . . . As with the poems and their maker, the word for this could be "other-world".'³

Cunard was herself an exotic figure, as Cooper recalled from their visit: 'Nancy arrived with a green face, and she had huge bracelets, absolutely huge. She looked as though she should wear a leopard skin. She came in with her black lover [the American jazz pianist Henry Crowder], an enormous man, very gentle. . . . I was so knocked out by Nancy, I'd never seen anything like it — green face, green cheeks, green eyes!'⁴ Later Lye recorded his impressions of Cunard: 'I saw a white praying mantis benignly clunking ivory bracelets praying her wheel clinking ice in her drinks. She was my idea . . . of Paris from London and any night was right to hear Mantis Prayer on arms of bone poised on the glass stem . . . white & black, ivory & glass, skin & bones. She was OK by me out of the corners of both eyes. As for the Hours Press it was part of the here we are ourselves.'⁵

From Paris the group took a train to Barcelona, where they stayed several days. Then having taken a boat to Mallorca they travelled by road to Deyá, a small fishing village well off the tourist track. To Riding and Graves it seemed a suitable refuge from the superficialities of modern life. Lye took an immediate liking to this rocky island, which reminded him in some respects of New Zealand. He reported to Eric Kennington: 'There are many things here unequalled — plants, rock formations, shapes of twigs, pebbles on beach. Sun is good, so is clear daylight and nightlight. . . . Mountains their own textures, a good stream below and trees with their own balance about them.'⁶ The other members of the party were less enthusiastic about Mallorca, which was having a very wet January. Thompson had brought only summer clothes since she expected Mallorca to be 'like the South of France where the English go to escape the dismal English winter'. Their house, Casa Salerosa, 'had stone walls, a concrete floor, and didn't receive any sun even on fine days'.⁷ Also 'Laura used to serve us dismal little meals with a base of salt pork or something, which caused considerable constipation, and she wouldn't let anyone — not even Len — into the kitchen'.⁸ Cooper was upset about the rats that ran over her bed.⁹ Thompson was more worried by Riding's talk of building Lye a film studio on the end of Casa Salerosa so he would become a permanent resident. 'She wanted to appropriate him intellectually!'¹⁰ Eventually Thompson insisted that she and Lye find a different house, but her attitude was viewed as highly suspicious: 'Laura put me through an inquisition that lasted for hours. Finally I broke the whole thing up by throwing a fake hysterical attack.'¹¹ Graves and Riding then arranged for their four visitors to stay in Ca'n Pa Bo, a pleasant cottage with a courtyard and almond trees and a well on the other side of the village.

This new situation eased the tensions and Lye and his partner stayed about four months on Mallorca. She served as typist for Graves and Riding, and he made a number of covers for Seizin and Hours Press books, 'celebration-type things'[12] with no direct connection to the particular texts. While these covers baffled many people they were very eye-catching, and together with the meticulous hand-printing of Graves and Riding they gave the Seizin books a distinctive house style. Some were examples of Lye's biological imagery — doodles that had grown into unknown forms of life which metamorphosed and danced energetically. The covers for Graves's *To Whom Else?* were an exception with their geometrical patterns in silver, black, and dark blue. One reader described the back cover as an abstract pattern of 'circles and rectangles in rows' and thought the front cover suggested 'a peacock's tail'.[13] In fact the starting-point for the front cover was the memory of 'a feather headdress' in the film *Pearls and Savages*.[14] But Lye's shapes were so abstract he could describe the same image on another occasion as 'a plant form going up, chasing vitamin C'.[15] With their striking colours and visual rhythms, these images also recalled the tribal textiles he had been studying for many years.[16] For the covers of Riding's *Twenty Poems Less* Lye again created strange living creatures but on this occasion he used collage. Stones, twigs, roots, pieces of bark, and other local materials were arranged on a background of burlap and rough planks of wood. This produced complex textures and was very evocative. For the back cover Lye had the idea of re-photographing a section of the same collage ('Earth Goddess') with the light source at a different angle.

He and the other visitors spent a great deal of time exploring the mountains around Deyá, occasionally getting themselves into dangerous situations. Cooper remembered being just saved from a serious fall by Graves. As a teenager Graves had gone on climbing expeditions in Wales with famous mountaineers such as George Mallory. In Cooper's words: 'I was astonished what a good climber he [Graves] was because he was so clumsy. If he came into a room you'd hasten to put all the china out of reach in case it went flying!'[17] Climbing was difficult for Lye — he felt as though his 'nuts and bolts were clattering and about to fall off'[18] — but he was excited by the Mallorcan landscape, which reminded him of his childhood at Cape Campbell. There was one experience in particular which made a lasting impression: 'The shallow water of the bay was so limpidly clear I began to examine the big boulders on the bottom and marvel at their water-magnified clarity. Then along came a school of great big fish. They traversed the entire bay as they glided along. There seemed to be more fish than there were because their shadows slid along the large white stones.'[19] This sight was so 'fleetingly and magically kinesthetic' that it left him musing about how to create an 'equivalent form in abstract motion sculpture'.[20] Two works of art that always reminded him of this scene were a 'big marble fish' by the sculptor Brancusi, and the song 'Full Fathom Five' in Shakespeare's *Tempest*.

Thompson remembered Lye becoming engrossed in 'collecting stones, combing the beach for oddments, and making constructions. . . . We all used to go down to the beach for our bath and we would have to collect pebbles. Judgement would be passed on them.'[21] Lye discovered there was nothing to stop him sending some of his favourite stones to friends as letters, though Post Office staff would frantically check their rule books. His friends would receive letters that consisted simply of an interesting stone bearing a stamp and their address in Lye's handwriting.[22] He kept some stones for his outdoor constructions, an extreme development of his collages: 'I would just take chicken-wire and put stone and wood in the chicken-wire, find a good piece of earth, the side of a cliff . . . or some spring running out, put the wire up against it and say "This is the [book] cover". But to make it more like a convincing type of composition I would do a cement job of . . . conduits and viaducts and stones.'[23] A local photographer was hired to record Lye's constructions and two of the photographs were then used as the covers of Graves's *Ten Poems More*.[24] Another photograph has survived which shows that these images were details of a larger construction which included some totem-like figures. Working with the landscape in this way Lye was thinking of the sacred sites of the Australian Aborigines. Aniela Jaffe has said: 'We know that even unhewn stones had a highly symbolic meaning for ancient and primitive societies. . . . Their use may be regarded as a primeval form of sculpture'. Sometimes touches of human shaping were added but the stone was mostly left to 'speak for itself'.[25] Lye saw his constructions in this way as a 'primitive-type shrine idea'.[26] By a small intervention — the grouping of stones, say, or the placing of strands of wire — he could convey his insight into a particular landscape (what James Joyce would call 'inscape', and Gerard Manley Hopkins 'instress'). In Lye's words: 'The rocks and other things, they are certainly always there timeless and it's not until some insighter comes along that they have any whatever.'[27] In another letter he wrote: 'What then is the reason for animal man to browse in amongst such [natural] phenomena, if not to state the reason for the arrangement . . . by showing that only a personal insight enables it to survive as a landscape. . . . And as paint holds no favour for me or for mine I do hereby declare it null and void hence insisting on the result not of paint but of the insight.'[28] If for some reason he had stayed in Deyá or gone back to New Zealand in the 1930s it seems likely he would have developed this form of art more extensively. His constructions anticipated the kind of 'earth art' that would emerge in the late 1960s — site-specific sculpture that consisted of some small addition to a particular landscape, leaving no permanent result except the photograph that documented it.

Before leaving Mallorca Lye worked with Laura Riding on his book *No Trouble*, a showcase for his doodling with words or what he called his 'zig-zag back-to-front type verbalising'.[29] 'I used to train my old Brain to forget everyday grammar and just let its word arrangements fall where they may. If you word-doodle after supper, you'll find that you begin to develop your own idiom, your own fingerprint stuff, in your own word arrangements. In any case you'll get a kick out of it because your wits get sharper.'[30] He admired the risk-taking of poets such as Rimbaud and Stein, and wanted translations of tribal sayings to keep as close as possible to the original idioms. For example, he was very struck by an Aboriginal description of a road that was translated as: 'What is it road for me there they are standing up hills'.[31]

Lye found it easier to doodle with words in a conversation than on a page but he sometimes could get into the right frame of mind when writing a letter: 'I would remember a letter long overdue, so to get pleasure out of at last writing, I would write it in this spontaneous way.'[32] For example: 'Hello Robert [Graves] up in Cumberland amongst the goats and springwater hills and mud. We all went to a show yesterday trusting to luck and the outside posters and inside golly it was nothing but a gully of dustbins: as usual the deadness: as usual up in the air thick and nasty: as usual it curled us up: as usual we slunk away not anything. Now I ask you! a little sparkle now and then is relished by all last-word men. . . . Anyhow, if we all stopped pushing away the garbage around work and concentrated on no trouble just easy and good to go . . . we'd certainly never want to kick our own dustbins young as we are in our own lives anyway. Yes you bet, any of us could float an easy haze enough to warm the cockles of anybody's nipples . . . .'.[33]

His letters would usually include doodling, both verbal and visual. Many letters were obscure, some were (in his own opinion) 'rather over-ebullient and therefore pretty corny', but almost all contained flashes of what he called 'old brain writing' and his friends valued them for their crazy wisdom.[34] Lye believed that inherently everyone had an individual way of handling words but society had many subtle ways of destroying confidence. He wrote: 'All English teachers should give their prior attention to each pupil's own distinctive idiom' before they imposed general rules.[35] Lye had developed his word doodling without any thought of publication but when Riding saw some of his letters she at once recognised their freshness and said: 'You'd better start saving these because we're going to do a book of them.'[36] She had a strong interest in letter-writing and would later publish an anthology, *Everybody's Letters,*[37] in which she argued that 'letters are the most anarchic activity tolerated as ungovernable in civilised experience'.[38] Letters were 'the very next-best thing' to poems,[39] especially those that made inventive use of the medium.

Riding outlined her views on *No Trouble* to Hugh Ford: 'Len Lye . . . was working to develop forms . . . for a primitivistic alternative to the visual experiences afforded by conventional art. . . . The book was . . . written in a style that was an informal verbal version of his technique in the visual field. . . . There was in Len Lye himself an instinctive sympathy with the devotion to chosen standards that was a strong component of the [Seizin] Press's critical atmosphere. In a sense that both books were uncompromisingly what they were, neither deviating anywhere from the adopted compositional "line", *No Trouble* was not a strange successor to [Gertrude Stein's] *An Acquaintance with Description*. But it held a very different personal character; for one thing, it produced excitements, and there was evident excitement in the writing.'[40] Riding also commented that 'there was a greatly appealing, loveable, good-feeling freedom in his letters'.[41] She selected and edited Lye's letters but took care not to iron out the idiosyncrasies.[42] This was Riding at her best as an editor, selecting twenty letters that Lye had written to 'Laura [Riding]', 'Robert [Graves]', 'Ben [Nicholson]', 'Eric' and 'Celandine [Kennington]', 'Cedric [Morris]', 'Norman [Cameron]', 'Jane [Thompson]', and 'Rose Ann [Lye]', among others.[43] There was also a letter addressed to 'God'! *No Trouble* had something of the character of a diary covering the years 1928 to 1930, vividly expressing the 'no trouble' or 'easy jazz' atmosphere of its Hammersmith milieu. While Lye wrote with special affection to his mother and expressed some nostalgic feelings about New Zealand and his 'friends of yore', he was blunt in asserting that staying overseas was essential to his work.

According to its usual procedure the Seizin Press produced 200 copies beautifully hand-printed on handmade paper, with gold covers by Lye. The book sold for 25 shillings, a reasonable price in terms of the production values but likely to restrict the audience mainly to collectors. Kanty Cooper, who returned to London two months before Lye and Thompson, had the job of distributing Seizin books. She made the rounds of all the booksellers in Charing Cross Road but none was especially sympathetic to avant-garde work. 'There were awful rows with Laura when the books didn't sell — not rows with me, she would write directly to the booksellers!'[44] In 1931 the Press sent review copies of *No Trouble*, Graves's *To Whom Else?* and Riding's *Though Gently* to a number of publications. Reviewers admired the look of the books, but their only way of dealing with the contents was to be either flippant or moralistic. These were still common responses to all forms of modernism. Even Graves's rather traditional writing raised eyebrows because it referred to arm-pits and dung-worms.[45] *Publishers Circular* began its combined review with the comment: 'We must confess right away that the contents of the [three] books are entirely beyond our comprehension' [1 August 1931]. *Time and Tide* lectured Riding on her 'lazy' style, and said of *No Trouble*: 'Mr Len Lye is a student of that school which Mr James Joyce was mainly responsible for founding . . . and of which you will find endless examples in the magazines which provide outlets for those young American writers who are still in their experimental stage and throwing off minor pieces.'[46] The *Manchester Guardian* began by observing sadly that 'There is no chance of getting an amusing evening out of these books' then launched into an almost incoherent tirade: 'Why did she do it? Why did she sit in Majorca and do it? Why did Len Lye do the cover? [etc.]'[47]

The *Times Literary Supplement* was the only periodical that made any attempt to assess *No Trouble* seriously: 'Mr Lye has a strong natural exuberance which he does not try to restrain. He gives exasperation an amusing gusto in a letter called "In Grim Determination", and we like his fable of the butterfly and the dragonfly. But a certain general looseness and apparent carelessness of form suggest an aptness in the title which may or may not be intentional.'[48] In general these reviews provided typical examples of the resistance to experimental work. As we have already seen from the Seven and Five Society, modernists found scarcely any audience outside of their fellow artists. From hard experience they had no faith in the average reviewer and no respect for the official art world. As Lye put it in the first section of *No Trouble*: 'I was dragged up among the tombstones and . . . learned that the most the monuments stand for is to be found at the foot of any lamp-post.'

nineteen a wedding

Back in London Lye's attention turned to film projects but it was difficult to find a producer willing even to listen to his ideas, particularly as the Depression had now set in. With her partner pouring so much time into non-paying projects, Thompson shrewdly managed the household budget and earned all she could as a typist and part-time fashion model. She still found Lye easy to live with for he never lost his gaiety despite money pressures and the many rejections of his work.[1] She made unusual clothes for him which were a sensation at parties. They shared a love of jazz and often went dancing; they took long walks through London, or dropped in to see their Hammersmith friends. But she still suffered from confidence problems whenever a group discussion turned intellectual. She knew that some bohemian acquaintances regarded her as too suburban and they were always suspicious of her attempts (no matter how justified) to help Lye become more businesslike. When she had a serious argument with her partner it was most often about fidelity, for while they had a sexual relationship that both found very satisfying he found it hard to understand why they should not both be free to have other partners. She kept such a close eye on him that other women tended to find her unfriendly. The freethinkers looked upon her 'possessiveness' as another middle-class hang-up. Lye valued his relationship with her and was willing to tone down his behaviour, but to him it seemed unnatural to be totally faithful. In particular he found it hard to stop seeing Liz Johnson who had been a special friend since his first year in London. In Lye's words: 'When Liz talked, the vibrancy of her cockney twang pinned back your ears. She had a trick of turning at you sideways and throwing her eyes at you, to connect with such force that you took a bosun's chair and swivelled over to her deck.'[2] He saw the sexually liberated Johnson as Thompson's opposite, and the fact that she lived nearby in St Peter's Square made her a constant temptation to him and a constant anxiety to his partner.

At the end of 1931 Thompson received a cable from her father asking her to accompany her grandmother on a boat trip from England to South Africa. She agreed to do so not only because of the family obligation but also because she wanted some time away from Lye to think about her future. Returning to South Africa also gave her an opportunity to get a divorce from the man she had once eloped with. During the long voyage she found herself showered with attention, in particular by a man in the British consular service who had been serving in South America.[3] While she was staying with her family he sent her a cable proposing marriage, and her parents tried to persuade her to accept.

Lye initially missed Thompson a great deal. He wrote a blues lyric 'My baby's gone left me' which was published in a local arts magazine.[4] But then Johnson moved in to The Barn and Lye became engrossed in her: 'She came home like the Mayflower visiting America.'[5] He was also intrigued by her social circle, a mixture of the fashionable rich and the London underworld, including prostitutes and criminals such as 'Henry the fence' and 'Spin the cat burglar'.[6] In Lye's words: 'This was the time when I couldn't care less for society at large nor any part of its conformity.'[7] Meanwhile Thompson prolonged her stay in South Africa. Her family's affluent lifestyle was a novelty and she had several suitors. But she was troubled by South African politics and she missed the excitement of her life with Lye, an excitement that seemed in retrospect to matter more than his careless attitudes to sex and money. She came finally to the realisation that she could not give him up.[8]

Neither Johnson nor Lye had ever wanted their relationship to be exclusive. One day, visiting the Ellitts on their barge, she met John Stuart-Wortley who was working as Ellitt's assistant on music projects. (Ellitt was trying to develop a business based on his many innovative ideas for use of the new sound-recording technologies.) Johnson and Stuart-Wortley began an affair which ended in marriage. He belonged to a wealthy South African family who were horrified by the news and disowned their son.[9] The couple left for Brazil, and the news that Johnson was out of the picture confirmed Thompson's decision to return.[10] She arrived back in London a few months later, and Lye was genuinely delighted to have her back. He had been going through a very frustrating period in his film work. On 4 April of the following year (1934) they were married in a brief, non-religious ceremony at the Hammersmith Registry Office. The witnesses were John Aldridge and his partner Lucie Brown, recently returned from Mallorca. Thompson wrote down her address as 9a Black Lion Lane ('The Barn'), but presumably to avoid embarrassment Lye gave his as the barge *Avoca*. He listed his occupation as 'Artist (designer)' and then in a touching exaggeration he recorded his father's occupation as 'Artist (painter)'. Neither his family nor Thompson's were represented at the wedding. Some of their Hammersmith neighbours were shocked to hear they had thrown away their bohemian principles by getting married but everybody was certain the idea was Jane's rather than Len's. Graves spread the inaccurate gossip that she was pregnant.

According to another observer, 'Jane wanted Len's name'.[11] Her new habit of referring to him as 'my husband' rather than 'Len' struck their friends as a bad omen; but they could understand why she might feel insecure in the relationship, and some guessed that she now wanted to start a family. Questioned years later about the marriage she remarked: 'We were flat broke. I said to Len, "If we get married, my father will probably give us some money". So we literally married for money.'[12] This gift helped them through a period of financial crisis, and their life together continued in a generally happy fashion, but Lye was later to comment to an intimate friend that after he had 'finally given in' to his partner's request to get married, he felt even less of an obligation to remain faithful.[13]

Jane Lye now embarked on a new career. In South Africa a professional dancer had said to her: 'You're the best natural dancer I've ever come across so why don't you teach?' Back in London she took a three-month course at the Imperial Society for Ballroom Dancers, then gained a job at Josephine Bradley's 'very respectable' school in Knightsbridge where she worked alongside a dancing instructor so fanatical she had cut off some of her toes in order to wear a narrower shoe. Jane became expert at dancing the rumba which she learned from a Cuban couple: 'It has a very tricky rhythm if you're doing it properly, it's sort of like getting in before the beat.' She won silver cups in rumba competitions and sent them to her mother-in-law in New Zealand. And she taught the dance to Lye who liked it so much he started thinking about ways of using Cuban dance music in films.

Her knowledge of South Africa also had an influence on Lye's approach to painting. During her visit to the Drakensberg mountains in Natal someone had told her about some ancient cave art that could be reached by a four-hour ride. Local residents took little interest in the art but she had managed to persuade a small party to accompany her to the caves where she took photographs. She brought the photographs back to Lye and they greatly heightened the interest he already felt in ancient African art.[14] He obtained a reader's ticket to the Victoria and Albert Museum Library and looked up a large number of books about prehistoric art, including those of Abbé Breuil whose illustrations were vivid and painterly.[15]

At the beginning of the 1930s Lye had gone through a period of rejecting painting as too traditional, devoting his energies instead to photograms and plans for films; but at the end of 1932, still blocked from making films, he had gone back to painting. Some of his gouaches had been accepted for the Seven and Five Society's exhibition in February. Developed from doodles they brought together protagonist figures representing various types of energy. In 'Cagn Who Made

Things' a creature with a strange triangular head, poised on three long stick-like legs, was emitting a stream of darkness from one of its dark eyes. As this stream reached the dark object on which the creature was standing, it became a bright splash. After completing the painting Lye decided to associate the creature with one of the gods of the San people (or Bushmen, as they were called by white South Africans). Cagn, a cross between a man and a mantis, was 'the originator and creator of things' who needed to be propitiated by dancing.[16]

Later Lye created his own remarkable myth, interpreting the image as the discovery of the sense of sight out of the sense of touch: 'Then there was the first great man of all trees who knew all things by feeling them with his feet. Now a tree has its heart in its roots. Because the first great man had his heart in his feet he found the world and it was a big black log. Then everything was black inside and out. The great man wanted to know more of the log than he could feel with his feet. He thought of what he felt so long and hard that he made a waterfall of seeing come out of his head and fall on the log. So he saw with his head what he felt with his feet and it was the earth in the shape of a black log. With his seeing he watered it and it grew green branches.'[17]

Other paintings that he exhibited in 1933 were based on doodles that seemed to have a family resemblance. Indeed, one was given the title 'Family' and Lye developed a whimsical story about a group of flora puzzled by their new offspring, a small creature who had a snake-like body instead of roots, and who refused to stay put. Lye imagined that the painting showed a family conference being held to discuss this mobile mutation who represented an entirely new species.[18] The theme of evolution was also suggested by other 1933 titles such as 'Earth Cools, Plants Arrive, and Fire Devil departs' (for a complex painting about the fire devil Lye had 'prised loose with a doodle' from the pattern of cracks in dry wood).[19]

Starting to feel that his approach was getting too predictable Lye stopped looking for totem figures and began experimenting with 'a method of colour notation in oils' that seemed closer to 'the actual activity of sensation'.[20] This change was reflected in his three paintings for the Seven and Five exhibition in 1934. Their abstract titles — 'Marks on Pink', 'Design on Buff', and 'White Wall Painting' — signalled the fact that Lye's interest had shifted from tribal art to prehistoric cave drawings, the most ancient and cryptic form of art. He had always been aware of this kind of art, but the photographs his wife had brought back from South Africa had provided a further push.

Lye was not the only avant-garde artist talking about cave art at this time, and there was a broader trend towards more extreme abstract forms of painting.

For Ben Nicholson this implied pure forms of geometrical abstraction, an approach he promoted through the Seven and Five Society. A tireless organiser, he sought to create an English equivalent of European movements such as Abstraction-Creation. In contrast Lye's version of abstract art was more doodley or painterly, resembling cave art whose signs seemed to float at the far edges of meaning. The Spanish artist Joan Miró was interested not only in cave markings but also in the richly textured walls of the caves (some of which were near his home), and he began giving his paintings a complex ground of layered glazes.[21] Although Lye was not aware of Miró's current work he was moving in a similar direction, emphasising the physical aspects of colour and line. His study of cave art helped him to narrow the gap between the raw energy of his doodles and the smoother brushwork of his paintings.[22]

One friend who shared this cluster of interests was Humphrey Jennings. Jennings, who was introduced to Lye by Laura Riding, was 'rather tall, very angular and bony, with a wild crop of straggly fair hair, usually quite uncontrollable. He had . . . an extremely prominent Adam's apple which jumped all over the place while he talked — which was a great deal of the time.'[23] Jennings was passionately interested in many subjects but above all in modernity.[24] While still a student at Cambridge University, Jennings had created the 'Experiment Gallery' with his friends Julian Trevelyan and Gerald Noxon, and had established direct lines of communication with the French avant-garde. There was room for the most ancient art in his definition of the most modern, and by 1933 when he settled in London he had already gathered an impressive amount of information on cave art.[25] In Lye's view Jennings 'was a fabulous person. Highly original, highly creative, but over-intellectual because once you got talking with Humphrey you went into a kind of drunkenness. You woke up with a hangover next morning, . . . your brain reeling with thoughts and words.'[26] Lye usually avoided such talkers but he admired Jennings not only as a source of information about art but also as an exciting painter in his own right. A painting given to the Lyes as a present was based on a postcard photograph of a horse and cart, reduced to 'a few brushstrokes of infinite delicacy of touch and subtlety of colour, on [a canvas] left largely bare'.[27] Lye saw affinities between this calligraphic approach and his own doodling, though he was also struck by how different the results could be. In 1934 he wrote an enthusiastic letter to John Aldridge nominating Jennings for membership of the Seven and Five Society: 'I met a lovely up-and-down Cambridge-Elton talk chap but thin and 22 but best he paints lovely blobs of ink or oil to be Constable but as quick as the sting of a china [he can] write [an ideogram] and so Humphrey Jennings. He's going over to P [Paris] soon so you won't see him till, but a good bet for 7 & 6.'[28] The fact that Lye's nomination was unsuccessful was a symptom of changes taking place within the Society. Nicholson, its most influential member, now specialised in austere relief paintings of geometrical shapes. Artists associated with a primitivist or painterly approach were voted out of the Society. Lye had always admired Nicholson's work but a gulf had opened up between their different conceptions of abstract art.

In 1935–36 Jennings got more involved with Surrealism, and his paintings became in Lye's opinion 'more and more literary',[29] leading to some fierce arguments between the two artists.[30] Nevertheless they still had common interests, particularly as Jennings became more involved with film-making. He worked for the local agents for Gasparcolor and Dufaycolor, the new colour processes, as an artistic adviser. Colour in films was still a novelty and it had the potential to become big business. Jane Lye served as Jennings's model: 'On one occasion I had to run round the top of an office building while Humphrey tested various types of colour film.'[31] Becoming an expert on film processes Jennings began using similar methods of colour separation in some of his paintings, experimenting with pointillist dots of colour.[32] Like Lye he kept up his avant-garde painting alongside his film work but film seemed more likely to provide him with a living.

twenty peanut vendor

What Lye called 'fine-art film-making' was still at an early stage of development. Since 1926 his membership in the London Film Society had allowed him to sample most of the work being done. He admired the German Expressionist film *The Cabinet of Dr. Caligari* (1919) as the first 'fine-art feature film' but its style was not sufficiently abstract for his own use,[1] and he was more interested in the short abstract animated films made in Germany during the 1920s by Viking Eggeling, Oskar Fischinger, Hans Richter, and Walther Ruttmann. Eggeling's *Diagonal Symphony* (1924) struck Lye as 'marvellous', and he was also very excited by one of Fischinger's films: 'Mighty good for some few seconds of it. It's all I aim for, myself, just a few moments of real kinesthesia — there's no other kick of its kind.'[2] Although Fischinger and Lye never worked together, each felt an affinity for the other's films. In the later words of Elfriede Fischinger: 'My husband Oskar was always aware of Len's [film] work; we saw most of it together and I know that Oskar liked and appreciated it.'[3] At the same time Lye was less interested than Fischinger and his German contemporaries in abstract images of a geometrical kind.

From Paris, still a centre of modern art in the 1920s, came films such as Man Ray's *Return to Reason* (1923), Fernand Léger and Dudley Murphy's *Ballet Mécanique* (1924), René Clair and Francis Picabia's *Entr'acte* (1924), and Marcel Duchamp's *Anemic Cinema* (1925). At this time many avant-garde painters were interested in making films but few projects were completed because of the costs and technical difficulties of the medium.[4] The few experimental films produced in England, by directors such as Kenneth Macpherson and Oswell Blakeston, tended to have closer links with literature than with painting (though there were exceptions such as *Light Rhythms* and *Tusalava*).[5]

In the late 1920s and early 1930s all existing types of art-film-making were overshadowed by the new style of narrative film developed in the USSR by directors such as Sergei Eisenstein and Vsevolod Pudovkin. Their work combined radical politics with dramatic imagery and innovative editing. In capitalist countries the attempts to ban films such as *Battleship Potemkin* merely added to their interest. Eisenstein visited London in December 1929 and delivered a typically high-powered series of lectures — combining art, science and philosophy — that made a deep impression on the young British film-makers who were later to create the documentary movement of the 1930s.[6] Eisenstein was accompanied by Hans Richter who led a film-making workshop in a small studio above Foyle's Bookshop in Manette Street.[7] Despite the opportunity to watch Richter and Eisenstein at work, Lye was disappointed by one aspect of this 'expensive' workshop — the particular film exercise selected by Richter who was at the time so strongly influenced by Russian films that he steered the group towards political themes.[8] The final result — later given the title *Everyday* — was an ingenious satire on the yuppies of the 1920s, showing the build-up to the stock market crash. Lye, who took part as an extra, felt uneasy about the extent to which Eisenstein's aesthetics were coming to dominate experimental film-making. Nevertheless, his meeting with Richter was the start of a long friendship between the two men.

Lye was now thinking of *Tusalava* as the first part of a trilogy: 'I wanted to do this great big film, taking about ten years to make.'[9] Oswell Blakeston described Lye's plans in an essay for *Architectural Review*: 'The second section . . . deals with the beginnings of geological shapes . . . and ends with a conflict between land and water shapes in a climax similar to the first. . . . Layer upon layer the earth builds up: sea corrodes. Earth figures turn into palpitating light, recessed circles of vibrations; sea figures in the eternal role of destroyer, form a contact. Anni-hilation comes in a violent series of electric sparks.'[10] In the third section, as Lye described it, the earth would continue to evolve as a 'ballet' between 'natural objects' and 'more humanized shapes'.[11] Finally there would be an apocalyptic 'Epilogue' with an explosion in which concentric circles would be combined with footage of ripples in water, and then the camera would 'dive down into their centre for an underwater take of nebulous dots and flickering light which is the complete circle back to the beginning, which is Uma — the end'.[12] Jack Ellitt saw the project as an opportunity to apply some of his radical ideas about music. His soundtrack would employ 'wire brushes, tap drums, [and] natural sounds, e.g. rushing water, crackle of high frequency current, etc'.[13] Anticipating later developments in electronic music, Ellitt saw film sound technology as an oppor-tunity for music to be reinvented. Composers no longer needed to limit their ideas to traditional instruments but could select and mix the entire range of possible effects. 'All world sounds of interest now come within a sphere of creative control which may be termed Sound-Construction. . . . Therefore we may say that music [as we know it] is ethnological and dated. . . . Musical forms are only the chrysales from which more beautifully conceived forms will eventually burst forth in complete freedom and independence.'[14] Sound compo-sition would also rescue composers from the frustrations of live performance (such as those associated with the premiere of *Tusalava*). Unfortunately both Lye and Ellitt lacked the money to realise their ideas. Blakeston noted in his 1932 report that although Lye had 'created hundreds of plans, diagrams, photograms, batiks, all relating to the other sections of his film, ... economic problems have not, so far, allowed him to transfer these moments to celluloid'.[15] The artist was able to exhibit some of this material separately but he could not find a sponsor. Apart from the esoteric nature of his project, a sound film was going to cost more than a silent one. This increase in cost and the drying up of funding put many independent film-makers out of business in the early 1930s.

Back on Mallorca, Riding had asked Lye to create the scenery for a large-scale masque, 'Fantasia', which evolved gradually into a film scenario, 'Description of Life'.[16] Riding wore Lye out with so many letters about the project that he finally had to ask her to stop writing. Meanwhile, racking his brains for a project commercial enough to pay the bills, he speculated that there would be opportunities for filmed ballet as part of the growing popularity of music in films.[17] Ballet was a suitable meeting-ground between art and commerce, and in the 1930s it was 'one form of entertainment which rapidly extended its popularity from high-brows downwards'.[18] Personally Lye was more interested in the traditional dance forms of Japan, Java, and other non-western cultures, but he and Jane Lye had been hugely impressed by the Diaghilev Ballet Company (formerly known as the Ballets Russes) when it performed at Covent Garden in July 1929, shortly before Diaghilev's death. Its month-long season, which included Stravinsky's *The Rite of Spring*, was seen by Lye as proof that a ballet company could gain success by employing avant-garde composers and designers. And wasn't there an equally wide range of talent among his own friends?

For a start, there was Jack Ellitt's music. At this time Ellitt was working on a sound-construction (on 78 rpm gramophone records) that evoked rocket travel to the moon. Then Riding suggested making a fantastical musical comedy on this theme. This was exactly the type of project Lye was looking for, since a science fiction story would be well suited to the new colour film stocks and it would give him plenty of opportunity to experiment with visual effects. He persuaded John Aldridge and Basil Taylor to help him prepare a portfolio of science fiction sketches that would astonish film producers in Soho, including beautiful women in costumes as exotic as anything dreamed up by Busby Berkeley. The images included a rocket ship (a theme already used by Lye in several batiks), with a whimsical picture of its pilot asleep on a cloud in the moonlight surrounded by such items as an alarm clock and a toothbrush. Another set of sketches portrayed life under the sea with fantastic women's costumes based on the shapes of shells, coral, sea anemones, sharks, etc. The two groups of images were linked by a rendezvous between the rocket and a submarine. The images recalled not only the world of modern ballet but also the whimsical fantasies of Georges Méliès (an early pioneer of special effects in films).

With 'Quicksilver' as its working title, the project was in a state of continual flux between 1930 and 1934. Lye spent a great deal of time planning special effects, including model and trick photography for rocket flight. He persuaded a number of artists, actors, and musicians to become involved and a complicated script grew and grew. Ellitt produced futuristic music and other friends contributed cabaret-style songs. The Lyes spent many weekends in Essex developing the portfolio with Aldridge and Taylor. Taylor, a particularly close friend, was only a year younger than Lye and had a similar reputation as a bohemian who was both wild and charming. His contribution to the project was especially valuable because he had worked as a designer for the Sadler's Wells Ballet. In Jane Lye's words: 'The portfolio was hawked around Soho among the unbelievers. Occasionally Norman Cameron would go along because Len was quite inarticulate. They would go from one film mogul to another, Norman would try to sway them to invest some money, but no luck whatsoever.'[19]

Lye had lost his job at the Lyric Theatre when he left for Mallorca, but through a friend in the London Film Society he found work at the newly built Wembley Studio of Associated Sound Film Industries. In July 1930 a reporter from the *Star* interviewed him among the cleaners whose job it was to sweep the floors and lend a hand with the props: 'The "odd-job-man", who figures on the company's pay-roll as a "cleaner", is a man of culture, an artist, a sculptor and a designer, whose genius has already won recognition. I asked him why he had left his own studio at Hammersmith to become, first an assistant carpenter, and later a "property-man". The tall figure said: "I wanted to know the technique of making films, the difficulties of production and lighting. One cannot hang about a studio in the ordinary way and poke one's nose into the producer's business. So I decided to take work as a 'hand'. I have in mind a ballet, and the information I am picking up will be invaluable".'[20] The job was poorly paid and consisted mainly of running errands but Lye was able to watch musicals being filmed such as the highly romantic English–Italian co-production *City of Song* (also known as *Farewell to Love*) about a Neapolitan singer in London. After Lye had been working at the studio for a year he was offered a job as assistant cameraman on a five-year contract at three times his current salary.[21] The prospect of a secure job was very tempting, but he declined because he was still hopeful that sponsorship for 'Quicksilver' would turn up at any moment. One company talked seriously about investing 400 pounds but the money remained a mirage. Lye was always puzzled by his inability to find sponsors but the fact was that even the proposals he assumed to be accessible and commercial still contained enough odd or experimental aspects to make producers smell a rat. Eventually, as Ellitt recalls, the 'Quicksilver' idea was 'taken up by a maverick New York producer-director, and a musical of sorts was made with Ben Lyon singing in it etc. etc., and away it went, all the way to the Moon, with no relation to the original idea' — and with no financial return to Lye or Ellitt.[22]

Next Lye switched his attention to puppets, one of the few areas of popular animation not yet dominated by Walt Disney. Some European film-makers such as George Pal had used puppets to achieve fantastic or surreal effects,[23] and in 1930 John Grierson had experimented with puppets designed by the Gorno family, who were linked with the Wembley studio where Lye worked.[24] In 1934 Lye completed a three-minute, black-and-white pilot film showing a monkey dancing to 'Peanut Vendor', a piece of popular jazz music by Red Nichols and his Five Pennies. His home-made monkey was two feet high with jointed limbs able to lock into any position and removable screw-pegs in its feet to fit the holes in the stage. There were 50 interchangeable versions of the mouth to suggest singing. He made a small set in a corner of the Footprints studio showing houses, clouds, and a palm tree that swayed to the music. As a guide to the monkey's movements he made a film of his wife dancing the rumba.

Animating the puppet frame by frame was a slow business but it was still easier than making drawings for *Tusalava*. Jack Ellitt helped Lye with the synchronisation. The results were sufficiently lifelike for some viewers to believe they were watching a real monkey — until its head began spinning and its tail floated away to become a walking stick. The filming was made possible by a donation from Sidney Bernstein, manager of the Granada cinema chain. To keep costs down Lye and Ellitt did their own processing. Then armed with *Peanut Vendor*, the completed film, Lye approached various companies to see if they would sponsor a series of musical shorts or advertising films. On 23 February 1935 *Melody Maker* reported that Lye had an arrangement with The Four Crotchets to provide music if he could find a sponsor for a film based on a 'bizarre' cast of puppets. But soon after this Lye wrote to Riding: 'I was all out on a film musical thing that now has fizzled out almost to a legal fight over some twisting [that a] producer wants to try on me.'[25] And to John Aldridge: 'I've been in an amazing maze lately with a film — all lined up — talent found — decent script . . . when phooey it fell flat and fellow trying to gyp me for script. . . . All wonderful experience in the art of learning to take it which is what the film packet consists of.'[26]

Five years had now gone by with almost no tangible results from Lye's proposals but he had at least gained hands-on experience in virtually every area of
film-making. He had also come to the conclusion that the only way unusual films
could get made was through a cooperative film studio. Today many cities have
film 'co-ops' but these are generally assumed to be a development of the 1960s, so
it is surprising to read the detailed plans drawn up by Lye in 1934–35: 'Get
Montagu, Bernstein, and through them several producing companies to contribute until 300 pounds reached. Then get studio for one year 52 pounds, lights 30
pounds and camera twelve pounds ten, renovations, table, stages, benches,
darkroom, tools [etc.] — 100 pounds ad lib. The studio is then a small film place
where any sculptor or painter can do any experiments he wants to in simple
abstract movement stuff. Have a secretary to do the contract stuff and sort out
whose turn. In the line up there would be a list of technical men available during
evening to give free help. For example I'd be free of an evening and weekends to
give help to anyone wanting to animate anything like bits of cardboard wire tin
curtain rings strings woolworth shops twigs leaves cloths sugar lumps etc. The
thing would be uncommercial and the more uncommercial the better. There is
absolutely no standard of comparison or criticism about visual abstract movement stuff and if one & all had a go at it there would be something not bad after
a year.'[27]

twentyone a colour box

Lye was a non-stop innovator who lacked the right sort of support group —
people who could find funding for his ideas and help sort out the practicalities. In
1935 he felt he had hit rock bottom in terms of 'capitalist film things', but then he
bounced back with one of the best ideas of his life. What had constrained him
was the fact that a film-maker (in contrast to a writer or a painter) needed access
to complex equipment and a sizeable budget to cover the cost of film stock and
processing. Now Lye found a new game to play: 'I used to go out to some friends
in Ealing Studios . . . and hang around. . . . I used to get the old n.g. [no good]
sound takes, that is, clear films with just a skinny [sound] track on one side. I
would then scratch and paint and mess around with these pieces of film. I would
join them together and take them up to the GPO Film Unit, where I had some
friends, and run it. All this was done under the counter, you know, on lunch
hours.'[1]

   He had first made scratches on film in Sydney ten years earlier. In London he
was reminded of this experiment by a sequence in a German film where
scratches were used to add emphasis.[2] Leon Narbey has suggested that Lye may
also have been influenced by the grease-pencil lines that film-makers draw on
workprints to mark optical effects or music cues. Whatever the catalyst, he now
began to explore the possibilities systematically. The artist Julian Trevelyan
remembers that Lye was preoccupied with painting on film when he met him
for the first time on Durham Wharf at Hammersmith: 'In the summer of 1934,
my wife-to-be and myself looked at the old sheds that were to become our
studio, and a man in shorts and nothing else glared at us from a deck chair, and
round him was a lot of coloured film drying.'[3] Lye's doodling and the
increasingly free brushwork in his paintings had prepared him for a new
approach to film. What had deterred artists from drawing images directly on
celluloid was the jittery effect caused by the slight differences between one frame
and the next. It took a special kind of artist to regard this jitter as an advantage,
as a display of energy, and as a visual equivalent of musical resonance.
Animators of all kinds from Walt Disney to the German abstract artists had
sought smooth movement and maximum control. Similarly, the long tradition of
tinting film and adding hand-painted areas of colour (by both brush and stencil)

had emphasised neatness and precision. Lye was well aware of these precedents, but he preferred (as Malcolm Le Grice has put it) to work 'with rather than against the "imperfections".'[4]

Painting films by hand allowed him to draw on his many memories of tribal art such as the patterns of *tapa* cloth.[5] Polynesian artists used brushes, sticks, or fingers to paint *tapa*, and there were also wooden forks to draw parallel lines in the wet paint. Stencil motifs included circles, diamonds, diagonals, and asterisk shapes which changed slightly each time they were repeated. Lye was delighted to use similar methods to transform the high-tech medium of film into something handmade. The main practical problem was to find types of paint that would not crack or peel off the surface of the film but were transparent enough to produce the right colours when projected. This was a slow process of trial and error, though Lye had had some experience in testing dyes for his batiks. He settled finally on a particular range of lacquer paints. As tools he used a camel-hair brush and various homely objects such as a fine-tooth comb which he wiggled through wet paint to make 'striated wavy lines'.[6] Later he made use of an air-brush to spray paint through specially made stencils such as 'stars, circles, triangles, and yin-yangs'.[7] There were also stencils he improvised such as a fish slice that was ideal for rows of dots. Though he was more interested in painting than scratching he also experimented with various types of needle.

A strip of film was only 35 mm in width, a tiny surface on which to paint patterns that would later be blown up to fill a huge cinema screen. To discover which figures of motion worked best he made and projected countless strips, a process not unlike his collecting and testing of doodles. This was time-consuming but at least it was cheap — there was no need for a camera or film crew. It is interesting to note that handmade or 'direct' film-making (as Lye came to call it) is the only form of film-making that literally fits the *auteur* theory, an approach that speaks of films as though they are the work of a single artist (usually the director). Whereas the *auteur* approach oversimplifies the orthodox film-making process, the touch or 'signature' of the artist is physically present in a direct film in every frame. Still, even Lye needed help to synchronise his visual ideas to music. Ellitt, who had already worked as his friend's musical arm on a number of other projects, had an exceptionally clear grasp of the way music could be analysed and edited for film purposes — 'the length of the phrases and the rhythm and all the emphases and changes of orchestration'.[8]

Their first direct film collaboration was not based on music but on a famous lyric from William Shakespeare's *The Tempest*:

Full fathom five thy father lies;
Of his bones are coral made;
Those are pearls that were his eyes:
Nothing of him that doth fade
But doth suffer a sea-change
Into something rich and strange . . .

The surreal mood of these underwater images, their associations with Cape Campbell, Samoan coral, and the uncanny 'water-smoothed rocks' he had seen in Deyá, and the theme of the missing father all contributed to Lye's fascination for these lines.[9] The choice of reader was settled one evening early in 1935 when Norman Cameron insisted on taking the Lyes to the New Theatre to see *Hamlet*. Though Lye seldom liked plays he was so impressed with John Gielgud (who directed the production as well as playing the title role) that he asked a mutual friend for an introduction. Gielgud agreed to record the poem, a generous gesture since he was already in great demand. Once his reading was recorded on film, Ellitt measured the phrases for Lye who then painted designs directly onto the same film strip. Robert Herring wrote an enthusiastic description of the first screening of *Full Fathom Five*: 'It is not true to say that it is an illustration of Shakespeare — unless you are willing to concede that a figure 5 floating across the screen is an illustration of the opening line. . . . Probably I don't know at all what it is, but it seemed to me a pouring out of image and association which leaves a feeling of magic, an underlit, underwater quality, which the verse has. . . . It is rather like the speech being made, there is mind-movement in the shapes, mind-pictures in the occasional flashes, inserts, of actual photography.'[10] These inserts were presumably offcuts of film from the editing rooms Lye visited, images that he had put through a filmic sea-change by colouring them and cutting them into his film. (We may never know for certain as the film has since been lost.)

Armed with *Full Fathom Five* as a pilot, Lye set out once again to do battle with the industry. This time he took his idea to John Grierson of the GPO Film Unit. Only three years older than Lye, Grierson was a producer fired with the idea of transforming the film medium from escapist entertainment into a vehicle for public education. His basic aims were political — getting the lives of working people on to the screen and raising serious social issues. Grierson persuaded young film-makers to think of documentary films as important in themselves, not merely as a training-ground for feature films. He also succeeded in persuading the civil service that it needed a skilled film unit, which ended up (by a series of historical accidents) being attached to the Post Office.[11] While the Unit had to attend to the prosaic needs of government departments, it seized every possible opportunity to explore broader social issues. The commercial film industry, whose limitations were exposed by the originality of the GPO films, did all it could to make trouble for the Unit and to stop it going beyond its brief, but Grierson was very good at defending his liberal interpretation of the job. As an admirer of Eisenstein and a collector of modern painting, Grierson wanted his film-makers to develop both a strong social awareness and an appetite for artistic experiment. He brought the innovative film-maker Alberto Cavalcanti from France to be second-in-command of the Unit. The Unit developed its own culture, as the writer J. B. Priestley observed: 'I had some dealings with the ordinary British film industry. But this was quite a different world, this of the documentary film producers, directors, and their assistants, whose social head-quarters appeared to be a saloon bar just off Soho Square. . . . I liked the enthusiasm of these rather solemn young men in high-necked sweaters. Most of them worked like demons for a few pounds a week, for less than some imported film stars were spending on their hair and fingernails. They were rapidly developing a fine technique of their own, so rapidly that if you wanted to see what sound and camera could really do, you had to see some little film sponsored by the post office.'[12]

Lye learned of the Unit from Cavalcanti who urged him to go and see Grierson. At first it took all of Lye's personal charm to persuade this producer that the idea of direct film-making was not simply crackpot,[13] but once Grierson had watched his film he said to Cavalcanti: 'This man is terribly important, we must get him going.'[14] Grierson knew enough about modern forms of art to understand the power of what Lye was doing. He also saw the possibility of using such films to liven up the Unit's packages of black-and-white documentaries. Colour was still a novelty, particularly the brilliant colours produced by the direct application of paint, and a successful film made without a camera was such a striking innovation that (in Cavalcanti's words) 'Grierson, that king of showmen, wouldn't miss this opportunity.'[15]

The problem was how to justify the use of government money. Grierson's solution was to stick a Post Office announcement on the end. He was prepared to buy *Full Fathom Five* for this purpose but Lye preferred to start again.[16] On 21 June Grierson provided a commission: 'I write to confirm officially that you will produce an abstract colour film . . . on the lines we discussed. For this work we shall pay you a fee of 20 pounds, plus the cost of the necessary materials.'[17] After more negotiation the payment was finalised four days later at 30 pounds, still a very modest sum.[18] In this way Lye began a three-year working relationship with

Grierson, who saw him as 'a wonderful odd ball',[19] and with Cavalcanti, whose two 'favourite boys' at the Unit were Humphrey Jennings and Len Lye.[20] He greatly valued Lye's ability to think artistically about the film medium in an industry dominated by the unimaginative.[21] He also recalled that: 'He [Lye] became my youthful godfather by calling me Cav' (his subsequent nickname in the British industry).[22]

Since the GPO budget did not allow Lye to commission music or to use well-known groups, he and Ellitt listened to hundreds of less well-known records before making their choice. In the case of *A Colour Box* the music was 'La Belle Creole', a *beguine* (a native dance of Martinique that had become popular in Paris) by Don Baretto and his Cuban Orchestra.[23] Ellitt made a detailed 'chart' (analysis), then the music was transferred to film and Lye made various cue marks along the soundtrack. Then he painted images directly onto the clear film alongside the soundtrack. Thanks to a year of experiments, it was not difficult for him to select and paint visual ideas of the required length. Only a couple of splices were needed and Lye was able to paint most of *A Colour Box* in five days, though the sequence of words at the end slowed him down.[24] Including planning and post-production the film took a total of two months, but that was a breeze compared with the years spent on *Tusalava*.

Lye told Laura Riding about his breakthrough: 'After many nights of working late painting film it's finished and pleased and loafing. . . . This thing I've just done is the only thing I've ever had the result that it faintly pleases me, this new film. It was made in 5 days is a simple toy to me is simply controlled time pattern far more than I had hoped it would be. I'm afraid only that it caused me no trouble and is slight not exacting throe, correct but happy go lucky alive stuff for the mind to see simple colour outline of about seven different flowers translated into music and pattern time. All who have seen corroborate it's something to mention anyway definite film notch. Simply means I can get near what I want without camera and expense. . . . Think how nice an apple must clean teeth judging how my mouth feels now after cigs all day. . . . Yes was just thinking how nice it is to satisfy your mind with a piece of work. First time I've ever done it. It's all right for you there to do so often. Me it's always had to be thoughts mainly instinctive never anything tangible for myself got near it at least by stinking christmas I'm pleased now I come to think of it jesus wept yes. Anyway I'm sleepy, only had a gin and lime yesterday . . . must utilise another soon.'[25]

Its lively dance music made *A Colour Box* a striking exception to the earnestness of many avant-garde films. Lye's aim was not merely to translate the music into images but to develop visual ideas in counterpoint. He liked to have enough synchronisation to keep the images in step with the music but not so much that their dance became predictable. He felt free to pick up ideas from any aspect of the music — the rhythm, the timbre, the style of a particular player, the general mood, or the look of the printed sound track. He was generally inclined to associate the sound of drums with dots and circles, the piano with a shower of tiny splashes of colour, and string instruments with lines that quivered and twanged, but this was not a strict code. The vertical line (drawn along many frames at a time) was a favourite motif that he would use for a variety of instruments. He learned to do many things with a line such as make it sway, wriggle, jump, or glide. The imagery of *A Colour Box* made Roger Fry's description of *Tusalava* prophetic: 'You really thought not of forms in themselves but of movements in time.' The new film had a much quicker tempo than *Tusalava*, a fact which was disconcerting to painter friends who wanted to linger over the images.[26]

Initially Lye's film was known as *Cheaper Parcel Post*, then it changed its title to *La Belle Creole* and finally to *A Colour Box* (presumably as a variation on phrases like paint box and music box).[27] It was first screened on 6 September for a preview audience of journalists and reviewers. Grierson, who had an eye for publicity, knew that Lye's film was an exceptional novelty. The preview produced a flurry of news stories about this 'first film made without a camera', yet cinema owners were reluctant to screen it. Quota regulations required cinemas to include a certain number of British films but the demand was for features rather than experimental films or serious documentaries.[28] Most cinema owners failed to see how an audience could be interested in a Post Office film. Grierson had therefore been forced to find other outlets for most of his films, such as libraries, schools, community groups, exhibitions, and so on, but he always seized any opportunity for a cinema release. In the case of *A Colour Box* most cinema owners were uneasy not only about its experimental style but also its Post Office slogans which seemed to put it in the category of advertising films, a genre likely to draw complaints from audiences of the period. Lye's old patron Sidney Bernstein came to the rescue and agreed to launch the film at the Granada. It was also picked up by the Tatler, a cinema specialising in short films. The Tatler management made a special announcement to the effect that it was against their policy to show advertisement films but they were making an exception because of the unique nature of the film.[29]

From its first screenings *A Colour Box* was controversial because of its abstract style. Responses were sharply polarised with some viewers laughing and applauding and other viewers regarding it as 'crazy' and shouting 'Take it off!'[30]

At a children's matinee 'the audience began by hissing, but caught up the rhythm as the film progressed, and ended by clapping'.[31] Such noisy responses for and against the film were so unusual that newspapers began to report them, and after that every film reviewer had to offer an opinion. All agreed that *A Colour Box* was extremely original or futuristic,[32] but some writers were madly fascinated while others hated it.[33] *Today's Cinema* remarked: 'Well, it's certainly a dovecote stirrer all right, but I don't expect to see Wardour Street rushing wildly to take it in its arms. Nor can I see the proletariat . . . asking the local to rebook it for a second week!'[34] The *Daily Herald* found it crazily amusing but added: 'After watching the waves, stripes, blobs of violent tints, suggesting tartan, bandanna, boarding-house wallpaper, fruit salad, chromatic spaghetti and an explosion in a cocktail bar, I half expected to find myself coming to in a dentist's chair.'[35] The *Daily Telegraph* dryly observed: 'The thing I liked best about this fantasy is the cutting. It only lasts a minute [sic]. You might suggest, as a further improvement, that Mr Lye should cut it up the middle.'[36]

Other reviewers recognised that it was an important breakthrough. Robert Herring in *Life and Letters Today* wrote: 'Colours flow over the screen. . . . They whirl, perfectly patterned, come near, seem to deepen as the music becomes more urgent, complicate as the tunes interweave, and make one realise, finally, that one is seeing the first ballet in film.'[37] (Lye must have been pleased by such a comment which suggested that the months he had spent on the 'Quicksilver' ballet project were not entirely wasted.) Anthony Vesselo remarked in *Sight and Sound*: 'The reinforcements of sound and colour have stirred the abstract film to a new vitality.' He saw *A Colour Box* as 'more profoundly effective than a horde of vacuous feature-films'.[38] Robert Fairthorne in *Film Art* praised the film but warned would-be imitators that it was all too easy to do such films badly.[39] (There were good reasons for such a warning, though it should be noted that Lye's discovery had for the first time made film-making open to all comers. A direct film could be a strip of celluloid covered with felt-tip designs by a group of small children, or — at the other extreme — it could be a complex art film based on years of experiment.)

The impact of *A Colour Box* on audiences was heightened by the fact that colour film was still at an early stage of development. As late as 1949 a film-maker like Paul Rotha would still be expressing his frustration at the way 'colours glow and pale at alternate moments (red are revolutionary, yellows are dirty, greens are sickly, grass like that in fruiterer's shops, skies like aluminium, and flesh tints jaundiced)'.[40] During the 1930s various colour processes made their erratic entry into the marketplace and, as Lye observed, there was considerable 'interest in seeing what [had been] fluked, applied, and generally achieved'.[41] By painting directly on to celluloid and having prints made from this original, he was able to narrow the margin for error. But the printing process could still go astray, and Dufaycolor (which he used for *Colour Box*) had a tendency to produce soft, desaturated colours which did not always suit his bold effects.[42] Trying out many processes he used to lament the loss of colour in the printing.[43] Despite these problems the impact of his direct films was so great that reviewers told their readers: 'You've not seen a colour film till you've seen a Len Lye effort.'[44] Art-house audiences continued to be sceptical of colour films in the late 1930s but a special exception was always made for Lye's work.[45]

At the end of October 1935 *A Colour Box* made its overseas debut by winning a Medal of Honour at the International Cinema Festival in Brussels. While the Festival's award for animation drawings went to Walt Disney, members of the jury were 'so impressed by this film [*A Colour Box*], for which there was no suitable category, that they invented the special category of "fantasy films" in order to give it a prize'.[46] Four GPO documentaries also won awards at the Festival — *Song of Ceylon*, *Coal Face*, *Face of Britain*, and *The Voice of Britain* — and the judges said they were astonished by the excellence of the British entries and amazed that such adventurous work had been sponsored by a government department.[47] British newspapers reported the awards under such headlines as 'Britain Sweeps the Board' or 'Awards Show Britain's Strength: Honour For P.O. Colour Film'.[48] This publicity helped to put the GPO Film Unit on the map and gave timely support to Grierson's crusade.

At the 1936 Venice Festival *A Colour Box* was 'met with such loud condemnatory stomping that the screening had to be stopped before the film was over'. The Nazi press gloated over the incident and William Moritz has suggested it was stage-managed by Nazi sympathisers who condemned the film as degenerate art.[49] Meanwhile *A Colour Box* rapidly gained cult status among the avant-garde in other parts of Europe.[50] The long-running controversy over *A Colour Box* did more to make the film famous than any straightforward critical success would have done. Some exhibitors continued to fear that Lye's work was aimed 'above the heads of average cinema audiences'[51] but there were so many requests for *A Colour Box* particularly in Britain that it came to be seen (as David Curtis has pointed out) 'by a larger public than any experimental film before it and most since'.[52]

A number of cinemas actually paid to rent *A Colour Box* because it created so much public interest.[53] *World Film News* saw this as a revolution in advertising films,[54] for it was difficult to get theatres to screen such material, let alone pay for it. As for the Post Office advertising slogans, Lye had done what he could to integrate them by stencilling the words in a style reminiscent of Cubist painting, constantly changing their colours, and sliding them onto the screen at various angles. This ingenuity helped audiences to accept the slogans with good humour. A *Daily Express* reporter wrote: 'We guarantee a good laugh when a blob totters on and says, "3 lbs for 6d".'[55] And Ernest Betts observed: 'I doubt if Ginger Rogers could make a more startling appearance.'[56] Lye was always uneasy about advertising and on one occasion he said angrily: 'You can't go and put a pack of Chesterfields on the brow of Michelangelo's "Moses" and call it fine art.'[57] But in 1935, for the chance to make a film after five years of frustration, he was willing to accept a few slogans. And after all he did not regard *A Colour Box* as in the 'Moses' category — it was 'happy go lucky' stuff, an experiment to pass the time until he found a sponsor for more ambitious projects. When this film went out into the world he was astonished to find that his previous audience of (at most) several hundred viewers had suddenly expanded into the millions. More important to him was his growing excitement about the potential of direct film-making — he had not merely made a film but introduced a new method.

Publicity for *A Colour Box* constantly stressed its originality, and this was a claim nobody disputed in the 1930s. But later historians have dug up precedents. During the 1920s Man Ray made film sequences without a camera by the photogram method, placing unlikely objects such as nails or a sprinkling of salt and pepper on unexposed film. This was certainly a type of direct film though it did not anticipate Lye's methods of hand-painting or his particular aesthetics. A stronger precedent was a series of experiments by Arnaldo Ginna and Bruno Corra around 1912. Unfortunately no films or reports of screenings have survived, but there is an essay by Corra that talks explicitly of hand-painted abstract films.[58] These Italian Futurist artists deserve to be honoured for their idea, and later there were other film-makers who experimented independently with painting or scratching on film in some form or other such as Hans Stoltenberg, Henri Storck, and Norman McLaren.[59] When sound arrived at the end of the 1920s several film-makers — including Jack Ellitt — discovered that sound-tracks could be painted by hand. We can acknowledge this rich body of experiment and still see *A Colour Box* as worthy of a special place in the history books. It was a breakthrough film because Lye and his audience were not aware of any precedents and because the film demonstrated the potential of the direct method in such a thorough and sophisticated way that the paint-brush had to be accepted, once and for all, as a viable alternative to the camera.

twentytwo the birth of the robot

John Grierson could offer him only one or two commissions per year, but the association with the GPO Film Unit helped Lye to find other sponsors. By 1935 there were signs of a new openness in British advertising as a small group of trend-setting sponsors and agencies started taking a serious interest in modern art. Early examples were a series of posters commissioned by Shell and Oskar Fischinger's advertising films in Germany. The newly developed field of public relations acknowledged the value of 'soft sell' advertising in such forms as the prestige film which collected prizes and good reviews and gained a warm welcome from cinemas and community groups.[1] Many companies remained sceptical, but Grierson and Cavalcanti did have some success in selling the idea with *A Colour Box* as prime example. As Cavalcanti said, 'it would have been futile to expect people to post more parcels after *A Colour Box*, but a Len Lye film brought a great deal of prestige to its sponsors.'[2]

Lye was commissioned by the Imperial Tobacco Company to make *Kaleidoscope*, a four-minute film advertising Churchman's Cigarettes. The job came from Jennings's friend Gerald Noxon who was working for a London advertising agency (F. C. Pritchard, Wood, and Partners). The project was probably inspired by the success of Fischinger's 1934–35 films for Muratti Cigarettes which used single-frame animation to show cigarettes marching and dancing like the legs of Busby Berkeley girls.[3] At the time these commercials had such a fresh impact that people bought cinema tickets especially to see them.[4] Lye's film also included a ballet of cigarettes, but his particular interest lay in extending the direct methods of *A Colour Box*. He designed a number of steel stencils which (in Jack Ellitt's words) 'gave him a yin-yang, a diamond shape, a wheel, or a star, and he animated these frame-by-frame to the music I'd marked out for him'.[5] Against rapidly changing backgrounds that were boldly painted in the style of *A Colour Box*, these stencilled shapes rocked or spun rhythmically like kinetic sculpture. The images were synchronised to music ('Beguine d'Amour' by Don Baretto and his Cuban Orchestra) more tightly than in the previous film, with drumbeats sometimes accented by dramatic splashes of colour. A pair of cigarettes circled each other in an elaborate dance against brightly coloured backgrounds. Lye had the idea of physically cutting out the cigarette shapes so that the light of the projector would hit the screen directly. This involved a pains-taking process of going through each print and punching out the cigarettes by hand. *Kaleidoscope* was premiered on 27 October 1935 at the London Film Society where — according to *To-day's Cinema* — it 'moved the audience to a state of sheer glee', with viewers 'amazed by the whiteness of the cigarettes'.[6] A week later the film opened in the West End at the Curzon Cinema, and Sidney Bernstein accepted it for his Granada chain. The film was both a public relations coup and a critical success (with special praise being lavished by reviewers on its use of colour).

With two popular films in the cinemas and a Brussels award, Lye's name began to appear in the newspapers. A feature writer for the *Sunday Referee* described him as 'the English Disney . . . a different Disney, but with all [Disney's] genius'.[7] Now Lye had to learn how to talk to reporters. When Tom Driberg (as 'William Hickey') interviewed him in November 1935 for his popular *Daily Express* column, 'These Names Make News', he was struck by the film-maker's mixture of confidence and reserve: 'We lunched . . . off hot eels with mash and gallons of parsley sauce. Lye, 33, bald, has a good self-contained oval face; talks a lot, well, in a diffident monotone, rarely finishing a sentence.'[8] Lye's connection with John Grierson also introduced him to a new film-making community. The GPO Film Unit provided a determined alternative to the commercial culture of the film industry. In Harry Watt's words, 'It was slumming to come and work for us. You've no idea how looked-down-upon we were by the trade. . . . We were badly dressed and going about in a pretty amateur way. The trade, the whole of the film business, had no respect for documentary.'[9] Despite the lack of glamour and the minimal wage (less than two pounds per week for some directors and editors),[10] there was a strong sense of solidarity within the Unit. After work, the pub talk had an edge of seriousness — 'like an English equivalent of cafe life in Paris', as Paul Rotha put it.[11] The staff would head for several pubs just off Soho Square (where the GPO Unit was based, along with several related news and documentary companies). Though always a light drinker Lye would meet with friends at the Swiss Hotel, or alternatively at the French Pub which was popular for its French aperitifs (which included absinthe until the police intervened).

In Rotha's view the vitality of this after-hours talk was one of the main reasons for the success of this period of the British documentary film.[12] Certainly there was a serious meeting of interests — technical, artistic and social — in a way that seldom happens in the specialised business of film-making. Grierson believed that film had to stay in touch with new developments in the other arts, and his Unit gave work to many experimentally minded artists such as W. H. Auden,

Benjamin Britten, Lotte Reiniger, and Humphrey Jennings, in addition to Lye. Morale did not depend on pub talk for they were often too busy for that, as Richard McNaughton recalled: 'We worked at the studio at Blackheath. Nitrate film was highly inflammable so we didn't edit in Soho. We didn't think of knocking off at 6 o'clock — we went on till the job was finished. Many times I've slept on the floor of the cutting room. Everyone was like that — we were so enthusiastic about the job, we lived there. When there were rushes being shown, we all used to go to see them. Not that we'd go every time but we always knew we could. Grierson would say, "What do you think of that?" We always knew what was going on there and we always felt part of it. And we could experiment.'[13] This sharing of ideas was well suited to the documentary genre, and some films were so much a group effort that individual credits had little meaning.

Lye was not a typical member of the Unit because his concerns were less political and his projects were mostly shaped by his own hand, but in McNaughton's words: 'We all knew him, we all liked him.'[14] John Taylor remembered his helpfulness to less experienced film-makers.[15] One way Lye stood out from the group was his interest in offbeat clothing: 'He was always immaculately dressed and in the summer wore pale casual clothes which were unheard of in those days, like safari jackets with outside pockets. . . . He didn't look like anyone else in the film units who were all as scruffy as could be.'[16] Some people assumed he was part-Chinese. His curiosity value for his colleagues may be gauged by the response to a greetings telegram he sent years later to a reunion of GPO film-makers. The message, written in Lye's word-doodling manner, was typically breezy and obscure. The audience instantly recognised the style, roared with laughter, and went on to swap anecdotes about one of the GPO's most vivid and most enigmatic personalities.[17]

Lye's work made a huge impact on one of the younger GPO film-makers. Grierson, with his remarkable ability to spot talent, had offered a job to a student named Norman McLaren whom he had met at the Glasgow School of Art. The young Scotsman, who was later to become one of the world's best-known experimental film-makers, started work at the Unit in the autumn of 1936. In his words:

> One evening every week or fortnight, there was a screening at Soho Square of the latest GPO films [and here] I saw my first Len Lye film. I was electrified and ecstatic. I wanted to see it over and over again. It was *Colour Box*. Here was the pioneer of the handpainted film. Apart from the sheer exhilaration of the film,

what intrigued me was that it was a kinetic abstraction of the spirit of the music, and that it was painted directly onto the film. On both these counts it was for me like a dream come true. I had dabbled with drawing and painting on film (because I couldn't afford a camera) and had turned out a small amount of footage but I had never succeeded in making a film. Len Lye had shown the way, and shown it in a masterly and brilliant fashion. I felt sure that I would follow this way, in the future as soon as I had an opportunity. . . . Soon after that first screening, I happened to be working for several weeks on a script at Soho Square in a small office outside the screening room. Almost every day the latest GPO films were screened for various outsiders. *Colour Box* was always included. As soon as I heard its title music I would sneak in and stand at the back of the theatre. By the second week, I felt like a drug addict. Len's other films of that period . . . also affected me greatly. . . . I am perpetually amazed at the wealth of technical innovation in them. And all this technical inventiveness is not just assembled in a plodding manner, but beautifully integrated into a fascinating filmic experience. The inventor in him never overwhelms the artist.[18]

Although McLaren did meet Lye, their personal contacts were superficial. As McLaren explained: 'I was new and very shy at that time, and even if I wanted to talk, I would have been too hesitant and over-awed.'[19]

Lye's next project after *Kaleidoscope* was a puppet film. John Grierson had persuaded Jack Beddington, the progressive publicity officer of Shell, to sponsor films as well as posters, and one of his ideas was a puppet film to incorporate Shell's robot symbol. Humphrey Jennings, who was working for Beddington, successfully recommended Lye on the basis of *Peanut Vendor*. Beddington arranged for an empty storehouse in Victoria to be available as a studio. Lye assembled a strong team including John Banting as designer of the puppets and Jack Ellitt who skilfully condensed *The Planets*, an orchestral work he had once performed in Sydney, to make a seven-minute soundtrack. Its composer, Gustav Holst, had died in 1934. *The Birth of the Robot* was one of several elaborate puppet films being made at this time by directors associated with experimental film-making. The genre of the animated cartoon had come to be dominated so completely by Walt Disney, and styles had become so slick and conventionalised, that animators were drawn to the puppet film as an alternative. Lye felt the *Robot* project was still too restricted, and he described it to John Aldridge as his 'penance . . . to someone else's version of the publicity angle Shell wants',[20] but he and his collaborators presented the story in such a tongue-in-cheek way that they added many flashes of humour and originality. The characters — doll-like figures a few inches high with flexible joints[21] — struck contemporary viewers as 'more grotesque' and 'more expressive' than previous film puppets.[22] These puppets were put through their paces as a playful kind of animated sculpture, like the characters of Alexander Calder's circus.[23]

The quaint storyline of *The Birth of the Robot* was basically an excuse for various animation ideas. The film began with Old Father Time being woken up by an egg-timer ringing like an alarm clock — he had to start work making the planets revolve. The solar system was a merry-go-round turned by an old-fashioned mangle, with the planets represented by gods and goddesses such as the glamorous Venus whose harp produced a shower of coloured notes. The scene shifted to Earth where a motorist was driving nonchalantly through the desert with his car engine singing. Then a storm blew up and the motorist searched in vain for a gas station. He died in a bizarre montage of symbols including a skull, a spinning egg-timer, and Father Time's sickle. The final section of the film began with Venus playing her harp over the driver's skeleton, until the notes changed to drops of oil and the skeleton was metamorphosed into a robot. As this cheerful figure set out across the desert, the passage of its shadow magically transformed the sand into a green landscape crisscrossed with roads. The sequence ended with a whimsical image of the robot driving a sports car through the sky, waving to the gods whose planet-turning mangle had been replaced by an oil-driven machine. Finally the robot returned to his familiar position on the Shell advertising sign.

After using Dufaycolor film for his last two projects, Lye decided to try Gasparcolor which had been invented by a Hungarian chemist, Dr Bela Gaspar, with the assistance of Oskar Fischinger.[24] Gasparcolor used a beam-splitter camera to obtain three separate images, each recording one area of the colour spectrum. These separate images were recombined on a single film stock when a release-print was made. The process was finicky and expensive and the results were somewhat unpredictable, but at its best it delivered brighter colours than any previous film-stock. An English agency was created in 1934 by Adrian Klein, an expert on colour film who impressed Lye immensely because he was not only a scientist but also a man with a strong interest in 'colour music' experiments (such as Aleksandr Scriabin's colour organ).[25] Klein for his part was intrigued by the originality of Lye's thinking and he agreed to give *The Birth of the Robot* special attention as a showcase for the new colour process. Humphrey Jennings, who also did jobs for Gasparcolor, joined the project as colour consultant and producer. Unfortunately the beam-splitter camera that the English agency had ordered from Europe was late in arriving and Lye and his team had to start with

an ordinary animation camera using three colour filters. This made the animation process even more nerve-racking since each frame had to be shot three times
and the change of filters had to be perfectly smooth.

Lye was fortunate to enlist the services of Alex Strasser, a brilliant cameraman
who had recently left the UFA film company in Germany. He was one of many
film-makers forced into exile by the rise of the Nazis. (Another was Fischinger
who would move to Hollywood in 1936.) Lighting the puppets and shooting
Lye's film in Gasparcolor with a modified camera called for all of Strasser's skills,
and despite the exceptional effort everyone put into the film, Lye was dismayed in
the end to see that no two release-prints had precisely the same colours.[26] The
film still astonished those who saw it on its release in 1936, particularly the colour
effects in the storm scenes. The reviewer for the *New English Weekly* wrote: 'The
colours are almost prismatic in range, and the shots over the car's bonnet of the
cavern of shifting varied colours . . . gave an illusion of sand storm for which Cecil
B. De Mille would have spent millions.'[27] *Life and Letters* added: 'We get skies so
unlike Disney's coloured cardboards, alive with shadows and suggestions.'[28]
Advertiser's Weekly proclaimed it as proof that the colour commercial film had
entered a new stage.[29]

Although this was a more obviously commercial project than Lye's previous
films, it was warmly received by the London Film Society[30] and by fellow film-
makers such as Cavalcanti who considered it more poetic than earlier puppet
films.[31] There were cynical comments about the oil industry (such as a later
review which suggested that 'Mars', one of the sections of Holst's *Planets* not
represented in the film, would have provided more suitable theme music), but
the film itself was widely appreciated. In June the film was released in West End
cinemas, followed by a run in the provinces.[32] It was eventually screened by 329
cinemas and viewed by more than three million people in Britain,[33] a staggering
result for a film of its kind.

twentythree rainbow dance

Lye's next commission, *Rainbow Dance*, was arranged by Grierson. In Lye's words: 'Every film I got from the GPO, I tried to interest myself in it by doing . . . something not previously done in film technique.'[1] His producer Cavalcanti was always excited by this approach: 'Len Lye could be described in the history of British cinema by one word — experiment. Perhaps the greatest of [his] experiments were with colour. But rhythm came very close nearby, and there were many other items such as camera angles and a very personal way of pursuing pure filmic expression.' *Rainbow Dance* grew out of Lye's interest in the new 'colour separation' processes such as Gasparcolor. Splitting up each image into three separate negatives (by the use of colour filters) and then re-combining them to produce a positive print was a complex business, but it gave more control over the final product by providing opportunities for fine-tuning. He was also intrigued by the fact that the three intermediate negatives were black and white, even though each represented a different area of colour. It occurred to him that any black and white material could be fed into this system and converted into colour. Such material might be new or old, positive or negative, filmed or hand-painted — there were no limits. This idea enabled him to see the technology as like a musical instrument waiting for a bold performer who could use it to create wild cadenzas of colour. Alternatively, it was a kind of cubist machine that could swallow bland documentary footage and convert it into vivid, multi-coloured fragments.

Why were others not using the technology as freely as this? Because they still thought about film in realist terms, devoting their energy to imitating nature and getting the colours right. Lye, on the other hand, came to film as a modernist interested in abstract shapes, dream images, and collage effects. Why not 'a strange yellow tree in a deep blue sky' with 'vibrant colour spots'?[2] Lye's lateral approach to colour processing was typical of his general attitude to technology. While he never learned to drive a car — and no one who knew him wanted to encourage the idea — he could display an intuitive understanding of technology that would astonish the experts. Lye took his colour processing idea to John Grierson and succeeded once again in arousing his interest. Having organised a commission for a five-minute film to advertise the GPO Savings Bank, Grierson asked Cavalcanti and Basil Wright to act as producers to keep this odd project on the rails. Wright later remarked: 'I loved Len Lye's films. I produced one of them without knowing what the hell it was all about. I must say, seeing it again (at a retrospective) I was frightfully impressed.'[3] Lye also won the support of the Gasparcolor laboratory, although Adrian Klein was initially sceptical that anyone would be able to juggle the three colour films (or matrices) in the complex manner proposed: 'It is a problem in non-Euclidean geometry to predict the results.'[4]

The story-line of *Rainbow Dance* is minimal: a city-dweller shelters from the rain under an umbrella until a rainbow appears and magically 'changes him into a colour silhouette'. He sets out on a holiday, travels by boat and train, goes hiking, and plays a game of tennis. These actions flow from one to another in the style of a ballet. Finally there is a voice-over announcement that 'The Post Office Savings Bank puts a pot of gold at the end of the rainbow'. Understandably some viewers saw the advertising message as an anti-climax,[5] but Lye's interest was focused on the earlier scenes, on the opportunity to film live action in the studio and 'break that motion right down and build it up again in cinema terms'.[6] Lye was not interested in technical experiment for its own sake but saw it as a way of achieving something he had dreamed of for years — a non-naturalistic style of story-telling that used live actors as freely as if they were cartoon characters.

Cavalcanti described *Rainbow Dance* as 'perhaps the first essay in film ballet',[7] and some of Lye's ideas for 'Quicksilver' were able to find a home in this film. The dancer was Rupert Doone, a key figure in the Group Theatre, one of London's most adventurous theatre companies which had produced plays by T. S. Eliot and W. H. Auden. Doone sought to revive theatre as 'an art of the body,' an approach reminiscent (as Ian Christie has observed) of Meyerhold's bio-mechanics.[8] He collaborated with Lye and Ellitt on the choreography of *Rainbow Dance* which was based on everyday activities such as walking and tennis-playing synchronised to jazz music ('Tony's Wife' played by Rico's Creole Band). As Richard McNaughton remembered the shoot: 'We had to rig up a white sheet in the studio without any creases in it to serve as the background because Len who was shooting in black and white wanted to use the dancer as a silhouette. Very difficult to do in those days because you had trouble with glare off the white sheet. . . . We had to play a gramophone while the chap danced — we couldn't use synchronised playback in those days.'[9] Even the sets were painted black and white since Lye wanted the colours created during the printing process to be as pure as possible. The filming was done by 'Jonah' Jones, later an expert camera-man but at that time a 20-year-old only recently promoted by Grierson from the position of messenger. He accepted Lye's odd procedures without surprise.

During the printing Lye gave full rein to his creative ideas. Complex stencil patterns were superimposed over the silhouette of the dancer. When the tennis player made a leap, he left behind a row of variously coloured images of himself, an effect which took the old idea of Lye's motion sketches or Balla's Futurist paintings a vivid step further. In such scenes Lye could also be seen taking his revenge on the English climate — transforming rain and gloom into outdoors scenes with a South Pacific sense of colour and sunlight.[10] The bold poster effects of *Rainbow Dance* have become familiar features of music videos today but in 1936 they were still a startling novelty. Some viewers were disconcerted by the lack of realism — for example, the transformation of the traveller into a pair of brightly coloured asterisks rolling across the screen. *Rainbow Dance* combined a whimsical sense of humour with a streamlined approach to story-telling. The railway train was blatantly toy-like, and the boat was in the style of a child's paper cut-out, superimposed over footage of actual waves. Rain was shown as darting dashes of colour accompanied by percussion sounds. This was typical of Lye's desire to replace the clichés of realistic representation with what he called 'moving hiero-glyphics'.[11] In a stunning transition near the end of the film, the tennis player settles down to rest on the tennis court which suddenly becomes a bed. Lye could switch backgrounds in this rapid way (as an alternative to editing) because he had filmed everything with the colour-separation process in mind. This was also a new way to use matte effects (masking and superimposition). The care with which he planned every aspect of the film's colour imagery was made unmistakably clear by the theoretical essay about it that he wrote for *World Film News*.[12]

Rainbow Dance was premiered at the 1936 Venice Film Festival and then screened by film societies in various parts of Europe. Critics sympathetic to experimental film-making, including the painter Paul Nash, cheered its innovations.[13] In January 1937 the film received its first cinema release as part of a controversial programme of 'Surrealist and Avant-Garde Films' at the Everyman Cinema in London. Only in 1938 did it gain a more general cinema release in Britain, and the reviews were proof of how puzzling and unfamiliar its effects seemed at the time. Many described it as 'an abstract film'. The *Evening Standard* reviewer commented: 'I was unable to follow it without my anti-dazzle glasses'.[14] *To-Day's Cinema* found it 'peculiar' and 'garish' but recommended it as a 'challenging' film for 'specialised' cinemas.[15] Although the public response was initially mixed, *Rainbow Dance* was eventually seen all over the world[16] and some of its visual effects entered the common vocabulary of film-making. Not every aspect has worn well but its colour and style still carry a strong impact, as Barbara Ker-Seymer noted years later when the film turned up on British television: 'The other evening there was a programme of 1930s documentaries, all very worthy and very dull films of miners down the pits and trains puffing through the night, when suddenly the screen lit up with a burst of colour, design, and movement. It made you sit up as though you had suddenly drunk a very strong cocktail, and I recognised *Rainbow Dance*. It was amazing, it was as though there had been a mixup in the projection room and an extract from a contemporary avant-garde film had got in by mistake!'[17]

A few months after completing *Rainbow Dance*, Lye obtained another commission from Grierson — *Trade Tattoo* — which allowed him to develop his colour-separation ideas in an even more extreme form. The brief, mundane script for *Trade Tattoo* read as follows: 'The rhythm of work-a-day Britain / The furnaces are fired / Cargoes are loaded / Markets are found / By the power of correspondence / The rhythm of trade is maintained by the mails / Keep in rhythm by posting early / You must post early to keep in rhythm / Before 2 p.m.' This time Lye chose to work with out-takes — left-over material — from GPO documentary films.[18] He selected shots of mail-sorting, welding, cargo loading, steel milling and other types of work. This black-and-white documentary footage was transformed in astonishing ways as though an energetic team of Cubists and Futurists had given it the once-over. There was no disrespect involved — in fact, Lye was treating the Post Office's message more seriously than usual because he was intrigued by the idea that work-a-day Britain had an underlying rhythm. Was there a figure of motion for an entire society? As one possible answer to this question, *Trade Tattoo* can be related to films such as Walther Ruttmann's *Berlin: Symphony of a Great City* (a 1927 documentary that Lye admired). While Lye was never as involved with working-class politics as some of the left-wing film-makers associated with Grierson, he was interested in their ideas and commented in a letter that he wanted *Trade Tattoo* to convey 'a romanticism about the work of the everyday, in all walk / sit works of life'.[19]

Not satisfied with the uneven results he had obtained from Gasparcolor, Lye decided this time to try the rival process Technicolor, which had just established a lab in England. At this time Technicolor was also a three-strip (or 'subtractive') process. Ellitt recalls that 'Len got a colour chart from Humphries Laboratories which showed 32 different colour changes which could be made on the printing camera. He worked out frame by frame what colours he wanted.'[20] The final prints were made from three strips or matrices, but Lye saw no reason why each of the matrices should not be itself complex. This re-working made *Trade Tattoo* one of the most intricate exercises in multiple-printing ever attempted. He sought to include as many different kinds of visual material as possible. At the beginning of the film a hand-painted drum sequence served to warm up the audience. Later there were cartoon-style drawings of letters and clouds, a green comet and a red planet Saturn. Much of the live footage was printed in a contrasty way or reversed as a negative so that figures and objects became silhouettes. Lye used those silhouettes as a background for brightly coloured stencil patterns so that a plane in flight was filled with a buzz of polka dots and a signalling railway guard had his arm covered with dashes like Morse code. The stencil patterns (dashes, dots, asterisks, and stars) were always in motion, growing larger or smaller, changing from one colour to another, dancing in counterpoint to other movements on the screen. During the steel furnace sequence, for example, a container of hot metal passed through a series of subtle colour changes as it swung gracefully through the air while a changing pattern of dots pulsed in the background.

Periodically the lab staff lost their patience and it took all of Lye's charm, together with John Grierson's negotiating skills, to talk the technicians into once more attempting the impossible. Bernard Happe and Leslie Oliver of Technicolor Ltd were struck by Lye's amazing ability to visualise in detail the effects that could be obtained by such complex printing procedures.[21] Lye saw the job as 'simply a matter of knitting — two pearls, one plain, etc'.[22] This knitting was shaped not only by visual ideas but also by the patterns of the music. For the soundtrack Jack Ellitt drew on five recordings of dance music by the Lecuona Band, a group which was then playing in England on the variety circuit.[23] *Trade Tattoo* was more wordy than most of Lye's films but it was also perhaps his most successful experiment in combining words with images. He avoided using a voice-over commentary by transferring the words in the script directly onto the screen, in a mix of styles from hand-painting to typewriting. He presented the words in rhythmic bursts, moved them round the screen, and kept changing their colours. In one sense Lye was returning to the use of words on screen in silent films but he found new ways to play with these intertitles.[24]

Ellitt received about 80 pounds for his three months' work on the film, and Lye about 200 pounds for five months' work. Although the laboratory costs of *Trade Tattoo* may have grown to several thousand pounds — a lot of money by Lye and Ellitt's standards — the two men must have roared with laughter when an American journalist was so impressed by the intricacy of the film that he estimated the budget at a million dollars.[25] During 1937 there were previews of *Trade Tattoo* for special interest groups. The film had several working titles — including 'Post Early' and 'In Tune With Industry' — but Lye liked the word 'Tattoo' because of its association with drumming and large rhythmic displays. In 1938 the film was released through British cinemas but it made its greatest impact at specialised venues in Europe. In Paris, for example, it was shown at the Palais des Beaux Arts, the Paris Exhibition, and the Cinémathèque Française.[26]

twentyfour public and private

The success of Lye's experimental work for the GPO occasionally brought him a commission for special effects. His most notable client was Alfred Hitchcock who asked him to do some hand-painting for the 1936 feature-film *Secret Agent*. Hitchcock liked Eisenstein's surprise use of colour in black-and-white films such as *Battleship Potemkin* where a new stage in the political situation was signalled by the hoisting of a red flag, or *The General Line* where the success of a farm cooperative was celebrated by a hand-coloured fireworks display. *Secret Agent* included a terrible train crash, and Hitchcock and his collaborator Ivor Montagu asked Lye to paint scarlet and yellow flames directly onto the preview print to help 'give a feeling of the complete, rending break that it [the crash] represented in the characters' lives'.[1] Lye painted flames then made it even more of a 'hot shot' by adding the impression that the film itself had caught fire in the projector, 'jerking off the screen and back on the melting emulsion', followed by a 'blackout'.[2] At the preview his warning somehow failed to reach the projectionist. These were the days of highly inflammable nitrate film, and as soon as the sequence appeared on screen, the projectionist shouted 'My god, the thing's on fire!' and threw the tripping device, which caused some damage to the projector.[3] Discovering his mistake, the projectionist stormed out of the box and threatened Hitchcock and Montagu with a punch on the nose.[4] Meanwhile the audience assumed there was a fire and hurried for the exit.[5] Since the film was about to go into general release, a special letter to projectionists was drawn up: 'In reel five of this feature there is an effect of fire in the gate — it's just an effect — it isn't real — please be aware of this and don't turn your projector off.'[6] But the front office of Gaumont-British was not willing to run the risk of audiences panicking. Montagu was for making a stand, but Hitchcock was willing to bow to pressure.[7] Montagu brought the bad news to Lye: 'It's a great idea but it could cost the film industry millions of dollars!'[8]

'Len was the only person I have ever known who certainly appeared to be completely happy,' recalled Barbara Ker-Seymer. 'He would not allow any setback to discourage him. I once said to him, "Doesn't anything ever get you down? Haven't you ever been depressed?" After a minute's thought, he admitted to being depressed once, so I asked him when. He said it was when he was trying to explain art to some communists.'[9] Ker-Seymer, who was four years younger than Lye, first met him in 1936 at a party hosted by Roland Penrose, and they immediately became friends. She had a flat in Soho and a nearby photographic studio and he would visit her while working at the GPO Film Unit. 'We were both hard up, and Len would buy some sausages and we'd fry them and share a simple meal.'

Ker-Seymer had been unexpectedly left in charge of a photographic business: 'There was a friend rather too fond of the bottle that I used to help out. She went to New York for a visit telling me I must pretend to be her in her absence. She never came back.' After a few disasters, Ker-Seymer (a former art student) became one of the most innovative photographers in London. Society and fashion work were her meal ticket but her most interesting work involved the many artists and writers she knew (such as John Banting, Edward Burra, Jean Cocteau, and Nancy Cunard). Her studio often became a playground. On a typical occasion after she had shot some advertising photos of 'a male model in copious Jaeger underwear, some chums arrived who tried on the heavy wool combinations and danced about the studio.'[10] Ker-Seymer was exactly the kind of free spirit Lye found attractive, and soon they became lovers. Lye liked to have a 'home' relationship but it was equally important to him to have adventures. He got on well with Ker-Seymer's wild friends and admired her experimental approach to photography and to life in general. He was also amazed by her knowledge of jazz. With the help of black friends who were jazz musicians she kept up with the latest American trends. Lye could not afford a record player and when he needed music for a film he would spend hours sampling her record collection and debating the possibilities with her. His favourite musicians were always black with the exception of Bix Beiderbecke, Red Nichols and Benny Goodman. He and Ker-Seymer were both dismayed by the growing shift in popular taste towards white musicians, big bands, and swing music.[11]

Ker-Seymer already had a steady relationship so she was happy to keep her affair with Lye on a casual basis. She was fascinated by his *joie de vivre* and 'all the marvellous plans he had for the future'. She recognised that he was instinctively a lateral thinker and breaker of rules, 'as all good artists are'. She added: 'He was a wonderful person to have an affair with, but he could have been a problem to someone who wanted a steady lover or provider.' He liked people to be relaxed and be themselves. If he came to see her one evening, and he wanted to make love but she felt like going to a movie, he would respect her choice without acting hurt or trying to manipulate the situation, but he would not necessarily accompany her to the movie. Ker-Seymer saw him as very self-absorbed yet not selfish in the usual sense — he could also be extremely sensitive and understanding.[12] It was an unusual mixture but she 'took Len as he was and enjoyed him very much as he was'.

For Jane Lye, her husband's relaxed attitude to affairs was the most serious problem in their generally happy marriage. He later wrote in a private note: 'I've lived a life rich in girls. Who hasn't, who has had an all-round satisfactory sex life? Every girl has her own basin of sex to offer. It always seemed full to me.' He claimed it was always the woman who made the first pass: 'My motto has been let sleeping dogs lie [but] when they arouse themselves let them go their own sweet way.'[13] If his wife suspected he was having an affair and questioned him, he would give her a direct answer. As she herself acknowledged, 'He was always honest.'[14] But she would always find the knowledge painful. On one occasion she went to see the woman concerned and had such a terrible row with her that the woman's husband got to hear about it. This turned into a financial as well as an emotional disaster for the Lyes since the husband was a film producer who had previously given him jobs.[15]

Late in 1936 Jane Lye found she was pregnant: 'It was quite unexpected because I'd been totally sterile for so many years.'[16] Since the news came at a time when there was steady work from the GPO Film Unit they decided they should find better living quarters. From their tiny 'Barn' they moved to 18 Black Lion Lane, a little white house with the luxury of five rooms and a back garden with apple trees. It was one of two semi-detached houses next to the church. For the first time Lye had his own workroom where strips of film could be hung up to dry without guests getting tangled up in them or cats treating them as a game. As the birth approached, John Taylor remembered there was a great fuss over the choice of name, with many film-maker friends becoming involved. 'For a while Len's favourite was "Moly" after "molecular steel", something that currently interested him.'[17] When the baby arrived on 19 February 1937 he was named Bix, because of the jazz cornet player Bix Beiderbecke and because his parents liked the sound of the name.[18] Rose Lye was excited to hear about her grandchild, though it was another reason to regret the fact that her son lived on the other side of the world. People commented on the likeness between father and son. Derek Waterman, a fellow film-maker, remembered Lye as a proud parent who would turn up with his son and ask to borrow the film company's camera to take snapshots.[19] 'He loved children because any child who could talk was his equal. He never approached kids or talked to them in any other way than equal to himself. And they felt this, they adored him because he was just like them.'[20] Lye loved the imaginative energy of children, their fresh way of looking at things, and the freedom of their drawings and constructions. But playing the role of a child was much easier for him than playing the role of a parent. He had always had a devoted mother but there had been no one to provide him with a role model of fatherhood. He left many of the everyday, practical details to his wife as he was often away on film jobs and even at home he would go through periods of total absorption in his art. When things were going well, Lye was a delightful, stimulating person to have as parent or husband, but when problems arose he would have difficulty negotiating the details. He was better at sorting out other people's conflicts than his own. Though Bix would grow up loving and admiring his father, he would also be well aware of his limitations.

At first things went along smoothly for the proud parents. There were presents from friends such as a hand-painted toy cabinet from Ben Nicholson. But the rent for their new home was 30 shillings a week, three times what they had paid for The Barn, and there were periods between film jobs when he received no income. For many years Jane had earned a steady income as a secretary and as a dancing instructor, but she had given up her job during her pregnancy. She sometimes quarrelled with Lye over his reluctance — or inability — to become more commercially minded. But they managed to scrape by with the help of occasional 'loans' from friends who were a little better off, or money from odd jobs. One transaction that turned out badly involved a painting on plywood bought by a friend, the historian A. J. P. Taylor. Jane Lye (who was pregnant with Bix at the time) remembers going with Norman Cameron to deliver it and discovering why people often teased Cameron about his driving: 'I thought I was going to deliver in the back seat of the car! The wind caught the picture underneath and broke it in two. Whether poor Taylor got his money back I can't tell you.'[21]

Cameron remained a close friend. He introduced the Lyes to a young poet, Dylan Thomas, who quickly became their friend. Thomas first visited London in 1933 as a 20-year-old prodigy who had already written some of the poems for which he would later be famous. Despite their difference in age, Thomas warmed to the Lyes and would 'drop in, sit on the floor and talk'.[22] According to Rose Slivka: 'Dylan certainly knew that Len was an intellect, a very unique intellect.'[23] Among many other topics they discussed Surrealism, and Lye's ideas about combining poetry and film. William Sansom, who worked in the same advertising agency as Cameron, described what it was like to socialise with them: 'I met a number of Norman's friends — an astounded cherub called Thomas, a clerky-looking fellow [poet] called [David] Gascoyne, egg-domed Len Lye like an ascetic coster in his raffish cap, and many others. . . . What impressed me most was that, unlike certain other writers *manqués* [in the advertising world], they did not discuss literary theory or whine about their souls and sensitivities — they made up things there and then, grabbed down extraordinary stories and myths from the air, wrote down doggerel and verse.'[24] The Horlicks slogan about 'Night Starvation' was reworked by this group into an elaborate saga about 'Night Custard', based on the fluff that gathers under beds. The group kept coming up with new ideas for collecting the stuff (as Lye had once collected soot for his stepfather) and making their fortunes from it.[25]

Thomas, who spent a lot of time at St Peter's Square, caused concern even among his bohemian friends about his careless behaviour. In the words of Jane Lye: 'Norman Cameron never got recognition for all the help and encourage- ment he gave to Dylan. Edith Sitwell got the credit but it was Norman who used to put Dylan up, accompany him round the pubs, supply him with pocket money, and finally buy him a ticket to Wales and drop him off at the station. Then, after Dylan had watched Norman leave he would cash in the train ticket and later be found drunk somewhere.' One small detail stayed in Lye's mind as an emblem of Thomas's lack of concern for his health. During a visit to a chaotic flat where his friend was living, Lye watched him search for a beer glass. In the bathroom Thomas found a glass encrusted with years of toothpaste and other deposits; he casually scraped off the top layer with his fingernail and poured himself a drink. That wasn't Lye's style; but in social and artistic matters he was totally in tune with the poet's contempt for the status quo.[26]

'Dylan's politics had always been on the far Left', observed Caitlin Thomas.[27] 'There was a period during the Spanish Civil War when Dylan seriously thought of going off to fight. . . . [Also] at one time Dylan thought quite seriously about joining the Communist Party.'[28] Most of Lye's other friends (including Ellitt) were also on the Left, and some were directly involved in the daily work of politics. There was much to do in the decade of the Great Depression and the rise of Fascism. Lye was sympathetic to his friends' aims but for him politics had to begin with the individual. Art was the deepest form of politics because it directly addressed the way people lived and felt, and that was the arena in which he chose to work for revolution. He saw good jazz (for example) as a mind-expanding experience and he urged earnest communists and anarchists 'to give us a jazz song as well as an anthem'.[29] Despite his scepticism Lye attended left-wing demons- trations such as the 1937 May Day March in London (which drew a crowd of around 100,000). He described the day in a letter to John Aldridge:

> I traipsed all over Victoria en route to [Hyde] Park for my May Day conscience.
> It was enjoyment: best amount of crowd they've about had, and I should think

that all that was sadly missing was some brass dance music instead of the dizzy words and music they use for work song. Cecily and Humph [Jennings] and a lot of other fellers there: priests raising fists, and sons of the trees sitting on newspapers in the middle of the road resting. My feet too got hot . . . the same as on a persistent dance floor. John Banting had a little camera. Passing Mummie Parliament he would dart ahead (about 2 yards) and beg us to raise our fists as a foreground effect for the austere buildings beyond.'[30]

Lye was shocked to receive a first-hand account of the Spanish Civil War from his friend Kanty Cooper (who had once worked alongside Len in Eric Kennington's studio). Cooper had joined a group of Quakers in Barcelona helping refugees and had ended up running a canteen for 3000 homeless children. When she returned briefly to England he found her looking thin and tired but with a new sureness of purpose. After relating Cooper's story to John Aldridge, Lye concluded: 'All pretty wild west for a good cause — and that's how the other half lives.'[31] He and Jane gave her some things to take back to Barcelona, including a framed picture by Aldridge that she wished to have as a reminder of her English friends. Lye had always tried simply to ignore the stupidities of the public world but now, as he admitted to Aldridge, things were no longer simple — 'All seems to be a race in time against Hitler.'[32]

twentyfive **surrealism**

'Surrealism had liberated my thinking. With Surrealism you could after all change anything into anything.'[1] This remark by Norman McLaren about *Love On The Wing*, a film he made for the GPO in 1938, is typical of the impact of Surrealism on many young artists in London during the 1930s. The event that 'knocked everyone off the rails' was the huge International Surrealist Exhibition in London in 1936.[2] This included almost 400 works, representing 69 artists from 14 countries. Among them were Salvador Dali, Max Ernst, Paul Klee, Joan Miró and Man Ray — and Lye who contributed a painting and two photograms. The exhibition also included examples of African, Aboriginal, and Maori art which were admired by the Surrealists. It was one of those exhibitions that turns up in the right place at the right time, for though the movement had been active in France for twelve years it was still controversial, and young English artists were now ready to take a close look. André Breton, a leading Surrealist, observed that the exhibition 'marked the highest point in the graph of the influence of our movement'.[3]

English artists such as Lye and his friends had been interested in Surrealism for years but they had resisted its collective approach and polemical tendencies. In the months leading up to the exhibition, however, they were sold on the idea of a united front by the painter Roland Penrose, the art theorist Herbert Read and the poet David Gascoyne. Julian Trevelyan remembers being visited by Penrose and Read: 'They came and selected three paintings from my studio, and so, overnight so to speak, I became a surrealist.'[4] Other friends of Lye who took part in the movement included John Banting, Edward Burra, Stanley William Hayter, Humphrey Jennings, Paul Nash, and Dylan Thomas. The English Surrealists were nowhere near as sectarian as the French, though Barbara Ker-Seymer remembers that 'they were always having meetings and trying to rope in more artists [and] once you were a member you were supposed to toe the line'.[5] The only avant-garde movement in England to give them serious competition was Ben Nicholson's Unit One, which championed abstract art.

As an artist Lye was temperamentally a loner, but the commotion that was going to be created in London by an international Surrealist exhibition was too interesting to miss. He admired the Surrealists as 'a rebellious bunch against stodgy Western art of the past and also against the academicians of the present'.[6] But from the start he had reservations, which he expressed strongly to his friend Aldridge just after the two principal organisers had looked through his work: 'The international surrealists (Mr Penrose and Herbert Read) came down this evening to look at my paintings and didn't like them. . . . I nearly got angry with them but why should I educate utter know-all surrealiste strangers, so avoided all art talk rather than risk it. Thinking about it later it was simple to solace my penchant for painting by thinking, well, I know of no one except myself who has an understanding of my line. Similar kinks are only in Papuan or early paleolithic cave stuff, only in a few African bushman cave things. All other people's visual kinks, except in pattern stuff, are derivative from realism in various degrees of distortion, and in surrealism there is literary distortion galore.' In Lye's view, the taste of Surrealists such as Penrose and Read was too literary and too much influenced by Picasso. While Picasso personally 'did not care fourpence' what people thought of his work, there were times when his images became facile, relying for their impact on a flirtation with realism. 'The Picasso kink is paint that does not know what to do with itself and overflows like so much sperm.'[7] Still the Surrealists continued to invite Lye to participate in their activities and he was happy to be involved: 'Not only was it good to be in the swim but it was good to be able to swim at all, with the Paris gang nabbing all the lifebelts.'[8] It was a typical situation for him — to be involved in an interesting group (such as the Seven and Five Society, the GPO Film Unit, the Surrealist movement) yet to remain always off-centre.

The International Surrealist Exhibition, held at the New Burlington Galleries from 11 June to 4 July, produced virtually no sales of paintings but broke attendance records. There were 25,000 visitors and they purchased 10,000 copies of the catalogue. The news media had a field day. The work of William Freddie was confiscated by the English customs authorities as 'an offence against decency'.[9] The 'Phantom of Sex Appeal' made an appearance in Trafalgar Square as a female figure with roses in place of a head. Dylan Thomas walked through the exhibition offering boiled string in teacups and politely asking, 'Weak or strong?'[10] Salvador Dali put on an old-fashioned diving-suit and began to deliver an inaudible lecture about paranoia in art, only to discover that the helmet had jammed and he was suffocating for lack of air. He was rescued just in time — the audience had assumed his frantic gestures were part of the performance. The exhibition was a great *succès de scandale* though most visitors were inclined to laugh. The sourest response came from the orthodox art magazines such as *The Studio* which hit back with a weighty editorial: 'The type of imagination shown is repellent. The

exhibition in London abounded in literal monstrosities and cheap horrors. . . .
They may be ascribed to a deluded amateurism, a striving for notoriety, or
genuine craziness.'[11]

Lye's contributions to the exhibition were a new painting, 'Jam Session', and
two early photograms, 'Self Planting at Night' (later 'Night Tree') and 'Marks and
Spencer in a Japanese Garden' (one of the 'Pond People' images he had hoped to
include in the sequel to *Tusalava*). Herbert Read seems to have particularly liked
this last picture, for he included it in his book *Surrealism* published later in 1936.
The whimsical title — which associated a pair of amoeba-like creatures producing
what seemed to be pearls with a popular chain of clothing and food retailers, or
perhaps with the two businessmen who founded it — was so uncharacteristic that
Lye may have been having a sly dig at the selection committee by using a Surrealist
title close to parody. 'Jam Session' was a striking oil full of energetic lines moving
over a background that had been freely painted in shades of yellow, brown, and
gold. The painting reflected Lye's interest in cave art, not only in its cryptic signs
but also in its weathered surface. Near the centre of the canvas was a shape with
bird-like claws, which helps to explain his later change of title to 'Snowbirds
Making Snow'.[12] The rest of the painting was abstract, able to hold attention
purely by the liveliness of its brushstrokes, as red, orange, and black lines flew and
wiggled across the canvas. A number of the artist's interests came together here in
a successful blend — doodling, graffiti, Bushman art, figures of motion (such as
those painted or scratched on film), and the energies of improvised jazz. More
abstract and painterly than most of the work being done by the English Surrealists, such a canvas was closer to the work of Joan Miró and André Masson or
to the style later known as Abstract Expressionism.[13]

Lye's growing success in bringing the energy of his doodling into his painting
can be seen in other works of the period such as 'The King of Plants Meets The
First Man'.[14] The title was an afterthought and the painting can be admired purely
for its abstract qualities, for its bright colours and what Lye called the 'electricity'
in its lines.[15] He remembered that the process of painting was very vigorous and
the green shape ran away with his hand ('My brush went right down — bonk!').
The painting 'Helium' was even more raw and extreme in its doodling.[16] It was
based on an 'adult kind of doodle, completely abstract' that Lye had copied from
the wall of a tube station.[17] In his words: 'One day I painted it and felt I was expressing something about my feelings in relation to forces of energy.'[18] The three
main shapes resembled stylised birds, but Lye was interested in them purely as
figures of motion. He enjoyed the free use of a brush to create swishy strokes and
tried out a number of variations, as though he was practising film animation.

In subsequent years Lye continued to be represented in Surrealist magazines, film screenings, and London Gallery shows.[19] He admired the ability of Surrealist images to evoke 'an uncanny, hypnotic mysterioso'[20] but remained critical of some tendencies within the movement. The best-known Surrealist artists such as Dali might use juxtaposition cleverly but he personally preferred 'the kinetic of the body's rhythms' to 'the literal look of the dream image'. In 1936 he attempted to stimulate debate within the movement by an essay in *Life and Letters Today* which advocated an art of 'pure visual impulse' or 'sensation stimuli' and argued that the best-known Surrealist films such as Dali and Buñuel's *Un Chien Andalou* were still too realistic, literary, and dependent on dream imagery.[21] Though he was trying to define an aesthetic that would beat the Surrealists at their own game, he continued to regard them as valuable allies in the general struggle — they had their 'hearts in the right place' and were helping to give the world of art a shake-up now that 'the stags at bay don't entertain no more'.[22]

twentysix the english walt disney

Frank Evans of the *Evening Chronicle* wrote in 1937: 'In the cartoon field Disney has lost a good deal of his pre-eminence to men like Len Lye and George Pal.'[1] This may have been true in terms of prestige among critics but the popular audience always associated animation with Disney. Yet the phrase 'English Disney' continued turning up in reviews of Lye's work, often as a way of cheering on the English side.[2] Almost all forms of English film-making were engaged in a fierce lopsided struggle with Hollywood. Some European animators such as Oskar Fischinger and later George Pal accepted invitations to work in Hollywood in the hope that they would gain access to its unique resources, but what they found there was a corporate culture with little serious interest in their experiments.[3]

Lye's only contact with Disney came about through an intermediary — Sidney Bernstein. While Bernstein was as well informed as anyone about the commercial side of the cinema business, he was also eager to see and support the work of experimental film-makers. As C. A. Lejeune noted in the *Observer* in 1936, Bernstein 'likes documentaries, Len Lye colour films, pictures from pre-Nazi Germany, and Russian cutting, and, if you let him, these are the things he will talk about. But he also knows to a penny the box-office value of Claudette Colbert and Greta Garbo.'[4]

In 1936 Bernstein made a trip to the United States. Typically he spent most of his time driving round the country trying to gain a grassroots sense of American film taste rather than talking to studio executives, but he did stop off in Hollywood: 'I recollect that one evening I was going round Walt Disney's studios. I hadn't intended to meet him because I was trying to duck meeting celebrities. I was being shown round by one of his associates and we were walking down a long corridor about three foot wide. We banged into Walt Disney. I was introduced to him and we started talking. One hour later we were still talking, but by this time we were sitting on the floor! Eventually I said we must meet again and added incidentally that I had some films with me by a young man of great talent and I thought he, Disney, would be interested in seeing them. He said he would, and I sent them over the following day. About a week later I was dining at the Brown Darby restaurant on my own while waiting for Fritz Lang to pick me up and take me to a preview of *Fury*. While I was eating, a man walked up and said he thought the films were most interesting. It took me a minute to realise what films and that it was Walt Disney who was talking to me. He was very impressed by Len's films.'⁵

Bernstein cabled Lye: 'DISNEY ENTHUSIASTIC AND SHOWING ARRANGED FOR HIS STAFF'. After Bernstein left Hollywood, he continued to promote Lye's work in other parts of the country. In New York he showed the films to Iris Barry of the Museum of Modern Art who at once placed an order. This was the beginning of a long-term relationship between Lye and the Museum's film department. When Paul Rotha was guest of honour at an elaborate reception at the Museum of Modern Art in 1937 he arrived two hours late but found the two hundred people 'still in a good mood, not only because of the drinks but also because Iris Barry had sensibly shown them Len Lye's *Colour Box* . . . three times with much success!'⁶

Disney never contacted Lye directly. Over the next few years, however, Lye noticed occasional effects in Disney films that seemed to derive from one of his ideas. Some British reviewers noticed this also — for example Dilys Powell who commented on *Fantasia* (the Disney Studio's most adventurous film): 'Let me say without more palaver that Len Lye used to do this kind of abstract decoration better.'⁷ In *Fantasia* the coloured silhouettes of orchestral players were reminiscent of *Rainbow Dance*, and the coloured sandstorm in the 'Rite of Spring' sequence matched the storm in *Birth of the Robot*. There were other shifts of colour and synchronisations of image with music that had parallels in Lye's work, but it would be difficult to prove cases of borrowing because Disney's artists appear to have taken ideas from the whole tradition of experimental animation, diluting or vulgarising many of them in the process. Oskar Fischinger who had initiated *Fantasia* left the project in a state of despair.

Meanwhile, Lye received another GPO commission, *N. Or N.W.,* a short film about the importance of using postal codes correctly.⁸ His producer was once again Cavalcanti who had taken over the GPO Film Unit in June 1937 when Grierson left to spread his ideas elsewhere. 'Len refused to repeat himself,' recalls Jack Ellitt. 'He wanted to try handling human beings and getting away from hand-drawn stuff.'⁹ Cavalcanti gave Lye the opportunity to do so on this project. Always excited by an experiment, Cavalcanti was later to say of the film: 'It was very, very good. In fact, I felt I could work with [Lye] very well. . . . Things like *N. Or N.W.* are very important.'¹⁰ The film's basic story-line could hardly have been simpler: a young man and woman plan to spend a weekend together but they have an argument. She writes to him demanding an apology. He puts one in the mail but carelessly writes 'NW1' on the envelope instead of 'N1'. The letter is eventually redirected but his tiny mistake almost wrecks their relationship. In the final scene, while the lovers are enjoying a passionate weekend, a postman appears to deliver the moral of the story. This would have to be Lye's most incongruous, tongue-in-cheek ending. He enjoyed working with Ellitt on the soundtrack, selecting three jazz songs which became an integral part of the film's structure — 'I'm gonna sit right down and write myself a letter' (by Fats Waller, one of his old favourites), 'Gimme a break baby' (Bob Howard), and 'T'aint no use' (a jazz curiosity because — according to Lye — it was 'maestro [Benny] Goodman's first, and last, essay at vocalising').[11] For actors he chose to use non-professionals, not merely to keep the budget down but because he considered most professional actors too theatrical. His choice of actress was a 15-year-old GPO assistant named Evelyn Corbett with no drama experience, and Tom Driberg enthused in the *Daily Express* about her 'charming natural London voice which I hope she won't have elocutionised away'. Indeed Corbett and her co-star Dwight Goodwin gave the film an interesting look but their acting was somewhat gauche.[12] The film survived such moments because its real stars were the editing and the camerawork.

N. Or N.W. was a conscious attack on what Lye called 'the D. W. Griffith technique' — the orthodox rules of editing and camerawork for film drama. Because those rules were first clearly formulated by Griffith in the early 1910s, and had been generally followed since then, Lye liked to make the provocative comment that 'all film is D. W. Griffith'.[13] He had always felt an outsider to the conventions of cinema just as he had to the conventions of painting. He had discovered several ways of avoiding Griffith — by painting directly on to film, and inventing new lab techniques — but he also wanted to challenge Griffith on his home ground which was camera-based drama. For this project he had a sympathetic cameraman, 'Jonah' Jones, who had shot *Rainbow Dance*, and was perfectly happy on this occasion to follow Lye's strange ideas about focus-pulling. But getting away from Griffith was not an easy business, as Ellitt recalls: 'Off Len went, and immediately found himself in difficulties. He kept on changing, kept on shooting and changing. I was absolutely astounded what caused Len so much trouble, because the project was so simple and so direct, with two practically static people talking occasionally.'[14]

The finished film was full of unexpected edits, extreme close-ups, trick dissolves, superimpositions, and other effects. The letter, decorated with doodles, was filmed from odd angles. The posting scene consisted of a strange, subjective close-up of the envelope in Goodwin's hand as he approached the postbox. The letter's travels were conveyed by cartoon-style superimpositions of maps, letters, and clouds (reminiscent of the play of symbols in *Rainbow Dance* and *Trade*

Tattoo). A sequence of the lovers on holiday began with a poetic shot of Corbett's body covered in leaves. Anyone entering the cinema in the middle of the story would have thought they were watching a Surrealist experiment rather than a Post Office information film. Not surprisingly a number of viewers were baffled and assumed that Lye was a trainee film director. But avant-garde audiences in many parts of Europe were delighted[15] and Cavalcanti wrote in *Sight and Sound*: 'It has a strange poetic quality . . . which is purely filmic'.[16]

Lye's favourite sequence was dropped from the final version of *N. Or N.W.* because even Cavalcanti thought it went too far. Lye accepted the decision at the time but later wished he had put up a better fight, particularly as the out-takes were subsequently lost. He wrote a description of the sequence illustrated by stills in the Summer 1939 issue of *Sight and Sound* as part of an essay about the need to escape from Griffith's rules.[17] He was critical of orthodox films because to his eyes the camerawork and editing were not sufficiently selective. He wanted to break motion down to its essential elements then build it up again 'in cinema terms, kinetic terms'.[18] In this way film could achieve a freshness of vision equivalent to modern paintings such as Duchamp's 'Nude Descending a Staircase'. The sequence removed from *N. Or N.W.* had attempted to present a walk in that way by an abbreviated series of images or signs of walking. When the young woman got dressed and went out she put on her shoes and suddenly the viewer noticed that the bedroom floor had become the street. This was similar to the sequence in *Rainbow Dance* when a tennis court suddenly became a bed. Lye wanted film-makers to find more imaginative ways of 'cutting on movement' and to experiment with the idea that motion is relative, an idea already developed in sophisticated ways by the cel animation method for cartoons.

The fluidity and freedom of the first animated films (by artists such as Emile Cohl) had been lost when Disney flooded the market with slick cartoons based on the Griffith technique. Lye saw a new opportunity to break loose with the arrival of television. During the 1930s the BBC was transmitting programmes to a small number of sets in London. In his *Sight and Sound* essay he used the discarded *N. Or N.W.* sequence to demonstrate that other conventions were possible and to argue that it would be a tragedy for television simply to adopt the ready-made language of film. He continued to write essays along these lines, such as 'In Search of a Technique for Television' published in 1940 in the *Journal of the Television Society*, but felt unable to advance further along this line in his own film-making without financial and technical support. As the first television studios were being planned, he published detailed proposals for movable props[19] which would allow programme-makers to experiment with new forms of visual continuity. He pleaded for some innovative thinking about how to present movement on the screen,[20] but he was fighting a losing battle since television institutions and directors were too busy with other problems. Over time television did create new idioms, but initially it was happy to borrow its basic editing and narrative codes from the cinema. During these years when Lye had few film jobs he was a frequent contributor to film, television, and art magazines. His essays illustrate the boundless energy with which he kept generating new ideas. Attacking the mainstream for its unadventurous realism, he championed many forms of stylised movement and representation. Besides explaining the new methods used in his direct films, he discussed ideas for films he could not afford to make. He wrote essays about colour which criticised the general run of colour films for not having advanced much beyond the scripting methods employed for black and white. To offer an example of what could be done he imagined a film based on Peter Fleming's short story 'The Face' about a man suffering from amnesia who could not even remember the colour of his hair. Was he the red-haired man the police were hunting as a murderer? In the climax of the story the man caught sight of himself in a mirror. Lye proposed various ways a film could use colour subjectively, for example by alternating colour flashbacks with black and white.[21]

Lye's prolonged experiment with the *N. Or N.W.* project had its costs, the most serious being the end of his working relationship with Jack Ellitt. Ellitt recalls that 'Eventually the cutting of the film was taken out of my hands because I was standing around too long doing nothing. Paul Rotha had offered me a job with Strand Films as Chief Editor and I decided to make a change because being Lye's sidekick wasn't getting me anywhere really. I wanted to move into film directing.'[22] Ellitt had made an important contribution to all of Lye's films up to this point. He would chart the music and help to match images with musical phrases. Since Lye had no technical knowledge of music, particularly in the early days, he relied heavily on the skills of his sound editor. He was fortunate to have a collaborator who was both a technical perfectionist and an artist excited by radical experiments. As a composer Ellitt had a disciplined sense of balance, contrast, and development, and he would suggest changes of order that seemed to him to enhance the overall form of his friend's films. This had been not only a working relationship but a close personal friendship. These two mavericks liked and respected each other but over the years the difference in their personalities had created tensions. Lye was more high-spirited, impulsive, outgoing, and risk-taking. Ellitt felt that Lye had been corrupted by London: 'When I first knew him he was a quiet person, very serious, very observant, and quite ascetic. He lived a very taut, clean and spare life, almost like a monk. And he was a good listener, a non-talker.' Lye had grown away from Ellitt's austere ideal — he mixed too much with the big talkers like Laura Riding. And according to Ellitt (who had a very stable marriage), Lye's sexual appetite was seriously out of control. Considering their temperamental differences, it was remarkable how long they had managed to work together. There was never a dramatic break between them — in the end they went their separate ways, with Lye finding a new sound editor and Ellitt relieved to have a full-time job since their previous projects had involved long hours for little pay. Now Ellitt directed his own documentaries, and in his spare time he continued to make sound-constructions and to experiment with direct (hand-drawn) soundtracks. In the field of *musique concrète* (music composed on tape by mixing and manipulating recorded sounds) he was an important pioneer. Yet he was never to gain much recognition for his work except from a few fellow composers and film-makers — another example of the selective vision of history which allows so many artists to slip through its net. He spent his later years in isolation, composing music for his own satisfaction, no longer interested in the effort required to find sponsors or audiences.[23]

N. Or N.W. was the last commission Lye received from the GPO Film Unit because the English film industry experienced a severe downturn in 1937.[24] He picked up as much freelance work as he could from newsreel companies. He was also commissioned to create two fantasy sequences for the British feature film *Mad About Money* (also known as *Stardust*), directed by Melville Brown.[25] The plot of this frivolous backstage musical starring Harry Langdon and Ben Lyon (from the popular radio programme *Life with the Lyons*) involved the theft of a colour process which was going to prevent some film-makers from finishing their film (entitled 'He Loved an Actress') in time to show it to a tycoon. Presumably Lye was expected to function as an English equivalent of Busby Berkeley, the director whose surreal song and dance sequences added colour and excitement to many American musicals of the 1930s. But Lye had to achieve this on a tiny budget. The two sequences he contributed to *Mad about Money* had a bizarre charm, particularly the spaceship sequence 'Stardust' which may have borrowed an idea or two from 'Quicksilver', the science fiction ballet he had never been able to make. In 'Stardust' a man falls asleep watching nightclub dancers and dreams that he and some of his fellow nightclubbers are travelling through space. They visit Saturn which conveniently changes into a bar. They sit on Saturn's rings, sip drinks, and watch the 'stars' perform in space — chorus girls in star costumes who do a Berkeley-style dance routine. Then one of the travellers falls off the rings and plummets through space until he is caught by the moon's safety net and bounces back up. The principal character then decides to try a similar

Above: Lye (seated on the right, with a hat) at a 1929 film-making workshop in London conducted by the Russian director Sergei Eisenstein (wearing a policeman's helmet). Other participants include Hans Richter (lower left, with scarf), Mark Segal (next to Richter, 'playing' a warming pan), Lionel Britton (with telephone), Jimmy Rogers (behind the camera), and then to the right of the camera: Towndrow, Basil Wright (with cigarette) and Michael Hankinson. COURTESY LEN LYE FOUNDATION

Left: Robert Graves (in a photo taken by Lye in 1929 which was used for the frontispiece of *Good-Bye to All That*) and his partner Laura Riding (photographed by Kay Vaughan, circa 1928). These writers became close friends of Lye. COURTESY BERYL GRAVES

Bottom left: The motif Lye designed for the Seizin Press, used on the title page of Gertrude Stein's *An Acquaintance with Description*, 1929.

Right: Lye designed these covers, printed white on clear blue, for Laura Riding's *Laura and Francisca* published by the Seizin Press in 1931.
COURTESY LEN LYE FOUNDATION

Below: This pencil drawing, circa 1930, is another example of Lye's 'doodling' style. The shape at the top left became the starting-point for his later painting 'Crustacean'.
COURTESY LEN LYE FOUNDATION

Right: An example of Lye's 'earth art' in Mallorca. Close-ups of this outdoor construction provided the cover pictures for Graves's 1930 book *Ten Poems More*.
COURTESY LEN LYE FOUNDATION

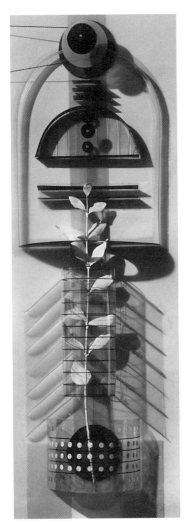

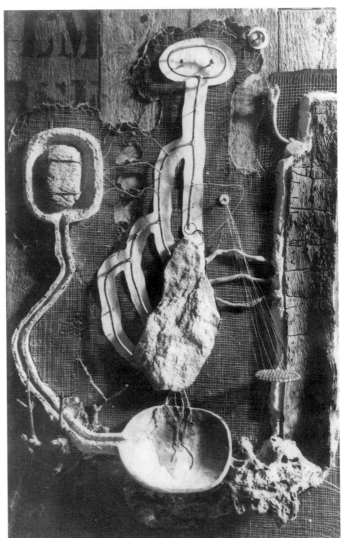

Left: Lye's construction 'Tomb Cylinder', used on the cover of the first edition of Robert Graves's *Good-Bye to All That* in 1929.
COURTESY LEN LYE FOUNDATION

Right: Lye's cover for Laura Riding's *Twenty Poems Less,* in 1929. The publisher, Nancy Cunard of the Hours Press, said this picture helped her to understand Riding's 'timeless' poetry.
COURTESY LEN LYE FOUNDATION

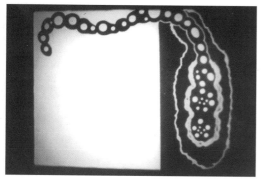 

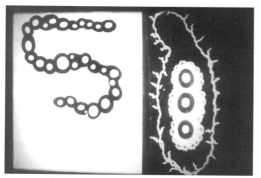 

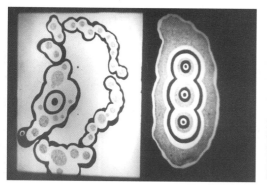 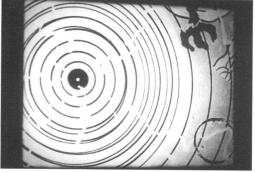

Frames from Lye's 1929 film *Tusalava* (the sequence runs down the page). COURTESY LEN LYE FOUNDATION

Above and previous page: Lye painting the film *Colour Flight* (1938). In the full-page picture he is holding an airbrush in his mouth. COURTESY LEN LYE FOUNDATION

Below left: Lye made this dancing monkey in 1934 for his puppet film *Peanut Vendor*.
COURTESY LEN LYE FOUNDATION

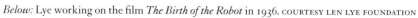

Below: Lye working on the film *The Birth of the Robot* in 1936. COURTESY LEN LYE FOUNDATION

Barbara Ker-Seymer, the photographer with whom Lye started a long-term relationship in 1936, and three of her many photographs of him. The bottom left shows Lye with Surrealist painter John Banting outside the French Pub in Soho. Ker-Seymer commented: 'Len was wearing his white cap which he nearly always wore. He and John were quite a pair.'
COURTESY BARBARA KER-SEYMER

Family photographs of Lye with his wife Jane and children Bix (born in 1937) and Yancy (born in 1940).
In the garden photo (above) there are strips of painted film hung out to dry on the clothes line.
COURTESY BIX LYE AND YANCY McCAFFREY

leap and at that moment he falls off his chair in the nightclub and wakes up. Lye's tongue-in-cheek sequence alluded to the early films of Méliès with their cartoon spaceships and pasteboard planets inhabited by music-hall characters. His contribution to the rest of the film seems to have been limited to some ghostly special effects. A Tin Pan Alley composer is seated at a piano writing a song reminiscent of 'The Blue Danube' when Johann Strauss and other composers turn up as ghosts to complain about the way their music has been stolen and vulgarised: 'They take our best creations / And turn them into trash / And for our inspirations / They are paid a lot of cash!' A court case ensues in rhyming dialogue with a woman putting the case for the defence. She argues that every composer does a bit of stealing and, in any case, the modern world is a racier sort of place. The court case ends with a blue version of the 'Blue Danube' with dancers in revealing costumes. Unfortunately *Mad About Money* (released in 1938) did not set the film world on fire and there were no sequels.

Lye racked his brains for other ways to use his skills. At one point he was recommended as 'a colour consultant for Olympia's North West Passage . . . an arid area ugly and uncoloured for many years'. He wrote to Aldridge: 'And so my first job may be to glamorise fire escapes etc. with such skill and psychological insight that visitors will be lured on through the area to find peace and plenty in a colour climax in yonder hall.'[26] Olympia, at the Hammersmith end of Kensington, was an exhibition centre, and Lye's plan was to 'colour box' the approaches to the exhibition halls, but his ideas were rejected as too radical. Eventually he was rescued from unemployment by a commission from Imperial Airways to make a hand-painted film. A sympathetic publicity manager, C. F. Snowden-Gamble, had to work hard to reassure his superiors that an abstract film would not damage public relations. Lye 'put nose to celluloid'[27] and completed the film in nine weeks on a total budget of 2500 pounds. This four-minute riot of colour displayed his hand-painting and stencilling methods at their best: 'Trumpet notes dance in greenish whirlwinds against a background of purple and violet' and 'a piano solo sprinkles the screen with mercurial beads'.[28] Although *Colour Flight* was rich in painterly effects of this kind, there were also linear images such as an animated wave (always one of Lye's favourite motifs). For the processing of *Colour Flight* he decided to give Major Klein and Gasparcolor another try, but he was shocked by the first answer-print: 'Colour printing holidays at the labs caused everything in the film to turn dirty green and double-dirty brown'.[29] Many adjustments were needed to restore the brilliant colours he had painted.

How to insert the advertising message? Lye came up with the elegant solution of using the Imperial Airways speedbird symbol. At the end of the film stylised aeroplanes and speedbirds emerged from a swirl of hand-painted shapes: 'Singly or in flocks, they drift and wheel across chromatic skies, shoot off on inter-planetary voyages, circling Saturn and his rings. Letter by letter, like a mechanical neon sign, the slogan FLY IMPERIAL AIRWAYS spells itself out in jazz time.'[30] In the process of selecting the jazz Lye visited the Decca factory and played 130 records before settling on a rumba by the Lecuona Cuban Boys and 'Honolulu Blues' by Red Nichols and his Five Pennies. He liked the latter because it reminded him of the Hawaiian records he used to listen to in New Zealand.[31] His new sound editor was Ernst Meyer, a talented German composer who had come to England to escape the Nazis. Like Ellitt, Meyer was a pioneer of *musique concrète*, and also someone who had experimented with surrealism in sound.[32]

Colour Flight was given an impressive send-off as part of an Imperial Airways film show at the Cambridge Theatre on 12 June 1939. Among the 1200 invited guests were members of the diplomatic community, airways executives, and government representatives. Jane Lye took her husband's place because he was in Hammersmith Hospital recovering from an emergency operation for acute appendicitis. The reviewer for *The Cine-Technician* observed coolly: 'We can only hope that this operation will not form the basis of [another] one of Mr Lye's phantasmagoric colour offerings.'[33] In general the film was well received — it was distributed widely in Britain and given prestige screenings at overseas venues such as the 1939 World Fair. Like Lye's earlier films, *Colour Flight* was not eligible for cinema distribution in the United States because of restrictions on any film that could be considered an advertisement,[34] but *Time* magazine ran a long, enthusiastic story about it: 'Last week in London an original artist named Len Lye, working on a shoe string budget, crashed through with an animated movie called *Colour Flight* which previewers hailed as art, as entertainment, and as the freshest stuff of its kind since Disney arrived.' The magazine went on to develop a vivid David and Goliath comparison between Lye and Hollywood: 'The Disney *Silly Symphonies* are the product of a big corporation employing 75 animators, 150 copyists and a gang of gagmen, musicians and technicians. . . . Len Lye, however, paints or stencils his designs by hand.'[35] The *Time* story was widely read but neither this international recognition nor the general success of the film brought Lye any commissions. He remarked to John Aldridge: 'When I look in my PO Savings Book I can't find even a bacon rind.'

twentyseven the world and ourselves

Riding and Graves were back in England, having been forced by the Spanish Civil War to leave their quiet corner of Mallorca. As owners of a press they had come under the suspicious gaze of Franco's supporters.[1] Riding now acknowledged the need to pay urgent attention to politics. Graves lent strong personal support but privately wished she would go back to creative work since it was one of his 'most fundamental beliefs that it was not a poet's job to become involved in politics'.[2] In 1937 Laura Riding sent a mimeographed letter to four hundred people asking them what they thought should be done about the state of world politics. If there was anyone who could get Lye involved in politics it was Riding. Though well informed about the issues, he had always been too much of an anarchist to join political organisations. But he wrote a thoughtful response to his friend's enquiry, which she found particularly congenial. It began: 'About behaviour politically . . . I don't do much thinking, until lately it has consciously become such a menace that my personal line of thought . . . may be interfered with so much that everything seems working to waste as well as myself . . .'.[3] Having warned the reader that his flair was 'for visual statement . . . not as a hard thinker in social values', Lye went on to explore the idea that politics should conceive of 'general well-being' in terms of 'making the best of what each has got'. In a Communist society 'it seems that individuality is sucked up for the short-sighted good of the average' with the exception of a few 'figureheads'. Fascism was even more aggressively mass-minded. The other alternative was Capitalism which did offer at least 'a bleak chance of individuality'. Its 'competitive anxiety' created good as well as bad individuals. Those with 'exaggerated individuality' in the positive sense — 'poets, philosophers, scientists and art workers (as distinct from entertainers)' — were forced to live as pariahs, yet ultimately it was their discoveries that enlarged the 'living pleasure' of both the individual and the mass. In a well-organised international society their role would be properly acknowledged and the time lag in accepting new creative ideas would be reduced. People such as politicians 'who have a grip on surface conditions should not lose touch with those who have a grip on inner stuff, for the sake of all of us'. Among other issues discussed by Lye were the dangers of a macho approach to politics: 'Fascism derives from one sex only, not the two. But people can't be jossed into accepting inferiority for ever . . . all he-man stuff must get muscle-bound and burst. And so must all stuff out of touch with the full range of human makeup.' After two pages Lye got uneasy: 'This letter is develop-ing into some sort of lip-smacking philosophy.'

Riding assembled the replies, together with her own detailed commentary, as *The World and Ourselves*. While working on the book she called her friends together for a series of meetings to discuss her ideas and to get them involved in putting those ideas into practice. She persuaded Lye that the political situation was so extreme he could no longer afford to keep his distance. He was impressed by her original approach to politics which was not about joining parties but about activism based on art. She saw artists as having a special role to play because of their ability to regenerate language and devise new forms of communication. *The World and Ourselves* began with the individual and the problem of how a 'private intelligence' could assert itself in a sick world without compromising its own sanity in the process. Her answer was based on a particular conception of work-ing together as a network of equal individuals rather than as a movement with a leader. Friends provided the perfect unit of association rather than the family or the state. Each person should think of himself or herself as a 'centre of contact' and try to purify the fields of communication in which he or she lived and worked. The 'private sanity' of those associated with the network — 'the inside people' — would start gradually to heal the public madness without recourse to the methods of mass politics. Riding's vision of a politics of personal trans-formation anticipated some aspects of the 1960s New Left and some aspects of 1970s feminism with its sense of 'the personal as the political'. She believed that women had a special potential for 'insideness', as did artists both male and female. With her emphasis on discourse, she proposed an exciting (if over-optimistic) role for writers and artists to play in the growing crisis. Though it was ironic that her strong appetite for leadership contradicted her own ideals, her book provided a brilliant statement of a possible politics (a politics of networking that seems highly relevant to today's World Wide Web).

Riding was one of the very few people to exercise a significant influence on Lye. Though his approach to art was very different from hers, she had a deep understanding of it. Valuing him for his strong sense of inner purpose, she had constantly encouraged him to write — first, in his word-doodling style in *No Trouble*, and then in an expository style she had helped him to develop for essays. He found their first collaboration — a 1935 essay on 'movement as language' — a gruelling experience, but in the end the 'work was something good . . . especially all that exactness that went into it. It means a lot that someone [Laura] can sort things out'.[4] Gradually he came to find the struggle to get his ideas into words so stimulating that he took up writing as a regular habit. Along the way he picked up ideas from Riding, such as her feminism which inspired his own critique of 'he-man stuff'. For her part she was dismayed that Lye could not find more sponsors for his films. She understood that film was a more expensive medium than writing so that issues of money, power, and ownership were involved, but she was always confident that problems could be solved by reasoned argument. She therefore decided to write a pamphlet to promote his work — *Len Lye and the Problem of Popular Film*, published by the Seizin Press in 1938. This was conceived as the first in a series of 'Literal Solutions', studies of contemporary specialists who had worked out a method for solving certain contemporary problems but who had not been allowed to practise that method because of 'forces of historical habit, of social or commercial prudence and inertia (vested interests)'.[5] In view of the excellence of Lye's work she asked why he had been unable to gain regular access to the funds and facilities he required. This question exposed the inadequacies of the present commercial organisation of films. Riding appealed to 'the knowing minority', the 'intelligent exhibitors', and other possible sponsors to remedy this unhealthy and illogical situation. No revolutionary changes were required, only 'the co-operation of the practical-minded people of high standards who want right ways of things *now*'. Tucked into each copy of the 46-page book was a note giving information about how readers won over by these arguments could help to sponsor Lye's films.

Though the biographical information about Lye was brief and based on his erratic memory, Riding's book was the most detailed account of his work up to that time. It was also a very generous attempt to help a film-maker who was out of work. Though it produced no practical results, the book at least offered a thoughtful discussion of his aims and methods. These had the potential, in her view, to form the basis of a new type of popular film, neither crudely commercial nor narrowly aesthetic. Lye was a film-maker 'unsnobbish' enough to offer the public a genuine education in feeling. She added: 'He has, in a more robust degree than anyone I know of, those sensibilities of social pleasure that in earlier times would have made the master of community ceremonies, and must now be the criterion for the film-master of public entertainment'.

In April 1939 Riding travelled with Graves to the United States — not to avoid the impending world war but to meet Schuyler Jackson, a writer with whom she had been corresponding. During the next few months Jackson's marriage came to an end, and his wife Kit suffered a breakdown, accusing Riding of 'being a witch' with power over people's minds.[6] Riding left Graves and began a new life with

Jackson. They made their living as farmers and focused most of their energies as writers on one vast project, the creation of a dictionary of 'exact' or 'rational' meanings. Riding renounced poetry and ceased promoting the network idea. There was a certain intellectual logic in her progression from poet to lexico-grapher, but as the years went by her former associates came to see her later career as a cautionary tale, a warning for poets to beware of getting too involved with philosophical questions.[7]

Lye had no wish to take sides in the break-up, but he and Riding gradually drifted apart, whereas he continued to see Graves after his return from the United States in August 1939. With Riding no longer encouraging him, Lye's friends expected his interest in politics and theory to decline, but this was not the case. There were several strong reasons — his mind had become deeply engaged with the problems, unemployment gave him more time to think about them, and most importantly, the threat of war continued to grow.[8]

twentyeight individual happiness now

In September 1938 Hitler's attempt to seize Czechoslovakia created a fear in London that the next move by the Germans might be a Guernica-style air attack. Hence London was blacked out and plans were made to move all children under five and their mothers out of the city. The Lyes' house was situated in a particularly vulnerable area because German bombers would use the river Thames on moonlit nights for navigation. Jane Lye went to stay with Naomi Mitchison in Scotland but she and Bix had been there only five days when the Munich Pact was signed, whereby the Allies agreed to abandon Czechoslovakia to Hitler. This week in 1938 gave her a foretaste of what her life would be like during wartime — urgent moves from place to place and separations from her husband.

On 1 September 1939 the German army invaded Poland, and two days later Britain declared war. On the same day she learned that she was pregnant. Lye was not drafted into the army because his age (38) made him a low priority and because his recent operation for acute appendicitis had involved complications that left him unable to stand for long. Hundreds of thousands of children were now being evacuated from the cities, and Sidney Bernstein offered the Lyes a cottage on his Coppings Farm near Leigh in Kent. Lye remained in London to look for work but made weekend visits to the farm. The family was desperately short of money until late in the year when some old Grierson associates came to their rescue and arranged for TIDA (the Travel and Industrial Development Association) to sponsor a new direct film with top-up funding from the British Council. The film was based on the Lambeth Walk, a dance introduced two years earlier, which (in the words of Robert Graves and Alan Hodge) incorporated 'a jerky swagger, the "thumbs-up" gesture, and the hand-spreading Jewish "Oi!". More copies of the song were sold than of any other since "Yes, We Have No Bananas . . .". In England its respectability was sealed when the Duke and Duchess of Kent were reported to have danced it in spite of protests against its vulgarity.'[1] Bureaucrats were surprised to hear that the Government's travel and industrial development agency was sponsoring a film of this kind.

To create the sound track Ernst Meyer skilfully edited together a number of different recordings of the dance music. His four-minute montage included solos by piano, drums, organ, guitar, violin, and double bass. As usual Lye's imagery linked the drums with bouncing circles, the piano with a sprinkling of coloured dots and rectangles, and the string instruments with vibrating lines, but he gave this film an unusually strong sense of contrast, associating each version of the music with its own style and colour. The many striking images included a vertical rainbow of colours (like a Morris Louis painting). Lye animated his favourite wave motif behind the title. And he made a dynamic sequence out of a double-bass solo with 'a spiffing sequence of twangs towards the end, yes! I mean Hoorroo, Hoooo-roooo, Hooooooooo'[2] — a passage of music he liked so much that he matched it very closely with a vibrating line.[3] Perhaps this was the music on his mind when soon after he wrote in the *London Bulletin*: 'Everything is XXXX cellent and the hum on the double-bass is so extreme that one's cord quivers in sympathetic response or should we say ecstatic response.'[4] *Swinging the Lambeth Walk* was his first direct film without advertising slogans. It began and ended simply with a jaunty 'Oi!' Completed late in 1939 the film was not released until 1940 when politically minded reviewers criticised it as pre-war and no longer relevant.[5] Still, Lye's old ally Robert Herring championed it in *Life and Letters Today*: 'I found it both the best Len Lye and the best Lambeth Walk I have seen and heard, and . . . how grateful we are that a new Lye appears in war-time.'[6] It was around this time that Charles Ridley selected footage of goose-stepping Nazi soldiers and slyly manipulated the images by optical printing and editing so the Nazis appeared to be dancing the Lambeth Walk. This satire — *Germany Calling*, or *The Panzer Ballet* — became justly famous, but by a freak of film history it was confused with *Swinging the Lambeth Walk* and many writers have attributed Ridley's film to Lye.

Lye continued to do some drawing and painting. In 1940 one of his doodles was selected for the series 'A Dozen Surrealist Post Cards' published by the English Surrealists. (Other contributors included Giorgio de Chirico, Matta, Man Ray and Yves Tanguy.) In the same year Lye had two paintings in the 'Surrealism Today' exhibition at the Zwemmer Gallery. The painting entitled 'As in the Arctic I Sieve the Sun with Thoughts' (later re-titled 'Ice Age') was produced by 'spraying pigment powder in a lacquer medium through stencils' onto plywood.[7] With its geometrical doodles it differed from paintings such as 'Helium' in the same way that Lye's stencilled film sequences differed from those he painted by hand. He came to associate the strange 'Klee-ish gang of images' in this painting with feelings of extreme coldness, and eventually he turned these associations into a prose-poem entitled 'Sun Thoughts':

> To get sharp clean alone feeling is a man in the arctic who sieves his thoughts
> with sunlight. He has above him a calendar of the sun of all colour. In an ice

bank is the idea of him waiting. A whale bone is company. Sunfish are in the air. Light is white and black keeps it white in the square. All here is the man's thoughts made clear by white sunlight.[8]

He also contributed woodcuts in 1940 to *London Bulletin*, the English Surrealist magazine. His untitled woodcuts demonstrated how visually strong and kinetic his abstract doodles could be.[9] The *London Bulletin* also published a prose-poem based on memories of his New Zealand childhood ('Soft toes stub hard rocks but the core remains: a most enjoyable apple').[10] In February 1940 the news arrived from his brother Philip in Auckland that his mother had died. Rose was 61 and had been suffering from pernicious anaemia. Jane Lye remembered this as the only time she had ever seen her husband sink into a deep depression. For sixteen years he had been exchanging regular letters with his mother.[11] She had never tried to pressure him into returning to New Zealand for her sake, though as the war approached she had suggested it would be a safer place for him and his family.

The first seven months of the war were surprisingly quiet in Britain, a phase that came to be known as 'the phoney war'. Around the end of March Jane Lye decided to leave the farm: 'Nothing was happening in London, I was pregnant and I wanted to be back in my own house.' The deceptive calm ended on 9 April when the Germans staged a surprise invasion of Denmark and Norway. On 20 May she went into a nursing home in Chiswick and gave birth to a daughter that day. Meanwhile there was no relief from the war news: 'First we heard of the retreat from Dunkirk, then on the 28th the matron announced that King Leopold of Belgium had surrendered. Everything was falling like sticks. For some reason the doctor wanted to keep me in the nursing home for three weeks but I was anxious to get back to my own house.' The Lyes named their new child Yancy Ning Lou Lye, with a nod in the direction of jazz pianist Jimmy Yancey and jazz record titles such as 'Yancey Street Blues' and 'The Yancey Special' (a boogie-woogie favourite). John Taylor also remembered Lye associating his daughter's name with the famous Chinese river the Yangtze Chiang. 'Ning' had been the name of a favourite cat.

The Lyes had so little money at this time that they often did not know where the next day's meals would come from. One day, with a German invasion imminent, Jane suggested hiding all the Gollancz Left Book Club books because she 'had visions of the Nazis lining all the intellectuals, including Len, up against a wall and shooting them'. Then Sidney Bernstein contacted the Lyes to offer the cottage on his farm again. Kent would be a safer place than London when the bombing started, though it was also closer to the coast where the German army was likely to land. When Jane Lye arrived at the farm with her children, Bernstein said: 'It would be best if you kept at least twenty-five pounds under your pillow because we're in the first line of defence for invasion, and you may have to bribe a lorry driver to take you away.' She was too embarrassed to tell him that all she had was one pound. The authorities considered it possible that the Germans would launch a gas attack, and so (in her words) 'I had some damn thing to put the baby in, which I was supposed to pump while I put my own gas mask on — and Bix had a Mickey Mouse gas mask.' The Battle of Britain began on 10 July with German fighter planes attempting to gain command of the skies while German bombers carried out massive raids to soften up the country for invasion. Hearing the sirens she would go outside and see German planes passing over perhaps on their way to London. Despite such threats she felt fortunate to be staying at the farm where there was fresh milk for the children. And there were cheerful weekends when Lye arrived from London, together with friends of Bernstein such as Edward R. Morrow, Quentin Reynolds, and a popular humorist named Nathaniel Gubbins. Bernstein was now working for the Ministry of Information (MOI) after a prolonged security check by MI5 which had initially been suspicious because (in Jane's words) 'he once had as a house guest a fellow organiser of the London Film Society, the Hon. Ivor Montagu, whose money subsidised *The Daily Worker*'.

The war became an everyday reality for both parents and children. There were days when Bix Lye could look out his window and watch the vapour trails of planes engaged in aerial battles. Once his father took him to see an amazing sight, a scarcely damaged German plane which had crash-landed upside down. On another occasion his father hoisted him excitedly on his shoulders so that he could look over a fence to where a German pilot who had landed by parachute was being taken prisoner. During the week Lye scouted London for film work. Because of the war the film industry had slowed right down — 'studios were requisitioned by the government, some of them for use as storage depots; British actors and technicians were called up; [and] the materials for film production were drastically cut'.[12] Film crews working outdoors were often accused of spying. An MOI Film Division was set up to make films for the war effort but there was a tremendous fight within the organisation between those who wanted to produce old-fashioned propaganda (along the lines of 'society ladies dressed as Britannia')[13] and those sympathetic to the Grierson tradition who championed the documentary approach (to record the vast social changes which were coming over Britain).[14] The Film Division became active at the end of 1939 when Kenneth Clark was put in charge, and gained further momentum in April 1940 when he was succeeded by Jack Beddington, former head of the Shell Film Unit. Beddington had always been a supporter of innovative work (such as *The Birth of the Robot*). He commissioned Lye to make *Musical Poster #1* as part of a series of 'short cautionary tales warning against the presence of spies and the dangers of careless talk'.[15] Consisting mostly of hand-painting and animation, the film had the advantage of needing not much celluloid or equipment. Generically *Musical Poster #1* harked back to the 'poster films' produced by the Empire Marketing Board in the early 1930s. Its main slogan was 'Careful! The enemy is listening to you.' And so:

> DON'T tell him where you come from.
> DON'T tell him where you go.
> DON'T tell him what you work at.
> DON'T tell him what you know.

Lye treated these and other slogans as though they were lines from a jazz song, snapping them on and off the screen like a musician playing with the phrasing of a melody ('C-CA-CARE-CAREFUL!'). As an extra reminder, 'SH!' kept popping up. Before these messages appeared, the viewer had been softened up (or woken up) by two minutes of direct film-making, synchronised by Ernst Meyer to 'Bugle Call Rag', with a rich visual texture ranging from single lines vigorously painted and scratched to complex stencil patterns. To accompany a drum solo Lye added a highly kinetic version of his favourite wave shape jumping this way and that. The film began and ended with a glimpse of live action — a bill-poster pasting up the title with his hand movements synched to music and the colours of the scene transformed in the poster style of *Rainbow Dance*. Released in July 1940, *Musical Poster #1* was screened in cinemas and taken round by MOI film vans to factories, village halls, and other locations.[16] The film received a rave review from *Variety*, which summed it up as 'a fantastic but effective blending of colour and sound to draw audience interest'.[17]

Almost a year elapsed before Lye's next film. Travelling to Kent or looking for jobs, he had spare time to fill which he would spend musing on politics rather than images. As he later put it: 'People's minds became removed from what lasted. Concern was how the hell could you stay alive? It felt like any second a flock of planes would be here, and there would be a lot of Guernicas — just holes in the ground. . . . At that point, when it looked like you'd have a bomb in your plate of cereal, I felt I ought to give some thought to what you could do about politics'.[18] His thinking was given direction by the essay 'Where are we going?'

by J. B. Priestley which he came across by chance in a back issue of the popular magazine *Picture Post*.[19] Priestley, writing just before the war, saw western civilisation facing a crisis that was a matter not only of everyday politics but of basic values: 'We have persuaded everybody, yellow men, brown men, black men, that we have the secret of the good life. No sooner did they join in than we began to show them very plainly that we possess no such secret . . . they found out that they were much worse off . . . and cursed us for persuading them out of their primitive way of life. We have all the world marching behind us, and we have not the least idea where we are going. . . . Nearly all politicians and diplomats are out-of-date men.' This lack of clear values affected people deeply: 'You cannot explain the present state of the world simply in terms of economics and politics. You have to go deeper, down into the mysterious dimly-lit realm of men's beliefs about themselves and their destiny and the nature of the universe.'

It was a theme Priestley carried into his other writing such as *English Journey* (1939), which asked 'where was our creative idea, what banner had we raised?'[20] Lye was puzzled by Priestley's lack of answers: 'Why didn't he come up with something? Then it struck me that if he could have he would have; he was passing the buck. I made up my mind to give it a go.'[21] In fact Priestley did develop some answers of his own, which he discussed in weekly radio talks that were so popular during 1940 and 1941 that they became a kind of national institution. He argued optimistically that the war had jolted the community out of the moral confusion into which it had sunk during the Depression. People had been forced to set aside sectional differences, and a new public spirit was replacing the old mood of cynicism and apathy. Despite their huge following Priestley's talks were dropped by the Home Service in 1941, apparently because leading Conservatives considered them socialist! Lye listened to the talks but came to dislike their 'pontificating' and 'sounding off on the character of the English'. Priestley was an independent thinker who drew attention to important problems but was then inclined to fall back on traditional common sense solutions. Lye hated this kind of cosy Englishness: 'J. B. Priestley was a merry old soul, a merry old soul was he.'[22]

Priestley's question ('where was our creative idea?') at least served to focus Lye's thinking. He could not agree that the war had stimulated answers: 'The stuff the war leaders told me was an utter bore. It was all "freedom FROM" stuff, not "freedom FOR".'[23] And: 'We were being covered over with rhetoric about freedom and democracy in almost a repeat form of the call of patriotism and the crap of World War One.'[24] Trying to formulate an alternative, Lye gave himself 'a migraine for three months'.[25] Some of his thinking was done during the long nights he had to spend in air raid shelters now that the Germans bombed London almost every night. By the beginning of September he felt he was starting to develop an answer to Priestley's question, but help was needed to bring his idea into focus — he was going 'through bloody hell trying to verbalise that stuff'.[26] And so he wrote a letter to Graves: 'Robert, I've got a workable idea for the well-being of the complete people in the whole world, and am getting interest out of planning it tidy in my mind, just for my self of course; but it's something you might like to listen to one of these waking days. It naturally has nothing to do with bread and butter.'[27] Lye wanted to focus on the idea of individuality as an alternative to the usual wartime appeals to nationalism or religion. He felt he had new things to say about individuality based on his long involvement with art. His other key word was 'happiness', referring not merely to pleasure or comfort or hedonism but to the kind of happiness derived from art, from intense experiences or 'stimulations' of individuality.

But in November there was a serious distraction, as he explained to Graves: 'I must get into a hospital soon. . . . My stomach wall needs sewing up, or a hernia . . . so the doc said. . . . Ain't told Jane this yet as wanted to [find a] job to get in the clear first.' But his hope of another film job remained a mirage. Jane Lye recalls: 'Len came back from London one day and said, "I can't keep quiet any longer, I have to go into hospital and have an operation for hernia." So I gave him the last ten shilling note we had in the house and he got on his bike and cycled to Tunbridge Wells Hospital.' He was there for the month of December while his wife had to survive on no money, robbing Peter to pay Paul. The hospital was a sobering place for him with its air raid victims from London: 'The quiet suffer-ing the bombees do with their legs strung up in the air . . . makes me shelter-conscious. One feller today came up from theatre . . . and in his chloroform . . . pleaded for his old girl. "My old girl, my old girl, where's my old girl." Then for his 15 year old daughter, both smoked flat with him, in a church. He was the only one out of 70 to come out of his part of it alive.'[28]

Lye had planned to write scripts but instead could not stop thinking about political philosophy. 'War' (he wrote) was 'what happens when mass moves for happiness get off the rails'. The Nazi was 'representing himself by the state, and hopping out of bed each morn with ideas of conquest, with the pseudo-spiritual sun shining in a great blaze on his world-oyster. He's got everything but himself.'[29] It was during this period in hospital that Lye added a third element to his theory — 'the now of time'. To attach special importance to the experience of the present was to challenge the many forms of war, religion, and economics that exploited nostalgia or the promise that 'happiness is just around the corner'. Back at Coppings Brook Cottage just after Christmas, he tried to condense his many thoughts into a kind of manifesto. There were conflicts with his wife over his obsession with the subject. And he continued to fret about his 'pretentious' style. When he tested the material on Graves, his friend replied: 'It makes sense, but the writing is just disastrous. Let Beryl and I sort it out and see how you like it.'³⁰ (Graves had just found a new partner, Beryl Hodge, the former wife of the writer Alan Hodge who had been working with him on a book about British social history.) While they revised the manuscript, Lye kept up a steady flow of letters to Graves that combined Krazy Kat comic strips, talk of jazz, and snippets of family news with new versions of his theory.

His greatest breakthrough came in March 1941 when he coined the slogan 'IHN' or 'Individual Happiness Now'. In his words: 'got the idea out of writing and writing and writing all sorts of ideas until the one I wanted brewed itself out of the mash. Then I was levitated onto my bike and biked around country lane corners shouting or bellowing "Individuality! Happiness! Now!" exuberantly exultant. I can in memory still match my bike spokes turning with an exultant larynx vibrating.'³¹ This wild ride round the village of Leigh was an experience Lye would always remember, his equivalent of Archimedes jumping out of his bath shouting 'Eureka!'³² A good slogan can count for a great deal in politics, but it can also lend itself to misunderstandings such as the notion that IHN simply means hedonism, or a 1960s-style injunction to 'Do your own thing'. In some respects Lye's philosophy does anticipate the radical politics of the 1960s but IHN needs to be understood from his own perspective. By stressing the relationship between the three words he hoped to rescue them from the clichés they normally evoked. These words represented 'the best in human experience'. People were inclined to take them for granted, but 'I think we could stimulate this dormant intensity . . . more than we do and create more evidences of it . . . yes by bloody Jesus I do'.³³ These three personal goals — to become a more distinct individual, to develop a greater capacity for happiness, and to live more fully in the present — were more difficult to falsify or appropriate than political abstractions such as freedom, democracy, or our country's way of life. At the same time IHN could be universal because it was independent of race, creed, class, or nationalist prejudices.

The theory was given a moral dimension by Lye's insistence that every individual should have an equal opportunity to pursue IHN. Most societies paid lip-service to the separate elements but in practice they promoted them only in a partial form. Lye stressed the necessity for all three to be present to achieve 'fullness of being'. He based his theory not only on his own happiness but on the evidence provided by the arts, which he saw as the great testing-ground of individuality. The freedom to produce and experience a wide range of art gave happiness to people all over the world, with the glaring exception of states such as Nazi Germany which had censored modern art as degenerate and had persecuted artists. (Lye had heard many details from refugee artists such as Ernst Meyer.) Art was Lye's personal answer to the question 'What would I die for?' As he put it on one occasion: 'I imagined for myself that I would be ready to go over the top and march into shrapnel . . . if I could see overhead a mirage of Brancusi's work, Turner's water-colours, hear the best African percussion, and so on. In other words, the beauty and durability of the arts.'[34] But he did not want to impose his own extreme taste. Trying to speak of happiness in a way that would include a wide range of human experience, he wrote in 1940 (in a version edited by Graves): 'It may seem cynical to speak of [individual happiness] in so cruel a year as this. But people have a new sense of what really matters, of what remains when all else is lost. They have learned, among other things, that loss of property does not matter much, if life is saved. They know, now, perhaps for the first time, how good a thing a cheese is, or an onion, or a peaceful night's sleep. This is not an argument in favour of war, but only of individuality.'[35]

twentynine going to the top

These themes had been present in Lye's writing for some time but now he had developed a clear distillation of his ideas and a new interest in politics. In a time of war people faced ultimate questions and needed serious answers. Graves agreed to lend his skills as a popular writer, and in April 1941 — a month after Lye had invented his IHN slogan — they completed the twelve-page essay 'A Definition of Common Purpose'. It began by noting that Britain's leaders were finding it 'difficult to express the national war aims beyond the negative one of crushing fascism'. The Germans had created the dramatic concept of the New Order and it was necessary that 'an alternative should be put into circulation, and pretty quick'. The essay proceeded to explain the basic conception of IHN and to show why each of its elements presented a challenge to the Nazis. The authors cited the American Declaration of Independence as a precedent in its concern for everyone's right to 'life, liberty, and the pursuit of happiness'.

The aim was to present Lye's idea to the public as 'a reasonable and modest enough concept', with Graves providing the right style and tone. IHN was thus transformed from an artist's ideal of intensity to a more general value similar to what politicians would later call 'the quality of life'. Even in this diluted form IHN was still a fresh and attractive idea, presented as the basis of a style of politics that respected the individual and valued 'variety of life'. Graves softened Lye's anti-religious attitude by suggesting ways the Church could 'adapt itself to the spirit' of IHN. Passages linking IHN with British tradition were unmistakably from Graves's hand: 'Good manners are the test of true national health. And by good manners we do not mean . . . insincere formalities but the good manners that imply a real respect for the individual character of every person in one's society. . . . And the code of sportsmanship which . . . has been Great Britain's most notable contribution to the world in the last hundred years, embodies good manners precisely in this sense.' By smoothing out the stylistic tangles Graves also got rid of some of the intensity and originality. As a professional writer with a clear sense of British culture he was providing Lye with exactly what he had asked for — a version of the theory that had a real chance to attract public interest. But there was a dilemma here that neither of them could resolve — how to translate individual intensity into the lukewarm language of mass politics?

184

Lye had mixed feelings about the revised version of his essay. Nevertheless he worked hard to circulate it to as many people as possible, hoping that readers would still recognise the underlying energy of his concept.

If his theory was most relevant to artists like himself, why was he spending so much energy trying to market it to the general public? Certainly the war was an extraordinary provocation. And a compelling precedent had been set by Laura Riding and by many of his friends from the documentary movement who had become deeply involved in politics.[1] Lye's new interest was driven by a particular mix of circumstances — the political situation, the lack of film jobs, and the new fluency with words and ideas he was working hard to develop. For the first time he was high on pure ideas. As an artist he had seen the public gradually come to accept new developments in painting and film, so why should it be any different with moral or political ideas?

He had reached the mid-point of his life, a time (according to W. B. Yeats) when a person was likely to be drawn to his or her 'anti-self', to previously neglected aspects of personality. In later years Lye saw a symmetry between the two halves of his career since each began with a flash of insight — the first about motion and the second about IHN.[2] He was only one of many modern artists and writers to develop a mid-life interest in theory. Riding withdrew from poetry to devote herself to the study of word meanings, and in 1943 Graves became engrossed in speculations about the 'White Goddess', as he reported in a letter to Alan Hodge: 'I have been worried by thinking about poetry and finding that all the poems that one thinks of as most poetic . . . are intricately connected with primitive moon-worship. This sounds crazy, and I fear for my sanity, but it is so. . . . This may not lead me anywhere and I am so anxious not to get dogmatic or psychological. But I find myself making the Bards into Moon-men. . . . Help!'[3]

The poet Malcolm de Chazal once issued a warning about theory and its seductiveness: 'Every artist makes the mistake of eventually wanting to turn his art into a science. Of doing what Adam did when, dissatisfied with his enjoyment of Paradise, he wanted to know "What made it tick" and how the formula was arrived at.'[4] While Lye's theory was not merely concerned with his own art, his new earnestness did not fit the image many people had of him. In May 1942 he remarked to Graves: 'Alan [Hodge] today helped me with my opening paragraph of the synopsis and very decently didn't say that IHN is making me a bore to all my friends. I know I've never been so miserable over anything . . .'.[5] Jane Lye tried to persuade herself that his theorising was necessary to his art. No one felt confident that they understood his central idea but friends gave what help they could. Lye remembered one day 'a telegram came right out of the blue [which] simply said, "Hurray for IHN". It was signed by Dylan Thomas and John Tunnard. It sounded as if someone was enjoying beer somewhere. It was the right kind of lift.'[6]

Lye had a lifetime habit of going to the top when he wanted something, and he had found support for his direct film-making more or less by walking in off the street to talk with John Grierson. Now he needed a sponsor for an idea. He began by sending the essay to Edward Hulton, prominent in magazine publishing, and was rewarded with an invitation to lunch. But afterwards he sent this report to Graves: 'If ever a man had pins and needles Hulton had at my lunch with him. He is . . . extremely unable to find out what I am talking about. . . . First remark was, what was meant by "low-bubbling point" [a minor detail at the beginning of the essay]. Jesus wept! . . . We were at variance over every single thing we spoke about. (He didn't like films. I didn't like English magazines)'.[7] This experience was to be repeated many times — people just could not 'tag it out'. The essay would initially catch their attention but when Lye met with interested parties to discuss his theory further, the idea of IHN soon ceased to seem 'reasonable and modest'. He talked to left-wing groups: 'Socialists say, well, that's what socialism is about. And I say, then why the hell don't they say so.'[8] He decided to approach the Quakers because he liked their sense of 'the present', their ability to 'do something and yet not ride the doing', but nothing came of those discussions. Then he gained an unlikely supporter in Dr George Bell, the Anglican Bishop of Chichester, who wrote to say he had 'read and re-read' the essay: 'There is much in it that appeals to me. . . . I have little doubt that in that phrase "the present" lies the main contribution which you would make to the education of human experience. . . . I am sure there is something in your programme which is in tune with much that is deepest in religion.'[9] Lye had what he considered a friendly meeting with the Bishop, and there was even talk of passing on a copy of the essay to the King, but then nothing more was heard.[10]

When the USSR became an ally of England in June 1941 Lye decided he might as well approach the Russian government, even though he despised Stalin whom he saw as an enemy of the arts. He sought the advice of Tom Driberg, a *Daily Express* columnist who had shown an interest in his film work. Driberg introduced him to the top English representative of the Russian news agency TASS (an interesting connection in view of the fact that Driberg would be accused after his death of having been a double agent working for the Soviet KGB as well as MI5).[11] The Russian listened to Lye's presentation then said: 'You're doing a lot of thinking on heights above the plains, but have you considered the thinking of other men up the same mountain?' Lye replied: 'I've tried to, but I don't like the route they took, nor what they reckon to find at the top.' The reporter then quizzed him about his knowledge of Marx. When Lye admitted there were some gaps he was told: 'Read Marx, comment on it, and if your comments are good I'll forward them to Stalin.' Lye insisted on help to find the particular passages where Marx discussed happiness. When the Russian could come up with only two pages on this topic Lye decided to call it a day.[12]

Towards the end of 1941 when Lye's friend Rita Vandivert of the *March of Time* left with her husband for New York, he asked her to take a copy of his essay and bring it somehow to the attention of Wendell Willkie, the unsuccessful Republican candidate for the American presidency. Willkie had made a much-publicised visit to Britain in 1940 to learn more about the probable social and economic consequences of the war and what form life would take after the war was over. Sending the paper to New York was a long shot and there was no immediate response from Willkie.

It was natural for Lye to think of promoting his idea by means of a film. He hoped the involvement of Robert Graves would help to sell the project, which he conceived in large-scale terms as an answer to Nazi propaganda epics such as *Triumph of the Will*. One of his proposals singled out Orson Welles's *Citizen Kane* — just released in London — as 'proof that a feature film of a new sort can be successfully produced'. (Unfortunately this brilliant film was not doing well at the box-office.) The few studios still active in London had difficulty visualising Lye's project in film terms and were not interested in spending money on development. Michael Balcon of Ealing Studios replied: 'I know from the amount of thought you have given to the subject it cannot be classified as experimental from your point of view, but it must be from ours.'[13] And John Sutro of Two Cities Films commented: 'It is not easy to see how such an idea could be worked on by a commercial concern unless they were prepared to regard it, in the first instance, as a piece of research.'[14] A theory that emphasised 'happiness now' appeared to lack conflict which was regarded as necessary for a strong narrative. Lye's interest in films had never had much to do with conventional forms of drama. He saw his ideal actor as Charlie Chaplin who had just made *The Great Dictator*, a brilliant satire on Hitler. In one of Lye's scripts (as Tom Matthews remembered it), 'The protagonist [Chaplin] makes his way around the world, in each country confronting the head of state. . . . As the outline of [a] film it seemed to lack drama . . . and I tried to say so, gently, in a way that would be acceptable to Len. It was not acceptable: the [IHN] idea bothered him, he admitted, and all he wanted to do was get rid of it; but he was sure that the only way of getting rid of it was through this film. . . . Talking with Len about individual happiness degenerated into a gloomy wrangle.'[15]

Why did the IHN campaign run into so many problems? Lye believed the main obstacle was the difficulty he had in articulating his ideas, in adequately expressing what art meant to him and the happiness it gave. He felt an endless tension between what he wanted to say and the ideas he was able to capture on paper with the help of Graves and other friends. He had no doubts about the ideas themselves because they were based on experience. In the words of Barbara Ker-Seymer: 'Len was one of the few people who really lived his philosophy. He always seemed to have a special happiness.'[16] IHN was based not merely on his temperament and his own powerful individualism but on a long Romantic tradition of thinking about the arts. It provided passionate answers to questions about the value of individual experience in a world at war where life seemed cheap — but were such answers for everyone? The war was being fought for many reasons. Religious and political leaders were likely to feel uneasy about his enthusiasm for individual freedom which seemed to extend all the way to anarchism. Lye's own life revolved round the connections between art, individuality, and happiness but not everyone attached such great importance to art. Where his ideas were most vulnerable was in their attempt to claim universal relevance. Graves and Riding were similarly inclined to minimise what was time-bound and culture-specific in their search for ultimate answers — indeed, looking for universals was a common trait of modernism. Its ideas were more usefully seen simply as probes opening up new territory. For example, the modernist idea that tribal artists were kindred spirits was a useful way of challenging the values and assumptions dominant in Western art, but it skated over the problems of projecting individuality on to a wide range of communal cultures.

IHN was a theory in progress, gradually expanding to cover more of Lye's interests. He found each of its three ingredients endlessly thought-provoking. Unfortunately the successive drafts of a theory do not have the same lasting value as (say) a series of drawings. And whereas making a picture had always been satisfying in itself, IHN seemed incomplete without an audience or a political application. When Lye moved beyond the art world to approach editors, politicians, and other influential people, most of them could not understand where he was coming from — he was not an Oxbridge intellectual, he lacked the popular touch of a Priestley, and he had no political group behind him. He had been a maverick for so many years that he lacked a sense of mainstream culture and its discourses. What he did have was a passion for a particular cluster of ideas, a stubborn belief that art had something important to say to politicians, and a lonely sense of once again having to trust his own instincts.

thirty war films

During 1941 Lye gained several jobs on war-time information films produced by the Realist Film Unit which was doing regular work for the Ministry of Information.[1] Realist had been in existence for five years as an offshoot of the GPO Film Unit. The films Lye directed for Realist had low budgets and their themes were often prosaic — for example, *When The Pie Was Opened* showed how to overcome the meat shortage by cooking vegetable pies — but he was never going to make a film without sneaking in some experiments. This was one of the reasons he was hired by John Taylor, head of Realist and an important figure in British documentary-making, who later remarked: 'I've been in the film industry for 50 years now, and I think he is probably the one truly original thinker I've met in that time. He had completely his own approach to every-thing.'[2] Taylor continued to defend Lye even when people were puzzled or shocked by his work because he believed that innovation was important at a time when a lot of wartime instructional films tended to be very straightforward.[3]

Lye worked on his Realist projects with 'Jeak' — A. E. Jeakins — a camera-man with an outstanding reputation for solving lighting problems and the ability to work quickly.[4] For many years Jeakins wrote the 'Technician's Notebook' section of *The Cine-Technician*, and his up-to-the-minute knowledge of technical developments was a great resource. Lye set him some extraordinary challenges. In Jeakins's words: 'I have very happy memories of working with Len. He was so stimulating and so full of ideas, with a wonderfully sunny temperament and not a trace of pomposity or "side". Always willing to discuss how one should tackle any problem that arose, and ready to welcome ideas no matter from how lowly a source they came.'[5]

Lye's script for *When The Pie Was Opened* was (in his own words) 'written by a mouse with a tongue in its cheek'.[6] He presented part of the film through the eyes of a child (Valerie Forest) hungry for a meat pie, with Fats Waller's 'In My Solitude' as accompaniment. The film is extravagantly playful and surreal, for example in the girl's dream of 'four and twenty blackbirds baked into a pie' which ended with the plate crashing to the floor leaving one grotesque blackbird still standing. When the mother (Hilda Masters) discovered a newspaper item about vegetable pie, a mouth appeared in the middle of the page and began

189

reading the recipe aloud. The most amusing sequence in the film was the making and serving of a vegetable pie accompanied by a collage of sound effects which included sawing and hammering as the pastry was cut, marching feet and train noises as the pie was carried to the table, and the sounds of cows, roosters, and other farmyard animals as it was savoured. Lye and his sound editor Ernst Meyer made a meal of this experiment in sound composition.

Like other Realist films, *Pie* was offered free to the many cinemas that the British public continued to attend even during the height of the German bombing. Unfortunately its soundtrack proved baffling to some viewers. One critic described the film as 'not so much "Realist" as surrealist', and cameraman George Noble remarked: 'The film is not only non-theatrical, it's non-showable.'[7] But Taylor recalls that Beddington was pleased with the film and it was generally well-received by audiences: 'People found it very amusing. There were a lot of references to things happening at the time that people wouldn't pick up today.'[8] The reviewer in *Documentary News Letter* observed: 'Len Lye is a director who cannot help communicating through his films a warm, friendly, and imaginatively lively personality. . . . It is the gayest short for many a day — and from the Ministry of Information too!'[9]

Before his next job for Realist, Lye was asked by the London office of the American series *March of Time* to direct several sequences for 'Britain's RAF', a programme about the war in the air.[10] From the end of June 1941 he and the cameraman Bob Navarro were based in Oban, Scotland, to film the air patrols that accompanied convoys. In Lye's words: 'The small port was an air base for large flying boats called Sunderlands. Nazi fighter pilots called the Sunderland a "flying porcupine" because it bristled with guns. We hit the time of year when there were mists and the days were short so we got back after dark. It was a regular routine for the crew to crowd up forward with the two pilots to watch as our heavy flying plane put her nose down, to find the red flashing beacon that would tell us we were coming down over the tiny harbour and not over its mountain ridges. There was an extreme simplicity in the way the boys did their breath-holding without saying anything while we got lower and lower without seeing the beacon, and rose up to try again. It was alright for me and Bob, we were not stuck with it, but they were. A lot of planes had missed the beacon and the boys referred to Oban as "Crackup Port".'[11]

Navarro and Lye spent their evenings at a restaurant drinking the local whisky (Oban Mist) and dancing with the waitresses, the customers, and eventually the proprietress.[12] During the day they shot some good scenes in the air but mist prevented them from filming a convoy. After several attempts Lye told the briefing officer that 'the next flight had to be lucky' because the *March of Time* urgently needed the footage. But that morning while he and Navarro were sitting in the Sunderland waiting to take off, there was a last-minute change of flight crews and they were required to leave the plane. This was a big disappointment because the weather was perfect for filming. Later they heard that their plane had gone down and their own names were included in the casualty list. People were astonished to see them alive.[13] Back in Kent Lye found that his family had also had a narrow escape. As Jane described it: 'We had eighteen bombs across the barn one night, and craters in the meadow just at the back. But no damage to Sidney's place, the bombs dropped in between the buildings — 250-pound bombs, jettisoned on a bad night to get away over the channel.'[14]

Lye now had regular work from the Realist Film Unit. One of the many unusual features of the Unit was the fact that the seventeen members of its production staff were all paid the same, directors and cameramen and editors, and given equal credits.[15] The pay was a modest ten pounds per week but it was the first steady income Lye had seen for a long time. John Taylor recalls that 'Len was ten or fifteen years older than us, but he didn't seem to be. He was always a very cheerful and amusing man. We worked very much as a cooperative unit — people discussed other people's work, went to other people for help with ideas — and Len was always very good on ideas.'[16] During the war more than half the Realist staff were women and the Unit seems to have been unusually free of the male bias typical of the film industry. Yvonne Fletcher, Dorothy Grayson, Rosanne Hunter, Jane Massy, Evelyn Spice and Margaret Thomson were among those who at some time directed films for Realist. Thomson was a New Zealand science graduate who had come to England because she could not find work during the early years of the Depression. Starting out making educational films for Gaumont-British, she had gone on to work in many areas of the British documentary movement.[17] She remembers Lye as friendly and genial on the surface, but she sensed that a part of his personality always remained private. One thing that impressed her was the fact that he read almost nothing but poetry. Lye's favourite book at this time was Norman Cameron's translation of Rimbaud's poetry. He painted the cover of his copy and carried it with him on film shoots as an 'anchor to reality' while 'overnighting in bleakness'.[18]

Derek Waterman, Lye's assistant, remembers him as a proud parent who would turn up at the office with Bix on his shoulders.[19] His clothing was always a talking-point, for example the unique plaid suit in greens and yellows that had been made to his design from material brought back from Scotland. Though the jacket had the same tartan pattern as the trousers, the pattern was in a smaller size.

'Len never wore a tie' recalls Maurice Lancaster, 'and that was most unusual in those days. He also didn't wear a hat, but perhaps some sort of odd cap like a fez.'[20] Taylor noticed that his sense of style extended even to small things: 'We couldn't buy cigarettes so we used to have Fruit Pastille tins to keep our tobacco in. Everybody just had a tin with a label, but Len's was beautifully painted with a Chinese motif on top. Everything he touched, he brushed with imagination.'[21] Waterman found him a tolerant and understanding director to work for, and the only trait that earned him a reputation for being difficult was his passion for editing which caused him to monopolise the Editola. Lye would test so many possibilities that he tended not to bother scraping the film before making a cement splice. On one occasion this shortcut led to disaster as his film, an edited workprint, fell apart in front of a preview audience. Editing could be a risky business because inflammable nitrate film was still in use. Waterman remembers that he and Lye were in the editing room one day when a film being cut by members of an American Army Film Unit caught fire. 'We rushed over to help, knowing that if the rapidly travelling flame reached the main rolls there might be an explosion. Len and I grabbed one each and managed to tear off the film in time, but not before quite a lot of film was destroyed and we were both slightly burnt.'

Lye was 'always prepared at the drop of the hat to discuss art, life, literature', but Waterman was struck by his down-to-earth style: 'There was nothing of the intellectual snob about Lye.'[22] Not surprisingly the discussion often turned to IHN. Thomson remembers Lye talking a lot about theory but she was struck by the laughter that went with it — he never treated theory as something solemn. Everyone tended to find IHN baffling with the exception of Frank Sainsbury (an influential figure at Realist), who got roped in to help with 'the latest writings and manifestoes',[23] after which he was known around the Unit as 'Len's official interpreter'.

Lye's next Realist film was *Newspaper Train*, a six-minute tribute to the people who continued to distribute newspapers even at the height of the German bombing.[24] With its shots of newspaper boys in Piccadilly Circus, the project must have reminded him of his old paper run in Wellington. Focusing on the Ramsgate newspaper train and ending with a newsagent in Ramsgate finding bullets embedded in his copies of the *Daily Express,* the film spoke of the importance of newspapers in keeping people informed and in countering Nazi propaganda. No air raid could be staged for the film, but Lye proved that symbols could be just as dramatic as realistic images. Determined to keep conventional voice-over narration to a minimum, he came up with many ingenious methods of conveying information in visual terms. For example, the guard on the train flicked through photographs of bomb damage accompanied by the imagined sounds of a bombing raid. The raid itself was represented by explosions and severed lines on a railway map. The drawback to this filmic approach was the problems it created for less visually oriented people who were used to a commentary telling them what to see and think.

Jeakins remembered Lye trying constantly to push the boundaries of what was possible or conventional:

> Len seemed to have a knack for charming the most extraordinary facilities out of people. For example, he had devised a sequence in which a couple of American newsmen climbed into a taxi and rode around Piccadilly Circus throwing off some (post-sync) remarks about the nippy way that London news vans darted around delivering papers to the kerbside paper sellers. In those days some London taxis had fold-down hoods over the back seats, and Len wanted a wide-angle shot with the lens poised over the back of the taxi showing the chaps getting in, sitting down, and the cab driving off, with the camera travelling along with it. The Model A Newman-Sinclair, by the way, couldn't take any lens wider than a 35 mm; so where do you mount the camera to get it far enough away to hold all the action? Len's solution was to put the taxi on a low-loading trailer so you can put the camera where you like. Yes, but won't you see bits of the trailer and the towing truck . . . ? No, not if you drive backwards round the Circus. This was all supposed to happen with the traffic flowing round the Circus too. I wasn't at all keen on the idea. However, it got as far as being discussed quite seriously in Ralph May's office at the MOI! Eventually we hired or borrowed a rather ancient taxi from a South London garage. The railway workshop at Nine Elms stripped off the hood and built a wooden platform for the camera out on the back of the taxi. I don't think it was the shot of the year, but it worked.

Lye's interest in exploring alternatives to Griffith-style editing now included the use of extended shots of this kind, partly inspired by his enthusiasm for *Citizen Kane*.

Another difficult shot was the interior view of a guard's van at the moment a Messerschmitt sent a burst of machine-gun fire through the roof. Jeakins recalled that 'Len asked for, and got an old guard's van provided by the Southern Railway and parked at a quiet and remote siding somewhere in Kent, overlooked by a handy embankment on which the machine gun squad, provided by the Army, could mount their weapon and fire into the roof of the van. I almost forgot to mention the large generator, also supplied by the Railway Station and probably capable of lighting Waterloo Station, from which we drew the modest amperage needed for our photoflood lamps. We mounted the camera on low legs at one end of the van and built a sandbag emplacement round it. When everything was ready, we switched on the camera, leapt out of the van, took cover under the arch of a nearby bridge and gave the signal to fire. A classic example of a one-take set-up.'[25] John Taylor was horrified to hear that one of his directors had done such a shot because of the possible risk to the camera (cameras being in short supply at the time). In contrast, the attacking Messerschmitt was evoked simply as a shadow seen from the train window. Lye and Jeakins laid out sheets of white cardboard on the floor of the Realist office, set up the camera at a similar angle to that at which they had already shot the fields going past from a moving train; then Lye whisked the shadow of a model plane suspended from a rod across the white card, and Studio Labs matted (superimposed) the resulting shot onto the travelling background.[26] The shot was so effective that at least one film-maker, Harry Watt, was deceived into thinking it was made with a real aircraft. *Newspaper Train* also became the showcase for a soundtrack invention by Lye, Taylor, Ernst Meyer, and Frank Sainsbury. The Association of Cine-Technicians took out its first patent on behalf of this method, which consisted of printing two separate soundtracks side by side, one for dialogue and commentary and the other for sound effects, to avoid the loss of definition that often happened when the tracks were mixed.[27] But there was one complication — the projectionist had to turn up the volume — and when *Newspaper Train* went round the cinemas, most projectionists ignored this instruction and the film's dialogue became difficult to catch. The problem was exacerbated by the fact that the principal voice was that of an American reporter (Merril Mueller) whose accent displeased some British viewers.[28] *Newspaper Train* was unlucky enough to be selected as one of four films followed through the nation's cinemas by an MOI study of audience response.[29] The study was contracted out to Mass Observation, an innovative organisation which Humphrey Jennings had helped to establish but which had become more opinionated and commercial over the years. Its report showed that an exceptional number of people considered *Newspaper Train* exceptionally bad.[30] The film had confused some viewers — a reasonable criticism — but the report added the simplistic explanation that this was because the film 'gave its information in an unprecise, "over-intellectualised" way'.[31] The report concluded that the war effort needed information to be presented as straightforwardly as possible,[32] and the film most favoured by the report was 'the least cinematographic'.[33]

Lye survived this bad report-card and went on to direct *Work Party* (or 'Factory Family'), which made an exceptionally strong impression on his associates at

Realist. John Taylor saw it as the model for a new kind of documentary: 'I think it's from *Work Party* that the idea of cinéma vérité came. . . . I've always thought that he [Len] probably took the idea . . . to America when he went, and it spread from there to people like [Richard] Leacock.'[34] This is to overstate Lye's influence since it was an experiment that he made once only. Still, it is clear that *Work Party* was regarded at the time of its release (May 1942) as highly original. Taylor recalled that the starting-point for the idea was a scene from a documentary he was making about the Canadian Light Infantry: 'We used to watch rushes together, and Len saw some rushes of two Canadian soldiers and two girls playing poker. Because the sound camera and equipment were all so big in those days, and the room they were in was very small, the camera was put outside the window, and the lights as well, and the microphone was hidden. So they more or less performed completely normally, without any consciousness of a camera being there.' Because of a problem with the content the scene was dropped from the film but Lye 'saw the possibilities — he was very quick on the uptake with things like that — and he made the film *Work Party* using the same technique.'

In Jeakins's words: 'The theme broadly was women working in a munitions factory (at Hayes), and the main protagonists were the Herrick family, a mother and her daughters who all worked at the same factory and all lived together in a semi-detached house in the neighbourhood. Mother drove one of those overhead cranes, a rather unusual job for a woman even in wartime.'[35] The women worked extremely long hours manufacturing guns and shells. Wanting to include a scene of them waking up early and talking as they got ready for work, Lye decided that the only way to achieve the genuine feeling and atmosphere was to shoot it at the actual time. To reach the house early enough, the film crew had to leave London the previous evening, sleep at a local hotel and rise at the crack of dawn. But (in Jeakins's words) 'we found on our arrival at the house, with all the paraphernalia of blimped 35 mm camera, that the girls had already risen, dressed fully, and then put their night dresses over their day clothes! We went ahead with the shot, but I don't think it was quite what Lye had in mind.'[36]

The title *Work Party* alluded to the fact that Mary Herrick was having a party in the evening to celebrate her twenty-first birthday. Her party was filmed as 'hand-held off-the-cuff stuff' with synchronised sound, but problems created by the cumbersome equipment of that period made it necessary to continue the party on a subsequent evening. Set to jazz, this delightful slice-of-life sequence documented the details from the food to the dancing. One part of the film in which Lye departed from this candid camera approach was a montage of various factory machining operations shot in close-up and cut to jazz. Jeakins thought the sequence was marvellous but the MOI did not and most of it had to be dropped.[37] (Lye would return to this idea in a later film.) Although *Work Party* ended with slogans ('The munitions industry needs more women now'), it was an unpretentious slice of wartime life rather than a slick piece of propaganda. The film was given an extensive cinema release but received an exceptionally sour review in *Documentary News Letter* from Basil Wright (the founder of Realist Films), who saw its 'propaganda value' as 'nil or even minus' because it had been 'shot in such a way as to give an impression of indescribable drabness and sordidity which is not merely unfair to the people in the film but also to the people that have to see it'.[38] Lye, who had grown up in a working-class family, found such middle-class attitudes patronising.

He also directed two of a series of 90-second 'trailers' or 'poster films' designed to follow newsreels. The first trailer, *Planned Crops*, featured up-and-coming comedian Ted Ray performing in front of a set designed by the *Daily Express* cartoonist Giles.[39] The second trailer, *Collapsible Metal Tubes* (also known as *Tin Salvage*) urged people to recycle tin because Japan now controlled much of the world supply. It included two voice-overs spoken by Lye. The term poster film is very appropriate for this extraordinary mixture of live actors, cartoons, models, and painted sets. By today's standards the cartoon treatment of Japan in the film was racist, with the enemy presented as a human skull on a spider's body creeping across the map towards Britain. In fact the body consisted of a painted tomato, and in the climax of the film a fist came crashing down on the spider splashing goo and pips in all directions. This cheap but stomach-turning special effect underlined the slogan 'Take back [your tin] — and hit back.' *Documentary News Letter* praised this propaganda film as 'imaginatively and excitingly done'.[40]

It was frustrating for Lye to be in such close contact with the Ministry of Information yet to be unsuccessful in his attempts to interest its top people in IHN. In a letter to Graves he described a typical conversation: 'I said to Walter, the MOI's job is to propagate an idea and principle. But there ain't no place to define the idea, and there ain't no idea. So tell me what the hell is the use of the MOI except to censor? And he said they [the Ministry] will say, we don't get fat on an idea.'[41] There was a school of thought within the Government that morale depended on material factors such as food, warmth, and rest, whereas ideas were potentially divisive.[42] Lye could not agree that films about vegetable pies or toothpaste tubes were more urgently needed than films about principles. But his MOI film job was at least putting food on his own family's table after several lean years. And there was always the possibility of sneaking one or two worthwhile projects through the Unit. Lye's favourite proposal, worked out in collaboration with Sainsbury and Taylor, was a survey of British society. In Taylor's words: 'The idea was that we would take twelve people — say, Bernard Shaw, J. B. Priestley, well-known writers or painters or sculptors or whatever — and do a cinéma vérité on them, shoot 10,000 feet, say, and put it away into a national archive as a record of these people. At the same time we should edit a two-reel version for public distribution. The scheme had four categories with twelve people in each, and it was meant to cover the whole spectrum of British life during the war period. It would include a coal miner, a farm labourer, a factory worker, an office worker, a scientist . . .'.[43] Taylor attempted to persuade the MOI to sponsor the scheme but it was judged too expensive. Considering the potential historical value of the footage, he felt it was a great tragedy that the project was turned down.

thirtyone kill or be killed

Kill or Be Killed, Lye's next project for Realist, was considered by some critics to be one of the best of all wartime films. It was a fictional enactment of the deadly contest between a British soldier and a German sniper hiding in a tree. The *Documentary News Letter* reviewer, who summed it up as 'without doubt one of the most exciting films ever made', wrote: 'There is no commentary, but the thoughts of both hunter and hunted are spoken, one by a Scots voice, the other in English with a German intonation, and this device adds enormously to the tension. Here warfare is reduced to a primitive, man to man contest, in which the colour of a leaf, the sudden movement of a horse, the keenness of one's eyes or ears, may mean life or death. . . . The film has the very magic of cinema in it, every legitimate device has been used with an integrity that is rare in film making. . . . It is well worth your while to hunt it out — that is if you don't mind being shaken up, frightened and fascinated'.[1] And Cavalcanti wrote in *Sight and Sound*: 'To praise without reservation is the critic's most difficult task and about this [film] I cannot but say that it has the weight of a classic Greek tragedy. *Kill or Be Killed* keeps also, in a slow tempo, the same sense of rhythm that we find in *Colour Box*.'[2]

Though the film's primary aim was to train soldiers, it was also shown to many groups of civilians who would have needed to take up arms if the Germans had invaded Britain. Since most army instructional films were so straightforward and didactic that even Mass Observation would have approved of them, *Kill or Be Killed* gained great impact from Lye's decision to replace commentary by drama. The film stayed close to the point of view of each protagonist — in fact for one sequence Jeakins fitted the equivalent of rifle sights on to the front of his camera. When a soldier was crawling through the woods, the camera was hanging by leather straps from a rifle being carried along by both Jeakins and Lye. This hand-held camerawork heightened the viewer's involvement. Alternating viewpoints gave the film a classic structure. Richard McNaughton, an editor who had worked on many films of the period, commented: '*Kill or Be Killed* is small-scale and very precise — each scene motivates the next. John Grierson used to say: "When you come to make a film, think in terms of boxing, and the famous film of the cobra and the mongoose. You saw the cobra doing his thing, and then you saw the mongoose attacking. That movement, where one attacks and the other reacts and hits back, was exactly what you'd get in boxing, so the actions were always motivated and always alive".'[3]

The film had absolutely no relevance to IHN but Lye did become very involved in its sense of body movement. He wrote to Graves: 'I just made a simple film — The War, as played by a Lovat scout versus a German sniper — and it is 18 minutes of crawling and jumping.'[4] Or as he put it years later: 'It exemplifies a slow unfolding rhythm, a rhythm that creeps into one's buttocks, as does Samuel Beckett's body imagery.'[5] The part of the British soldier was played by Duncan Chisholm, a Scotsman with no experience as an actor but many years of experience as a soldier and as a deer stalker. In civil life he had been head gillie in a large estate. Lye was excited by his agility — 'his movements are smooth and rhythmic like a cat'. Chisholm had to do so much crawling for the film that his trousers wore thin and it was difficult to avoid showing his shirt through his breeches in the final scenes.[6] The part of the German sniper was played by another Scotsman (Alistair McIntyre), an actor who had become a captain in the Army. His voice was dubbed in for Chisholm's, while the thoughts of the German soldier were spoken by Marius Goring (who had played Hitler in the BBC series *In the Shadow of the Swastika*).

The film's presentation of warfare was so matter-of-fact and lacking in sentiment that today it shocks viewers who have grown up on conventional war (or anti-war) films. Even in 1942 it ran into problems. The first problem was minor, as Waterman recalls: 'There was quite a stir over the line, "I'll get that Jerry bastard if it takes me all day." The War Office or MOI objected, and a post-sync session had to be organised to change it to: "I'll get that Jerry, blast him, if it takes me all day." Everyone at Realist felt that if the word was good enough for Noel Coward's *In Which We Serve* it should have been good enough for our film.'[7] As for the second problem, Tom Matthews remembered attending a preview of *Kill or Be Killed* in the company of American army officers who found the film so stark that they resolved to prevent its proposed theatrical distribution in the United States.[8] Some prints of the film in circulation today tacitly omit the brutal last few minutes which show the British soldier setting up the body of the German as a decoy to pick off members of a scouting party that come to investigate.[9]

Lye's final project for Realist was *Cameramen at War*, a 17-minute compilation film about the sacrifices and achievements of wartime cameramen (including a shot of D. W. Griffith in the trenches with a camera). What the film does well is to make sure that viewers pay attention not only to the dramatic events shown on screen but also to the skills of the people who filmed them. The cameraman's ability to keep objects in frame was likened to the precise aim of the marksman or bombardier. The film included an unforgettable sequence where the camera followed the descent of a stick of bombs while Raymond Glendenning commented: 'Put yourself in the cameraman's place. These bombs, gleaming white against the blue of the sea, plunging down relentlessly on the Italian fleet. Directing his aim all the time, his eye glued to the viewfinder, he follows the tiny specks down and down. Is this the target coming into view on the left? No, it is only a destroyer between the torpedo nets. The light seems pretty good down there. Now! What is this? Yes, there she is. One of the Littoria class. But where are those bombs? The camera pans again as the pilot banks. Target just in picture. There go the bombs!' Besides promoting an awareness of the film-making process, *Cameramen at War* paid tribute to cameramen who risked their lives on the front lines and seldom received individual credit for their work.

Unfortunately the project got bogged down in an argument between departments as the War Office insisted that more prominence be given to their cameramen. Apart from some shots of the AFU School at Pinewood, *Cameramen at War* was made entirely on the editing bench, and in the end Lye found the project too restricted. He wrote to Graves: 'I'm making a knitting sort of film and can't cast off.'[10] And: 'The film is not myth — just newsreel I can't control, but only edit towards myth.'[11] IHN remained at the centre of his thoughts. For Lye the war was the ultimate proof that a new set of social values had to be put in place and it was not enough for society merely to celebrate heroism on the battlefield. He was puzzled that others did not share his sense of urgency about the need for new political ideas, or his belief that the end of the war would give politicians a once-in-a-lifetime chance to set new directions. To move closer to where those decisions would be made Lye took a new job in July 1943 at the *March of Time*, exchanging the documentary genre for the 'weekly news magazine'. He left Meyer and Waterman to do the final tidying up of *Cameramen at War*.[12] Ironically some of the footage left over after editing the film was destroyed by a German bomb.[13]

At the beginning of 1942 Jane Lye and the children had to move out of their Kent cottage to make room for farm workers. Bernstein had been given an ultimatum that if he did not bring the farm into full production he would have to turn it over to the government. Both Lye children had a bout of whooping cough, a serious illness. Jane's parents had been urging her for some time to escape with the children to 'the sun and oranges' of South Africa and this now seemed an attractive option. After lengthy negotiations with the South African embassy she

Lye with his steel kinetic sculpture 'Storm King'. COURTESY ERIK SHIOZAKI

Above: 'Polynesian Connection', Lye's 1979 acrylic painting based on a batik he first exhibited with the Seven and Five Society in London in 1928. COURTESY LEN LYE FOUNDATION

Below: The 'Pond People' in this 1930 batik were among the creatures Lye planned to animate in a sequel to his film *Tusalava*. This batik had the alternative titles 'Fresh Water Things' and 'Marks and Spencer in a Japanese Garden'. COURTESY LEN LYE FOUNDATION

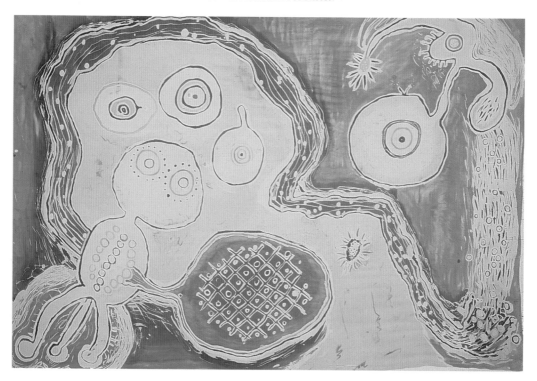

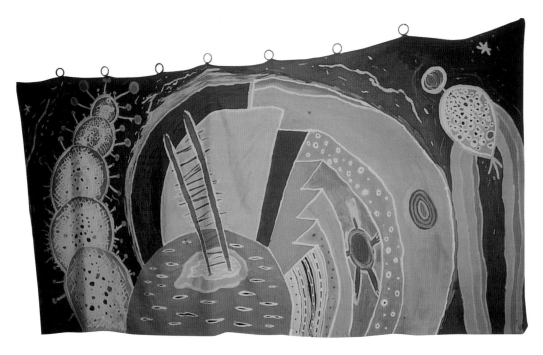

Above: The batik 'Laura Riding Shawl', also known as 'Jacob's Ladder', seen on the wall of Robert Graves's home in Deyá, Mallorca. The batik was reproduced in the international avant-garde magazine *Transition* in 1928.
PHOTO SHIRLEY HORROCKS

Below: 'Land and Sea', a 1977 oil painting based on a batik made 50 years earlier. COURTESY LEN LYE FOUNDATION

Right: 'The King of Plants Meets the First Man', a 1936 oil painting.
COURTESY LEN LYE FOUNDATION

Below: 'Tree People', a 1947 oil painting.
COURTESY LEN LYE FOUNDATION

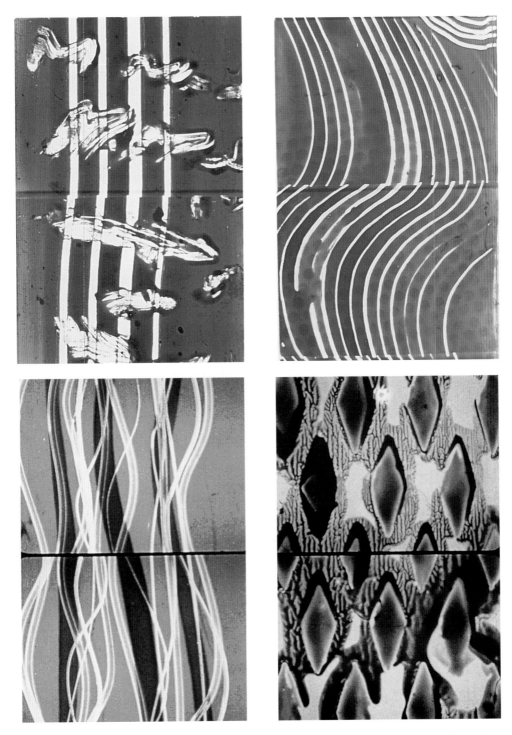

Frames from Lye's direct films *A Colour Box*, 1935 (top) and *Swinging the Lambeth Walk*, 1939 (bottom).
COURTESY LEN LYE FOUNDATION

Images from Lye's film *Rainbow Dance*, 1936. In both *Rainbow Dance* and *Trade Tattoo* Lye used colour printing methods to transform the colour and texture of black and white footage. COURTESY LEN LYE FOUNDATION

Images from *Trade Tattoo*, 1937. COURTESY LEN LYE FOUNDATION

Above: Lye's letters were always free-wheeling. This one to his daughter Yancy shows him at his typewriter and Ann in the garden. It is signed 'Love, L & A'. COURTESY YANCY McCAFFREY

Opposite: Strips of direct film from *Color Cry* (1953). Lye would sometimes make a composition out of strips of film to hang on the wall of a gallery. COURTESY LEN LYE FOUNDATION

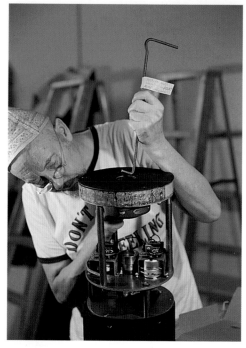

Above left, top: Jane Lye, photographed by Humphrey Jennings circa 1936, as a test for a new colour film stock he was promoting. COURTESY JANE LYE

Above left, bottom: Lye working on a direct film in his Greenwich Street studio in 1976. COURTESY LEN LYE FOUNDATION

Above: Assembling a small 'Fountain'. Lye is wearing one of his favourite T-shirts which carried the slogan 'Don't Fight The Feeling'. COURTESY LEN LYE FOUNDATION

Left: Len and Ann Lye in Toronto in 1967 inspecting a 25-metre 'Wind Wand'. (The artist was dismayed to find that his instructions had not been followed.) COURTESY LEN LYE FOUNDATION

Top left: Lye with Robert Graves in Deyá in 1968. Lye is wearing 'Tiki', his 1922 carving, which Graves also liked to wear. COURTESY LEN LYE FOUNDATION

Bottom left: The Lyes outside their house in Warwick in April 1980, a few weeks before Lye's death. COURTESY LEN LYE FOUNDATION

Below: A late photo of Lye with his son Bix. COURTESY LEN LYE FOUNDATION

Right: John Matthews working with Lye in his Greenwich Street studio in 1974. COURTESY LEN LYE FOUNDATION

The 1977 version of 'Fountain' at the Govett-Brewster Art Gallery.
PHOTO BRYAN JAMES. COURTESY LEN LYE FOUNDATION

was able to make reservations, but the only possible ship was sunk on its way to England. She had no alternative but to move back to London where Lye found them a house in the Golders Green district at 65 Southway. In her words: 'Hampstead Heath which was near us was very noisy and I had to put the children in a shelter every night. I would stand on the porch with a tin hat on and hear all the lavatory cisterns being pulled as soon as the air-raid warning went — a gut-rotting noise!' In the morning Bix would search the street for pieces of shrapnel to add to his large collection, and on one occasion he came home with a live incendiary bomb. Like many of his peers Bix was not unhappy about the fact that schools were often closed during the war.

For the allied countries 1942 was a particularly grim year because Japan had entered the war and was advancing far into the Pacific. In August Wendell Willkie, who had lost one presidential election but seemed a strong contender for the next, set out on an international fact-finding mission. In Chungking, China, he made a widely reported speech which argued that: 'Men need more than arms with which to fight and win this kind of war. They need enthusiasm for the future and a conviction that the flags they fight under are in bright and clean colours. The truth is that we as a nation have not made up our minds what kind of world we want to speak for when victory comes.'[14] Such comments confirmed Lye's interest in this politician, as did his discovery that Willkie had connections with the Twentieth Century Fox film studio. Trying to find an intermediary Lye turned to Tom Matthews, a journalist based in New York who had once been a member of the group around Riding and Graves. Matthews was given an IHN essay during a visit to London, and in January 1943 he phoned Willkie and asked if he could show him something written by 'a friend who is a bit of a crackpot'. Willkie invited him to send it over but somehow the essay got lost. Matthews had more urgent things to worry about because in February he was appointed managing editor of *Time* magazine, but eventually he cabled Lye for another copy. By then *One World*, Willkie's account of his two-month trip round the world, had been published and had become a surprise bestseller (with three million copies sold in the first eighteen months). Willkie wrote: 'In every country I found worry and doubt in the hearts and minds of people behind the fighting fronts. They were searching for a common purpose.'[15] *One World* argued that the challenge was not only to win the military struggle but to establish a lasting peace, and the precondition for that was a global sense of common purpose. Politicians had failed to provide such a vision at the end of the First World War and now there was an urgent need for 'new men and new ideas'.[16] Willkie saw the United States as the ideal facilitator because it provided living proof of how a diverse, democratic society could be held together by shared ideals (particularly a belief in individual freedom).

Lye wrote to Graves: 'He's my best bet against the other office holders',[17] but the months went by without any sign that Willkie had read Lye's essay. Towards the end of 1943 the *March of Time* sent Lye to Eire (the Republic of Ireland) to collect material for 'The Irish Question', a programme which examined that country's refusal to enter the war despite pressure from the Allies. Lye had grown up in the midst of Irish Catholic culture but this was his first visit. He shot some vivid footage of farms, schools, politics, craft activities, horse races, and football matches, along with his old adversaries, the priests. The documentary explained Irish neutrality in a sympathetic way in terms of an historical struggle for independence. During his month in Ireland Lye got to know members of the IRA and gained confidential information about their smuggling activities. When the film crew returned to England they decided to do some smuggling of their own by bringing a case of prohibited food, liquor, and clothing back for their families and friends. The Customs officers at the port of entry were so suspicious that Lye had to use diversionary tactics: 'I started raising a storm about taking pictures of the port, and red-herringed the thing furiously. Bob and I were so winded when we finally got on the train we could hardly light a cigarette.'[18]

Arriving home Lye found a letter from New York waiting for him. 'My dear Mr. Lye,' it began. 'Our mutual friend Tom Matthews gave to me your memorandum "Foreword to an Idea of Freedom". It interested me enormously. I can see you are thinking somewhat along the same lines I am. I do hope it is possible in the not distant future for us to have a talk. You don't happen to be coming over this way, do you? Why don't you try. It would be a great trip for you.' The letter was signed 'Cordially yours, Wendell Willkie'.[19] Receiving such a letter from the man who might become the next President of the United States was a moment Lye would never forget. He opened a contraband bottle of Tio Pepe and he and Jane drank a toast to Willkie and IHN. A few days later he received a letter from Tom Matthews which confirmed the good news: 'I finally got the chance about a month ago when some of us had dinner with him [Willkie]. I delivered your letter by hand, and he called me up the next day, apparently quite excited. Says he: "Why this fellow Lye is talking about the same thing I'm trying to talk about. How can I get hold of him?"'[20] From this point on Lye's thoughts were consumed by the problem of how to get to New York, a difficult task because of wartime restrictions. If he was reading too much into Willkie's letter, this was natural enough in view of his long period of frustration. He was not seeking personal success, he simply wanted to find a public figure able to put the idea of IHN to work.

Endlessly knitting his theory, he had been frustrated by his inability to 'cast off'. Willkie's interest seemed to offer the ideal conclusion and Lye now invested all his hopes and dreams in this politician and his talk of the great trip.

After unsuccessful attempts to set up a visit to the United States through institutions such as the BBC,[21] he tried his luck with the head office of the *March of Time*. Richard de Rochemont who had seen and admired Lye's work while managing the *March of Time*'s European operations explained that there were many problems but he agreed to watch out for an opening. Meanwhile Lye was asked to do some more filming for 'The Irish Question'. Charlotte Shaw, the wife of the famous playwright George Bernard Shaw, had died in London in September 1943 leaving money in her will for the improvement of the Irish people, whom she regarded as sadly illiterate and uncivilised. Over the following months Maurice Lancaster sent a number of letters to her husband asking for a statement on the subject. In the end the only reply was a brief postcard: 'No, no, no. You've got Shaw on the brain.' It occurred to Lancaster that he had one staff-member who might succeed in catching Shaw's interest. Lye had just had an extraordinary suit made up from tweed material he had smuggled back from Ireland, and dressed in this way with a fez-like cap on his head he knocked on the playwright's door. As expected, Shaw took a fancy to him and they sat talking for some time. Though Lye was most interested in discussing IHN, he eventually steered the conversation round to Ireland and Charlotte's controversial will. Then he said to Shaw: 'These remarks of yours are exactly what I need. I've got a film crew waiting outside, it would take only a minute to record you.' The result was a flaming row that ended with Shaw rushing out of the house and locking himself in the garden shed.

Soon afterwards Lancaster received a letter from the playwright which (as he remembered it) began: 'Why did you send Mr Lye to me when you knew perfectly well you were trying to exploit a valuable commodity?' Having assumed that Lancaster was American, Shaw added: 'The last cameraman who came to me commanded my respectful attention by presenting me with a cheque (but I then questioned him because it was not in dollars). As you don't know your way around this country, for what you may receive — may the Lord make you truly thankful.' Since the *March of Time* was not interested in buying interviews it fell back on its usual method of re-enactment: the great man was portrayed with his back to the camera as one of a group seated round a table listening to Mrs Shaw's will being read out.[22]

During February there was another setback for Lye's IHN campaign. For two years he had been writing to J. Arthur Rank and having occasional meetings with him about the possibility of a film that would communicate 'a common inspiring purpose in Democracy',[23] but the conversations between the two men kept wandering off track into arguments about religion. Rank's Christian beliefs gave him an interest in projects of an inspiring kind but Lye's secular attitudes made him uneasy. Finally on 29 February Rank ran out of patience: 'I cannot see my way to be interested in the proposition which you put before me.' There was more bad news for Lye early in April when Willkie gained so few votes in the Wisconsin primary that he abandoned his attempt to become a presidential candidate. The Republican Party went on to select Governor Dewey of New York for the campaign against Roosevelt. Though Lye was confident that Willkie's career would quickly recover, he felt an increased urgency. He sent Willkie a cable asking if he would back his application for a Twentieth Century Fox Skouras Scholarship. The cable also asked if he was still interested in Lye's ideas. On 30 April Willkie offered the cryptic reply: 'HAVENT AS YET DECIDED ABOUT MY FUTURE PLANS THANKS FOR CABLE'.

A few days later Lye's luck began to change as a friendly letter arrived from the film producer Filippo Del Guidice to say that he had read and thought a great deal about some proposals Lye had sent him. He was sufficiently impressed by Lye's basic ideas — and by his track record as a film-maker — to request further details and even to risk some money, though as yet he found it difficult to imagine how his ideas would work on the screen.[24] Since arriving in England as a refugee from Fascist Italy, Del Guidice had established the Two Cities Films Company and backed many of the best British directors such as David Lean, Carol Reed, Anthony Asquith, and Laurence Olivier. Olivier's million-pound film of *Henry V* had just been a huge box-office success for Two Cities. J. Arthur Rank then purchased the company but left Del Guidice to make his own decisions. Lye replied to the producer's letter immediately, and after some discussion he was offered a feature film in colour to direct. Unfortunately the script was not his own and it had nothing to do with IHN. Del Guidice needed a director for 'Creation', a script based on the first book of Genesis with a musical score by Darius Milhaud. Impressed by the brilliant colours and silhouettes of *Rainbow Dance*, Del Guidice saw such techniques as a way of making this biblical film less naturalistic and more like a medieval masque. Lye said: 'I'll do that, if you let me do my little philosophical thing first with Willkie',[25] but Del Guidice explained that his 'Creation' could not be delayed because he had obtained an agreement from the British government to use film studios in Rome as soon as they had been liberated. Lye went away and discussed the offer with his friends who all encouraged him to accept it because the film would be a great display of his technical skills, likely to outshine Disney's *Fantasia*. Dallas Bower, the script-writer of 'Creation', pointed out that Lye would make enough money from the job to be able to finance his own IHN film.

At this moment Lye received an invitation from Richard de Rochemont in New York, offering him a trip to the United States to direct four one-reel films about 'Basic English' in collaboration with I. A. Richards, a famous literary critic and one of the inventors of the new 'basic' approach to language teaching. Lye would be away from London for 'six months maximum including travel time'.[26] He saw the series as no great challenge but he was excited by the idea of getting to New York. The choice between the two film jobs struck him as a choice between the past and the present — on the one hand there was 'Del's reviving of faith via the Bible', on the other hand there was the struggle to develop new values such as Willkie's One World and his own IHN. He had always followed his dreams and ambitions, however risky, but first he sought his wife's permission. Wartime regulations made it impossible for her and the children to accompany him to the United States. In her words: 'Of course it was a blow when Len wanted to go off to America because the war wasn't over yet. And he would certainly have profited by the chance to direct a feature film. He asked me about it and I said "If you don't want to do that film, don't do it". I had long been accustomed to the fact that his work was the most important thing in his life, and I never raised a squeal about whether he was going to make a particular film or not. He had the tendency, if anything looked as though it were going to be a commercial success, he would be off it and on to something else.'[27]

And so Lye was scheduled to leave for New York in July. His last assignment for the *March of Time* in England was filming the effects of a V-1 flying bomb for a programme that aimed to educate Americans about 'the efforts and sacrifices made by the British people'. Many Americans who had not experienced the war directly had no sense of the casualties and shortages in Britain. The first flying bomb had fallen in London on 13 June, followed by hundreds of others that caused so much damage and so much anxiety that by the end of July one and a half million people had left or been evacuated from the city. Lye obtained some horrific news footage. A few days later he came back to Lancaster with a request that he be allowed to follow up the story: 'It would be interesting to find out what those chaps who were pulling the bodies out of the ruins thought about the war and what life would be like after the war.'[28] Since there was a growing public interest in the theme of recovery from the war Lancaster gave Lye the go-ahead, provided he could locate the same rescue workers. This proved a difficult task since there was no record of who the volunteers had been, but Lye managed to track down four or five of them and recorded their thoughts on the war and their hopes for the future. Lancaster was very impressed with the footage — 'That was the sort of thing Len was very good at' — but there was room in the programme to use only a small sample.

Before leaving the country Lye wanted to find a new place for his family to live away from flying bombs. The search seemed hopeless until Dallas Bower suggested Ruthven Todd who had a house in Essex. Todd — brilliant, generous, and disorganised — was a poet, an expert on William Blake, and a former Surrealist. Some years earlier the Lyes had given him accommodation for a fortnight as a small favour to their friend Norman Cameron. When they phoned Todd at Zwemmer's Bookshop, his response was immediate: 'Yes, you can share it. Now I have to look after a customer, goodbye.' This was an enormous relief to Jane Lye, for though the house turned out to be 'a rather primitive, cold, stone affair' it was safely out of London and the rent was nominal. In later years Todd was to figure importantly in the lives of both Jane and Bix.

As the time approached for the trip to New York, a friend who worked at the Summerhill School took charge of the children so that Lye and Jane could have a holiday in Scotland. At the end of ten days she saw him off at Victoria Station, then headed back for her last bleak evening in Golders Green. Bombs fell that night. As the air raid sirens began to sound, she had a polite exchange with the punctilious woman who had been her next-door neighbour for several years: 'Mrs Copley said to me, "I believe you're alone, Mrs Lye, would you like to come and use my shelter tonight?" I said, "Yes, thank you." I'd sold my own Morrison shelter. So I went over there, and as we crept into this tiny thing, to share the same mattress, I said: "Do you think, Mrs Copley, the time has come when I might call you Catherine?" That was the English style.'[29]

When Lye set out for the United States he was 43, an age that might still be described as mid-life. He was heading for a very different country. This crucial juncture in his career had presented him with clear choices — he might have stayed in London, directing the feature film 'Creation' as his first taste of large-scale film-making. When the film business picked up after the war he would have been well placed to get similar jobs, building on all the groundwork he had laid. This was his wife's dream — the hope that after many years of paying dues, she and the children could start to reap the rewards as he turned critical success into commercial success.

Alternatively at the end of the war Lye might have gone back to New Zealand, something that New Zealand expatriates were expected to do. His mother had urged him to return in 1939 to shelter from the war. He could have come home as an artist and film-maker who had won many overseas distinctions. Although he would have found a more sophisticated art scene than he had left, the public galleries would still not have known what to make of art like his. In 1949 Frances Hodgkins's painting 'Pleasure Garden' was rejected by the Christchurch City Council even though it had been offered as a gift to the public gallery. The first Film Society was created in Wellington in 1946 but there was still not much film-making in New Zealand. Margaret Thomson, his colleague at Realist Films, returned to Wellington in 1947 to work for the National Film Unit, which had been established six years earlier after a visit by John Grierson. She made some notable documentaries but was frustrated by the lack of freedom for directors and went back to England after two years.[30] An alternative for Lye would have been working as an art teacher since his old friend Gordon Tovey had taken up the position of National Advisor of Art and Craft in 1945. There were a number of progressive developments in New Zealand in the post-war period, such as Tovey's crusade to introduce modern methods of art teaching in schools, but in general the country still had a long way to go before it was ready to welcome the kinds of skills and energies that innovators such as Lye, Hodgkins, or Thomson had to offer. It might have been a good place for retirement but Lye did not have the slightest interest in slowing down and taking things easy.

A trip to the United States was the biggest gamble and the highest stakes. Lye had always trusted his instincts and taken huge risks. His main artistic interests — modernism, tribal art, motion, and the unconscious mind — had been his consuming passions for more than 20 years. Now his IHN philosophy had become a similar passion and one of his favourite mottoes was 'Don't Fight The Feeling'. Focusing purely on ideas, this passion was a wild card so far as his future was concerned. But it was not the only reason he refused to settle down or repeat himself or rein in his energies for the sake of sponsors or audiences, for he felt he had still not fully realised his ideas for an art of motion.

One of the surprises that awaited him in New York was the city's potential to become the post-war centre of avant-garde activity. In 1944 modernism in Europe seemed well on its way to becoming settled and predictable, qualities at odds with its own experimental spirit. But New York would turn out at this historical moment to have the right mix of ingredients to ignite the next creative explosion in art.

part three free radical

thirtytwo willkie

Though the American war effort was in full swing, Lye's first impressions were of a country less tired and grim than England. To allow Lye to 'catch his breath before plunging into the whirlpools of New York', Tom Matthews invited him to his summer house at Boothden (near Newport, Rhode Island) for two weeks of 'squash, hot tea on ice in hot weather, whizzing back in a wooden station wagon to fry sprats, and every eve the ritual of clinking ice in the cocktail mix'.[1] When the Matthews family held an all-night dance to farewell a group of young men going off to the South Pacific to fight the Japanese, Lye took charge of the decorations and turned the large room into a fantastic environment. Among 'the various Len-jokes', as Tom Matthews described them, were 'odd bits of flotsam and sea-shells summoned by his sharp eye from various beaches', bottles and glasses 'hung tipsily together', plaster nymphs repainted for the occasion, and a 15-foot trail of red silk towed by a toy aeroplane. At Boothden Lye also began making oil paintings on wood, interpreted by most viewers as abstract but not by the artist who explained one picture as 'what happens to the rocks at sunset when the light leaves them'.[2]

Lye was fortunate to have an influential friend like Matthews on his case. After a phone call from Matthews, Willkie said he would be happy to come to Boothden for the weekend to meet Mr Lye. This caused a flurry of excitement in the household but at the last moment urgent business caused the politician to change his plans. Willkie invited the artist to come to his office several weeks later. By that time Lye was established in Manhattan at 791 Lexington Avenue, in a second-floor apartment passed on to him by Humphrey Jennings and left by agreement under Jennings's name so it could still qualify for rent control. While the front of the building was a busy city street, the windows of this back apartment offered an unexpected view of trees with birds and squirrels. Lye's general response to New York was 'love at first sight'.[3] Not weighed down by its history as London was, the city seemed more energetic, more open to the spirit of 'individual happiness now'. The best jazz musicians played in its night clubs. There was a great ethnic diversity, reflected in the many inexpensive restaurants where Lye could sample new kinds of food. He was delighted with the sense of informality, especially in Greenwich Village where he found a community as lively as the best days of Hammersmith. Over the past decade many European avant-garde artists had moved to New York. Although rationing was in force, the city's shops were still full of items scarce in England such as painting materials and razor blades, and he mailed as much as he could back to family and friends, though he discovered later that many of his parcels never reached their destinations.

Since his final days in London Lye had been busy studying Basic English to prepare for the film project with I. A. Richards. The Basic approach had grown out of C. K. Ogden's belief that a small set of words, if chosen with sufficient care, would be sufficient 'for all the purposes of everyday existence: the common interests of men and women, general talk, news, trade, and science'.[4] Ogden arrived at a Basic English vocabulary of 850 words and then set out with the help of Richards and other collaborators to show that virtually any complex idea could be broken down into a combination of these words. One of the virtues of Basic English was its potential as an international second language. Unlike other world languages such as Esperanto, English was already spoken in a number of countries. Because Basic English retained the normal structures of the language, a native speaker would hear or read a well-written passage of Basic English without even being aware of its limited vocabulary.

Richards concluded from his own research that people learned English more rapidly if words and sentences were combined with pictures, in the form of a film or a comic strip. He was determined to discard the clichés of educational film-making and explore new methods. Not that he was interested in novelty for its own sake — he worked from the assumption that there was an ideal order by which any language structure could be most clearly presented: 'It is our business to find this ideal order. And success in our quest gives us the design of our teaching picture. Conversely, film is the ideal medium in which to record our attempts and test their efficacy.'[5] Words and pictures were so rich in possible associations and 'distractions' that it was no easy matter to control the range of meanings and to develop a suitably basic screen language. In one respect Lye was the worst possible choice for this assignment since his approach to language had always been quirky — his idea of straight talk was a poem by Rimbaud, or an ancient tribal myth. Nevertheless he and Richards got on well together.[6] Richards's advocacy of Basic English had a moral dimension because he saw wars as largely the result of insularity and poor communication; and like John Grierson he saw films as having great power either to confirm or to challenge prejudice. He shared Lye's belief that the end of the war was a crucial time to campaign for new international values. Winston Churchill had given strong support to the idea of Basic English as a world language in a speech at Harvard on 6 September 1943, but his enthusiasm proved something of a liability since politicians in other countries immediately became suspicious of the system as a British ploy.

The *March of Time* film project addressed itself modestly to the needs of the classroom rather than those of the political world. Richards had already supervised one film, a ten-minute pilot based on simple outline drawings made by the Walt Disney studio. This had allowed him to test various speaking and editing speeds. Next he had made a selection of the 500 most basic words within Basic English and illustrated them by matchstick drawings. This list became *The Pocket Book of Basic English* and provided a starting-point for the *March of Time* scripts. During the planning stage Lye's friends were amused by the thoroughness of his attempts to immerse himself in Basic. Tom Matthews remembered that on his first night at Boothden:

> My two oldest sons . . . had arrived home late from a party in Newport to find this bald-headed stranger, who greeted them with an unseeing stare, pointing a finger at himself, and uttered in molasses-slow accents: '*I-am-a-man*', with slow sorceror's gesture of pulling the words with difficulty from his . . . mouth. Then pointing at one of them: '*You-are-a-woman*'. They thought he was a madman, and were so alarmed they almost took to their heels.[7]

In late August Lye had his long-awaited meeting with Willkie, in a large office with windows that looked out over Wall Street. To Lye's eyes the politician 'was a sturdy bovine guy, kind of massive, quite a coper'.[8] While waiters were serving lunch, the conversation got off to an awkward start: 'Willkie gave me a lecture on the history of Wall Street. I wasn't a bit interested in that topic. I don't think he was either. He had to say something.'[9] After lunch Lye managed to introduce the idea of making a film but the initial discussion went badly. Then Willkie seemed to change direction, stepping outside 'his world of moguls', and joined Lye in a brainstorming session. By the end of the meeting a proposal had taken shape. First, a number of world leaders such as Churchill, Roosevelt, Stalin, and Gandhi would be separately interviewed on film to clarify each person's view of 'what the allies were fighting for and what was freedom all about'. Each would have an opportunity to check his own sequence and to comment on the views of the others. Willkie as 'master of ceremonies' would try to identify common ground and lead the discussion as often as possible towards the kind of ideas he and Lye valued. If disagreements occurred — and there were bound to be some with Stalin — the film would represent them as accurately as possible and leave viewers to make up their own minds. Most viewers would presumably see Willkie himself as the clearest thinker in the film.

At the end of the meeting Willkie asked Lye to write a detailed proposal which he could pitch to Twentieth Century Fox. Lye knew that the politician's greatest successes in the past had involved the media — his magazine articles, his radio talk to the nation after his world tour, his bestseller *One World* — and so it seemed only natural that he should be interested in an innovative media project from which he would emerge as (in Lye's words) 'a great organiser of ideology'. And so, while there was a world of difference between their personal styles, Lye decided that their meeting had been basically successful.[10] Matthews was unconvinced — he had always assumed that when the politician came face to face with the artist he would consider him a crackpot. He therefore interpreted Lye's account as proof 'there was no meeting of minds, only the brief encounter of two strangers who at first glance had taken each other for a long-lost brother but who soon discovered that they were only strangers after all'.[11] Determined to disprove this cynical view, Lye went to work on the proposal. Matthews warned him: 'Don't go near Twentieth Century Fox until your scenario is word for word, or the Hollywood buzzsaws will cut it up and you won't recognise a thing.'[12] And so Lye sweated over the details, impatient because the *Basic English* series was now taking up so much time.

Basic English took shape as six ten-minute films employing only six actors. They would space out their remarks so the viewer had time to repeat them. All dialogue was to be captioned, and each reel was to introduce around 45 new words. As a whole the series would carry the learner forward on 'an organically graded advance' into the language.[13] Lye's growing interest in logical argument, necessary to develop his IHN theory, helped to attune him to Richards's approach. The project was a technical challenge precisely because the style of the films had to be so simple — timing was crucial and the captions had to be easy to read.

Early in September the 52-year-old Willkie had a heart attack. Confident of a rapid recovery, he and his aides managed to hush up the fact that he was confined to hospital, but a throat infection led to his death on October 8th. Many people were shocked by the news; in Lye's case the hopes he had been building up for years came crashing down. The loss of this man who could have carried his ideas to the world was one of the worst moments of his life, in some respects as disorienting as the loss of a father. Lye described it as his 'wailing-dog day'.[14]

But he was never down for long. The technical problems of *Basic English* continued to provide him with interesting challenges and at the end of November he was pleased to report to Robert Graves: 'Been inventing new film styles and [am] now ready to simple the job nearly out of existence.'[15] The results were totally unlike anything Lye had done before but also somewhat weird — the farm families who exchanged common sayings in slow motion were rather like a combination of the Beverly Hillbillies and Ionesco's Theatre of the Absurd. Nevertheless the films were very effective in the classroom, as Richards noted in a later essay: 'Beginners with a dozen different native language backgrounds, and of every degree of educational preparation from complete illiterates upwards have been initiated into the sounds and constructions of English with their help. . . . The pictures have been used with classes of all sizes up to 500. The last was composed of seamen of the Chinese navy undergoing instruction (through English) at the U.S. Naval Training Centre.'[16] Researchers from Harvard University monitored the effects of the films and judged them to be a great success. 'So far from audiences finding repeated screenings dull and regarding them as merely mechanical drills, heightened interest and pleasure due to improved command of the material and forms [are] frequently very marked.'[17]

Lye had found New York so stimulating that by the end of 1944 he could not bear the idea of returning to England. He described the city in glowing terms to Jane and suggested that she and the children come over to make a new life. She was sceptical and wondered how he was going to get a visa or make a living. Lye asked the *March of Time* if he had any prospects of a permanent job. Richard de Rochemont had justified his visit on the grounds that he would bring a special creative flair to *Basic English*. Some of the New York staff found his 'sweet, happy-go-lucky style' so different from theirs that at first they 'could not take him seriously',[18] and most of the films produced by the *March of Time* had such a strict house style that there seemed no point in employing an avant-garde artist. But he had directed *Basic English* successfully and had also designed a striking new logo for the *March of Time*. When teased about Lye's 'artiness', de Rochemont's favourite reply was: 'There's an old Irish saying: "It's a poor family that can't afford one gentleman!"'[19] He told Lye that provided he could handle the everyday assignments as well as the unusual ones, the *March of Time* would keep him on the payroll.

This was not good news for Jane Lye, for though England had been a harsh environment during the war she thought of it as her home. She only agreed to come to New York because she wanted to be with her husband. Unfortunately she could find no way round the wartime travel restrictions and his attempts to pull strings on her behalf in New York also failed. The months dragged on, and in September 1945 he had to rescue his own position by making a quick trip to

Canada to reapply for entry into the United States. His application — to become a permanent resident — was successful thanks to strong support from Richard de Rochemont and the *March of Time*. He would become a full American citizen in 1950. Many years later De Rochemont commented: 'Len was undoubtedly the most purely creative genius I was ever associated with, and I have always felt pride in the fact that I brought him in to the March of Time. . . . I was a sponsor for his naturalization, and I think in doing so I did the U.S.A. a favour, rather than Len. Maybe not as many cities will claim him as they say claimed Homer, but surely New Zealand, London and New York will long remember.'[20]

thirtythree a rorschach test

Each monthly episode of the *March of Time* was a 15- to 20-minute documentary whose topic was often unpredictable because the series had such wide-ranging interests. More opinionated and controversial than most news and current affairs programmes, the *March of Time* was determined to be noticed and talked about and it usually succeeded in that aim. A budget of $50–75,000 per episode made it possible to film in a variety of locations, and the pace was brisk. A distinctive feature of the series was its use of re-enactment, with no inhibitions about setting up representative scenes for the camera or using actors to recreate important events. Its directors therefore needed drama as well as documentary skills. Occasionally a detailed script would be provided but often the director was sent out simply with a list of suggested people and locations. The *March of Time* had a very definite house style. The director knew that head office would make its own editing decisions and write its own commentary so it was important to use a straightforward filming style and to supply plenty of coverage. As Richard de Rochemont put it, 'This was group film-making — we had no auteurs'.[1] In some cases the voice-over commentary became so dominant that the images were treated as mere illustrations (or what film-makers call 'wallpaper'); but the best of the *March of Time* programmes were rich in visual as well as verbal information.

Lye found it a curious experience to be working at the heart of the mainstream, reporting on the latest developments in American life. *Teen-age Girls* (June 1945), apparently his first *March of Time* assignment after *Basic English*, provided a lively survey of a new social trend — the emergence of teenage girls as a distinct group with their own music, fashions, and attitudes. The programme included comments by girls, parents, and 'experts', and various scenes of teenage life from a classroom to a pyjama party. Despite some detours into cuteness the programme did a good job of encouraging parents to be understanding. Then came *Life with Baby*, a programme based almost entirely on Lye's footage, which turned out to be very important to him in personal terms. Its topic was the Clinic of Child Development at Yale University. The clinic's studies, such as *The First Five Years of Life* by Dr Arnold Gesell and Dr Louise Bates Ames, gave new insights into the psychology of children and were later to become standard manuals for American parents, making the Gesell Institute as much a household name as Dr Spock. Lye visited the clinic for the first time on 25 October 1945 and found the staff 'thrilled at the prospect of a *March of Time*'.[2] While engaged in pre-production work for the film he spent a great deal of time with Dr Louise Bates Ames, associate director of the clinic, and her friend and colleague Janet Learned. The women found Lye exotic and attractive. He had his eye on Learned and after two weeks asked her out. Ames was surprised that a film director would mix work and social life in this way, and also felt a tinge of regret he hadn't asked her.

Lye had now been apart from his wife for more than a year and had always had difficulty understanding the value of sexual fidelity. As he saw it, society made a great rigmarole about jealousy and possessiveness but such feelings only existed because people were insecure. He could not understand why the happiness of one relationship should make any difference to another. He offered Jane as much freedom as she wanted, but this was one topic they always argued about. After his arrival in the United States he had been introduced to the editorial staff of *Time* magazine by Tom Matthews and had spent a great deal of time playing tennis or partying with this group. Lye was a popular guest: 'He was bursting with spirit. He loved New York, he was so delighted with everything — he was like a cricket hopping around!'[3] He had what a friend described as several 'little adventures' but one of them turned serious. He and the wife of a senior editor were getting along so well that she felt her marriage was at risk. She made the choice to stop seeing him, but there was serious conflict when her husband learned what had happened. Lye found himself no longer welcome in *Time* magazine circles.

His friendships with Learned (who was unmarried) and Ames (who was divorced) were less risky. But the triangle situation did get awkward, as Ames noted in her personal journal: 'Len said he guessed he was in kind of a thing and ought to discuss himself/me/Janet. I said did he mean that he liked her best but that I liked him better than she did. He said yes he really did have kind of a case on her but he did like to talk to me. I rather carried on and told him why I was really more the one for him, and he was quite interested and surprised and said "I didn't know you had such a case on me." . . . He stayed late and we discussed it at length.' After that, Lye paid more attention to Ames (whom he always called 'Louis').[4] His conversations with her were very important to him because she was one of the first people to take his IHN theory seriously. Today she remembers Lye as 'one of the nicest, kindest, most lively, warmest, and most multi-talented men I ever knew'.[5] From the beginning she was 'fascinated by his manner of talking and thinking' and enjoyed the zest that went into his film-making. She noted in her journal: 'Len's crew very lively and friendly. They obviously think a lot of him and he is good with them. They make jokes like, "Let's have about a thousand feet of that" (sign on door).'[6]

Lye already knew his way round aspects of New York that came as a surprise to Learned and Ames. In contrast to the 'formal, strait-laced' Connecticut atmosphere in which they worked he introduced them to Greenwich Village with its tolerance for 'unmarried couples and even casual sex (by nice people too)!'[7] Also it was rare for white and black to mix as freely as they did in certain downtown locations. Lye took both his friends to dance at his favourite jazz club, the Stuyvesant Casino at 140 Second Avenue where the resident band was led by Bunk Johnson, and to hear jazz concerts by Sidney Bechet, Cow-Cow Davenport, and Art Hodes, all of whom Lye had got to know personally. He introduced 'Louis' to his friend Fred Ramsay, a collector of early blues, and to artists and curators associated with the Museum of Modern Art. A night out with Lye was always unpredictable. On one occasion he took Ames to a political meeting where Julian Huxley was giving a laudable but lengthy talk about the dangers of the atom bomb to the International Council of Artists, Scientists, and Professionals. In her words: 'We had to sit on the stage and suddenly it was so boring we could bear it no longer and left the stage, we thought. But what we thought was the exit was only a coat closet, so we had to stay in the closet till the meeting was over. Had some fun writing each other left-handed poems. Finally got out and sat on the steps talking about his life in Samoa and waiting for Janet — then all went to the Taft for drinks.'

The death of Willkie had put a damper on Lye's political theorising. Friends who saw the IHN campaign as a drain on his creative energies hoped he would now abandon it, but the interest shown by Ames and Learned, specialists in developmental psychology, gave him a new angle. Establishing a base in politics was too difficult, so perhaps he should try science? There seemed to be an increasing public respect for science. Ames suggested that IHN be put forward as a challenge to science to take account of human happiness. The time had come for scientists to admit they had 'a responsibility toward improving general human welfare and not simply toward increasing knowledge without caring what the result is.'[8] Lye was excited by this idea but also wondered whether a place for IHN could be found within science itself. He started to read scientific books and began to see IHN more as a research project. Though he would still write letters to politicians and journalists, he became more interested in talking with scientists who (like artists) tended to take a long-term view.

Ames knew that Lye's ideas had little to do with logic or science but she was fascinated by his creative, lateral thinking. She saw that his elaborate line of argument was a problem for readers and so she offered to 'get the theory down to the shortest possible form'. But here she found herself pursuing an elusive goal, one that kept disappearing behind new revisions and 'daily communiqués from Lye'. He once described Ames to a friend as 'my guide, mentor and compass' — he might also have said 'my long-suffering editor and typist'. Though he continued to expand his ideas faster than she could condense them, her comments did influence his general approach, nudging him in the direction of science. Over the next few years she introduced Lye to experts such as Nina Bull, Robert Grenell, C. Judson Herrick and Herbert Spencer Jennings. She helped him to write an application to the Guggenheim Foundation and later to the Viking Fund for a grant to make a film about IHN, conceived now as a scientific rather than a political project. Both funding bodies expressed interest in the idea but after further discussions with Lye they backed off.

As a psychologist Ames was intrigued by Lye's story of how, as a child, he had 'thought' his way free of religion. How to define his unique personality and style of thinking? In 1948 Ames talked him into coming to the Gesell Institute to take a Rorschach test, administered by a psychologist who did not know him. She remembers that he was not very interested in the test and went through with it merely as a friendly gesture to her,[9] but the findings were highly relevant and full of insights. The Rorschach test involves the analysis of a subject's responses to ten seemingly random ink blots, five in black and white and five in colour. This is a 'projective' test because each individual projects (or reveals) their mental habits, their ways of responding to shape, colour, implied movement, etc. When a subject talks about the ink blots in a way that is not 'popular', the psychologist tries to decide whether those interpretations are sufficiently coherent to be described as original or whether they are merely bizarre and inaccurate.

To Lye nothing could have been more natural than chatting about random ink blots because of his old habit of making up myth stories about doodles. Each blot triggered off a flood of comments such as his response to the fourth card of the series:

> This is a beautiful pelt, a lovely rug of some very nice animal that has 28 eyebrows. . . . Very nice listening thing, still has life, happy drooling wonderful texture of softness. . . . Well, I could go on and say on the other hand there is a beautiful sloth who learned to prance on hind feet, he started climbing trees. As if he thinks the steam comes out of his mouth, it's a frosty day, very nice looking animal. In fact it could be a nice village idiot in disguise, quite wise about big like he is. . . .

Or the fifth card:

> That is the damned bat stuff again. . . . Two girls with long headgear embracing.
> Most batty looking bat you ever saw, must be in a ballet. . . . Texture good and
> terrific black depth in it, wonderful edge. . . .

Or the eighth:

> Oh that's the best for art so far. This way, or upside down. Flowers very petally
> and beautiful, rose and orange. Here luminosity and depth in sea pools, green
> center. This big line is in keeping with the sea, it's coral, but more like salmon
> bones, kind of tinned salmon, to take away the prettiness. Gray below has
> primitive animal life quality . . . a kind of flying pterodactyl . . .

Ruth Metraux's analysis of the responses yielded a 'Psychogram' of the subject's
personality. It was obvious to her that this was an exceptionally original mind at
work. Her summary seems as shrewd a rapid assessment of Lye as anyone could
hope to make:

> A subject of high intelligence. . . . This is an introversive individual with high
> interest in himself though his extratensive [outward-looking] components are
> also quite strong. His psychic activity is dynamic, creative, and the result is highly
> euphoric. He undoubtedly has a great interest in the theatre, in dancing, and art
> in general, and is very sensitive and critical towards fine nuances of color and
> shading. He is certainly a very sensuous individual, with warm, unrepressed
> feelings toward others ('men embracing', 'women embracing'), a person to whom
> sensations are paramount, and his imagery type is probably kinesthetic. He is
> either a very productive creative artist, or has the capacity of one. He often takes
> the most banal resources and by his imagination and good constructive ability he
> transforms them into a dynamic new creation. It must be said here, however, that
> this same ability can sometimes be carried to such lengths that he loses touch with
> reality.
>   There is a preoccupation with 'fossil' which may coincide with his interest in
> beginnings, in the primitive, though further interview with the subject would be
> necessary to discover its meaning for him.
>   The philosophic, abstract . . . realm undoubtedly has a great fascination for
> him and he is quite conscious of thinking and thought processes. . . . However
> strong the fascination . . . is, his best performance is in the active, sensational

sphere. He expresses it himself when he says 'Having lost their head in thought they get sensation from their feet.'

Metraux summed Lye up as a person 'inclined toward good adaptation' with his strong sense of 'fantasy and magic' combined with a lively interest in the world around him. But she still noted some deep reserves of anxiety. He interpreted the third ink blot with its sharper, more differentiated shapes as a group of 'anxiety things'. He then saw it as a 'fossil insect' with 'mouse legs'. Those legs — which he could tell 'quite a story against' — had kneecaps with 'phallic' shapes. Lye had always regarded certain doodles as sinister, such as the attacking octopus figure of *Tusalava* or the 'sharp needles', 'zig zag spikes' and 'gargoyle creature' in his painting 'Polynesian Connection'.[10] Metraux speculated about Lye's underlying problems:

> There is a deep seated inner conflict which he attempts to master, occasional doubts in himself, occasional opposition to his environment, which, when they appear, reduce the quality of his performance. There is ambivalence towards his more profound problems and he makes a cautious, sometimes egocentric adaptation to them — though he is more often adaptable and there is a free flow of emotions in general.

thirtyfour ann hindle

A party on New Year's Eve 1945 was to represent a turning-point in Lye's life. Late in December at the *March of Time* he had met and chatted with Tommy Hindle, a British journalist who had once lived in St Peter's Square, Hammersmith. When Hindle told his American wife Ann about this encounter she said: 'You should have invited him to our New Year's Eve party.' She phoned the *March of Time* and gave Lye the address. It was a boisterous party which ran all night 'with the whole house wide open — there was dancing on one floor and games on another, and food and draught beer'.[1] Lye's New Year's Eve had already included a conversation about science and IHN with the psychologist Nina Bull, cocktails and talk about art at the home of the critic James Johnson Sweeney, and jazz dancing at the Stuyvesant Casino with Learned and Ames. When Lye finally turned up at the Hindles' party at 2.45 a.m., Ann was very struck by 'this tall, slim man in marvellous clothes who arrived with a woman on each arm'. Though she was suffering from a bad cold and traipsing round in old slippers, she livened up as soon as she started talking to Lye. To Ames 'it was perfectly obvious that those two hit it off very well'. It was equally obvious to Tommy Hindle, who was 'not pleased'.[2]

Lye phoned Ann Hindle next day to see if she would come with him to Bunk Johnson's club. She accepted his invitation for she had already drifted far apart from her husband. In her view their 16-year marriage was little more than a formality. She and Lye started going to the Stuyvesant Casino almost every night, amazed to discover how well attuned they were both on and off the dance floor. In her words: 'He had a style. His dancing was jerky, syncopated, a little off the beat. No one could really dance with him except me.' She had been born Annette Zeiss in 1910 in a mining town in Minnesota, but had grown up in Chicago, Illinois, and San Diego, California. Her parents, middle-class and politically conservative, were often baffled by the views of their independent daughter. During a trip to Europe in 1928 she met Tommy Hindle, a 26-year-old journalist. As she was about to leave London, a week after their first meeting, he proposed marriage. She said: 'Don't be silly!' but with romantic determination he followed her to San Diego and ten days after his arrival they were married. He brought her back to Hammersmith where she felt 'young and innocent' but delighted to be living in such a lively community of artists and intellectuals. Her husband's thriving career as a journalist and leader-writer for *The Times* was mostly concerned with politics, but he also took a strong interest in the arts. One of the first groups to which he introduced her was the London Film Society. In December 1929 they attended the premiere of *Tusalava* and though she knew nothing about Lye or his views on art the film gave her 'goose pimples'.

Later she occasionally saw the film-maker walking through St Peter's Square, conspicuous in the summer because his clothes were white and his face and bald head were darkly tanned. Once when he was working on *Peanut Vendor* he visited the Hindles to pick up scraps of material for his puppets. She liked the look of him but their acquaintance remained superficial. She had many close friends in Hammersmith, in particular Alan Herbert, who took her sailing on his boats (including the barge that Lye had lived on), and Elfriede Cameron, who had been involved with Robert Graves (and with Lye), before marrying Norman Cameron. Another coincidence that linked her life with the film-maker's was that she was living just round the corner from St Peter's Square in an apartment previously occupied by his girlfriend Liz Johnson.

Tommy Hindle's newspaper career flourished but it demanded long hours and frequent travel, leaving his wife to look after their two daughters Gillian and Jane. Having to move many times, Ann Hindle discovered she had a talent for selecting and decorating old apartments, an activity that would later become an important part of her life in New York. As the war approached the British Government recruited journalists as intelligence agents, among them her husband who carried out some dangerous assignments in Europe. Ann spent time with him in Prague but during the war there were long separations, including a three-year period when he was posted to Iran. By the time they moved to New York in 1945 they no longer had much in common, and Ann was coming round to the opinion that divorce was the only realistic option. She now found him stuffy and conventional and at 35 she was eager to start a new life. When she got together with Lye, both saw the relationship as something unique because of the shared ease and happiness they were feeling. This experience was not the main cause of her divorce but it did strengthen her resolve.

Ann Hindle was similar to Jane Lye in some respects, since both loved dancing and both enjoyed living among artists and being involved in art, even though neither regarded herself as an artist or an intellectual. A friend said of Ann: 'She seldom reads a book straight through, but she's streetwise, quick to pick things up through conversations or reviews.' Ann was a more enthusiastic, more natural bohemian than Jane, and as Lye saw it, she had a more confident personality which allowed her to enjoy closeness without becoming clingy or possessive or trying in subtle ways to change the other person.

She also shared his enthusiasm for New York, particularly Greenwich Village. Its culture was very different from that of other parts of the United States, and (as New Yorkers were proud to proclaim) it took a special type of person to relish living there — tough-minded, high in energy, attracted to a wider-than-usual range of experience. In Lye's words, 'New York is a fantastic merging of people, of all sorts, shapes, sizes, dispositions and what not . . . in which you get the absolute worst and the absolute best.' Though real-estate prices have today risen so high that Greenwich Village is now dominated by yuppies, the area was for many decades a haven for artists, bohemians, and political radicals, and at the same time a working-class neighbourhood with a large Italian population. As one of the oldest areas in New York, with early nineteenth century houses in an irregular pattern of narrow streets, the Village offered a more human scale and a more relaxed ambience than the concentration of skyscrapers and expensive stores uptown. In 1945 Ann Hindle was living in 'the West Village', a neighbourhood roughly bounded by 14th Street to the north, Christopher Street to the south, Hudson Street to the east, and the busy docks of the Hudson River to the west. Irish longshoremen drank at the local bar, the White Horse Tavern. This run-down area included old brownstones, industrial buildings, and a red-light district on Washington Street. It was a particularly lively example of the type of neighbourhood Lye had became familiar with in London and Sydney where artists could, if they searched carefully, find low-cost studio space. As he explored the West Village with Ann, he felt totally at home with its unpretentious style, in sharp contrast to what he was hearing from friends about the revival of formality in England after the war. In the words of one Londoner: 'During the war no one worried about wearing a tie or a dinner-jacket, no one could have cared less. People talked to one another. But then as soon as the war ended, the city went back to its old regimented way of life.'[3]

Since his arrival in New York Lye had been making oil paintings, experimenting with photography, and writing poems, as well as working on his IHN theory. This exceptional burst of energy was obviously helped along by the stimulation of a new city, new friends such as Louise Ames, and his relationship with Ann Hindle whom he described as 'the best and most wonderful and logical and practical and generous person I've met since I left New Zealand'.[4] At the same time he felt guilty about his wife and children and the failure of his attempts to find transport for them. The last year and a half had certainly been a hellish time for Jane Lye. The German bombing of England by V-1s and V-2s had continued until February 1945, and though Ruthven Todd's house was in a relatively safe location the war still cast a grim shadow over daily life. The house was cold in winter and the children were often sick. She had problems with the education authorities because Bix did not want to start school and was still unable to read at the age of eight. She arranged to send him to a Quaker boarding school which offered special remedial teaching, but Lye objected to this because religion was involved. Eventually Bix was diagnosed as a 'mirror reader' and once the problem was taken into account he was able to make excellent progress, but this breakthrough did not come for several years.

Meanwhile Jane Lye made frequent visits to travel agencies but for some time the only women with children able to obtain tickets and visas to the United States seemed to be war brides. Finally Maurice Lancaster of the *March of Time* managed to arrange a flight for the Lyes in May 1946. Because it was necessary to travel light she had to leave behind furniture and many other possessions which were later vandalised.[5] Her son was disappointed he could not take his collection of bomb fragments to the United States. Jane Lye did manage to send her husband's collection of 400 rare recordings of jazz and African music by boat, but in New York the collection was stolen as it passed through Customs. On 15 May when Louise Ames visited Lye in his Lexington Avenue apartment, he had just heard about his family's imminent arrival and was in a spin trying to get ready. Always a true friend to Lye, the long-suffering Ames swung into action: 'We ran out to Bloomingdales and got him some sheets and a new suit. Scrubbed his apartment spotless.' But the reunion between Len and Jane was already doomed, in part because their experiences during the past two years had been so different. Jane, worn down by problems, was inclined to see the negative side of everything, and she took an immediate dislike to New York. After another visit to Lexington Avenue on 29 May, nine days after the family's arrival,[6] Ames noted in her journal: 'Jane attractive but HATES America. She also hates Len's apartment. Thinks it is small, dark and dirty and hot. Says of the children in her English voice: "I keep bathing their brows every twenty minutes but it doesn't do any good." Says she would rather send Bix to Alcatraz than to the New York public schools. Said she couldn't imagine how I could wear a WHITE raincoat in dirty New York.' Nothing would change her fierce preference — England had its problems but they were minor compared with the crude, ugly way of life she saw in New York. Besides suffering from culture shock, Jane found the New York climate hard on her asthma. If her hostility to the city was in some respects an attempt to persuade her husband to return to London, the attempt seriously backfired.

Though Lye felt he was trying hard to make her welcome, he could not fully understand the problems she had had to face during their time apart. In an effort to 'work things out', he took her and the children away from the city in July to Castine, Maine, and to Martha's Vineyard, Massachusetts. But a month's holiday with his wife made it clear to him that he was really in love with Ann Hindle. Lye was a person who never found it easy to ignore or disguise his feelings. His wife was angry with him when he admitted to having had affairs but the news did not surprise her. What did shock her was the way he talked about Ann as a woman he not only liked but loved; and she recognised that here was an affair she might not be able to ride out. Jane had felt badly treated even before she arrived, and now her dream of a better life after the war was in danger of being cancelled out by another woman. Lye understood happiness better than unhappiness, and his wife's negative view of things perplexed and distanced him further.

When Jane Lye informed Robert Graves of the situation in August, he replied: 'Though I knew that Len, being Len, would make some temporary hookup in the U.S. as he did when you were away in S. Africa that time, it never occurred to me that it wouldn't be dissolved the moment you three turned up. . . . What the hell will you do? I can't see Len's income being enough to raise a second family and pay out alimony.' Graves was one of several old friends who strongly endorsed her criticisms of the United States: 'Len seems to have succumbed to the American Way of Life, and how I agree with you — "Better fifty years in Europe / Than five weeks in U.S.A!" . . . Then [there is] the education problem: the American boy apart from vice is exactly 4 years behind his . . . British counterpart as proved by children who temporarily emigrated during the war. . . .'[7] Graves did not write to Lye for three years but then resumed their friendship in this way: 'I was very sorry about the break; but I am not the one to judge who's to blame etc. We're all miserable sinners . . . and life's like that. I only hope Jane finds someone, and that you and Ann continue happy.' (Not that Graves had softened his social critique, for the same letter made tart comments about Laura Riding's American attitudes.)

While the Lyes were away, Ann Hindle decided independently that she wanted a divorce. Her husband had mixed feelings but eventually gave his agreement and the legal process began. By 20 September Lye had explicitly left his wife, turning the Lexington Avenue apartment over to her while he moved in with Ann Hindle at 739 Washington Street.[8] Ames noted on 27 November: 'Ann is having a very hard time, everyone raising hell: Tommy Hindle, Gillian, Ann's mother, the Matthews. Ann for the first time says perhaps she made a mistake having Len move in. . . .' Many of Lye's friends were shocked. As one Londoner remarked: 'This was a recurring saga with those *Time* people during the war —

film-makers and journalists went off on jobs and met someone else. It happened all the time. But I felt bitter about that for Jane because Len's great slogan was "universal happiness".'⁹

Although Lye tried hard to make friends with Ann Hindle's two daughters, the 11-year-old Gillian was greatly disturbed by the break-up of her parents' marriage. This was a situation many families were going through because separations during the war had estranged husbands and wives while increasing the desire of their children for stability. As a parent Lye had always been a mixed success, as Ann explained: 'He loved children but found it hard to take responsibility.'¹⁰ Bix and Yancy Lye came to stay every other weekend. Their father liked taking them to Coney Island but the children found his choice of rides too scary. Yancy scarcely knew him and clashed with Ann Hindle over household rules. The children's relationship with their father was also complicated by the distress of their mother, who could not adjust to what had happened. Len and Ann's suggestion that she leave the children with them and go back to England made Jane even more grimly determined to hang on.

By the end of 1946 Ann Hindle had obtained a divorce but Lye had not. She recalls: 'We didn't want to get married — ever — but it got so difficult with Len's children and my children and the way my family felt and the way Jane felt and everything else, it seemed the only way we could stabilise it.'¹¹ Advised by lawyers that the quickest place to obtain a divorce was Nevada, Lye made a trip to Reno in May 1948 and stayed for six weeks at the Silver Dollar Hotel to establish legally that he was a bona fide resident of the state. It was a miserable period because Lye suffered a serious bout of illness; then, with his typical lack of attention to legal matters, he almost torpedoed his own court case by answering 'New York' when the judge asked his address. His lawyer just managed to rescue the situation by arguing that Lye had not heard the question correctly. The divorce agreement (finalised on 4 June) required him to pay 25 per cent of his income to Jane and another 25 per cent to the children, with a minimum of $150 per month in each case. He was also to help with 'extraordinary medical, surgical, and dental bills'. Jane Lye, who accepted the divorce reluctantly, retained custody of the children and was able to control access.

Len and Ann got married in Reno on the same day as the divorce — a simple ceremony performed by a Justice of the Peace, followed by a wedding breakfast that consisted of 'a tuna casserole with a wedding decoration on top'. They had a strange night on their honeymoon trip. When the train stopped at a station, they got off to look at something and the train started again, leaving them stranded on the platform in their nightclothes. Back in New York they moved to

739 Washington Street in the West Village, a house that was initially 'a wreck' but one they worked together to remodel. The basement became Lye's film studio, the top floor was rented out, and the rest of the house — a duplex — provided living space. Though their relationship had come under much stress over the past two years, it had survived because of their shared conviction that each had found the perfect partner. They conspired together to live life to the full. Lye's countless love letters celebrated Ann Lye as his 'wagon-pusher, color-fixer, and all general around shape and shaper of delight', his 'darling of a Robert Burns barley lass', his 'clicker of serene sailings on moonlit bays', and his 'throat-clear romantic always speaking clearly her mind'.[12]

Meanwhile Jane Lye had settled in to the Lexington Avenue apartment, profoundly bitter about what had happened though she kept a stiff upper lip and generally did not let her feelings show. In 1949 she returned to London but was disappointed by it — rationing was still in force and the people she had known had died or moved away. And so she reconciled herself to living in New York, perhaps still hoping that one day Lye might come back to her. Part-time clerical jobs barely kept food on the table, yet she managed somehow to enrol her children in a prestigious private school. Friends wondered how she had pulled this off — had she exploited her Englishness, perhaps, or her connection with artists? Sometimes her social ambitions — her belief that she was meant for better things — grated on Bix and Yancy, though they appreciated how hard their mother was having to struggle. Meanwhile their father was troubled to think he had saddled his children with the same problem of the absent parent as he had known during his own boyhood, yet he also believed that in some ways that situation had made him freer and more independent. One thing he and his new partner were clear about was the need to avoid having any children of their own. In later years Ann Lye liked to quote a comment by the widow of the painter Hans Hofmann: 'Every artist is a child, and a woman married to an artist should not have children because her own husband is her child.'[13]

thirtyfive paintings and poems

Although Lye's first two years in New York were very eventful in personal terms, and he had a full-time job as a director, he also completed a great deal of painting and writing. His burst of painting in the late 1940s was based on the free-wheeling style he had developed just before the war. These 'oil doodles' (as he sometimes called them) were painted on board rather than canvas and ranged in size up to three by four-and-a-half feet.[1] The brushwork was vigorous, so that the lines were full of movement and the pictures tended to have a raw, unfinished look, as though Lye had thrown away the final traces of his art-school training. Despite this bold style his approach was still slow and self-critical; he would often get up in the middle of the night to change a detail, and he threw away pictures he was not satisfied with. He was trying to combine oil painting with the energy of doodling, producing restless lines and curious shapes that hovered at the edge of meaning. The colours were earthy and the eye needed time to tune in to the paintings, to their apparent looseness of form. The imagery was so abstract that halfway through a painting Lye would sometimes generate new ideas by turning it upside down (as he had done with the Rorschach ink blots). Still, he always associated the finished paintings with natural forms and processes such as rain, sunlight, seeding, and growth.

The late 1940s were an exceptional time for painters in New York. Before the war Europe had been so firmly established as the home of modern art that New York seemed peripheral, but with the rise of Fascism many European artists had fled there. Their presence acted as a catalyst, particularly on the emerging paint-ers who would later become known around the world as the abstract expression-ists or the New York School. These American artists were not drawn to the geometric style of abstraction championed by Piet Mondrian, or to the 'literary' imagery of the better-known surrealists, but took as their starting point the more 'painterly' or 'plastic' forms of surrealism, the kinds of abstract art based on doodling that they saw in the work of Matta Echaurren, André Masson, and Joan Miró. This had long been Lye's aesthetic preference. In the late 1930s he had found himself isolated as an artist because most of his English friends were drawn to other types of surrealism or to geometrical abstraction. Now American artists felt (as Barnett Newman put it) that 'only an art of no-geometry can be a new beginning'.[2] Many of these artists (such as Arshile Gorky, Adolph Gottlieb, Barnett Newman and Mark Rothko) were close in age to Lye, though some (such as Robert Motherwell and Jackson Pollock) were a decade younger. Lawrence Alloway has described this phase of American art as 'the Biomorphic Forties'[3] because the paintings contained so many doodled shapes suggesting biological forms.

Periodically modern art had felt compelled to return to basics — 'To be original is to go back to origins', as Antonio Gaudí put it[4] — and it was in this spirit that the New York avant-garde of the late 1940s jettisoned as much artistic ballast as possible, including a great deal of what had come to be recognised as modern art. These artists were more interested in nature than culture, more interested in ancient myths than in fashionable new work from Paris. To quote Robert Motherwell: 'We replaced the nude girl and the French door with a modern Stonehenge, with a sense of the sublime.' The ideal was to create 'an abstract picture as rich as nature'.[5] This aesthetic bore striking similarities to the one Lye had been pursuing for years. His work also anticipated the increasing emphasis these artists placed on the physical act of applying paint, an approach later described as 'gestural' or 'action' painting. Lawrence Alloway's observation that 'There is a psycho-sexual content in biomorphic art, which abounds in visceral lyricism full of body allusions' could be applied to Lye's art throughout his career.[6] In the 1950s painters such as Jackson Pollock moved away from biomorphic imagery and concentrated on purer or more painterly forms of abstract art. Lye did not join the trend to larger canvases nor did he feel any need to abandon biomorphic imagery. At the same time he enjoyed the physical energy of Pollock's paintings, their links with jazz, and the way they sometimes suggested the flurry of subatomic particles. Lye's hand-painted films had always included patterns of an abstract expressionist type, blown up to a huge size on the cinema screen. His exceptional ability to control the process of painting and scratching on celluloid was comparable to Pollock's control of the drip technique.

How much contact did Lye have with 'the New York School'? The community of vanguard artists was small in those days and between 1949 and 1955 many of its activities revolved around 'The Club' (or 'Artists' Club') at 39 East 8th Street. Lye often took part in 'the cackle and crack of the brain functions' at this venue,[7] as he later recalled: 'I met all the abstract expressionist boys before they expressionisted. I met all the good artists of NYC at The Club and showed my films there. We'd meet and talk art, then dance and dance, good old day's stuff. I saw them later when abstract expressionism grabbed the ball from Paris. I liked all their stuff and I think they liked mine.'[8] During the 1950s Lye also spent time at the

Cedar Tavern at 8th Street and University Place, which functioned as a neighbourhood bar for the downtown art community.⁹ He made other contacts through
the Museum of Modern Art, which held screenings of his films, and through his
old friend Stanley William Hayter, who was his next-door neighbour in Washington Street. Hayter's Atelier 17, transferred from Paris to a loft above Rosenthal's
art supply store on East 8th Street, became an important centre of print-making in
New York, frequented by the leading young American artists as well as by
European émigrés.

   Although Lye found the art scene congenial and knew most of its members,
and his films and paintings had anticipated some aspects of the abstract styles
now being developed, he preferred to stay on the margins. Accustomed to
working in isolation, he did not look for a group to exhibit with. He was also
reluctant to spend time chasing publicity or negotiating with dealers and
collectors. Other New York artists accepted that kind of hustling as part of the
job, but Lye felt he had wasted too much of his energy in London and he was
happy simply to give paintings away to friends. By not linking his work more
directly with abstract expressionism — the art movement poised to 'grab the ball
from Paris' — he passed up one of the best opportunities of his life to acquire a
prestige label and thus command the attention of critics, museums, and buyers.

   Clement Greenberg, the influential art critic and champion of the abstract expressionists, liked what he saw of Lye's paintings and considered his films 'ahead
of their time' but was surprised by the artist's 'lack of drive': 'I felt he came out of
the 1920s in his way as a person, and that he was Anglicized in this respect. The
British writers and artists we saw in New York in the 40s and 50s all seemed to
come out of the 20s: their bohemianism, their unstudied free-and-easiness, their
desperate dissipatedness. But Len didn't dissipate as far as I know. What he did
do was expect the world to be as un- and informal as he himself was. By that time
Americans of my generation — which hadn't come out of the 20s — were ever so
much grimmer. My retrospective impression is that this was why Len didn't
make real contact with the New York art world. Not that he seemed to mind, he
was so much more at ease with himself than the inhabitants of that world.'¹⁰ New
York may have been more informal than London in its style, but it also had a
more competitive, business-minded culture. Greenberg's comments are highly
perceptive but we should note that Lye's 'free-and-easiness' was not merely
British — it had its roots in Australia, Samoa, and New Zealand. It was related to
his sturdy sense of independence. While he got on well with other artists, he liked
to keep some space round himself, and he was indifferent to fashion. These
frontier values — which also harked back to the heroic days of modernism —

kept him strong and self-sufficient but they would be increasingly out of place in post-war American society.

Besides meeting American artists at Hayter's Atelier, Lye renewed his acquaintance with Ruthven Todd, the poet and engraver who had made his house available to his family. It was through him that Lye met Joan Miró when the Spanish artist came to the United States in 1947 to paint a mural for a hotel restaurant.[11] Staying in New York's Spanish Harlem, Miró would go downtown to the Atelier to collaborate on prints with Todd. He visited Lye at his current home at 278 West 4th Street, and despite his limited English and Lye's total lack of Spanish or French, the two artists felt a very strong affinity for each other's work. Miró left an artist's proof of one of his prints signed: '*À Len Lye, affectueusement* [To Len Lye, affectionately]'.

Besides being a fruitful period for Lye's painting, the late 1940s brought new developments in his poetry. He developed the habit of writing a prose-poem on the back of each new painting before giving it to a friend. Though triggered off by a specific image, the prose-poem was always surprising, seeming to reveal a strange tribal mythology concealed within the abstract patterns of the picture. The simple structure of the sentences was deceptive, for the poems followed a strange logic as though objects and words were undergoing a kind of sea change. For example, 'Silver Sea Valley':

> There is a valley of pure silver and sand without earth where moonbeams drain down to silver the sea at night. Pearls have taken root in silver cracks and hollows filled with dew. They have grown into trees that live on moonlight and sea mist. The trees have blooms that only unfold from their stalks in the moonlight. Crabs climb the trees and go from flower to flower to eat the moon seeds in them. At the centre of each seed is a speck of silver sand. The crabs take sea smells from one flower to another. The trees know the crabs will carry the moon seeds down to the sea. And they will become pearls again.[12]

Colours are simple and strong, as in 'Frost Dance':

> A red moon is the start of frost. . . . All eggs in earth turn to black stone if they are caught. . . . Veins of trees and rocks come out and dance in the green fields.

Intensely active and physical, Lye's poems brought all the senses into play. He described the earth responding to the touch of sunlight, lightning, snow, and hot lava. Marine creatures led a vivid sex life:

> It is night-time 60 feet deep by a coral reef. A coral king leaves his skin of rock. A queen of starfish leaves her shell. They meet as they really are and make ideas of the sea. He puts red and she puts yellow. That makes phosphorus and they see. Some finished phosphorus by that stem of seaweed will float to the top and be their memories. They make a lot of memories and go back to their shells. They always are new to each other out of their shells.

The poems evoked an animistic world in which darkness, thunder, and fire were as much living beings as seeds or fish. The most common theme was metamorphosis — a snake started standing on its tail, plants learned to walk, branches became birds. Human beings appeared occasionally in these poems but were still very much part of nature:

> They plant all things and grow their own blood and iron. They don't need the Seer any more but sometimes he helps them with rain. . . . Today when people stand up straight and still on hills and feel the earth with their feet they are most like a tree because a tree has its heart in its roots.[13]

These poems varied in length from a single sentence to the three pages of 'A Tree Has Its Heart In Its Roots' (1948) which combined a number of incidents and images into an evolutionary 'fable'. Such myth-making was informed by Lye's memories of New Zealand and Samoan landscapes, by his lifetime study of tribal cultures, and by his own paintings and films such as the unfinished *Tusalava* trilogy. While the poems were complete in their own right they provided a kind of verbal parallel to biomorphic abstraction in art. It is a pity that Lye made no attempt to publish them, not even after the 1960s when the growth of interest in 'deep image' writing and 'ethnopoetics' (stimulated by magazines such as *Alcheringa* and the poetry anthologies of Jerome Rothenberg) enlarged the audience for work of this kind.

Some of his experiments went even further than 'Song Time Stuff' in their self-conscious questioning of language and the writing process. The work of the Greenwich Village poet E. E. Cummings may have provided a model for the intricate wordplay of poems such as 't w i':

> why should writ (y) ing should i
> we when word say sign not
> it its is me world its
> my. . . .

Though 'Knife Apple Sheer Brush' was explicitly a tribute to Stanley William Hayter, written after seeing an exhibition of his work in January 1948, it provides a vivid expression of Lye's own aesthetic. The first draft was little more than a piece of didactic prose ('Paintings state / Enduring qualities / Of individual experience / Isolated as art'), but Lye developed it into a sensuous lyric:

Take a	knife
To an	apple
The pith lies	sheer
With the mind take a	brush
Peel the skin of your own	pith
See the sinews of	feeling
Traced in the glow of vegetable	dyes
Pinioned by the black	action
Of the cadmium	sun

HAYTER

The poem then described his visit to Hayter's exhibition as an encounter with a unique vision:

> mind stands confronted with mind
>
> Not by museum label or institution
> But by the work of one man
>
> Seeking responsibility for his version
> Of the transparent skin of the universe

Hayter's pictures were celebrated as 'hypnotic mind juice', as 'living candescent signs', and as 'priceless scarecrows / Guarding the seeds of experience'.[14] In March 1949 this poem was published in *The Tiger's Eye* alongside Hayter's 'White Shadow', a painting whose lines were charged with kinetic energy. *The Tiger's Eye*, which took its title from William Blake, was edited in Greenwich Village by Ruth and John Stephen. One of the most important avant-garde magazines of the period, it published poetry alongside the work of European artists such as Joan Miró and Paul Klee, composers such as John Cage, and new American painters such as Jackson Pollock, Clifford Still, Mark Rothko, Mark Tobey, and Barnett Newman (who worked as associate editor). As a showcase for biomorphic painting, the magazine explored such topics as prehistoric art, mythology, surrealism, and the Sublime. 'Grass Clippings' and another piece of Lye's poetic prose, 'Am Thing', were also accepted for *The Tiger's Eye* but unfortunately it ceased publication in 1949 with its ninth issue and there was no other magazine for which he felt impelled to write.

Writing was not the only area of experiment during the excitement of his first years in New York. Ann Lye recalls: 'Len was getting into all kinds of things, such as finding old doorknobs and painting them in weird ways and giving them to friends.' In 1947–48 he was busy making photograms, silhouette photographs produced without a camera. His photograms of the 1920s and 1930s had been based on curious combinations of objects, or abstract shapes moulded in plasticine; now he focused on people's heads. He persuaded visitors to lie on the floor of a small dark room, on a sheet of unexposed photographic paper,[15] then he would make the exposure with a flick of the light switch. With his current interest in signs of the self — a theme explored in poems such as 't w i' — Lye was intrigued by the idea of someone leaving a direct imprint, a physical profile. But then, to complicate this reality, he would flip the image, reverse positive and negative, or add words and visual symbols (as he had done in his 1937 film *N. Or N.W.*). This involved making additional exposures so that a piece of fabric, say, or a fern, or a necklace could be superimposed over the silhouette. His photograms included many friends such as the artists Joan Miró, Hans Richter, and Georgia O'Keeffe. In the case of O'Keeffe the superimposed shape was a pair of deer antlers she had given the Lyes as a present. Other participants included the architect Le Corbusier, the scientist Nina Bull, Roy Lockwood from the *March of Time*, and the plumber Albert Bishop who had come to do repairs. (Bishop's silhouette was ringed with tools and washers.) When a couple arrived with their newborn baby it was positioned naked on the floor but foiled the first attempt by wetting the photographic paper. The second attempt was a success and the parents framed and hung the result. Wystan Hugh Auden, a fellow expatriate from England, also submitted to the photogram ritual, and Lye superimposed a wry stanza from a poem Auden had just written over his distinctive profile:

> Caesar's double-bed is warm
> As an unimportant clerk
> Writes I DO NOT LIKE MY WORK
> On a pink official form.[16]

Perhaps the most striking picture in the series was Lye's 'Self-portrait', made by superimposing the complex photogram 'Night Tree' (included in the 1936 International Surrealist Exhibition)[17] onto the silhouette of his head, creating what he called an 'x-ray'. Soon Lye would find a new way of applying these techniques to film-making.

thirtysix **shoe of my mind**

In August 1951 the *March of Time* came to an end. Although it still had a loyal following the monthly news magazine of the cinema could not hope to compete with the speed and novelty of television. During the late 1940s Lye had directed sequences for a number of *March of Time* episodes including 'Night Club Boom', 'Wanted — More Homes', 'Problem Drinkers', 'Farming Pays Off', 'Watchdogs of the Mail', and 'T-Men in Action'. Perhaps the most important episode he worked on was 'Atomic Power', which traced the development of the atomic bomb and the decision to drop it on Hiroshima. Scientists such as Albert Einstein and Robert Oppenheimer agreed to re-enact key scenes, and the scientific aspects were explained by a three-dimensional model of the atom spinning like a kinetic sculpture. 'Atomic Power' acknowledged the dangers of the new atomic age and the need for international cooperation, a cause to which Einstein as chairman of the Emergency Committee of Atomic Scientists gave his support. Einstein's interview broke the record for brevity — his only words were 'I agree' — but the implications of the documentary were clear, summed up on screen by the title of a pamphlet, *One World or None*.[1]

For seven years the *March of Time* had provided Lye with a regular pay cheque. Though he was well liked by his fellow film-makers and journalists, he was considered the most offbeat or flamboyant person on the staff. Cecile Starr remembers catching sight him for the first time as he was shooting a sequence in the *March of Time* office: 'His billiard-ball head was bouncing up and down by the camera. He had so much vitality he couldn't stand still. His appearance and voice were so unfamiliar to me he was like a man from Mars. After I left the room I remarked to someone, "It's like an alien world in there", and the person replied: "Oh, you must have met Len Lye"!'[2] James Merritt, who was assigned to Lye as assistant because he had less trouble than most in understanding him, was often amazed by his clothing. On one cold day when they went to New Jersey to film a farmer with a herd of cows, Lye turned up dressed in an extraordinary tweed suit (without sleeves) topped by an ancient fur-trimmed black coat he had bought for $10 from an East Village thrift shop. The scene became a farce because the cows were obsessed with Lye's appearance and kept following or chasing him. On another occasion Lye and Merritt thought they had obtained permission from the owner of a house to use it to film interviews, but halfway through the shoot they discovered they had been the victims of a practical joke when the real owner walked in — a burly prison guard furious about the invasion of his house. While there were plenty of surprises involved in working for Lye, his crew-members liked and respected him. Having to dissuade him now and then from spending too much time on a complicated shot, Merritt used to think: 'Sending Len out to direct ordinary newsreel footage is like using a race horse to pull an ice wagon.' But Lye was not temperamental — basically he accepted the house style and brought his work in on schedule and within budget.

When the staff had lunch together in the office Lothar Wolff remembered Lye as a good mixer: 'He stood out but he didn't stand apart.' Lye was never an intellectual show-off but he would occasionally bring up his theories. In Wolff's words: 'He was always having new ideas — about art, film, God, or the world. A very searching mind.'[3] One day he handed Merritt his poem about the Hayter exhibition with the comment: 'Maybe this will explain my ideas better than my essays.' But Merritt found Lye's poetry as enigmatic as his prose. Lye was never daunted — he was sure the problem lay not in the ideas but in his limitations as a writer, and this made him determined to try again.

Receiving severance pay from the *March of Time*, he delayed looking for another job and embarked on a period of full-time writing. The work he had done on IHN up to Willkie's death had been a huge workout for his intellectual muscles. The more thinking and writing he did, the more he enjoyed those activities and the more hours he devoted to them. What spurred him on was his belief that the theory not only offered a key to his own experience but touched upon a universal truth. Thinking in universal or archetypal terms was a tendency he shared with the theorists he had studied such as Freud and Jung. But to do the job properly he needed to find a new way of communicating his ideas, because his own way struck people as too individual and quirky. (Riding has struggled similarly to forge a discourse of 'truth'.) After his unsuccessful attempts to insert his ideas into the discourse of politics he now focused mainly on science which also saw things in universalist terms. But scientific thinking and writing did not come naturally to him and he would often feel — as he had with politics — that scientific discourse was distorting his original insight.

Back in December 1945 Louise Ames had introduced him to Nina Bull, a woman who had educated herself in psychology with so much energy she had been given an honorary research position at Columbia University despite her lack of formal qualifications. She was committed to a behaviourist approach, relating mental to physical states. Discussions with Bull fired Lye's interest in theoretical aspects of the mind's relationship with the body. His approach to art had always been distinguished by its emphasis on feelings of physical empathy. The essay and poem which shared the title 'Shoe of My Mind' were triggered off by the sight of a shoe floating in the sea. Lye was fascinated by the human ability to 'put yourself in someone else's shoes' with physical feelings providing the bridge. In 'You Be Me' he wrote: 'Empathy is the sweat in the soles of your palms when you walk in the shoes of the tightroper as you sniff his height from down here in your seat. No image is formed without a bit of projection spatially relating your bodily sense to it.'[4] Lye had always contrasted his approach with Descartes's famous phrase 'I think therefore I am', which seemed to him typical of the narrow way many intellectuals focused on the mind. He preferred the approach of ancient Greek philosophers who linked individuality with body processes such as breathing. He was intrigued to learn from Bull about behaviourism and the ways it was giving more weight to the body, but his discussions with her usually ended in an argument because she would go too far in eliminating the concept of mind.

To argue such issues Lye saw that he needed to develop a more scientific version of 'Individual Happiness Now' grounded in physical reality. This would also enable him to link his theory with evolution, a field of enquiry in which science could not so easily ignore questions of value since evolution seemed to be propelled by something more than just the survival instinct. Lye was fascinated by evolution, which he saw as a drive to develop ever richer and more complex forms of individuality, from an amoeba to an Einstein. Experimental art was an important evolutionary force because it sharpened the sense of self, whereas Fascists and other book-burners wanted to regress to the psychology of the herd.[5] By speaking of IHN in the context of evolution Lye could make it clear that he was not celebrating selfishness but talking about what furthered happiness and individuality for all human beings. In his vision of an ideal society there would be so many strange, stimulating individuals that everybody's wits would be sharpened.[6]

He summed up his scientific version of IHN by the slogan 'Identity-Degree-Act'. 'Identity' could be applied not only to human beings but to any form of life. 'Degree' referred to our ability to recognise different degrees of intensity so that we could ask and answer such questions as 'How happy are you?' The third term, 'Act', emphasised the kinds of activity — including movement — that we need to survive and to express ourselves. Because IDA was a more 'objective' version of IHN it was less disturbing to a biologist or psychologist, but it was still based on the intense vision of an artist to whom everything in the world seemed alive. Lye could celebrate individualism not only in the grace of a dancer but in the energy of an atom spinning to maintain its complex identity. In 'The Identity of Value' he found wit everywhere in nature: 'We perceive this quality in the bouquet of a wine, the spirit of Bach's works, or in the nicety with which a bird builds a nest.' This way of thinking was too heady for most scientists. But in 1951 Lye did receive a long, friendly reply from Dr Ray Lepley of Bradley University, a leading 'axiologist' (philosopher specialising in the study of value) after an essay about IDA came to him out of the blue. Lepley began: 'I have read your paper once rather quickly, once carefully, and several times in spots. It strikes me as being well worked out and unified — a work of art, which has more meaning than is explicitly expressed. In general, your point of view seems to be akin to that which a number of people have arrived at recently.'7

Encouraged by such responses, Lye sent many applications to funding bodies asking them to sponsor films about IHN or IDA. He described his projects as experimental research, experimental in scientific as well as in film terms — 'uncommercial' work that would be understandable to an intelligent layperson but not necessarily to the general public. Not one of his appeals to groups such as the Viking Fund (1946), the Guggenheim Foundation (1946 and 1948), the Rockefeller Foundation (1952), and the Ford Foundation (1953) struck paydirt. Despite advice from friends such as Ames, he could never complete an application without at least one dangerous digression into theory. To those who did not know Lye, his style was an unclassifiable mixture of science and art, technical language and racy colloquialisms, certain to freak out at least one person on any committee. Replying to a submission from Lye, two Directors of the Rockefeller Foundation commented: '[We] might as well say candidly that neither of us could make much of it. This is probably a defect in us, but we simply do not see what you are driving at.'8 One scientist whom Lye hoped to get on side as a referee agreed to spend a weekend discussing a proposal, but the visit ended in acrimony because he could not stand the jazz records Lye kept playing.9 Bull, who was extremely wealthy, was very interested in one of his film projects but she wanted to have some influence on the script. As Ames recalls: 'If Lye had just been a little more flexible Nina would probably have given him funding for a substantial film. But he was the sort of person who wouldn't change a sentence even if someone offered him $10,000.'10

One project for which he shot some footage at his own expense focused on the work of the psychologist William H. Sheldon whose research had established a correlation between temperaments and body types. Sheldon's categories — ectomorph, endomorph, and mesomorph — stirred up debate even in the popular press. Lye wondered whether such categories could also be applied to an individual's empathy for particular types of image, and he went to see the psychologist to discuss the making of a film on this topic. Discovering that Sheldon was not expected to live long because of cancer of the throat, Lye began immediately to shoot the documentary. Sheldon pulled through with the help of radiation treatment but the film was not completed.[11] In June 1949 Lye wrote to George Orwell to express his belief that *Animal Farm* would provide an excellent basis for a film about individualism. It was difficult for Orwell to reply — 'I'm frightfully ill (T.B.) so can't write much of a letter' — but he was very cordial: 'Of course I remember you!. . . . I'd love it if you had anything to do with filming my book.'[12] But Lye could not raise the money, and Orwell died in January 1950.[13]

In July 1950 Lye sent a letter to Dwight Eisenhower, President of the United States, who had just given a commencement address at Columbia University about democratic values. As Ann Lye observed: 'Len was in the habit of writing to anyone he'd read about that he had a question for. He might not get an answer, but he would always give it a try.'[14] His letter to the President outlined his own ideas on the subject and argued that a nation that promoted democratic values ought to be sponsoring more 'objective' research on the subject. (In one of his grant applications he had asked: 'When will research on values be considered as important as research on nuclear physics?') Eisenhower's reply was not as warm as Wendell Willkie's but it did hold some promise: 'Thank you for an extremely stimulating and provocative letter. Unfortunately, I do not feel that I am competent to advise you. However, immediately after my return to the University, I shall talk to some of our faculty members.'[15] But that was the last Lye heard of it.

He wrote incessantly. Some of his most interesting writings from this period are in the form of an elaborate 'stream of consciousness', tracking the mind's dialogue with the body. He said of his long work 'Chair': 'It is in honour of the wandering sitting resting unlimbering body's body.'[16] This physical awareness in his writing paralleled the work of Charles Olson, the 'projective' poet and theorist of 'proprioception', whose poetry has been described as the closest literary equivalent to abstract expressionist painting. Unfortunately neither writer was aware of the other's work. Though Lye's starting-point would be something commonplace, a small event of the day, he would bring it to life by elaborating on all the mental and physical processes involved in it. For example, 'Brown Paper Bag' described walking along a busy New York street and crossing to the other side:

> I paddle along back to my shaded cove of a room while the objective imagery of
> me and the street is being transmitted to me by senses of weight and muscle and
> nerve action helped out by senses of light and sound . . . [with] kerb and street
> and sidewalk and traffic lights and people as interesting craft with laws of tides

and navigation all synchronised in my spatial relationship with them by mind and body work each to each. I am now completely myself, a canoe on the sidewalk, a swimmer in a sea of crocodiles to traverse the road of a river. . . . And this organism that possesses my name got me out into the sunshine to experience being alive . . . a body with a name on its prow.

Lye was always fascinated by the act of walking, the 'I' moving through space with a heightened sense of feet feeling the ground while eyes weighed up passing objects. He also liked to describe the partnership of mind and body in the activity of writing itself. For example:

> To think words 'individual happiness now' means [an] experience of immediacy . . . feeling alive with wattage from [the] senses. I have to stop writing to feel it in me as the enjoyment of sitting and feeling the pressure of a good weighted leg across the thigh near the knee on top of the other and the bread-board on the slope of the crossed leg's thigh with the left hand's fingers holding the plain yellow note-paper, and the pen-nib ink flowing on it as the nib makes a pleasant rubbing sound on the sounding board of the bread-board and I can feel its vibrations transmitted to my thigh bone and I'm dealing with sensation and . . .

This unfinished sentence became a drawing of his own hand writing the word 'bone' on a piece of paper on his thigh.

Despite Lye's struggle to be more scientific and more analytical, it was the pleasure of 'feeling alive with wattage from [the] senses' that gave his writing its most distinctive flavour. And at the deepest level his thinking still followed the logic of poetry or myth rather than science. The experience that most strongly reassured him about the truth of his ideas was a dream. He had been worrying about his obsession with theory: 'I was crazy, it was all I could think about, I'm afraid I bored a lot of friends.' Then one night: 'I dreamt I had my work under my arm and had set out with it to find my father. He had died when I was four [sic] but I felt sure I would find him and that he would know whether I was on the right track with my philosophical idea or not. I found him in New Zealand and he was glad to see me and very interested in knowing what I was up to. He read [my work] and got the hang of it but said he couldn't tell me whether it was right or not. He said that I had better ask his father. I found my grandfather in some place in Sussex, out in a field. He looked at my work and said I would have to go further back, that perhaps my great-grandfather would know and if not, try his father — that someone down the line would be sure to know. So back and back along my ancestral line I went, meeting all sorts of interesting forebears, all pleased to see me, but all non-committal about my work. At last I came to one old white-bearded man in Cornwall and I felt that this was it. He sat on a stone chair near some trees covered in mistletoe. Stonehenge stood some way behind him and I took it for granted he was one of the main Druids. We stood looking at each other and neither of us moved. Then he said quietly, "My boy, you are right." I woke up right away.' Lye added: 'Had I been Greek I would have ended up at Delphi, but Stonehenge suits me. I still don't know why I saw Stonehenge in Cornwall when its bones stand [on Salisbury Plain]. But if I could do work to stand like Stonehenge it would suit me pretty good!'[17]

thirtyseven gracious living with little money

Lye's severance pay ran out and he and Ann now faced serious money troubles for in addition to their own expenses each had two children to support. They rented out their duplex and moved into the crowded cellar. This left them with a toilet but no bathroom so when their tenants were out they would sneak up to their old apartment to take a shower. Lye's unemployment also created a crisis for Jane. She was able to find occasional part-time jobs as proofreader, secretary, or teacher but there were periods when she was desperately short of money. On one occasion when Len and Ann met Jane, Bix and Yancy, the children refused to acknowledge their father, leaving him deeply shocked. Jane threatened him with legal action over support payments until Ann managed to convince her that Lye had absolutely no income.[1] The children's contact with their father was eventually restored but the situation remained volatile.

Realising she must (in her own words) 'become the maintenance man', Ann Lye took a job as a model, appearing in advertisements for home appliances, tools, and crockery. She also began working as the assistant to a Frenchman who owned property all over Greenwich Village. 'He was insane — someone would fall in love with a property and the lease would be all ready to sign, then he'd ask them who they'd voted for in the last election and start a big argument. It wasted all my working time fighting with this madman — he'd write me these long letters even though he was just in the next room, and I'd write long letters back.' Having found she had a flair for selling as well as for renovating old houses, Ann Lye decided to go out on her own. 'Space is the most valuable thing in New York city. I worked mostly in the Village with creative people who needed space — artists and writers and theatre people. I discovered that if you bought a house, one of those small four-storey houses, rented two floors out and lived and worked in the rest, it still cost you less to pay the mortgage than to rent. With this logic I sold houses to two people and they recommended me to four of their friends, and so it grew. I never advertised. People knew me as "the seller from the cellar" — the basement of our home in Bethune Street which became my office, painted white with a pink floor!' She obtained a broker's licence in 1958. Over the years she played a key role in maintaining the Village as a place where artists could live and work. She was involved in many Village campaigns to save old buildings from demolition, an activity that brought her into conflict with other brokers and major property developers. She was a leader of the protest movement that persuaded the city's planning board not to demolish large areas of the West Village under the National Slum Clearance Act. As a broker Ann Lye had the satisfaction of helping to defend the presence of artists in the Village as well as generating a steady income for herself and her husband. She could drive a hard bargain, but with people she liked she was capable of great generosity. Because some bohemians in the Village were automatically suspicious of success in business, there were two conflicting images of Ann Lye — to some she was 'the ruthless wheeler and dealer', to others 'the honest broker, the only one in New York'.

Close friends agreed that her combination of practicality and zest for life made her the ideal partner for Lye.[2] There were countless anecdotes about his problems with money such as the time he was called in to justify his tax return. He turned up at the IRD with a mess of papers and explained: 'I don't understand any of it.' After a lengthy conversation with Lye the tax inspectors were so perplexed they closed the file and asked him to leave. 'He had no concept of money', said Ann Lye. 'Even when we had enough, he still assumed we didn't have a nickel. We operated a joint account but he would never cash a cheque without asking me. As for being "maintenance man" I didn't mind going out to work as long as he got on with his art. He was helpful in the house — he cleaned and cooked. Some people thought I was nuts to put up with him, and occasionally I wished he were different but I never expected him to be. I understand that artists are a special breed — if they can't create they will go crazy. Len was always a happy person, always very loving. We agreed on everything.'

She got used to his cartoon sense of time and space: 'Any time he went out of a door he would turn in the wrong direction. For years I tried training him to go out of a door. Going uptown he'd get on the wrong train and land in Brooklyn. He didn't like finding himself in wrong places but he accepted it as a way of life. He had to.'[3] He would sometimes get around by bicycle 'but he couldn't ride anywhere except on the left side. . . . He used to think red lights were for everyone else to stop and let him go. He could have killed himself any minute. I [used to wonder] if it was something to do with coming from the Southern Hemisphere.'[4] Good-humoured herself, she admired Lye's insouciance: 'I think he was born happy. He would never panic as a lot of people do under stress. On the other hand, because he wasn't a tense person he was not always reliable with deadlines. If he had something more important to do he could slide — he just had his own priorities and that was that.'[5]

Friends from England who visited them in 1949 found their Village lifestyle unfamiliar: 'Len and Ann lived in one room — a "loft". And people were smoking marijuana — we'd never struck that before.'⁶ Dancing was an important part of their life: 'We'd be starting dinner when something came on the radio that Len liked. We'd start dancing and forget the dinner.'⁷ There was plenty of socialising — at the White Horse Tavern or in one another's apartments. Anaïs Nin wrote in her *Journals*: 'Another life I like is Len Lye's. He has a house by the waterfront in New York. . . . It is an old house (1800). When they scraped the paint off they found beautiful wood underneath. . . . Several artists have bought houses in the same block. It is a community. It is near cheap workmen's bistros, Spanish restaurants, Dutch restaurants, Irish bars, and near the market where they buy fresh and cheap food. I admire those who live graciously with little money.'⁸

In 1954 the Lyes purchased their first home, moving round the corner to 41 Bethune Street, another early nineteenth century house to repair. In the words of a reporter from the *Newark News*: 'The old house at No. 41 would have frightened off one with less courage, tenacity and know-how than Ann Lye. The stained marble staircase, the collapsed ceilings and the cobwebby walls would have sent a less capable lass fleeing. . . . Ann tore into the west wall, ripping down not only the paper but the plaster and found, as she knew she would, wonderful aged brick. . . . Old floors were torn up, exposing the original random width, long leaf yellow pine.'⁹ Whereas the tendency of the time was to modernise Ann Lye argued that anyone who bought an old place should keep it as such. Their liking for bare brick and wood helped to change the local fashion. But they were not purists and there was room for a few startling innovations such as covering a floor at Bethune Street in pigskin. A special oak seat was made for the toilet, and friends were invited to a 'Bathroom Opening' celebration when it was installed. To solve the problem of a crumbling ceiling they put up an aluminium one which Lye painted gold. He was a conscientious helper, though on occasion Ann would come home to find he had not only finished a wall but also painted a mural.

In summer they and their friends vacationed at Martha's Vineyard, an island in Massachusetts. Subsequently the Vineyard become chic and expensive and also somewhat notorious, but in the 1940s and '50s artists and writers from the Village were attracted by its privacy (which made nude beaches possible) and by the opportunity to 'live graciously with little money'. In 1947 the Lyes bought a 1926 Model A Ford for $75 and each year drove it to the Vineyard. In the 1950s they moved up to a 1936 Ford beach wagon, its 'square and elegant' sides made of maple wood. They could camp in it and Lye liked painting the panels. Then they started renting an old house near a beach which they called 'Quauk Cottage' after 'the night-flying herons in the cedar woods who streaked all over everything and made this terrible noise: quauk, quauk, quauk!'[10] Lye worked there during the summers, writing essays and poems and making paintings such as 'Lagoon Life' and 'Clay'.

In Ann Lye's words: 'Once you get to the Vineyard you go out of your head a bit, you want to stay for ever, you forget the outside world — it's rather like New Zealand in that respect.' Once she began to make steady money out of real estate she and Lye decided to build a house next to Quauk Cottage. 'Tony Smith [a sculptor and architect who had worked with Frank Lloyd Wright] made a design for us but we'd never seen anything so dull — square, made of cinder-blocks, flat-roofed. So Len came up with a pattern — a trapezoid figure. His design had no right-angled corners at all — it was narrow facing the road but widened out as it went back towards the water so it gave the most amazing feeling of space. A two-storey thing built out of cedar — we used the trunks of cedar trees as a staircase, and in the middle of the house as the main support there was a cedar tree-trunk with all its bark on, and a branch going up to the balcony. We called it "the Trap" because of the trapezoid figure. The whole thing felt open and natural. The problem was that after we got it built we realized we'd been suffering from the Vineyard madness — how could we make a living there?' She opened a second-hand shop called 'Things and Stuff' which bought things from people when they left and sold them to new arrivals. She described it as junk of good taste, and Lye was the assistant buyer. But living at the Vineyard created too many problems: 'The Trap was built with a big studio room with film-making in mind, but we found there was no place Len could get film developed closer than Boston. So we had to rent out the house and return to New York. After four or five years of renting it and cleaning it up we sold it and started looking for a summer place in up-state New York.'

Among the many old friends from London who looked Lye up in New York, one of the most enjoyable visitors was Dylan Thomas. On the first day of his first American reading tour in 1950, the poet invited the artist to lunch at a Third Avenue bar. Also present were Ruthven Todd, who now lived near Lye both in the West Village and at Martha's Vineyard, and John Malcolm Brinnin, organiser of the tour, who later said of this reunion: 'the smoky air was soon loud with Rabelaisian reminiscence — of prodigious drinking bouts that had laid everyone under the table, of literary parties that had not so much ended as disintegrated, of pub-room ribaldries that had shocked the fatuous and famous, of escapades that had brought wives, mothers, and the London police running.'[11] When Jane Lye came to join the group at the invitation of her friend Todd, she (in Brinnin's words) 'took one look at Dylan, whom she had not seen in ten years, and said in a sinking voice, "O Dylan — the last time I saw you you were an *angel*"'.[12] For Brinnin who later highlighted this remark in his book *Dylan Thomas in America*, the poet's 'rueful' response was 'the first real evidence' of how painfully he was aware of his own decline. Jane Lye acknowledged that her remark had been reported accurately but she found Brinnin's interpretation melodramatic: 'I don't really believe Dylan minded at all. He and his friends never wasted time fretting about their sensitivities.'[13] In the course of the lunch she remembered the talk getting very bawdy, creating problems for a writer who had joined them to interview Thomas for the Book Review section of the *New York Times* — he could not 'get a word out of it "fit to print"'.

Lye had always been enthusiastic about his friend's poetry, admiring its extreme individuality. He also had a personal respect for Thomas as someone who refused to compromise, who liked to embarrass rich and famous people at dinner parties. As for the poet's chaotic life and work habits Lye had no wish to be 'a moralistic prig'. He knew from his own art that 'It is far more difficult to discipline yourself not to discipline yourself than it is to discipline yourself!'[14] Not that the two men always saw eye to eye, as Stanley Hayter observed: 'He [Len] was a friend of Dylan Thomas [but] I remember in the '50s them bickering in my house — Dylan objecting violently to Len's highly allusive and elliptic speech — remarking that he never understood the half of what he (Len) was saying!'[15]

During his New York visits of 1950 and 1952, Thomas spent time with Lye discussing a possible poetry film. 'We ran all sorts of coloured abstract film in my studio (at Washington Street) accompanied by all sorts of poems (including Dylan's) on phonograph, but Dylan agreed with me that none seemed to work. He offered to write something that he thought would work — such as something about a bicycle.' (The 'bicycle' idea may have been a spinoff from the film script 'Me and My Bike' written recently by Thomas.) Lye continued to work on the problem independently: 'I was not to be beat by the idea that direct film had a place in presenting poetry. Then I tumbled: as one can't gild the lily (the lily being a perfect poem) the thing would be not to garnish but to emphasize the *words*. I did this by doing direct-film-technique words that moved three-dimensionally, two-dimensionally, and with the cadences, oscillations, dips, flutters, etc., etc., of the vocalised accentings of the heard words. Being done in direct film, the words vibrated in a way that seemed to go with the resonance of their delivery.'[16] At this time Lye was experimenting with many ways to scratch designs on film using a strange assortment of instruments — gravers, various kinds of needles and nails, paper clips, dentist's tools, surgical tools, and saw blades whose teeth were just the right size to fit a strip of film. He also — 'for romanticism'[17] — used Native American arrow heads. To experiment with the animation of words Lye made a new version of 'Full Fathom Five', scratching Shakespeare's poem on to black film to accompany the recording that John Gielgud had made for him in 1935. The words came to life — they changed size, swung back and forth like a bell, flew apart and went through other changes in keeping with the poem's theme of transformation.[18] He saw this as a possible method not only for poetry but for filmed opera since it matched the vibrancy of sung words.[19]

Lye talked further with Thomas about a film when the poet returned to New York in April 1953. A month before this third reading tour Dylan had written to John Malcolm Brinnin: 'I am hoping that perhaps my old friend Len Lye, who lives in Greenwich Village, near Ruthven Todd, will put me up: I am only small after all, and alone, though loud.'[20] But the Lyes were still living at Washington Street with scarcely enough room for themselves, so Thomas went once again to the Chelsea Hotel on 23rd Street, a hotel popular among writers and artists of the West Village. Thomas would walk down Hudson Street to the White Horse Tavern, his favourite New York bar, where artists and writers mingled with truck drivers, stevedores, and seamen. The Lyes' neighbourhood was still at this time an industrial area with busy wharves, and the White Horse was (in Thomas's words) 'as homely and dingy as many a London pub, and perhaps just as old'.[21] As Ann Lye described it: 'Everybody would be there, and sometimes the Clancey Brothers would be practising their Irish singing in the back room.'[22] The sculptor Joellen Rapee (who was married to Ruthven Todd) remembers that when Hayter's Atelier closed at 10 p.m., he and the other artists would come regularly to the White Horse for beer and hamburgers. When Thomas was there he 'mostly told jokes, he was a great joketeller, he had us all in stitches. Rarely anything very literary or very deep.'[23]

The group at the White Horse often included the Slivkas who were later to play an important role in the poet's life. Rose, a writer, and David, a sculptor, lived next door to the Lyes in Washington Street. Rose Slivka enjoyed her contacts with Lye, who 'looked a bit like a pristine and arrogant Fu Manchu. There was a mysterious quality about him, I never really knew what he had up his sleeve — some marvellous work of art without a doubt.' She was also impressed by his relationship with his wife: 'Each was so distinctly different. They would come back from the country and, even before they had unpacked, Ann would be out there digging over the garden and Len would be off doing *his* thing. It was really such a pleasure to see two people who were absolutely uniquely themselves, who did not impinge on each other, and yet were totally cooperative.'[24] During Thomas's first visit in 1950 the Lyes called the Slivkas over to their house to meet him. On that occasion the poet 'made his routine proposition' to Rose but she 'fended him off without difficulty'.[25] On his 1952 tour Thomas was accompanied by his wife Caitlin who struck up a strong friendship with Rose. Caitlin was not with him, however, on his third tour, or his fourth and final tour which began in October 1953.

By this time the poet's fame and notoriety were at their height. He was drinking harder than usual and suffering from severe bouts of depression, a condition which alarmed those who saw him at a party given by the Slivkas to celebrate his thirty-ninth birthday. Through the following week he sank deeper into depression, then on the morning of 4 November he left the Chelsea Hotel around two o'clock, returning an hour and a half later with the comment: 'I've had eighteen straight whiskies. I think that's the record.'[26] The details of what actually happened on this final binge have since become the subject of widespread speculation.[27] Ann Lye added one detail to the record, for she remembered Len receiving a phone call in the small hours of the morning from Thomas who was apparently at the White Horse. The ostensible reason for the call was a tuxedo the poet wanted to borrow for a trip to California where he was going to work on an opera with Igor Stravinsky. Ann's first husband Tommy Hindle had given a tuxedo to a young friend of the Lyes named Mark Mitchell but it had been too large and was now stored in a box in the Lyes' basement. Various friends knew about it and one of them had mentioned it to Thomas. When the telephone rang, Lye was still awake working in his basement studio but was not in the mood for visitors. In Ann's words: 'Dylan was obviously very high. He mentioned the tuxedo and Len said, "Well, I'm working in the cellar", and Dylan said — in a drunken voice because he was in a bad way — "Well, I'm way down below cellar!" Once they had started this they went on for about ten minutes — "I'm in the cellar", "I'm lower" — a very goofy conversation. As for the tuxedo they never got down to cases. When Len talked with Dylan they were always in the clouds — or in the cellar — one or the other.'[28]

Back at the Chelsea Hotel Thomas slept for a few hours then walked back to White Horse and had a few more beers. On his return to the hotel he became seriously ill and a doctor was called. It was later alleged that the doctor's choice of medication made the condition worse. By 2 a.m. on the following day Thomas was in St Vincent's Hospital in a comatose state that would continue more or less unchanged until his death four days later. Notified by Rose Slivka, Caitlin Thomas flew immediately to New York and stayed at the Slivkas' home in a situation that Rose found 'terrifying' because the Thomases were the target of what would today be described as a media feeding frenzy. Not only journalists but numerous so-called friends of the poet were 'fighting for a piece of the corpse'.[29] Caitlin Thomas was beside herself with grief and anger. As Rose Slivka recalls: 'She had not wanted Dylan to come on this trip. It was a marriage in which there were a lot of battles but they really did love each other, they needed each other very much. In the hospital I think it was such a shock that she could not believe it was real — an unconscious form, with tubes coming out of his nose, eyes, ears. . . . She really had the feeling that this was an American plot. She lunged at John Brinnin. And there was one of those little statues of the Virgin there which she smashed. The nuns got very angry and finally Caitlin was put in a straitjacket.'[30] There was talk of sending her to Bellevue — a grim prospect because Bellevue was the hospital where New York City police take suspects for psychiatric observation — but after appeals by friends the destination was changed to a private institution in Westchester. It took Rose Slivka and Ruthven Todd two days of negotiation to get her released.

Rose Slivka later spoke of the help she received from the Lyes before and after Thomas's death: 'Ann would come over bringing food, and she and Len were so calm.' He spent time with Caitlin trying to quieten her down. In Ann's words: 'He was marvellous with anyone in distress. When Hayter's wife Helen [had a breakdown], Len was the only one who could feed her. He used to look after her for days at a time, playing phonograph records. He never got upset. He was the same with Caitlin, when everybody else seemed to be going nuts.' Slivka notes that Lye was one of the few people who kept out of the spotlight: 'There was so much competition — who knew Dylan best, to whom did he say what, etc. Len did not enter into this. He had his own history with Dylan but Len is a completely unpossessive person. The others kept coming, hordes descending all day on Caitlin. Ann and Len would sit there and laugh — they had an incredible capacity for laughter. And Caitlin turned to me and said: "What would we do without them?" for they [the Lyes] were absolutely down-to-earth. Though Len could be "way out there," he was anchored.'

thirtyeight madison avenue

There seemed to be a great deal of prosperity in New York in areas such as television and advertising, so Lye was hopeful of supporting himself by freelance work. There had to be a market in New York for new ideas and he always had a number of experiments on the go. In 1952 he wrote to an old friend Marcus Brumwell who worked for a London advertising agency: 'I have been trying to find an easier way to make direct films. I got very excited when I found that muslin dot fabrics made great patterns and I dashed round looking for more and more fabrics'. In addition to these shadowgraph experiments: 'My painted film technique has been developed so I now get a languorous rhapsodic effect to off-set the more syncopated stuff. . . . I'm onto new forms and movements.'[1] He proposed making a series of 'art films' to be sold through galleries. Since the abstract expressionists were now getting good prices for their canvases, why not create a market for artists' films? The galleries could attract customers by having screenings in one room and displaying strips of the films on the wall in another.

Another new idea to which he devoted a large part of 1951 and 1952 was the dancing atom, an animation invention that made linear shapes with dancing electronic dots of light. Lye had a large backlog of other ideas, his favourite being the proposal to break out of the Griffith style of editing by applying animation methods to live action. He was excited to see the popular UPA cartoons adopting increasingly streamlined transitions and he believed it was only a matter of time before films started to take the same short cuts. The possible customers for his idea included advertising agencies and television companies. Lye had tried without success to persuade British television to sponsor experiments during its formative years, and in 1945 he gave up a part-time job as consultant to CBS because the network kept ignoring his suggestions. In the early 1950s he saw the impending arrival of colour television as another chance to introduce a spirit of adventure to the medium. He started a new paper war, sending proposals and theoretical essays in all directions. An impressive array of people involved in broadcasting or classical music wrote letters of support for Lye, but none was prepared to commit money. For years he kept bouncing back with new ideas — another was the use of three-dimensional abstract mobiles, manipulated by hand on small animation stages as an inexpensive accompaniment to music[2] — but after some consideration his proposals were always considered too offbeat. When colour television arrived he was dismayed by the quality of the colour and the banal ways it was used, but he could not find anyone in television to sponsor an alternative. Trying a different tack, Lye approached the State Department to fund a series of direct films to be distributed worldwide as a showcase for American jazz. He presented his case strongly and was invited to Washington DC to show his films, but that screening appears to have brought negotiations to an end.

Finally Lye turned his attention to the advertising industry, which in the 1950s was booming. He began his assault on Madison Avenue by sending out a letter about why agencies needed an experimental artist to freshen up their methods. This gained him several interviews. Alastair Reid recalls: 'On days when Len had to get dressed up and go uptown to see someone in the big world, that was painful for him.'[3] The ritual consisted of carrying all his film cans over his shoulder in a nylon bag on the end of a hickory broomstick handle. Balancing this hefty load he would take the subway uptown. In Lye's words: 'When I got to the 30th or 40th floor of Rockefeller Centre I would put my bag down near the doors of the reception room and go inside and say to the handsome girl, "Hey, will you get someone to take my films to the projection room? My boy has just left them outside".'[4] But despite all Lye's efforts to act the part, advertising executives still came away from meetings with the uneasy feeling there was something weird or subversive about him. What the agencies wanted were high-tech special effects or slick animation in the style of Walt Disney, not hand-painted films which struck them as oddly primitive.

Finally Harry Harding, the executive vice-president of Young and Rubicam, gave Lye a one-day-a-week job advising the agency on how to achieve special effects on television. Lye saw the consultancy as 'money for jam', but 'tried to fig-ure out a way to make it even more jammy'.[5] He persuaded Young and Rubicam to offer his film-making services to their clients. He also created some sample animated advertisements, using the technique of scratching words on film that he had developed for Dylan Thomas. He could make words dance or spin, an anticipation of the video effects now produced more mechanically by computer. Experimenting in this way with phrases such as 'The Magic of Life' and 'Life's Musical Moment' he tried unsuccessfully to get *Life* magazine to sponsor a television ad. He synchronised his sample ads to the drum solo by Buddy Rich from 'The Golden Wedding (La Cinquantaine)' by Woody Herman's Orchestra, one of the most popular jazz records of the period. Another striking experiment was 'Station Prime Time,' a generic promo for a television channel, which he synchronised to African drum music.[6] When Young and Rubicam gained the account for Cheerios, a breakfast cereal consisting of small oatmeal rings, Lye discovered that Cheerios were just the right size to fit on film frames, and by means of the shadowgraph method he could turn a line of them into an animated film sequence. Because no two Cheerios were exactly the same size, they seemed to shiver, an effect he matched up with resonant jazz music. He got very excited about the results — the colours were brilliant and the effect was highly kinetic — but the client simply could not see the point.

Ann Lye recalls that 'Len had two girl-friends at Young and Rubicam, who practically lived in our basement at Washington Street while he worked on commercials'.7 His last commercial was for Apple Jell-O. To avoid paying for expensive music rights Lye had the idea of using an old music-box rendition of 'In the Shade of the Old Apple Tree', a song composed by Ann's grandfather. The metal disc with its perforated notes had been hanging on their wall for years, assumed by many visitors to be a mysterious work of art. When Lye heard the disc play, he decided that the resonance of the music would go well with his direct film. The overall effect was so odd that viewers roared with laughter. Young and Rubicam agreed to test the commercial as a possible novelty item but the results were extremely mixed. After that, both he and the agency were glad to part company.

Lye could not comprehend why the advertising agencies in a city as up-to-the-minute as New York should have so little appetite for taking risks or sponsoring experiments. His old boss at the GPO Film Unit, John Grierson, had been similarly disappointed by New York, which he had hoped to be 'a big wonderful hunting ground'. The city's initial impression of openness was deceptive, as Irving Jacoby has pointed out: 'This is a power town, a tougher town [than London]. The energy is more controlled. It is set in little boxes, and he [Grierson] wasn't quite aware of that. . . . The advertising agency is an old and established barrier. . . . The agency people feel they know best; they are paid a great deal of money to know what . . . will succeed best for the business.'8

But Lye's experiments were not all wasted. In 1953 he made a return to non-commercial or fine art film by selecting some of the many shadowgraph test strips he had created for his colour television campaign and editing them into a three-and-a-half-minute film. After a long search for suitable music he hit upon something that 'fitted like mad' — 'Fox Hunt' by the blues musician Sonny Terry, a sequence of wordless yelps and howls interspersed with harmonica phrases. In Lye's words, 'The fox chase is simulated by repetitive yelps of hounds, the pounding of horses' hooves and, once in a while, by Terry emitting a blood-curdling, high-pitched cry of pain and fright.'9 Knowing that the musician came from the South, Lye assumed that this eerie music evoked a lynch mob hunting a black fugitive. He did not want the film to be interpreted too literally; but for many viewers the music did carry sinister associations, and though some of the images were a riot of colour there were enough black lines to convey an anxious sense of being blocked or enclosed. When Lye returned to the film years later, however, he had a different interpretation — now the images seemed to him more organic, suggesting 'blood cells, nerves, bone and marrow, rib-cage, sinews'.[10]

The shadowgraph method involved a slow process of experimentation in the dark: 'One stretches out a length of film on a bench; lays a perforated strip of metal over the unexposed film (still in the dark); then a coloured sheet of gelatine is spread over both and the film is quickly exposed by the on-off switch. When developed the strip of film shows up as a length of coloured patterned footage. If one shifts the perforated (dots, triangles, etc.) strip of metal on the exposed film and changes the coloured gel, one will get a three-colour complex formal pattern.'[11] In addition to metal stencils Lye used thin saw blades, spoons, wooden dowels, spiral wires, string, ribbons, mosquito netting, muslin and many other fabrics — an extraordinary range of templates. He learned to control his kinetic effects precisely: 'You twist a ribbon and that produces a turning effect. Working in the dark you get into a very inventive mood. Your fingers arrange shapes across this strip of film which will unreel whatever energy you can put into it.'[12] This was Lye's first 16 mm film, and he built most of it up from strips 16–40 frames long. The wide range of abstract images, based on hundreds of hours of experiment, was a startling expansion of the range of what direct film-making could do. The images had a complex sense of space because layers were superimposed, with the illusion of depth suddenly opening up as though one were looking at a landscape from the air, then concentrating back to a flat surface. Maintaining the parallels between Lye's film-making and the latest developments in American painting, *Color Cry* was in some respects reminiscent of the large abstract paintings by artists such as Barnett Newman, Morris Louis or Kenneth Noland. But the film added a physical sense of movement to such images and the music added a strong dimension of feeling.

Lye described *Color Cry* as a production by the Direct Film Company, a company that consisted of two people — himself and Ann. The film was shown informally to groups of friends. Though experimental film-making in the United States did develop vigorously after the war, it began on a very small scale with few screening venues.[13] One of the catalysts for film-making as for painting was the arrival of experienced artists from Europe such as Oskar Fischinger, Hans Richter and Lye. Lye's contacts in New York included film-makers such as Maya Deren, Arnold Eagle, and Francis Lee. Lee, who had first seen Lye's films around 1940 when Norman McLaren had screened them in New York at the apartment of Marie Mencken and Willard Maas, remembers his first meetings with Lye in 1945 as a great turning-point because 'At that time I was completely alone — I didn't know a soul who was making my sort of independent or avant-garde film'.[14] Another artist who valued Lye's technical advice was Ian Hugo who turned to film-making after working as an engraver with Stanley William Hayter. In 1952 Len contributed 'abstract colour effects' to Hugo's *Bells of Atlantis*, a nine-minute dreamlike colour film based on the opening pages of Anaïs Nin's *The House of Incest*. Nin, who was married to Hugo, appeared in the film and read passages from her book on the soundtrack. Some of the imagery of the film suggested a Dali-esque or literary surrealism that Lye had never felt comfortable with, but he liked the underwater theme and Hugo's sensuous approach to movement. The impact was heightened by Bebe and Louis Barron's remarkable soundtrack, an early form of electronic music. Lye's contributions to the film included the title sequence, 'the glass globe over the introductory scene', and the technique of super-imposition used towards the end to create the illusion that Nin was ascending.[15] The effects looked like expensive laboratory work but were actually made in the camera. Hugo commented: 'Len was most generous in the help he gave me, and which I am sure contributed to the testimonial which Abel Gance (of *Napoleon*) expressed after he saw *Bells of Atlantis*.' The film was less kindly received by the New York reviewer Dwight Macdonald who described it in *Esquire* as 'a paradigm of corny avantgardism'.[16]

During this period there was a strong surrealist influence on American film-making, as there was on American painting. One of its sources was *Dreams That Money Can Buy*, a film made by Hans Richter in New York in 1947. Lye turned down an invitation to participate in the film because he considered its approach too literary, but he remained friends with Richter whom he had known since Eisenstein's film-making workshop in 1929. In 1953 when Herman G. Weinberg asked Richter in an interview for *Cinedrama* magazine 'which of the American experimenters he actually liked best, he replied without hesitation: "Len Lye"'.[17] Richter was the director of the Institute of Film Techniques at the City College of New York, a film-making school whose students would later play an important part in the 1960s 'underground film' movement. Richter introduced Lye to teaching by asking him to take a weekly night class. Lye kept it up for two terms but then 'got fed up because I had to spend almost all the time checking the equipment out of the safe or back into the safe!'[18] Later — in 1956–57 — he taught Saturday morning classes at Columbia University,[19] and over the years he helped and advised many young film-makers who approached him on an individual basis.

thirtynine rhythm

In 1953 Cecile Starr, a former *March of Time* employee, became involved in programming for an early morning CBS television show hosted by Will Rogers Jr. Impressed by Norman McLaren's *Neighbours* the producers asked Starr to find other unusual short films. She was able to offer Lye $300 to make a film specially for the programme, selecting footage from the travel film collection of the National Film Board of Canada and editing it to 'Autumn Leaves' (a popular song of the day). Starr, a lifetime supporter of experimental film-making, was hopeful that 'this rather mundane assignment' could lead to other jobs for Lye. As she recalls: 'He came up to our office to meet with a group of my employer's staff — men who knew very little about the kind of films he had made. . . . Len was snorting and tearing at the bit, to try to get these guys interested in the jazz cut-out films he was working on at that time. I knew the staff people well enough to realize that they couldn't imagine what they were doing with "Autumn Leaves", and they definitely weren't ready for Len's next step. When we recessed at one point I took him aside and told him that everything would fall through if he didn't stick to the one subject before us. . . . He agreed, but when the meeting took up again, he really couldn't keep quiet. Finally, we agreed that I would do all the talking . . . until he had some sort of film in hand that looked like the thing he had been commissioned to do. Well, he finished it, and it did go to air, and was reasonably well received — but by that time, I was on my way out of CBS-TV.' The producers had decided to stop looking for 'original ideas' and to concentrate on a talk-show format.[1]

As William Baldwin recalls, 'Len was never downcast for more than 50 seconds. He was a source of great comfort and joy to all his friends. If you got depressed you went and hung around with Len for a while and it cheered you up. He always had some non-hurting but tough-minded statement about your problem. Ann Lye put it very nicely: "Len's greatest creation was himself", and it was.'[2] During the 1950s the Direct Film Company kept a wide range of experiments on the go. If a potential sponsor failed to respond, it made no difference to Lye's own enthusiasm, except on rare, unpredictable occasions when he would have an intense burst of anger, anxiety or depression. To everyone's relief such black moments passed rapidly. But on one such occasion, 4 October 1955, Lye was sufficiently depressed to write a suicide note: 'Ann Zeiss is to get on without me and *not* to be influenced except to be twice as happy. . . . Until lately I felt I could always in some way adapt my talents . . . to getting bread and butter for me [and] my kids and responsibilities like Jane Lye who used to stake me, and repaying Ann Lye who is staking me now. I have now come to hate being staked.' He also felt frustrated in his work: 'My work is of no value because it has never been resolved.' He would 'die by disappearing in mid-sea somehow'. Later he scribbled across the letter, 'This is all postponed because Ann would finish her life too and that's silly.'[3] He hid the letter away in a personal file and never told her about it.

Restored to his normal good spirits, Lye began a productive collaboration with the composer Henry Brant who lived nearby in Horatio Street. Brant admired Lye for his spirit of total independence: 'It didn't seem to him to matter what anybody thought or how the world went, he remained good-humoured about it. It was possible to talk to him on any subject and get a good-humoured comment. He had very pronounced opinions but nothing that sounded like a personal bias so that made his company very enjoyable.'[4] Like Lye, Brant was an artist that the critics found hard to label because he was so versatile and so independent. In the 1930s and '40s he had composed and conducted for radio, ballet, jazz groups, and films (including music for more than 50 documentaries), using highly original combinations of instruments.[5] Today he is best known as a pioneer of spatial or site-specific music, in which the positioning of the performers around the hall is an integral part of the composition. As soon as Brant had seen Lye's direct films he proposed a collaboration. They decided not to attempt to synchronise their work closely but to allow the images and the music to proceed side by side, separate but similar in spirit. For this project Lye decided to use some 'languorous rhapsodic' imagery, hand-painted footage produced by lacquer paint and felt-tip marker pens (a new product that delighted him). He had created complex patterns of dots in wet dye by using a rubber pad with bristles, the kind of pad found next to cash registers from which customers picked up change. His washes, blobs, and bands of colour were reminiscent of the painterly styles of abstraction being created by contemporary artists such as Sam Francis, Philip Guston, and Helen Frankenthaler.

Lye made a 16-minute compilation of his pulsating and vibrating images[6] and Brant wrote the six-part suite 'All Souls' Carnival', incorporating some ideas from earlier ballets. Scored for piano, flute, violin, cello and accordion, the music was energised by a colourful use of instruments, quick changes of tempo, and a wry sense of humour. There were affinities with Stravinsky's *The Soldier's Tale* or the chamber music of Les Six, but Brant's carnivalesque music had a distinctive life of its own. He had developed this style during the Depression years because it was so difficult to get performances of experimental work: 'I wrote pieces that were satirical or caricatures, because that was a middle-ground I could get away with. I wrote ballet scores, or concert music that sounded like ballet scores, using satires on other music and ideas of that kind.' Brant decided that 'All Souls' Carnival' should be played live when combined with the film because 'Len's work was so direct with the actual paint on the film — so I wanted the organic sound of acoustic music'. Lye liked this idea because he had collaborated in a similar way with jazz groups at the Five Spot, a run-down Bowery saloon at 5 Cooper Square which in 1955 had become a centre for new jazz and a meeting place for vanguard artists and poets.[7] His friend Alan Morrison had also arranged for Lye to provide 'a light show' for a concert by Count Basie's band, which at the time had seemed a very original event.[8] Lye's other mixed media experiments had included 'projecting colour abstract films over a large black-and-white blow-up of Charlie Parker playing his music, trying out abstracts as accompaniment to vocalised poetry, and projecting a scene on the powdered belly of a belly dancer'.[9]

The Brant–Lye premiere took place at the Carnegie Recital Hall on 3 March 1957 in a programme that included music by Igor Stravinsky and Darius Milhaud. The performers included members of the Beaux Arts String Quartet. The lights were turned off and Lye's film was back-projected on to a highly luminous screen behind the musicians. The *New York Herald Tribune* reported that 'the film was quite ravishing, its iridescent shapes and forms aburst with vivid colours; and no less vivid were the sonorities conjured up by Mr. Brant to assist the images as they danced by'.[10] The *New York Times* observed that the music and the film 'were not indissolubly synchronized' but in combination 'they made an effect which, by turns, was charming, poignant, playful and often faintly mocking'.[11] Brant recalls that his four-year-old daughter was delighted by the colour and movement of the film, and after the concert her way of describing the images to her mother was to make vigorous Lye-type gestures with her arms. The work had at least one other performance, at Bennington College in Vermont, where the composer was teaching.

Around June 1956 Lye had obtained some commercial work. On one of his occasional visits to the agencies with his khaki bag of films he had encountered a producer with a genuine interest in experimental films — James Manilla of McCann-Erickson. Manilla had been hired by the agency to provide approximately five minutes of film footage every week for the Chrysler Corporation, which had a one-hour television programme in prime time featuring suspense dramas and musical shows.[12] Manilla's films were essentially advertisements for Chrysler cars, but he made them fresh and varied by using independent directors including animators and model makers. His interest was caught not only by Lye's work but also by his manner: 'He was an odd-looking duck and he did nothing to minimise his oddity. From his accent I thought he was some strange form of Britisher.' He invited Lye to come up with an idea for 'an experimental something', one or two minutes long. The budget was $2000 ($1000 up front and the other $1000 on delivery). Lye selected a half-hour film directed by Tom Marker for Chrysler's in-house film unit, which showed the making of a car from start to finish, and asked for the out-takes. Manilla managed to obtain approximately one-and-a-half hours of black-and-white footage consisting of alternative shots or unused scenes. Lye narrowed this down to shots with 'a good, definite, contrasty quality',[13] then sampled some favourite recordings of traditional African tribal drumming and chanting,[14] and made up a one-minute soundtrack. He then began editing the footage to match. His idea was to reduce the process of assembling the car to a minute not by speeding up the footage but by a series of jump-cuts. The editing was a huge challenge because he was working with shots only a few frames long and had to cut the original footage (he could not afford to make a copy). He succeeded in creating some brilliant synchronisation between the images and the syncopated drumming, for example when a tire bounced down the conveyor belt, or a drill-like machine twitched rhythmically. Although the film had a playful sense of humour it never poked fun at the workmen. Lye later described his film as 'an attempt to kinetically convey the vitality and romanticism of efficient workers in their everyday jobs'. In this respect the film was a sequel to *Trade Tattoo* in which he had re-edited documentary footage of the workplace. He was also drawing on many years of editing experimentation in his search for alternatives to Griffith.

At the beginning and end of the film Lye showed the exterior of the Chrysler plant, punching holes through the image to add impact. Alastair Reid remembers trying to help Lye to come up with a clever title but their suggestions were far too colourful. Lye's favourite was 'Jesus Chrysler'. In the end he simply scratched 'Rhythm' with a diamond stylus.[15] When the film was delivered to the agency James Manilla was very pleased: 'Beautiful jump cuts. It was everything the title said it was, the rhythm of the Chrysler Corporation. But when I showed it to the directors of the agency they were so shocked they pleaded with me not to take it any further. They refused to show it to the Chrysler Corporation. But they didn't castigate me for having commissioned it because generally I was doing well in my job. "If Manilla wants to do some damnfool thing like this, well, I guess we can indulge him" — that was their attitude. You know, in this business you can ruin your career by doing something very good that no one wants.' They were mainly troubled by the use of African tribal music, but were also worried about a brief shot of a black worker on the assembly line winking at the camera which seemed out of keeping with the serious business of making Chrysler cars.

Lye's style of rapid jump-cutting was not as familiar then as it is today. Manilla was so impressed that he entered *Rhythm* in the 1957 New York Art Directors Festival competition for the year's best television commercial.[16] Lye received an unexpected telephone call informing him that *Rhythm* was one of the 25 finalists out of a field of 850 entries. Then there was an excited call to let him know his commercial had won first prize so that he could expect Madison Avenue to be beating a path to his door. Unfortunately the head of the Festival was an art director from McCann-Erickson, 'a painfully honest Irishman' (as Manilla put it), who knew that this commercial had never been broadcast and therefore disqualified it. When the awards were given out, there was no mention of *Rhythm*.

A year later *Rhythm* won a prize at a European film festival.[17] Manilla recalls: 'One day Len phoned me up and said, "Jim, we won!" He said "we" not "I". Most people wouldn't even have called me, but Len said: "I've got a medal and we should share it — you can have it for six months and I'll have it for six months." Nobody else in the film business would have done a thing like that — the attitude is, "I'm all right Jack, fuck you!"' When the Chrysler Corporation heard through their newspaper clipping service that one of their films had won a prize they got in touch with Manilla to ask what was happening. When he showed the film to them they were interested in using it but in the end rejected the idea because the car in the film was no longer their current model.

Although screenings of *Rhythm* have been few and far between, the film has made a deep impression on film-makers and critics. In an interview with Peter Kubelka in *Film Culture* Jonas Mekas asked: 'Have you seen Len Lye's fifty-second automobile commercial? Nothing happens there . . . except that it's filled with some kind of secret action of cinema.'[18] Film-maker Francis Lee remembered *Rhythm* as 'very advanced for its time, so far ahead it could not be shown on the air'.[19] Editor Paul Barnes has spoken of it as a 'tour de force' of editing — 'Just taking that scrap film and turning it into this unbelievably vital one minute film!'[20] And P. Adams Sitney writes: 'Although his reputation has been sustained by the invention of direct painting on film, Lye deserves equal credit as one of the great masters of montage.'[21]

forty free radicals

The last-minute disqualification of *Rhythm* fuelled Lye's desire to 'chuck up [Madison] Avenue and go straight',[1] to make the best films he could rather than pander to 'any cake, soap or tooth-paste-seller'.[2] The opportunity to concentrate his energies on art would be like 'swimming over to the sunny, clear, sparse side of the river'.[3] Just at this moment (mid-1957) he received a letter inviting him to submit a film to an International Experimental Film Competition in Belgium. The World's Fair was to be held in Brussels in 1958, and the Belgians had decided to give experimental film a high profile — an important decision for a genre that was still marginalised even by the world's leading film festivals. Lye's old friend Cavalcanti persuaded the organisers to send him an invitation. The idea of submitting a film was attractive to him because there was a 'new scratchy figure of motion' over which he had been 'salivating holy water'.[4] But could he afford to spend months on a high-risk project on the remote chance of winning a prize? Ann Lye knew that Lye was uneasy about being 'staked', but she was also concerned about his state of mind as a frustrated artist. In her words: 'I was crazy about the proposed film and I really made him do it.' She said to him: 'I'll work overtime at real-estate and you just make the film. But look, the money is going to be spent only on that and nothing else.'[5]

And so for eight months Lye scratched strips of film. The idea went back to his first film job in Sydney in the early 1920s, and during the 1930s he had included scratched as well as painted sequences in films such as *Swinging the Lambeth Walk*. In the film business at large, accidental scratches were a fact of life, but film-makers and projectionists were always horrified to see them. A few film-makers had made conscious use of scratching on film but usually only as a special effect. One problem with the process was the difficulty of controlling it. In the 1950s Lye added to the challenge by shifting to the 16 mm film format, but his favourite tools were better suited to the smaller size and he had refined his hand and eye through decades of doodling and film-painting. A burst of experiment in 1953 had given him tantalising glimpses of a new type of imagery which inspired him to 'mess around' for four or five months with a film he called 'Anions'. He had finally put this aside because 'I could not make a "jump" image that matched up with the ephemeral image-feeling I felt at the back of my skull'.[6] He had included some scratched titles and linear designs in his commercial films of the 1950s, but it remained to be seen whether this method was strong enough to sustain a complete film.

He began by seeking advice from Francis Lee. In Lee's words: 'I'd never have dreamed of giving such a master artistic advice, but I could tell him the best labs and the best places to get raw stock. I was a past master at getting film cheap — scrounging, begging, borrowing, stealing and God knows what — but I managed to get it and I made films!'[7] He helped Lye obtain samples of black leader (black film without images) and black exposed film on various stocks. The final choice was Du Pont leader because the black emulsion peeled away cleanly. Then Lye went to work full-time, scratching his way through thousands of feet of film. In his words: 'You stick down the sides [of the film] with Scotch Tape. You spit on or dampen the celluloid with a sponge. Now the question is register [but] you've got sprocket holes to guide you. When you hold the needle you dig it in through the black emulsion into the film and then start doing pictographic signatures.'[8] And: 'My wife said one day when passing me working at my bench, "Len, I didn't know you were spastic." She saw me crouched over a piece of film with my etching needle stuck in it. I wriggled my whole body to get a compressed feeling into my shoulders — trying to get a get a pent-up feeling of precision into the fingers, and with a sudden jump I pulled the needle through the celluloid and completed my design. So, I called to Ann on her way back, "Hey, I'm not spastic; but wait till you see these things." On film they are very controlled, yet very kinetic.'[9]

It took a great deal of concentration to draw on such a small scale vigorously without tearing the film. As Norman McLaren later said of cameraless animation in general: 'The artist will find that the small scale on which he is working will force him to simplify all his shapes. . . . This is a real advantage and it should be encouraged. It will force him to make his point primarily by means of the movement, action and gesture itself.'[10] As Lye held the scriber with both hands he could not see the separate frames distinctly, and so when he scratched his images down a strip of film he was spacing them largely by instinct. (This was Lye practising Zen in the art of animation, so to speak, like the Zen archer who closed his eyes before shooting.) The film-maker Hilary Harris watched Lye at work: 'I admired the way he really got into it, he gave himself over to the process completely. When I saw the results I was amazed at what could be done with scratch film. Len had developed a kinetic use of his hands. It reminded me of when I was editing film, I'd get into a similar rhythm of work. But his hands had developed such a keen rhythm there was a real coherence in the way things progressed from frame to frame. His films are outstanding in terms of kinetic

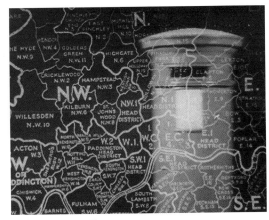

Frames from the film *N. or N.W.* (1937). Evelyn Corbett and Dwight Goodwin play the two lovers trying to communicate by letter. The two bottom frames are from a sequence using animation methods to streamline the process of the young woman getting dressed. This sequence had to be dropped because the GPO Film Unit considered it too experimental. COURTESY LEN LYE FOUNDATION

These untitled woodcuts by Lye were published by the Surrealist magazine *London Bulletin* in 1940.
COURTESY LEN LYE FOUNDATION

Left and below: Lye at work during the war years directing for the March of Time.
COURTESY LEN LYE FOUNDATION

Right: The Herrick family are having a party — a frame from *Work Party* (1942), a documentary Lye directed for Realist Films which anticipated 'cinéma vérité' methods of hand-held camerawork. COURTESY IMPERIAL WAR MUSEUM

Above: Lye in his office at the March of Time, circa 1945. On the left is a new logo he designed for the series. COURTESY LEN LYE FOUNDATION

Right: Socialising with March of Time staff in New York. The man on the left in a bow tie is Richard de Rochemont. COURTESY LEN LYE FOUNDATION

Above: Lye with his new wife Ann, circa 1948. The photo on the right, taken by Ann's daughter Jane, shows them outside their new home, 739 Washington Street in the West Village. COURTESY JANE HINDLE BAMBERG

Left: The Lyes with their friend Ruth Richards (centre) at a Harlem jazz club. COURTESY LEN LYE FOUNDATION

Previous page: Lye in New York in 1946, making spiral shapes out of wire. In the 1960s he was delighted to learn that the DNA 'double helix' resembled the spiral patterns he had always been fond of making and drawing and that he had observed in indigenous forms of art (such as the Samoan tapa cloth hanging behind him on the wall). PHOTO WILLIAM VANDIVERT. COURTESY LEN LYE FOUNDATION

Top: Lye christening an old beach house they rented at Martha's Vineyard in the early 1950s. COURTESY LEN LYE FOUNDATION

Above: 'Things and Stuff?', the Lyes' second-hand shop at Martha's Vineyard. COURTESY LEN LYE FOUNDATION

Left: Len and Ann visit a photo booth at Coney Island in the early 1950s. (Their caption: 'I'm making a love potion. See, it works!') COURTESY LEN LYE FOUNDATION

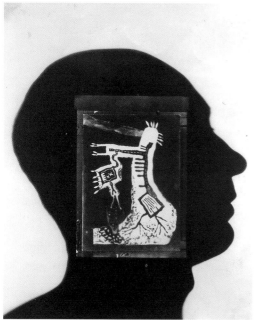
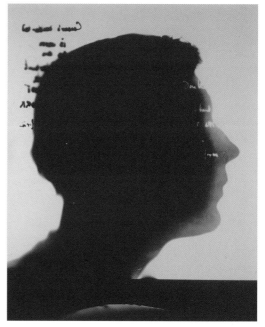

Photograms, 1947. *Top row:* the architect Le Corbusier and the artist Georgia O'Keeffe (including a pair of deer antlers O'Keeffe had given the Lyes). *Bottom row:* Lye's 'Self Portrait' (incorporating his 1930 photogram 'Self Planting at Night') and the poet W. H. Auden (including lines from one of his poems printed in reverse).

integrity and what I call aliveness.'¹¹ Lye produced his best results when he entered a kind of rhythmic trance.¹²

Not only Lye's imagery but his film-making process were strongly reminiscent of the 'action painting' or abstract expressionism of artists such as Jackson Pollock, with their emphasis on intuition, physicality, gesture, and the basic energies of the medium. Making scratches that penetrated the black emulsion so that the light of the projector flashed through the clear celluloid base, Lye created effects as dramatic as lightning in the night sky. He enjoyed reducing the film medium to its most basic elements — light in darkness. The thousands of years that separated modern technology from the scratching of designs on cave walls fell away. Perhaps he was also reminded of nights at Cape Campbell watching the great lighthouse flashing out its signal. He would begin each session with a particular figure of motion in mind — the feeling of a table rocking, for example¹³ — which he would draw for hours, checking the results with a jeweller's eyepiece or through the projector. 'Usually when you look at it you're disappointed. You draw a bit, then go to sleep, then draw a bit more.'¹⁴ When he liked something he would keep trying to control and refine it further. But he was also open to chance, quick to seize on interesting accidents. The best bits were made into loops and run through the projector over and over. Gradually the strips and loops of film accumulated, hung all over the walls. Now music was needed to accompany his 'little zig-zags of electricity',¹⁵ music with a similar physical energy. 'I came across an absolutely marvellous field tape of the Bagirmi tribe. It had the same kind of feeling to it, the same resonance, the same attack.'¹⁶ Its singing and drumming could 'rattle the marbles in your skull'. Lye was delighted to learn later that this African music was part of a tribal homage to Yoruba, the god of thunder — an ideal accompaniment to lightning. As usual Lye had the music printed as an optical sound-track since it helped him to understand the structure. The sound-track patterns would occasionally give him ideas for images – 'I like this because it does a lot of busy things here, then it goes straight along for a while, then it extends out' – but he would never copy a pattern directly, preferring to use it as 'a little seed in the brain for germination.'¹⁷

The finished film ran for five minutes, made up of hundreds of pieces about a second in length together with a few longer sequences. The imagery of the film has many connections with Lye's earlier paintings, drawings, and doodles – with the repertoire of zigzags, asterisks, dots, dashes, and other 'energy signs' he shared in some respects with Joan Miró. But here these signs were set in motion. An asterisk, for example, struggled to stay in place then split in two like a couple separating. Broad banner-like scratches made a particularly graceful sequence as though rippling in the wind. The film had a very fluid sense of space — '3, 2½ or 2D', as he put it.[18] Though the images were basically abstract they occasionally suggested figures or letters. When some random frame enlargements were made, the Lyes were delighted to see the initials of their names — 'L' and 'A' — not only visible but linked together! In trying to think of a title Lye had felt from the start that the imagery symbolised some kinetic aspect of energy.[19] He was excited by a story in the *New York Times* science section about free radicals — atoms or molecules that are highly reactive and unstable because they contain an unpaired electron. He was not interested in the question whether free radicals had positive or negative effects but in the fact that they were fundamental particles of matter present in all chemical change. And they were like a compressed spring ready for release.[20] *Free Radicals* was thus the perfect name for his film in a scientific (not to mention political) sense. He scratched the title on to black leader, using the method of twisting letters he had developed for the Dylan Thomas poetry film. With a dexterity refined by months of practice he was able to give the letters a tense vibration.

He began to think that his imagery would be even more dramatic on 35 mm film, with some controlled use of colour. This involved additional cost, but Lye was hopeful that a sponsor would respond to the strength and novelty of his film. He applied to Kodak, Bell and Howell, Du Pont, and other companies without success. He also approached the television networks. To improve his chances he enlisted the aid of William C. Seitz, a friendly curator at the Museum of Modern Art. Seitz described the film to Alfred H. Barr Jr, a top man at the Museum, and asked him to recommend it to a chief executive he knew at CBS. When Barr heard the title *Free Radicals* he said to Seitz, 'That's a hell of a film for me to go to a millionaire with!'[21] When no money was forthcoming for colour or 35 mm, Lye concentrated on getting the best possible 16 mm black-and-white print. What he wanted was a pure black background so that the images appeared to be floating in space, and at the same time some grey tones within the scratches to add a subtle hint of three dimensions. The images were meant to be as 'scratchy' as his earlier films had been 'painterly'. No processing lab had ever seen a film like this before and Lye had to try a number of companies to find what he wanted. The amount of money and time involved kept on growing, but Ann continued to give full support.

Lye despatched *Free Radicals* together with *Rhythm* to the competition in Brussels; they were among the 400 entries received, which represented almost all the well-known experimental film-makers in the world, together with a number of newcomers. The jury that met in May was a remarkable group — Man Ray, John Grierson, Norman McLaren, the famous animator Alexander Alexeiff, and the composer Edgard Varèse whose *Poème Electronique* (a pioneer work of electronic music) was another high point of the World's Fair. As Grierson remarked a few months later on television: 'A lot of years have gone by [since the days of the GPO Film Unit] and Len Lye has been wandering the world. You can imagine then what a delight it was for me to find him turn up all over again at the Brussels Experimental Film Festival this year — young in spirit and experimental as ever.'[22] The Grand Prix was awarded to Polish film-makers Walerian Borowszyk and Jan Lenica for *Dom*, a film of animated objects and extraordinary optical effects. The Second Prize (donated by the Belgian firm SIBIS) went to *Free Radicals*. The Lyes were woken at 3 a.m. in New York by a phone call: 'You've just won $5000.'[23]

In the world of experimental films the choice was widely endorsed. One reviewer after another used the word 'masterpiece'. For example John Adams of *Film Quarterly* saw *Free Radicals* as Lye's 'most austere, direct, simple, and successful' work, a demonstration of the power of animation in its purest form: 'It is a rare accomplishment in a genre so essentially amorphous and beset by the trivial. If proof had ever been needed that Lye, the pioneer in this field, is the real — and for some the only — master, here it is.'[24] The title of the film inspired some ingenious interpretations such as Parker Tyler's comment that it 'seems a morally motivated pun on the Marxist dialectic as formulated in montage by Eisenstein'.[25] In a discussion of abstract films Jonas Mekas drew a useful contrast between Lye's approach and that of film-makers with a more intellectual orientation: '*Free Radicals*, though highly formal and pure, is charged with emotion. The drawings and scratches have a spontaneous quality of powerful impact upon the viewer.'[26]

Lye's abstract imagery, driven along by the drum music, always maintains a strong sense of physical intensity. Lines stretch, spin, wriggle, and sway, constantly reminding us of the human body in movement. Who can sit still while watching such a dynamic film? The music is directly related to his old interest in African tribal dance, and the most frequent association in this film is dancing, but its figures of motion are sufficiently abstract to invite other analogies — such as the glide and spin of a skater, the physical act of handwriting, the inner workings of the body (like the urgent patterns of an electrocardiograph), flashes of lightning in the night sky, or the collision of atomic particles. Such analogies do not contradict one another, for throughout his career Lye liked to interrelate different forms of energy. *Free Radicals* is a dance of natural energies. Lye himself stressed the film's carnivalesque spirit by adding these comments at the beginning: 'Brancusi said: "Do not look for obscure formulae or mystery, it is pure joy that I bring you." I say: "Film is advanced art, not science, education, nor box office . . . but utopia."'[27]

fortyone going on strike

The 3 a.m. phone call from Brussels joined what Lye called his 'lifetime collection of happy moments' and vindicated his wife's struggle to keep him on the job. But the elation did not last long because the $5000 prize money did little more than cover the lab bills and other costs of making *Free Radicals*. The key question was whether Lye could continue to make such films. His initial hopes were high because in 1935 the prestige of the medal he had won in Brussels had certainly helped to attract sponsors in London. But when he offered *Free Radicals* as a short to New York art cinemas such as the Sutton and the Paris, they were not interested at any price.[1] The only taker was Amos Vogel's Cinema 16 series which gave unfailing support to the avant-garde but offered only $50 for five screenings. Lye then sent applications for film grants to various foundations including the Guggenheim, but had no success.

His natural exuberance had been worn down by the frustrations of recent years. He felt that the battle to open up some space for art in film and television had virtually been lost. The 1950s were a conservative time for Hollywood and the initial promise of television had disappeared in a flood of advertising and cheap entertainment. When James Breslin interviewed him about his Belgian prize in the *Village Voice* (28 May 1958), he used the opportunity to speak out on behalf of experimental film-making and the fact that it faced greater obstacles than other arts because the medium was expensive and film culture was almost entirely commercial: 'The two great film industries, television and movies, are too busy gearing their programs to mass taste to concern themselves with financing the screen artist.' Lye added a personal note: 'My best films will never be made.'

He launched a campaign of letters to prominent people challenging the lack of public support for experimental film making. He started with President Eisenhower, which at least brought him a reply from the President's assistant. He extended his campaign to the Under Secretary of State and a number of other officials associated with the USIA (US Information Agency) and cultural exchange programmes. At this time a substantial amount of money was being spent by government agencies on programmes of American films as a cultural weapon in the cold war. Although these agencies supported experimental work in some areas such as painting, their interest in films was limited to Hollywood features and documentaries. Lye argued that experimental film-making was a form of advanced research, a source of new techniques vital to a healthy film industry. In 1957 the success of the Russian space satellite programme had created an uproar in the United States about the need for more to be spent on research. Lye emphasised the fact that the Communist countries, along with other parts of Europe and Canada, gave strong support to film as an art. For example, *Dom*, the Polish film which had won first prize at Brussels, had received massive state support, as had *The Cranes are Flying*, the Russian film that had won first prize at the last Cannes Film Festival. Lye liked to end his letters with the provocative comment that, since he had found it so difficult to fund experimental films in the United States, he was now planning to apply to the Iron Curtain countries. Although he presented a strong argument, his letters were invariably too long and too theoretical for the busy executives who received them. He spoke not of specific USIA programmes but of large principles. His letters did, however, include vivid comments on the problems of film-making, for example: 'The poet with his old envelope, the painter with his pencil, the musician with his notation can record the germ of his creative conception while he is hot. But the experimental film maker can only experiment in film itself.'[2] That was the nub of the problem for Lye, that he was simply not able to get on with his work. He was dependent on a medium so costly that it demanded both compromise and business expertise, neither of which came easily to him.

His campaign and his thinking on the subject culminated in the 1959 essay 'Is Film Art?', published in *Film Culture* in 1963, which announced: 'As an experimental film maker I have gone on strike. . . . I will no more chase after sponsorship for fine art film.'[3] His own situation occupied only a few lines of the essay — the rest of it was a brilliant overview of the state of experimental film-making. Despite all its prestige and popularity the medium of film remained 'the Cinderella of the fine arts' still 'waiting for her glass slipper in order to enthral with her unique kinetic beauty'. Even the best films tended to remain at the level of 'good folklore fun', and the artistic shaping of movement was crowded out by 'roller-coaster sensations.' The essay evoked the untapped potential of film by describing the kinetic or kinaesthetic effects that had been achieved even within static forms of the visual arts: 'A Hiroshige woodcut makes us aware of the power and weight of a curled mighty wave about to break; . . . we respond to the taut spatial relationships of a Cézanne painting; we may almost quiver to the ecstatic stillness of a Zurbaran stilllife.'[4] The sense of movement had been further developed in art by Futurists, Dadaists, and action painters, and in literature by writers such as Hopkins, Rimbaud, Stein, Cummings, and Thomas. Lye made it clear in this essay that a kinetic artist could work in other media besides film, which implied that he was personally considering a change.

This period was the first time his friend Alastair Reid had ever seen him succumb to frustration: 'Len really felt let down. He'd got his badge as a film maker and yet nobody would give him the money he needed to make films.'[5] The conflict was intensified by the ability he had developed to theorise any situation — he saw big principles at stake and was ready to speak his mind. Lye's prickly manner led to him being stereotyped by advertising agencies as a temperamental artist.[6] The Museum of Modern Art also saw him as difficult because when it wanted a print of *Free Radicals* Lye set the 'unrealistic' price of $4000 as though they were buying a painting. He was grateful for the Museum's interest in his work over the years but angry about never having received any money from its distribution of his earlier films. (Any revenue for those films was claimed by the GPO.)[7]

During this 'strike' period, Lye was among the 20 New York film-makers on stage for a disastrous Cinema 16 event to celebrate the winners of Creative Film Awards. In reply to the question: 'For what audience are experimental films made?' he gave the cryptic reply: 'None.' No one challenged this comment and the subject was dropped.[8] The audience was equally cold to the other 19 film makers and after a restless half hour they started shouting that they wanted to see films. According to the report by Jonas Mekas in the *Village Voice*: 'Len lifted his hand, ready to slap the audience. "I hate you," he said, and left the stage. Willard Maas followed, and soon after so did the others. War was declared.'[9] As soon as Lye read Mekas's account he wrote a letter to the editor to make what he regarded as an important correction: 'No one on God's earth has ever heard me say I "hate" anything or anybody. . . . One thought, though: If anyone tries to really put me down I might get irritated and tell them to go to hell. This happened. . . . I didn't want to be on stage in the first place. And *was* I right. I got off the stage and stood by the pit in front of the audience and really shouted, "Now you see why I said I don't make films for any audience. Audiences can go to hell!" Then, in the middle of the audience I found my moral support, my wife. Joining her I soon merged in with them.'[10] Soon after this, Amos Vogel of Cinema 16 referred in the *Village Voice* to Lye's 'well known bitterness'. Lye replied that 'resentment' was a more accurate word than 'bitterness'. What he resented was the general state of the film culture — 'the critics; the Museum of Modern Art (dear hearts in the right but inadequate place); foundations; the twatty Hollywood Academy of Fine Arts; the pratty television spokesmen — the whole shooting match of dimness concerning what fine art film making is all about'.[11]

When Stan Brakhage first met him in 1958 Lye was pushing his 'free radical' attitude to the limit. The New Jersey company On Film Inc. was working on a commission for the Pittsburgh Bicentennial. In Brakhage's wry account: 'I was director of a film to try to show how Pittsburgh is beautiful. Not in that sense of the great films of the 1930s — the beauty of its smoke and so on — but the clean-up of the city. And that was such a desperate circumstance that they turned it over to me, the arty one in the company, and they told me to hire whomever would be necessary to [beautify] this union footage of Pittsburgh, which did not look at all beautiful. . . . So I hired Stan VanDerBeek and Len Lye and Weegee to come up to Princeton, New Jersey, and help beautify Pittsburgh. And Len Lye was very grumpy about this. . . . He knew that all they were after was his name . . . and some tricks, and he [made it] very clear at the table, at the board meeting, that the techniques he used through the Grierson GPO were so expensive that they couldn't afford it. Then he explained to them *in detail* how expensive they were and how they couldn't afford it. And therefore that was his only contribution to this miserable film.'[12]

But some film commissions proceeded more smoothly. Lye's strike was never total — basically what it meant was that he no longer put any effort into chasing film jobs or maintaining his public persona as a film-maker. He still experimented with the medium when he felt like it and he was sometimes in the mood to accept a job that came his way. In 1958–59 he contributed a sequence to *The Sign of Plexiglass*, a promotional film made by Dan Klugherz for the Rohm and Hass Company. Plexiglass was a tough new form of plastic well suited to sign-making, and Klugherz, a New York director knowledgeable about the arts, decided that an abstract sequence by Lye could give it some up-to-the-minute excitement. In his words: 'When we first met it seemed unlikely that we could work together. Len felt that advertising was tawdry and they didn't respect his work. But in any human situation he would respond to the individual and forget his prejudices.'[13] Lye agreed to make a sequence in which abstract pieces of coloured plexiglass would fly around, occasionally arranging themselves to spell words. When he ordered numerous pieces of plexiglass to be cut Lye 'was very particular, a perfectionist'. Working with the cameraman Ken Snelson (himself a sculptor), Lye created a brilliant animation sequence to the rhythm of 'Opus de Jazz,' elegant modern jazz with Milt Jackson on vibes. Klugherz was excited by Lye's sequence and wanted to make the whole film abstract but the sponsor felt that was going a bit too far. At the end of the job the two film-makers parted as friends, with Klugherz charmed by Lye and his zest for things: 'In the middle of a meeting he would tinkle the ice in his glass and say "Just listen to that!"'. He was also impressed by Lye's 'gut feeling for rhythm, his sure sense of whether an effect would work or not', and his clothes ('black and white checker-board patterns, mixing checks that were different sizes, a strange vision!'). Lye was paid $4000 and he and Ann took a trip to Puerto Rico.

Though in general he did move his best creative energies out of the film medium, he would return from time to time to make another experiment. Around 1960 he produced a 'geometrical scratch' sequence based on jazz by Sonny Rollins and Clifford Brown, but the film was not completed. Nor was a similar film of parallel lines and symmetrical patterns inspired by jazz guitarist Tal Farlow. He also made some tests of *Free Radicals* imagery with added colour — trying out orange, red, pink, yellow, and blue in place of white. There was also a highly ambitious project he worked on intermittently through the 1960s: 'I kept messing around running my original "Anions" scratch kinetics [from the early 1950s] with leftovers from *Free Radicals*, and at last got that going too.'[14] It was based on 'a zizzy-looking little figure of motion, a smaller, more compact zizz of energy than I'd ever got before on film'.[15] The title went through many changes: 'Sun Particles', 'Galaxy Particles', 'Rays in Space', and 'Particles in Space'. Lye gave some versions a public screening but still regarded the film as work in progress.

It was somewhat ironic that in the decade after 1958, when film-making became a secondary interest for Lye, there was an increase of public interest both in European 'art films' and in 'independent' or 'underground' American films. In New York and California public debate raged not only over the work of the French New Wave but over local films such as Jack Smith's *Flaming Creatures*, Andy Warhol's *The Chelsea Girls*, Ken Jacobs's *Little Stabs of Happiness*, or Kenneth Anger's *Scorpio Rising*. Lye enjoyed the energy of this work but from his perspective it was more literary than filmic, concerned more with issues like sexual freedom than with the aesthetics of movement. He remarked to Jacques Ledoux in 1964: 'How do you like the last lot of US "Beat" films? They are too "poetic" and amateur for me but I like the spirit in which they're made — one of utter freedom.'[16] During the 1960s there were several attempts by the great Austrian film maker Peter Kubelka to organise a Lye retrospective, but though Lye was impressed by Kubelka he kept insisting that he had given up film production. He did not want to take time out from his current passion: 'I now make kinetic sculpture.'[17]

fortytwo **tangibles**

Lye had started making kinetic constructions in the 1920s, animating shapes based on Aboriginal boomerangs and shields by using the parts of a hand-cranked gramophone. Over the years he had continued to experiment with motion gadgets of one sort or another, and in the early 1950s his interest intensified. One of the reasons for the Lyes' move to 41 Bethune Street in 1954 was to provide Lye with a larger workroom. While still devoting his best energies to film making and writing, he created objects such as 'Eye of the Storm', a tribal mask with eyeballs protruding on long springy stalks that swivelled on a bent shaft,[1] and 'Pineal Flutter', a motorised construction that dangled from the ceiling and shivered madly when touched by black (ultraviolet) light.[2] He played with pieces of metal in much the same way he doodled with a pencil or scriber: 'Once I'm impelled to mess around I don't know what's going to happen. I pick up a band of steel, one end — the rest lying on the floor — and just whip it, whip it up and down [until] it undulates like a snake.'[3] When pieces of flexible steel were shaken vigorously, they produced a variety of wave-like patterns. A handsaw, for example, produced an elliptical shape that reminded him of the streamlined fish sculptures of Brancusi.[4] He also liked the complex sounds and light reflections associated with metal; he had first experienced these as a child kicking a kerosene can.

Constantly experimenting with different forms of metal he became a connoisseur of their characteristic figures of motion. Having spent a lifetime studying how things moved, he saw a piece of metal as no different from a tree or an animal in having a unique physical personality. He would observe the metal's weight, tensility, and bounce, together with its sound and reflective properties. He had always been interested in patterns of vibration and oscillation. His direct films had taken full advantage of the way hand-painted lines quivered with tension,[5] and he had studied vibration in all its forms from the strings of guitars to the muscles of athletes. He had also focused on repetitive movement like the 'perpetual motion machine' which had first given him the idea of kinetic sculpture, or the rhythms of pistons, clock pendulums, rocking chairs, swings, seesaws, and boats at sea. Cyclical movement created form and rhythm, although — as chaos theory acknowledged — nature always added some surprises and syncopations. Friends used to joke about the similarity between Lye's favourite figures of motion in his art and the bouncy, quirky rhythms of his own walking and dancing.

When he needed metal for his experiments he would wander downtown to Canal Street where manufacturing coexisted with a crowded marketplace of shops and tables selling cheap goods. He would go 'looking for metals and springs and motors and mechanical tools and gadgets galore which are stalled out on the pavement for all the young Einsteins and Edisons to pick and choose and put two and two together and make a wonderful press-button affair out of scraps and rejects'. His most valuable purchase was a sanding machine with a flat plate for sandpaper which moved back and forth in a reciprocating stroke.[6] This eight-dollar motor could shake a strip of metal more rapidly than his hand, releasing from the metal an astonishing amount of energy and noise and a new range of wave-like patterns. The smallness of the motor was appropriate since Lye wanted to reveal the character of the metal rather than to force it into unnatural shapes. A Veriac motor connected to the sanding machine allowed Lye to vary the current and modulate the speed so that he could work like an animator, controlling the sequence of events. At certain speeds there were dramatic changes in the behaviour of the metal, which would for example suddenly assume an S or double-S shape.

Once he had identified a particularly striking figure of motion — 'something that looks kind of magical, that keeps fascinating me' — he would spend many days figuring out how best to develop it into a work of kinetic sculpture. His relaxed approach to doodling had always been complemented by his perfection-ism in finalising the details. He would decide on the size and shape of the steel and plan the sequence of speeds. He would gradually increase the speed to the point at which a change of shape occurred, and hover there for a few seconds, before accelerating to the limits of what the metal could sustain. He would experiment with different ways of ending the sequence, bringing the metal shuddering to a halt or leaving it to coast under its own momentum. His aim would be both to hold a viewer's interest and to explore a figure of motion thoroughly. Although he regarded the visual dimension as primary, he also saw himself as composing a sequence of sounds.[7]

Two of the first sculptures he completed were 'Storm King' and 'Blade', which grew out of his doodling with a handsaw. In both sculptures a long strip of very flexible stainless steel was held by a clamp and shaken vigorously at various speeds, but whereas 'Blade' rose up from the floor 'Storm King' hung down from the ceiling. The original 'Storm King' was approximately 9 feet long, 9 inches wide, and about 1/32nd of an inch thick. Lye concealed the motor in a wooden mounting because it might distract a viewer from what the sculpture was really about — the patterns of movement and sound it generated. Like Lye's other sculptures, 'Storm King' looked rather simple, even a little bland, when it was stationary. But then the hanging strip of metal would start to shake, creating various curves and ripples, together with various pitches of metallic sound.[8] As the speed increased the metal would bend into S shapes and shower the spectator with light reflections. Because the steel was very resonant it produced eerie swishing and flapping sounds as though a storm were brewing.[9] In developing the sculpture Lye decided to attach two smaller pieces of steel as a counterpoint — a small strip at the top shaped like an S, and a slightly thicker strip in the middle shaped like a 6.[10] Parts of these strips hung free and as the work gathered speed they shook like the clothes of a dancer. As the climax approached, the movements and light effects became less predictable and the sounds more urgent as the 'storm king' danced to its self-generated metallic music. The noise rose to a terrifying crescendo and then the energy was suddenly withdrawn and the quivering of the metal subsided. The title 'Storm King' was added as an after-thought, and with a touch of humour. While Lye did not want viewers to re-spond to the sculpture in a literary way, what interested him was not technology but nature and natural energies. Despite his growing interest in science and mechanics, his imagination still harked back to the ancient world of pantheism.

'Blade' was a shiny, upright strip of cold rolled steel standing 5 feet 4 inches high, just under 8 inches wide, and 1/14th of an inch thick.[11] The height was established by testing the strip of steel to see how high it could go before it bent under its own weight. The base was fixed in a clamp and then vibrated by a motor which released an astonishing display of energy. At first the strip would quiver gently, making sounds like a knife swishing through the air. Then it would develop a spring-like tautness, and when a certain speed was reached it would start to make 'S' shapes, flashing light in all directions. After working with this sculpture for some time, Lye decided to add a supple steel rod (about 20 inches in height) with a cork ball on top. The rod and the blade stood side by side, emerging from the same circular base (or plinth). The fun would start when the blade picked up speed, bellied out, struck the cork ball and reverberated like a gong. It would then proceed to pound the ball in a frenzied rhythm. The ball bounced back and forth so vigorously that it looked as though the rod was as active a partner as the blade.

Lye then had the idea of adding a second motor which would slowly rotate the circular base. This created a counterpoint and allowed the highly reflective surface of the blade to flash light from different angles. He choreographed a five-minute sequence of events that resembled (among other possible analogies) a strange, non-human mating dance. The dance of the blade and the striker would begin with no contact between them, then there was a first series of encounters, then the blade would slow down to stand quivering just short of the ball. After this period of tension, the blade would speed up, bending ecstatically back and forth until the 'S' shape became a blurred '8', accompanied by shuddering sounds as though it were breaking some kind of sound barrier. The pounding rhythm of the ball would rise to an unbearable intensity and the floor would shake. Suddenly the energy would ebb and the blade would re-emerge from the blur of light, to quiver gently for a few seconds before stopping. After the climax the silence and stillness were almost tangible.

Lye gave 'Blade' the alternative title of 'Plinth' because he liked the ancient Greek associations and the interesting sound of the word. A plinth was a base supporting a statue or column, but whereas the classic examples were square, his was round. The movements of the steel strip were so violent that the work needed to be bolted to the floor. Although its size and colour were among the many finishing touches to which he devoted endless attention, his aim was not to make his sculptures more decorative and elegant but more streamlined and intense.

The year 1958 saw a major change of direction for Lye. After 'going on strike' he had transferred his best energies from film to kinetic sculpture, and the result was an immediate explosion of ideas. Withdrawing from film-making did not leave him bitter and frustrated — he simply created a new vehicle for his skills as an artist, a new way to apply his lifetime study of motion. In Ann's words: 'It was a thrilling time. He was working out the feasibility and we all got into the act with suggestions, and he would listen very patiently and then do exactly his own thing! With sculpture I felt that a lot of things had come together in Len.'[12] He himself was not happy with the term sculpture because its history and aesthetics were based on static objects. The look of a kinetic work at rest was of little importance. Lye sometimes used the term 'kinetic steel' but his favourite at this stage was 'tangible motion sculptures' or 'tangibles'. He thought of his constructions as ways to make motion (and energy) tangible. 'Tangible' did not imply that the metal was to be touched — rather, it encouraged viewers to make sense of it in physical or kinaesthetic rather than intellectual terms.

To many of the people who knew his films, Lye's shift to tangibles was a surprising change of direction but he saw it simply as another aspect of his art of motion. Typically his tangibles had a programme — a composed sequence of motion and sound — similar in length to his films, and his work in both media suggested dance analogies. Some friends continued to prefer his films but others found the tangibles more dramatic. Although the basic sequence or master pattern was choreographed, each time the motor was switched on there was an element of unpredictability, like a piece of music receiving a live performance.[13] Even a small motor produced feedback effects that could add up to a happy accident or a disaster — small variations and nuances of movement that kept the works fresh even for their creator.[14] Standing close to them could be both exhilarating and alarming. (Lye's description of 'Blade' as 'an Aztec ritual to the sun' was hardly reassuring.) Unfortunately, performance also involved a great deal of strain and there was a frequent need to repair motors and replace metal. If Lye were working on something new he might have a very precise idea of the effect he wanted to achieve but lack the equipment or technical skills to realise it. Since money was scarce he relied on finding an electrician or mechanic sympathetic to the problems of an artist.[15] Paul Barnes remembers Lye searching the whole city: 'He'd get a motor from some little company down in SoHo, he'd get the steel from a little company in the West Village — the pieces came from all over, which was partly a money-saving device and partly a social thing on Len's part. He'd run across these individuals, old machinists who could modify the motors for his needs, there'd be some sort of crazy interchange and amusing relationships would develop. They looked on Len as an oddball, an alien from outer space, but as much as they thought he was crazy it was the event of their day when he came to see them. And he really loved these people, he had such respect for the work they could do, it was amazing the rapport that could develop.'[16]

On 11th Street Lye found a particularly important ally who combined technical expertise with creative imagination. This was Louis Adler who ran a radio and television repair business. In his words: 'It was a small shop with a small apartment above it. There was little chance of becoming rich, but it gave me a lot of freedom and I got to know the rich human theatre known as Greenwich Village. It was here, one quiet morning, that this man came in. . . . He asked, "Do you repair electric things?" "Well," I said, "that has been going on for some time in this shop." He was standing it seemed on one foot, vibrating with something unsaid, something very urgent, he was always dancing, and laughing.'[17] Discovering that this modest repairman had wide-ranging interests in music and philosophy as well as electronics, Lye invited him to his studio for a demonstration of 'Plinth' and 'Storm King'. Adler was attracted to the work immediately, recognising that the artist had found ways 'to get the material into motion so as to express its inner nature and character'. He astonished Lye by supplying a scientific explanation of the patterns he had been working with. Many forms of energy moved in wave patterns called 'harmonics'. Musical instruments vibrated in that way, as did the sound waves they produced. There were certain points or plateaus where a qualitative change occurred — for example, increasing vibration added a second harmonic curve (or fish shape) exactly at the point at which the frequency became double the first or fundamental frequency. Lye had intuitively worked out the programmes for his tangibles in terms of those progressions but he lacked a vocabulary for them. In Adler's words: 'When I told him that his "Plinth" was vibrating and producing a second harmonic, he laughed in the delight of a man who is not enclosed in the tight concepts of classical physics. The thing was a joy to him whether it obeyed the laws of wave mechanics or any other laws. He laughed — that was Len's secret. I felt he understood wave mechanics better than my oscilloscope.'

Adler was the ideal person to talk to the artist about science because of his poetic approach to harmonics, his belief that a principle of harmony informed all things natural or well-made.[18] Lye took Adler's physics seriously enough to begin using the term harmonic in the titles of sculptures. The term was in accord with his conception of nature as a shapely force and his sense of a strong affinity between music and visual motion. Adler made frequent visits to the studio: 'I became aware of this man's enormous creative force and knew it was a privilege to work with him. I knew I was present at the birth of a new art form. And when he told me he could not pay on time, I said, "It's all right, Len. We'll get around to it".' He was amazed by the artist's discipline — his ability to become totally absorbed in a project — and by his energy. 'Len had the most expressive body I've ever seen. He had a dancing vibrating way of standing still. After our day's work, we usually sat down before the huge wood-burning fireplace and roasted huge chunks of beef and drank mulled wine from ancient mugs. And all accompanied by his ebullient talk and the acting of his expressive body. Sometimes he jumped up to try a new idea. He was impatient with the human slowness to implement an idea. If only the action were as fast as the thought. And when he did complete a mechanism successfully, he chuckled at having out-manoeuvred the fates and wrested one of nature's secrets from her.'

One day when they were working in the studio, two NBC researchers came to the house hoping to talk Lye into appearing on a television programme devoted to 'surrealist artists'. He had never liked ostentatious forms of surrealism and was exasperated by the media's inability to deal with art except through labels and 'isms'. Adler was astonished by the speed of Lye's reaction: 'Len was so incensed at being categorised in this way that he shouted and almost physically escorted the two young men downstairs and out of the house. It was the only time I saw him in such an angry mood.' The one topic on which Lye disagreed with Adler was spiritualism. Adler, drawn to discussions of mysticism and life after death, was surprised by the intensity of his friend's suspicion of anything religious, particularly as Lye had always seemed to him in other respects a priestly figure with a 'spiritual power'.

The artist would often drop in to Adler's shop. On one occasion he placed a projector and rear projection screen in the window so that he could see how the man in the street responded to his films. With a devilish grin Lye sat watching the pedestrians along 11th Street stopping to view the abstract films, providing Adler with a running commentary: 'Look, that's a truck driver. I know him. Look at him laughing, isn't that great.' The two men thrived on each other's company, and when Adler emigrated to Israel (to teach electronics at a university), Lye sent him a warm letter: 'I think of your presence often and the many voluble talks we have had, and I use your teachings about energy and harmonics in my descriptions of my kinetic stuff. I want to give you credit for all your ideas.'[19]

fortythree dance of the machines

In playing with metal Lye was 'interested in the business of energy and getting a feeling of zizz'.[1] Many of his discoveries involved pushing a piece of metal to its limits so that the intensity was almost overwhelming. But he was also interested in a variety of slow, gentle, sensuous movements — which he called 'lethargic or euphoric'[2] — and these provided the basis for a different range of tangibles, including 'Roundhead', one of his smallest and most ingenious sculptures. Developed with the help of Lou Adler it consisted of four concentric metal rings on a round base. The outside ring was attached to the base by a steel shaft whereas the three smaller rings were suspended, one inside another, by black cords. Movement began with the shaft giving a push to the outer ring, which passed this energy on to the inner rings. In Lye's words, 'The whole biz spins on a torsion pendulum principle.' The four rings went through an ingenious set of variations, with rings turning clockwise and counter-clockwise as they were pulled and tugged. Because of the different size and weight of each ring and the tension of the cords, each part had some independence of movement and the viewer could never predict exactly what was going to happen next. 'Roundhead' was such an attractive and harmonious work that Ann Lye likened it to having a fireplace in one's home, always restful and absorbing to watch.[3]

The rings were made of high-tempered steel coated with nickel and under strong lighting their highly polished surfaces created dazzling reflections and produced beautiful trails of light in long-exposure photographs.[4] The patterns created by 'Roundhead' suggested musical forms such as canons and rounds. Although the motor and the rings produced their own sounds, Lye decided to heighten the musical effect by incorporating a music box (by Reuge of Switzerland) in the base, timed to produce a quiet sequence of sounds when the outer ring stopped. The sight and sound relationships were meant to 'engender both harmony and counterpoint depending on whether they [were] in or out of phase'.[5] The music box played 'Silent Night' but Lye removed so many of its pins that the melody was reduced to fragments.[6] At first he had called the sculpture 'Orrery' in reference to old mechanical models of planets in their orbits round the sun, but later he came across an electron-microscope photograph of the roundhead chromosome.[7]

When the first 'Roundhead' was being built, Ann Lye remembers she was just leaving their home in Bethune Street to go shopping when her husband appeared at the window: 'I heard him yell, "Ann! Ann! I'm doing a work and there's something that I need and I know that you've got it." So he ran down and caught up with me, and he had to have a gold ring for the centre of this little piece of sculpture. So I said O.K. and gave him my wedding ring.'[8] Ann had never been sentimental about rings and both the men she married had forgotten to bring one to the wedding service. Hindle had had to borrow a ring from her mother; but several years later he made amends by buying Ann a gold ring. When Lye forgot to bring a ring to their wedding, she lent him the one from her previous marriage. Finally, after losing this ring to a tangible, she went off to Woolworths and bought another ring for $2.98 which she wore for the next quarter of a century. Meanwhile the gold ring still functions today as part of the 'Roundhead' prototype.

'Fountain', another exquisite work based on gentle movement, consisted of approximately one hundred stainless-steel rods fitted tightly into a socket like stems squeezed into a flower vase. From the base these long rods spread out in a symmetrical pattern, the metal strong enough to keep them pointing upwards but flexible enough to curve gracefully. When the work was tested outdoors the wind made the rods sway like tree branches, creating a rustling sound as they brushed against one another. But Lye was more interested in the controlled patterns he could create indoors by using a Bodine motor to rotate the base. The stainless-steel rods rotated slowly for about ten seconds, then the motor was stopped, leaving the rods to swing under their own momentum. The rods would rebound, then just as they were slowing down the motor would start again, repeating the action.[9] Each rod responded in the same basic way but with subtle differences. As the light played subtly on the rods, all their movements added up to a gentle but complex dance. Like most of Lye's titles, 'Fountain' was intended as no more than a metaphor, and the work could variously evoke the patterns of spray in a fountain, the glimmer of a fire, or the play of wind in a wheat field.[10]

The sculpture looked particularly striking against a flat black background. With its graceful lines, its gleaming metal, its quiet, rustling noises, and its hypnotic movements, 'Fountain' had a powerful sense of presence. The NBC television programme *Today* made an item about the sculpture and *Newsweek* published a dramatic time-lapse photograph.[11] In 1959 the United Nations decided to use the work, along with some of Lye's other tangibles, as the basis for a one-minute film, *Fountain of Hope*, to publicise United Nations Day (24 October).[12] The film was screened worldwide in cinemas and on television and was one of the reasons why 'Fountain' became Lye's best-known tangible. His work was selected because the United Nations wanted to overcome language barriers, using visual images with a strong emotional impact and 'universal appeal'. He was delighted to be associated with a message of world peace and called off his strike temporarily to direct the film. Maxwell Dunn, the producer of the film, remarked: 'Lye is as unlikely a character as one might find around the dignified halls of the United Nations. His crisp beard bristles with enthusiasm, his shirts are as bright as his mind.'[13] The worldwide publicity for the film even reached New Zealand, where the general news magazine *Free Lance* ran the first local story about Lye for many years, describing him as a former Wellington art student who had become 'a well-known figure in the movie and art world in New York'. Interviewed by the magazine, he explained he was looking for money to make large-scale tangibles and added jokingly: 'Who knows, perhaps some sheep-farmer in New Zealand has just sold his station.'[14]

With 'Fountain' receiving so much publicity, it seemed likely that sooner or later museums or private collectors would want to purchase it. Lye saw limited editions as the most appropriate format for work of this kind. In anticipation he began designing a metal plate that could be attached to the base, but he got so involved in the engraving of his name that he drew dozens of possible signatures, each more abstract than the last. 'Noone could decipher the wriggling worm-shape that stood dancing to the right of a banana, its body wiggling downwards to its tail. This banana-worm dance was arrived at after several hours of evolution.'[15] He was so pleased with his abstract expressionist-style signature that he decided to use it on an everyday basis. As a precaution he registered it with his bank, but the pattern was so complex he sometimes forgot the details and the bank would reject his cheques. Lye went to the bank manager with an impassioned argument about how 'an artist represents a certain type of individual freedom; his craft demands he practise spontaneity; his signature is his most personal expression, and seen philosophically, this cooperation between the artist and banker can be as good a symbol of freedom in a capitalist society as any.' Accustomed to the peculiarities of Greenwich Village, the bank manager finally agreed to treat Lye as a special case.

Although he was yet to sell a 'Fountain', Lye continued to develop new variations such as a faster, noisier version called 'Fire' or 'Firebush'. With a stronger motor and more rods, its movement rose to a crescendo. He also planned a number of ingenious ways to combine his idea with a literal fountain — using jets of water at the base, for example, and hollow tubes instead of rods.[16] Since turning his attention to kinetic sculpture he had had an endless flood of ideas, but many of them were dependent upon sponsorship. One idea he was able to realise was 'Grass', which consisted of two parallel rows of slender, flexible rods about three feet high, set into a wooden board about five feet long. The rods ran the length of the board in a gentle curve. Underneath in the centre of the board was a spring and a small cam motor which created a gentle seesaw (or teeter-totter) movement. As one end lifted, the rods would lean, swing, and bounce back in a slow-motion dance, with light gleaming on their stainless-steel surfaces. Before they came to rest, the base would tilt the other way and the motion would be repeated. The rhythms of the work suggested grass stalks bending in the wind or underwater plants swaying in the current. Once again this was a sculpture that made its own music, as the 'strings' swished together and the board was (in Lye's words) a 'fantastically weathered, seasoned piece of mahogany that made a beautiful, Stradivarius-type, resonant sound'.[17] All details of the work were designed to maximise the most interesting visual and sound patterns. Lye wanted his sculpture to seem simple even though a great deal of complex, technical work was needed to produce it. 'Grass' had a classic simplicity of this kind and viewers described the work as calm, meditative, and hypnotic.

In 'Fountain' and 'Grass' the particular figures of motion — or patterns of rhythm, energy, weight, and balance — that Lye wanted to explore were best controlled by a motor. But in 'Wind Wand' he set out to work directly with the wind in all its moods. He designed a hollow aluminium rod, rising more than twenty feet in height from a metal base, which would curve in an elegant way. On top was a small globe (or in one version 'a suspended red ball in a clear plexiglass sphere').[18] A wand could be set up in isolation or there could be a cluster of wands. Lye said: 'Their weight is so lightly balanced that if a bumble bee stood on the ball at the top it would dip a bit, and the more honey he carried the more it would dip. In a strong wind they oscillate from side to side, but no matter what distance they swing it's always at a slow seven-and-a-half seconds period of time from side to side.'[19] He had some wands built with the help of an engineer named Maurice Gross, who was as generous a supporter of his work as Lou Adler.[20] The wands were first tested in 1960 in a vacant lot on the corner of Horatio and Hudson Streets, with Robert Graves, the Lyes' current house guest, lending a hand. In the following year the wands were exhibited as part of an art show organised by the Committee to Save the West Village. Ann Lye was one of the most active members of this group which campaigned against New York City's plans to 'redevelop' the area by demolishing old houses, houses in which many artists had their studios. When the *Village Voice* reviewed the event, it focused on Lye's wands under the headline, 'Swaying Mobile Is Art's Ode to West Village Battle':

Although the exhibit of paintings and sculptures by such artists as Franz Kline
. . . drew large crowds, the main attraction proved to be outside, in the playground of St Luke's School. It consisted of eight giant wands erected by West
Village sculptor-movie maker Len Lye. The wands, ranging to nearly 30 feet in
height, were made of aluminum tubing. . . . As the afternoon breeze came up
they began to nod and sway rhythmically, like beings from another planet
conversing with each other. A local physiologist who stood puffing on his pipe
and watching the objects for over an hour finally commented: 'They're as graceful as dancers. It's like making the motion of the wind visible.' For the children
in the playground, the wands became ultra-modern May Poles just right for a
junior bacchanal. They shook the wands until they quivered like immense car
aerials. They knocked one over. Then the junior among them began dancing
around them, bending backward and forward in imitation of their constant
swaying. Lye himself puttered nervously among his tubular creations with
wrenches in hand . . . a thin, tall man wearing what looked like a Mongolian
army vest.[21]

The wands were also exhibited on two university campuses — Southern
Illinois University at Carbondale (in its Reflecting Pool) and at New York
University (on the terrace of the Loeb Student Centre).[22] Lye enjoyed the contrast
between the university context and his own conception of the wands as the kind
of work an artist or magician might have created in prehistoric times. While the
wands were on display at New York University he attempted to persuade this
institution to purchase five for the Loeb Centre and to commission a giant wand
35 feet high for some other location on the campus,[23] and he was deeply disappointed when they said no. After that he and Ann attached the existing wands to
the roof of their own building.

Finding sponsors had become a matter of urgency, as Lye needed larger
versions to magnify the power of his tangibles and to rescue them from the
assumption that they were merely toys or games. In small versions people saw a
shiny elegance whereas the true aim was intensity. Lye's ambition was to 'really
get the utmost, to get the god-damn utmost out of the fundamental image'.[24] As
he explained in a radio interview: 'When you look at a [small-scale model], it's
the equivalent of looking at a five inch wave turning over very gently on a calm
day on the beach. The difference between the empathy you feel for this little
furling wave — so minute that you hardly notice it — and the empathy you feel
when you are watching a huge comber — a 15 or 20 or 25 foot comber — is
increased in ratio to the size of the thing, the energy involved in it.'[25] He drew a

similar contrast between the falling motion of a small shrub and that of a giant redwood tree, emphasising that each involved the same natural laws and the same figure of motion but that the 'empathic tension' felt by the spectator increased with scale.[26] His ultimate ambition was to build a kinetic equivalent of Stonehenge. For now, he wanted to make a modest start by finding an architect, real estate developer, university, or corporation willing to sponsor one of his sculptures.

Living in Bank Street near the Lyes was William Baldwin, a former journalist currently involved in public relations work for well-known politicians such as Adlai Stevenson. Around 1958 Baldwin became deeply interested in Lye's ideas on motion and over the next five years did what he could to help him in his search for sponsorship. He enjoyed Lye's company and was very impressed by his freedom from self-pity, depression, and the other common foibles of artists. Baldwin knew the work of other kineticists such as Jean Tinguely but concluded that Lye's was the only work conceived totally in terms of movement. From the beginning the artist told Baldwin that he wanted his sculpture to be monumental. '60 feet seemed to be the magic number — everything was to be 60 feet high.' When the Time–Life Building on Sixth Avenue was completed, Lye decided to show 'Blade' to Henry Luce, the head of the corporation for which he had once worked. Baldwin recalls:

> I went over to Len's one day and he had this new six-foot working model. There was a wand with a copper ball which was actually from a toilet. Inside the ball were two of Ann's pearls from a necklace. The motor had a timer on it so the blade didn't just get up there and hit the ball, it worked up to it. The ellipse got bigger and bigger — it was very suspenseful — until finally there was this very satisfying crash, with the pearls rattling around. Then it went back down again and became still. Len was very excited and said he had an appointment to talk to Henry Luce about putting a 60 foot version on the top of his new building. So he went up to Luce's penthouse office, which had a huge area outside on the roof, and Len was just watering at the mouth to get at that space. But when he came back he said, 'Well, Luce didn't go for it.' I said, 'Well, Len, you know, Henry Luce is the son of a Presbyterian missionary and I don't know how you expected to sell him an orgasm on the top of his building.' Len said, 'Of course, I didn't present it like that, I explained that the thing could go off and mark every hour.' 'But my god, Lye, an orgasm every hour on the top of the Time-Life Building!' Len said, 'Well, I don't think Luce saw it that way.' But I thought perhaps Luce was more perceptive than Len took him for.

With Baldwin's help in making contacts and setting up meetings, Lye tried unsuccessfully to sell the idea of a giant 'Fountain' as part of the Lincoln Center plaza which was then under construction. Baldwin knew a number of developers and was initially hopeful that at least one project would adopt a Lye sculpture.

> But they all said, we've got to talk to our architect, and the architect would say, it won't work. I think the real reason was the architect didn't want something that was going to upstage his work. Those buildings always ended up with something puny in front. Also, I think Len was just too wild for them. He was this funny guy popping in — they thought he was very visionary, but they refused to believe he had checked out the engineering problems. They were scared his things would fall apart and kill somebody! Originally Len had thought that New York was going to be better than London because it was free of the old boys' network. But this city is also full of connections. All the big real estate developers have their favourite architects, and the architects have their favourite engineers and so on. Art dealers have a connection with one museum or another, and with art critics, and they have a group of investors who buy in at a good price just before the publicity machine starts. New York is a whole network and Len just wasn't in on it. Still, I never saw him downcast for more than 50 seconds. He was just like champagne, just bubbling with this stuff, he'd be off to see someone else.

One of the ideas Lye liked kicking round with Baldwin was the possibility of hiring Carnegie Hall and giving a performance of all the tangibles built to date. In 1927 Carnegie Hall had been the venue for one of the great scandals of modern music, 'Ballet Mécanique', which George Antheil had written for an experimental film by Fernand Léger and Dudley Murphy. Lye and Baldwin wanted to use a more contemporary piece — 'Le Marteau sans Maître' by Pierre Boulez — and as this music played the sculptures would perform a ballet. In Baldwin's words, 'I had this vision of the steel fountain springing to life and swooshing away, then that would shiver into silence and something else would start, and we would just go round the stage, having the sculptures react to one another!'

Although Lye had not been discouraged by the failure so far to find sponsors, it was difficult for him to sustain even the cost of making small-scale prototypes, to keep up with his constant stream of ideas. It had become a race to find buyers or sponsors before the artist ran completely out of money. Fortunately his work was starting to attract interest in the art world, helped along by an enthusiastic report in the 24 August 1959 issue of *Time* which described his tangibles as a new art form. Lye found himself being courted by two art dealers, Leo Castelli and

Howard Wise. Castelli, who had opened his gallery in 1957, represented rising stars such as Jasper Johns and Robert Rauschenberg and he would eventually become one of New York's most influential dealers.[27] It was his assistant, O. K. Harris, who first drew his attention to Lye. The dealer exhibited 'Fountain' in his gallery as part of a group show and advanced $500 for the right to represent his work. Baldwin remembers that 'Castelli was fascinated by Len, he was very flattering, but it seemed to me that he just gracefully didn't do anything. I think at that time they were looking for paintings, that was what they could market. As for kinetic sculpture, I'm sure Castelli didn't want to start a maintenance division.'[28] Howard Wise, on the other hand, saw the working relationship between artist and technologist or scientist as an important direction for art.[29] As the leading American dealer of multimedia work, his gallery was a launching pad for everything from high-voltage electrical installations to the latest forms of video and computer art. Regular exhibitors included Nam June Paik, Agam, Pol Bury, Hans Haacke, and Group Zero, together with two of Lye's old friends, Stanley Hayter and Frederick Kiesler. There was an exhibition of 'Unidentified Fluorescent Objects' by the New Zealand expatriate Billy Apple. Wise believed that developments such as kinetic and 'op' (optical) art had the potential to bring new vitality and new audiences to art museums. In some respects the growing popularity of high-tech art in the early 1960s encouraged the wrong sorts of response to Lye's work. But Wise understood its distinctive character: 'I think that Len Lye is the king of kinetics. He is going down in history. This idea of energy is imbued in him, and he is so full of it he is literally a bouncy fellow. . . . By the way, he is no scientist whatsoever. He doesn't even drive a car. But he has an intuitive feeling for the qualities of his materials, which are mostly metal. . . . You wouldn't think that steel could be so sexy.'[30]

Lye was very pleased to gain the support of this enthusiastic art dealer, and he saw this as potentially the New York equivalent of his relationship in London with John Grierson. Wise had started his art career in the 1950s, running a gallery in Cleveland, Ohio. Screening experimental films on a regular basis, he had begun a correspondence with Lye. In December 1959 he reported that he was opening a gallery in New York at 50 West 57th Street and was 'going to try to make it one of the best galleries in town'. In the new year he paid a visit to Lye's studio with his son David who had already done some hand-painting on strips of film. It was the relationship that sprung up between the artist and the 5-year-old boy that cemented the friendship between the two men. Lye screened *Free Radicals* and immediately David began a serious discussion with him. Wise was startled to hear his son explaining what he thought should be done to improve the film, but Lye always took children's comments about art very seriously. In the end he gave David some tools he used in scratching his films, and the boy went away and made a short film which was a parody of *Free Radicals*, creating his own soundtrack by means of an egg-beater. After Lye had seen the film he said to Wise: 'Listen, you have equipment, you should give him anything he needs.' He continued to take an interest in David, who eventually made a career in Hollywood.[31]

In March 1961 Wise reached an agreement with Castelli to finance and promote Lye's work jointly. They would pool proceeds from any sales on the basis of 50 per cent to the artist and 25 per cent to each of the two galleries. In the same month Wise presented 'Fountain' in his Cleveland Gallery alongside the work of Tinguely and Agam. Entitled 'Movement in Art', this was one of the first of a new wave of exhibitions devoted to kinetic art. Next, Castelli and Wise were successful in persuading the Museum of Modern Art in New York to sponsor a demonstration by Lye of his 'tangible motion sculpture' on the evening of 5 April. The Museum was a prestigious venue for introducing his work to the opinion leaders of the New York art scene. The auditorium with its 480 seats was quickly booked out. This was not an expensive event for the Museum to sponsor because no new tangibles were built — instead, Lye displayed ten of his small-scale models. The Museum provided three assistants and the total budget was $660, with half of this being contributed by Leo Castelli. Lye's costs increased and in the end Castelli and Wise each contributed $510.

The details of the evening had been worked out at a visit to Lye's studio on 15 February by Wilder Green and William Seitz (who was in charge of the evening), and Ivan Karp representing Castelli. Also at the meeting was Peter Selz, a curator then visiting New York, who would prove to be a key supporter in the future. Selz had curated Jean Tinguely's 'Homage to New York' at the Museum of Modern Art in 1959, a great *succès de scandale*. Tinguely's giant kinetic machine had splattered the elegant guests with paint during its frenzied performance, and the Museum could not dissuade the Fire Department from hosing and axing it. Selz remembers being tremendously impressed by his visit to Lye's studio: 'We had been looking at all those new pop paintings and colour field paintings, and suddenly here was something extraordinary. There was very little kinetic sculpture being done at this time. There was Calder and George Rickey, both of them doing objects that move freely in the air, but Lye's sculpture driven by motors was a very new kind of thing. I was reading about new kinetic work being done in Paris by the Groupe de Recherche d'Art Visuel, and in a way I was prepared, when I came to see Lye, for something kinetic but totally different from Tinguely.'[32]

On the night of the show the audience passed three sculptures in operation on their way into the auditorium. The seats were arranged in two groups, one facing south and one facing west. The other seven sculptures were lined up under coloured spotlights against a black cloth background. The evening began with a screening of *Free Radicals* and then the tangibles were put through their paces. Like the machine ballet planned for Carnegie Hall, their performance was accompanied by a variety of records from African drumming to Pierre Boulez. But 'Roundhead' and 'Grass' were left to provide their own sounds, with a microphone to amplify the swishing sounds of 'Grass'.

The evening was a great critical success but did not provide an immediate solution to Lye's lack of sponsorship. Peter Selz said of the event: 'People loved what they saw. Everybody was extremely enthusiastic.' Bennett Schiff of the *New York Post* wrote a glowing account of Lye's 'sculpture of light and movement which is truly innovatory and magically expressive'. He also chided the Museum for giving the work only a one-night stand and advised it to make amends by purchasing a tangible for its collection.[33] Inside the Museum both Selz and Seitz made the same suggestion but nothing came of it. John Canaday wrote a rave review for the *New York Times*, being particularly impressed by the way movement 'dematerialized' the steel sculptures, transforming them into gleaming lines and planes. Canaday quoted Seitz's suggestion that a new work by Lye entitled 'Ring' would make 'a staggering and beautiful and appropriate symbol for the 1964–65 World's Fair instead of the pedestrian skeleton globe that has been adopted' — but there was no official response to this idea.[34]

Lye's own performance seems to have made as strong an impact on the audience as his tangibles. He spent the evening in the midst of his machines making adjustments. In Ann Lye's words, 'Len was alone on the stage among all those gadgets, a leather belt with a tool kit hanging on both sides of his behind, with a stepladder. Everything was going on and he was absolutely deadpan — he never cracked a smile through the whole thing, it was so serious to him! Something would start going wrong and he'd climb up his ladder and fix it. It was very impressive — and moving.'[35] Lye's friend Douglas Newton, an art historian and curator, recalls: 'As usual the sculptures didn't work at first but eventually they got going. The fountain went into motion slowly then worked up to a fine frenzy, thrashing around in a way that was hallucinatory, very beautiful, and seemed quite dangerous. Len liked that bit I would imagine. When it was over he said in an offhand way, "It would be better if it was forty feet high."'[36] The person working the gramophone kept putting on records at the wrong time but it scarcely mattered.[37] The tangibles were so novel and dramatic that this one evening was enough to establish Lye's local reputation as an important sculptor. This was a big step forward in critical terms for he had found, in moving from film to sculpture, that the two fields were surprisingly separate, obliging him to deal with a new set of curators, critics, and collectors who in many cases had no knowledge of his previous work.

fortyfour sartorial thrift-shop style

Around the end of 1956 the Lyes had put their trapezoid house at Martha's Vineyard on the market and started to take their holidays near the village of Warwick in upstate New York. One-and-a-half hours by car from the city, it was more convenient for 'quick dash-a-ways'. They purchased a wooden house in Milford in the mountains. The house was small and in such a primitive state that they called it the 'Hen House'. Both put a great deal of work into the house, adapting it for the harsh winters. Lye described their country life in a letter to his brother Philip and sister-in-law Wynne, inviting them to come from New Zealand to sample it: 'Deer pass our bedroom window. . . . Pheasants scoot about and whirr off from the "Hobbit" area of our lands. Local cider is terrific, especially when laced with vodka. . . . We grill the most delectable [meals] on our wire grid over the fire's red hots of ember.'[1]

By 1960, the Lyes were spending more and more of their time there. It was their dream house and they filled it with their treasures, their favourite books and paintings from friends, and much of Lye's own work.[2] Then an arsonist struck. In Ann's words: 'We had packed the car and were ready to leave for our country place when friends from London phoned, they were on their way to Hollywood, and wanted us to have dinner with them. So we decided to stay in New York over night. At about 2 a.m. we were called with the news that the house was gone. The police caught the arsonist who'd burned two barns and a house before ours. The head of the volunteer Fire Department was our plumber, and he'd noticed that this guy was the first to be at all these fires, so he told the police. The arsonist was sent for life to the state institution for the criminally insane. The fire was a terrible tragedy for us. One of the few things we found in the ashes was the head of an assegai, a gorgeous Zulu assegai, one of Len's favourite things, which had run along the centre beam at the top of the house. . . . Two days later, when we were up there, I got a call that my father had died. All that happening together — it was too much. But we survived. After the fire I think we both had a different feeling about possessions. Len had always *said* he never put a lot of stock in possessions, but actually he'd had a lot of things he was fond of.'[3]

They eventually found a replacement in the mountains just over the New Jersey state line. The house was nearly half a mile off the road and the setting was idyllic — in the woods, in a clearing, with huge boulders. They shingled the house with cedar shingles and put in two large picture windows for light. There were two rooms in an L-shape, and one room became Lye's studio for painting. He spoke of the place as his 'thinking house' or 'Walden' (since it was near a pond). Ann, meanwhile, would stay in a caravan which she left parked next to a three-acre garden in Milford. In her words, 'We'd go shopping on Monday morning and buy food for the week. I'd drop him off at the house, making a date with him for Friday night. I'd make a reservation somewhere. So at the end of the week I'd arrive all dressed up and ready to go, and there he'd be in his *lavalava*, and he'd say, "Oh! what day is it?" He had no radio, no telephone, no clock, and he had no sense what time it was. Sometimes, though, I'd drive up and there would be this beautiful kerosene light in the window with goblets on either side — very romantic — and he'd have a dinner ready for us. That was marvellous. At first when we told people about it they would look strangely at us — "Imagine going away separately!" — but in the end everybody decided that maybe that was one reason our marriage was so strong — being able to have separate interests and to pursue them without being interrupted. I know it worked for us.'[4]

Their friend Alastair Reid, a poet, translator, and staff member of the *New Yorker*, would sometimes look after their place in Bethune Street. He recalls: 'I learned most about Len by staying in his house. I used to sit up in his studio and do my work. Looking around I'd see his tools and the way he kept them. His studio was an entire expression of the joy he felt all the time. He had an intimate relation with everything — the objects were precious to him, he had a sense of how beautiful tools were. I'll never forget coming across a box of nails and it was white like those big boxes of matches, but he had covered it with paper on all four sides and written over it with magic markers of different colours: "Thanks, thanks, thanks, thanks." That was so characteristic of him, if I had to pick one image of Len that would be it: "Thanks!"'[5]

Another friend observed that while outwardly the studio was immaculate, Lye's filing system often gave way to chaos once the relevant box was opened. In contrast, Ann appeared outwardly less tidy but the things she put away were arranged in a more logical order. He spent a huge part of his life in the studio — working on sculpture or film, doodling, painting, writing, or simply pottering around. He hated going out to do business in the art world and saw most of that time as wasted. Not that he had consistent work habits. When Robert Graves came to stay, Ann was amazed at the writer's regular routine — starting at 7 every morning and working until 1 p.m., leaving the rest of the day free. Lye could never organise himself in that way. He was not regarded as a very productive artist because he completed only a few works each year. His greatest interest was always the process of discovery rather than the end-product or the potential audience or market. The most extreme example of this attitude was the way he endlessly revised and added to his theoretical essays even though he had no publisher. Though Ann sometimes complained about his 'absent-mindedness', she understood that the source of his problems was rather his extreme 'present-mindedness'.[6]

Lye would leave the studio once or twice a day for a walk round the Village. To quote Susan Maxwell: 'Anyone who knew him could spot him a mile off, hopping, dancing, crossing on the red lights . . . dressed in sartorial thrift-shop style.'[7] Every day he would walk along Bleeker Street to the far side of Sixth Avenue to get fresh Italian bread — it was the only shop that made bread he liked. In the outgoing manner of many New Yorkers, he would often get into conversations with strangers. For example: 'I was sitting on a kerb down the way to the river writing some ideas that couldn't wait; it was near a bus terminus on East 59th and a busdriver had given me a stub of a pencil before he pulled out. I had got the idea set down, when a friendly man smiled and said, "Hello, sketching?" . . .'[8] According to Ann, 'Len was a street person, so many people knew him that I knew nothing about. It was the same in all the places we stayed. Everybody knew him in Warwick, but that was a small place and a lot were nervous because of how different he looked.'[9] Alastair Reid remembers going for walks with him: 'He lived in his senses more than anybody I've ever known. Smells and tastes just as much as the other senses. Walking in the Village we would decide that instead of just looking at people that passed, we would look entirely at their noses. If you just keep noses in mind and don't look at anything else, it's mind blowing! Then we'd do ears. He educated my senses a lot. The day to day life was great, it was some of his best work.'[10] This included weekly expeditions in search of clothing: 'Len was a monument of sartorial splendour. He'd turn up in some extravagant outfit and he would have bought all of it in Klein's basement. S. Klein was a big cheap department store at Union Square and 14th Street. Len would go into their bargain basement which was a jumble of cheap clothes. He had an unerring eye for what was his style, his wavelength. He would always find something incredible that cost only a few dollars. It was always something that only Len could have done. His clothes are a good example of what he had more than anybody, and that is style.'

His wife did share his wavelength and bought many of his clothes for him. In Ann's words: 'Len's clothes were first of all dependent on the fact he had a marvellous figure, he was tall, he was thin, he moved elegantly in his own way, he enjoyed finesse in everything. He had absolutely no knowledge of what was fashionable ever. But he wore things that always looked unique and marvellous. I knew exactly what he liked. He refused ever to wear a tuxedo but I bought him a dress suit on 14th St in purple velvet, with the trousers lined in silk. I got the whole thing on sale for $20. He had many marvellous outfits. One of them had blue and white striped trousers going up and down this way, and a T-shirt with stripes going that way, and on top of that he wore a white shirt and a hat with navy polka dots.' Caps were a specialty, including scarlet berets, Nehru hats, fezes, smoking caps, railway boilerman's caps, and many other types. At home he would sometimes wear his Samoan *lavalava*, a costume that puzzled callers. Lye championed the *lavalava* and would give demonstrations on how to wear it.

Some of his walks would end up at the Greenwich Theatre on the corner of West 12th and Greenwich Avenue. However devoted he was to fine art, he could still get something out of any movie. He had a weakness for melodrama, as Reid recalls: 'It was the sinful thing we did, artists of one kind of another, to sneak in to the movies in the afternoon instead of working. And if the movie was a tear-jerker of some kind, suddenly we'd hear the sound of someone not only sobbing but howling — "Hooooooo!" — and three people would stand up and call "Len!", and he'd say "Here." He blubbed constantly at movies, it was very endearing, and when we heard him we'd all go and join him.'[11] Once when they came in to a movie late and he started crying, he turned to Ann and said, 'It wouldn't be so bad if I only knew what it was about!' In Hollywood movies he tended to concentrate on the movements of actors, which he saw in cartoon terms — for example, 'the knobbly cast of the star Elliott Gould, bemused, his mouth full of marbles, finally flapping his foot-flippers enroute insouciantly to some horizon or other' or 'the celery stick walk of that stick of celery, *High Noon* star Gary Cooper' or 'the molasses of a James Dean spreading his bodily attitudes all over the armchair' or 'the nifty Balinese hand motions of a James Cagney'.[12]

Lye was reluctant to go to social events, claiming always that he had too much work to do; but once Ann had dragged him there, he would become the life of the party. He had a reputation as a great dancer although he was hard to follow, his steps were so original.[13] Reid remembers him inventing 'think dancing' which meant stopping in the middle of a dance: 'He used to say, "You move for a while and then you dance internally." So he'd stand still and the dance would be taking place through him.'

Lye was on friendly terms with many artists, writers, and jazz musicians but there were few that felt they knew him closely. In Douglas Newton's words:

'We've met at various intervals but I can't say I know Len well — I wonder if anyone does. He has always seemed both tough and elusive.'[14] His self-contained personality and the hint of something oriental in his appearance often led people to describe him as 'inscrutable', either a Zen master or a rogue. Gretchen Berg gained a vivid impression of his enigmatic qualities when she interviewed him for a 1963 issue of *Film Culture*:

> I was used to hanging around the Experimental or 'Underground' film circles in those days. Unlike many of the other film-makers, he seemed without any kind of pretension about himself or his work, and while possessing a healthy ego he seemed oddly at home with himself. He also had a good sense of humor, something also unusual among that crowd then. He was more like a sorcerer or wandering gypsy than the others. Of course, not being American may have given this impression too; his voice had that rather strange Australian or New Zealand drawl which sounded almost harsh to your ears until you got used to it. He was given to sudden, short bursts or guffaws of laughter and seemed to be enjoying himself hugely. I just assumed that he happened to look like a Chinese. My drawing of him in *Film Culture* as an Emperor on some servant's backs was half a joke and half a feeling of something demonic and potentially fierce about him; it could be seen when he laughed in those short bursts and his eyes almost disappeared in his face. I felt he was capable of strange thoughts and metamorphoses.

Despite this sense of strangeness Berg liked him very much. She saw him as keeping to himself 'only in the way a sage might do — not because he didn't get on with people.' The two aspects of Lye she remembered most vividly were 'his feeling of being at peace with himself when many of the people around were either failures and embittered, or aggressive pushers; and his laugh: "HA!" he would go, bending backwards at the knees, holding his breath, eyes shutting, right hand stroking the top of his head, then again — "HA!"'.[15] Lye liked Berg's interview but told her he was worried about one aspect, the way she had included the phrase 'BIG LAUGH' so many times in her transcript that no one would take his ideas seriously.

Throughout this period Lye kept up his own sage-like theorising. Around 1960 he delighted his friends with a burst of writing that was more personal and down-to-earth, a series of 'Moments' which recorded his most intense memories of childhood. These were not what an adult would regard as major events but moments of special importance from a child's point of view. Lye had had many of these experiences when he was alone, like the youthful epiphanies collected by poets such as Wordsworth. They ranged from lyrical encounters with nature, to homely excitements such as the discovery of chewing gum, to bitter defeats such as a fist fight with the local bully. Lye wrote in punchy, rhythmic sentences full of colours, smells, tastes and kinaesthetic feelings:

> Not quite four and in a tantrum I kicked that can around to make the most god awful racket my lungs and kicks on the can could. (from 'Flash')

> The big moment was settling down on my own, up in the weeds overlooking the yard with houses in the distance, all set to clamp my teeth onto that big square white biscuit. (from 'Biscuit')

> Here's a moment with a strong flick. It's one that's no good for me to try to get by simply thinking about it. It's only when I see a pool in the country with a puffy wind skidding over it, then I'm back at a rainpool I found on the flat top of a hill. To see the sky and the sea and the sheep and this huge grassy pool of rainwater and feel the breeze and see it make riddlings in silver scurrying patterns was something to soak up, so I stood there and did. (from 'Rainpool')

> My mother threw a fit and made me bathe my face in cold water. I can still see and feel that water in the white china hand-basin as I bent down into it. One eye was completely closed when I looked at my face in that mirror through a slit where the other eye was. The pain of that water in the cuts on my hot face gave me a moment of realization — it was the first time I had felt defeat. (from 'Victory')

One stimulus for writing about childhood was the time he had spent with Howard Wise's 5-year-old son David. Since Lye's theoretical speculations focused on the development of individuality, it was natural for him to be interested in children's art and experiences. By this stage his own son Bix, in his twenties, had become a sculptor. When Lye started to consider his own life as a case study he found that his memories were vivid but fragmentary. He had not seen New Zealand for more than 30 years but was still in close touch with his brother Philip. He began working systematically through his memories, selecting those that were most intense. Feeling that he had hit a rich lode, he showed samples to Alastair Reid. Reid had previously tried to help Len with his theoretical writing but had always found that task depressing because 'Len belonged in particularity. Particulars were so vivid to him that he had no need for abstractions. Unfortunately he kept feeling he had an obligation to theory.'[16] Reid summed up his very different response to the 'Moments' in a letter to Lye: 'I was always gloomy when you read me the pieces on value, because your own speaking language was wondrous — your letters, too — but when it was boiled down to theory, all the wonder went. But tonight, I just felt such delight from these pieces. . . . They are so beautifully transparent and heart-stopping that I just feel thankful for them. And I will do everything in my power to see a book out.'[17] With Reid's encouragement Lye continued to record moments and soon had twenty.[18] He also described a number of adult moments but recognised that they were different in style, less sensuous and more ruminative. He assembled the youthful ones under the title 'Moments', changing it to 'Happy Moments' after he came across a book about two Chinese sages who exchanged their 'hundred happy moments' while they sheltered in a mountain hut during a rain storm.[19]

Lye created an exercise out of his happy moments which he described as an alternative to yoga or drugs: 'So there's me now flattened out as a body breathing with eyes closed sorting out its life's best moments. It finds itself pleased to be the same skin full of tension and bones . . . with the clean warm sheets on smooth skinned feet in the cool-as-a-cucumber weather'. Running through his memories was like 'the way a drowning person sees his whole life',[20] but with pleasure rather than anxiety. Even if some of the experiences had originally been painful, he could now savour them with a kind of aesthetic detachment. He played with them both as moving images and as frozen moments, as in 'Wave", a memory of his first visit to Australia:

> On Coogee beach there was this glass-clear twenty-five-foot-high walking wave of green sea. Twenty-five-foot! Alive and swimming along its curling middle was this huge shark. What's the frantic magic? Simply feeling, hey, there's a mighty rising mass of energy forever gathering, never stopping, preserving a fish in amber, gone greeny forever. That big slow curling wave never comes down.

He also began analysing some of the moments in terms of his theories, particularly his earliest moment (the flashing kerosene can) around which he wove an elaborate myth in which the sun represented life and energy in contrast to the death threatening his father. In the end he took such speculations out of the 'Happy Moments' manuscript, simply describing the flash and not explaining why the image was for him a powerhouse of associations. This understatement owed something to his current admiration for Ernest Hemingway's novel *The Old Man and the Sea*.

Late in 1961 Reid started using his contacts to try to get some of Lye's manu-scripts published. First, one of his more accessible philosophical essays ('Why Art Is Great and Ideology Isn't') was submitted to the *Saturday Evening Post*. The magazine gave it careful consideration, but the verdict — as reported to Lye by Senior Editor Richard Thruelsen — was that the essay 'wandered considerably' and this was likely to create 'a great deal of confusion for the general reader'. He added: 'I think you are on occasion unnecessarily cryptic. Categorising [Samuel] Beckett's boys, for example, as, "hardly contemplating navels because they them-selves are navels," may be clever but it will miss the mark with many readers.'[21] Thruelsen offered to help with a 'what-do-you-mean-here?' session, but Lye in his eagerness submitted a re-write of his own a few weeks later. This time the editor threw up his hands in despair: 'your . . . piece is improved but it still wanders . . . in such a wide-ranging fashion that the average reader would, I'm afraid, be completely lost. . . . It seems to me that you light two fuses here and each theme sends out its own little skyrockets (a hell of a metaphor) in different directions.'[22]

Would the 'average' or 'common' reader find 'Moments' more accessible? Reid took some samples to friends at the *Atlantic Monthly* and enlisted the help of a literary agent (Constance Smith Associates) who sounded out various book publishers. A typical response was that of Fred Birmingham, an editor at Fawcett Publications, who wrote this in-house memo: 'I am ashamed of myself, but I can't for the life of me think how "Magic Moments" could be marketed. There is no doubt that the stuff is good, in certain moments quite touching. But I am afraid it strikes me that unless this type of sentiment is contained in a package like *Where Have You Been? Out* [a current bestseller], it is just amorphous.' The moments lacked a sufficiently clear (or cute) organising principle. Knox Burger of Gold Medal books thought he had found a solution when he advised Lye to pair up with a photographer: 'I could see a feature in *Horizon* or perhaps in *Holiday* consisting of beautiful colour photographs which suggest the moods and places you write about, with some of your "Moments" run as accompanying prose poems in lieu of captions.'[23] Burger was trying to be helpful but Lye was not interested in a glossy spread on behalf of New Zealand tourism. When publishers kept worrying about the lack of unity he assured them there was an underlying philosophy and proposed adding an essay as the second half of the book. From their point of view, this suggestion was the final straw. Reid recalls: 'I went away to Europe and when I came back I was astonished that nothing had happened. When I asked Len about it he said, "Oh, well," and brushed it aside.' The sequence had been rele-gated to one of his many boxes of unpublished manuscripts. Yet his lack of success in finding a publisher never stifled his pleasure in the activity of writing, and 'Moments' provided the seeds for much subsequent work. The project had also reawakened his interest in a return visit to New Zealand.

fortyfive the movement movement

In the same month as the Museum of Modern Art event, one of Lye's tangibles was being exhibited in Europe as part of the first major international survey of kinetic art. Although the works assembled for the exhibition were extremely various, the packaging of them as a movement — as an avant-garde — attracted large amounts of publicity, pushing the European interest in kinetic art to a new level and lending valuable support to Lye's attempt to get his work noticed in the hope of finding sponsors. The name of the exhibition was 'Bewogen Beweging', a complex wordplay exploiting different meanings of 'move'. One possible translation into English was 'motivated movement' but most reviewers preferred 'The Movement Movement',[1] a term said to have first been used by Hans Richter. The exhibition, curated by Pontus Hulten, opened on March 10 1961 at the Stedelijk Museum in Amsterdam. It toured over the next two years to the Moderna Museet in Stockholm, the Louisiana Museum near Copenhagen, and the Musée d'Art Moderne de la Ville de Paris.

Planning for the exhibition had begun in 1957 centred round a small but significant range of European artists who had been working in this area, including Tinguely, Takis, Pol Bury, Nicolas Schöffer, and groups such as Zero in Düsseldorf and the Groupe de Recherche d'Art Visuel in Paris. In its final form 'Bewogen Beweging' was remarkably comprehensive with 74 artists represented from around the world. Kineticism was presented as a logical outgrowth of modernism and as the art most relevant to today's science and technology. Billy Kluver, a Bell Laboratories scientist as well as a sculptor, tracked down 20 American artists (although very little of their work would have been categorised by Lye as kinetic). Lye was represented by a 7-foot 'Fountain' and by several films. Newspapers described the exhibition as 'bizarre' and the police ordered an enigmatic work by Robert Muller (a bicycle resembling a home trainer with a 'widow's veil' covering the seat) to be removed because they saw it as 'obscene and shocking to decency'.[2] The public turned out in record numbers, evidence that kineticism was one form of modern art that could achieve popular success. Although the exhibition emphasised the work of Alexander Calder and Jean Tinguely, *Newsweek* illustrated its report with a photograph of 'Fountain', commenting that its 'variable, sinuous motion makes one of the show's loveliest images'.³ And at least five newspapers published photographs of Lye's work.

The critical response to this show initiated the kinds of arguments that would accompany most exhibitions of kinetic art over the next decade. Some critics worried about whether this was really art or merely a gimmick. Others hailed it as a populist victory, a rebellion against austere forms of abstract painting. In the 1960s art was branching out in a number of new directions — pop, op (optical), kinetic, and conceptual. These tendencies tended to be jumbled together and seen as evidence that a 'new generation' had emerged, which was characterised as the space age or television generation. The new artists were contrasted with the previous generation as 'more playful', 'more optimistic', 'more technological', etc. One of the ironies of this debate was the fact that Lye, now 60, actually belonged to their parents' generation. Granted, some of the critics who remained suspicious of the new art (such as the reviewers of *Artforum*) did recognise the special qualities of his work.

In general, American critics and artists tended to see kinetic art as a European tendency, a challenge to their home-grown forms of modernism. Clement Greenberg was particularly worried about the threat to what he regarded as the great tradition in American art: 'In the spring of 1962 there came the sudden collapse, market-wise and publicity-wise, of abstract expressionism as a collective manifestation. The fall of that year saw the equally sudden triumph of pop art. . . . Assemblage art came along almost simultaneously, and now optical art and kinetic art have appeared, to swell the reaction against abstract expressionism.'⁴ Other critics and artists were reluctant to ally themselves with science and technology, or with the related European tradition of Constructivism. Paradoxically, op art and kinetic art also came to be associated in the later 1960s with the anti-rationality of the counter-culture. The fact that hippies might see the new art as psychedelic was another reason for serious critics to regard it with suspicion.

These controversies helped to attract public interest, and so it was fortunate for Lye that he had just recently returned to kinetic sculpture. It was one of the few times in his career when he found himself close to the charmed circle of art-world fashion. Yet his position was a complex one, because he could not fully identify with either the American or the European mainstream. His attitude to high-tech forms of European art resembled the classic jazz attitude: 'It don't mean a thing if it ain't got that swing.' In the United States kinetic art tended to be associated with Alexander Calder, an artist three years older than Lye who also used the term 'composing motion'.⁵ Calder had been exhibiting 'mobiles' since 1932, and Lye greatly enjoyed and respected his work but felt that ultimately it grew out of a different sense of movement. Although Calder was trained as an engineer and made use of hand-cranks and electric motors in his early constructions, his best-known work was set in motion by wind currents. The movement of its brightly coloured cut-out shapes connected by wires was gentle and somewhat random. In contrast Lye's sculpture was machine-powered, it often moved rhythmically at high speed, and it played with the sense of space by creating after-images and complex patterns of light. In those and other respects his work was more closely related to the film medium than Calder's. One of Lye's main reasons for adopting the term 'tangibles' was to distinguish his work from 'mobiles'.

Among contemporary European artists Lye was most interested in Takis and Tinguely because they used motors, though he knew their approach to art was different from his. Tinguely he enjoyed because his scrap-metal art made so much fun of technology — 'a fantastic anarchic dadaistic marvellous freedom loving guy who shakes the rafters'.[6] Howard Wise exhibited work by both these artists. Although Lye was sceptical about some of Wise's enthusiasms, he was impressed by the dealer's solid commitment to kinetic art. A dealer specialising in this field had to be determined, because, in addition to the tricky art politics, machine art was expensive to make, awkward to market, and difficult to maintain in working order. By August 1961 Wise was so enthusiastic about Lye's work that he asked if he could represent him exclusively. Lye replied by letter: 'You're the best agent I could ever get. . . . It's your attitude of first for the artist's work for the artist's sake.' Wise then wrote to Leo Castelli who gave his consent. Because Castelli was a friend Wise reimbursed him for the $500 advance he had paid to Lye and also for the money he had contributed to the event at the Museum of Modern Art. Ann Lye recalls: 'Len got on well with Howard, he liked him a lot. Len wouldn't kowtow to anybody, he treated everyone exactly the same. Rather than him going into Howard's game, he felt that Howard was in his game. That was very much the relationship.'[7] Clement Greenberg had a somewhat more guarded opinion. He agreed that Wise did the best he could for Lye, but felt that Wise 'was "advanced" in his gallery in too dogmatic a way, too mechanical a way. Over the long run Len would have fared better maybe elsewhere. But this is only a surmise. [And] Len's lack of drive had to have something — a lot — to do with the way the world treated his art.'[8]

Lye's work was included in group shows at the Wise Gallery in July 1962 and January 1964. The latter show, 'On The Move', was a particularly impressive survey of kinetic art by seventeen artists including Agam, Pol Bury, Alexander Calder, George Rickey, José de Rivera, Takis, and Jean Tinguely. Lye was represented by a 7-foot version of 'Fountain' and a large new sculpture which became

the most talked-about item in the show. This was 'Loop', which consisted of a
22-foot strip of polished steel. The oval loop rested on a flat base which concealed
electromagnets, timers, and other equipment. The magnets would suddenly tug
at the loop then release it, causing the steel band to lurch sideways then spring
upwards, eventually striking a ball suspended from the ceiling. The work looked
simple — a loop and a ball — but produced the most complex effects. The
movement of the loop was unpredictable, wobbling from side to side like a fat
stomach, shivering like a jelly, or bouncing violently. Photographs with a long
exposure time produced dramatic patterns and became a popular image for
reviews and posters. Viewers would wait expectantly for the loop to hit the ball,
producing a variety of percussion sounds. Lye attached special importance to the
sound aspect and demonstrated it for the *New Yorker* who described 'Loop' as
one of the most beautiful kinetic works to date: "'Listen" [said Len]. He pushed
down on top of the ring, released it, and as the steel sprang into motion, rapped it
smartly with the flat of his hand. A clear fluctuating tone rang out. He tapped it
with a cigarette lighter, and a different tone joined the first. "We'll get these in
parks and gardens, and have tapes of the sound they make playing along with
them — have them dancing to their own music, you know.""⁹

Although Wise's 'On The Move' show was a critical success for Lye there had
been a huge struggle behind the scenes which typified the practical problems
involved in kinetic sculpture. Four days after the opening Lye wrote a record of
what had happened:

> Howard has given up giving me money as he's not selling anything and I owe
> him $2000 — but he has my 'Fountain' as equity. When I heard he was satisfied
> to just show my old 'Fountain' in the group show, I wanted to make something
> new. So I showed him 'Loop'. He took a look and liked it, and said go ahead and
> make it, but not to exceed the $500 which I had quoted. Well, in the end, the job
> cost $440 for the mechanic's work hours, $60 for steel, $60 for five weldings, $75
> for five goes at getting the right magnet wound, $200 for technical wiring of
> transformers, rectifiers, condensers, timers, etc. Ann sprang in with some extra
> money to enable me not to have to ask Howard for it. When we were five days
> off from the opening date I saw that the 'Loop' was not only going to work, but
> also saw that the steel could be thicker and higher, and two magnets would be
> better than one. We went out to the steel warehouse for sprung steel, and then
> tried to find welders and so on. After working all night we had everything ready.
> The 'Loop' was set up in the gallery all ready for the show when — guess what
> — it conked out! So opening night came and went, but everyone was satisfied

because, if the 'Loop' was pushed by hand — which everyone seemed to like trying — it would roll back and forth on its own, in perpetual motion style. Next day, Friday, we worked at the magnet mechanism and got it fixed by five p.m. O.K. Saturday it worked, now comes Monday and I hope it will continue to behave . . .

Lye and Wise had kept their cool up to this point but now the artist got into a fierce argument with the dealer over the price of 'Loop'. Lye insisted that it had to be the most expensive work in the show, $5000 more than the $30,000 price of José de Rivera's large 'steel serpent'. In his words: 'Howard hit the roof. He said it was his job to fix prices. He knew the market. He was out to get the most he could. Too high a price would kill any sale possibility. And lots of other telling points. I replied, too bad. It would only sell to one in a million who liked kinetic art plus having lots of coin, and unless I sold one work a year [in that way] it was impossible to [finance] others. It was the only way I could operate. He could not finance me, nor could Ann.'

The conversation ended in a state of war with Wise refusing to pay the last $100 of his $500 advance, and Lye determined to pull 'Loop' out of the show. ('And, who knows, I'll put it on my grave in memoriam to art galleries!') But next morning Wise phoned and said, 'Len, I couldn't sleep all night thinking how great the "Loop" was. I've decided to let you have the $100, plus whatever your debts are, and put the price at $35,000 for it. O.K.?' Lye was not ready to make peace but he did agree to leave his work in the show. At the end of the three-week season 'Loop' remained unsold but Lye and his dealer were back on friendly terms. The price of 'Loop' was later dropped to $20,000, but the tensions remained — Lye continued to be known as a wilful artist whose attitude to the art market sometimes made no sense at all to potential customers or to his dealer. But he desperately wanted money to finance large-scale works. He felt he had already paid his dues, albeit in a different medium. Creatively he was at his peak and his reputation as a sculptor was growing steadily, but it was anyone's guess whether buyers and sponsors would come along in time for him to be able to realise his most ambitious ideas.

fortysix a flip and two twisters

Major American museums were now beginning to seek him out. The 1965 survey of American sculpture at the Whitney Museum in New York included Lye's new work 'Zebra' or 'Spin', made up of nine-foot-high stainless-steel rods with black tape wound around them in a spiral pattern. With motors in the round bases of the rods spinning them at various speeds, the rods went through a series of metamorphoses as a combination of silver cylindrical forms and black horizontal lines.[1] *Newsweek* praised the exhibition as a 'landmark' for 'its brilliant opening up of potentials of movement'.[2] More specialised reviewers such as Barbara Rose in *Artforum* used it as an opportunity to debate the fashion for kinetic sculpture, challenging most of the work as little more than a display of 'engineering know-how'. But Rose made an exception for Lye's tangibles because of their great variety of movement and their success in equating movement with form. She said of 'Zebra': 'Lye's spinning steel rods, which . . . seemed to make the space they traversed almost palpable, transcended mere ingeniousness to become truly inventive sculpture.'[3]

Around this time the Ford Foundation made a grant to the Whitney enabling it to buy works from exhibitions. Howard Wise recalls: 'The Whitney wanted "Fountain". Well, they pleaded poverty, they wanted to make the Ford grant stretch as far as it could, and they finally got "Fountain" for a very low price. This was not what I felt a museum of that stature should do. And then later on, when they put it on show, it was really pretty miserably displayed. What irked Len was the base which he wanted to be more in keeping with the "Fountain" itself. So he offered to build another base, for what I felt was a very reasonable price, about $2000. But they turned us down, they just wouldn't do it. You know, that's the sort of treatment from a museum — buying work cheaply and displaying it badly — that artists just never get over.'[4]

Two 1965 exhibitions went some way towards solving the problem of Lye's sculptures being seen only one at a time in group shows. The Wise Gallery gave Lye a solo show (from 6 March to 3 April), and the Albright-Knox Gallery in Buffalo not only included him in its large exhibition of 'Kinetic and Optical Art Today' (from 27 February to 28 March) but gave him and Nicolas Schöffer top billing, with separate rooms for the two artists. Thus, at the age of 63, Lye was getting what were virtually his first solo exhibitions. He presented five works in Manhattan and seven in Buffalo. Because the two exhibitions took place at virtually the same time they were planned together. Wise agreed to put up $10,000 towards the cost of his gallery's show and $6000 towards the Buffalo show. As its contribution the Albright-Knox agreed to buy 'Grass' for $3000 and to refund half of Wise's $6000. This was not exactly a windfall but the Albright-Knox did represent an important venue for contemporary art. Late in 1964 Lye had discussions with the Design Service Company about manufacturing one copy each of eight works. When the company quoted a figure around $34,000, he reduced the order to 'Blade' and two copies of a new work — 'Flip and Two Twisters' — to be made for approximately $7000. He was thus obliged to use existing versions of the other tangibles and as usual the cost of getting them into running order proved greater than expected. Wise's contribution eventually rose to $19,000. As compensation Lye gave him two of the sculptures.[5]

Douglas McAgy wrote a lively, provocative catalogue for the exhibition at Wise's gallery. He argued that Lye's approach to kinetic art was different from that of either European or American artists because he had never studied at the Bauhaus or at an American university but was a self-taught artist from New Zealand. McAgy's account was warmly sympathetic but leaned rather heavily on the old stereotype of Lye as a noble savage. The artist contributed a striking comment: 'Perhaps I'm for magic carpets over flying saucers, and would rather be heir to the Australian aboriginal with his boomerang and bullroarer than an heir to constructivism and mechanics.'[6] Wise's publicity for the exhibition used theatre analogies to describe the tangibles as 'the cast' who would 'perform to music of their own making, first in succession, then in concert'. The intention was to coordinate their activity for the entire period of the exhibition. This proved difficult, but each day did end with the entire group shaking and roaring together as a chorus.[7] A mixture of red, orange and blue as well as white lights shone on the highly reflective metal surfaces. These colour effects were worked out by Wise in association with the artist. In addition to 'Loop' and 'Blade' there was 'Ritual Dance' (or 'Bell Dance') — a tall steel rod dancing up a storm, surrounded by six shorter rods with bells on top swaying in counterpoint.

The exhibition also included the 'Gateway Model' or 'Universe Walk'. This was a tabletop model for a sculpture park in the mountains. It had first been proposed on a more modest scale for a site in Arizona, but Lye now saw it as a proposal for an art gallery of the future, a 'Mecca of art' dramatic enough to 'shiver the pilgrim's timbers'[8] set in the mountains or on the desert floor of Death Valley. This aimed to combine many of Lye's sculptural ideas into a single work of art. The visitor would enter through a gateway consisting of 'Loop' wobbling and banging overhead, which would ensure that 'the shoulder blades and thigh sinews of the gallery-goer got the resonant message'.[9] He or she would come next to 'Walk', a slow escalator moving past a series of kinetic displays based on knee and leg actions. These images (a development of the lost 'Walk' sequence that Lye had made for *N. or N.W.*) would be synchronised to music (such as 'the bamboo dance music of the Philippines').[10] After being thus encouraged to reflect on the physical sensations of walking, the visitor would arrive at giant versions of Lye's tangibles.

As early as 1959 Lye had told a *Time* reporter he wanted 'story-high versions of his Tangibles in public parks and plazas', and soon after he had started playing with the idea of a sculpture park as awe-inspiring as an Aztec temple, an Egyptian pyramid, Stonehenge, or other ancient monuments. In the course of the 1960s his concept became increasingly specific as well as increasingly more expansive. It was evidence of the way his imagination was working at full stretch, and also reflected his contempt for what he saw as the small-minded, ungenerous attitude of many institutions. His 'temple' would upstage the museums. By going on strike as a film-maker in 1959 he had indicated he would no longer play the game of art by the usual rules. And as a sculptor he was increasingly attracted to utopian think-ing. If artists turned their backs on the art world and got on with their utopian planning then museums and collectors could no longer exploit them. Since the art market was ultimately dependent on their creative ideas, it would eventually have to meet the artists' demands. Lye raised these possibilities in a playful, provocative way but there were times when he became so passionately involved with them that his dealer and friends feared he was simply wrecking his career.

Meanwhile, the sculptures he was producing were among his very best. The highlight of the Wise exhibition was 'Flip and Two Twisters' (later known as 'Trilogy'). This was his wildest kinetic work to date and he saw it as a possible climax to the experience of visiting his temple. The energy of even his small prototype was terrifying and Wise had to rope off the area for safety. The work consisted of two 'Twisters', 9-feet-long vertical steel strips, flanking a loop of steel called 'Flip'. All were suspended from the ceiling. The performance began with the two twisters dancing a duet, spinning so fast they produced single and double harmonic curves. Then they would suddenly brake to a stop, straightening out in a shudder and crash of metallic sound. Then the loop would slowly begin turning itself inside out. This was a tense, protracted process. At last the metal would flip over in a thunderous cascade of sound. The sequence ended with the loop and the twisters doing their dance together.

The metal was Swedish stainless steel, the type used for surgical blades, which was highly flexible and cast dazzling reflections. When the twisters moved fast they seemed too fluid to be metal, making S shapes or dissolving into a blur of energy. The work had a strong sense of progression, and its sound effects were as varied and dramatic as its movements. Many viewers were reminded of sex, particularly in the sequence where 'Flip' strained to reach a climax, finally twisting inside out with a great shudder of sound. Ann Lye judged 'Flip' to be 'the sexiest sculpture Len has ever made'.[11] The critic Dore Ashton spoke of 'erotic undulation' like 'a belly dance' and saw Lye's work as unique within kinetic sculpture because of its human quality.[12] Emily Genauer of the *Herald-Tribune* regarded 'Blade' in the same exhibition as so erotic that its value as art was compromised. She reported that her friends had laughed at her when she said she had never seen anything in an art gallery or museum 'as realistically orgiastic'. One replied: 'Mere Freudian fantasizing! Abstract kinetic op art is what it is. Don't go reading things into a flat, shiny shaft that casts such lovely reflections when it moves.' But Genauer knew very well what sort of 'paroxysmal shudder' was being evoked, and this spoiled the sculpture in her judgement because she saw true art as something that should transcend the physical and reach out to 'the spirit'.[13] Lye was amused by the review, and happy to admit that his sculptures might have a sexual dimension; but he was also confident that his art went deeper than Freud, tapping natural energies and archetypes at an even more elemental level.[14]

The show attracted considerable public interest and there were enthusiastic reviews by well-known art critics. Lucy Lippard in *Art International* saw Lye's work as 'far more inventive' than Tinguely's and added that his ideas were 'probably the most advanced in the kinetic field at the moment'.[15] There was even a favourable comment from the sculptor Donald Judd, a hard-to-please critic who was an influential figure among young artists: 'So far, mechanical motion hasn't been used much more clearly. . . . It will be an important aspect of art but it isn't yet. . . . [But] there is less wrong with Len Lye's use of movement than with anyone else's in the United States. . . . Subsidiary movement is all right but motion can be the whole work. It is pretty much in Lye's pieces.'[16]

The Buffalo exhibition, 'Art Today', gave an even greater boost to Lye's profile. The room devoted to his work contained versions of 'Fountain', 'Roundhead', 'Zebra', 'Flip and Two Twisters', 'Grass', 'Sky Snake', and 'Loop'. In the judgement of critic Sam Hunter, Lye's work 'was without any question the main attraction'.[17] The city was a centre of contemporary work in the arts and the Albright-Knox Art Gallery had an excellent reputation for keeping up with the play. There was an unusually high level of media attention because the exhibition was part of a two-week 'Festival of the Arts Today'. Kinetic and optical art still had novelty value. The 'Art Today' exhibition was visited by more than 300,000 people, easily breaking the previous record set by a large Van Gogh show. Indeed, it was so popular that some reviewers became worried about the 'funhouse' atmosphere,[18] a suspicion that was constantly cropping up in some form or other when critics discussed the popularity of kinetic art.

One piece of feedback on the exhibition that made a big impression on Lye came from Neddy, a six-year-old watching 'Loop'. He turned to his mother and asked, 'What is it mum, the universe?' Asked why he had suggested this, the boy replied: 'I think it's the sound.' Lye was amused by this comment, and when he later read George Gamow's account of the 'big bang' theory of the origin of the universe, he decided to change the name 'Loop' to 'Universe'.[19] Another strong contender for Lye's park or temple of giant sculptures was 'Sky Snake', a long suspended chain of polished steel balls set in motion. It would begin spinning slowly and gracefully, then as the speed increased it would twist and writhe. After the snake had gone through a series of rapidly changing shapes its energy was withdrawn and with a series of diminishing shudders it would go back to being merely a chain of polished steel balls.[20] Lye liked the snake's 'range of play', the distinct figures of motion it produced as different amounts of energy were fed in. To ensure that these figures did not blur one into another, the motor was turned off at the end of each figure and the snake was allowed to coast for a few moments before the next began. To enhance his own viewing Lye liked to add an accompaniment of African percussion music. For the temple he imagined a number of large-scale snakes dancing round the roof, with louder sculptures such as 'Storm King' in the middle 'making all the various harmonics and all the thunderous noises you can possibly imagine'. The effect would be 'hypnotic — you'd feel like a rabbit with a cobra!'[21]

Buffalo's Festival was a huge public success, as much for its shock value as its innovation. A performance of John Cage's *Concert for Piano and Orchestra* ended in uproar. *Life* magazine ran a report on the festival entitled 'Can This Be Buffalo? Dancing Nudes and Sculpture'.[22] *Newsweek* devoted a complete story to Lye which linked his Buffalo and Wise Gallery exhibitions, describing his work in poetic terms as 'a futuristic dance of automatons flexing . . . metallic muscles'.[23] Lye and Wise were pleased with the popular and critical success, but, behind the scenes, both exhibitions were plagued with technical and financial problems. At both venues there were stripped gears and short circuits for 'Flip and Two Twisters'. Wise blamed the manufacturer of the machinery, the Design Service

Company, and a protracted argument ensued. In Buffalo one reviewer offered the sympathetic comment: '[Lye's] sculptures require a great deal of engineering to function and fairly often they don't function at all. This is all rather endearing, for Lye's imagination outstrips his means.'[24] Problems were solved through the unstinting help of Pierre Broquedize, an IBM executive who happened to be a board member of the Albright-Knox Gallery. Help of this kind was a novel experience for Lye. He dreamed of becoming the ward of an electronics company who could take over his everyday struggles with money and machines. He wrote to Thomas J. Watson of IBM: 'I need the help of your corporation . . . in programming motion sculpture. Without it we will lag behind the contemporary kinetic sculptors in Europe. . . . The hit works at the Albright-Knox [exhibition were] by Nicolas Schöffer and myself. Mr Schöffer's programming was sponsored and executed by Philips of Europe. He is now designing a one-thousand-foot kinetic tower which has been commissioned by André Malraux [French Minister of Cultural Affairs].'[25] IBM was not interested.

Schöffer, who had gained sponsorship in both France and Belgium (where Philips had helped him to construct a 'luminodynamic tower' in 1961) was an intellectual artist well informed about the latest technologies. Eleven years younger than Lye, his interests had been shaped by constructivism and other forms of geometrical abstract art, and by the ideas of László Moholy-Nagy. His current work focused on the application of computers and electronics to art. Since 1956 he had exhibited 'spatiodynamic sculptures' made up of aluminium and plexiglass parts, which incorporated electronic music and projections of coloured light. Lye was interested in his work but saw it at the opposite pole to his own: 'Nicolas is a very *new* brain kinetic artist. . . . I balance him up with my old.'[26] They met in 1966 and became friends. Despite his own successes, Schöffer shared Lye's contempt for the establishment. He was later to write a generous tribute to Lye in his book *Perturbation et Chronocratie*, describing him as a pioneer in both film-making and sculpture. 'Len Lye . . . came into sight . . . as the forerunner of programming, prototype-making, and taking stock of time, of which he was the first great and subtle explorer.' He added that Lye was an artist of integrity who 'represented, along with Marcel Duchamp, the reduced group of incorruptibles who never gave in to the demands of economics or the art market. Both preferred to halt their artistic production rather than give in and compromise themselves.'[27] He described Lye's work vividly in terms of form (how 'simple means' were used to produce 'extremely complex results') and psychology (how a new sense of time and rhythm could be learned from his work). In this passionate account, Schöffer saw him as one of the 'principal victims' of the current 'bourgeois era' because of the lack of support his work had received. Certainly in practical terms Lye was now under great pressure, for while each exhibition boosted his profile, it left him and his dealer with more financial and technical problems.

Sam Hunter, an art historian and curator associated with many successes such as the first exhibitions by Jackson Pollock and David Smith at the Museum of Modern Art, attempted to help Lye by writing a letter on his behalf to wealthy patrons and corporation executives. In contrast to the urgent, earnest tone that the artist usually adopted, Hunter's letter was relaxed and down-to-earth. After spelling out the artist's importance and his popular success in Buffalo, Hunter concluded: 'Lye's requirements are ambitious, and possibly unrealistic . . . [but] an imaginative businessman in the computer or space industries would, I'm sure, see the value of such creative expressions in creating a better public atmosphere and understanding of contemporary technology. Lye himself is a very refreshing and original character, remote from the art marketplace, and content to go on working without much public attention, as he did for some thirty years prior to his first one-man show this season at the Howard Wise Gallery. He is also an extremely charming and articulate man, and I would say this because I think an executive of some related industry would find him quite enchanting. . . .' Lye needed a lot more letters of this kind, letters that could mediate and translate between his ideas and the world of executives, patrons, and politicians. Hunter's letter did help to open doors, though no sponsorship deal came of it.

Howard Wise received frequent requests for the loan rather than the purchase of Lye works. 'Fountain' was the work in greatest demand because it was the cheapest to ship and install. (The rods could be dismantled and packed in a tube.) The artist got grumpy about servicing such requests because they were time-consuming and brought in little money. In 1965, for example, an oil magnate had offered to sponsor a large 'Fountain' for the World's Fair in New York where it would be exhibited at the Christian Science pavilion. Rufus Stillman, whose company helped Lye to solve engineering problems, remembered the artist turning up to the negotiations wearing extraordinary Ben Franklin-style glasses and being very temperamental: 'During lunch Len started to come up with absurd demands. He wouldn't be involved unless the World's Fair put up $100,000. Howard turned to me and said, "Oh Christ!".'[28] Eventually the World's Fair rented a 'Fountain' for $1000. Wise remained confident that Lye was on the edge of a major breakthrough in terms of recognition and sales, but when he entered any negotiation he was always nervous that the artist would start reaching for the stars, attempting to solve his problems with a single deal.

Artists who took a more customer-oriented, businesslike approach were able to achieve a higher public profile. Nevertheless there continued to be a demand for Lye's work. It was exhibited for example at the Art Institute of Chicago, the William Nelson Gallery and Atkins Museum in Kansas City, the Rhode Island School of Design Museum, the Los Angeles County Museum, the Philadelphia Museum of Art, the Huntsville Museum of Art in Alabama, and the Cincinnati Contemporary Art Center (which sponsored a solo show). In 1966, the invitation that interested Lye most came from Peter Selz who had left his job at the Museum of Modern Art to become director of the University Art Gallery (later the University Museum) at the University of California at Berkeley.[29] This was a small gallery but Berkeley was a lively place (a centre of hippie activities, among other things). Selz's first exhibition was to be 'Directions in Kinetic Sculpture', the largest survey of its kind in the US, an American equivalent of 'Bewogen Beweging' with 40 works by 14 sculptors. Lye was represented by 'Loop', 'Fountain' and 'Flip and Two Twisters' (now entitled 'Trilogy'), with a selection of his films being screened at the Pacific Film Archive. The exhibition turned out to be a high point in Lye's career. The *San Francisco Chronicle* reported that on its first day the gallery 'which clocks in 200 people on an average abstract-expressionist day, almost burst its bricks prematurely as 4200 fascinated, sceptical and excited people came to look, listen, pedal and push'.[30] In six weeks the exhibition attracted more than 80,000 visitors, a phenomenal number for a campus institution.[31]

By chance the San Francisco Museum of Art opened a similar but smaller kinetic exhibition at the same time and the combined impact of the two events gained national publicity. The *New York Times* ran a story entitled 'Moving Art Moves Viewers On Coast',[32] and *Newsweek* suggested that the two exhibitions 'made the laboratory of a mad-movie scientist seem as sedate as a church confessional. Thousands of spectators surged amid whirling lights, stuttering speakers, clanking cogwheels and spiky sculptures crackling like bowls of Rice Krispies'.[33] The mid-1960s was the peak period for public awareness of kinetic art, with magazines such as the *New Yorker* running frequent cartoons on the subject (such as a worried art collector asking his dealer, 'But what about spare parts?', or a family argument about 'Who left the sculpture on all night?')[34] Lye was always reluctant to leave his studio and Selz had to work hard to persuade him to come to Berkeley. When he did arrive, he was amazed at the public reception he received as the artist whose work was creating the most interest. (The next most talked-about artist was Takis, followed by Rickey.)[35]

Lye took part in a symposium on the campus with an overflow audience of

850.[36] Peter Selz chaired the panel which consisted of Lye, Takis, Rickey, and the sculptor and film-maker Harry Kramer. Between them, these four artists illustrated the variety and internationalism of kinetic art. Apart from mutual respect, they appeared to have little in common except the use of movement, and even 'movement' held different meanings for them.[37] In the *San Francisco Chronicle*'s account of the evening: 'Lye [is] a feisty, goateed charmer, . . . popping up from his chair to make a point or a joke with ebullient vigor. . . . Lye fills the air with invisible bobbing exclamation points. "There are two dichotomies here. Art and science. And in the end, they are after the same thing. Truth!" Cries of "yes! yes!" fill the room. Lye beams. An old *March of Time* director himself, he grandly directs the TV cameraman: "Take a cutaway here of this marvellous-looking audience."'[38]

The artists enjoyed one another's company, with Lye and Takis forming a close bond. One evening Selz took them and Howard Wise over to San Francisco to see more of the counter-culture. Lye and Wise were 'tremendously impressed' by the Fillmore Ballroom with its new style of music, light show, and dancers with fantastic clothes or painted bodies. The excitement matched the buzz they had felt around the Berkeley exhibition. At the end of the evening, Wise congratulated Selz on the success of his exhibition and offered to make a permanent gift of 'Trilogy' to the Gallery, conditional upon the sculpture being kept in working order.[39]

Meanwhile the exhibition continued to be packed out day after day. As Selz recalls: 'People had a lot of fun. They would keep coming back, they would bring their children.' It was a curator's wildest dreams come true. The public confirmed their interest in kinetic art, finding it challenging but also curiously entertaining. Reviews were also enthusiastic, though *Artforum* published an attack by Philip Leider which expressed the magazine's usual concerns. Kinetic art was more relevant to Europe, and in his opinion the best American artists were too sophisticated to take it up. Leider went from one scathing comment to another. Kinetic art was the 'dumb imitation of machines', as out-of-date as the 'dumb imitation of nature'; movement was exploited as a gimmick and dressed up in pseudo-scientific rhetoric; and kinetics as a whole stood in the same 'sterile relationship' to real sculpture as Op art did to 'real painting'. Yet Leider made one exception:

> The single artist in Dr. Selz's exhibition who seems to transcend all the confusion — esthetic, mechanical, rhetorical — of kinetic sculpture is Len Lye, whose work manages to compress so ferocious an energy that the viewer stands paralyzed,

gripped by an emotion almost of terror. Lye's elements are supremely simple: hanging strips of stainless steel, six or seven feet long, are set to spinning around at very high speeds. The whiplash strain on the steel produces a series of frightening, unearthly sounds in perfect accord with the mood of barbaric energy that seems to have been released. Installed by itself in a black-painted room, the viewer comes upon Lye's 'Trilogy' as he would upon a volcano. The effect is beautiful, frightening, utterly beyond the petty limitations of the other artists in the exhibition.[40]

fortyseven life in the sixties

Lye's own art and ideas could be seen in some respects as a forerunner of the new 1960s culture he had encountered in Berkeley. His ease with the body and his commitment to sexual freedom were 1960s values. Though he had moved on from 'Individual Happiness Now', Lye saw affinities between his old philosophy and hippie slogans such as 'Do Your Own Thing'. In his words: 'As Jerry Rubin's book title goes, *Do It*, don't talk about it, just in your own sweet slow sure maddened insidiously fanatical confident time-biding way — Do It!'[1]

In the 1960s the East Village took over from the West Village as the heart of the counter-culture. In 1966, its first year of publication, *The East Village Other* published a story about Len as 'The Free-est Radical': 'At 60, Len Lye is one of the youngest and most creative members of the Avant Garde. . . . Last year Howard Wise invested $15,000 in Len . . . but there were no commissions. I find it hard to believe that our society is so blind as not to see the worth of Len Lye's work. However, the sad fact is that America is a death oriented country. . . . [With money Lye] could make things of joy and light which would trigger Love in the hearts and souls of all who saw his works.'[2] The profile ended with a comment by Lye about his plans for giant sculptures: '"Art is replacing religion," he said, and as if to prove his point [he] talked about the Indian raising his arms to the sun each morning in recognition of the source of light and life — of the T.V.A. turbines and generators, of their power to produce and their lack of ability to inspire — about electricity being to us what the sun is to the Indian — about the necessity for us to be awed by this energy — about the blueprint he's working on now for a Temple of Lightning. . . .' Lye reported proudly to his brother that *The East Village Other* had interviewed him 'because they're wild and rather woolly like yrs true'.[3] Over the next few years other counter-culture papers ran similar stories.

When LSD became popular, Lye's attitude was that he did not need drugs because he already had his sense exercises.[4] Nevertheless he and Ann accepted the invitation of a poet friend to try mescalin. Both the poet and Ann were curious to see whether it could help Lye's art. Sitting under a seven-branched candelabra with a supply of fresh fruit brought by the poet, they took the mescalin in silver eggcups that Ann had purchased in Hungary many years ago, eggcups that had once belonged to the Hungarian royal family. The mescalin was slow to act but eventually Ann and the poet got extremely high. In her words: 'The grapefruit was breathing when I held it up. I fell in love with the grapes. I took three grapes and I was going to taste them but instead I just held them up in front of the candelabra and started crying! Our old oak tavern table was alive, everything was alive. The smell of the fresh open bottle of milk was terrific, you couldn't drink it because that would have been too much.'

She and the poet also got wildly excited about the art in the studio. At one stage he suggested that she make a phone call to prove to herself that she was capable of coming down from her high; but on the way to the phone she found that 'the whole of our pigskin floor was moving!' (In redecorating the house, she and Len had covered the floor with square tiles of pigskin.) While his wife was having what she later described as the most exciting day of her life, Lye said he did not feel any different. He continued to function as a good host, checking that the other two were all right. Ann later commented: 'I still salivate thinking about that day! But it just didn't work for Len. He didn't have the revelations we were having because that's where he lived all the time. It was such pure sensuous experience and joy, we had simply gone in to Len's territory!'

Talking later with William Baldwin, Lye admitted that the mescalin had affected him: 'For some reason I had to go on the subway after taking this stuff and it was a weird experience — all the noises were magnified and the seats were melting away. There was a woman with a bag of oranges and the pores of the oranges kept getting bigger, then getting smaller, and so forth. Some of it was terrifying, some of it was wonderful, but after it was over I could hardly remember any of the stuff. What I saw on mescalin wasn't that different from what I see normally and it's better when I see it normally because then I can remember it.'[5] In contrast Ann continued to have memory flashes for years: 'I would find myself holding a grape up to the window to enjoy the light and colour instead of eating it. The mescalin was so powerful that I didn't want to take it again for three years.' Eventually the three of them tried mescalin again in the country but this time even Ann was disappointed: 'Even though it was spring and the flowers were out, they felt gross, everything was too big, everything felt threatening. I went down to the stream and the stream was going in the wrong direction. I walked home and went to bed!'[6]

The Lyes continued to maintain their open marriage, which was unusual even by Village standards. In Ann's words: 'When I told a friend about it she said, "You obviously don't give a damn about your husband." She was mad because I think she was still interested in Len. Most people just couldn't understand, they thought we didn't care that much for each other, but really it was the other way round — we could do this because we cared.'⁷ In their previous marriages they had both had extremely jealous partners but felt so confident about their own relationship that they 'didn't need possessiveness'. When they had affairs, 'It didn't ever get too heavy because we saw other relationships as not too serious. I don't mean that we treated them casually but that Len and I always knew our love for each other came first.'⁸

Ann did admit to feeling disconcerted at times. On one occasion when she came back from a trip to Reno to finalise her divorce and asked Lye what he had been doing, he freely admitted he had spent the night with a young woman (a film-maker) who was scheduled to visit the Lyes later that day. 'I was surprised,' says Ann, 'but I reminded myself it was fair enough — we were not obliged to keep clear of friends.' They did, however, have some ground rules: normally they never talked about an affair while it was happening but would inform their partner afterwards, not for voyeuristic reasons but to prepare them for any gossip. They also agreed to be brutally honest if a lover did ever become more important to them than their partner. Both took advantage of the open marriage. In Ann's case, there were 'two serious relationships that lasted about six months' and various 'fleeting affairs', particularly during her late forties. She was grateful to her husband for the way he made himself scarce with no questions asked when someone who was important to her (such as Alan Herbert) visited New York. Both always insisted that their affairs did not create problems. 'It was natural to Len, he was so free about sex, he had no hangups, no tieups — I never ran into anyone else like that in my life. Some women may have wanted more from him than an affair but he took it so naturally and lightly, he would just say, "I've had a marvellous time, I've loved knowing you."' His former lovers seem to have continued to think well of him. Meanwhile he and Ann both felt that their own relationship was growing stronger over the years. He constantly wrote her love letters and poems such as this one:

I have lain in bed with you
both of us listening to the
waves on many beaches
to the rain on many roofs
and to streams and rivers
on many beds
as you wake you smile
I remember all
your waking smiles⁹

Over the years Lye had occasionally taught film-making and given guest lectures at colleges and universities.[10] His lectures were generally popular despite a tendency to marathon length and startling leaps of thought. For James Manilla, 'He was so far from the mainstream, he walked to such a different drummer, that you had to be somewhere on his wavelength to follow him.'[11] Yet most audiences found him compelling because of his energy and originality. Professor Howard Conant, chairman of the Department of Art and Art Education at New York University, regarded Lye as 'one of the great under-recognized talents of the twentieth century' and observed, on a visit with his students to Lye's studio, that he had great potential as a teacher. In Conant's words: 'His gnome-like, elfin prancing about and toying with his sculptures created an everlasting impression on all of us. I can just see Len's Mephistophelean grin and pointed beard, turning his head to one side, winking and laughing as he agreed on some philosophic or artistic point or other.'[12]

Subsequently Conant did his best to persuade the famous architect Marcel Breuer to place a large version of one of Lye's sculptures in the plaza of one of his buildings. An agreement was almost reached for the IBM Building in Paris but there was a last minute change of plans. Conant seized another opportunity when early in 1966 New York University set up a Creativity Cross-Over Program within its new School of the Arts. The program grouped media with performing arts courses and encouraged students not only to learn craft skills but to develop their creative imagination broadly. Certain artists on the cutting edge of contemporary art were invited to join the staff on a salary of $10,000 per year. With a studio supplied and only two-and-a-half 'class contact' hours per week, the artists were encouraged to keep their usual careers going. When Howard Wise started to lobby for Lye, he found that Conant had already laid the groundwork. A job offer was made on April 26 by Robert Corrigan, Dean of the School of the Arts, who wrote to the artist: 'I see this association as a way for the University to help one of the most creative men I've ever met. Your presence here will provide a quality of mind and spirit which I believe is essential for a School of the Arts.'[13] Corrigan hoped that Lye would be able to make links with other parts of the University such as the Computer Center and the Department of Metallurgical Engineering. His title was 'Master Artist' and the appointment was for three years. (It would run to the end of 1969 since he did not teach in 1968.)

Lye was in charge of a course entitled 'The Art of Vision' which met twice a week. He made unprecedented efforts to be on time, spent hours in preparation, and would always buy cider and cookies to offer to the class. He wrote to his brother: 'I'm teaching 165 students the sensory approach to art, particularly to kinetic art. A bit of a drag as there's no good books on kinetics and I have to prepare a new lecture twice a week, wow! But the coin is useful to get some machine work done.'[14] Lye's approach to lecturing was eccentric and inspiring, comparable to famous mavericks of the 1960s such as the poet Charles Olson or the architect Buckminster Fuller. In some respects Lye remained sceptical of the whole idea of teaching and would continually urge students to develop their own theory of art. No assignments were set because he wanted each student to find the exercise that best suited them ('I would like you to shape your own shoe as you and only you know where it fits best'). To help his lectures to be received in the right spirit, he quoted Zen sayings such as: 'A Chinese sage said that words were only for meaning, and that when you got the meaning, you best kept it by throwing the words away.'

Although Lye always came prepared with notes it seems he was inclined to throw those words away. Cecile Starr watched him lecture: 'One word would lead, in mid-sentence, to connect up with another thought that would in turn lead somewhere else, and Len provided the punctuation by waltzing around the room, twisting and turning himself around in a kind of syncopation to the ideas. . . . These were not random ideas, but rather ones he was familiar with. When he brought them out, however, there was a newness in the way he let them arrange themselves. . . . They were ideas he never got tired of, ideas he shared joyfully with others. One felt that these ideas were all over the room; he had only to look up in one direction and there came an idea; if he stumbled as he talked it was because another idea lay at his feet; when he swung his arm to help make a pivoting turn, he fairly knocked into another idea; he gave each of them a nod of recognition. . . . Underneath it all, there lay a beat of ideas, a rat-a-tat of the brain at work.'[15]

Lye explained to students that whereas most university courses aimed to strengthen the New Brain, his course concentrated on the Old Brain which was associated with the body and the senses. He described various exercises, such as concentrating for a day on one sense, analysing which sensations are the most interesting and why, observing a moving object in minute detail (such as a door or a tree branch), studying each part of your own body, and thinking about the activity of breathing while your eyes are shut — to mention only a few of his suggestions. Everyone was encouraged to doodle with words, and Lye handed out strips of film to paint. He would also bring pieces of metal to class to show how he played with them to generate kinetic ideas. He urged students to practise such exercises constantly, like pianists and athletes working out every day to 'ensure that the body got together with the brain at crucial moments'. Lye strongly encouraged students to have confidence in their own ability and intuitions but he also expected them to work hard. In a metaphor he borrowed from *The Old Man and the Sea*, he would say: 'Right now you should be building your boat to go way out there and catch some really big ones.'[16]

When Philip Lye visited New York he found his brother writing a textbook about kinetics. After Philip had read the manuscript, he was asked what he thought of it. He replied: 'The only thing I can fault is that sometimes you sound tentative, almost apologetic, and you don't have to, Len, because *you're* the authority!' Ann said to Philip a week later, 'Remember that book? He's ditched the whole lot because you said that.' Philip was horrified, but thought: 'Well, that's Len. He never saw what he made as good enough.'[17] Books that Lye did use in class included Marshall McLuhan's *Understanding Media* and a book about the development of 'happenings' as an art form. He was drawn to happenings by artists such as Claes Oldenburg because of their kinetic aspects and emphasis on physical presence.[18] Other contemporaries discussed in class included Robert Wilson, Meredith Monk, and Samuel Beckett.

Paul Barnes who was then a student in the class recalls: 'Multi-media was the oddball department — a crazy conglomeration of Len's kinetic course, a composer of electronic music, an artist who did light sculptures, and a man from the Esselin Institute — a strange meeting of the West Coast with the East Coast. Definitely a "counter culture" group of people. Other departments looked on them as very bizarre and far out.'[19] In the hothouse atmosphere of the School there were students pretending to be artists carrying round camera cases or film cans which actually contained sandwiches. Erik Shiozaki, another of Lye's students, remembers that 'His reputation as a film maker would attract people off the street, or students from other departments, who came to see his films and to get some idea of the man.'[20] Since this was the height of the 1960s there were also a number of nonconformists who (in Barnes's words) 'were drawn to Len because he was such an odd character, they liked his personality and his philosophy. The whole counter-culture part of him was very attractive to them.'[21] Lye liked the radicals and had no objection to people skipping class to take part in a protest action so long as it really meant something to them. Barnes saw that 'as an artist and as a person Len was always aware of what was happening and he was supportive of the civil rights movement and the campaign against the Vietnam war'.[22]

His students responded in a variety of ways to the unfamiliar freedom of his class: 'Though he would ask students to sit in the same seat each time, everybody shifted around. Sometimes people would get bored, and do a little dance, or go out in the hall and smoke a joint, or just leave. . . . Those who'd come in off the street would ask ridiculous questions, which he was always patient about trying to answer. Student opinions of him ranged from "Here's this very creative film maker" to "Who is this eccentric guy who just babbles on and makes no sense, and why don't we have any tests or assignments?"".[23] Many students stopped coming but a small committed group formed around the lecturer, spending time with him after class in a Bleeker Street coffee house or in his campus studio which was above the Bleeker Street cinema. Lye was approachable and encouraging. Barnes recalls: 'I'd help Len get materials together for the next day's class. We'd be working on something when all of a sudden he would say, "Let's sit down for a minute," and he'd go off into a spiel for twenty minutes — about kinetics, about his gene theory, about film, about anything. The topic was always very unpredictable, and for me this was the best part of the day.' Barnes, who is today a noted film editor, had begun his studies with a love of narrative film, but Lye gave him an interest in experimental forms, not only in film but also in music, dance, theatre, and the other arts. Lye's film taste ranged across all genres, but he was seldom enthusiastic about complete films, only about brief sequences where the editing had a kinetic quality. For example there were Samurai films in which he admired the choreography and editing of the fight scenes. This taught Barnes to look at films in a different way: 'I'd been attuned mostly to naturalistic or realistic film making, and Len sold me on stylisation.'

Frustrated because he could not interest the computer and engineering departments in helping him with his sculpture, Lye was often close to throwing in the job. There were also times he felt that teaching took up too much energy — 'it completely sucks every goddam bit of yourself out of you'.[24] But as well as providing him with a steady income the job gave him a great deal of experience in talking to audiences and presenting his theoretical ideas orally. It marked another stage in his progress from an extremely diffident young man to a highly articulate theorist, a development that would astonish old friends.

During January–February 1967, Lye took time out from the university to join a group of artists touring campuses around New York State. Organised by his friend John Hightower, Director of the New York State Council of the Arts, the tour also involved John Cage (composer), Robert Creeley (poet), Merce Cunningham (choreographer and dancer), Jack Tworkov (painter), Stan VanDerBeek (film-maker), and Billy Kluver (electronic engineer). Kluver, who had selected Lye's work for the Stedelijk exhibition in 1961, was currently the organiser of EAT (or Experiments in Art and Technology, Inc.). The seven artists all knew one another from the New York art world. Robert Creeley remembers that when some of the group were waiting at La Guardia airport at the beginning of the tour, they were having difficulty finding a place to be comfortable until Lye solved the problem: 'Len led us into a rather formal restaurant where a waitress immediately gave us large menus and waited for our orders. We simply wanted to talk and so Len with a lovely avoidance kept the whole scene in confusion. . . . There is a lag in the situation of the eye's response to projected film image . . . that lets the eye see a continuous image. . . . Just so in the proposal of the restaurant, the assumption of a *necessary order* let [us] use it in quite another manner, and we were thus able to enjoy the lag of their adjustment to the fact that we were there to do nothing more than sit comfortably and talk.'[25]

This was to be the first of many 'performances' on the tour. The basic schedule at each campus was a day of classroom talks — such as energetic attempts by Lye to explain to science classes why 'Art has got to be a magical business, absolutely' — plus an evening group event (usually in a packed auditorium) where the artists performed simultaneously. As Grace Glueck of the *New York Times* described such an evening: 'On comes a multisensory blast of "media mix" that feels like a message directly from McLuhan. While some ten projectors bounce Stan VanDerBeek's "movie mural" off the walls and ceiling, John Cage's whiney electronic "white sound" throbs relentlessly through the room. . . . The collegiate audience was rocked. It giggled, applauded, whistled, stomped and twisted in its seats. "Oh, you're too far out," yelled a scornful sophomore, storming up the aisle.'

Glueck summed it up as perhaps 'the most exotic intellectual road show ever to hit the College Belt'.[26] The aim, as Kluver expressed it, was to present the students 'with a kind of exploratory confusion that's very different from the structured, logical patterns of their lives at school'. Lye relished the idea of addressing all the senses at once and creating performance situations so busy that viewers had to divide their attention or keep making choices. Creeley saw the multiplicity as 'a whole new order for us to move in — we're used to apprehending only one thing at a time. Our environment is multiple now — we can't any longer escape it. We can't be single-channeled any more.' All these artists were tough old veterans with no interest in playing safe. As Cage observed: 'We're widening our sense of syntax. We feel expanded by the relationship — and furthermore, we're enjoying each other's company.'[27]

Some professors as well as students were disturbed by the 'primitive randomness' of happenings. How did Lye handle such situations? Creeley saw him as a 'wild, heroic figure' who was 'always impatient with any *located* place, . . . walking around somewhat like a carnival barker, trying to get hold of the audience directly and admonishing them to admit the fact of their own feelings'.[28] Lye would screen films and demonstrate 'Jump Fish', a very springy strip of steel suspended from the ceiling on a black cord. In his words: 'It swings out and straightens and swings back and forth on its suspension cord and it makes a terrific resonating sound, for about 30 seconds to a minute.'[29] He would hold the steel at each end, bend it outwards, then step back as it burst into action. Lye saw this 4-foot-long model as a prototype for giant versions that would be mechanically set in motion. In his sculpture park the 'Fish' would leap dramatically out of the water and dance to its own resonant sounds, then slide back into the water where it would be compressed ready for its next leap.

The tour ended in Manhattan on 25 February with a gala public performance at the 92nd Street YMHA. The event was called 'TV Dinner: Homage to EAT (Food for Thought)'. The artists sat around a well-stocked dinner table, some with their backs to the audience, getting up in turn to talk or perform. They wore microphones and were supposed to answer questions from the audience. Cups, glasses, and other objects were also wired for sound thanks to an intricate system engineered by Billy Kluver and Robbie Robinson (an engineer from Bell). There were television cameras and a number of film and slide projectors. Merce Cunningham danced behind a swinging strobe light. VanDerBeek projected images on the walls. Lye, wearing a strange pair of dark glasses with a cross-shaped opening for each eye, attempted to screen three films at once but only two projectors would start and one dropped out before the end. He then demonstrated his model for 'Jump Fish', and Cage improvised beautiful bell-like sounds by rubbing a contact mike along the suspended sculpture.[30]

To the audience these activities added up to chaos. No one could make out what the panellists were saying. The audience threw paper aeroplanes and coins, and tried to grab the microphone.[31] Erik Shiozaki (whom Lye had invited along with other students from his class) recalls: 'People were screaming out "We want our money back!" and "What is this?" They didn't understand any of it. Len called it a happening, and the audience became part of it.'[32] The audience seemed to find the food especially provocative. Ann Lye remembers her friend Ruth Richards walking over to the table and saying to the artists, 'I'm hungry and I'm not going to just stand here and watch all you people eating.' In Creeley's account: 'At one point apparently the Y's stage manager came up to Robinson and said, "You've got to do something, the crowd is very restless." Robinson continued with his own preoccupations. They were literally more interesting.'[33] Ann summed up the evening with the phrase, 'It was such a fiasco, it was a great success.'[34]

fortyeight the snake god

From late 1958 to 1966 Lye had devoted his best energies to kinetic sculpture. (Though he had coined the term 'tangibles' to emphasise the distinctive nature of his approach, he became more relaxed about describing his medium as 'kinetic sculpture' once that term gained general acceptance.) His work had received consistently glowing reviews and had been singled out as remarkable by some of the country's most influential critics and artists.[1] The public had been as enthusiastic as the critics, with his work attracting huge crowds in Buffalo in 1965 and Berkeley in 1966. Yet for some reason this critical and popular success had never been translated into sales. Five of Len's sculptures had gone to museums ('Loop' to the Art Institute of Chicago, 'Grass' to the Albright-Knox, 'Flip and Two Twisters' to Berkeley, and 'Fountain' to the Whitney Museum and the Tel Aviv Museum in Israel), but one had been a gift and the others obtained cheaply. Three small models and one larger work had gone to private buyers. No wealthy collector had developed a passion for Lye's work, though Wise did sell a 'Blade' and a 'Thundersheet' to one of his regular customers, Pat Lannon from Florida. The dealer was perplexed by the slow response from the marketplace. If quality and critical acclaim were what counted in art, there should have been a crowd of eager purchasers. Many more sales were needed to recoup what he and the artist had spent in developing the sculptures. Lye's difficulties revealed serious limitations in the ability of the art market and the art establishment to support innovation.

What had held things back? Certainly he had plenty of work on offer for he was overflowing with ideas, and multiple copies of each of his sculptures could be produced on either a small or a large scale. But Lye was too much of a loner to endear himself to the market. The qualities that made him heroic as an artist — his single-minded focus on his work, his self-contained life style, and his refusal to kowtow to rich and important people — worked against him in the post-war world of art fashion and art politics. There were also problems associated with kinetic art as a genre, with some important American critics continuing to sound warnings about it because they saw it as a European fad. Museums valued its popular appeal but were not equipped to provide the necessary technical support. Also, some kinetic art was noisy. A work such as 'Flip and Two Twisters' tended to dominate a museum and staff-members wanted to preserve the traditional peace and quiet. Dealers were afraid that buyers of kinetic art would keep returning it when it broke down. In Ann Lye's words: 'People were spending more on their cars than on Len's sculptures. Though they knew they would have some running costs to maintain the cars, they didn't expect to have to maintain the sculptures. Neither galleries nor buyers were geared for that.'[2]

Ironically there was now a fashion outside the art world for small kinetic works treated as decorative objects or chic toys, and the ideas behind Lye's works such as 'Roundhead' and 'Fountain' were frequently ripped off. William Baldwin recalls: 'I would see those imitations in offices, small "fountains", sometimes two or three feet high, without Len's conceptual cleverness or artistry. He used to be so careful with the height, the size of the rods, the material they were made of, and exactly how the motor stopped and started and reversed direction in order to make a composition — it was those details that made all the difference.'[3]

Lye's university job provided a personal income for three years but could not finance the new and larger sculptures he longed to make. And so the years 1966–68 were full of conflict for him. They should have been the high point of his career as sculptor, but at times he was uncharacteristically troubled and impatient. He was, however, obviously in good spirits during the week that a CBS crew spent with him in 1967, shooting a 10-minute film segment for their *Eye on Art* series. (After its television screening, the segment became part of *The Walls Came Tumbling Down*, a film about innovative artists of the 1960s.)[4] This provided a valuable record of 'Len Lye at 66', an artist who 'refuses to stand still', and it was evidence of how much more articulate he had become since his television appearance five years earlier. His confident assertion (as his sculpture thundered in the background) that he was really an artist for the twenty-first century was partly serious, partly tongue-in-cheek. This was a wry, provocative stance he came to adopt more often as the hope of financial deliverance grew more remote.

By now he had acquired a certain reputation as a lecturer. Artist Hans Haacke persuaded the Philadelphia College of Art to invite Lye, and in March 1968 he was asked back to Buffalo for its Second Festival of the Arts Today to give a lecture entitled 'A Saga of the Creative Imagination'. Other idiosyncratic speakers at the festival included poet Charles Olson, composer Iannis Xenakis, and architect Buckminster Fuller. Typically Lye delivered a barrage of ideas, films, slides, and audio tapes, which listeners found baffling but fascinating. Meanwhile, with Wise's help, Lye continued to make grant applications to funding bodies such as the Guggenheim Memorial Foundation. The well-known artist

Frederick J. Kreisler wrote strong letters of support, emphasising the contemporary importance of his work and its relevance to 'large architectural schemes'. Despite such backing, Lye's applications were unsuccessful. This was the third time he had been rejected by the Guggenheim Foundation (twice as a filmmaker, once as a sculptor).

There were times when Lye became impatient with any sort of application or negotiation. Wise was always afraid of him switching to his 'artist for the twenty-first century' stance at the wrong moment. The greatest disaster of this kind occurred during negotiations with the Jewish Museum, a Manhattan museum interested in avant-garde art. Sam Hunter had suggested an exhibition that would bring together the work of Nicolas Schöffer, Jean Tinguely, and Len Lye. Wise remembered taking Vera List, one of the patrons of the Museum, to Lye's studio where she was deeply impressed by a 30-foot-long sculpture called 'Snake God' which undulated its way to a loop where it delivered a load of thunderous sound. Though List did not make a firm offer, she indicated to Wise that she would be willing to advance the $100,000 which the artist had estimated as the cost of solving engineering problems for the exhibition. Wise was delighted. But when he went back to see Lye the price had gone up — now it was going to cost four times as much.[5] The exhibition went ahead in 1966 without Lye, as a survey of 102 works by Schöffer and Tinguely. Lye's friends were baffled by his unwillingness to seize the opportunity. Was it (as Wise believed) that Lye did not want to be grouped with two artists whom he saw as having a different approach to kinetics? Had List said something that annoyed him? Was it still not the opportunity he was waiting for, the big one-man show (which the Jewish Museum had at least discussed with him as a possibility)? Was there a deeper reason, a fear of being compromised by success (as though the snake god demanded a sacrifice)? Or did the proposal simply come at a time when he couldn't be bothered, when he wanted to concentrate on some new idea he was developing?

Sculpture such as Lye's needed all the exposure it could get at this particular time. In 1968 the exhibition 'Primary Structures' at the Jewish Museum focused attention on a new group of American sculptors known as the minimalists. With links to conceptual art, their work came to be seen by American critics as the cutting edge of sculpture. Kinetic art retained its popular appeal but critical interest waned. One of the dangers of a high-powered art scene is that each tendency gets only a short time in the spotlight before it is pushed aside, despite the amount of unfinished business or unrealised possibilities. Kinetic art, which had no well-known critic to defend its position, was rapidly upstaged by minimalism.

Lye's bursts of cranky behaviour (or so people interpreted them) did not occur often and he remained tireless in his search for sponsors for monumental sculptures. He was grateful for the help of sympathisers such as William Baldwin and Howard Conant who tried to translate his ideas into the language of real-estate developers and architects. This was difficult because, as one observer put it, 'Lye just wasn't in the right group shows and he wasn't represented in the Museum of Modern Art sculpture garden. It was nothing personal, they just saw him as a bit too far out on the periphery.'[6] Lye gained one of his strongest supporters in Allan Temko whom he met during his visit to Berkeley in 1966. He caught Temko's attention in the Faculty Club by asking the enigmatic question, 'How's corners around this place?'[7] Temko had wide-ranging interests in art, architecture, and city planning, and the two men hit it off. Lye was deeply impressed by Temko's 'thoughts for getting the best out of shaping city and living environments on a humanity scale'.[8] Over the next few years Temko helped the artist to seek commissions, and when he visited New York — staying at smart uptown hotels thanks to the clients for whom he was working — Lye would turn up for hilarious champagne breakfasts. The ambience of a luxury hotel seemed to bring out the artist's anarchist streak and Temko was alarmed by Lye's tendency to help himself to things. One of the projects for which he put Lye's name forward was the upgrading of Pennsylvania Avenue (the area near the White House). There was to be a large square and Lye proposed a sculpture — 'Timehenge' — dedicated to Franklin D. Roosevelt that would sound the hours in the most dramatic way. This would consist of twelve versions of 'Blade' increasing proportionally in size (to represent the hours) and an additional version which sloped like the hand of a clock. On the hour, this hand and the relevant hour would do a flashing, harmonic dance together, ending with the bell-like sound of metal striking metal. A black granite base would carry Roosevelt's saying: 'Time Reveals Man's Stature'. The project was under serious consideration until the overall budget was slashed and the membership of the advisory panel was changed.

In 1967 New York gained a new Parks Commissioner, Thomas Hoving, who was very open to new ideas for upgrading the parks. Coney Island which had once had universal appeal was now shabby and dangerous after dark. Wanting an outsider to take a fresh look at the situation, Hoving brought in Temko who saw the possibility of turning Coney Island into a kind of permanent World's Fair, a spectacle offering education as well as fun. Raising the topic with Lye, Temko discovered that his friend loved Coney Island and often took its para-chute jump, an exciting free fall on wires. They came up with the idea of building the giant snake god as a sea serpent pointing out to sea, able to shoot high-voltage electricity from its mouth like a giant fireworks display. Temko was confident of finding a large corporation to sponsor it. Lye did plenty of planning for the project but Temko noted there was always a touch of unreality in the way the artist talked about it, as though he had been disappointed so often that he did not really believe it was going to happen. Sure enough, when Hoving left the Parks job to become director of the Metropolitan Museum of Art, his replacement rejected Temko's proposals as too extravagant.

Late in 1966 Lye had received an invitation from the city of Toronto to build a giant sculpture to become a permanent part of its High Park. Along with eleven other sculptors he was offered a budget of $10,000 and a $2000 honorarium. He decided that the site would be ideal for a giant 'Wind Wand'. Since 1960 Len had been testing 20- to 30-foot versions. The wand was like a yacht mast swaying from side to side in a swell though it was more flexible than a mast. Despite its simple, streamlined look, the wand involved many engineering problems, growing in complexity as the height increased. It needed to be neither too rigid nor too floppy and the base had to withstand a great deal of stress. Lye wrote excitedly to Temko in September 1966: 'I might go to Canada to put up a 150 foot "Wind Wand," full of wow. It would be a good test-out to debug in readiness for any large "Fountain" that eventuated.' He expressed the hope to his brother Philip that the Toronto wand would once and for all demonstrate the feasibility of his large sculptures.[9] By the start of the 1967 Toronto International Sculpture Symposium, the size had gone down to 90 feet but local papers were predicting that the wand would be a great hit with everyone, including children.[10] The project got off to a lively start with 'bearded Len Lye of New York, as bald as a bullet . . . the continent's leading kinetic metal sculptor' (as the *Toronto Daily Star* described him) being flown in to his first press conference in Nathan Phillips Square by helicopter.[11] Mayor William Dennison proclaimed: 'This is going to be a great adventure for the city, and, I hope, for the sculptors.'

The first of the dozen projects to go off the rails was Armand Vaillancourt's sculpture 'Je Me Souviens'.[12] Vaillancourt was so unhappy about the standard of work done for him that he left the sculpture unfinished, a rusting pile of metal blocks. Then Lye's project ran into problems. He was told that metal was too expensive and the only possibility was glass fibre. When the Protective Plastics company took the job, Lye gave them detailed drawings to scale. Ann Lye, who had come to Toronto with him, remembers that 'he had the whole thing absolutely down pat. But when we went round every day to inspect it, they would never let us see it. They made one excuse after another. When it finally arrived, it

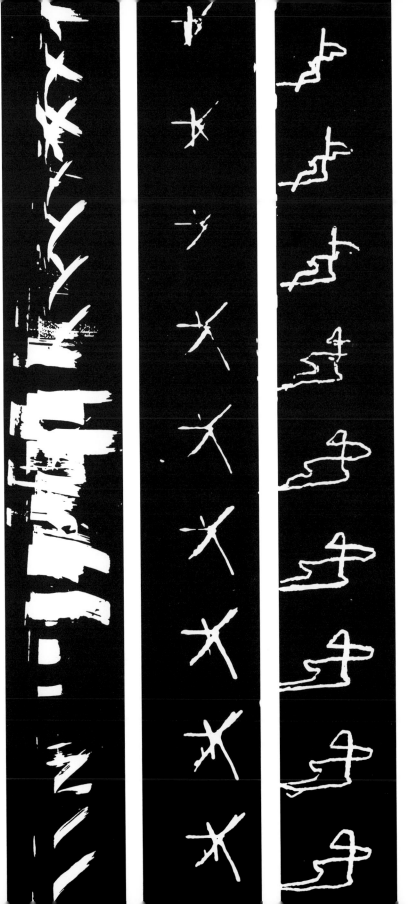

In *Free Radicals* (1958) Lye scratched white designs on black film. Each of these strips consists of nine frames and represents just over one-third of a second of screen time.

Lye scratching strips of 16-mm direct film and testing them on his projector.
(A proof sheet from a photographic session by Gin Briggs, circa 1966.)
COURTESY LEN LYE FOUNDATION

Left: After Lye's job at the March of Time ended in 1951, his wife Ann went to work as a model, appearing in ads such as this for tools and home appliances. COURTESY LEN LYE FOUNDATION

Below: The Lyes owned a 1928 Model A Ford Coupé for their trips to Martha's Vineyard. (She was the driver, he was the decorator or customiser.) COURTESY LEN LYE FOUNDATION

Below: The Lyes at home at 41 Bethune Street in 1958, showing Ann's restoration of the original brick walls and wood floors. Furniture was purchased cheaply at auctions. Behind Ann is a small painting given to Lye during his Seven and Five days by Ben Nicholson. COURTESY LEN LYE FOUNDATION

Above: Lye making the film *Fountain of Hope* for United Nations Day 1959. He is combining the word 'peace' in five languages with his kinetic sculpture 'Fountain'. COURTESY LEN LYE FOUNDATION

Right: The kinetic sculpture 'Loop' (or 'Universe'). The striker ball swings above the steel loop which has just rolled over to one side. PHOTO BRIAN EASTWOOD

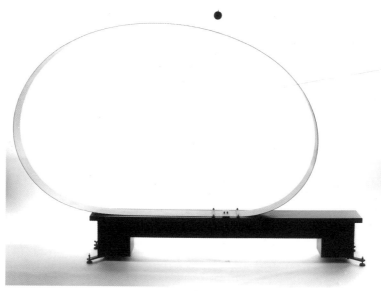

Above and previous page: The Lyes setting up a 40-foot aluminium 'Wind Wand' in 1960 on a vacant lot in the West Village (on the corner of Horatio and Hudson Streets). The helpers include mechanic Morris Gross, and Robert Graves (in a light-coloured suit), who was staying with the Lyes at the time. PHOTOS MAURIE LOGIE. COURTESY LEN LYE FOUNDATION

Right: Lye (upper left) at a meeting of artists called by the Art Workers Coalition in 1969 to challenge the policies of the Museum of Modern Art and other museums. PHOTO © FRED McDARRAH

Bottom right: 'TV Dinner: Homage to EAT (Food for Thought)', a performance at the 92nd Street YM-YWHA in New York at the end of the 'Contemporary Voices in the Arts' tour in 1967. At the table behind Lye are (L to R): David Vaughan, Robert Creeley and John Cage. On the far side of the table are (L to R): Stan VanDerBeek (standing), Jack Tworkov, Billy Kluver and Merce Cunningham. The man in a tweed jacket standing behind Lye and speaking into a microphone is John B. Hightower. PHOTO ADELAIDE DE MENIL

Lye with 'Grass', 1965 (above) and (below) with 'Fountain' in 1960.
PHOTOS ALBERT GRUEN (ABOVE) AND BURTON KRAMER (BELOW)

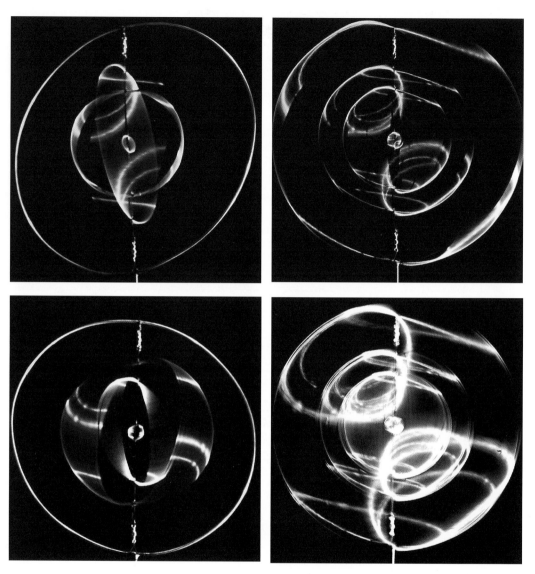

Successive time-lapse photographs of 'Roundhead' in motion.
COURTESY LEN LYE FOUNDATION

was all wrong.'[13] In Lye's words, the stem was 'fabricated to their view of their concept, not mine'.[14] The wand was meant to have the same width from bottom to top so that the only tapering was in the eye of the beholder. If the base needed to be reinforced, this was to be done on the inside. But the manufacturers had found these requirements too difficult and instead had built the wand in three parts, thickest at the base and thinnest at the top. They defended their three-step wand on the basis that the difference in width was only an inch. Lye retorted: 'The difference between the oscillation of a telescoped tube and a straight tube is most marked.' And: 'If the Greeks in carving their columns had said to hell with the architect's concern with the aesthetic appearance, [and had not gone] to the trouble of slightly sloping columns to a grading of three-quarters of an inch in 34 feet . . . then we wouldn't have had the perfection of the Parthenon. [It's] those little touches of perfection which make the difference.'[15] As well as stepping the wand, they had made the top section solid so that it did not move in the correct way. To Lye it was now no more artistic than 'a car aerial'.

Angry as he was, he was persuaded there was no alternative at this stage but to allow the wand to be erected. The artist felt vindicated when the engineer in charge of hoisting the wand said, 'Len, don't you think the bubble on top of the stem is just a little small?' Lye replied: 'Gordon, I'd like to quote you in parliament. That sphere looks small because your eye travels from the [too] thick base of the stem'.[16] Ann recalls: 'Before we left Toronto I remember driving around there again, and Len wanted to knock it down.' At the beginning of May 1968 the wand developed cracks. City officials, in the midst of an embarrassing public argument with Vaillancourt, tried to hush up this new problem. A Parks Department crew took down the wand and hauled it away.[17] A Toronto friend noticed that the wand had gone and wrote to inform the artist. Lye's first reaction to the news that it had gone to a rubbish dump was 'Fine, that's just where it belongs!',[18] but later he wrote to the city council twice to ask what they intended to do. No reply was received. To a friend who expressed sympathy Lye wrote: 'It seems to me that Art is the only hope we have of ever getting perfection but, to get it, we have to make a kind of war. If so, it's the only war worth fighting.'[19]

fortynine genetics

Through the 1950s and 1960s a series of dramatic discoveries in genetics had an impact on many intellectual fields, particularly on the study of evolution. Lye followed those discoveries with intense interest and began searching for a way to relate them to his own conceptions of art and individuality. As he became increasingly frustrated with the field of kinetic sculpture, he shifted his best energies back to the field of research and theory. He found it a huge relief to be immersing himself once again in words and theories, but as his ideas multiplied he felt strongly compelled to share them with others, bringing him once again into collision with the common-sense limitations of the public world. Such conflicts occupied only a small part of his life, however; he was usually bubbling over with excitement about some scientific idea he had just encountered or some original way he could apply it to art.

Genetics, the scientific study of heredity, had been growing since the beginning of the century, helped along by the development of the electron microscope in the 1930s. By that stage Lye was already in the habit of comparing his imagery with things seen in a microscope. Many of his paintings belonged to the tradition of abstract art that used biological or biomorphic imagery and he had often associated his images with evolution. Playfully he would speak of shapes he had painted as 'a fossil', 'solar tadpoles', 'an earth-type thing rooting and sprouting', and so on. In *No Trouble* (1930) he described *Tusalava* as 'life among the microbes',[1] and evolution was a central theme of the film as it progressed from 'the beginnings of organic life' to the 'development of an anxiety all human'.[2] Not that Lye's interpretations were ever definitive — he described the protagonist of his film variously as 'microbe', 'grub', 'python', 'octopus', etc. Over the years his creative writing often included evocative phrases about plumbing the depths of the mind to get in touch with the inner workings of nature.[3] In the 1950s he began to associate his biological imagery with genetics. In 1953 Francis Crick and James Watson discovered the double helix model for DNA, the stuff of which genes were made. The artist was excited by this news because he had always been interested in double spirals. Ann Lye recalls that when he grew a beard, 'he tried to plait it as a double helix'.[4] A photo from the late 1940s showed him standing in front of a tapa cloth with helix patterns, fashioning similar shapes out of wire. He also put spiral patterns into his 1952 film *Color Cry*. In December 1961 Crick and Watson made world news with another discovery — they had cracked the genetic code. The code appeared to be universal and it made possible a new understanding of evolution through the study of genetic mutations.

Lye was fascinated by the idea of DNA, and his curiosity about all areas of contemporary science expanded.[5] His information came from popular science writing in magazines such as *Scientific American* and the science section of the *New York Times* (which he read eagerly every week). In 1966 he discovered a new way of linking his interests. While developing his sea serpent sculpture, Lye had looked to see if there were any relevant ideas in his 1920s batik 'Land and Sea'. This batik was (in his words) 'derived from one pencil doodle of an oval figure rising up out of the sea, wet and dripping. The creature looked like the cross-section of an onion but I knew it had nothing on earth to do with onions. I decided it was a kind of sea god loaded with resonance and vibrancy, quite a protagonist of natural energy. I balanced him up with a cave goddess firmly enthroned in an arched strata of earth and rock. A stroke of lightning from the sea god joined them.'[6] Then a couple of weeks later Lye came across an item he had cut out of the *New York Times* in 1964, which began: 'What may be an important link in the food chain that maintains life in the ocean depths has been discovered.' A chemical reaction had been identified by which particles of organic matter were created from bubbles — a crucial step 'by which the raw materials of life aggregated and concentrated into the huge complex molecules that are the essence of all living things'.[7] Lye made a sudden intuitive leap between this 'bubbling' and the mysterious process evoked in his batik. He had always enjoyed inventing stories around his images as a way of relishing their strangeness. Now science had come up with a dramatic new story for 'Land and Sea' — the creation of life on earth by a chemical reaction in bubbles, triggered off by some kind of electrical charge. The batik was full of relevant details including bubbles, lightning, and shapes like complex molecules.[8]

The parallels continued to multiply. Lye came across an electron microscope photograph of a 'pinwheel cell' which had just been discovered for the first time in a human organism, and was struck by how closely it resembled the oval figure in 'Land and Sea', particularly the original doodle.[9] Other items of scientific news also attached themselves to the painting, such as a *Time* story about 'horizontal lightning' associated with the emergence of the land from the sea[10] and a *New York Times* story about how, during early periods of the earth's history, the earth's magnetic poles had sometimes reversed themselves, promoting the evolution of life by causing some species to mutate.[11] Lye had always developed his images in a very intuitive way, putting each batik or painting through an intense process of trial and error until the image seemed to have arrived at its most powerful and coherent form; yet this sense of rightness could never be explained rationally. He remembered that his decision to flip 'Land and Sea' — to reverse the positions of the two main figures buzzing with energy — had been an important creative decision. Could it be that some kind of natural logic had underpinned the workings of the imagination? Could it be that the parallels with prehistory were more than mere coincidence? If so, what mechanism could have given the human mind access to the inner workings of nature all the way back to prehistoric times? One possible answer was the pinwheel cell which had carried genetic information since the beginnings of life.

Lye became absorbed in these strange speculations about how he might have tapped into a collective evolutionary consciousness. At a time when scientists were making so many amazing discoveries about genetics, were not artists entitled to their speculations also? And a scientist had explicitly suggested that 'the whole story of man's evolution is contained within man himself'.[12] Lye had already found a basis for his conception of the 'old brain' in the contemporary scientific view that the human brain encompassed three systems, each corresponding to a different stage of evolution. The most primitive was the reptilian brain, now largely vestigial. Surrounding it was the old mammalian brain or limbic system (something that mammals possessed in addition to the brain they had inherited from their reptile forebears). This was surrounded in turn by the new mammalian brain or neocortex which was the source of reasoning and, in human beings, the source of language. The three systems operated together but the two deep-lying regions were responsible for the human body's most basic functions and rhythms, and were the source of the strongest emotions.[13] Lye, who had always sought to link his art with the body, associated the 'old brain' with those two regions. As the place where primal data was stored, the brain-stem to the body was likely to be the source of any 'throwback' genetic images.[14]

What he was creating was his own version of C. G. Jung's idea of the collective unconscious (which had had a strong influence on avant-garde art in the United States since the 1940s).[15] Jung believed that the unconscious went deeper than Freud had imagined, and he stressed the need to distinguish between dreams on a personal level and the few extraordinary dreams that tapped archetypes. Lye felt similarly that only a few images came from the old brain, or in terms of his current speculations, only a few were 'genetic' or 'evolutionary'. Jung wrote: 'The deeper layers of the psyche lose their individual uniqueness as they retreat further and

further into darkness. "Lower down", that is to say, as they approach the autono-
mous functional systems, they become increasingly collective until they are uni-
versalised and extinguished in the body's materiality.'[16] While Jung was interested
above all in the level of the mind that contained archetypes, Lye wanted to
investigate the mind's descent into 'the body's materiality'. While he continued to
have great respect for both Freud and Jung, Lye felt that both were new brain
thinkers unable to grasp the wilder energies of the old brain except in an intellectual way. His own speculations strongly renewed his interest in the batiks and
paintings he had made during the 1920s and early '30s because he could see a
myriad of possible parallels between those images and the deep structure of nature
and of the human body as revealed by recent scientific discoveries. In contrast, his
films of the 1930s seldom included imagery of a biological kind and he began to
think of them as operating on a less profound level.

On 9 September 1966 he wrote to his brother: 'I'm working on an analysis of
the subject-matter of one of my own paintings. It appears it's full of scientific
information about evolution. . . . Anyway, I did a lecture on the subject to the
States' Arts Councils boys the other day. Ann there, and wish you were, as it went
mighty wow.' Lye had little success bouncing his ideas off scientists[17] until he met
Dr Oscar Hechter of the Institute for Biomedical Research in Chicago, who told
him that the imagery of 'The King of Plants Meets the First Man' bore an
uncanny resemblance to cells and other microscopic forms associated with the
brain. Here was a scientist interested in art and willing to speculate. However,
when Lye wrote an essay on the subject, Hechter made it clear he could not see it
getting published in any scientific journal.[18]

In 1967 the artist was visited by Guy Coté of the National Film Board of
Canada and invited to be a keynote speaker at a huge festival in August to celebrate the history of the animated film. This 'World Retrospective of Animation
Cinema' was a Canadian contribution to the 1967 Expo to be held in Montreal.
Coté surprised Lye by asking him for permission to screen *Tusalava*, which he
considered one of the slowest, weirdest, and best animation films he had ever
seen.[19] This was good news for Lye as he had not seen *Tusalava* for years and
thought it had been lost. He was also pleased that the festival would enable him to
renew his acquaintance with Norman McLaren, now Canada's leading animator.[20] The two artists had always felt a strong affinity for each other's work.
Lye would speak of McLaren as an animator who could produce a real 'meat-
cleaver of a film effect'.[21] McLaren had been too shy to get to know Lye when
both worked at the GPO Film Unit, and it was not until the 1950s that they had
had their first serious discussion. This had happened (as McLaren recalled) after

an event at the Museum of Modern Art: 'We talked in the taxi and at his [Lye's] home later that evening. He seemed very relaxed, and down to earth; extremely funny and serious at the same time; philosophic wit and humour kept popping up in a delightful way; he was intensely hooked on certain ideas that seemed to be the pivot of his creative existence at that time. He was fresh and inventive in his thoughts, as he had been in his films. That evening lingered in my memory for a long time.' They had more time together at the Montreal festival and McLaren was intrigued by Lye's presentation, as he later wrote: 'Our theatre was jammed mainly with artists and animators. Everyone was impressed by his movies; the personality that appeared in them came across even more when he started to speak. Once again his seriousness was shot through with an extremely casual whimsy and wit. He was very absorbed by the idea of mobile sculptures. The one he brought for us to see was very elegant and shimmering. He talked about building them a city block high. He talked about many remarkable things.'²²

At the festival Lye also met Elfriede Fischinger, widow of Oskar Fischinger, whose German abstract films set to music had closely paralleled the films he had made in England during the 1930s. Although both film-makers had followed each other's work with enthusiasm, they had never met. When Coté introduced Lye, Elfriede Fischinger was strongly reminded of her husband. In her words: 'Len's eyes . . . seemed at that time to be much like Oskar's; somewhat very friendly, contentedly cloudy at the end of a fulfilled life, somewhat at the same time sadly warm and old. I recall thinking about many similarities and could not stop making comparisons about him and Oskar.'²³

The screening of *Tusalava* at Montreal produced a strong reaction from another film-maker. As Lye later told the story: 'It was coffee break for us film boys. A chap named Sen asked me, "Where did you get your dope on the macro-phage?" "What's that?" I asked. "It's a sort of virus. It attaches itself to the wall of a cell, darts its hollow needle-like tongue at it, pierces the wall, and injects its own genetic juices into the cell. And then you get the shivers, or whatever." "Oh," I said. [He continued:] "Your figure, there at the end of the film was not only the spitting image of a 'phage', its action was similar."'²⁴ Sen was shooting a documentary on the subject for a scientist at the University of Toronto. In 1932 an article about *Tusalava* written by a friend, in close association with Lye, had said of the film's images: 'Life cells form the actual motifs of the diagrams: biology is their inspiration.'²⁵ But Lye was certainly not aware then of the macrophage, a type of large white blood cell which helps the body to defend itself against invading micro-organisms and to get rid of damaged and senescent cells. The term 'phage' denotes a creature that devours other creatures. When a macrophage senses the presence of an alien cell, it moves towards it, sticks to it (with antibodies serving as a kind of glue) and then engulfs it, secreting enzymes to promote digestion.[26]

This process paralleled the strange sequence of events in *Tusalava* in a striking way. But if the macrophage was part of the body's immune system, why did it seem so sinister, like a monstrous 'octopus-spider'? Lye was troubled by this discrepancy, as though his old brain had 'got its signals crossed'. In 1978 the problem was solved for him when he came across a story in the *New York Times* announcing that scientists had just discovered that 'antibodies and microphages used by the body to attack invading viruses and microbes sometimes turn around to attack the body's own tissues instead'. This account gave a new lease of life to Lye's speculation that the mysterious sequence of events in *Tusalava* might have been inspired by some biological imagery from the depths of the mind.[27]

Lye would never have thought in such terms in his twenties or thirties. While he sometimes spoke of biology he wanted his art to remain a mystery, even to himself. But now the idea that genetics might provide an explanation for the curious affinity with nature that he felt when making art brought him a surge of excitement, an electric shock, a sense of magical power — not merely the cool satisfaction of logical explanation. Whatever the scientific implications might be, the artist was still a seer, a shaman. Talk of the 'old brain' did not diminish the artistic qualities of the work but simply helped to explain how the artist had obtained his source material — by hitting the mother lode. Lye did not claim to have a precise understanding of the process but he felt certain that something important had been uncovered, and he was desperately eager to find a scientist interested enough to investigate. In 1969 he told his brother: 'I am still messing around with the genetic stuff and will be for a year or two yet until a scientist takes over.'[28] Lye was well aware that his essays lacked the rigour of scientific writing, and he sometimes got scientific details confused, but he was cheered to read about scientists and mathematicians who also made discoveries by leaps of intuition. For example, he often quoted a report that 'Einstein's first intimation of his fabulous Theory of General Relativity took the form of a doodle'.[29]

Lye was not alone in believing that recent genetic discoveries had relevance for those interested in art. During the 1970s a number of writers and film-makers speculated about their possible implications.[30] Lewis Thomas's 1974 popular science book *The Lives of a Cell: Notes of a Biology Watcher* became a surprise best-seller. Thomas articulated the excited mood of this period: 'There are fascinating ideas all over the place, irresistible experiments beyond numbering, all sorts of new ways into the maze of problems.' In his essay 'Some Biomythology' he wrote: 'Our most powerful story, equivalent in its way to a universal myth, is evolution.

Never mind that it is true where myths are not; it is filled with symbolism, and this is the way it has influenced the minds of society.' And: 'I suggest the need for a new bestiary, to take the place of the old ones. I can think of several creatures that seemed designed for this function, if you will accept a microbestiary, and if you are looking for metaphors. . . . The story told by myxotricha [a single-celled creature] is as deep as any myth and profoundly allusive.'[31] Neither of the two men knew the other's work, but Lewis's 'universal myth' and 'microbestiary' were perfect terms to describe the way Lye had begun, some years earlier, to think about his art.

Other artists of Lye's generation had already attempted to create a theory of art. There was Riding's theory of language and Graves's myth of the White Goddess. Like those projects Lye's genetic theories may be seen unsympathetically as a vast folly, or sympathetically as an epic achievement. Ann Lye felt that his genetic ideas absorbed too much of his time and energy, and she and some of his artist friends would try passionately to persuade him that his art expressed his ideas more successfully than any theory. Lye would reply, 'It's near the end, in just three weeks the ideas will be fully resolved and I won't have to worry about them any more.' But his temporary withdrawal from kinetic sculpture left him free to keep researching. Douglas Newton has offered a more positive view, suggesting that Lye's ideas have a poetic coherence, adding up to something like the Renaissance conception of the world as the Great Chain of Being: 'Lye talks about things which are ultimate: pure motion and genetic structures. . . . The artist, socially a "maverick", finds his place in this hierarchy through his creative powers, which are attuned to the basic structures of nature.' The proposal to create a temple of giant sculptures that represent the energies of nature fits perfectly into this scheme. Newton concludes that Lye's overall conception may be valued as one of the purest and most ambitious myths created in his time.[32] If we approach Lye's theoretical writings in this way we need not share the artist's hope that he has discovered something scientifically true; rather, we can appreciate his cosmology for having the richness and complexity of a great myth or a work of art.[33]

fifty the absolute truth of the happiness acid

One day when Ann Lye was in the studio she noticed a letter from England on the floor — an invitation to attend an animation film festival in Cambridge with an offer of accommodation and return fares for them both. When she asked Len what he was doing about it he replied: 'Nothing, I haven't got time.' Ann had heard that excuse once too often. She said, 'I think it's about time you got to New Zealand again. You haven't been there in over 40 years and I'm going to see if this Cambridge trip can be used to get us started on a trip round the world.' He was pessimistic about the prospects but with Ann's urging he started trying to set up some lectures.[1] She knew that the idea of seeing New Zealand again was the only possible way of persuading him to make a long trip. Despite his antipathy to nationalism he had always bristled when he heard this small country described in a condescending way. He had never lost (or tried to change) his New Zealand accent, and if he was asked whether he 'came from England or Australia', he always made a point of setting the record straight.

Lye's most positive memories of the country had to do with nature rather than culture. From the religious prejudice faced by his parents in the 1900s to the conservatism of the official art scene of the 1920s, he had found New Zealand's mainstream culture claustrophobic, but he was certain that the natural environment had profoundly influenced his work, as had the indigenous art of the region. He had observed in 1946 in a poetic passage of 'You Be Me': 'This style is from me in my quest — kid to adult — [growing up around] the coasts the hills the trees the plains. . . . Biographically then was bone and mind knitting far from the visual imagery groove of continental cubic walls of coffee surrealist human split-strewn-spent-match-used sidewalks of café. Instead, as an ant with a brush, I was alone in the Australasian wides, with pilgrimages to towns like Wellington and Sydney to homage a plethora of Polynesia and Melanesia ritual works of art that had been swiped off to the museums.'[2] Writing 'Happy Moments' had made him curious to see New Zealand again, and in 1965 he had had his first meeting with his brother for more than 40 years. During Philip's visit to New York they compared notes on their childhood and Lye said he would like to return to exhibit his sculpture and give some talks. The artist was also interested in finding a quiet location in New Zealand, Australia, or the Pacific Islands where he could paint.³ His interest in painting had been rekindled by his speculations about genetic imagery in his early canvases and by his difficulties with more expensive media such as film and sculpture.

Philip Lye worked as a dentist and a part-time musician, playing the saxophone in dance bands. Although the brothers felt very close, Philip was not involved with the visual arts. His letters offered no hint that the art scene in New Zealand had been going through some big changes. Lye was surprised, then, when a new generation of well-informed New Zealanders started contacting him. First there was Peter Tomory of the Auckland City Art Gallery who came to tell him in 1964 'that New Zealand was going modern in its culture'.⁴ Tomory, born in England, had a strong interest in international art. At the Auckland Gallery he had survived fierce public controversies over exhibitions of Henry Moore sculpture in 1956 and British abstract painting in 1958. The mayor of Auckland had denounced the Moore exhibition as 'repulsive' and a 'desecration' of the gallery, and a leading member of the city council had campaigned against the purchase of Barbara Hepworth's 'Torso II' because it looked to him like 'the buttock of a dead cow washed up on a beach'.⁵ These were heroic years for the struggle to gain public acceptance for modern forms of art. Some artists and art schools had promoted modern styles for many years but there were still many New Zealanders who had hardly ever come into contact with it. With Tomory as director and Colin McCahon as keeper, the Auckland City Art Gallery's exhibitions were creating extremes of scorn and excitement.

Tomory had been delighted to get to know a New Zealander who was an avant-garde artist, and Lye had been impressed by his visitor and intrigued by his suggestion of a return visit to New Zealand. Unfortunately, when in 1965 Tomory had taken the proposal for a lecture tour by Lye on 'fine art film and kinetic art' back to the Queen Elizabeth II Arts Council (the recently created arts funding body in New Zealand), the organisation was not interested. In 1966 Lye was sorry to hear that Tomory had left for a job overseas, and observed wryly that New Zealand was still not able to hold on to its talented people.⁶ But the seed of the idea continued to grow. In October 1966 he wrote: 'I think I'd like the climate, vegetation and general topography of New Zealand so much if I ever got back . . . that I could stick, especially if I didn't care [about] the typical non-support attitude for non-traditional art . . . like in the reaction of the Queen Liz Arts Council [which was] exactly the kind of attitude that drove me out of New Zealand in the first place. Now . . . I could afford to not get any support — because my work has matured enough for me to not even need the moral support one gets out of being in the world's cultural center, NYC. Although I'd need all sorts of technological do-dabs for my films and steel types of motion composition I would not mind to just settle down and paint fantastic paintings.'[7]

Other lively New Zealanders began writing to Lye, such as Hamish Keith who had taken over as keeper of the Auckland City Art Gallery. As the New Zealand art scene sought to strengthen its links with international contemporary art, its far-sighted members took great pleasure in the rediscovery of an artist who had successfully bridged the two worlds more than 40 years ago. Having first heard of him from Tomory, Keith was astonished to see *A Colour Box* for the first time: 'I was shocked to discover that Lye had preceded Norman McLaren in the production of direct films. McLaren's films had been the staple diet of the National Film Library, they were shown to us at school. And of course everyone here was led to believe that McLaren was the pioneer of drawing on film. It's another example of how New Zealanders undervalue and misunderstand their own culture — we defer to other people and don't believe in our own powers of innovation.'[8] In 1967 Keith visited New York with the help of a Carnegie Fellowship, lectured on New Zealand art at the Museum of Modern Art, and visited Lye's studio. Since Keith knew nothing of his work as a sculptor, the visit was an astonishing introduction: 'In no time at all every single piece in the whole studio was working, including the snake that unrolled between two rooms. The whole house was chugging and banging and thumping. It was extraordinary, Len just kept turning on other pieces. At the same time as he was hurling his ideas at me nineteen to the dozen, he was wanting to find out from me what was really going on in New Zealand. And trying to discover whether there was any sort of New Zealandness left in him. What do you think of this work? Is this strange to you? Does it belong to you? Is this my part of you?. . . I had a really strong sense that he had got to a time in his life when he was asking himself: where do I belong?'

The two men had long conversations in various artists' bars. 'Len used to dance along the streets. He literally would be dancing, dancing around you while he was talking. He would dance from sentence to sentence, and walking with him was always an adventure. I always felt comfortable with him. To me he was a New Zealander — as long as he'd been away, they couldn't take New Zealand out of the man.' Keith came to see him as 'a great example of the kind of generous, innovative, ad hoc, radical genius that New Zealand seems to produce from time to time. Our culture does have a radical imagination, even though we also have an army of people trying to suppress it. All our radical writers and artists were concealed from me when I was growing up. I was led to think books were only written by dead foreign people. When I saw Colin McCahon's paintings for the first time, they absolutely rocked me. And Len to me was another of those extraordinary visionaries, like people in cartoons with a light bulb in their head. I could see his idea of the temple translate so easily from Death Valley to the volcanic landscape of the Central Plateau. I discussed that with him — I said, "Re-do it for the pumice plateau under Mt Ruapehu!"'

The two kept up a lively correspondence after Keith returned to Auckland. When Lye announced that he was planning to visit, Keith did his best to organise lectures, as did the art dealer Peter McLeavey in Wellington. However, as Keith recalls, 'Until people had actually met Len and seen his work, it was hard to generate any enthusiasm.' The fees Lye was offered were paltry by American standards. He agreed to do a lecture in Auckland out of loyalty to friends and relatives, but said no to the rest. ('Ann is mutinying on the others as they take so much damn preparation — rehearsals and all that'.)[9] Despite such disappointments, the Lyes managed to find the money for their round-the-world tickets and on 30 October they flew out of New York.

Their first stop was London, where they spent a wonderful week revisiting old haunts such as Hammersmith and the Black Lion Pub, and socialising with friends such as Barbara Ker-Seymer, Gwen and Alan Herbert, Ivor Montagu, and Sidney Bernstein. Lye revisited the British Museum. Then they moved to Cambridge for the Animation Festival which began on 6 November. In Ann's words: 'We adored Cambridge. Goose pimples at everything. We fell in love with England all over again and immediately wanted to live there!' Lye had put a huge effort into his lecture for Cambridge. For some time now he had been trying to find a way of combining all his current ideas in one package. He had tested this in Buffalo and Berkeley, but was particularly pleased with the version for Cambridge. He gave a crowded three-hour lecture in two parts — 'Art and the Body' and 'Art and the Genes', illustrated by films, slides, and audio tapes (coordinated with the help of three assistants). Film-makers Arthur and Corinne Cantrill who were in the audience remember it as 'a marvellously untidy talk but terribly strong, personal and dynamic'.[10]

Lye's overall title for the lecture, 'The Absolute Truth of the Happiness Acid', alluded not to LSD but to DNA (that is, to nucleic acids). His all-embracing theory was based largely on visual parallels, displaying the logic of a visually oriented thinker. A witty series of 'lookalike' slides pointing to similarities between artists and their images amused the audience even if it didn't persuade them that an artist's unique gene pattern shaped his or her art. Lye was never discouraged by the scepticism of his audiences — he was so excited about the intricate web of visual correspondences he was able to weave. *Films and Filming* said of the event: 'Lye himself [is] a slim wiry man looking like a close relative of Ho Chi Minh, dressed in a jolly red sort of kaftan and tripping over his microphone cable. His intelligence is immediately apparent, his sense of humour engaging and, like much of his work, faintly surrealist. But, as with many artists totally absorbed in their own creativity, he has difficulty in communicating clearly to his audience the complex thought processes and impulses which have led him to his present state of development.'[11] For the *Observer* Lye was 'a legend', as other-worldly in his appearance as he was in his thinking: 'Len Lye, a lean, bald, goblin of a man, pushing 70 . . . looks, in fact, exactly like the traditional cartoon Martian.'[12]

After the talk the Lyes returned to London. In Ann's words, 'We spent time on buses and walking, looking at everything. I was struck by all the things growing in the streets, all the coloured things that grow in the dampness of London. We went back to Eric Kennington's studio on the river, and Julian Trevelyan and his second wife were living there, and he was putting up some studios. We were so much in love with London that we applied for one of the studios. But it was November — and in the end we had second thoughts about the climate!' Next the Lyes made a two-day trip to Edinburgh University where a famous biologist, Professor C. H. Waddington, had invited the artist to lecture. This was a rare opportunity to address a science rather than an arts audience, at a leading research centre. As Ann recalls: 'It was a classroom going straight up, very steeply banked, and way down below there was this big desk behind a kind of fence. Len got very involved in demonstrating something, he wanted to get higher to communicate with the people in the high seats, so he just climbed up on the desk and gave most of the lecture from there! He had everybody in hysterics — those animal scientists didn't have much sense of humour, but they were roaring. His ideas didn't relate to anything they were studying and they were just amazed by him — he was so entirely unscientific as far as they were concerned. It showed them an entirely different mentality, one they had never run into and weren't even aware of, and they were completely nonplussed. But as an event, it was a great success. Some of Len's lectures were very successful and some were absolute flops. In its own way Edinburgh was a success.'[13]

On 18 November the Lyes flew from London to Mallorca, where they were met by Robert and Beryl Graves and taken to their home, Canellun, at Deyá. Ann Lye wrote in her diary: 'Heavenly setup — oranges ripe — our own little house. Climbing mountains like goats — Majorcan soup and thin bread — sweet rolls for breakfast — more climbing around — best squid ever for dinner'. Lye and Graves had remained friends despite the huge difference in their interests.

As Ann saw it, 'Robert had a tremendous classical education, whereas Len couldn't have cared less about that, he was for the pre-classical! I was walking up a mountain-side one day with Robert when he said out of the blue, "Ann, I just can't understand why you married Len!" He and Len thought so differently. Len never knew what Robert was, and Robert never knew what Len was at all — and yet they always had such a great affinity.'[14] They regarded each other as 'old myth men'. When Lye had told Graves in a letter about the apparent discovery of ancient evolutionary information in his paintings, the latter had replied: 'Yes, chum, you and I do things in a weird [way] certainly inherited from Ireland or Scotland or some place which enables us to work in the fifth dimension and so by-pass time, and be considered geniuses for anticipating strange facts and phenomena. I'm accustomed to it now after writing *The White Goddess* in perfect ignorance of history.'[15]

The Lyes left Mallorca on 21 November, and over the next eleven days they visited Rome, Venice, Athens, and Delphi. They were seeing Italy and Greece for the first time. While Lye may have retained mixed feelings about classical art from his student days when classes had to copy replica statues, the experience of walking around the ancient sites fired his imagination. Ann recalls: 'One Sunday he went out and spent the whole day in the drizzly rain at the Parthenon, transporting himself back. He empathised so much. He got the biggest kick of the trip, I think, at Delphi. He just became one of the people with this goat going to the Oracle.' Such experiences strengthened his commitment to the idea of a temple, and reinforced his belief that the ancients had brought art and architecture together more successfully than anyone since.

The Lyes flew from Athens to Sydney via Bangkok. They found the flight disturbing because it took them over Viet Nam. In Ann Lye's words, 'We're anti any war, and most of all *that* war'.[16] Arriving in Sydney they made contact with Daniel Thomas, assistant curator of the Art Gallery of New South Wales, who had written to the artist for information about the marble portrait head that Rayner Hoff had sculpted in the 1920s. The head was on display in the gallery and Lye was amused to see that — like Van Gogh — it had lost one ear.[17] Parties, press interviews and visits to Sydney galleries took up the rest of their week, except for a day spent driving north to the mouth of the Hawkesbury River where he wanted to revisit a favourite beach. Then on 13 December the Lyes flew to New Zealand, where the artist's first priority was to revisit the places of his early childhood. They had planned to fly around the country but changed their minds as soon as they saw Christchurch. Instead they got up at five and caught an early bus to Blenheim, through the landscape he remembered as 'bosom hills'. In Ann's words, 'It was a gorgeous trip — how anyone could bear to fly it I don't know. At Blenheim we had tea in a little store where everybody seemed to think we were funny or something. Then we rented a car and drove along the tracks to Cape Campbell.' At the Cape Lye was delighted to find the lighthouse unchanged, except that the light no longer burned oil and the keeper's house now had electricity and a washing machine.[18]

In Wellington the artist revisited his old schools, and then he and Ann went to meet Peter McLeavey whose dealer gallery was an important centre for New Zealand art. McLeavey had become curious about Lye's work several years earlier when he had learned that he was a New Zealander. Obtaining Lye's address from Howard Wise, he had struck up a correspondence. He found his films and kinetic sculptures 'astounding' and reported his discovery in a Wellington newspaper ('New Zealand Born Artist Has Won Renown in Unusual Idiom').[19] The Lyes had dinner with McLeavey and he held a party in their honour at his gallery. He found Ann 'charming and very attractive' and Len impressive for 'his intelligence, his vigour, and his wonder at being alive. Every day when he got out of bed he seemed to confront the world with the eyes of a child. The way he responded to nature was a kind of pantheism, and he celebrated this in his art. He was interested in so many things. He had met so many famous people. You could have a conversation with him on any topic, from Ezra Pound, say, to the colour theories of Rodchenko.'[20] McLeavey was struck by Lye's New Zealandness after 44 years away: 'It's like the case of Picasso. If you know Picasso is Spanish, and you know Spain, then you can see the Spanish element in his work. It's the same with Len — he transcended his nationality, but there is a New Zealand element if you know how to look for it.' Lye was equally impressed by McLeavey: 'I think it is fabulous of Peter to stick it out and try to keep art moving in so meagre an art collecting place as Wellington. It would break anyone else's heart.'[21]

It was through this gallery that Lye met Gordon Walters, one of the country's most important artists. Born in 1919, Walters appears to have been the only New Zealand artist aware of Lye's career from the early days, thanks to his extensive reading of overseas art magazines. He wrote: 'I first became aware of Len Lye in 1936 through a copy of Herbert Read's *Surrealism* which had a reproduction of one of his paintings. Round about this time I made the acquaintance of a Wellington commercial artist, Keith Hoggard, who had been a student with Len at the Wellington Technical College School of Art under Linley Richardson. I got from him a good picture of what Len was like. Richardson told Hoggard that Len was an exceptional student. As I learned more about Len I found that his interests in art in many ways paralleled my own. We were both interested in tribal art especially Bushman art via the books of G. W. Stow, Aboriginal art and Melanesian and Pacific art styles.'[22] Around 1946 Walters's art went through a profound change, setting aside some of its technical virtuosity (as Lye's art had done) under the influence of surrealism, tribal art, and cave art, and in that year he made a first-hand study of Maori rock art in the South Island.[23] Walters's paintings marked a new stage in the development of modernism in New Zealand art.[24] He spent time with Lye during his visit to Wellington and was particularly struck by 'an inspiring talk right off the cuff' that the film-maker gave to the National Film Unit. Lye put this institution on the spot by passionately arguing the case for newcomers to have 'bread and space to work' and access to its film library and film equipment 'after hours if necessary'. If this was not forthcoming, then 'the young chaps have got to get off their arses and agitate, picket, and vibrate some walls till the glass quakes'.[25] Lye's advocacy was timely since the next few years would see the emergence of a new wave of film-makers and the creation of the first 'film co-ops' in New Zealand.[26]

The Lyes spent Christmas with Philip and other family members. Although the brothers had lived their lives in such different worlds — a dentist in suburban Auckland, an artist in Manhattan — they were totally at home with each other, sharing the same accent and the same droll sense of humour. (When Philip had visited New York and met Bix and Yancy for the first time, they had been astonished by his likeness to their father.) Around this time the Lyes also visited artists such as Jim Allen and Don Binney. Binney lived at Anawhata on the West Coast, not far from the area later used as a location for the film *The Piano*, and this was one of several landscapes that impressed Lye deeply. In a radio interview with Hamish Keith he said that as far as he was concerned the most distinctive aspect of the country was its topography, which kept its inhabitants always aware of the force of nature. He could imagine expatriate artists returning at the end of their lives to New Zealand 'like salmon coming up the old river', as the place to create 'their final messages'.

As usual the Lyes went to check out the ethnographic art at the local museum. In Ann's words, 'I had to go to the ladies' room. I was directed down a hallway to some stairs. Along the hallway I passed a marvellous figure. I went back to Len and said, 'Come and see this!' He absolutely fell in love with that figure. We were shocked that this figure wasn't more prominently on display so we went straight to the office of the director of the museum. Len said, "This is the most beautiful thing you have in this whole museum, something has *got* to be done with her!"'[27] As he later described her in a letter to Keith: 'Along with a Brancusi fish and a couple of African [sculptures], she's one of the sculpture-half-dozen-humanity-forever jobs!'[28] This tall, dark figure carved from a single log of wood was Kawe (or Kave) de Hine Ali'gi from the small island of Nukuoro in the Caroline Islands. Within the matrilineal culture of the island, Kawe was a goddess. Since arriving at the Auckland Museum in 1878 this figure had moved from prominent display to banishment in a store room, perhaps because someone had decided that she was 'lacking in artistic merit, or her pronounced breasts and tattooed pubic area were unsuitable for general exhibition'.[29] When the Lyes saw her she was back in public, displayed in an obscure corner but already scheduled to occupy a more prominent place when a new gallery was completed.[30] Lye's outburst was natural for someone who had been protesting against the conservatism of museums for half a century. Kawe was later to become one of the Auckland Museum's most treasured exhibits, receiving international attention in 1984 when it was borrowed by the Museum of Modern Art for its controversial exhibition '"Primitivism" in 20th Century Art'.[31]

By the time their visit ended on the first day of 1969 Ann Lye had come to see New Zealand as a country in which 'the general standard of everything is maybe 30 years behind, but the young people are just the same as in New York. They are right in the groove of art. Len would go somewhere like the Barry Lett Gallery in Auckland and the young artists would sit around on the floor and ask questions. The young New Zealanders are terrific — the old ones are stodgy!'[32] Although Lye had come to New Zealand not to see contemporary art but to renew his acquaintance with his family and with the landscape, he was struck by the energy of the local art scene. In a letter to photographer John Turner he wrote: 'Say hello to all the crazy young artists I met and tell them they inspired me to know there was the right stuff at long last in the old joint.'[33]

Following the same route he had taken 45 years earlier when he left New Zealand, Lye headed for the Pacific Islands. He and Ann visited Fiji, Tonga, and Samoa. In Samoa he located the area near Mt Vaea where he had once lived, but the region had changed so much it took him several days to find it. He learned that his Samoan friend had died six months earlier. After delaying their departure because of a hurricane in the area, the Lyes flew on to Hawaii, where they spent a relaxed three weeks staying with friends on various islands. On 5 February they arrived back in New York. In contrast to the places they had been visiting, Manhattan now seemed full of noise and dirt. Ann in particular found herself 'resisting New York like mad'[34] and wondering if the time had come for them to sell their place and move, particularly as Lye's job at New York University was coming to an end. In the wake of the trip he continued to receive letters and enquiries from New Zealand. The National Film Library ordered copies of *A Colour Box* and *Trade Tattoo*. Owen Jaine, a lecturer in architecture at

Auckland University and an admirer of Buckminster Fuller, told Lye that his students were working on the design of a kinetic temple. And Hamish Keith was hopeful that the Auckland City Art Gallery could purchase a Lye sculpture for its new wing. Lye suggested 'Universe' or 'Storm King', and offered to keep the cost down by getting it built at the same time as the versions needed for an exhibition in Cincinnati. But Gil Docking, the new Director of the Auckland Gallery, had different priorities and Keith resigned. When Docking then wrote to Lye to ask if he had any sculpture that was not motorised, the artist realised that Auckland was still not ready for the real thing.

Meanwhile in Wellington McLeavey was doing his best to persuade the Arts Council to sponsor a lecture tour. Although the Arts Council gave the idea a better reception in 1970 than they had in 1966, the tour could not be finalised. Lye was still thinking seriously about settling in New Zealand, and though he continued to have doubts about the climate, he kept in close touch with his contacts. He was delighted to hear that the country had just produced a vigorous new political movement called the 'Values Party'. Meanwhile several New Zealanders came up independently with the idea of making a film about Lye as a way of introducing the public to a remarkable expatriate.[35] Lye kept saying he was too busy, but eventually in 1972 he agreed to let director Tony Rimmer make a half-hour documentary for the NZBC (New Zealand's public broadcasting network). A television crew flew to New York and shot some excellent footage of the Lyes in Greenwich Village and at Warwick. Entitled *Len Who?*, with narration written and spoken by Hamish Keith, the documentary began by admitting that Len Lye was completely unknown so far as New Zealand reference books or people questioned in the street were concerned. But what if this unknown figure were actually one of New Zealand's greatest artists? Peter McLeavey put that case strongly: 'Of all the creative people in this country, he's probably made the most important contribution to any of the arts internationally.'[36] As part of the evidence of this achievement there was an interview in New York with the art critic Clement Greenberg, who said: 'He's made the only kinetic sculpture that has any real value — real value, artistic value, that moves you — and Lye's kinetic sculpture happens to move me.'[37] With its unusual camera angles, clever juxtapositions, and playful humour, the documentary was a good example of the new energies emerging in New Zealand film and television in the early 1970s. Lye liked the film crew but was disappointed with what they had produced, perhaps because of cheeky (but good-humoured) details such as the cartoon-style music added behind one of his speeches. But then it was never easy for film-makers to satisfy him — their work always seemed to him too conventional, mere 'television fodder'.[38] The documentary received enthusiastic reviews in Lye's home town of Christchurch where *The Press* saw it as 'a fascinating study' of a 'prophet without honour in his own country'.[39] Unfortunately a single television programme could not rescue Lye from obscurity — he continued to be ignored by the New Zealand reference books. And even the art world had mixed feelings about him because — as one artist explained the problem — 'We weren't all that keen on making space for the expatriates because it was hard enough to find space for ourselves.'[40]

fiftyone **utopias**

Back in the art world of New York Lye continued to grapple with the problems involved in scaling up his sculptures. 'Kinesthetics', an exhibition which opened at the Howard Wise Gallery in December 1969, provided him with an opportunity to exhibit a new, enlarged version of one of his earliest and most dramatic tangibles. 'Storm King', a tall blade of glistening steel, was now accompanied by a large metal 'Thundersheet' suspended from the ceiling behind it. As they rippled and vibrated it was as though each part vied with the other to achieve the greatest possible intensity of movement, sound and reflected light.[1] Lye was very excited to be able to realise this large version which had been in the planning stage for years. Paul Barnes, who helped him build the 20-foot-high sculpture in his Bethune Street studio, recalls: 'The thing shook you to your roots. When we finally got it working somewhere near to what Len wanted, he got so excited he said: "That's what art needs, we have to go back to the Aztecs. They'd get sacrificial victims and march them up their huge pyramids at night with torches and ceremonial robes!" And Ann laughed and said, "Len, you know, we can't go round cutting people's hearts out nowadays." And he said, "Well, we've got to find *some* form of art that will move people as deeply as the ancient rituals and ceremonies did in those cultures!"'

As usual there was a tempest of technical problems. In Barnes's words: 'Because of a lack of money Len worked with a hotchpotch of different sources — the parts came from all over the city — and it was a great frustration for him that he couldn't solve all the mechanical problems himself. It was something he often talked about, how he'd love to find an engineer, a solid collaborator, who would work with him to realise his sculptures without the snags and problems that came from part-time, half-interested helpers. For "Storm King" there were a couple of young men who had some engineering experience, and one or the other would come in for a few hours and fiddle with this and that, but they would wind up doing things in a half-assed way, and he didn't appreciate that sort of work at all. Despite all the problems "Storm King" was an incredible piece and when it was turned on, everyone in the gallery would leave whatever else they were looking at.'[2]

Lye hoped that one day his sculptures could be computerised but the possibility of finding an adequate support system now struck him as remote. He never became bitter or angry with particular people, but (in Alastair Reid's words) 'he would sometimes get very bothered, he would get very tall and thin when he was fussed, he'd wave his hands as though to wave the trouble away. If people were not on his wavelength and were argumentative he'd dig in his heels and say "You don't understand". He'd make this gesture of scrubbing away the trouble — swish-swish — and disconnect!' Lye turned increasingly to philosophy and utopian writing, such as his plans for kinetic parks and temples. Leaving his ideas to the future became an attractive choice for an artist who had bumped up against so many obstacles in the present. The last time he exhibited at the Wise Gallery was September–October 1970 when some temple plans were included in the group show 'Propositions for Unrealised Projects'. The theme of the exhibition (which included Billy Apple, Marcel Breuer, Buckminster Fuller, Frederick Keisler, and Claes Oldenburg, among others) had a special appropriateness for Lye. The Wise Gallery closed its doors at the end of 1971 with Wise redirecting his attention to the new medium of video.

Lye saw planning as a valid art activity. For a long time he had believed that 'art and happiness will be the basis of a final religion'.[3] Temples of art, made possible by new technologies, would offer spectacular entertainment but they would not be merely a high-brow Disneyland — they would help people to rediscover the sense of awe they experienced as children when confronted by the energies of nature. Lye's playful sense of humour eased the solemnity — for example, visitors to the temple were promised an aerial view from a flying saucer and Lye assured them there would be a good cafeteria with coffee and croissants.[4] There were many variations on the idea of a temple but each involved a large natural setting — a lake, say, or a desert, or a mountain. To develop the sound dimension Lye worked with New York composer Ann McMillan, a former assistant of Edgard Varèse, who came up with the idea of a 'Symphony of Thunder'. As Lye described it, 'There would be horizontally suspended sheets of metal, magnesium, copper, zinc, and tempered brass. They would all give different sounds when struck and mechanically shaken to make a live performance of this thunder composition she's doing.'[5] Although the 'Symphony' was never realised, McMillan did complete 'Earth Song Metals', a tape composition based on the recorded sounds of his sculptures.

Meanwhile Lye had never entirely given up film-making. Though he was still officially on strike, and tended to be uncooperative when museums and archives wrote asking for his films, he derived too much pleasure from the act of doodling on film to keep away from it entirely. 'Particles' continued to be a work in progress, an ongoing experiment with forms of scratched imagery that he had not been able to develop fully in *Free Radicals*. With wire brushes he was able to create clusters or swarms of dots — 'nests' he called them — moving across the screen with the sense that every detail was constantly moving and changing. The rough, scratchy texture of the images set them at the opposite extreme from the neat styles of line drawing that characterised so much animation. The nests were like a wild abstract expressionist painting come to life. After a long search for music Lye came across two compatible tracks, some *bata* drum music by the Yoruba of Nigeria and 'Jumping Dance' music from the Bahamas. He subjected these tracks to a good deal of editing, but the end result sounded like a continuous piece of drum music, even though the tempo changed every 20 or 30 seconds in line with the imagery. In February 1963 Lye reported to Alastair Reid that the film was 'more than half done'. He described it as 'particles in space that spin and change momentum and speed and go "thrang thrup" between galaxies'.[6] Money was needed to carry the film through to completion and so Lye applied in 1963 to the Ford Foundation which was offering fifteen grants of $15,000 to finance non-commercial projects. In the application the film was now called 'Rays' and he described it as conveying a 'feeling of the nature of energy and the vastness of space'. When neither Lye nor Stan Brakhage received a grant, other film-makers questioned the credibility of the selection process. For example, Robert Breer protested on Lye's behalf in the magazine *Film Comment*.[7] When Lye was asked to reply, he said graciously that the winners were 'all worthy recipients' and that the Foundation's funding was 'the best of a very bad bargain experimental film-makers have got'.[8]

Despite the lack of sponsorship he continued to work on the project. In 1964 he told his friend Jacques Ledoux of the Cinémathèque Royale of Belgium that he 'would rather not have copies of *Free Radicals* on the loose' because he was thinking of expanding it to include the 'Particles' material. But by the following year he was again talking about it as a separate film; and when he was invited to Berkeley, he tried unsuccessfully to persuade Peter Selz's museum to fund the completion of a film that he now described as 'Kinetic Particles In Space'. Soon after that, he dropped the word 'Kinetic' and made the definitive title sequence, scratching the letters in the same way he had spelled out *Free Radicals*.[9] He had become so skilled at this process that he could make a letter rotate like one of his sculptures. He also had the idea of using the dramatic sounds of his sculptures 'Storm King' and 'Twister' to accompany the beginning and end of the film, thus linking the two main aspects of his art.

Lye screened a five-minute version of *Particles in Space* as part of the 'Absolute Truth of the Happiness Acid' programme which he presented at various venues in 1968.[10] On those occasions he talked of happy accidents of which he had recently become aware. He had learned that the Nigerian drum music he had intuitively selected for its sound was part of a ritual to celebrate Shango, the god of the sky and accordingly the god of thunder and lightning. This perfectly matched the associations of his sculptures 'Storm King' and 'Twister'. Furthermore he had learned that the music from the Bahamas reflected the Shango tradition (which had spread through the West Indies). Lye felt that his old brain had responded to these deep affinities.[11] In 1971 he also discovered a scientific parallel when the *New York Times* reported that the crew of the Apollo 14 moon mission were startled to see energy particles in space. There were 'three types — pinpoint or starlike lights; explosive flashes; and thin streaks of light'.[12] This sense of space as a field full of energy particles or free radicals was exactly what his film expressed. But despite his pleasure in having captured new figures of motion, the film still seemed to him incomplete. He continued to make additions and deletions and other changes including a 35 mm blow-up. A 1971–72 version ran for six minutes. Like his theoretical writing, *Particles in Space* was a perpetual work in progress.

fiftytwo **homes**

Through the Sixties the Lyes had spent several weeks each year in Puerto Rico, and this was the one place where they always vacationed together. Their friend Eve Scott ran a school in an old villa where they could stay during the Christmas break, sleeping on a foam mattress on the floor. It gave them a break from the New York winter and an excuse (as Ann put it) 'to avoid all the family business that went with Christmas'. Later they started staying at Ocean Walk, an unpretentious hotel on the beach. The Lyes liked the tropical climate and general ambience of Santurce, especially when they moved outside the tourist or condominium areas. Though they were troubled by the widespread unemployment and poverty, the growing pollution, and the onslaught of American commercial culture, they were amazed to encounter so much personal warmth and generosity. Lye spoke of Puerto Ricans as 'intuitive insighters to whom the bell tolls, who know the tones from the overtones'.[1] The various places in which the Lyes had lived — Hammersmith, the West Village, Martha's Vineyard, and now Santurce — had all offered lively, informal neighbourhoods where they could live cheaply and feel free of middle-class proprieties.

At the end of 1970 when they discussed where to spend what they jokingly described as their 'retirement years', they decided to make Puerto Rico their first choice. The day before their annual visit ended, they saw 'a very tiny, very ugly, very funny little house in terrible condition for sale in the barrio neighbourhood off Loiza Street'. This was 169 Diez De Andiano and there was something about the high ceilings and general shape of the house that appealed to them. The price was $12,000 and Ann Lye (who took charge of such negotiations) offered $10,000. The vendor said, 'Forget it.' Back in Warwick the Lyes saw a house advertised at 20 Church Street. This was the town where they had always planned to retire provided they could live near their favourite building, 'the beautiful old Baptist Church'. Dressed in their snow suits (since it was a very cold January), they went to look at the house; it had no electricity and its water pipes had burst. For Ann, 'It was an impossible little place but we loved the location and for some reason we loved the house'. She offered $12,000 but the owner wanted a lot more. In May the owner of the house in Santurce called to say he would accept their offer, and a few hours later the owner in Warwick called to say the same thing.[2]

The Lyes resolved that somehow they must try to buy both houses. Ann sold their home in Bethune Street at such a good price that they were able to buy another New York home — the two top floors of 801 Greenwich Street in the West Village — and still have money left over for Santurce and Warwick. Artist friends purchased the lower floors of 801 (painter Selina Trieff and sculptor Phyllis Mark and her husband Bud), while Eve Scott moved in next door at 803. The Lyes now faced the huge task of making their houses liveable. For the next year Ann commuted between Warwick and Puerto Rico while keeping her real-estate business going in New York. With some help from her husband she again displayed her remarkable flair for transforming houses on a minimum budget. In Santurce, as the local paper reported, the Lyes created 'a kandy-coloured pink-tangerine house . . . with shiny white trim, shaded by a thick wall of deep green tropical foliage. . . . They liberated the staid brown and beige façade, and carried their joyful palette inside.' Six tiny rooms were turned into one L-shaped space, including a studio for Len in case he returned to painting. When the walls were painted in such colours as tulip yellow and Iroquois orange, Ann commented: 'I consider it very Puerto Rican to have each space a different colour, but my Puerto Rican friends consider it very American.'[3] The Lyes stayed true to their tradition of not owning a television set. Behind the house Ann transformed a trash heap into a garden where once again she experimented in growing vegetables without the help of chemicals. A local reporter summed up her innovative methods of gardening and her broad range of vegetables and herbs (including some usually regarded as weeds) as a crusade to revive 'flavours and textures 20th century man is forgetting ever existed'.[4]

Despite the fact that neither of the Lyes spoke Spanish, they got on well with their neighbours — 'visiting, touching, partying' — with the help of a few words and plenty of gestures.[5] The artist Jean Matos remembers that 'Len was a striking figure, tall, thin, with his bald head and bright coloured clothes — black and yellow shirts and yellow pants. He caused a stir by wearing his *lavalava* in public. He was always interested in colours and would be sure to wear the right coloured jellies to match his *lavalava*.'[6] ('Jellies' were cheap plastic sandals, brightly col-oured, which the Lyes always referred to as 'fuckies'.) Bob McCoy adds: 'Len dressed like an artist but not like an artist who was dressing to make sure people knew he was an artist.'[7] He charmed the shopkeepers on Loiza Street which had something of the ambience of 14th Street, his old haunt in New York, and on occasions when he absent-mindedly forgot to bring money they were happy to give him credit. Local resident Jim Frye saw him as 'the archetypal artist, so uncommercial and so specialised. That could make him difficult but he was never pretentious. He could get on with all sorts of people.'[8] Friends were always impressed by his zest for life, his ability to make something sensuous and emotional out of the smallest happening. Lorraine Blasor remembers once at a dinner she noticed that his eyes were closed. He explained that he particularly liked the food and wanted to concentrate all his attention on its taste and texture — he was making this a Taste Day. In the end, all the dinner guests tried eating with their eyes closed. 'Len did this sort of thing all the time — there was nothing phoney about it. Ann had the same *joie de vivre.*'[9] For McCoy, 'What I liked about the Lyes was the way they always had an adventurous attitude, an experimental attitude. They would suddenly decide to do something or try something. They were not bound at all by convention.'[10] Ann felt very much at home in Loiza Street but Len sometimes found the music and noise in the area distracting when he was trying to work. He did, however, respond strongly to Puerto Rican music and attended concerts. He was interested in local music wherever he went, particularly when it had a down-to-earth energy and emphasised rhythm.[11] The language barrier remained — even for Ann who made an attempt to learn Spanish — and most of the Lyes' friends were expatriate Americans. However, one friend, Joanne Baker, who spoke fluent Spanish and had worked for many years in rural communities, was able to introduce them to many aspects of the culture.

The town of Warwick, 55 miles from New York, was in some respects the opposite of Santurce but the Lyes enjoyed the contrast. In this quiet neighbourhood they made a point of keeping to themselves. To avoid friends from New York City descending on them they were reluctant to give out their address. But it was inevitable that Ann should get involved in the local historical society for the area was full of landmarks, some going back to the period of the American revolution. She initiated a fund to encourage private restorations. She helped to rescue the first brick building in Orange County, 24 hours before the wrecking ball was due to swing into action. In the course of her work she was sometimes surprised by stodgy local attitudes: 'Some of the local oldies thought Len was attractive but they couldn't understand him. Once he wore a jacket made of a flour sack to a fancy cocktail party. In New York they would have said "What a marvellous jacket, where did it come from?" but in Warwick they never even mentioned it! In the Village that's one of the things parties are for, to wear something offbeat, and everybody comments on everybody else. I'd go in outrageous things. It's only above 42nd Street that a cocktail party means that everybody wears basic black.'[12]

Setting up new studios in New York City, Warwick, and Santurce meant that Lye no longer thought of returning to New Zealand to spend his final years. But meanwhile several New Zealanders continued to campaign for a major exhibition of his work. After a visit to New York, artist and educator Ray Thorburn took the idea of an exhibition to the National Art Gallery in Wellington in January 1972 but was shocked by its lack of interest. He then decided to look for a provincial gallery which might have 'less red tape, more imaginative thinking, younger people and a greater chance of a commitment'.[13] He found it in the Govett-Brewster Art Gallery in New Plymouth, converted from a cinema in 1970, which had been exhibiting a wide range of contemporary art despite demands that it should be supporting more traditional and more local work. Its current director was a Californian, Bob Ballard, who had seen Lye's sculpture 'Trilogy' (or 'Flip and Two Twisters') at the University Art Museum in Berkeley and was aware of his reputation as a film-maker. Although Lye had no previous connection with New Plymouth, Ballard was intrigued by Thorburn's suggestion and willing to explore the possibilities. A member of the Gallery committee also expressed interest — John Matthews, the owner of Fitzroy Engineering Ltd, who remembered seeing some years earlier 'a colourful maverick named Len Lye shaking pieces of steel in *The Walls Came Tumbling Down*'. Having responded strongly to the film without realising that the artist was a New Zealander, Matthews was now excited by the idea of bringing such sculpture to the Govett-Brewster with its high studs, sheer walls, and good acoustics, and also by the thought that he might gain a personal opportunity to 'work with such an artist outside the mundane concerns of conventional engineering'.[14]

So Ballard wrote to the artist to ask if he had a project suitable for the gallery. Lye replied: 'Yes, but I'll need a very clever engineer.' Tired of wrestling with technical problems, he was reluctant to get involved unless the gallery could find him 'a genius engineering designer and technical motion programmer'.[15] Matthews found Lye's criteria daunting but felt that someone had to accept the challenge. Aware that engineers often received a bad press for what they did to the environment, Matthews was happy to be involved in such a positive project. In his next letter Lye said he would like two works to be built, 'Fountain' and 'Trilogy', representing the two poles of his kinetic sculpture (the gentle and the powerful). He had drawings but he could not provide detailed plans. Matthews had an engineering workshop that was well equipped for sophisticated work, but was so busy with other jobs that he hoped he could delay the project for a couple of years. When he phoned Ray Thorburn — who had returned to New York on a Fulbright Scholarship — to discuss the timing, Thorburn gave a blunt reply: 'No! The time to act is now.'[16]

In September 1974 Thorburn picked up Matthews at Kennedy Airport and took him to meet Lye. Matthews was full of trepidation because he knew from past experience that such a project would never work unless the artist and the engineer were on the same wavelength. In his words: 'We went to his studio. He wasn't there but I immediately had a feeling, hey, this is going to be all right. There were little boxes all over the place with notes on, labelling his kinetic work. Ray said, "You've got to put the saucer back in the right place, and make sure you put the sponge in the corner of the shower, because that's how he likes it," and I thought: "This guy is as difficult as I am about these things." I wandered around his studio and I found pinned on the wall a framed cartoon out of the *New Yorker*. It showed two rats in a laboratory and one is looking at the other and giving him a dig in the ribs, and saying: "Hey, have I got these guys fooled. Every time I pull this handle, they drop in a piece of cheese." I was delighted because on the wall of my office in New Zealand I had exactly the same cartoon!'

Lye had been similarly worried about getting on with his visitor. He feared that the New Zealand interest in his work was merely a nationalist reflex, as he remarked to Robert Graves: 'They are after me as a fox — the tallyhoo to tally the total — they who do not know my old brain significance of work are keen to preserve it, why? . . . that snooky stuff of being lo and behold a native son of home grown chlorophyll.'[17] But with Matthews he developed an easy rapport — at last here was an engineer with the knowledge and commitment needed to grapple with the operational problems of kinetic sculpture. Matthews stayed for two weeks and was impressed as much by the artist as by his art. 'Len had great energy and was busy from the time he got up to the time he went to sleep. You could always see him coming down the street because he had this gait about him, he moved at quite a fast clip and at the same time there was a jauntiness. He walked tall, stood tall, and was a very dapper dresser. He had a lovely outgoing personality, he laughed a lot, with a raucous laugh. Len was a warm sort of character and he appealed to a lot of people. He really attracted attention, and I think he knew it, but in a pretty nice way.'[18]

Matthews returned to New Plymouth with the aim of making an 8-foot-high version of 'Trilogy' and a 10-foot-high version of 'Fountain'. The former required Swedish surgical stainless steel which was only rolled once a year, and the latter involved 120 high tensile steel rods of a material also difficult to obtain. The engineer was greatly impressed by the artist's approach to motors: 'The motivation force is a sophisticated little DC unit that uses fractional horsepower. The wonderful thing is that Len never mounts so much power that the motivation force dominates. The work goes through all its various harmonics and those sources of energy get controlled by the work — there's a lot of feedback. The art always dominates the motors, the motors only just cope.'¹⁹ The gallery committee also continued to feel enthusiastic about the project and it was given the green light by the local city council. A budget of $18,250 seemed sufficient because various companies and individuals were prepared to donate their time (in particular John Matthews and Fitzroy Engineering). This figure had to include the cost of bringing the Lyes to New Plymouth. Because of his good feelings about the people involved and the idea of his work returning to New Zealand, the artist himself asked for only a nominal fee, thus making the sculpture virtually a gift.

In July 1975 Ron O'Reilly, the Govett-Brewster's new director, made a successful application for half the amount to the Arts Council, which was now headed by Hamish Keith, a long-time supporter of Lye's work. By November Matthews had been working for nine months in the Fitzroy engineering workshop in New Plymouth developing a full-scale working model of 'Trilogy'. Confident he had overcome the technical problems, he wrote to tell Lye he was returning to New York. But he was disturbed by the artist's reply: 'Terrific, John, bring me some plans for the art gallery so we can get the scale right.' Matthews recalls: 'I went to New York with photographs and sound recordings and I said to Len, "Here it is." And then I really got to know this man because he put me down in a chair, poured a stiff rum and orange juice — got me all relaxed, you see — and he said, "Now John, now that we've mastered this, we're gonna build the real one." And I looked at him with amazement. "What do you mean?" He said: "I want one twice the size." And I thought, oh my god, here we go again, because I knew that he had a history of this sort of scaling up. I said, "Well, Len, that's not the way we all agreed to do it." But that didn't seem to matter. He didn't seem to hear, he just went on and on about the scale. That's really when the end of the fun came for me.'²⁰

To get the scale right for the gallery, Lye wanted 'Fountain' to have 15-foot rods and 'Trilogy' to be 25 feet high.²¹ Matthews knew this would involve a whole new set of engineering problems. To make a sculpture twice as large was not simply a matter of doubling the size of all components because as the weight increased, so did the energy required. There was no longer any certainty that the steel would hold together or that the twisters would produce the desired shapes. Matthews, who had heard of the disaster in Toronto when a large, expensive sculpture had been built and then rejected by the artist, began to have nightmares about the New Zealand venture ending similarly as a heap of rusting metal.²² Nevertheless he returned to New Plymouth and said he was prepared to continue, though he made it clear that there were now doubts about whether the project could be achieved from an engineering point of view. One way to keep the cost down was to buy uncut steel. Because of its hardness the metal was very difficult to cut but Matthews believed his workshop could handle it. The artist agreed to buy the steel, and Matthews and many other individuals were prepared to donate their work to the project. The Arts Council agreed to increase its contribution to $12,500, and the gallery matched this figure, which was a large and potentially controversial amount for a provincial gallery to risk.

Matthews turned to his former university teacher, Cliff Stevenson, who was now dean of the Engineering School at the University of Canterbury in Christchurch, to help with the mathematical work required. Stevenson decided to make it an exam question. But even after some of the best students in the school had made a computer analysis, the problems appeared to be mathematically insoluble, and Matthews began to have serious doubts about the project. The artist might know what shapes and sounds he wanted, and might display an intuitive understanding of metals, but he could not offer any help with the engineering problems. But Matthews did not give up. He spent the next twelve months working on it. He imported all the materials — the motors and the steel — and enlisted the help of Colin Corcoran's engineering firm to plan the electronic control aspects. That was a challenging task as the artist required a very precise sequence of movements. Matthews and his team spent many nights and weekends in the engineering shop, experimenting with ordinary stainless steel because of the high cost of the Swedish steel. Despite the small size of the motor the movement would sometimes twist the metal horribly out of shape.[23] Finally the work seemed to be performing satisfactorily, and Matthews again felt a deep respect for Lye and his intuitive sense of what was possible.[24]

Conscious that the aesthetics of the work still had to be approved, Matthews sent regular reports to the artist who turned out to be much easier to get on with than his reputation had suggested. A typical response from Lye was: 'Well, if you think it looks all right, and it has that sort of tingling business about it, then it's all right with me.'[25] So Matthews prepared the final designs. By now there were strong time pressures since the exhibition had already been delayed for a year. The Lyes were booked to come to New Zealand in October 1976. The critical moment arrived when the scarce Swedish steel had to be cut. Previously the team had proceeded by a lengthy process of trial and error, aware than a difference of half an inch, or even less, could make a huge difference to the way a strip of metal performed under speed. There was also a whole set of variables associated with the motors, which was why the Engineering School had given up — too many variables to give any clear answers. Finally Matthews took a deep breath and gave directions for the cutting of a 'Flip' and two 'Twisters'. When the cut strips were set up on crane rails in the roof, and the motors were turned on, the work went crazy, almost slicing off the workmen's heads. It was a moment of great drama and despair for Matthews who now realised that the Swedish steel behaved in a completely different fashion from the steel used to date.

Again the team went through a long process of testing. Finally they found the magic numbers and all three parts of the sculpture began to perform perfectly. The mayor came down to the workshop and was very impressed. Matthews' doubts were at last resolved — Lye was 'a bloody awful engineer but a genius when it came to handling steel!' Even the more gentle work, 'Fountain', presented its own technical challenge, such as how to polish 120 stainless-steel rods to produce the glitter required by the artist. The team tried pumice, sandpaper, polishing, and buffing machines but nothing seemed to work. There was neither time nor money to get more rods shipped over. Finally Tony Smale of Cambrian Engineering in New Plymouth pointed to a grinding machine under a dusty canvas in a corner of his workshop. In Matthews' words, 'It was an ancient cast-iron machine that looked as though it had come out with Captain Cook. We had one of those magical moments when we fed a rod into the machine and it came out the other end looking absolutely perfect.'

Lye agreed to lend a 5-foot-high version of 'Blade' from his studio, but when it arrived it was not working properly and the task of adapting it from the American to the New Zealand electrical system was not at all straightforward. 'Trilogy' still had to be mounted in the gallery, and so great was the energy of the work that the main roof beam cracked and had to be braced.[26] Fortunately the director, Ron O'Reilly, continued to give enthusiastic support. And John Maynard, who had been the first director of the gallery, did an outstanding job of designing the exhibition to ensure that works were seen to their best advantage. At last, early in 1977, everything was ready.

fiftythree new plymouth

During this long struggle to scale up the sculpture, Lye had made another overseas trip with Ann as guest of honour at the 1975 Annecy Festival of film animation. A postcard to Philip summed it up: 'A great life we gypsies live — here for a film festival where they're paying homage to yours truly — food, wine, song and friends'.[1] Next they visited Paris, so charmed by the city that they spent all the first night strolling along the Seine.[2] Next day they met up with their old friends Bernard and Judith Childs. In Judith's words: 'We were running around like kids. We took them to see this incredible exhibit of seashells from all round the world in the anthropological museum, the Musée de l'Homme. There were shells of every kind and description — shells as money, shells turned into musical instruments, shells encrusted with gems, a whole universe conducted on the basis of shells. We were the only people there and they were playing music to illustrate certain aspects of the shells. There was a very catchy waltz version of a melody from Verdi's *Nabucco* and we all started to dance, we had a ball. As we waltzed we knocked over some of the furniture, but the guards didn't mind — they were West Indians who liked music. Everybody had an hilarious time.'[3]

Then Lye searched out the exhibit he had been wanting to see for more than 20 years since reading about it in the *New York Times* — the oldest known musical instrument, a 'Stone Age marimba' more than 5000 years old. Back in 1954 he had tried unsuccessfully to fund a hand-painted film to be based on a piece of music composed especially for the instrument. When he finally saw the marimba it seemed to him that 'a stone-age Brancusi' had carved the stones. He wrote a poem to describe his reaction:

> The flesh on my bones
> Warmed with such resonance.
> Have you ever felt your gene-pattern
> Light up [like] the ringings and buzzings
> Of a pin-ball machine? . . .

While in Paris Lye spent time with the artist Nicolas Schöffer, and later wrote: 'If I can't get a temple project going in New Zealand I will try France and

360

Left: Lye revisits the Cape Campbell lighthouse on his 1968 return trip to New Zealand. COURTESY LEN LYE FOUNDATION

Below: Lye with kinetic sculptor Nicolas Schöffer in Paris, 1975. PHOTO ANN LYE

Bottom: A panel of kinetic sculptors at the Berkeley campus of the University of California in 1966. L to R: George Rickey, Len Lye, Peter Selz (chairman), Harry Kramer, and Takis. PHOTO RON CHAMBERLAIN. COURTESY LEN LYE FOUNDATION

Right: One of Lye's many designs for a 'temple'. Here the Temple of Lightning is located at the centre of a cinquefoil lake, ringed by giant sculptures. Clockwise from the top they include a 'Water Swirler', 'Wind Wands', 'Flying Discs', a 'Steel Fountain' rotated by water jets, and 'Twisters'. On the left there is a 'Swayer' viewing platform. COURTESY LEN LYE FOUNDATION

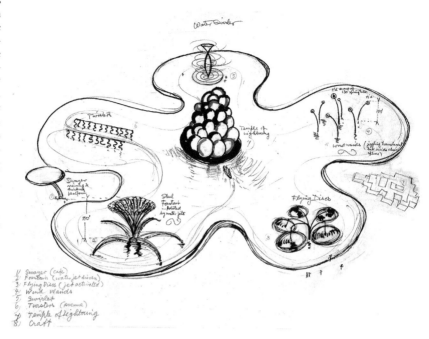

Right: 'Timehenge' or 'Steel Henge', Lye's 1960 design for a kinetic clock sculpture on Pennsylvania Avenue near the White House. The drawing shows the tenth 'Blade' from the left doing its dance for ten o'clock, demonstrating the double-harmonic '8' shape. The caption is a famous saying by Franklin D. Roosevelt: 'Time reveals man's stature.' COURTESY LEN LYE FOUNDATION

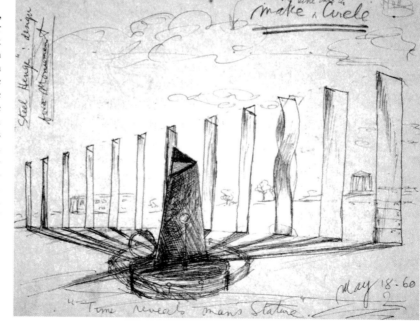

Left: Lye's 1978 acrylic painting 'God of Light', also known as 'The Big Bang Man', based on his 1933 watercolour 'Cagn Who Made Things.' Lye spoke of the painting as a myth about the discovery of seeing.
COURTESY LEN LYE FOUNDATION

Bottom left: The Lyes at the Govett-Brewster Art Gallery in New Plymouth in 1977 for the opening of his exhibition.
COURTESY TARANAKI NEWSPAPERS

Below: After 43 years Lye comes face to face again with Rayner Hoff's portrait head (in Sydney, at the Art Gallery of New South Wales, 1968). COURTESY LEN LYE FOUNDATION

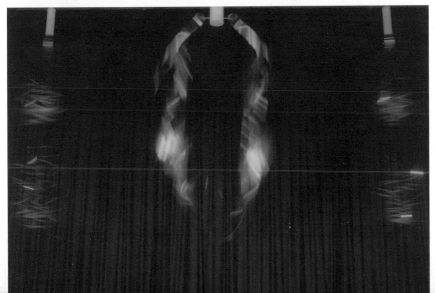

Left, top to bottom: Three phases of 'Trilogy' in motion at the Govett-Brewster Art Gallery.
COURTESY LEN LYE FOUNDATION

Opposite page: 'Trilogy' under construction at Fitzroy Engineering, New Plymouth, in December 1976. Ron O'Reilly is standing on the left next to a 'Twister' (the vertical metal strip) while John Matthews walks past 'Flip' (the metal loop).
PHOTO BRYAN JAMES. COURTESY LEN LYE FOUNDATION

Right: Lye in his painting clothes taking a break from work on a canvas (Santurce, 1979). COURTESY LEN LYE FOUNDATION

Above: In a familiar pose at the typewriter revising one of his theory essays (Santurce, 1977). COURTESY LEN LYE FOUNDATION

Right: In his attic studio at Warwick in upstate New York working on a slide-tape programme (1976). PHOTO NANCY BUNDT

Top: Lye in front of his 1979 painting 'Witchetty Grub' (based on an image from his 1929 film *Tusalava*). PHOTO ROBERT DEL TREDICI

Bottom: Two of Lye's ever-changing signatures (which created problems with his bank).

Top: Ann Lye in 1980 with the portrait of Lye she commissioned from Selina Trieff. She is standing beside the prototype of the sculpture 'Blade'. PHOTO SHIRLEY HORROCKS

Centre: At Lye's wake (15 June 1980) Ann talks with David Horton, Lye's photographer in Warwick, and his wife Katha. COURTESY LEN LYE FOUNDATION

Bottom: New Zealanders Max Gimblett (left), Roger Horrocks and John Matthews (right) stand with Ann Lye outside 801 Greenwich Street, having just finished clearing out Lye's studio and getting his work ready for shipping to New Plymouth where it will become the Len Lye Foundation's core collection. (Photo taken by Shirley Horrocks, another member of 'the removal crew'.)

start with Nicolas Schöffer.'[4] The Lyes also went to London for nine days to see old friends. One was Tom Matthews who was then writing *Under the Influence*, a passionate account of his struggle to escape from the intellectual influence of Laura Riding. Since Matthews could see traces of the same mind-set in Lye's theorising, he added a description of this meeting to his book: 'I went up from the country to have lunch with [Lye]. He must have found me much aged, but I could see no change in him. What an innocent old con man he is! His besetting notion is still with him (he'll never let go of it) but the key word now is "body" (genes?). Even his clothes — what *was* he wearing? — reminded me of those Irish tweeds in which he had appeared when he first arrived in New York. We looked at each other sideways, and talked of old times. His rolling, watchful, evasive eye! *The Guardian* had a piece the next day in which he was mentioned as "the legendary Len Lye" — and that's what he is. I'm glad we met again. I think it was our last time.'[5]

Then, in February 1977, the Lyes headed for New Plymouth. They stayed in a house owned by John Matthews's mother Mary right on the beach at Ohakura. This extraordinary setting conjured up youthful memories for Lye who wrote in the Visitors' Book: 'Just a sang-song-ting at twilight for Mary and her bach by the sea. As I said it in 1928: "Ye yea you gentle South E breeze . . . take me to Poneke shore and to the friends no fried eggs and friends I loved so well in days of yore yoke or gone by."'[6] The Lyes rambled round happily, enjoying the local pub and the fresh food from the local fish and chip shop. Philip Lye and his wife Margaret came to join them, then John Matthews took the Lyes on their first visit to the Govett-Brewster Gallery. The artist was very pleased with the engineering work, producing great sighs of relief all round. He also liked the gallery for its 'temple' feeling. But he had some suggestions, enough to keep the team busy for several frantic days making adjustments. It was characteristic of Lye to be forever standing back to take another look, coming up with new ways to improve the sound or the lighting. He wanted the sculptures at the Govett-Brewster to be dramatically spot-lit against dark backgrounds, maximising the effects of light on their highly reflective metal surfaces.

Lye reported to his old friend Barbara Ker-Seymer: '[Monica Brewster] left a bequest to request the town to get themselves an art gallery devoid of too much interference from the town's councillors. John and the artists there decided not to let the town pull down an old movie house but convert it into a gallery instead. This they did perfectly and it happened to show my film and my steel cracker-jacks perfectly as if made for the job. Perfect is a word to write a hundred times and it was, I mean, perfect.'[7] Around 200 people turned up to the opening of the exhibition on 5 March 1977. Hamish Keith said in his speech: 'Once again New Plymouth has beaten everybody else. What has happened here is the realisation of a dream that was Len's many years ago, but to which many other New Zealanders have now contributed.' He mentioned supporters such as Peter Tomory, Peter McLeavey, Ray Thorburn, Bob Ballard and John Matthews, then added: 'All I can say as Chairman of the Arts Council is that this is for me perhaps the most import-ant occasion I've ever been asked to speak at.' Recalling *Lye Who?*, he added: 'The prophet *is* with honour in our land!' Ann Lye wept at the sight of her husband's sculpture realised on a giant scale after so many years of conflict and frustration. Astonished by the resourcefulness and commitment of all the local people who had worked on the project, she later commented: 'It's like we found New Zealanders to be still members of a tribal society where every man takes pride in his own work. It was very stimulating. With John Matthews supervising and with a local electrician actually inventing electronic controls for the sculptures, it was the first time they'd ever worked all the way through a show — they never broke down and they're still running, it's magic!'[8]

The first work encountered by visitors to the gallery was 'Fountain'. Then they climbed the stairs towards 'Blade', which attracted them with its insistent rhyth-mic sound. 'Trilogy' was timed to follow 'Blade'. Visitors moved to a balcony and looked out into a black space two storeys high (a space once occupied by a cinema screen). From the roof hung the two 'Twisters,' 20-foot strips of gleaming steel, with a great 30-foot steel loop between them. In Wystan Curnow's vivid des-cription, 'something very theatrical is about to happen. The twisters begin to turn, to curve into scimitars, scythes, twirling and slicing the dark air and flicking light across the curtains.'[9] On this scale the struggle of 'Flip' to turn itself inside out and its ecstatic release of sound became an astonishing experience. Matthews recalls: 'People were at times quite frightened about the energy, and sometimes I was too. You start to wonder what might happen with this whole raging piece. I remember a child crying, and I asked Len about this, and he said: "Oh, that's quite normal. They cry when they're born and they're crying now!"'[10]

A television crew came to New Plymouth to record the opening and to inter-view Lye. He was wearing one of his classic outfits which included hexagonal dark glasses, a hat with large blue polka dots, and a white shirt with an optical explosion of blue polka dots over a T-shirt with blue stripes. For the benefit of the camera he waggled a saw to illustrate his habit of doodling with steel. He also gave an interview to the arts magazine *Spleen* in which he argued for the local mountain Mt Egmont to be given back its Maori name Taranaki, and for the local cricket ground (Pukekura Park) to become a site for art rituals because it looked Aztec.

The interviewer from Wellington added a personal comment about how weird it felt to be having a conversation about temples with an avant-garde artist from New York in a prosaic region of 'cow-farms and broken-down dairy factories'; but then as he drove home after the interview he found himself seeing the landscape with new eyes. Thinking of the Maori prophets of Taranaki he ended with the comment: 'Men have had visions before between the mountain and the sea!'[11]

Before leaving New Zealand at the beginning of April Lye had a meeting with John Matthews, Ray Thorburn, and Hamish Keith to discuss the possibility of creating a non-profit foundation in New Zealand to which he could bequeath his work — his paintings, films, manuscripts, sculptures, and plans and models for unfinished projects. A foundation in New Zealand seemed to offer the best chance of his work being preserved and kept in working order so that eventually his big projects might be realised. The Govett-Brewster exhibition was the first time in his career he had received adequate technical support, and he liked the idea that returning his art to New Zealand would be a way for things to go full circle. An agreement was drafted in principle, though there were still many details to resolve. Lye was certainly transforming his old reputation for being difficult to deal with or fiercely possessive of his work. He told Barbara Ker-Seymer about the foundation: 'This is miraculous as it lets Ann off the hook when I peg out maybe sooner maybe later the sooner the better if there's plenty of gorgeous angels soaring round.'[12]

He did have an increasing sense of urgency. For ten years he had been think-ing about returning to painting, and a room in their house in Puerto Rico had long ago been set up as a studio. Lye was himself puzzled about why he was not able to paint, a procrastination he compared with the creative block he had once experienced in Samoa. To friends he wrote: 'I'm in Puerto Rico where the mañana lurks waiting to throw a mosquito net over my work.'[13] Ann Lye was afraid he might have 'lost his touch', and perhaps he felt the same anxiety. Then the success of the New Zealand trip and the promise of a Foundation to look after his work gave him a new energy, and one day in June 1977 he returned from Warwick to New York with his first painting. In Ann's words: 'It was so good that I cried for half an hour after I saw it. Len was very impressed by my response! After that he painted steadily, and achieved what he'd set out to achieve. It was a huge relief.'[14] There were fourteen large paintings in the series, almost all acrylics.[15] Lye saw them as a return to roots and a way to assemble images as parts of a single mythology, like the sacred images or totems of some long-lost culture. What the images had in common was their origin in the old brain and their potential (in terms of Lye's theories) to symbolise natural evolutionary values.[16]

The canvases were mostly around 7 feet high, varying in width from 6 to 10 feet. He painted 'Land and Sea', 'Family Conference', and 'Fire Devil, Leaving' in New York, then did the other paintings over two winters in Puerto Rico. Lack of space in his Santurce studio forced him to paint at least one of the larger paintings ('Polynesian Connection') turned on its side.[17] After each canvas was completed, the Lyes would have an 'opening' — friends would view the new work and there would be sandwiches and champagne and dancing, and the artist would be very relaxed. At other times, as Jean Matos recalls, 'he was so engrossed in his work, he was like a monk'.[18] In 1978 Ernest Smith, the director of the Auckland City Art Gallery, wrote to him to discuss an exhibition, and this gave him deadlines to aim at. Though Smith resigned in 1979, the planning for the exhibition was carried on by the gallery's enthusiastic senior curator Andrew Bogle. Lye saw himself as racing against time, not only because the event was scheduled for 1980, but because of his age. He told Wystan Curnow: 'I am way behind. I've got about ten more of these things *starving* to get done. Christ!'[19] He still agonised over the quality of his work, and his failing health gave him good days and bad days. Still, he kept driving himself along.

Some of the paintings were based on batiks that had become badly faded and others were reconstructions of canvases that now existed for him only as photographs or memories. 'Witchetty Grub' was derived from the film *Tusalava*. Three of the paintings ('Night and Day', 'Rift Fish', and 'Rain Tree / Earth') were basically new, but for the most part the series was a gathering and reworking of his favourite images. He kept close to earlier versions but he would make small changes of composition or colour or title.[20] His method of working was to select an image, make a slide of it, and then project it on to a large hanging canvas. As Bogle observed: 'By manipulating the slide projector he was able to control the size and position of the figure or figures in the composition. With charcoal he then sketched in the details of the design, finally painting it in with flat colour.'[21] Lye felt that the larger size of the paintings increased the impact of the images, as was also the case with his sculpture. He spoke of a painting as 'like a freshly caught fish',[22] and saw his art as a kind of deep-sea fishing. He would not allow the new brain to take over the catch and dress it up in a showy way. Yet aesthetics did creep back into his work — he would, for example, agonise over colours and was in the habit of hanging a plastic sheet over part of a painting as he worked so he had a surface on which to test colours as well as brushstrokes.[23]

Most paintings had a protagonist figure or figures at the centre. To the artist each of these powerful protagonists had its own unique sense of movement. There is an amusing sequence of photographs showing Lye adopting various poses in front of the paintings as he responded to their implied movements. He considered turning 'God of Light' into kinetic sculpture as 'a big figure with three legs and prongy feet. It was very spastic and it compressed its three legs and sharp elbows all together, then suddenly they sprang out. This springing side-ways action would cause it to sidle sideways like a crab. A very spectacular figure with its three eyes gradually turning round and blinking.' He also liked the idea of stylised performances in front of the paintings, to highlight their implied movements and their symbolic or mythic elements.[24] Such performances might resemble tribal rituals, Japanese Noh dramas or Javanese marionette plays. In the case of 'Rain Tree' he planned a happening that involved mounds of black earth, red and black stylised arrows, rotating white tubes (symbolising bones), and the reading of an Aztec poem.

When Bogle visited him in November 1979 to finalise the details of the exhibition, Lye was able to show him thirteen canvases. He also wanted some of his early paintings to be included in the exhibition such as 'Ice Age' and 'Snow Birds Making Snow'. There were two giant canvases that he still hoped to paint — a 13-foot by 20-foot blow-up of his faded batik 'Watershed,' and a 20-foot by 30-foot version of 'Galactic Core', the batik he had given 50 years earlier to Robert Graves. Lye associated this image with the beginnings of the universe and joked that his painting would represent 'the First Supper as a match for the Last Supper — not quite so much a match as a companion piece'.[25] This painting would be as big as his New Plymouth sculptures. He planned to paint it like a mural with the help of a cherry picker, but for the time being there was not enough money.

While he was rounding off his life's work in painting he was also struggling to sort out his theoretical work. His constant note-taking and essay-writing had filled dozens of boxes in his New York studio. Whenever he completed a new manuscript he would take it to the photocopying shop at 380 Bleeker Street where the staff enjoyed his conversations so much they would usually refuse to charge him.[26] He continued to spin his ideas into an ever larger and more intricate web. His philosophy cohered around the idea that art was the source of 'myth', by which he meant something more serious than the myths of popular culture but less absolute than the myths of organised religion. To leave behind a curriculum for teachers, Lye sought to complete a series of approximately 30 slide–tape programmes. Although the topics were diverse — children's art, tribal art, cave art, 'cracks, stains and other energy signs', doodling, and interpretations of his own work — all the programmes highlighted the power of the old brain which educators tended to neglect in favour of the new brain. Though Lye kept running into problems with his slide–tape equipment and longed for a chance to transfer this material to a fully automated system, he still retained a certain affection for the jerky action of slide-changing, which seemed to him to have more impact on a viewer than watching a slick educational film.

In 1975 he had produced a 70-page manuscript, 'Somewhat Autobiographically' which covered some of the same ground as 'Happy Moments' but in a more analytical way, reinterpreting his life in the light of his theories. As the 'Somewhat' in the title suggests, he was more interested in exploring ideas than in recording facts. He mailed copies of this and other essays to old friends and to any scientist or academic mentioned in the newspapers who appeared to take a broad-minded view of genetics or evolution. Lye knew he had allies in the art world but he yearned to establish more links with science. His strongest supporter in this project was Gerhard Brauer, a Canadian medical researcher he met in Wellington in 1977 who later moved back to British Columbia. Brauer was a consultant in epidemiology and community health who went on to write about Lye's art and theories. Noting how momentous it would be if any of the artist's claims were verified, Brauer argued that even the faintest possibility of such confirmation made it imperative that his ideas should become the subject of wide-ranging debate.[27] Lye's theorising was always the aspect of his work that people found most difficult to accept or evaluate. Most continued to regard the theories as a waste of time and energy that he should have been devoting to art, but some saw his new paintings as evidence that the theories at least stimulated him as an artist, or found the best of the manuscripts and slide lectures striking enough to be regarded as artistic creations in their own right. A few (such as Brauer) were seriously prepared to entertain the possibility that the artist had intuitively stumbled on new information about the complex interaction between body and mind.

fiftyfour relationships

Lye was always proud of his son and daughter but their closeness was complicated by the fact he had missed so much of their childhood. Also, their mother's
undiminished bitterness sometimes cast a shadow over their contacts. He would
have liked his children to be as relaxed about personal arrangements as he was,
but not surprisingly their feelings were more mixed, and it did not help that he
had difficulty remembering details such as birthdays. It took time for Bix and
Yancy to come to terms with his some of his unconventional aspects. Yancy
remembers a vivid moment when she had looked out into the audience at her
high school graduation, caught sight of her mother conservatively dressed and
her father in a mustard-yellow jacket wearing his strange little Ben Franklin
glasses, and thought 'Why can't I have a normal father?' When the children came
to see him, he was sometimes so preoccupied with his theories he would keep
bringing the conversation back to that subject and fail to notice that his visitors
were getting bored. In Bix's words, 'There were days we wished he would just
show us his films! Still, we had some good times with him. And we did accept the
fact that our father was a special sort of person, an original.' Yancy came to
respect her father as 'someone 30 or 40 years ahead of his time'.

Jane Lye had her own ways of being unconventional. She too was a product of
the bohemian world of the 1920s, and could be so engrossed in her own concerns
that she was an equally distracted parent. After the marriage break-up Jane had
formed a relationship with Ruthven Todd, and while the poet's drinking habits
sometimes created problems, Bix accepted him as a surrogate father and grew
close to him. Jane kept her emotional life very private and though she was said to
have had affairs with several old friends from England, this remained only a
rumour. She often struck people as cool and remote. Money was a constant worry
for her, especially during the years when her former husband had no steady
income and was struggling to keep up with child support payments. She retained
a strange optimism that Lye would one day get rich from his discoveries, often
reporting to her children: 'He's got a new idea and I think this one's going to work
— at last we'll have some security!' Bix and Yancy remembered being given
excited previews of various projects such as the Chrysler ad, and recognising immediately that their father was going to horrify the sponsors, as he always did.

One aspect of Lye that the children always enjoyed was his unique style of letter-writing. Some letters were weighed down with theoretical discussions but most were exuberant, affectionate, and rich in doodles. A typical letter thanked Yancy (then married and living in Greece) for a teapot and box of tea she had sent him: 'It makes me think I am sipping the tassle-dryings of Benedictine monks and the box is supreme . . . a repository for Alexandrian hashish-hasish-shiskabashis possibly. In fact the entire cube was a utopian gesture where finesse of simple leaf ceremonies are tokens of nerve sensibilities. . . . So the box sits like a pandora of Hemingway's scrubbed wood table in the Old Man of the Sea's china sampans catching flying fish. . . . Xmas has flitted and New Year's to come is a round of red eye & sweat dance prance gin fins. Has Dick got work going, has Yan got her writing lurking, has the bracing air got nostrils quivering, has the sea got some sounds, does the sky open?'[1]

Becoming a mother helped Yancy to understand her parents and to 'reconnect'. Lye proved to be a popular grandfather. She remembered one of her sons explaining why he had enjoyed an afternoon with his grandfather so much: 'Oh, we just leaned against a building and watched the world go by!' Bix felt that he had only in the late 1970s started to understand his father's theories and this reflected the fact that the author had himself 'got them into clearer focus — he could finally hone them down to a few paragraphs'. When the Lyes bought 801 Greenwich Street he accepted their offer of an apartment and a workshop which he shared with his father. Bix had completed a Bachelor of Fine Arts degree at Boston University, and now — while supporting himself as a specialised carpenter — he was producing prints and sculptures, some of which were selected for group shows at the Whitney Museum. His sense of humour brought him to the attention of a leading architectural magazine which described in detail the elegant plexiglass 'house' he had designed for Lloyd, his pet cockroach. Although the style of imagery was different from his own, Lye was delighted with his son's achievements as an artist. And while Bix had felt closer over the years to Ruthven Todd, he came to accept that it was 'better to have had two fathers than one'.

Meanwhile the relationship between Len and Ann was as exuberant as ever after more than 30 years. He wrote notes to her constantly to express his pleasure:

> Dearest longest lasting darling. I went to Mathias Goretiz's show of lacquered columns and plain-gold leaf of shapes on walls, and met Rose there who said the one clear image of the whole of Dave's evening was how miraculous you looked. I know the look and your greek-nosed forehead's eyebrow for your lovely eyes too. But it's the sashay of your walk in bones I like so much. . . .[2]

Dear green-thumbed white goddess. You know how *The Old Man and the Sea* man thought of lions and beaches? Well, in the same way, I think of you, barefoot, with that grey cotton skirt with the colored 'seminole' tape braiding, walking along with me. Love, my dear old red-toe-nailed Roaring Camp heart![3]

Friends were always amazed at how youthful they both seemed. At the same time, they were puzzled by how well their relationship had survived several decades of open marriage. Lye was still exercising this freedom in 1978 when a young woman (known today as a leading experimental film-maker and writer) came to spend the night with him during a period when his wife was away. One of their neighbours saw the woman arrive in the evening and leave the next morning, and was shocked. In Ann Lye's words, 'Len told me about it later. I thought it was a big joke. In fact, I was proud of him!'[4]

Both Lye and Ann always loved to dance. Margareta Akermark of the Museum of Modern Art remembers a party in 1978 where 'Len was so spry, he was disgusted with me because I wouldn't try to cha-cha with him! I don't think he liked parties *per se*, but he was so happy that evening because there were lots of people that he knew.'[5] In the same year, a staff member of the New Zealand Consulate in New York described his first contact with the artist: 'Len Lye and his wife Ann had a small social occasion recently in honour of a visit by John Matthews. . . . Len has painted large canvases of all sorts of early doodles and hung them on runners on the ceiling and gave a great little lecture on them while flying high on his edgy 77 years, the occasion, and a soupçon of champagne. Afterwards he merrily performed a risqué joke called the one armed piccolo player. We all lined up as if on a picture-show queue while he whistled an entertainment then held out his hat for small change, sticking his piccolo in his fly to keep the tune going, which was memorable for the sheer goat-glee beaming on his face.'[6] The consulate had sought out the artist after his return to New Zealand in 1968 and since then there had been a great deal of contact, particularly in the early Seventies with the consul Paul Cotton and his wife Gill who socialised with the Lyes as friends and exchanged letters with them.

Another New Zealander that Lye grew close to in his later years was Max Gimblett, a painter who had made an extensive study of Eastern traditions of art and thought. Gimblett lived in Manhattan but maintained close links with the New Zealand art scene. In the early 1970s he made his first sighting of the artist at a social event at the New Zealand consul's house: 'A sort of king figure, very royal and very relaxed, with a lot of cushions around him, in brightly coloured clothing, with some sort of funny little hat on, and a very distinctive voice —

definitely the top person in the room.' Later Gimblett was taken to Lye's studio by Ray Thorburn, and the two artists clicked so strongly they continued to exchange visits. Gimblett recalls: 'We spend the evenings talking art. He was completely encouraging about my work and this was very exciting because I had never had a mentor with his stature. He would bring me his essays — always there were new versions — and there were books he wanted me to read. I could listen to his kind of rap endlessly — it never seemed to repeat itself.' He was fascinated by the colours Lye wore: 'orange cardigan, blue-violet and red-violet trousers, high-pitched and utterly clear and pure cadmium red beret, cobalt, sky-blue and cadmium, grass-green and white rugby shirt and bee-buzzing gold and black socks'.[7] For his part Lye admired Gimblett's calligraphic brushwork and his spiritual conception of art which he saw as parallel to his own idea of art as a final religion. In a letter he wrote: 'Holy Smoke Max! You . . . emanate the essence of art and its individuality. You are my idea of a high priest of art. I have only met two others, Hans Richter and Frederick Keisler. (If we had to have a pope I suggest Brancusi)'.[8]

Gimblett said of Lye:

> In terms of the tradition I've adopted in my life, he was a guru, a Buddha. In Japanese he would have been my sensai, my teacher. Len was way down the track, as fine a person as he was an artist and vice versa. First off he didn't gossip and he didn't make small talk and he didn't bullshit and he didn't lie and he wasn't very interested in manners other than the ones he'd come up with himself, so that's already quite a package. He never carried much extra weight, he was very spry and a completely positive person. He had a complete vision of the world — Len had it all together. He didn't need fame and fortune. He knew how to mind his own business and how to stay out of other people's heads and that I think is some indication of how he was with his own creative processes. Like Picasso he was fascinated by thoughts and he didn't bring a judgement in on them and so start to close them down. In the entire time we spent together, he offered me only one piece of criticism — this was a very different kind of father figure from my own father. And in New Zealand art I feel in my way that it would be good to balance Colin McCahon's grip on our culture by a more feminine, all-accepting figure like Len so that we wouldn't just be a land of dark fathers! (I don't want to stereotype McCahon but the art market is a bit out of whack there.)

fiftyfive direct film apprentices

Despite his good spirits and the amount of work he was producing, Lye had felt since 1977 that his energy was steadily draining away and he had a sensation of coldness, which reinforced his sense of time running out. A cystoscopy in July 1978 failed to identify the problem. Meanwhile, Ann Lye was diagnosed with skin cancer on the top of her head and in August she had a successful operation with a skin graft from her thigh. Lye's health continued to decline until 13 March 1979 when Dr. A. A. Cintron-Rivera in Puerto Rico made a diagnosis of chronic leukaemia — a cancerous disorder which involves the excessive production of white blood cells leading to anaemia. Ann wrote to Philip: 'Len has been so exhausted and thinner and thinner (now 128 lbs) for two years. He always put it down to old age. It's such a relief to *know*.'[1] Lye speculated about the original cause of his leukaemia since this condition was often the result of exposure to something toxic. In England he had smoked two packets of Pall Mall cigarettes a day, but there were other possibilities also such as the benzine he had used in London (the gallons of gas used to make dye-resist fabric paintings) and his work as stoker: 'The ship would be rolling and we would go head over kite into the soft coal, and inhale it. No wonder you come out of these sorts of industrial jobs with leukaemia.'[2]

There was no known cure, and while there were various ways to prolong life, the treatment could have unpleasant side effects. Lye began a course of chemotherapy. When he left Puerto Rico, Dr Cintron-Rivera sent medical details to Dr D. Connel in Warwick, commenting that his patient was 'mentally alert and surprisingly young for his age of 77'. He added: 'I trust that his condition goes into a complete remission. Thank you for your help in taking care of this exceptionally gifted man.'[3] The leukaemia was successfully brought under control for the next few months; but in August the white cell count zoomed up again and Lye suffered from bone tenderness, particularly in his back. Taking painkillers led to further complications. For him the most frustrating aspect was loss of alertness, as he observed to Gerhard Brauer, 'I'm too weak — wack — wock — to apply my mind to forwarding much.'[4] But he would never talk about his pain, and the poems he wrote in his notebooks were still sensuous and playful.

In the course of his career he had divided his best creative energies between four areas — sculpture, painting, film, and theory. He was now sorting out each

371

of these areas — for example, by documenting his sculptural ideas for his supporters in New Plymouth, who needed as much information as possible if they
were to accept the challenge of building giant versions. And he began to archive
his large collection of film cans, distinguishing between completed films, offcuts,
and experiments. Friends helped him in these tasks, with particularly valuable
support coming from three of his former students, Paul Barnes, Paul Fiondella,
and Erik Shiozaki. In Lye's words: 'my power of attention is pretty waney. I can
direct a couple of chaps what to do alright but can't always get up to show them.'[5]
Working with him was not without its problems. One assistant was so eager to be
helpful that, knowing Lye's history of unsuccessful applications, he applied
secretly on his behalf to an American fund and succeeded in obtaining a grant;
but Lye's response was extremely cool because though he needed the money he
felt he had been tricked.

Those who worked on the films and slide–tape programmes were sometimes
used as a sounding board. As a film editor Paul Barnes was accustomed to a colla-
borative role and he enjoyed the positive energy Lye always brought to his work:
'His humanism was rich and deep. Cynicism is so widespread today that it's a
hard mind-set to counter, but I think of him whenever that cynicism threatens to
engulf me.'[6] Lye's first priority was to make new versions of the films *Free
Radicals* and *Particles in Space* which he saw as still unresolved. He was able to
obtain a grant from the newly created New Zealand Film Commission for *Free
Radicals* and two grants for *Particles* — one from the National Endowment for
the Arts and the other from the Queen Elizabeth II Arts Council of New
Zealand.[7] With Barnes's assistance Lye re-edited *Free Radicals*, removing various
short sequences that he had come to regard as imprecise. They were (in Barnes's
words) 'kind of squiggley or messy — he wasn't happy with the clarity of the
line, or the way the images were synched to the music seemed to him too arbi-
trary'.[8] The drum music was relatively easy to edit since there were no phrases or
measures, just beats. No new material was added and the film was ruthlessly
condensed to four minutes. Lye required his wife to give her final approval since
it had been her remark that the film was too long that had led him to re-edit it.

Once the new version had been passed, Barnes took on the challenge of finding a laboratory that could make good prints. He recalls: 'There were not many
technicians around who still understood black and white or were willing to
spend time on a small job. I investigated smaller labs where there were older
technicians. Len was as fussy with the printing as he was with everything. You
would think a white on black image would be relatively easy to achieve but one of
the things Len liked about etching was the fact that at times there was a certain

depth to the lines. There were gradations of grey within the etched-out areas and that gave the lines a bit of substance. There were some lovely qualities in the old prints which he wanted to achieve again. The first prints that came back from the labs didn't have the delicacy he was looking for and he just felt like throwing them away.' Finally they found Control Lab which succeeded in producing both solid black backgrounds and textured lines.[9]

Next Lye shifted his attention to *Particles*, a more complex job. The film existed in many forms because over the years he had worked on it whenever he felt the impulse. The most recent version ran for six minutes but there were some sections he was not happy with. He chopped these out but wanted to keep two 20-second sequences of music. He and Barnes combed through reels and reels of experiments to see if there were any images that suited the music. In the end Lye decided reluctantly that new sequences needed to be made. A lot of the etching tools he had used in the 1950s and '60s had been lost or misplaced after he moved from Bethune Street to Greenwich Street, and so the pair embarked on an extensive search through hardware and junk stores to find old dental tools and saw blades that would fit 16 mm film.

Barnes recalls: 'Generally Len never wanted a sequence of images to run longer than a second. The sequence would be ten frames, twelve frames, eighteen frames. In *Free Radicals* there are sections of long straight lines that run for a number of seconds in counterpoint to the shorter, more staccato sequences — they work that way rhythmically in the film — but in *Particles* he wasn't interested in that kind of imagery. What he wanted now were shorter, tighter, more precise sequences.' One effect he particularly wanted to achieve was a kind of elbow movement jutting out from the body. He would start with a dot and stretch the dot sideways for twelve frames or so. He wanted the lines to be like the action of rowing but with a snap to it. When he tried to do it himself he found he could no longer trust the precision of his hands or eyes, and so asked his assistant to try. In Barnes's words: 'It didn't bother him that he couldn't do it, he just hoped I might be able to create something more precise. For the first few sessions my imagery was just disastrous, it took quite a while to achieve control. Then I got to be such a fanatic about it that my lines started coming out too precise-looking. I had tried to clean them up so they were smooth and straight, but now they came out synthetic looking compared to Len's, they lost the energy he was looking for. He liked a little bit of raggedness. So then I tried precision with a touch of imprecision, to get that spark he wanted.'

Scratching images was a complex dance of hand, arm, and wrist movements. It took a great deal of concentration to work on such a small scale, to cut and scrape so delicately that the tool did not score the whole frame or cut too deeply into the emulsion. Barnes was also struck by the unusual state of mind that developed from the intense concentration required — his scratching became more instinctive, driven by the old rather than the new brain. This 'Zen state' gave Barnes a new insight into how intimately Lye's use of tools was related to his respect for the old brain. By the end of the summer, when Barnes had to shift to another job, he had produced a satisfactory 'elbow' sequence. Work on the project had greatly increased his respect for Lye's direct films: 'Now when I look at them the complexity of the imagery and his control over the movement is absolutely astonishing. I still can't figure out how he made some of the images in *Free Radicals*. When I asked him he'd just laugh and say, "I don't know — saw blade or dental pick, something like that!" What will stay with me was his passionate involvement, the degree of perfection he brought to his work.'[10] Lye was equally impressed with Barnes's meticulous approach, and paid him his ultimate compliment: 'You're like one of those old Shakers struggling away diligently to invent a better broom — applying spiritual tactics to a practical invention.'[11]

The second sequence was yet to be done so Barnes found another assistant, the film-maker Steve Jones. It took Jones two months to develop a feel for the process. As he summed up the experience: 'If you move the saw blade too hard the film will tear, and if you don't do it hard enough you won't create a image that has a feeling of flow and commands a certain power. But if you practise enough you can learn to squiggle your hand and make images that are a direct extension of the movement in your arm, your hand, your shoulder. It's like learning to dance. When you're a kid and you're dancing with a girl, you're stuck-up and uptight, whereas twenty years later you've had some champagne and you're doing a tango and you can really *breeze*. To scratch film you have to let go of your inhibitions and let your body move. Then you look at the images you've scratched to see if any of them look stuck-up, as though they're merely the product of you trying to make them do something. You can tell when they have a real elasticity to them, a movement that's more like muscle. Len looked funny to me at first but he was very good at simulating motion. He had an interesting-shaped body because you could almost see the raw movement in his arms. He'd say, "You've got to go like *this*, and like *this*!" and whenever he described something, he would move. He had a way of detaching himself and just doing a motion for you — you didn't see him, you saw the figure of motion. And then you'd look on a piece of film he'd scratched and there was the same sort of figure, the same feeling.'

The sections Jones worked on were described by Lye as 'the nests and the climbing things with the nests under them'. A nest was 'a molecular nest of energy floating around in space' though Jones preferred to think of it as 'a funny little box of sparks'. To create more of them he found a suede brush with three-inch wire bristles — this was his 'personal contribution to the tools of direct film making'. He also took a small paint brush and replaced its hairs with wire bristles so that it could flake the emulsion away in tiny speckles.[12] Though *Particles in Space* incorporated the work of Barnes and Jones, the film was made under Lye's close supervision. The final four-minute version (completed in January 1980) had a sustained energy that made it a worthy companion to *Free Radicals*.[13] While one section was like a direct extension of *Free Radicals* with its spinning, three-dimensional shapes, the other sections created a whole range of new textures, starting with a single particle that was joined by a glittering swarm of other particles. There were dynamic sequences of horizontal lines jumping from side to side in an incredibly vigorous dance, or flying up to the top of the frame ('climbing' or 'reaching', as Lye described them), or being violently stretched sideways (in what he called the 'rowing' or 'elbow' sequence).

fiftysix quitting the lot

As the effects of his leukaemia intensified, Lye realised it was unlikely he would be able to paint the two large canvases he had planned or to travel to the Auckland City Art Gallery exhibition. In November 1979 the curator, Andrew Bogle, came to New York to finalise details. It was agreed that the exhibition would include 37 items — paintings, sculptures, and films.[1] The artist explained that he wanted each painting installed in a separate alcove, to help spectators adjust to the changes in style from one painting to another,[2] but more importantly to heighten their encounter with each image. Helping to create an old brain ambience the paintings and sculptures were to be surrounded by darkness.[3] Bogle was very responsive to the artist's ideas, as Ann Lye reported in a letter: 'The young [curator] came here and they planned the show together, and Len *knew* it was going to be right.'[4] Lye wrote a statement for the exhibition catalogue under the title 'Slow but Sure', a favourite phrase which he used to describe himself as a slow developer. While this statement was not one of his best pieces of writing it gained emotional power from its sense of finality as he looked back over his life from the imprint of nature during his New Zealand years to his 'messing with metal' in the United States. He paid tribute to three women who had been his 'greatest staunches' — 'Rose Ann Cole to start with, Jane Thompson to help the stuff's launchings, and Ann Zeiss by my side to egg my ego on. They put the tick in my art's tock.'[5] He urged New Zealanders not to make too much fuss about him because young artists could easily feel intimidated by the canonisation of older artists, as he remembered from his own student days. (He also worried that the rhetoric being used by some of his supporters in New Zealand might produce a backlash.)

Details of the 'Len Lye Foundation' had been under discussion since 1977 and now John Matthews arrived with a final version of the deed signed by the New Plymouth City Council.[6] The Lyes were happy to add their signatures. By this agreement they transferred ownership of all Lye's work to the Foundation, a charitable trust, for the public benefit of the people of New Zealand. The collection would be stored at the Govett-Brewster Art Gallery in New Plymouth, so long as the gallery was able to display and maintain them in good order. The deed referred specifically to the need for the late paintings always to be kept together as evidence of his theory of 'myth and the genes'. The Foundation was also expected to seek to obtain the rights to other Lye films such as those owned by the GPO Film Unit. Through Allan Highet, Minister for the Arts, the New Zealand Government gave $20,000 from lottery funds as a contribution to the cost of transferring the collection to New Zealand.

In making such a bequest Lye wanted to make it clear that he was not a simple nationalist: 'It isn't crucial to me where I live or where my work goes. I'm concerned about people and art, not about countries.'[7] At the same time he was optimistic about New Zealand because it was one of the few countries that had not wrecked its natural environment. Over the last few years Lye had increased his links with the New Zealand art world. Barry Brickell, one of New Zealand's leading potters, paid a visit, and Lye said he had his eye on Brickell's area in Coromandel as an ideal site for a utopian experiment. Art writers such as Wystan Curnow and Anne Kirker came to interview Lye about his early years. Hamish Keith spent an evening with him at the White Horse Tavern in December 1979 to discuss the creation of the Lye Foundation. Keith recalls: 'It was very cold. When we said good night, we both sort of knew it was goodbye, we were exchanging a farewell. Later he wrote to me about how he was ready to go on his last big adventure, looking forward to it as though it was just another journey somewhere. I've got a rather different view of death — for me it's a little more finite than that, so I was really quite upset.'[8]

Early in 1980 I arrived in New York. I had been corresponding with Lye for several years, discussing (among other things) the idea of putting together a selection of his writings. Curnow and I had managed to track down all his published essays, and Lye seemed as surprised as we were to discover how many he had written. The book project fitted well with the tidying-up he was trying to do in other areas, and he was eager to get some of his theories into print at last. He was, however, horrified by our proposed title — 'The Essential Len Lye' — because it made him sound 'too important' and his ideas 'too definitive'. He reminded me that he had spent his life trying to avoid tidy compartments and labels, and his theories were only speculations, so a better title would be 'Len Lye Sort Of'. Not wanting to take up too much of the artist's time, I had imagined that a day or two of discussions would be enough to finalise the book. My plans changed abruptly when I discovered that Lye knew his life was coming to an end and was desperate to complete a whole range of other projects. I began working full-time as his assistant.

Though his talk was always lively, he was thin and fragile, having recently had several bad falls, and chemotherapy put him out of action for several days a fortnight. He began each day with a sense of urgency and would start delivering instructions as soon as he saw me. One of his current priorities was a film he had abandoned in the 1950s, consisting of elegant vertical lines scratched on black film which danced to 'Rock 'n' Rye', a piece of lyrical jazz music by guitarist Tal Farlow. While this was a much lighter work than *Particles* it illustrated an area of imagery he had fully developed but not yet put on record. (In one of his slide lectures Lye had noted that while most of his doodling had produced free, irregular forms there had always been some geometrical patterns.) Since the making of new designs was out of the question, Lye wanted to select and edit together approximately two minutes of highlights from the twenty minutes of relevant scratch material. Steve Jones was asked to do the editing and synchro-nising, with some help from his friend Gwain Gillespie. Gillespie, a talented musician, smoothly edited Farlow's piece down from four minutes to two. After initial discussions Lye had to withdraw from the editing process because of his health. Jones then proceeded to sort out the hundreds of short film strips, using the approach he had learned from *Particles* which was to classify both the images and the musical phrases in kinetic terms: 'This is an expansion-contraction, this is a tradeoff, this is a twist, this is someone walking with a walking stick, this is an explosion. . . .'[9] From this starting point he experimented to see which strips of film corresponded most closely to particular passages of music. In some cases the relationship was obvious, but others required a lengthy process of experiment.

Meanwhile Ann had commissioned Selina Trieff, an old friend who lived in the same building, to paint a portrait of Lye. This was something to which he had never previously agreed despite many requests from artist friends. Now because the request came from his wife he consented to sit for Trieff. The artist later said of her subject: 'Len always had a little smile, and there was the sense of a curious wisdom, he knew so many things. He was also very independent, very well centred. And I gave an elfish emphasis to his ears.'[10] When Ann looked at the completed portrait for the first time she was shocked because of its cool colours and sense of distance. 'My only comment was, "That's not *my* Len!" But then I sat there for more than an hour and in the end I completely accepted it. Selina has caught his pointed ears — which are devil's ears, absolutely wicked ears — and she got his beautiful delicate hands. The thing that bothers me is the angle of the stripes in his jacket which imply that he's got a belly, and Len never had any belly at all.'[11] She was struck by the fact that while Trieff had tended in her previous portraits to project traces of her own features onto her subjects, giving them what Lye would call a 'lookalike' quality, there were no signs of it on this occasion, as though Lye's personality were too distinct and self-sufficient to allow anyone to impose.

Lye did not want to see the portrait — he said he was too busy. His doctors continued to try different drugs and dosages. Interferon was said to offer a new miracle treatment but it was extremely scarce because of the controls on genetic production methods. John Matthews, who felt it was crucial for the artist to live long enough to see the Foundation fully established, explored all possible sources without success. Lye accepted this philosophically: 'I knew this wasn't for my generation.' The beginning of May was a turning point, as Ann recalls: 'The doctor said, "You have to take twice as much medicine twice as often," and Len cocked his characteristic little half-smile and said, "OK, doc, then I'll quit the lot." The doctor replied, "You know, you may not last more than two weeks." And Len said, "Fine," with another smile.'[12]

A few days later Ann walked into Bix's studio and found herself face to face with Jane Lye. After more than 30 years there was still unfinished business between them. Then Ann held out her hand, Jane accepted it, and they began to talk. Their conversation lasted for two hours. Later, when Ann reported that she and Jane had met on common ground, Lye was delighted. By now he had stopped his medicine and within a week he had grown thin and weak and his legs bled easily. He had difficulty with food, even with the marijuana cookies Ann had baked in the hope they might help as painkillers. Still there were no complaints and he continued joking with everyone. 'That's the Irish blarney', commented Ann. When she too made an amusing play on words, he said: 'Hey, she's not trite, *she* can still dive!' She took a series of photos of him 'in some of his finest Lennery — a woven robe with red lining, red beret, red socks and red piped slippers and a day-wear night shirt topped with a Nehru hat'.[13]

Lye was now based at Warwick. Taking time out from archiving his work at Greenwich Street, my wife Shirley and I spent a day with him making plans for a book of his poems to be entitled 'Night Tree'.[14] He described a vivid dream from the previous night. 'Dreams have never been important to me,' he said; 'my art isn't dream stuff. But this was a good dream, I was thinking things out in it. Isaac Bashevis Singer was in a subway train with me and Ann, and I had a good discussion with Singer about the need for myth and how each generation needs to contribute to it and keep it going.'

When Andrew Bogle phoned him on 12 May they talked business for a while and then Lye said matter-of-factly: 'I only have a week to go.' On the same day his two close friends John Maynard and Max Gimblett came to see him. Gimblett recalls a quiet farewell at the end of the afternoon: 'When we got to the front door, he shook my hand firmly and said "Sleepy time down south!"' For the next few days the Lyes were alone at Warwick. He was determined not to be rushed to hospital where his life would be prolonged in an artificial way. He slept for most of the 14th and Ann thought he would die in his sleep, but he woke on the 15th in a lucid state of mind and they spent the morning talking. Selina's portrait came to her mind because his skin now had the same colour. He still had his old impish sense of humour, making comments such as: 'I'm going to enjoy the ride back to New York even more than usual.' Lye cracked his last joke as she was sitting down on the bed: 'Don't sit on my glasses, I might need them in heaven.' He died around 11 a.m. Ann, who had not slept for three or four days, felt strangely elated for a long time afterwards. 'Len died in a special way. He chose his own time and it all went exactly as he wanted it to go. Only he could have died like that. It was such a beautiful experience, I wanted to shout about it from the housetop — it was like being high on drugs.'[15]

She accompanied the body back to New York City where it was delivered to the College of Physicians and Surgeons at Columbia University because Lye had wanted to donate his body to science. The death certificate described him as: 'Artist, self employed.' Max Gimblett explains that 'Len actually believed he had one of the original pinwheel cells in his head and he was sure that when they opened him up after he died they'd find it'.[16] But the results of the dissection remain a mystery. A week later at Warwick, Ann came across a note that her husband had left her to find when she started sorting out his papers: 'Dear One of my one and only Ann: just to let you know dying is no problem & I feel I'll soon be dead so to let you have my last breath of love is all I want. No one has had a better life and it was had with your love and unselfish help.'

epilogue

Under the headline 'Len Lye Dead at 78', the *New York Times* art reviewer Grace Glueck outlined his pioneer work in film and kinetic sculpture and added some personal impressions: 'Bald as an egg, with a pointed goatee, Len Lye was a sprightly man who, despite his fascination with technology, referred to himself as "an old-brain guy who can't even drive a car".'[1] Cecile Starr, an historian of experimental film-making, said in her tribute: 'Every age has a few truly great artists whose worth is known only to a few associates and *amateurs*. I believe that the foremost "unknown" artist of our time is Len Lye.'[2] Film-maker Stan Brakhage organised two memorial programmes of films, one at the Telluride Film Festival and the other at the University of Colorado. When he saw the revised versions of Lye's last films for the first time, Brakhage described *Free Radicals* as 'an almost unbelievably immense masterpiece (a brief epic)' and *Particles in Space* as 'its contemplative equivalent'.[3] A comment in one of Brakhage's letters summed up the challenge facing the Foundation and others who cared about these films: 'We must now fight very hard to get Len Lye's work anchored in the EYES of this society (as distinct from simply shelved in the institutes of Art or somesuch).'[4]

There was an obituary in the local paper: 'In Warwick Mr Lye kept a low profile, though he was an exotic sight here with his gleaming bald head, white goatee, antique green "Ben Franklin" glasses and startlingly bright clothes.'[5] In the West Village Ann Lye was amazed by the number of people who wrote to her with anecdotes about their contacts with him. She had not realised he was quite such a local identity, a true 'street person'. She was also startled when a friend said to her: 'I just don't know how you were able to live with him. I only saw him once a year and he was always so full of energy I felt exhausted!' Ann had always thought of her husband as unusual but had never imagined that anyone would think of her as unusual too. The fact of his death was now hitting her hard, though she kept her feelings to herself. There was no funeral, but on 15 June — a month after Lye's death — she organised an Irish-style wake. This was an eight-hour party with champagne and Dixieland jazz (with records by Louis Armstrong, Scott Joplin and others). A few people left early because they were not comfortable with the cheerful atmosphere (though there was also plenty of crying going on). The other hundred or so people settled in to drink and dance and exchange anecdotes. A few were attending more for Ann's sake than Len's, for he had struck them as such a self-contained person they had never felt as close to him as to her; but the guests included many of Lye's old friends including Alastair Reid, Bernard and Judith Childs, Max Gimblett, Ann McMillan, Ray Thorburn, Howard Wise, many film-makers such as Francis Lee, people who had assisted or collaborated with Lye such as Paul Fiondella, people from the Museum of Modern Art, and well-known residents of the West Village such as Rose Slivka and Ruth Richards. Tim and Sheerah Francis came from the New Zealand Consulate. Ann's daughters Jane Hindle Bamberg and Gill Cintoli were there, and so were Bix and Jane Lye (although behind the scenes Jane had gone back to regarding Ann as an enemy — the truce was over).

The party paused to watch the performance of four kinetic sculptures and then a selection of films. Lye himself appeared in the last film, *When The Walls Came Tumbling Down*, making bold predictions that giant versions of his sculpture were going to be built one day, which the crowd greeted with delighted laughter. There was a storm of applause after his final statement to camera: 'I'm for ever!' Later Jane Lye — who saw this documentary for the first time at the wake — told me she was absolutely astonished by the confident way he had talked about his work. She could not reconcile this persona with the man she had known in England who had distrusted theory and preferred to be a listener rather than a talker. Like Ann Lye seeing Trieff's portrait for the first time, Jane felt this was not *her* Len.

In New Zealand, the Auckland City Art Gallery's board of management announced in June that it was interested in erecting a memorial to Lye.[6] This triggered off the first public signs of a backlash. Objecting to this use of 'rate-payers' money', art consultant Peter Vuletic said that 'the New Zealand public has been misled into thinking Lye had a considerable international reputation', and this over-valuing was a case of 'misplaced nationalism'.[7] The local newspaper published a number of letters supporting Vuletic, but there were also letters in favour of the memorial from Wystan Curnow and Hamish Keith. In the end the idea ran into practical problems and nothing came of it; but the gallery's exhibition 'Len Lye: A Personal Mythology' opened in August and received a positive response from reviewers and the public. The gallery brought Ann Lye to Auckland for the opening, at which she wore a black and red woven evening dress that Lye had selected the day before he died. As she recalled the way it had happened: 'My daughter [Jane Hindle Bamberg] brought in a box of stuff from a rummage sale. I modelled for him to tell me what he liked.'[8] Jane was surprised by Lye's insistence that Ann should wear a particular dress to the opening because 'It was the first time I can ever remember him telling her what to do!'[9]

Back in New York Ann supervised the final stages of the Tal Farlow film.
Lye had always brought his films to her for final approval and she was an
extremely critical viewer. As she kept sending Steve Jones back to do more
editing, the level of tension escalated. Jones talked of leaving the project and I
was kept busy as an intermediary. At last on 13 November he presented a two-
minute version which Ann felt able to accept. We all knew that Lye would have
gone on fine-tuning the film for years in his perfectionist way, probably wanting
to redraw some sequences; but no new material was possible now and Ann
agreed that the editor had made the best possible use of the existing footage. The
film could therefore be released as 'Len Lye's *Tal Farlow* synchronised by Steve
Jones' (the formula Lye had suggested). A copy of the film was sent to Farlow
who had been generous with the music rights. Later Farlow told Judith Hoffberg
he 'loved the film' and was sorry he had never met Lye.[10]

In the same month we finished clearing out the studio and packed everything
to send to New Plymouth to become the basis of the Foundation's collection. Lye
would have ditched much of the material as junk but John Matthews, with
proper archival caution, insisted on taking everything. In the flurry of packing,
how could we hope to distinguish precious starter doodles from random scrib-
bles? Matthews then approached a shipping company to see if he could talk them
into providing a large container free. Extolling Lye's importance as an artist and
film maker, he had almost won over the tough New York executives of the
shipping company when he made the mistake of showing them the Auckland
exhibition catalogue. They were horrified — they had not realised Lye was a
'modern' artist and they could not make head nor tail of his art. Fortunately
Matthews had the bright idea of asking them: 'Do you remember the *March of
Time*? Well, Lye was one of the directors!' This restored him to normalcy in their
eyes and Matthews got his free container.

Some of Lye's film material was given to the Film Department of the Museum
of Modern Art which was willing to do restoration work. On 5 January 1981 the
museum presented a special memorial programme of Lye's films to a full house
that included an impressive array of New York film-makers and artists who
applauded each film. Sadly absent from this event was Jane Lye, who had died in
New York a month earlier. After the Museum event, Ann Lye left for Puerto Rico
where she decided she would live permanently: 'It's so colourful and active and
noisy (including being wakened by roosters). My street is a theater. Len hated all
the noise and music because it hurt his work — and so I hated it — and I now
realise I was protecting him, I *love it*! Warwick at this point seems dull as ditch-
water — although I love what we put together there.'[11] She kept one apartment in

Greenwich Street and returned to New York for brief periods. In 1982 she formed a close relationship with 'Ernie', a scientist and engineer who lived on Puget Sound near Seattle. She wrote: 'This intense "affair" was very good for me, it broke my block. As Ernie said, Len would be the most pleased of all.'[12] She described her new partner as Lye's opposite because of his practical, scientific habits of mind, but he too was a highly intelligent man with wide-ranging interests who loved books. She brought a wild new energy into his life and it was an extremely happy relationship for both. But he died early in 1988, and this second loss was hard for her to absorb. In 1990 she decided to sell her New York apartment and settle in Puerto Rico. Making the arrangements was exhausting for her, and the finality of the move released a flood of memories. Friends in Santurce were shocked by her decline into a state of depression. She became apathetic, started drinking heavily, and one day had a bad fall down the back stairs of her house. She was not expected to recover, but Joanne Baker and other friends nursed her through the crisis and were greatly relieved when she emerged with her old zest for life renewed. She continued to live in Santurce until her death on 26 September 2000 at the age of 90.

Curating the Museum of Modern Art's film programme brought my own work in New York to an end. I spent my last night sleeping in Lye's studio, now empty of its sculptures, waking up to his enigmatic smile in Selina Trieff's portrait. Was it enigmatic or mischievous? Back in New Zealand, the image chosen by the Len Lye Foundation to put on its letterhead was not Trieff's but a 1920s photograph of the artist laughing heartily. Some people thought the Foundation needed a more serious image but others felt it was ideal for the philosopher of Individual Happiness Now. John Maynard and Bridget Ikin as director and deputy director brought their remarkable energy and resourcefulness to bear on the business of the Foundation. This had now come into focus as a daunting set of tasks which threatened to outstrip the powers of an underfunded organisation and a provincial art gallery. But there were good reasons for Lye's laughing image on the letterhead — for his work would not be dumped or dispersed like the collections of some of the artists he had mixed with in London in the Twenties and Thirties.[13] And while many of the kinetic sculptures of the Sixties would fall into disrepair overseas, John Matthews and his team would keep Lye's in working order. The Foundation was posthumously to provide the kind of support the artist had lacked for most of his life, while the Govett-Brewster Art Gallery would serve as a secure home base.

Judith Hoffberg came over from the United States on a Fulbright Fellowship to lay the groundwork for the huge task of archiving Lye's papers. The collection provided a rich documentation of Lye's work in the United States but was somewhat thin in earlier material (since he had left much of it in England and never recovered it). In association with the Govett-Brewster, the Foundation offered exhibitions of Lye's art to other galleries and drew up long-term plans for building giant sculptures according to the specifications left by the artist. But how to fund these expensive activities? The Foundation could sell works of sculpture because they were not one-of-a-kind but produced as editions, albeit with a limited number of copies. The Foundation could also hire and sell film prints, though many institutions preferred to use cheap video copies. There were occasional gifts such as a timely grant from the Stout Trust and another donation from Ann Lye (proceeds from the sale of an early painting given to Lye by Ben Nicholson). In return for the privilege of gaining a major collection, the Govett-Brewster Art Gallery provided exhibitions, storage, and professional services but frequently its resources were stretched. Some New Plymouth artists questioned the time and money the gallery committed to Lye's work, and some jumped to the mistaken conclusion that his art glorified machines and was therefore hostile to the natural environment.[14]

The Foundation has had many difficulties since 1980, but it has continued to make progress with the help of a steady stream of artists, curators, and engineers intrigued by Lye's work. Max Gimblett, still an active member of the trust board and an artist whose own reputation has continued to grow steadily, has suggested that 'A very good artist is forward-projected about 50 years, and I think Lye is just starting to come into his own. He didn't waste too much time building [his sculpture], he really put his time into imaging it.'[15] John Matthews, chairman of the Foundation, has continued to offer engineering support through his Technix Group Ltd and has quietly made personal donations when required. In recent years the other key figure has been Evan Webb, a Christchurch sculptor able to bring the ideal combination of practical skill and aesthetic judgement to the task of keeping the sculptures in working order. He is now executive director of the Foundation. Webb and Matthews have made use of new technology to avoid the breakdowns that the artist used to find so frustrating. Lye always welcomed new technology — the type of motor was irrelevant to him provided it produced the right figures of motion. Film footage has left the Foundation with an exact record of how his sculpture should move, with other details available from his notes and interviews and the memory of engineers he worked with. If the Foundation had not had such information the sculpture might have changed its character subtly over the years, gradually speeding up or slowing down.

A think tank in New Plymouth has worked on the complex technical problems involved in enlarging the sculptures, and Dr J. K. Raine has enlisted the help of senior students in the Department of Mechanical Engineering School at the University of Canterbury.[16] In 1994 the Foundation was able to tap research on the design of yacht masts (a study that has become highly sophisticated because of contests such as the America's Cup) to arrive at the right combination of glass fibre and exotic resins to produce a 25-metre 'Wind Wand' strong enough to stand up-right yet pliant enough to respond to the slightest breeze. A new set of engineering problems had to be solved for the construction of a 45-metre 'Wand', also in New Plymouth, completed just in time for an opening ceremony at midnight at the turn of the millennium. This work was jointly funded by the Government's Towards 2000 Taskforce and the New Plymouth District Council. Some initial technical problems have reignited controversy about local funding for Lye's work, but the 'Wand' has become a popular icon, with homemade versions springing up in many New Plymouth backyards. In addition, the Foundation has successfully built a 7-metre 'Blade' (four times larger than the existing prototype) and is now working on a 'Universe' so large that it could function as the gateway to a temple. Although assisted by a number of researchers and sponsors, John Matthews and Evan Webb have been the key figures behind these remarkable engineering feats.

Meanwhile it takes a long time to establish or re-establish the reputation of an artist. Lye would have more rapidly become part of the canon of New Zealand art history if he had been a straightforward nationalist. Nevertheless there have been several exhibitions each year and many local painters have come to acknow-ledge his influence, particularly those attracted by the freedom and energy of his work — Stephen Bambury, Philippa Blair, Max Gimblett, and Paul Hartigan, to name a few. An avant-garde jazz group has called itself Free Radicals, and his work continues to inspire experimental film- and video-makers. Several striking documentary films have been made about him such as *Flip and Two Twisters*.[17] His work has also had a strong grassroots influence on New Zealand popular culture, with copies of his films being screened at night clubs and his imagery being borrowed for music videos and rock concert posters. It was not easy to re-plant Lye's ideas in a different culture, but they have now vigorously taken root.

But this home base has its limitations. As Lye's reputation becomes more esta-blished in New Zealand, there is a danger it will decline internationally. Overseas exhibitions are crucial if the influence of his work is to reach its full potential. Museums are nervous about large motorised sculptures because of the cost of shipping and installing them. The fact that films travel easily has helped maintain Lye's international reputation as a film-maker, but it is hard to persuade audi-ences overseas that he is the greatest of all kinetic sculptors when they are not able to experience the power of his large works at first hand. Yet there have been breakthroughs, such as the inclusion of 'Universe' in 'Territorium Artis', the opening exhibition of the Kunst- und Ausstellungshalle der Bundesrepublik Deutschland, a new contemporary art museum in Bonn. This 1992 exhibition was based (in the words of curator Pontus Hulten) on the idea that 'one can recognize in the art of our century . . . a certain number of decisive moments', and at these moments certain works of art have come to mark decisive points or 'points of no return'. Each of those 'extraordinary creations' indicates 'a road, a direction of investigation' which 'has to be explored to its end', though the importance of these works has not always been recognised immediately.[18] In these terms Lye was given a place among the hundred artists who had created masterpieces or seminal works of twentieth-century art — Picasso, Duchamp, Kandinsky, Brancusi, Ray, and others — whose work Lye himself had admired. Such an exhibition (which included Naum Gabo and Alexander Calder as well as Lye) reminds us that kinetic art has always been best understood in Europe. Also, in April 2000, the Centre Pompidou in Paris exhibited a selection of his paintings, photograms, and works of sculpture, together with a full retrospective of his films, curated by Jean-Michel Bouhours.[19] At the same time the museum published a book of essays, *Len Lye*, by an international roster of critics.[20]

What is needed now is a comprehensive exhibition to tour overseas museums.[21] The impact of Lye's large kinetic sculptures would be profound. This next stage has been delayed by a catch-22 situation in which major museums remain nervous about making such an investment in a less-well-known artist, even though such an exhibition is the only way to confirm his 'major' status. At every stage along the way, the career of this artist has illustrated the limitations of the cultural machinery of art — with all its museums, funding bodies, art markets, critics, and art historians — in terms of its flawed ability to recognise 'extraordinary creations' and to provide enough support for artists to keep producing and exhibiting such work. Lye is a particularly interesting case because so many of his decisions as an artist left him institutionally at a disadvantage. He had little interest in self-promotion. His move from film to kinetic sculpture showed how compartmentalised those fields were — few critics and few audiences were aware that he had done outstanding work in both media (even though Lye regarded the two media as part of the same art of motion). His move from England to the United States demonstrated the separateness of the two art scenes and of the discourses associated with them. Again, the fact that Lye was temperamentally a loner who came into contact with a number of art movements (such as surrealism, abstract expressionism, and European kineticism), but felt no desire to become deeply involved, has led to a situation where writers make brief references to his work but seldom discuss it in detail. It has been convenient to map the history of modern art as a succession of movements, but this has pushed some highly creative individuals out to the edges of the map.

Once the many aspects of Lye's art and life are reassembled, we can see the strong coherence of his interests and the scope and originality of his achievement. He stands out as a figure of great energy, for his remarkable, one-of-a-kind life, and for the unique understanding of movement he embodied in his films and sculptures — those 'extraordinary objects' we are only just beginning to come to terms with.

acknowledgements

I was able to have many discussions with Len Lye during the time I worked as his assistant in 1980, and he and his wife Ann strongly endorsed my project. After his death Ann continued to be an invaluable source of information (as well as a dear friend). She listened to parts of the manuscript when I visited her in Puerto Rico in 1996, confirmed her general support, and made useful suggestions.

Other relatives have also been helpful. I had many conversations with Philip Lye, the artist's brother, a rich source of information on the early years. Jane Lye, Len's first wife, provided new perspectives on the years in England. I have also had the pleasure of getting to know Bix Lye and Yancy McCaffrey, Len and Jane's children. Jack Ellitt (who was the artist's closest friend for many years) and his wife Doris provided much unique information. I have attempted to write a history that these participants would regard as accurate, and I am deeply sorry that Ann, Jane, Philip, and Doris all died before the book could be completed.

My biography grew out of the work Wystan Curnow and I were doing for a collection of Lye's writings (published in 1984 as *Figures of Motion*). Wystan's research helped to lay the foundations for the present book, and over the years he has continued to play a very important role for me as a supportive friend and intellectual influence.

It is difficult to express adequate thanks to the two hundred or so individuals who agreed to be interviewed for this biography, sent detailed replies to my letters, or donated photographs. I must single out a few who made particularly significant contributions: Lou Adler, Louise Bates Ames, William Baldwin, Paul Barnes, Yann Beauvais, Andrew Bogle, Stan Brakhage, Henry Brant, Arthur and Corinne Cantrill, Kanty Cooper, Joe Davis, Sarah Davy, Robert Del Tredici, Richard and Jane de Rochemont, Jonathan Dennis, Max Gimblett, Beryl Graves, Keith Griffiths, A. E. Jeakins and his son Alec Jeakins, Steve Jones, Hamish Keith, Barbara Ker-Seymer, Anne Kirker, James Manilla, John and Lynda Matthews, T. S. (Tom) Matthews, John Maynard and Bridget Ikin, Ann McMillan, Richard McNaughton, William Moritz, Alastair Reid, Peter Selz, Cecile Starr, John Taylor, Ray Thorburn, Evan Webb, and Howard Wise. Five people in this list who had unpublished interview material generously made it available to me — Bogle, Griffiths, Kirker, Matthews and Thorburn. And Ann

Lye's daughters, Jane Hindle Bamberg and Gillian Cintoli, provided valuable perspectives.

I also want to mention some other people who were notably helpful: A. O. Aitken, Margareta Akermark, Jim Allen, Billy Apple, Joanne Baker, Priscilla Baker, Joe Barnes, Sidney Bernstein, Lorraine Blasor, Jean-Michel Bouhours, Eileen Bowser, Robert Breer, Ron Brownson, Alberto Cavalcanti, Bernard and Judith Childs, Pip Chodorov, Howard Conant, Gill and Paul Cotton, Robert Creeley, Janet Davidson, Elfriede Fischinger, Monica Flaherty, Tim and Sherrah Francis, Jim Frye, Peter Gaines, Gwain Gillespie, Grace Glueck, William Graves, Tony Green, Sophie Hahne, Robert A. Haller, Hillary Harris, Stanley William Hayter, Dorothy and Stitch Hemming, F. W. (Frank) Hempleman, Carol Henderson, Bob Henry, Judith Hoffberg, Warren Hope, Ian Hugo, Larry Kardish, Barbara Kirshenblatt-Gimblett, Dan Klugherz, Mr and Mrs Maurice Lancaster, Janet Learned, Francis Lee, Jeanne Macaskill, James Manilla, Bud and Phyllis Mark, Jean Matos, Bob McCoy, Dennis McEldowney, Miles McKane, Peter McLeavey, James Merritt, Naomi Mitchison, Leon Narbey, Roger Neich, Douglas Newton, Merv and Françoise Norrish, Paul O'Prey, Merania Paroa, Priscilla Pitts, Wally Popolizio, Joyce Porter, Joellen Rapee, Ruth Richards, Enid Richardson, Pam Riding, Simon Ryan, Kinsley Sampson, Howard and Duffy Schoenfeld, Eve Scott, Erik Shiozaki, Rose Slivka, Bill Sloan, Alan Smythe, Kenneth Snelson, Nancy Sommerschield, Rufus Stillman, A. J. P. Taylor, Allan Temko, Margaret Thomson, Julian Trevelyan, Selina Trieff, John Turner, Albert Douglas Tutt, Walter Tutt, Rita Vandivert, Gordon Walters, Derek Waterman, Gretchen Weinberg, Joyce Wexler, Rodney Wilson, and Lothar Wolff. This is still only a partial list of those I have consulted over the past 20 years. I add a warm thanks to everyone else who assisted my enquiries. Since there are many people who knew the artist that I have not yet talked with, I welcome additional information. I hope this first biography encourages others to expand or correct the record.

Among organisations, the Len Lye Foundation deserves particular mention. The Foundation (with John Matthews as chairman and Evan Webb as director) funded some of my travel costs and gave me permission to quote from the unpublished Lye manuscripts in its collection. Its cooperation has been crucial for my biography. In New Plymouth the staff of the Govett-Brewster Art Gallery (under its director Greg Burke and earlier directors John MacCormack, Priscilla Pitts, and Cheryl Sotheran) have been consistently helpful. I have also had excellent research assistance from archives and libraries — the Film Archive in Wellington, the National Film Archive in London, the Department of Film and

Video at the Museum of Modern Art in New York (with particular thanks to Steven Higgins), the John Grierson Archive at the University of Stirling, the Alexander Turnbull Library in Wellington, and the University of Auckland Library. I have attempted to track down the sources of all photographs. I apologise if any have inadvertently been used without correct clearance, and would be happy to make any corrections of that kind to future editions.

At the University of Auckland Greg Bennett has been tireless in providing technical assistance, and Brian Donovan and Gottfried Boehnke have skilfully restored old Lye photographs. My colleagues in the Department of Film, Television and Media Studies have always taken a thoughtful interest in my work on Lye, as have old friends such as Alan Loney, Susan and Leigh Davis, Terry Sturm, Michael Neill, Susan Bee, and Charles Bernstein. Also Steve and Tony Heim, Louis Spitz, Simone, Dylan and Nigel Horrocks.

During 1981, when I took a year of unpaid leave from my job to work on this project, I received a grant from the Minister of the Arts (Allan Highet). This was a modest amount ($2000) but as a gesture of public support it was extremely helpful and encouraging at that time. The other institutional support received for this project was research leave from the University of Auckland during 2000 which enabled me to complete the book. I owe special thanks to Dr John Hood, the vice-chancellor, and Professor Doug Sutton, the dean of the Arts Faculty, for their informed interest in my project and their generous decision to extend one semester of paid leave to two semesters.

Arthur and Corinne Cantrill, David Curtis, John Matthews, and Evan Webb read sections of the manuscript and made expert suggestions. Over the past year it has been a great pleasure to work with Elizabeth Caffin and her staff at the Auckland University Press — Katrina Duncan, Christine O'Brien, and Annie Irving — who have been exceptionally supportive and efficient. I was also fortunate in having my manuscript edited with great care and expertise by Simon Cauchi. I have saved my last and deepest thanks for my wife Shirley, who has lived with the project for 20 years and helped with so many aspects of it.

endnotes

introduction

1 Letter to the author, 26 March 1981.
2 Interviews with Ann Lye, Alastair Reid, and Kenneth Snelson, 1980.
3 For example, when Lye was asked about something he had made or done as an artist before his move to London, he would offer a date between 1917 and 1926 that was usually two or three (or more) years off the mark.
4 See Lye's comments in 'Slow but Sure' in *Len Lye: A Personal Mythology*, Auckland City Art Gallery, 1980.
5 Peter Greenaway interviewed by Jonathan Dennis on 'Film Show', National Radio (New Zealand), 5 October 1997.

one the flash

1 'Happy Moments', unpublished manuscript. See *Figures of Motion: Len Lye, Selected Writings*, ed. Wystan Curnow and Roger Horrocks, Auckland, Auckland University Press and Oxford University Press, 1984, p 29, for one complete version of this 'moment'. Because of the complex state of Lye's unpublished manuscripts — with many variant versions — this book was in danger of becoming overloaded with scholarly footnotes, ellipses, brackets, etc., and in the end I decided the only way to create an accessible biography was to standardise punctuation and get on with making my own editorial choices. When Lye gave his support to my biography in 1980, he also gave me permission to do as much editing as necessary. (This was on the strength of the editing I had done for him previously, plus the Lye collage I had made for the February 1979 issue of *Alternative Cinema*.) I hope that one day there will be opportunities to produce scholarly editions of the artist's writings to document and discuss the manuscripts in their full complexity.
2 Cecile Starr, letter to Stan Brakhage and Roger Horrocks, 27 December 1980.
3 Untitled note. (Unless otherwise stated, all unpublished notes and manuscripts are by Len Lye and are from the collection of the Lye Foundation.)
4 Interview with Philip Lye, 1981. (Unless otherwise stated, all interviews were conducted by the author.) See also note 11 below.
5 'Names', unpublished manuscript.
6 ibid.
7 For example Protestants in Christchurch 'actually came to blows in the streets with Roman Catholics', according to J. P. Morrison in *The Evolution of a City*, Christchurch City Council, 1948, p 154.
8 Untitled note.
9 This figure includes the suburbs.
10 Also born in 1901: Walt Disney, Jean Dubuffet, Albert Giacometti, Stanley William Hayter, Jacques Lacan, André Malraux, Margaret Mead, and Laura Riding. Compare these New Zealand birth dates: J. C. Beaglehole (1901), M. L. Holcroft (1902), Frank Sargeson (1903), A. R. D. Fairburn (1904), Rita Angus (1908), M. T. Woollaston (1910), Colin McCahon (1919).
11 Born on 9 May 1903 in Lyttelton. His birth certificate gives his name as Phillip John Lye, but as an adult his first name tended to be spelt 'Philip', and his brother always referred to him as 'Phil'.
12 'Miscellaneous note', unpublished. Harry died 16 May 1904, aged 27, with the cause of death listed as 'phthisis pulmenalis'. He was buried in the Lynwood Cemetery.
13 Letter from Len Lye to Philip Lye, 25 August 1975.
14 'Miscellaneous note', unpublished.
15 Interview with Philip Lye, 1981.
16 Quotations from *No Trouble* ('self-raising flower') and 'Rose Ann', unpublished ms.

two cape campbell

1 'Powell', unpublished ms. The maiden name of Powell's mother was Emily Cole; it is not known whether there was a family connection.

2 *Figures of Motion*, p 29.
3 'Dead Eye Dick', unpublished ms.
4 Draft of commentary for 'Wave', slide–tape programme.
5 William Eric H. Creamer, 'The Tall White Tower', qMS-0586, Alexander Turnbull Library, p 72. This memoir of growing up at various New Zealand lighthouses, including Cape Campbell, provides a valuable source of information.
6 'Black Sun' from 'Happy Moments', unpublished ms. The present chapter makes extensive use of Lye's 'Happy Moments' as background.
7 'Octopuses', unpublished ms.
8 'Black Sun'.
9 See 'Happy Moments' and 'Notes re Somewhat Autobiographically (Sacrifice)', unpublished mss.
10 'Somewhat Autobiographically', unpublished ms. (Henceforth cited as 'S.A.')
11 'Powell'.
12 Albert Tutt, quoted by Joyce Porter (one of the members of the Tutt family that I interviewed for this chapter), 1981.
13 Interview with Walter Tutt, 1981.
14 I cannot confirm this suggestion since records are subject to medical confidentiality. There is a listing for 'Frederick Ford Powell, Labourer' at a Masterton address in the 1910 edition of Wise's *Directory*. Was this Rose Lye's husband, or her father-in-law?

three the first sketchbook

1 'S.A.'
2 'The First Bite on the Hook of Art', unpublished ms. Lye would later guess his age at the time he started drawing seriously as 9.
3 'Note re kid drawing, his own discovery', unpublished ms.
4 'Misc. note', unpublished ms.
5 'S.A.'.
6 'The First Bite . . .'
7 Interview with Philip Lye, 1981.
8 'The Watch', unpublished ms.
9 *Figures of Motion*, p 30.
10 'Nightly', unpublished ms.
11 'S.A.'
12 'Happy Moments'.
13 'Nightly', unpublished ms. Lye's account of learning to draw mentions William S. Hart and Norma Talmadge as his original models, but as he could not have known these actors

in 1909–10 he must have been getting his early memories out of order.
14 Interview with Philip Lye.
15 'S.A.'
16 'Biographical Notes', unpublished ms.
17 'In Arcadia People Are Talking About . . . Len Lye', *Spleen* (Wellington), No 7, 1977, pp 4–7.
18 'Sundays', unpublished ms.
19 Interview with Philip Lye.
20 Philip Lye.
21 ibid. (Cf. 'Launch', unpublished ms.)
22 ibid.
23 'The Watch', unpublished manuscript.
24 'The Watch'.
25 Interview with Philip Lye.
26 'Note', unpublished.
27 'S.A.'
28 Letter, 20 July 1981.
29 Interview with Philip Lye.

four composing motion

1 Noel Harrison, *The School That Riley Built*, Wellington, Wellington Technical College, 1961, p 39 (a book which provides detailed information on the College).
2 Letter to Rose Lye from the College, July 1917.
3 Letter from Joe Davis, 20 July 1981. (Unless otherwise noted, all letters were written to the author.)
4 David Low, *Low's Autobiography*, London, Michael Joseph, 1956, pp 28–29.
5 Gordon H. Brown, *New Zealand Painting 1900–1920: Traditions and Departures*, Wellington, Queen Elizabeth II Arts Council of New Zealand, 1972, p 39.
6 Janet Paul, 'Painting 1920–50', *New Zealand Heritage*, No 84, 1973, p 2333.
7 A painter such as Cézanne 'wasn't generally acceptable [in New Zealand] until well into the nineteen-fifties' says Toss Woollaston in *Sage Tea: An Autobiography*, Auckland, Collins, 1980, p 100.
8 Gordon H. Brown, *New Zealand Painting 1900–1920*, pp 39–40.
9 Howard Wadman, *Year Book of the Arts in New Zealand*, No 3, 1947, p 12.
10 Deborah Shepard, *H. Linley Richardson*, Education Supplement, Manawatu Art Gallery, 1986.
11 Confirmed by both Joe Davis and Gordon Walters (who had heard it from one of Lye's

fellow students). Also see 'Writing', unpublished ms.

12 *New Zealand Heritage*, No 84, 1973, p 2331.

13 Draft version of 'Slow but Sure' for *Len Lye: A Personal Mythology*.

14 'Inspiration', unpublished ms.

15 'Two Grand Illuminations/ Illuminated Turn Ons/ My Best Ideas', unpublished ms.

16 The painting is the 'celebration of a fleeting moment' according to Seymour Slive, *Frans Hals*, London, Phaidon, 1970, Vol 1, p 92.

17 Letter from Joe Davis, 20 July 1981.

18 'Helix', unpublished ms.

19 *Figures of Motion,* p 33.

20 ibid, p 34.

21 'Helix', unpublished ms.

22 Interview with Philip Lye. See also 'Len Lye — through the eyes of his "kid brother"', *Auckland Star,* 4 August 1980.

23 'Two Grand Illuminations', unpublished ms (one of Lye's many and varying accounts).

24 ibid. It is interesting to compare Lye's accounts of this incident — for example, Gretchen Weinberg's 'Interview with Len Lye' in *Film Culture*, No 29, Summer 1963, p 40, and 'Ray Thorburn interviews Len Lye' in *Art International*, XIX (April), 64–68, 1975.

25 'Inspiration', unpublished ms.

26 Draft version of 'Slow but Sure'.

27 'A Kinetic Biography', unpublished ms.

28 'Ray Thorburn interviews Len Lye', p 64.

29 'Inspiration'.

30 See Wordsworth's *The Prelude*.

31 This and the next quotation come from an interview with Carol Henderson, 25 February 1998. See Henderson's interesting book on her father, *A Blaze of Colour: Gordon Tovey, Artist Educator*, Christchurch, Hazard Press, 1998. Henderson's account (p 17) is based on her memory of conversations. While her wording may have been influenced by later reading about Lye, she was clear about the main points, including the strong impact Lye had made on her father, particularly in his talk of motion. Those points were confirmed by Jeanne Macaskill who had also discussed Lye with Tovey.

32 Phone interview with Jeanne Macaskill, 2 March 1998. (Macaskill recalled the words as closely as she could.)

33 Anne Kirker, unpublished interview with Len Lye, 19 August 1979. (My thanks to Kirker for allowing me to use this and other passages from her interview.) Compare Lye's comments in Robert Del Tredici, 'Len Lye Interview', *The Cinema News* (San Francisco), Nos 2–4, 1979, p 35.

34 'My Model', unpublished ms.

35 'My Model'.

36 'In Arcadia People Are Talking About . . . Len Lye', *Spleen* (Wellington), No 7, 1977, pp 4–7.

37 ibid.

38 ibid.

39 'The New Muses — Aesthetic Kinesthesia', unpublished ms.

40 'My Model' (a variant version).

41 'The New Muses — Aesthetic Kinesthesia', unpublished ms.

42 ibid.

43 Robert Russett and Cecile Starr, *Experimental Animation*, New York, Van Nostrand Reinhold, 1976, p 7.

44 'A Kinetic Biography', unpublished ms.

45 Sources include Russett and Starr, *Experimental Animation*, and 'A Kinetic Biography'.

five modernism

1 Wystan Curnow, 'An Interview with Len Lye', *Art New Zealand*, No 17, 1980 (henceforward cited as 'Wystan Curnow interview').

2 'My Model', unpublished ms.

3 ibid.

4 'Len Lye — through the eyes of his "kid brother".'

5 Quoted by Bernard Rosenberg & Norris Fliegel in *The Vanguard Artist: Portrait and Self-Portrait*, Chicago, Quadrangle, 1965, p 60.

6 There is no evidence that Lye saw reproductions of these 1912 paintings and so we can only speculate. Balla was influenced by the motion picture (or 'chronophotography') experiments of Etienne-Jules Marey. Another forerunner was the photographer Eadweard Muybridge. In 1911 Anton Giulio Bragaglia was experimenting with 'fotodinamismo' (photographs of superimposed images showing the successive stages of a movement). For more details, see *Futurism and Futurisms*, the catalogue for an exhibition at the Palazzo Grassi in Venice, published by the Abbeville Press, N.Y., 1986. I include Duchamp as an artist whose interests included Futurism. Reports of his 'Nude Descending A Staircase' were certainly

published in Australian newspapers and may
have similarly appeared in New Zealand.
(See John F. Williams, *The Quarantined
Culture: Australian Reactions to Modernism
1913–1939*, Cambridge University Press,
1995, pp 71–73.)

7 The prizes were one pound per category.
See *New Zealand Times*, 21 September 1922,
p 12; and the Alexander Turnbull Library
collection of New Zealand Academy of Fine
Arts records, which include a letter from Len
Lye. (Thanks to Janet Horncy for alerting
me to this.)

8 'My Model', unpublished ms.

9 ibid.

10 Interview with A. O. Aitken, 1981.

11 Note beginning 'As an artist I kicked off . . .',
unpublished ms.

12 'Len Lye — through the eyes of his "kid
brother".'

13 'My Model', unpublished ms. Cf. 'Len Lye
through the eyes . . .'.

14 Letter to Cora Wilding, quoted in
Gordon H. Brown's *New Zealand Painting
1900–1920*, p 46.

15 'Ray Thorburn interviews Len Lye', p 65.

16 Interview with A. O. Aitken, 1981.

17 ibid.

18 Letter from Joe Davis, 20 July 1981. Cf. Leo
Rosten, *Hooray for Yiddish!,* London, Elm
Tree Books, 1983, pp 162–63. The phrase is
sometimes spelled 'Ish ki bibble' or 'Ish
kabibble'. Compare Lye's later slogan 'No
trouble'.

19 Ann Lye, his future wife, remembered
learning the phrase 'Ich gebibble' from 'the
funnies' read to her by her father (letter to the
author, 12 September 1981).

20 Letter from Len Lye to Philip Lye,
25 August 1975.

21 Interview, 1980.

22 'Len Lye — through the eyes of his "kid
brother".'

23 'Rose Ann', unpublished ms.

24 Letter from Joe Davis, 20 July 1981.

25 Interview with Philip Lye, 1981.

26 'Boats', unpublished ms.

27 'Butterfly', unpublished ms.

28 'S.A.'

29 *Figures of Motion*, p 84.

30 Press Release, The Contemporary Arts
Centre, Cincinnati, 1965.

31 'Hello / Orgone', unpublished ms.

32 'S.A.'

33 'S.A.' Cf. A. J. P. Taylor *English History
1914–45*, London, Pelican, 1970, p 219.

34 'S.A.'

35 Notes for 'Mechanical Me', unpublished ms.

36 Stan Patchett, 'Handpainted Swing',
Rhythm, February, p 68, 1939.

37 Wystan Curnow interview.

38 Interview with Jack Ellitt, 1983.

39 'Ward', unpublished ms.; also interview with
Philip Lye, 1981.

40 ibid.

41 ibid.

42 Interview with Jack Ellitt, 1986.

43 Kanty Cooper, diary entry, 4 October 1927
(recording Lye's words).

44 Interview with Philip Lye, 1981.

45 'Mail Boat', unpublished ms.

46 Interview with Philip Lye, 1981.

47 'Notes for S.A. re development stages',
unpublished ms.

48 Cf. Gordon Brown, *New Zealand Painting
1900–1920,* p 49.

49 Cf. Kanty Cooper diary, 4 October 1927.

six hei-tiki

1 Thanks to Evan Webb for checking the date
in the school records.

2 Gordon H. Brown and Hamish Keith, *An
Introduction to New Zealand Painting
1839–1967*, London, Collins, 1969, p 74.

3 D. J. Ramage, 'A Century of New Zealand
Painting, 1850 to 1950', MA thesis, Victoria
University College, 1953, pp 45–46.

4 'A Kinetic Biography', unpublished ms. See
also *New Zealand Free Lance*, 21 October 1959.

5 'S.A.' p 65.

6 *New Zealand Heritage,* No 71, 1972, p 1978
Cf. 'S.A.'

7 'Note', unpublished ms.

8 *Since Cézanne*, London, Chatto & Windus,
1923, p 113.

9 ibid.

10 Note 'For S.A., re: my old brain imagery',
unpublished ms.

11 *African Art in Motion: Icon and Art*, Los
Angeles, University of California Press, 1974,
p xiv.

12 'Film That Needs No Camera . . .', *The
Australian*, 21 December 1968.

13 Compare Rosalind E. Krauss's description of
Brancusi's 'The Beginning of the World': 'the
smooth shape of the top half is contorted by
myriad and changing visual incidents. . . . It

is this differential [between the upper and lower halves] that gives to the geometry of the form something of the kinesthetic quality that recalls the feeling of the back of one's head, resting heavily on a pillow, while the face floats, weightless and unencumbered, toward sleep.' *Passages in Modern Sculpture*, Cambridge (Mass.), MIT Press, 1994, pp 86–87.

14 Curnow interview, p 54.

15 'Ray Thorburn Interviews Len Lye', p 65.

16 Note 'For S.A., re: my old brain imagery', unpublished ms.

17 Curnow interview, p 54.

18 Stow, p 21.

19 'From 9 on . . .', unpublished ms.

20 The evidence for this statement is not conclusive. Lye said — for example — that the idea for the painting 'Polynesian Connection' came from a 'carving once seen on the gable of a Maori pa' (*Len Lye: A Personal Mythology*, p 74).

21 'Note, Dec 6', unpublished ms.

22 Faber and Faber, 1916.

23 p 22.

24 p 23.

25 Quoted by Anne Kirker, 'The Early Years in London', *Art New Zealand*, 17, 1980, p 50.

26 p 126.

27 pp 134–35.

28 p 88.

29 Interview with Philip Lye, 1981.

30 i.e. like a Bolshevik.

31 'Note 6/10/75'. According to Jack Ellitt, Lye also made a larger version and in London he made a metal cast of it, but the wooden tiki was charred in the process. My own inclination was to assign this work to Lye's return visit to Auckland in 1924 but Philip Lye supported the earlier date. Lye admitted that he himself had difficulty separating memories of New Zealand from Australia during these years. (Cf. Curnow interview, p 55: 'No, it was . . .')

seven sydney

1 Note: This date can be only a best guess.

2 Interview with Stitch Hemming, 1981.

3 *Low's Autobiography*, p 19.

4 ibid, p 146.

5 Interview with Dorothy Hemming, 1981.

6 'Len Lye — through the eyes of his "kid brother".'

7 'Canoe', unpublished manuscript.

8 p 15.

9 p 130.

10 Christchurch during Lye's childhood had a population of around 50,000, Wellington had 200,000, and Auckland had 370,000 at the time he left. (These figures include outer suburbs.)

11 Letter from Lye to Daniel Thomas, 1966.

12 George Blaikie, *Remember Smith's Weekly?*, Adelaide, Rigby, 1966, p 77.

13 Kenneth Slessor, *Bread and Wine: Selected Prose*, Sydney, Angus and Robertson, 1970, p 29. The cafe was active from 1922 to mid-1924.

14 pp 29–30.

15 Peter Kirkpatrick, *The Sea Coast of Bohemia: Literary Life in Sydney's Roaring Twenties*, Queensland, University of Queensland Press, 1992, p 254.

16 There are Cumine manuscripts in the Mitchell Library in Sydney.

17 Quoted Smith, p 201. On the conservative nationalist attitudes of the period, see John F. Williams, *The Quarantined Culture*.

18 See Ria Murch, *Arthur Murch — An Artist's Life*, Avalon Beach, Australia, Ruskin Rowe Press, 1997, pp 23–28. My thanks also to Arthur and Corinne Cantrill for background information.

19 Letter from Jack Ellitt, 5 May 1981.

20 Interviews with Philip Lye and Walter Tutt, 1981.

21 Interview with Walter Tutt, 1981.

22 ibid.

23 'Outrigger', unpublished ms.

24 Lye's own recollections of when he first saw the book were uncertain. He thought it was in New Zealand but I have evidence that the notebook into which he copied *Totem and Taboo* was purchased in Sydney. (The cover bears the trademark of W. C. Penfold and Co. Ltd, Stationers, of 88 Pitt Street, Sydney, and the early drawings appear to be derived from Australian sources. The cover has since become separated from the notebook but I saw it intact in 1980.) The State Library of New South Wales in Sydney did have a 1918 edition of Freud's book.

25 As quoted in Lye's notebook. He was using the translation by A. A. Brill. Other reasons *Totem and Taboo* would have had a particular impact on him were its references to Maori culture and its exploration of the theme of the dead father.

26 *The Psychopathology of Everyday Life* also

became an important book for him.

27 'S.A.'

28 Curnow interview, p 57. (Lye's comments about Freud in this interview, made near the end of his life, are more negative than earlier comments.)

29 'The Scorpion', unpublished ms.

30 Roger Neich commented to me on the 'accuracy' of Lye's drawings which made it relatively easy for him to identify their subject.

31 p 127. Compare Ezra Pound's favourite story about the zoologist Agassiz requiring his student to study a fish for days on end.

32 Curnow interview, p 54.

33 'S.A.'

34 Unpublished ms.

35 Curnow interview, p 55.

eight kinetic theatre

1 Published by Paul, French, Trubner in 1922.

2 St. Louis, C. V. Mosby, 1921, p 423 and p 426.

3 p 431.

4 'A Kinetic Biography', unpublished ms.

5 ibid.

6 Sources: 'A Kinetic Biography' (unpublished ms.); 'Happiness Acid' lecture notes; 'Ray Thorburn interviews Len Lye', p 64; 'Len Lye speaks at the Film-makers' Cinematheque', *Film Culture*, No 44, Spring 1967, reprinted *Figures of Motion*; Robert Del Tredici, 'Len Lye Interview', *The Cinemanews*, Nos 2–4, 1979; Russett and Starr, *Experimental Animation*, p 66; and 'The Berkeley Art Symposium', *Art and Artists*, I, February, 1967, p 29. (Lye's date of 1920 seems too early — my own guess is 1923.)

7 Gretchen Weinberg, 'Interview with Len Lye'.

8 'Len Lye speaks at the Film-makers' Cinematheque'.

9 Quoted in *Terratorium Artis*, p 116.

10 Rachael Low, *The History of the British Film 1918–1929*, p 289. See also Andrew Pike's essay in *Cantrills Filmnotes*, Nos 31–32.

11 'Frances Calvert on Frank Hurley', *Metro* (Australia), No 112, 1997, p 14.

12 The date when Lye saw it is a guess based on the evidence available to me.

13 'Frances Calvert on Frank Hurley.'

14 Curnow interview, p 56.

15 Russett and Starr, *Experimental Animation*, p 66.

16 Len Lye, 'Biographical Notes' (unpublished

ms). Lye did not remember the name of the company but he did recall the name of his supervisor, Garnet Agnew, and this enabled me to identify it.

17 'Ray Thorburn interviews Len Lye', p 65.

18 Joseph Kennedy, 'Len Lye — Composer of Motion', *Millimeter*, Vol 5, February 1977.

19 From a résumé by Lye.

20 Interview, 1980.

21 'A Kinetic Biography', unpublished ms.

22 Russett and Starr, *Experimental Animation,* p 67.

nine samoa

1 This and the following quotations are from an interview with Dorothy and Stitch Hemming in 1981.

2 Interview with Frank Hempleman, 1981.

3 Interview with Philip Lye, 1981. See also 'Len Lye — through the eyes of his "kid brother".'

4 See Bronwen Nicholson, *Gauguin and Maori Art*, Auckland, Godwit in association with the Auckland City Art Gallery, 1995, and Douglas W. Druick and Peter Zegers, *Paul Gauguin: Pages from the Pacific*, Auckland City Art Gallery in association with the Art Institute of Chicago, 1995.

5 I hypothesise this trip on the basis of the notebook, which includes several pages of drawings of objects at the museum.

6 Letter from Lye to Bill [Nelson], 26 May 1973.

7 'Biographical Notes.' Also see Russett and Starr, *Experimental Animation,* p 67.

8 Alva Carothers, *Stevenson's Isles of Paradise*, San Diego, Mallory, 1930, p 8.

9 'Names', unpublished ms.

10 Untitled and unpublished 'happy moment'.

11 'Ray Thorburn interviews Len Lye', pp 64–65.

12 'Outrigger', unpublished ms.

13 'Ray Thorburn interviews Len Lye', p 65.

14 'Outrigger'.

15 Curnow interview, p 55.

16 *New Zealand Heritage,* No 80, 1973, p 2235 and p 2233.

17 The figure of 35,000 is approximate and does not include American Samoa (only the New Zealand territory).

18 Carothers, p 71.

19 'Outrigger'.

20 Lye remembered the name as So'olevao

Tauai (or Tauui), but he was never a reliable speller of names, and he was trying to remember it many years later. Vavoa Fetui of the University of Auckland has suggested to me that the name might be 'Sola i le Vao' (from 'to run away into the bush'), condensed (either in fact or in Lye's memory) to 'Solavao'. Other notes by Lye suggest that the father's village may have been Vailu'utai but I have not been able to confirm this. Lye was sad to hear that his friend had died in mid-1968, about six months before his return visit to Samoa.

21 Curnow interview, p 55.

22 Lye remembered the name of the village as 'Vaia' or 'Vaea' but I have not been able to confirm its accuracy.

23 'Scorpion', unpublished ms.

24 Kanty Cooper's diary, 4 October 1927. (Cooper, an English artist, was recording what Lye told her. She obviously confused 'Samoa' with 'New Zealand'.)

25 Curnow interview, p 57.

26 'Sir Galahad', unpublished ms. The *lavalava* would continue to be one of his favourite forms of clothing for the rest of his life. To quote one of many stories, Alastair Reid remembers Len dancing in a *lavalava* at New York parties and giving guests a demonstration in how to wear it.

27 'Names', unpublished ms.

28 Kanty Cooper journal.

29 Carlos Baker, *New York Times Book Review*, 3 September 1950, p 5.

30 'Outrigger'.

31 Mead was in Samoa from August 1925 to May 1926, and Flaherty from May 1923 to around the end of 1924. For critiques, see Derek Freeman's *Margaret Mead and Samoa: The Making and Unmaking of an Anthropological Myth*, Canberra, Australian National University Press, 1983, and Albert Wendt's review of Freeman's book in the *Auckland Star,* 26 March 1983. A later generation of Polynesian writers (such as Wendt) have fought back against the myths of 'paradise' and 'Polynesianism' imposed on them by European culture. The assumption made by European artists that Pacific cultures were at their best and most authentic when they were at their most 'primitive' overlooked the ability of local cultures to adapt and innovate.

32 Curnow interview, p 57.

33 ibid. Some years later Lye became friendly

with the Flahertys and surprised them with his story — they did not even remember having met him.

ten deportation

1 Quoted in J. W. Davidson's *Samoa Mo Samoa*, Melbourne, Oxford University Press, 1967, p 112.

2 Interview with Monica Flaherty, 1983; and Michael J. Field, *Mau: Samoa's Study for Freedom*, revised edition, Auckland, Polynesian Press, 1991, p 68 and photo facing p 62.

3 'Here I was leaving Samoa . . .', unpublished ms.

4 'Outrigger', unpublished ms.

5 Curnow interview, p 55.

6 ibid, p 56.

7 ibid.

8 'Outrigger'.

9 Interview with Monica Flaherty, 1983.

10 'Here I was leaving Samoa . . .', unpublished ms.

11 'Outrigger'.

12 'Samoa', unpublished note.

13 See 'Tapa', unpublished note. In the 1920s some patterns were still done with leaf (rather than wooden) *upeti*.

14 'Samoa'.

15 Roger Neich and Mick Pendergrast, *Pacific Tapa*, Auckland, David Bateman and the Auckland Museum, 1997, p 15.

16 Curnow interview, p 56.

17 'Scorpion', unpublished ms. This dream curiously duplicated a trick he had once played on his sleeping brother (an anecdote Philip Lye liked to tell). According to Robert Mackenzie Watson, 'Venomous snakes do not exist [in Samoa]; the centipede and scorpion are there, but one hardly ever hears of their bites' (*History of Samoa*, Wellington, Whitcombe and Tombs, 1918, p 13).

18 'Samoa'.

19 He is described by C. G. R. McKay in *Samoana* as 'Chicago born, extrovert, and much loved by his congregations in Apia' (Wellington, A. H. and A. W. Reed, 1968), p 125.

20 'Art', *Time*, 10 March 1924, p 15.

21 28 May 1923, p 15.

22 5 November 1923, p 13.

23 'Theater', 17 March 1923. Lye remembered *Time* but could not specify particular issues or articles. He spoke of 'Stanislavsky and

Meyerhold in the Moscow Theatre' ('Outrigger' ms.) and may not have been clear about the relationship between Meyerhold and the Moscow Art Theatre.

24 Huntley Carter, *The New Theatre and Cinema of Soviet Russia*, London, Chapman and Dodd, 1924, p 70.

25 Russian title: *Velikodushnyi rogonosets*.

26 Popova quoted in Robert Leach, *Vsevolod Meyerhold*, Cambridge University Press, 1989, p 96.

27 Comment by Leach, p 96.

28 'Outrigger'.

29 Curnow interview, p 56.

30 'Outrigger'.

31 Curnow interview, p 56.

32 Laura Riding wrote in 1931 in *Laura and Francisca*: 'Len once lived in Samoa for six months.' Jane Lye told me that Lye had said he lived there about eight months. Both figures seem to match the other evidence. Late in his life Lye remembered it less accurately as a period of one or two years.

33 Interview with Ann Lye, 1995. ('Len talked a lot about Samoa all his life — it made a big impression on him.')

34 'Outrigger'.

35 'Tapa' and 'Outrigger'. The phrases describing the smell of cocoa beans and copra have been borrowed from Richard A. Goodman's essay 'Journey into Samoa' in *Samoa*, Auckland, Collins, 1973, p 98.

eleven jack ellitt

1 'Ocean Liner', unpublished ms.

2 The farm was in New South Wales — perhaps Cooley Arbour near Bourke or Coolamon, a centre of wheat growing?

3 'Biographical Notes'. See also 'Eight Aussie Horses', unpublished ms.

4 'Hats', unpublished ms.

5 ibid. (At the time Lye would probably have said 'pancakes', not the American 'flapjacks'.)

6 'Len Lye — The English Disney', *Sunday Referee*, 10 November 1935.

7 'Hats.'

8 Interview with Jack Ellitt, 1993.

9 In some interviews Lye said he was on the farm for six months, but an early source — 'Len Lye — The English Disney', *Sunday Referee*, 10 November 1935 — spoke of three months. There are so many inconsistencies of

this kind in Lye's interviews that no dates in the Australian and Samoan chapters can be definitive. Perhaps the missing collection of Lye's letters to his mother will turn up one day.

10 The author conducted many interviews with Jack Ellitt and his wife Doris, between 1982 and 1999. Any quotations from the Ellitts not otherwise acknowledged come from these interviews.

11 From Jack Ellitt's sound composition about Lye, 'Homage to Rachel Carson No. 2'.

12 From a 1987 interview with Ellitt conducted by Keith Griffiths, for his documentary *Doodlin'*. My thanks to Griffiths for making interview material available.

13 ibid.

14 Interview, 1996.

15 ibid.

16 Interview with Margaret Thompson, 1988.

17 This was the first concert by the Conservatorium Orchestra (31 March 1926). A decade later Holst's music would provide the soundtrack to *Birth of the Robot*.

18 Interview, 1996.

19 ibid.

20 From 'Homage to Rachel Carson No. 2'.

21 From a filmed interview with Lye in *Len Who?*, 1973. Lye's other girlfriends in Australia included Edna Dixon and 'Sybil' (to whom a letter in *No Trouble* was later addressed).

22 Commentary for 'Matisse' slide programme. Lye offers no date for the change, but I would guess it was late 1925 or early 1926.

23 Interview, 1980 ('That was the clincher, convincing me that tribal art was the way to go').

24 *Primitive Negro Sculpture*, 1926, reprinted in New York by Hacker Art Books, 1968.

25 For example, Lye wrote: 'When art has become humanity's final religion ... I would build a mound comparable to the ancient Mexican. And what would the pilgrim find at its summit? Why, the Black Gabon Goddess.' Letter to Violette de Mazia, Director, Barnes Foundation (owner of the sculpture), 5 April 1970.

26 Paul Radin et al., eds., *African Folktales and Sculpture*, Bollingen Series XXXII, New York, Pantheon, 1952 (illustrations 51 and 52).

27 Barbara Tribe, one of his students of the 1920s, remarked: 'During the period of G. Rayner Hoff, Modern Art had hardly

reached these shores — as students, Brancusi, Picasso, etc. and works of other countries were unknown to us' (quoted in Ken Scarlett, *Australian Sculptors*, West Melbourne, Nelson, 1980, p 264).

28 Letter from Lye to Daniel Thomas, 1966.

29 Lye also said that Hoff's brother 'took some photos of my head so he could work at it when I wasn't around' (letter to Daniel Thomas). One of these photos has survived.

30 T. J. McNamara, 'A Kiss in a Paris Cemetery', *New Zealand Herald*, 3 January 1998, section D, p 7.

31 *Len Lye: A Personal Mythology*, p 74.

32 ibid., p 74 (the photo is printed upside down). Another example is a carving on a food store named Te Puawai-o-te-Arawa from Maketu, Bay of Plenty, in the collection of the Auckland Museum.

33 In contrast, Clive Bell's 1919 essay on 'Negro Sculpture' in *Since Cézanne* saw industrialism as a direct enemy of African sculpture.

34 *Gaudier-Brzeska,* p 116

35 'Ocean Liner', unpublished ms.

36 Quoted from Sinclair's *A Destiny Apart: New Zealand's Search for National Identity*, Wellington, Allen & Unwin in association with the Port Nicholson Press, 1986, p 87.

twelve stoker sculptor

1 'Ocean Liner', unpublished ms.

2 ibid.

3 ibid.

4 ibid.

5 The *Euripides* was eventually taken over by Shaw Savill and converted from coal to oil fuel. Rebuilt and renamed the *Akaroa* (a New Zealand place name), it sailed between New Zealand and Australia.

6 'Ocean Liner'.

7 *St John's Evening Telegram* (Newfoundland), 12 November 1937.

8 Rosalind E. Krauss, *Passages in Modern Sculpture*, p 99.

9 Robert Graves and Alan Hodge, *The Long Week-End*, London, Faber & Faber, reprint 1950, p 124.

10 Anne Kirker interview with Lye, 1979.

11 Kanty Cooper journal.

12 Reported in Cooper's journal.

13 *Studio*, CXII, August 1936, p 80.

14 *Daily Chronicle*, 18 February 1928

15 Perhaps the choice of play was ironic (Lye as Eliza?).

16 Cooper journal, 12 January 1927.

17 ibid.

18 Cooper journal, 19 May 1927.

19 Cooper journal, 12 January 1927.

20 Curnow interview, p 60.

21 Interview with Doris Ellitt, 1993.

22 Ortega y Gasset, quoted by John Berger in *The Success and Failure of Picasso*, New York, Pantheon, 1980, p 40.

23 Letter, 26 March 1981.

24 Quoted by Laura Riding in *Len Lye and the Problem of Popular Film*, London, Seizin Press, 1938.

25 Transcript of talk on Lye by Stan Brakhage, 1981.

26 Cooper journal, 12 January 1927.

27 ibid.

28 30 June 1927.

29 4 October 1927.

30 Cooper's sculpture is among the most exciting work of the period, but in the mid-1930s she was forced to stop carving because the jarring of the hammer had given her neuritis. She went to the Spanish Civil War and began an important new career helping refugees. (See her book *The Uprooted*, London, Quartet, 1979.)

thirteen batiks

1 Interview with Jane Lye, 1980. Lye continued to make batiks till the end of the 1930s. Adrienne Rooke recalls that Footprints used 'ICI dyes, diluted to various strengths, combined with gum tragacanth. Linen, cotton and rayon materials were used [and] occasionally pure silk.' The blocks were made of 'thick plywood and thick cork lino stuck firmly together with a casein glue' (letter, February 1984; Lye Foundation collection).

2 *The Long Week-End*, p 180.

3 'The Ark'. Unfortunately some of the batiks have since faded.

4 The title was added many years later. It was originally exhibited as 'Wall Decoration'.

5 *Len Lye: A Personal Mythology*, p 74.

6 ibid., p 36.

7 Direction is ambiguous since the image is visible on both sides of the batiks. However, Lye made later versions of some of the batiks as paintings on canvas (as he did in this case).

See *Len Lye: A Personal Mythology*, p 37 and p 75, which shows them as reversed. (There are small changes within the two versions — such as the 'anxious' zigzag shapes being shifted around.)

8   Interview, 1980.

9   Jack Ellitt reports there was a cardboard construction with the same motif as this batik. It has not survived.

10 Also known as 'Jacob's Ladder', this batik has sometimes been thought to allude to Riding's scar after a near-fatal fall; but that is not possible in view of its date.

11 The colours have faded so it is difficult to be precise.

12 See *No Trouble*, p 2.

13 *No Trouble*, p 8. Cf. a letter of 18 May 1938 to his mother when he sent her a scarf and a batik from a Seven and Five Society exhibition.

14 Quoted Hamish Keith in *New Zealand Yesterdays*, Surrey Hills (NSW), Readers Digest, 1985, p 48.

15 Obituary of A. P. Herbert in *The Times*, 12 November 1971.

16 'You Know the Kind of Weather', *Figures of Motion*, p 103.

17 Kirker interview, 1979.

18 Curnow interview, p 58.

19 The film was not made on the *Avoca* but on the *Ringrose*, the larger barge later owned by the Ellitts. The Ellitts were angry with the film-makers because they built an ugly structure on top which made it look more like a houseboat.

20 'The Ark', unpublished ms.

21 ibid.

22 ibid.

23 Sir Alan Herbert, *A.P.H.: His Life and Times*, London, William Heinemann, 1970, p 153.

24 Interview with Jack and Doris Ellitt, 1996.

25 'Thames-Side Reverie' in *Occupation Writer*, London, Cassell, 1951.

26 Interview with Jack and Doris Ellitt, 1996.

27 Curnow interview, p 60.

28 'The Ark', variant version.

fourteen tusalava

1   From Jack Ellitt's sound composition, 'Homage to Rachel Carson No. 2'.

2   ibid.

3   Lye, 'The Tusalava Model', in Russett and Starr, *Experimental Animation,* p 70.

4   'No Trouble', *Figures of Motion*, p 105.

5   Robert Del Tredici, 'Len Lye Interview', *The Cinema News* (San Francisco), Nos 2–4, 1979, p 36.

6   Griffiths interview with Jack Ellitt, 1987. The studio described was in Brewer Street.

7   'The Ark'.

8   'No Trouble', *Figures of Motion*, p 103.

9   ibid.

10 ibid., p 109.

11 Russett and Starr, *Experimental Animation*, p 70.

12 Joseph Kennedy, 'Len Lye — Composer of Motion', *Millimeter*, Vol 5, February, 1977.

13 Curnow interview, p 54.

14 Griffiths interview with Jack Ellitt, 1987. Lye remembered it as a hand-cranked camera but Ellitt has a clear memory of it as a Moy camera with a motor, which he later purchased for his own experimental work.

15 See, for example, *Remembering Iris Barry*, New York, Museum of Modern Art, 1980, or Lord Bernstein's account, 'The Fans Who Made Film History' in *The Times*, 23 October 1975, p 11.

16 Jay Leyda in *Remembering Iris Barry*, p 7.

17 'The Ark'.

18 Curnow interview, p 54.

19 No Trouble', *Figures of Motion*, p 105.

20 Curnow interview, p 54.

21 G. B. Milner, *Samoan Dictionary*, London, Oxford University Press, 1966, p 102. The film imagery does not appear to have any other Samoan connections. It may be relevant that there is an octopus-like demon or *aitu* in Samoan mythology, but Lye's most vivid encounter with an octopus was at Cape Campbell.

22 Del Tredici interview, p 37.

23 *Leicester Mercury*, 6 March 1939.

24 Interview, 1980.

25 See 'No Trouble' in *Figures of Motion,* p 105. Also 'The Ark' and many of Lye's other writings. There is also a Lacanian interpretation by Lani Hunter in *Stamp* (Auckland), No 22, August 1991, p 12.

26 Relevant contemporary examples of rhythmic piano music included George Antheil's *Ballet Mécanique* (1926), Igor Stravinsky's *Les Noces* (1923) and his versions of *The Rite of Spring* for two pianos and for pianola. Lye told me in 1979 that if Ellitt's music was not available, his next choice would be a two-piano work by Eugene Goossens. I assume he meant *Rhythm Dance*

(1927), though the film is more than twice as long as Goossens's piano work.

27 Griffiths interview with Jack Ellitt, 1987. 'Over the course of two years' was reported to me by Doris Ellitt.

28 See 'No Trouble', *Figures of Motion,* p 105.

29 The composer told me in 1982 that the film was screened without any music and the silence helped this strange film to 'create a terrific impression'. On another occasion he said that his music was played but he was prohibited from being the pianist because he was not a union member. In response to enquiries, he has always insisted that the score has been lost (e.g. Griffiths interview). Such comments reflect the fact that the premiere was a traumatic experience for him. Fortunately I was also able to obtain an account by Doris Ellitt in 1996. Jack was present during this interview and ended up confirming that her memory of the event was more reliable (and so I have based my account on it).

30 2 December 1928.

31 *Close Up*, February 1930, p 156.

32 ibid., p 155. Also see *Close Up*, January 1930, p 74 for another review.

33 Cf. Lye's letter to Cavalcanti, 21 November 1947.

34 In 1930 and again in 1932 at the London Film Society, and in 1939 at the Leicester Film Society (cf. 'In the Abstract', *Leicester Mercury*, 6 March 1939). These screenings disprove the often repeated myth (repeated even by Lye in later years) that *Tusalava* was screened once only.

35 3 December 1929 (Lye Foundation collection).

36 Dorothy Knowles, *The Censor, The Drama and the Film 1900–1934*, London, George Allen and Unwin, 1934, p 237.

37 See Knowles, and also Ivor Montagu, *Film as Art,* Harmondsworth, Penguin, 1964, p 260. *Close-up*'s general summing up of the board's activities was 'Puritannia Rules the Slaves'!

fifteen jane thompson

1 Based on interviews with Lye and the Ellitts. Robert Graves spelled her name in a letter as 'Lizz'.

2 See Phyllis Grosskurth, *Havelock Ellis: A Biography*, New York, Alfred A Knopf, 1980, 348 ff.

3 Interview with Jane Lye, 1980.

4 ibid.

5 ibid.

6 Interview with Ann Lye, 1986.

7 Interview with Jane Lye, 1980.

8 ibid.

9 ibid.

10 ibid.

11 Kanty Cooper's journal.

12 Interview with Jane Lye, 1980.

13 ibid.

14 Kanty Cooper's journal.

15 'No Telling', unpublished ms.

16 'The Seizin Press of Laura Riding and Robert Graves', *The Black Art*, Vol 2, No 2, Summer 1963.

17 William Sansom, 'Coming to London (XI)' *London Magazine*, Vol 3, No 12, 1956, p 32.

18 Deborah Baker, *In Extremis: The Life of Laura Riding*, London, Hamish Hamilton, 1993, p 248.

19 Interview with Jane Lye, 1980.

20 Curnow interview, p 61.

21 ibid.

22 *Daily Express,* 2 November 1935.

23 Cf. Reginald Pound, *A P Herbert: A Biography,* London, Michael Joseph, 1976, p 120.

24 Letter to Wystan Curnow, 8 July 1981. Hayter also commented: 'Furthermore his [Lye's] poetic and literary work was not negligible.' And: 'I am aware of the debt I owe to a great number of splendid friends I have been privileged to know, Len among them, with whom I have exchanged experience over half a century, certainly receiving at least as much as I was able to contribute'. Hayter moved to Paris where he established an important print-making workshop, Atelier 17, and then to New York where he lived next door to Lye in Washington Street from 1948 to 1950.

25 See 'In Arcadia People Are Talking About . . . Len Lye', *Spleen* (Wellington), No 7, 1977, pp 4–7.

26 *You May Well Ask: A Memoir 1920–40,* London, Victor Gollancz, 1977, pp 79–81.

27 Naomi Mitchison, letter (undated).

28 Interview with Alastair Reid and Ann Lye, 1988.

29 Wystan Curnow interview, p 60.

30 T. S. Matthews, *Jacks or Better,* New York, Harper and Row, 1977, p 133.

31 Sibyl Moholy-Nagy, *Moholy-Nagy*, New York, Harper, 1950, p 117.

sixteen the seven and five society

1 At the 26 January 1928 AGM of the Seven and Five Society, Lye was nominated by Nicholson and seconded by Christopher Wood. (Minute books, Tate Gallery.)

2 Kirker interview, 1979.

3 *The Land Unknown*, London, Hamish Hamilton, 1975, p 138.

4 Quoted by Anne Kirker in *Art New Zealand* 17, 1980, pp 51–52.

5 Surprisingly there is no record of any meeting between Lye and the other New Zealand-born member, Frances Hodgkins, whose work he had once admired in Wellington. She was admitted to the Society in 1929, a year after Lye, and it seems inevitable that their paths would have crossed. By this time their interests had diverged, but in later years Lye continued to talk about how excited he had felt when he had come across examples of her work back in New Zealand (in Anne Kirker's 1979 interview, for example).

6 *Studio*, No. 452, May 1928, p 344.

7 Quoted in *The Long Week-End*, pp 193–94.

8 February 1931, p 135.

9 Paul Nash, 'The Colour Film', *Footnotes to the Film*, ed. Charles Davy, 1937, p 133.

10 These apparently no longer exist except in the form of photographs and written descriptions. I have no image of the butterfly construction which was made of cardboard. (Ellitt considered it the best of Lye's constructions.) Cardboard was also used by Picasso and Braque to make sculptures but few examples have survived. Many of Lye's batiks have also disappeared. See his account of making constructions, 'In Grim Determination', in *No Trouble* (in *Figures of Motion*, pp 110–111).

11 *Gaudier-Brzeska,* p 88.

12 The myth is reported by Jack Ellitt and the teasing by Kanty Cooper (journal entry for 4 October 1927).

13 18 February 1928.

14 22 February 1928 is the dateline on the story but I have not been able to confirm the date of publication. (The Lye Foundation has Lye's copy of the clipping.)

15 *Auckland Sun*, 19 May 1928 The dateline on the *Evening Post* story is 21 March 1929. The other news clipping (in the Lye Foundation collection) has no details.

16 Russell Reeve, 'London Letter', *Art in New Zealand*, Vol 5, No 20, p 238.

17 Interview with Carol Henderson, 1998 Also, phone interview with Jeanne Macaskill, 2 March 1998 (who mentioned the impact of Samoa). Cf. Henderson's book, *A Blaze of Colour: Gordon Tovey, Artist Educator*, Christchurch, Hazard Press, 1998, p 17 and p 25.

18 *Len Lye and the Problem of Popular Films,* p 39.

19 Interview with Lye, 1980.

20 *Webster's New Twentieth Century Dictionary*, 1980.

21 'Did Einstein's Doodles have a Genetic Source? (6 December 1973)', unpublished note.

22 Del Tredici interview, p 36.

23 See Camfield and Dierdre Wills, *History of Photography: Techniques and Equipment,* London, Hamlyn, 1980, p 16.

24 'Night Tree' has the date 1928 on the back (along with alternative titles such as 'Water Life in Small' and 'Fresh Water Protozoans').

25 See Kirker in *Art New Zealand,* No 17, p 52; and Herta Wescher, *Collage*, New York, Harry N Abrams, 1968, p 246.

26 *Len Lye: A Personal Mythology*, p 63.

27 Del Tredici interview, p 38.

28 'Fire Devil', slide programme.

29 'Words', slide programme.

30 Ray Thorburn, unpublished interview with Lye, p 14.

31 See Andrew Bogle in *Len Lye: A Personal Mythology*, p 18.

32 Interview with Kanty Cooper, 1988. The visitors included Brancusi.

33 'Song Time Stuff', *Figures of Motion*, p 116.

34 He no doubt visited the first London exhibition of Miró's paintings in 1933, though there is no proof of this.

35 Sandra Stich, *Joan Miró: The Development of a Sign Language*, St Louis, Washington Gallery, 1980, p 38.

36 'The Significance of Miró', *Art News*, May 1959, p 66.

seventeen robert graves and laura riding

1 Tom Driberg, *Ruling Passions*, London, Cape, 1977, p 63. For Graves's own description see his poems 'The Face in The Mirror.'

2 T. S. Matthews, *Jacks or Better*, p 127.

3 Quoted by Randall Jarrell in 'Graves and the White Goddess', *Yale Review,* Winter–Summer, 1956, p 473.
4 Interview with Alastair Reid, 1980.
5 Driberg, p 63.
6 Cunard, quoted in Hugh Ford, *Published in Paris*, New York, Macmillan, 1975, p 274.
7 Quoted in Joyce Piell Wexler, *Laura Riding's Search for Truth*, Athens, Ohio University Press, 1979, p 7.
8 Curnow interview, p 60.
9 Quoted in the 'Laura Riding' entry in *Contemporary Poets*, ed. James Vinson, London, Macmillan, 1980 (3rd edition), p 922.
10 'No Trouble' in *Figures of Motion*, p 107.
11 *Four Unposted Letters to Catherine,* Paris, Hours Press, 1930, p 18.
12 It is ironic to note that the once 'timeless' Polynesian culture of the Australs was dragged into European history so violently that by 1880 European diseases and slavers had very nearly wiped out the native Polynesian population — but this was not Riding's point.
13 Interview with Lye, 1980.
14 *Figures of Motion*, p 99.
15 Curnow interview, p 60.
16 See T. S. Matthews, *Jacks or Better*.
17 Interview with Jane Lye, 1980.
18 Interview with Doris Ellitt, 1986.
19 Interview with Jack Ellitt, 1986.
20 *Jacks or Better,* p 133.
21 Interview with Jane Lye, 1980.
22 See Martin Seymour-Smith, *Robert Graves: His Life and Work,* Paladin, 1987, p 146.
23 Richard Perceval Graves, *Robert Graves: The Years with Laura, 1926–40*, London, Weidenfeld and Nicholson, p 62.
24 Interview with Doris Ellitt, 1986.
25 Deborah Baker, *In Extremis: The Life of Laura Riding,* London, Hamish Hamilton, 1993, p 105.
26 Laura Riding and George Ellidge, *14A: A Novel Told In Dramatic Form,* London, Arthur Baker, 1934.
27 Interview with Jane Lye, 1980.
28 *Goodbye to All That.*
29 *In Broken Images: Selected Letters of Robert Graves 1914–1946,* ed. Paul O'Prey, London, Hutchinson, 1982, p 191 (letter from Graves to Stein).
30 *In Extremis,* p 178. Also interview with Jane Lye, 1980. Miranda Seymour in *Robert Graves: Life on the Edge* (New York, Henry

Holt, 1995) speaks of a 'mural' (p 180), and Richard Perceval Graves, *Robert Graves: The Years with Laura, 1926–40*, explains that this was a composition on Riding's bedroom wall in coloured distemper and chalk (p 117).
31 Wexler, p 54.
32 *In Extremis* p 180.
33 *In Broken Images,* p 192 (letter from Stein to Graves and Riding).
34 Martin Seymour-Smith, p 204.
35 Prologue, *Goodbye to All That,* London, Cassell, 1957, p vii.
36 Martin Seymour-Smith, p 186.
37 Interview with Jane Lye, 1980.
38 ibid.
39 *In Broken Images,* p 216.
40 ibid.
41 Interview with Philip Lye, 1981. (He is remembering his brother's account of the incident.)
42 Graves later wrote to the Society insisting that such thanks were undeserved (perhaps a case of modesty on his part).

eighteen mallorca

1 Interview with Kanty Cooper, 1988; and Cooper's Journal.
2 Ann Chisholm, *Nancy Cunard*, New York, Alfred A Knopf, 1979, p 147.
3 Quoted Joyce Piell Wexler, *Laura Riding's Search for Truth,* Athens, Ohio University Press, 1979, p 60.
4 Interview with Kanty Cooper.
5 *Nancy Cunard: Brave Poet, Indomitable Rebel* ed. Hugh Ford, Philadelphia, Chilton, 1968, p 36.
6 'No Trouble', in *Figures of Motion*, p 111.
7 Interview with Jane Lye, 1980.
8 ibid.
9 Interview with Kanty Cooper.
10 Interview with Jane Lye.
11 ibid.
12 Interview, 1980.
13 *A Bibliography of the Works of Robert Graves,* p 56.
14 Undated letter to John Aldridge (1930s).
15 'Did Einstein's Doodles Have a Genetic Source? (6 December 1973)', unpublished note.
16 See, for example, George W Stow, *The Native Races of South Africa*, London, Swan Sonnenschein, 1905, facing p 546. (This was a book Lye knew.)

17 Interview with Kanty Cooper.
18 'Five Dogs', unpublished ms.
19 'Big Fish', unpublished ms.
20 'Big Fish.'
21 Interview with Jane Lye.
22 He had, in fact, already started doing this in England.
23 Interview with Anne Kirker, 1979.
24 Interview with Jane Lye.
25 'Symbolism in the Visual Arts' in *Man and His Symbols* by C. J. Jung and others, New York, Dell, 1968, p 258.
26 Bogle interview with Lye, 1980. Unknown to Lye, Joan Miró had begun to use natural materials in some of his sculptures, and in 1935 in Switzerland Max Ernst wrote: 'Alberto [Giacometti] and I are afflicted with sculpturitis. We work on granite boulders, large and small.... Wonderfully polished by time, frost, and weather, they are in themselves fantastically beautiful. No human hand can do that. So why not leave the spadework to the elements, and confine ourselves to scratching on them the runes of our own mystery?' Quoted by Jaffe in *Man and His Symbols*, pp 259–60.
27 'No Trouble', *Figures of Motion*, p 111.
28 'No Trouble', *Figures of Motion,* p 112. One might also compare Wallace Stevens's 1926 poem 'Anecdote of the Jar'.
29 Curnow interview, p 61.
30 'Words', slide programme.
31 'Poneke Shores'. See Jerome Rothenberg's anthologies *Technicians of the Sacred* (New York, Doubleday-Anchor, 1967) and *Shaking the Pumpkin* (New York, Doubleday-Anchor, 1972) for examples of the kinds of 'ethnopoetics' that would have interested Lye.
32 'Writing (Nov. 1962)', unpublished note,
33 'No Trouble', *Figures of Motion*, pp 100–101.
34 'Writing (Nov. 1962)'.
35 Note on 'John Bond (Jan. 2 1972)'. As a lecturer at New York University in the 1960s Lye encouraged students to: 'untie mental shoelaces' so their thoughts could 'go barefoot' and 'trip the light fantastic'. He was also interested in 'body English', the physical or kinetic aspects of the writing process: 'the nib makes a pleasant rubbing ... on the sounding-board of the bread-board [under the paper] and I can feel its vibrations transmitted to my thigh bone' (unpublished notes).

36 Curnow interview, p 61.
37 London, Arthur Barker, 1933.
38 ibid., p 231.
39 ibid., p 253.
40 *Published in Paris*, p 393.
41 ibid.
42 *Chelsea*, No 35, p 189.
43 Martin Seymour-Smith makes a perceptive comment on Riding's editing in *Robert Graves: His Life and Work*, Paladin, 1987, p 204.
44 Interview with Kanty Cooper, 1988.
45 *Time and Tide*, 12 September 1931.
46 12 September 1931.
47 14 October 1931.
48 15 October 1931.

nineteen a wedding

1 Interview with Jane Lye, 1980.
2 'Liz', unpublished ms.
3 Interview with Jane Lye.
4 Interview with Jack Ellitt, 1986.
5 'Liz', unpublished ms.
6 'Liz (23 Oct 1962)', unpublished ms.
7 'Liz (23 Oct 1962).'
8 Interview with Jane Lye.
9 John's mother, Edith Stuart-Wortley, had been Ben Nicholson's fiancée, but in the end she had married Ben's father, William Nicholson (a well-known artist). John's grandfather was the South African magnate Sir Lionel Phillips.
10 One of the couple fell ill and died soon after arriving in Brazil. One of my informants thinks it was John Stuart-Wortley, the other is equally sure it was Liz.
11 Interview with Barbara Ker-Seymer, 1988.
12 Interview with Jane Lye. Cf. *The Long Week-End,* p 304.
13 Interview with Barbara Ker-Seymer.
14 Interview with Jane Lye.
15 The ticket is dated October 1933.
16 Lye had read about him in such books as George W. Stow's *The Native Races of South Africa*, London, Swan Sonnenschein, 1905, p 19 and p 118. (N.B. 'Cagn' is sometimes spelled 'Kaang'.)
17 See *A Brief Description of the Whole World* (Auckland), No 3, June 1996. A different version appears in *Figures of Motion,* p 123.
18 *Len Lye: A Personal Mythology*, p 72.
19 'Fire Devil', slide–tape programme.
20 ibid.

21 Sidra Stich, *Joan Miró: The Development of a Sign Language*, St Louis, Washington Gallery, 1980, p 18. Miró also liked Breuil's books.

22 By 1934 he was also looking closely at accidental marks such as cracks, stains, and scratches. An essay he wrote in 1935 (with the help of Laura Riding) included the comment: 'For examples of movement in shapes we might use paleolithic paintings; but marks just as good as cave marks can be found on walls or pavements. . . . Such marks are the nearest visual contact with moving life' ('Film-Making', *Figures of Motion,* p 40). Georges-Henri Loquet had suggested a few years earlier that prehistoric people may have come up with the idea of making art after observing accidental marks on cave walls such as cracks or the scratches of bear claws.

23 Gerald Noxon, 'How Humphrey Jennings Came To Film', *Film Quarterly*, Vol 15, No 2, Winter 1961–62, p 20. (Noxon was a friend of both Lye and Jennings.)

24 Raine, *The Land Unknown*, p 50.

25 Noxon, p 21.

26 Kirker interview with Lye, 1979.

27 I am borrowing Kathleen Raine's description of such paintings from her essay 'Humphrey Jennings' in *Humphrey Jennings 1907–1950,* London, Institute of Contemporary Arts, undated.

28 Letter from Lye, undated. He drew the 'ideogram' which is perhaps a play on the initials H J.

29 Interview with Lye, 1980.

30 Letter from Barbara Ker-Seymer, 14 July 1980.

31 Interview with Jane Lye, 1980.

32 Interview with Richard McNaughton, 1988.

twenty peanut vendor

1 Kirker interview with Lye, 1979.

2 Letter, September 1979.

3 Letter, September 1981.

4 Wasily Kandinsky, Kazimir Malevich, and Arnold Schoenberg were among other modernists who made 'considerable plans' for films but 'were unable to realize them' (William Moritz, 'Non-Objective Film: The Second Generation' in *Film as Film: Formal Experiment in Film 1910–1975*, London, Hayward Gallery, 1979, p 59).

5 Cf. Duke Dusinberre, 'The Other Avant-gardes', in *Film as Film*, pp 53–55.

6 See, for example, Marie Seton, *Sergei M. Eisenstein: A Biography,* London, Bodley Head, 1952.

7 See Hans Richter, *Hans Richter,* London, Thames & Hudson, 1971.

8 ibid., p 150.

9 Kirker interview with Lye, 1979.

10 *Architectural Review*, Vol 72, July 1932, p 25.

11 'No Trouble' in *Figures of Motion,* p 105.

12 ibid., p 106. ('Uma' is the Samoan verb 'to end', as in the phrase 'Ua uma le ala', the story is ended.)

13 ibid., p 105. Cf. Jack Ellitt's essay 'On Sound' in *Life & Letters Today*, December 1935, pp 182–84.

14 Jack Ellitt, 'On Sound', pp 182 and 184.

15 *Architectural Review*, p 25.

16 See *In Extremis*, p 258 and p 447.

17 'An Artist Turns Floor Sweeper', *The Star*, London, 9 July 1930.

18 *The Long Week-End*, p 348.

19 Interview with Jane Lye, 1980. The finished artwork for the portfolio was by Taylor.

20 9 July 1930.

21 See Del Tredici interview, p 7, and 'Handpainted Swing', *Rhythm*, February 1939.

22 Letter from Jack Ellitt, 4 May 1988.

23 For example, see *Close-Up*, Vol 7, No 6, December 1930, pp 393–95.

24 *Close-Up*, Vol 6, No 6, June 1930, pp 493–95.

25 *Focus*, No 3, April–May 1935, p 36.

26 Letter from Lye to Laura Riding, undated.

27 Letter from Lye to John Aldridge, undated. Cf. *Focus,* No 3, April–May 1935, p 36.

twentyone a colour box

1 Joseph Kennedy, *Millimeter,* Vol 5, February 1977, p 20.

2 Perhaps this was the 1927 silhouette film by Oskar Fischinger that included a fight scene with scratches to express raw energy or force. See William Moritz, *Film Culture*, No 58–60, 1974, p 95.

3 Letter, 26 March 1981.

4 *Abstract Film and Beyond*, London, Studio Vista, 1977.

5 Lye pointed out this connection in an early newspaper interview ('Len Lye — The English Disney', *Sunday Referee*, 10 November 1935), and Alberto Cavalcanti

noted it in 'Presenting Len Lye', *Sight and Sound*, Vol 16, Winter 1947–48, pp 134–35. Subsequently the connection seems to have been forgotten.

6 *Millimeter,* p 20.

7 Letter from Jack Ellitt, 12 September 1981.

8 Griffiths interview with Jack Ellitt, 1987.

9 As noted earlier, Lye had come across them in the early 1920s in Freud's *Totem and Taboo*.

10 *Life & Letters Today*, Autumn 1937, Vol 17, No 9, p 152.

11 See Rachael Low, *The History of the British Film 1929–1939: Documentary and Educational Films of the 1930s*, London, Allen and Unwin, 1979, p 88.

12 Quoted in Paul Rotha, *Documentary Diary*, London, Secker and Warburg, 1973, pp 135–6.

13 Cavalcanti, 'Presenting Len Lye'.

14 Reported by Basil Wright in G. Roy Levin, *Documentary Explorations,* New York, Anchor, 1971, p 39.

15 Cavalcanti, 'Presenting Len Lye'.

16 *Rhythm,* p 70.

17 Lye Foundation collection.

18 The overall production budget (including processing, music rights, etc.) is said to have been set at £400.

19 *This Wonderful World,* Programme No 347, 18 August 1965, produced by Scottish Television. (John Grierson Archive, University of Stirling.)

20 Cavalcanti, 'Presenting Len Lye'.

21 Quoted by Laura Riding in *Len Lye and the Problem of Popular Film*, p 10.

22 ibid.

23 Many reviewers described it as a rumba.

24 Roger Whitney of the National Film and Television Archive (London) rediscovered the original in 1997 among a batch of films from Rank's labs. There were only two splices in the body of the film. There were, however, about a dozen splices during the head titles and a similar number during the Post Office advertising slogans, and there is no way of knowing whether Lye had made an earlier version (a trial run). When I inspected this copy myself I was very struck by the bold painting style.

25 *Focus*, No 4, December 1935, pp 60–61. 'Utilize' is presumably the joking catchphrase from Ernest Hemingway's *The Sun Also Rises*.

26 This difference in taste was reflected in a comment by the art critic Herbert Read: 'When I see [Len Lye's colour films] I always have a strong desire to arrest them, to fix them at selected moments. I would, therefore, prefer to have the static picture … or better still, a series of static pictures which I connect in imagination. This is just what Ben Nicholson provides.' (*London Bulletin*, No 11, March 1939).

27 See, for example, *Newspaper World*, 28 September 1935.

28 Cf. Rachael Low, *The History of the British Film 1929–1939: Documentary and Educational Films of the 1930s*, p 69.

29 *Newspaper World*, 28 September 1935.

30 Interview with Ann Lye, 1985, and *Rhythm,* p 68 ('Take it off!').

31 'Where Children May Hiss', *World Film News*, May 1936.

32 *Yorkshire News*, 25 September 1935.

33 Interview with Jane Lye, 1980.

34 *Today's Cinema*, 16 September 1935. *Yorkshire News* (25 September 1935) similarly saw it as 'highbrow'.

35 20 September 1935.

36 18 January 1937.

37 Robert Herring, 'Technicolossal', *Life and Letters Today*, Vol 13, No 1, September 1935, p 195.

38 Autumn 1935, Vol 4, No 15, p 117.

39 *Film Art,* Vol 2, No 6, Autumn 1935.

40 *The Film Till Now*, London, Vision, 1949 (revised edition), p 399.

41 'Color & the Box Office', *Life and Letters Today*, Vol 13, No 1, September 1935, p 197.

42 In 1934 Ilford Laboratories had put Dufaycolor on the market as a reversal process — the version with negative was not available until 1937. Dufaycolor was an 'additive' process using a mosaic of minute colour filters.

43 'NY Times: John Bond (2 January 1972)', unpublished note.

44 For example: Harold A. Albert, 'Diary of a Young Man', *Sunday Mercury* (Birmingham), 8 December 1935.

45 See, for example: 'Artists and Colour Films', *Cinema*, 4 March 1936; 'Development of Colour', *Edinburgh Evening Dispatch*, 24 February 1936; 'Academy Manager Rejects Colour', *World Film News*, May 1936; Robert Herring, 'Technicolossal', *Life and Letters Today,* September 1935.

46 'High Praise for Manchester Films',

Manchester City News, 7 December 1935.

47 'British Films Win Prizes', *Daily Mail*, 31 October 1935.

48 See Wystan Curnow and Roger Horrocks, 'The Len Lye Lists', *Bulletin of New Zealand Art History*, vol 8, 1980, for a bibliography of these and many other news items about Lye.

49 *Film Kurier*, 16 August 1936 — quoted by William Moritz in his essay, 'Len Lye's Films in the Context of International Abstract Cinema', in *Len Lye*, ed. Jean-Michel Bouhours and Roger Horrocks, Centre Pompidou, Paris, 2000, p 194.

50 See 'The Len Lye Lists' for 1936–38 reports of European screenings. The film was later 'chosen as a culminating point in the cavalcade of films at the Paris Exposition' ('The First Swing Film', *Melody Maker*, 18 September 1937).

51 'New Zealand Boy Makes Good', *St John's Evening Telegram*, 12 November 1937. Cf. 'For Avant-Garde Houses Only', *Cinema*, 13 January 1937.

52 *Experimental Cinema*, London, Studio Vista, 1971, p 36.

53 Reported by Basil Wright in G. Roy Levin, *Documentary Explorations*, Garden City (New York), Anchor Press, 1971, p 39.

54 April 1936, p 29.

55 'Made a Film Without a Camera', *Daily Express*, September 1935 (precise date unknown).

56 'Coloured Novelty', *Daily Express*, 22 September 1935.

57 Gretchen Weinberg, 'Interview with Len Lye', p 44.

58 See Carra's 'Abstract Cinema — Chromatic Music' in *Futurist Manifestos*, ed Umbro Apollonio, New York, Viking, 1973, p 68.

59 Norman McLaren's experiments are covered in our next chapter. There are interesting discussions of the history of direct film by William Moritz in *Film As Film*, p 59, and by Jean-Michel Bouhours in *Len Lye*, pp 202–220. There are other possible precedents such as *Colour Abstract*, a film by 'Mr Jen' described in the London Film Society programme of 11 December 1932, but such an example illustrates the need to be cautious when interpreting the word 'hand-painted'. The fact that it is linked here to the phrase 'exact control' suggests the colouring of details via stencil — a process very different from Lye's.

twentytwo the birth of the robot

1 Cf. Paul Rotha's comments in *Documentary Diary*, p 143.

2 Cavalcanti, 'Presenting Len Lye'.

3 William Moritz, 'The Films of Oskar Fischinger', *Film Culture*, Nos 58–60, 1974, p 149.

4 ibid., p 35.

5 Griffiths interview with Jack Ellitt, 1987.

6 29 October 1935. Confirmed by Richard McNaughton.

7 10 November 1935.

8 *Daily Express*, 2 November 1935.

9 Elizabeth Sussex, *The Rise and Fall of British Documentary*, Berkeley, University of California Press, 1975, p 60.

10 Interview with Richard McNaughton, 1988.

11 Quoted Sussex, p 90.

12 ibid.

13 Interview, 1988.

14 ibid.

15 Interview, 1988.

16 Letter from Barbara Ker-Seymer, 25 March 1981.

17 Interview with John Taylor, 1988.

18 Grierson later said that he 'put him [McLaren] with Len Lye to learn, as an apprentice' (see Sussex, p 84) but in fact the connection between the two artists was much less direct, as McLaren explained in his letter to television producer Tony Rimmer (30 June 1972) while Rimmer was doing research for the documentary *Len Who?: Into An Unknown*. This letter (now in the Lye Foundation collection) is very helpful in clarifying a situation that has often been misunderstood, and so I have quoted it at length.

19 ibid. It was not until the 1950s that there was any personal exchange of ideas.

20 Undated letter, circa November 1936.

21 'Colour Film Sets New Standard', *Advertisers Weekly*, 2 July 1936.

22 E.g. *The English Weekly*, 2 July 1936.

23 Cf. Jean Mitry, *Le Cinéma Expérimental: Histoire et Perspectives*, Paris, Editions Seghers, 1971, p 182. The Calder analogy was suggested by Jim Hoberman in the *Village Voice*, 31 December 1980, p 40.

24 Moritz, *Film Culture*, Nos 58–60, 1974, p 55.

25 See Lye's review of Klein's *Coloured Light* in *The Cine-Technician*, December–January 1937–38, p 186. (In this tribute to Klein's expertise, Lye remarked: 'I myself am no technician and designate myself . . . a colour-playboy'!)

26 Klein discussed Lye's hand-painted Gaspar-color films in his book *Coloured Light: An Art Medium*: 'Mr Len Lye began his work . . . by hand painting with dyes upon clear film. The painted film was then placed in the negative head of an optical printer and three prints made on panchromatic film, through the standard trichromatic [three-colour-separation] filters. These . . . negatives were then used for printing upon Gasparcolor film. Thus accurate reproduction was effected of his hand-painted original' (London, Technical Press, 3rd Edition, 1937, p xxxviii).

27 2 July 1936.

28 Robert Herring, *Life and Letters Today*, Vol 14, No 4, Summer 1936, p 178.

29 2 July 1936.

30 26 April 1936. Cf. Rachael Low, *A History of the British Film 1929–1939: Documentary and Educational Films of the 1930s*, p 104.

31 'Presenting Len Lye'.

32 *Advertiser's Weekly,* 2 July 1936.

33 *Len Lye and the Problem of Popular Film*, p 43.

twentythree rainbow dance

1 Gretchen Weinberg, 'Interview with Len Lye', p 42.

2 See ' Experiment in Colour' and 'Voice and Colour', *Figures of Motion*, pp 42–49.

3 Quoted in Elizabeth Sussex, *The Rise and Fall of British Documentary*, p 84.

4 *Coloured Light*, p xxxix. Another Gasparcolor project that Lye began around this time (October 1936) but did not complete was 'Fireworks' (of which a few frames have survived).

5 E.g. *Kinematograph Weekly,* 28 January 1937.

6 'Len Lye speaks at the Film-makers' Cinematheque'.

7 Cavalcanti, 'Presenting Len Lye'.

8 See Christie's essay, 'Colour, Music, Dance, Motion: Len Lye in England, 1927–44' in *Len Lye*, p 189.

9 Interview with Richard McNaughton, 1988.

10 Compare Pat Hanly's 'Figures in Light' series of paintings (after his return to New Zealand from England).

11 'Voice & Colour', *Figures of Motion*, p 45.

12 See 'Experiment in Colour', *Figures of Motion* (first published in the December 1936 issue of *World Film News*).

13 'The Colour Film' in *Footnotes to the Film*, ed Charles Davy, London, Lovat Dickson, 1937, p 133.

14 'The L.C.C. Permits', 16 January 1937.

15 2 October 1936.

16 Edgar Anstey, *Experiment in the Film*, London, Gray Walls Press, 1949, p 249.

17 Letter, 25 March 1981.

18 Such as *Night Mail*, 1936.

19 Letter from Lye to John Halas, 15 January 1958.

20 Griffiths interview with Jack Ellitt, 1987.

21 John Happe, quoted in a letter from John Halas to Len Lye, 2 January 1958.

22 Letter from Lye to John Halas, 15 January 1958; see also Happe's memories of the film in John Halas & Roger Manvell's *The Technique of Film Animation*, London, Focal Press, 1976, pp 87–88.

23 Letter from Barbara Ker-Seymer, 29 June 1981. The recordings were: 'Anacaona', 'La Havane à Paris', 'Conga dans la Nuit', 'Pour Toi Madonne', and 'Adieu Mon Amour'.

24 During the silent period, film makers such as Eisenstein used to experiment in various ways with the rhythmic use of intertitles.

25 The original source is not known but the figure still gets quoted from time to time — e.g. *University Art Museum Calendar* (Berkeley, California), Vol 3, No 7, February 1981, p 3.

26 A review in January 1938 by the Amsterdam newspaper *Het Volk* illustrates the enthusiastic reception of the film by audiences interested in experimental films: 'The chief attraction of the evening was undoubtedly Len Lye's *Trade Tattoo*. . . . All the advantages of the trick film from Méliès and Murnau to Ruttmann, Richter, Moholy-Nagy and Fischinger were used in an amazing manner. . . . Geometrical figures, photographic fragments and typographical material mixed and flashed past in a wild race, but at the same time with a steady and clearly defined rhythm, combined with the most cunning sound effects. . . . Absolutely amazed, we . . . ask if after this there are still new inventions possible in the field of film technique' ('An Evening of Short English Films', *Het Volk*, evening edition, 27 January 1938 — English translation). We may add that the historical importance of *Trade Tattoo* and *Rainbow Dance* also rests — as Malcolm Le Grice has pointed out — on the 'extraordinarily versatile and accomplished way' in which they

advance one of the major tendencies in later experimental film-making — 'that based on the transformation of film images through printing and developing techniques' (*Abstract Film and Beyond*, p 71).

twentyfour public and private

1 John Russell Taylor, *Hitch: The Life and Work of Alfred Hitchcock*, London, Faber and Faber, 1978, p 137.
2 This is from the comment Lye wrote in the margin of his copy of Ivor Montagu's *Film World*, Harmondsworth, Penguin, 1964, p 124. (He was correcting Montagu's account.)
3 Based on interviews with James Merritt and James Manilla, 1980.
4 *Film World*, p 124.
5 Barbara Ker-Seymer, letter to John Matthews, 14 December 1980.
6 Interview with James Manilla (remembering what Lye had told him).
7 Taylor, *Hitch,* p 137.
8 Interview with Manilla.
9 All quotes by Ker-Seymer (unless otherwise credited) are from letters to the author (in the 1980s) or interviews with the author (in 1988).
10 'Queen's Counsel', article about Ker-Seymer in *Harpers Bazaar*, October 1986, p 341.
11 In a review of Louis Armstrong's autobiography Lye described jazz as 'the best popular art form we've got' ('Note for "Moments", January 1964'). Ker-Seymer recalled that Lye always preferred jazz with 'a strong beat or pronounced rhythm — for example, Fats Waller, "Stuff" Smith (who sang "If you're a viper"), Willie (The Lion) Smith, and of course the more obvious Louis Armstrong and pianists like Jimmy Yancey, Earl Hines, Jelly Roll Morton, Art Tatum, Teddy Wilson, etc. etc.'. The British jazz magazine *Rhythm* reported that 'Lye would rather listen . . . to a battered favourite by the Jungle Town Stompers than the smooth — "syrupy" he calls it — perfection of a Shep Fields, a Tommy Dorsey or a Larry Clinton' (Stan Patchett, 'Handpainted Swing . . .', February 1939).
12 Letter, 22 December 1981.
13 'Note re Sex (18 July 1962)', unpublished ms.
14 Interview with Jane Lye, 1980.
15 Interview with Jack Ellitt, 1986.
16 Interview with Jane Lye, 1980.
17 Interview with John Taylor, 1988

18 Patchett, 'Handpainted Swing . . .'.
19 Letter, 21 September 1981. (Waterman worked on documentary films with Lye.)
20 Interview with Ann Lye, 1985.
21 Interview with Jane Lye, 1980.
22 ibid.
23 Rose Slivka, in an interview by John Matthews, 1981.
24 'Coming to London (XI)' *London Magazine*, Vol 3, No 12, December 1956, p 33. Admittedly Sansom's description is not set in Hammersmith but somewhere like Hennessy's in the Strand; however, my emphasis here is on the group dynamics.
25 Interview with Jane Lye, 1980.
26 Interview with Ann Lye, 1980.
27 Caitlin Thomas with George Tremlett, *Caitlin: Life with Dylan Thomas*, New York, Henry Holt, 1986, p 71.
28 ibid., p 44.
29 'Jazz', *Life and Letters Today*, Vol 17, Autumn, 1937, p 198.
30 Letter from Lye to John Aldridge (undated; my guess of '1937' is based on internal evidence).
31 Undated letter from Lye (Aldridge collection, Tate Gallery).
32 7 September 1938 (Aldridge collection, Tate Gallery).

twentyfive surrealism

1 *Film as Film*, p 85.
2 An artist quoted in Donald Hall's *Henry Moore: The Life and Work of a Great Sculptor*, London, Victor Gollancz, 1966, p 87.
3 Quoted in *English and American Surrealist Poetry*, ed. Edward B. Germain, Harmondsworth, Penguin, 1978.
4 Julian Trevelyan, quoted in *The Surrealist Spirit in Britain,* ed Louisa Buck, London, Whitford and Hughes (catalogue for a 1988 exhibition), note on painting 42.
5 Interview with Barbara Ker-Seymer, 1988.
6 Note 'For S.A., re: my old brain imagery', unpublished note.
7 Note, 14 May [1936].
8 Note 'For S.A., re: my old brain imagery', unpublished note.
9 Herta Wescher, *Collage*, New York, Harry N. Abrams, 1968, p 235.
10 *English and American Surrealist Poetry*, p 39.
11 Geoffrey Holme, *The Studio*, Vol 112, August 1936, p 55.

12 There was an intermediate title, 'Snowbirds in Conference'.

13 One British artist that Lye did acknowledge was Humphrey Jennings who had encouraged him to play with 'brush-fulls of colour' (note by Lye on an envelope containing a reproduction of a Jennings painting).

14 Its date is circa 1937.

15 It is not surprising that Clement Greenberg, a critic who championed abstract expressionism, was impressed by 'The King of Plants' when he eventually saw it in New York.

16 Its date is circa 1938.

17 *Len Lye: A Personal Mythology*, p 63.

18 Thorburn interview with Lye.

19 For example, in January 1937 *Colour Box* and *Rainbow Dance* were included in 'A Season of Surrealist and Avant-Garde Films' at the Everyman Theatre in Hampstead, alongside Jean Vigo's *Zero de Conduite*. (Vigo's film was described by the *Daily Herald* on 15 January as 'poisonous drivel', while the *Evening Standard* commented the following day: 'Nought for behaviour, nought for story, and nought for direction. Also . . . noughts to Surrealism'!) During April and May, 'Jam Session' (now retitled 'Snowbirds in Conference') was part of the Surrealist Section of an exhibition organised by the Artists' International Association, and in November Lye contributed 'Long Strips' and 'Colour Cuts' to 'Surrealist Objects and Poems', an exhibition at the London Gallery which was now the centre of the movement's activities. These works were made up of strips of hand-painted film illuminated from behind.

20 Note 'For S.A., re: my old brain imagery', unpublished note.

21 Winter 1936, p 163.

22 *Life and Letters Today*, Vol 18, No 11, Spring 1938, p 79 and p 81.

twentysix the english walt disney

1 'Picking the Best Films of the Year', *Evening Chronicle*, 1 January 1937.

2 The phrase is used as early as 1935 (*Sunday Referee*, 10 November 1935).

3 See William Moritz, 'The Films of Oskar Fischinger' *Film Culture*, Nos 58–60, and 'You Can't Get Then From Now', *Journal: Southern California Art Magazine*, Vol 3, No 9, 1981.

4 'Films of the Week' *Observer*, 28 June 1936.

5 Letter, 11 September 1981.

6 Paul Rotha, *Documentary Diary*, p 174.

7 'The New Disney', *Sunday Times,* 27 April 1941.

8 The film was ready just in time to be included in the British Film Institute's 1937 retrospective of Lye's work.

9 Griffith interview of Jack Ellitt, 1987.

10 Sussex, pp 83–84. Lye was paid eight pounds per week for two months, and Jack Ellitt six pounds.

11 *Rhythm*, p 70.

12 'Wide-eyed Starlet', *Daily Express*, 18 January 1938.

13 'Len Lye speaks at the Film-makers' Cinematheque'.

14 Griffith interview of Jack Ellitt, 1987.

15 See reviews in the Lye Foundation collection. British film-makers who liked it included Basil Wright ('The Cinema', *The Spectator*, 25 February 1938) and Paul Rotha (*Documentary Diary,* p 221).

16 Winter 1947–48, p 135.

17 'Television — New Axes to Grind', *Sight and Sound*, vol 8, Summer, 1939, pp 65–70.

18 'Len Lye speaks at the Film-makers' Cinematheque.'

19 'Television — New Axes to Grind', p 68.

20 ibid., p 69.

21 'The Man Who Was Colourblind', *Sight and Sound*, Vol 9, Spring, 1940, pp 6–7.

22 Griffiths interview with Jack Ellitt, 1987.

23 Cf. my essay 'Jack Ellitt: The Early Years', *Cantrills Filmnotes*, December 1999–January 2000, Nos 93–100, pp 20–26.

24 See, for example, C A Lejeune, 'How High Is the Public', *Observer,* 28 February 1937.

25 This film was tracked down by Sarah Davy of the National Film Archive who has done much valuable Lye research over the years. Ian Christie suggests that the film was actually made in 1936 (see *Len Lye*, p 191, footnote 23).

26 May 1938. (Aldridge collection, Tate Gallery)

27 The phrase is from a letter to John Aldridge, undated.

28 The first phrase comes from an Imperial Airways pamphlet, 1937, and the second from 'Film Painter', *Time*, 12 December 1938, p 51.

29 Letter from Lye to John Aldridge, undated.

30 Imperial Airways pamphlet, 1937.

31 Patchett, 'Handpainted Swing . . .'.

32 See John Huntley, *British Film Music*, New York, Arno Press and New York Times, 1972, p 217.

33 T. S. Lyndon-Haynes, in *The Cine-Technician*, July–August 1939, p 63.

34 *Time*, 12 December 1938.

35 *Time*, pp 50–51.

twentyseven the world and ourselves

1 Hugh Ford, *Published in Paris*, New York, Macmillan, 1975, p 403.

2 See Richard Perceval Graves, *Robert Graves: The Years with Laura Riding 1926–1940*, London, Weidenfeld and Nicolson, 1995, p 269.

3 London, Chatto & Windus, 1938, pp 269–71.

4 *Focus*, No 3, 1935, p 36. Cf. No 4, p 61.

5 P 44.

6 Deborah Baker, *In Extremis: The Life of Laura Riding*, London, Hamish Hamilton, 1993, p 393.

7 Some of the results of their labours were finally published in 1997, posthumously, as *Rational Meaning: A New Foundation for the Definition of Words, and Supplementary Essays*, by Laura Jackson and Schuyler B. Jackson, ed. William Harmon, University Press of Virginia, 1997.

8 Other artists such as the English Surrealists also felt compelled at this time to transfer some of their energies from the avant-garde to more orthodox politics. See, for example, Edward B. Germain's 'Introduction' to his anthology *English and American Surrealist Poetry*, Harmondsworth, Penguin, 1978, p 39.

twentyeight individual happiness now

1 *The Long Week-End*, pp 389–90.

2 Letter, 28 February 1979.

3 'Len Lye speaks at the Film-makers' Cinematheque'.

4 Nos 18–20, June 1940.

5 See, for example, *Documentary News Letter*, March 1940, p 6.

6 Vol 25, 1940, pp 75–76.

7 *Len Lye: A Personal Mythology*, p 42. The painting is dated 1938.

8 From 'Night Tree', *A Brief Description of the Whole World*, No 3, June 1996. (Originally written in the mid-1940s.)

9 These and other images of the period look forward to the powerful kinetic shapes he

would one day create in sculpture and in the great film *Free Radicals*.

10 Nos 18–20, June 1940, p 33.

11 Unfortunately, with a very few exceptions, all the letters appear to have been lost.

12 Dilys Powell, *Films Since 1939*, The British Council and Longmans Green, London, 1947, p 7.

13 Arthur Elton, quoted by Elizabeth Sussex, pp 119–20.

14 Powell, p 10.

15 Powell, p 12.

16 Cf. Powell, pp 38–39.

17 This 1941 review is quoted by Denis Gifford in *British Animated Films, 1895–1985: A Filmography*, Jefferson, N.C., McFarland, 1987, p 117.

18 'Biographical Notes', unpublished ms.

19 17 June 1939 issue, p 67. When I discussed the article with him in 1980, Lye could not remember the exact title or date. My identification is an informed guess, based on circumstantial evidence. *Picture Post* had begun publication in October 1938.

20 *Rain Upon Godshill* (1939), quoted by John Braine in *J. B. Priestley*, London, Weidenfeld and Nicolson, 1978, p 102.

21 'The Spinning Coin', unpublished ms.

22 Unpublished note by Lye on a *New York Times* story about Priestley, 6 April 1974. See also Lye's letter to Graves, 19 March 1941.

23 'The Spinning Coin.'

24 'Paul F[iondella] and Len L[ye] at Talk Time', unpublished ms.

25 'The Spinning Coin.'

26 Curnow interview, p 61.

27 Letter from Lye to Graves, undated. (I would guess September, based on internal evidence.) My thanks to Beryl Graves and Paul O'Prey for passing on letters from this period.

28 Letter from Lye to Graves, 3 December 1940.

29 ibid.

30 Or so Lye remembered his friend's reply (Curnow interview, p 61).

31 'The Body English of Myth Art and the Genes: Somewhat Autobiographically', unpublished ms (February 1975).

32 ibid. Lye's sense of having a special bond with this village in Kent was later confirmed when he came across an old map in which the village's name was spelled 'Lye'!

33 Letter from Lye to Graves, 30 November 1941.

34 'Note (for biography?)', unpublished note.
35 'A Definition of Common Purpose', unpublished ms.

twentynine going to the top

1 Stan Brakhage has suggested that working with Grierson's film group was a mixed blessing for an artist such as Lye because it was hard to resist the group's belief that good art could be successfully combined with utilitarian aims: 'There was a gathering at this time ... in London of people who ... were thinking in terms of one world — that now the world is a tribe, one tribe, where art could be something that helps people to understand each other, and be in touch with each other.' Lye 'was the wildest of this group' but he too could be made to feel 'a tribal responsibility'. Brakhage adds: 'This impulse gets you into trouble; it got Len into the GPO' (from a talk on Lye at the University of Colorado, 13 October 1980).
2 See, for example, 'Two Grand Illuminations', unpublished ms.
3 *In Broken Images: Selected Letters of Robert Graves 1914–1946,* ed. Paul O'Prey, London, Hutchinson, 1982, pp 315–16.
4 *Sens-Plastique*, trans. Irving Weiss, New York, Sun, 1979.
5 Letter from Lye to Graves, May 1942.
6 'The Spinning Coin'.
7 Letter from Lye to Graves, 12 April 1941.
8 Letter to Graves, 1 May 1941.
9 Letter to Lye, l April 1942 (as Lye transcribed it).
10 Letter from Lye to Graves, 22 June (1942?).
11 See Chapman Pincher, *Their Trade Is Treachery*, London, Sidgwick and Jackson, 1981.
12 'The Spinning Coin', and interview with Len Lye, 1980.
13 Letter to Lye, 1 June 1943.
14 Letter to Lye, 16 December 1943.
15 T. S. Matthews, *Jacks or Better*, p 233.
16 Interview, 1988.

thirty war films

1 For additional background, see Sarah Davy, 'Len Lye: The Film Artist in Wartime', in *Len Lye*, pp 196–98. Davy also wrote an MA thesis in Film Studies and Film Archiving on the same topic at the University of East Anglia, 1992 (also entitled 'Len Lye: The Film Artist in Wartime').
2 Letter from John Taylor on tape, 1981.
3 ibid.
4 Jeakins (1907–81) entered the British film industry in 1928, first in newsreels and then in documentaries, a genre of film-making to which he was strongly committed throughout his career. He was staff cameraman for Realist and later Anvil Films. He was Basil Wright's favourite cameraman, a partnership that lasted from *Children at School* (1937) to *A Place for God* (1959).
5 Letter, 6 August 1981.
6 Letter from Lye to Graves, 12 April 1941.
7 John Taylor tape.
8 John Taylor tape.
9 August 1941, p.147.
10 *March of Time*, 6th year, No 6, released November 1942. Lye shot the footage on 'the Coastal Command'.
11 'Flying Boat', unpublished ms.
12 ibid.
13 After Oban, Lye went to film a lumber camp in another part of Scotland, then more scenes with the RAF in England. See letters to Graves, 26 June and 1 July 1941.
14 Interview with Jane Lye, 1980.
15 John Taylor tape.
16 ibid.
17 Margaret Thomson completed a New Zealand university degree in zoology but because science jobs were scarce during the Depression, she moved to London where she found a job making science films. Her impressive film-making career was mostly in England, the main exception being a period with New Zealand's National Film Unit (1947–49).
18 Letter from Lye to Warren Hope, 9 May 1973. The book was *Selected Verse Poems of Arthur Rimbaud,* translated by Norman Cameron, published in London in 1942.
19 Letter, 21 September 1981.
20 Interview with Maurice Lancaster, 1988.
21 ibid.
22 Letter, 21 September 1981.
23 ibid. Also interview with Margaret Thomson, 1988.
24 Released in December 1941.
25 Letter, 6 August 1981.
26 ibid.
27 'A.C.T.'s First Patent' in *The Cine-Technician*, November 1941–January 1942, p 129.
28 See *Mass Observation at the Movies*, ed. Jeffrey Richards and Dorothy Sheridan, London,

Routledge and Kegan Paul, 1987, p 453, and *Documentary News Letter*, vol 3, March 1942, p 37.

29 *Mass Observation at the Movies,* pp 445 ff.

30 ibid., p 452.

31 ibid., p 457.

32 ibid., p 455.

33 ibid., p 454.

34 John Taylor tape.

35 Letter from Jeakins, 6 August 1981.

36 ibid.

37 Such enforced changes were presumably the reason why Lye took his name off the credits. The final version was 8 minutes long.

38 June 1942. Rachael Low notes some similar comments in *The History of the British Film 1929–1939: Documentary and Educational Films of the 1930s*, London, George Allen and Unwin, 1979, p 152. (My thanks to Sarah Davy for drawing my attention to this passage.)

39 Letter from Jeakins, 6 August 1981. No copy of the film appears to have survived. Perhaps it was the Lye/Ray trailer listed in filmographies as *Planned Crops*, reviewed by *Documentary News Letter* in February 1943 (p 182).

40 Based on information from John Taylor and Derek Waterman. Waterman, the cameraman for this film, had great difficulty removing the paint Lye had applied before returning the borrowed skull! The *Documentary News Letter* review was February 1943, p 182.

41 Letter from Lye to Graves, 3 May 1941.

42 From a 1941 report by Dr Stephen Taylor, Director of Home Intelligence, quoted in *Mass Observation at the Movies*, pp 11–12.

43 John Taylor tape.

thirtyone kill or be killed

1 January 1943, p 165. (There is some evidence that the film was screened in British cinemas.) Realist received 1456 pounds for the production of the film, plus 50 pounds for script development. There was a final 27 pounds for a change to the soundtrack (discussed below).

2 Vol 16, Winter 1947–48, p 134.

3 Interview, 1988.

4 Letter from Lye to Graves, late 1942.

5 Letter, September 1979.

6 These and other production details are from Lye's three pages of publicity information.

7 Letter from Derek Waterman, 21 September

1981. There is also an interesting account of the incident by Clive Coultass in 'British Cinema and the Reality of War', *Britain and the Cinema in the Second World War*, ed. Philip M. Taylor, Houndmills, Macmillan, 1988, p 88. Coultass quotes the dialogue differently but both accounts agree on the main points.

8 Interview, 1983.

9 *Palaestra* (Amsterdam), Nos 6–7, 1948, p 155 (My English translation.)

10 Letter from Lye, 2 July 1943.

11 Letter from Lye, 16 [July?] 1943.

12 Letter from Waterman, 21 September 1981.

13 Interview with John Taylor, 1981.

14 Wendell L. Willkie, *One World,* New York, Simon and Schuster, 1943, p 181.

15 p 170.

16 p. 15.

17 Letter from Lye, undated.

18 'Biographical notes', unpublished ms. ('Bob' refers to Bob Lavarro, Lye's assistant.)

19 29 December 1943.

20 15 January, 1944.

21 See, for example, Lye's letter to Dallas Bower, 26 August 1942.

22 Interview with Maurice Lancaster, 1988. Other film-makers also remembered the argument. 'The Irish Question' was released in April 1944.

23 Letter from Lye to Rank, 11 February 1942. (Thanks to Judith Hoffberg for drawing my attention to this and related letters.)

24 Letter to Lye, 2 May 1944.

25 Curnow interview, p 62.

26 Cable from Richard de Rochemont, 30 May 1944.

27 Interview with Jane Lye, 1980.

28 Interview with Maurice Lancaster, 1988.

29 Interview with Jane Lye, 1980.

30 Cf. Deborah Shepard, *Reframing Women: A History of New Zealand Film*, Auckland, HarperCollins, 2000.

thirtytwo willkie

1 Unsent letter from Lye to T. S. (Tom) Matthews, 2 May 1975.

2 Letter from Matthews, 7 March 1983.

3 Letter from Matthews, 23 March 1981.

4 C. K. Ogden, *Debabelization*, London, Kegan Paul Trench Trubner, 1931, p 9.

5 I. A. Richards, 'English Language Teaching Films and Their Use in Teaching Training',

English Language Teaching, Vol 2, No 1, September 1947, p 2.

6   Interview with Richard de Rochemont, 1980.

7   T. S. Matthews, *Jacks or Better*, p 236.

8   'Somewhat Autobiographically', unpublished ms.

9   'Paul F[iondella] and Len L[ye] at Talk Time', unpublished ms.

10   The account in this chapter draws on (and attempts to reconcile) several of Lye's accounts. His later (1979) claim that Willkie had 'loved the idea' of the film (in Curnow's interview in *Art New Zealand*) is more positive than his earlier reports.

11   *Jacks or Better*, p 237.

12   'S. A.'

13   'English Language Teaching Films . . .', p.5. It is interesting that Richards says 'off-stage' rather than 'off-screen'.

14   'On the Day Willkie Died', in *Figures of Motion,* p 129.

15   Letter from Lye to Graves, 27 November 1944.

16   'English Language Teaching Films . . .', p 6.

17   ibid.

18   Telephone interview with Nancy Sommerschield (Richard de Rochemont's assistant), 1988.

19   Interview with de Rochemont, 1980.

20   *Art New Zealand,* No 17, p 63.

thirtythree a rorschach test

1   Interview, 1980.

2   Louise Bates Ames's personal journal, 25 October 1945. (My thanks to Ms Ames for permission to use this source in this chapter.)

3   Interview with Priscilla Baker, November 1988.

4   The Library of Congress (Manuscript Division) includes approximately 200 letters to or from Lye, written between 1945 and 1975, as part of the Louise Bates Ames papers. My thanks to Wystan Curnow for bringing them to my attention.

5   Letter to Curnow, 16 January 1982. Later quotes are from Ames's personal journal or her letters to Curnow. (The qualities she admires here in Lye seem to be equally present in herself, judging by her lively correspondence and generous support for his work.)

6   7 December 1945. I received a similar account of Lye's good rapport with crew and actors from Priscilla Baker, who watched

him direct a sequence of *Basic English*.

7   This and other phrases are from interviews with Louise Bates Ames and Janet Learned in New Haven, 1988.

8   Letter from Ames to Lye, 9 July 1946.

9   Letter to Curnow, 16 January 1982.

10   See *Len Lye: A Personal Mythology*, p 74.

thirtyfour ann hindle

1   Interview with Ann Lye, 1985.

2   Interview with Louise Ames, 1988.

3   Interview with Mrs M. Lancaster, 1988.

4   Letter to Ann Lye, undated (1950s).

5   The Lye Foundation's collection of Lye's papers gives better coverage of his American period than of earlier periods. One reason for this is the fact that so much was lost when the family moved to the USA.

6   Jane Lye remembered the date as 13 May — she later thought the 13th ironically appropriate — but Ames's diary gives the date as a week later.

7   Letter to Jane Lye, 29 July 1946. Graves expresses sympathy for Jane in other letters in *Between Sun and Moon: Selected Letters of Robert Graves 1946–1972*, ed Paul O'Prey, London, Hutchinson, 1984.

8   From 1946 until he moved in with Ann in 1948, Lye had been living at 278 West 4th Street.

9   Interview with Mrs M. Lancaster, 1988.

10   Interview with Ann Lye, 1985.

11   ibid.

12   Letter to Ann Lye, undated (1950s).

13   Such a comment leaves one wondering how many women artists have been fortunate enough to have husbands with a similar willingness to play the supportive role.

thirtyfive paintings and poems

1   There were also a few painted on card. It was characteristic of the paintings of this period that many had poems on the back.

2   Quoted *Artforum*, November 1973, p 38.

3   'The Biomorphic Forties' in *Artforum,* September 1965. Other relevant texts include the catalogue of the exhibition *Vital Signs: Organic Abstraction from the Permanent Collection* at the Whitney Museum of American Art (New York) in 1988.

4   Antonio Gaudí, quoted by Russett and Starr in *Experimental Animation*, p 13.

5 Motherwell, quoted *Artforum*, September 1965, p 46.
6 'The Biomorphic Forties', p 20.
7 Letter from Len to Ann Lye ('Dearest of all leaves'), undated.
8 Letter, September 1979.
9 Larry Rivers, 'The Cedar Bar', *New York*, 5 November 1979. The present Cedar Tavern is a few blocks north of the original location.
10 Letter to Wystan Curnow, l June 1981.
11 See Ruthven Todd, 'Miró in New York: A Reminiscence' in *Malahat Review,* No. 1, January 1967, pp 77–92. The mural was at the Gourmet Restaurant of the Terrace Palace Hotel in Cincinnati, Ohio.
12 The painting is owned by Louise Bates Ames. Here I have used one of Lye's variant versions of the poem.
13 'A Tree Has Its Heart in Its Roots', *Figures of Motion*, p 125.
14 *Figures of Motion*, pp 127–28.
15 Approximately 50 x 60 cm in size.
16 From 'The Fall of Rome'.
17 Also known by other names such as 'Self Planting at Night'.

thirtysix shoe of my mind

1 Exactly which sequences Lye contributed is not known. Was he responsible for the model of the atom in motion?
2 Interview, 1988.
3 Interview with Lothar Wolff, 1980.
4 'You Be Me', unpublished ms.
5 For Lye 'evolution' was not to be equated with 'progress'. Similarly, he had his own conception of 'individualism' which enabled him to say — for example — that individuals were more fully developed in some ancient tribal societies than in some modern urban societies.
6 'The Identity of Value', unpublished ms.
7 Letter from Lepley to Lye, 1 October 1951.
8 Letter to Lye, 23 July 1952.
9 Louise Ames journal, 7 July 1946.
10 Interview, 1988.
11 Letter from Ames to Wystan Curnow, 16 January 1982. Perhaps Lye hoped to persuade the March of Time (which was still in business at this time) to do an episode about Sheldon.
12 Letter from Orwell to Lye, 20 June 1949. The book was not specified and this is my guess as to the title. Lye had contacted Orwell previously in the 1930s about the possibility

of a film collaboration, to judge by a comment in one of his letters to Aldridge.
13 Halas and Batchelor completed a feature-length animated version of Orwell's *Animal Farm* in 1954.
14 Interview, 1995.
15 Letter from Eisenhower to Lye, 22 August 1950.
16 Letter from Lye to Wystan Curnow, 9 July 1979.
17 'Somewhat Autobiographically (Stonehenge)', unpublished ms.

thirtyseven gracious living with little money

1 Letter from Ann Lye to Jane Lye, 14 September 1953; and Jane Lye's reply, 28 September.
2 Interview with Joellen Rapee, 1980. Her comment was echoed by others.
3 Interview with Ann Lye, 1985.
4 Susan Maxwell, 'An Artist with a Whirring Mind', *New Zealand Herald*, 6 August 1980, Section 2, p 1.
5 Interview with Ann Lye, 1985.
6 Interview with Mrs M. Lancaster, 1988.
7 *New Zealand Herald*, 6 August 1980.
8 Anaïs Nin, *The Journals of Anaïs Nin,* London, Peter Owen, 1974, p 107. (His name is printed as 'Ly'.)
9 Guy Savino, 'This Avant-Garde "Films" Music in the Abstract' , *Newark News*, 29 January 1959.
10 Interview with Ann Lye, 1980.
11 *Dylan Thomas in America: An Intimate Journal*, Boston, Little, Brown, 1955, p 13.
12 ibid., p 14.
13 Interview, 1979. Jane Lye borrowed the last phrase — with acknowledgement — from William Sansom's essay in the *London Magazine,* December 1956.
14 'Some Comment (Notes by Joe Levy out of an interview)', unpublished note.
15 Letter to Wystan Curnow, 8 July 1981.
16 Letter, September 1979.
17 Russett and Starr, *Experimental Animation*, p 68.
18 An electronic sound effect was added at the end. Many years later he gave *Full Fathom Five* the date 1955, but this was not conclusive as Lye's dating was always erratic. If it was 1953 then this would have been the sample he showed Thomas.

19 Letter, September 1979. Lye made unsuccessful attempts to find sponsorship for opera films that would break away from naturalism. Besides using direct animation of words, he intended to conceal the singers behind 'Cycladic masks'.

20 *The Collected Letters of Dylan Thomas*, ed Paul Ferris, London, J M Dent, 1985, p 880.

21 Quoted by Andrew Sinclair in his book *Dylan Thomas*, London, Michael Joseph, 1975, p 164.

22 Interview by John Matthews with Ann Lye and Rose Slivka, 1981.

23 Interview, 30 September 1980.

24 Interview by John Matthews with Ann Lye and Rose Slivka, 1981.

25 Paul Ferris, *Dylan Thomas*, New York, Dial Press, 1977, p 272.

26 Quoted by Rob Gittins in *The Last Days of Dylan Thomas*, London, Macdonald, 1986, p 148.

27 ibid., p.146.

28 Interview with Ann Lye, 1980. Although this is a second-hand account — since she heard about Thomas's call from her husband — her memory is usually reliable.

29 Interview by John Matthews with Ann Lye and Rose Slivka, 1981.

30 This and other quotes from Rose Slivka are from the Matthews interview, 1981.

thirtyeight madison avenue

1 Interview, 1980.

2 Letter to Dennis Forman of Granada Television, 31 December 1956.

3 Interview, 1980.

4 'S. A.'

5 Interview, 1980. Lye worked for Young and Rubicam in 1954.

6 He would use the same music for his later film *Rhythm*.

7 Interview, 1988.

8 Quoted by James Beveridge in *John Grierson*, New York, Macmillan, 1978, p 94.

9 'Sight Sound Consanguinity', unpublished ms.

10 ibid.

11 Letter, September 1979.

12 Unpublished note.

13 Amos Vogel's Cinema 16 series and the Museum of Modern Art were the most important regular outlets for avant-garde films in New York in the early 1950s. Lye was a member of Cinema 16's 'Committee of Sponsors' (*Wide Angle*, Vol 19, No 2, 1997, p 170).

14 Interview with Francis Lee, 1980.

15 Letter, 22 April 1981. In describing one of Lye's contributions Hugo spoke of 'the wire contraption over the straight shots towards the end (the sequence where Anaïs was ascending)'. In another letter (13 November 1980) Hugo expressed his enthusiasm for Lye's film *Rhythm* ('a masterpiece'). Also see Hugo's essay 'The Making of *Bells of Atlantis*' in *Mosaic*, Vol 11, No 2, Winter 1978, and R. A. Haller's 'The Films of Ian Hugo', *Pittsburgh Film-Makers* (programme notes), May–July 1976.

16 *Wide Angle*, Vol 19, No 2, 1997, p 157.

17 'Hans Richter — 30 Years of Experimental Films' in *Cinedrama* (Buenos Aires, Argentina), No 2, December 1953.

18 Interview, 1980

19 Lye's recollection of the date.

thirtynine rhythm

1 Letter, Cecile Starr to Stan Brakhage, 27 December 1980. Later when Starr interviewed Lye for the *Saturday Review* ('Ideas on Film: Men in Movement', 22 September 1956) in a friendly attempt to find him 'some ingenious sponsors', he was working on a new project: 'I'm crazy about the islands of the South Pacific. To me no one has filmed their romanticism and social "feel" and certainly not in relation to the world as a whole'. (This was another unrealised project.)

2 Interview, 1988.

3 Lye wrote another note about suicide in May 1964 but that referred to Ernest Hemingway's suicide (in 1961).

4 Interview, 1989. (Other quotations from Brant are taken from the same interview.)

5 For example a brass choir, a gamelan group, a jazz combo, a percussion ensemble, a bluegrass group, three pianos, an organ, a boys' choir and ten vocal soloists, all incorporated into the work 'Millennium 2'.

6 Referred to by Lye as 'Carnegie Abstracts', 'Henry's Paint', and 'YMHA'. Lye worked on other films in this 'lyrical' style such as 'Colour Clouds'. None appears to have been completed to his satisfaction but various versions have survived. This is dazzling footage with brilliant colours and extremely rich, varied textures. Some colour has unfortunately faded.

7 See 'Last Horn is Blown at Bowery Jazz House', *Village Voice*, 30 August 1962, p 3 and p 13.

8 Letter from Barbara Ker-Seymer, 29 June 1981.

9 'A Note on Dance and Film', *Dance Perspectives*, No 30, Summer 1967.

10 *New York Herald Tribune*, 4 March 1957.

11 *New York Times*, 4 March 1957. This review suggests there had been an earlier collaboration between Brant and Lye.

12 Interview with James Manilla, 1980.

13 'Len Lye speaks at the Film-makers' Cinematheque.'

14 According to Lye, the music was by 'the Zeetzeektula and Zinkil tribes'. I have identified one source as the Ndlamu or Mgido Dance by the Zingili Clan of South Africa.

15 The 1962 television programme on Lye included what it describes as 'the first screening of *Rhythm* on American television'. That version was one minute and seventeen seconds, longer than today's official version because Lye had added a scratched intro and outro. Also, the title was given as 'The Rhythm of the Forward Look'.

16 This is how Lye usually cited the name, though he referred to it on one occasion as the New York Art Directors' Festival.

17 The International Experimental Film Festival at Brussels, where Lye also won a prize for *Free Radicals* (see below). Manilla assumes that Lye had made a reversal master of *Rhythm* from which he could print his own copies.

18 *Film Culture Reader*, ed P. Adams Sitney, New York, Praeger, 1970, p 293. (Kubelka replied that he had seen the film in 1958.)

19 Interview with Francis Lee, 1980.

20 Interview with Paul Barnes, 1980.

21 *Visionary Film*, New York, Oxford University Press, 1974, p 269.

forty free radicals

1 'S. A.'

2 James E. Breslin, '"My Best Films Will Never Be Made," says $5000 Winner', *Village Voice*, 28 May 1958.

3 'S. A.'

4 ibid.

5 Interview with Ann Lye, 1985.

6 Letter, September 1979.

7 Interview, 1980.

8 Russett and Starr, *Experimental Animation*, p 68.

9 Quoted in Adrienne Mancia and Willard Van Dyke, 'The Artist as Film-maker: Len Lye', *Art in America*, Vol 54, No 4, July–August 1966, p 105.

10 Norman McLaren, *Cameraless Animation*, Information and Promotion Division, National Film Board of Canada, 1958, p 7.

11. Interview with Hilary Harris, 1980.

12. Cf. 'Len Lye Speaks at the Film-makers' Cinematheque', p 51.

13. Letter from Lye to John Halas, 15 January 1958.

14 Russett and Starr, *Experimental Animation*, p 69.

15 'Sight Sound Consanguinity', unpublished ms.

16 Russett and Starr, *Experimental Animation*, p 69.

17 Interview with Steve Jones, 1980.

18 'A Note on Dance and Film' (1967), reprinted in *Figures of Motion*, p 56.

19 'The Artist as Film-maker: Len Lye', *Art in America*, p 105.

20 Letter to John Halas, 15 January 1958.

21 The incident is described in 'Somewhat Autobiographically' and 'Len Lye Speaks at the Film-makers' Cinematheque'.

22 *This Wonderful World,* Programme No 33, 30 October 1958, produced by Scottish Television. (John Grierson Archive, University of Stirling.)

23 *Art in America*, p 105. Other American film makers praised by the Jury included Stan Brakhage, Kenneth Anger, and Hilary Harris. Of the 400 films, 133 were screened at Brussels.

24 *Film Quarterly*, Vol 12, No 3, Spring 1959, pp 57–58.

25 Parker Tyler, *Underground Film: A Critical History*, Harmondsworth, Penguin, 1974, p 146.

26 'Movie Journal', *Village Voice*, 15 April 1959, p 6.

27 Thanks to Yann Beauvais for this information. The title, which was later removed, is evidence that Lye was thinking in utopian terms as early as 1958. Compare 'When the Venutians Sing "Auld Lang Syne"', his contribution to *Film: Book 2,* ed. Robert Hughes, New York, Grove Press, 1962.

fortyone going on strike

1 Letter to the Editor, *Village Voice*, 2 February 1961; reprinted in *Film Culture*, Nos 22–23, 1961, p 165.
2 Draft of letter to the *Village Voice* (unpublished?), Lye Foundation collection.
3 *Film Culture*, No 29, Summer 1963, pp 38–39.
4 Perhaps Francisco de Zurbaran, the 17th century Spanish Baroque painter.
5 Interview with Alastair Reid, 1980.
6 Interview with Dan Klugherz, 1980.
7 Interview with Margareta Akermark, 1980.
8 Letter to the Editor, *Village Voice*, 2 February 1961.
9 'Movie Journal' in *Village Voice*, 2 February 1961.
10 Draft of letter to the *Village Voice* (unpublished?), Lye Foundation collection.
11 ibid.
12 Interview in the film *Doodlin'*, 1987. (Thanks to Keith Griffiths for permission to quote this.) For other information see 'On Shelf 22 Years, Pittsburgh Premieres', *The Pittsburgh Press*, 10 June 1979, Section E, p 1.
13 Interview with Dan Klugherz, 1980.
14 Letter, September 1979.
15 'Excerpt', unpublished manuscript.
16 Letter to Jacques Ledoux, 24 August 1964.
17 Letters in the Foundation collection include Kubelka to Lye, 14 June 1961 and 30 January 1964, and Lye to Kubelka, 1 June 1961.

fortytwo tangibles

1 Sometimes known as 'Swivelling Eye Mask', this was part of a wall mural in the bedroom of their apartment at Washington Street. Ann Lye guessed the date as 1953.
2 He made a paper model and hoped to build it in steel. Lye remembered the date as 1958.
3 Curnow interview, p 61.
4 Interview with Hamish Keith, 1995.
5 Gretchen Weinberg, 'Interview with Len Lye', p 45.
6 'S. A.'
7 Lye's programmed sculptures could be regarded as musical compositions. At times the patterns of sound they produce are reminiscent of today's electronic or techno music. The sculptures can also be related to the tradition of home-made musical instruments or the tradition of sound installations.
8 Len Lye, 'Art and the Genes', unpublished ms.

9 'Storm King' provides the soundtrack for the opening credit sequence of *Particles in Space*, and is seen as well as heard in *When the Walls Came Tumbling Down*.
10 The top strip was 5/8 of an inch wide and the other was 3 inches wide and about 2 feet long.
11 The striker was 20 inches tall and the cork ball 3 inches in diameter.
12 Interview with Ann Lye, 1980.
13 Cf. 'Tangible Motion Sculpture', *Art Journal* (Wagner College), Vol 20, Summer, 1961, pp 226–28.
14 Letter from Lye to Yusing Jung, 11 October 1967.
15 Those mentioned in Lye's notes, besides Lou Adler, are 'Fairchild', Maurice Gross, Maury Logue, Carl Schulmann, Harvey Sleighton, and Bert Stanleigh. (This is how Lye spelled the names.) Rufus Stillman and the staff of his engineering company also helped Lye. No doubt there were others.
16 Interview with Paul Barnes, 1980.
17 Letter, 16 June 1981.
18 See 'The Visionary Art of Len Lye' in *Craft Horizons*, May–June 1961, p 30.
19 Letter, 17 December 1973. In terms of Lye's acknowledgement of Adler, see the caption for 'Roundhead' in 'Tangible Motion Sculpture', p 228. Adler commented to me: 'When Len couldn't pay me, he gave me half credit for one of his creations ... he was a person of great and real kindness' (letter to the author, 16 June 1981).

fortythree dance of the machines

1 'The Berkeley Symposium of Kinetic Art', *Art and Artists*, Vol 1, February 1967, p.31.
2 ibid.
3 *Len Lye — Two Studios*, documentary, 1980.
4 Lye had been trying for years in his film-making to achieve similar 'orbital whip' effects. Cf. 'Roundhead', unpublished ms.
5 'Tangible Motion Sculpture'.
6 Thanks to Evan Webb for this information. He adds: 'A drum with pins, driven by an electric motor, revolves so that the pins strike or pluck the steel reeds of an 18-reed tuned comb. Len had extracted striking pins from the drum leaving eight which in turn plucked or struck five separate notes from the tone comb' (letter, 23 September 2000).
7 In his words it was 'a magnified picture of a male hormone with its concentric circles'. By

'hormone' I assume that Lye meant chromosome since 'roundhead' refers to the Y (or male) chromosome.

8 Interview with Ann Lye, 1985.

9 He also used other programmes — for example, with the motor on and off for three seconds alternately.

10 John Matthews's interview with Lye, 1978 Also Lye's setting-up instructions for 'Fountain' (1969). Early versions of 'Fountain' ranged from 3 to 7 feet in height (though there were also some miniature models). He kept the base black and unobtrusive but tried out various shapes such as a cylinder, a cube, a cone, and a spheroid. He used strong lighting so that the rods gleamed in a constantly changing pattern of highlights.

11 Newsweek, 13 March 1961.

12 The film was screened during the week leading up to UN Day. It was also available in an abbreviated 20-second version. I have never been able to track down a copy. The following attempt at reconstruction is based on publicity material, production stills, an interview with Brant, and a storyboard. The film apparently began with the rods of the 'Fountain' opening out in a beautiful fan-like movement (a movement re-enacted whenever this tangible is set up for exhibition). Then the word 'peace' appeared in five languages — like fruit on the branches of a tree — followed by close-ups of the gently swaying rods catching the light. The 'Fountain' (a symbol of unity in diversity) was followed by two rotating rings at right angles with 'United Nations' in various languages revolving independently inside the rings. Finally 'Blade' was used to echo the shape of the United Nations Secretariat building in New York, a distinctive 39-storey tower built in 1952. Though 'Blade' and its striker were stationary, they revolved slowly on their base, with the two rings from the previous sequence superimposed, revolving in the opposite direction. In response to Lye's request for music Henry Brant composed a choral work for the United Nations Singers. 'They were office workers who had a choir that met every day at noon. They were the only performing organization the United Nations could furnish but they were willing to do it so I wrote it just for them.' The music was built up from the word 'Peace' sung in every language known to the choir members

with 'many recordings dubbed together for tonal richness'. The soundtrack also included the rods of 'Fountain' brushing gently together, a sound Lye called 'spinkling'.

13 Maureen Hill Broom, 'A New Zealander's Contribution to Message of Peace', New Zealand Free Lance, 21 October 1959, pp 3–4.

14 ibid.

15 'Names' and 'Moments', unpublished mss.

16 For example, water could provide the energy for 'a 150-foot job designed to have five powerful jets aimed at the retracting and protruding fins at its base. When water engages the fins, the fountain rotates; when the fins retract, it coasts to a stop. The result is what counts: out of the crash and splash and spray at its foot, the fronds of the fountain sway and oscillate.' Lye also planned a 'Swaying Steel Fountain' in which the usual rods would be replaced by hollow tubes sitting in a cone-shaped base. 'Retractable water vanes move in and out of this cone and alternately engage and disengage streams of water causing the fountain to rotate.' The work would create an interplay between 'the fluidity and power of water' and 'the strength and flexibility of steel'. Another outdoors fountain project, 'Swirling Harmonic', was a single large tube designed to rotate rapidly, 'leaving the jets of water trailing behind it in various designs' (unpublished notes).

17 Matthews interview, 1978.

18 Letter from Lye to Yusing Jung, 11 October 1967.

19 'Spear', unpublished ms.

20 Lye's spelling.

21 8 June 1961.

22 The 1963 WCBS-TV (New York) television programme about Lye includes a photo of the Southern Illinois installation. Thanks to Stephen Chodorov for providing a copy of this remarkable programme.

23 Interview with Howard Wise, 1980.

24 Matthews interview with Lye, 1978.

25 Hamish Keith radio interview with Lye, 1968 (New Zealand).

26 'The Art that Moves', in Figures of Motion, p 80.

27 See, for example, Castelli's memoir in Studio International, July–August 1969.

28 Interview with William Baldwin, 1988.

29 Howard Wise, in Stewart Kranz, Science and Technology in the Arts: A Tour Through the Realm of Science/Art, New York, Van

Nostrand Reinhold, 1974, p 59.

30 ibid.
31 Interview with Howard Wise, 1980.
32 Interview with Peter Selz, 1981.
33 'In the Art Galleries', *New York Post*, 16 April 1961.
34 'Sculptures Spin in Recital at Museum', *New York Times*, 6 April 1961.
35 Interview with Ann Lye, 1985.
36 Letter to Wystan Curnow, 20 January 1979.
37 Interview with Margareta Akermark, 1980.

fortyfour sartorial thrift-shop style

1 Letter to Philip and Wynne Lye, circa 1 January 1957.
2 Interview, 1980.
3 ibid.
4 ibid.
5 Interview with Alastair Reid, 1980.
6 'Practising', unpublished ms.
7 Susan Maxwell, 'An Artist with a Whirring Mind', *New Zealand Herald*, 6 August 1980, Section 2, p 1.
8 'Brown Paper Bag', unpublished ms.
9 John Matthews interview with Ann Lye and Rose Slivka, 1981.
10 Interview with Ann Lye and Alastair Reid, 1988.
11 ibid.
12 Unpublished note.
13 Interview with Joellen Rapee, 1980.
14 Letter to Wystan Curnow, 20 January 1979.
15 Letter, 1 November 1982.
16 Interview with Alastair Reid, 1980.
17 Letter from Reid to Lye, 9 December 1962.
18 As in the case of many of his other writings, Lye never produced a definitive version. Numbers and other details are a best guess (based on my own editing attempts).
19 Quoted by Andrew Bogle in *Len Lye: A Personal Mythology*, p 16.
20 'Turn On', unpublished ms.
21 Letter, 4 December 1961.
22 Letter, 19 January 1962.
23 Letter to Lye, 17 October 1963.

fortyfive the movement movement

1 Literally 'moved movement'.
2 As reported in the French newspaper *Libération*, 18 March 1961.
3 'For Movement's Sake', *Newsweek*, 13 March 1961.
4 'America Takes the Lead 1945–1965', *Art in America*, August–September 1965, p 109.
5 Quoted in Richard Marshall, *Alexander Calder: Sculpture of the Nineteen Thirties*, New York, Whitney Museum of American Art, 1987, p 6.
6 'Ray Thorburn Interviews Len Lye', p 67.
7 Interview with Ann Lye and Alastair Reid, 1988.
8 Letter to Wystan Curnow, 1 June 1981.
9 25 January 1964.

fortysix a flip and two twisters

1 John Matthews interview with Lye, 1988.
2 'Possible Futures', *Newsweek*, 18 January 1985, p 55.
3 Looking at American Sculpture', *Artforum*, Vol 3, No 5, February 1965, p 31.
4 Interview, 1980.
5 'Flip and Two Twisters' and 'Loop'.
6 Douglas McAgy, 'Len Lye', leaflet, Howard Wise Gallery, 1965.
7 Douglas Davis, *Art and the Future*, London, Thames and Hudson, 1973, p 48.
8 'Mecca Art and the L.Y.M.', unpublished ms. Also see Stewart Kranz, *Science and Technology in the Arts,* p 35.
9 'The Universe', unpublished ms.
10 'The Walk', unpublished ms.
11 *Len Lye: Two Studios*, documentary, 1980.
12 'Vision and Sound: Today's Art At Buffalo', *Studio International*, May 1965, Vol 169, pp 211–12.
13 Emily Genauer, 'Sensation and Sensibility', *Herald Tribune*, March 1965 (Lye Foundation collection — day of month not known).
14 See, for example, the Matthews interview with Lye, 1978.
15 'New York Letter', *Art International*, May 1965, Vol 9, No 4, p 58. For another example, see Lawrence Campbell, 'Reviews and Previews', *Art News*, Vol 64, No 1, March 1965, p 14.
16 'New York Notes', *Art International*, May 1965; reprinted in *The Complete Writings*, 1975, p 180.
17 Letter from Sam Hunter to Mr and Mrs Albert List, 28 April 1965.
18 E.g: Dore Ashton, 'Vision and Sound: Today's Art in Buffalo', *Studio International*, No 169, May 1965, p.213.
19 First reported in 'Timehenge', *Newsweek*, 22 March 1965.

20 Wise Gallery publicity leaflet.
21 Matthews interview with Lye, 1978.
22 *Life*, 23 April 1965. See also 'Avant-Garde', *Time*, 19 March 1965.
23 'Timehenge', p 58.
24 Dore Ashton, p 211.
25 Letter, 10 March 1965.
26 Note by Lye on photocopied pages from Schöffer's book, *Perturbation et Chronocratie*, Denoel, 1978.
27 *Perturbation et Chronocratie*, pp 192–93 (English translation).
28 Interview with Rufus Stillman, 25 November 1988. Stillman's company Torin made other copies of 'Fountain' for Lye, and one was on display at the factory for many years. Stillman worked out a way to electrify the sculpture so it would not get iced up outdoors.
29 Tom Freudenheim, whom Selz hired as his assistant, was a curator who had once described Lye as the 'most sophisticated of the kinetic sculptors' (Tom L. Freudenheim, 'Kinetic Art', *Albright-Knox Art Gallery: Gallery Notes*, Vol 29, Autumn 1966, pp 7–12).
30 Judy Stone, 'Sculpture and Science Meet', *San Francisco Chronicle*, 21 March 1966.
31 The figure is given in *Art and Artists*, Vol 1, February 1967, p 27. The exhibition moved on to the Museum of Art in Santa Barbara.
32 21 March 1966.
33 'Art in Orbit', 4 April 1966, p 92.
34 The first is reproduced in *Time*, 28 January 1966, p 65. The second is described by Alfred Frankenstein in 'Art's Most Moving Moments', *San Francisco Chronicle*, 27 March 1966.
35 Interview with Peter Selz, 1981.
36 'Sculpture and Science Meet.'
37 For a transcript, see 'The Berkeley Symposium' in *Art and Artists*, Vol 1, February 1967, pp 26–31, and March 1967, pp 46–49.
38 'Sculpture and Science Meet.'
39 Interview with Selz, 1981; also interview with Lye, 1980.
40 'Kinetic Sculpture at Berkeley', *Artforum*, May 1966, pp 40–42.

fortyseven life in the sixties

1 Unpublished note.
2 'Preston Presents: Voyeurama Voyeurama, The Free-est Radical', *The East Village Other*,

Vol 1, No 14, 15 June–1 July 1966, p 11.
3 Letter, 22 January 1966.
4 'Accordion', unpublished ms.
5 Interview with William Baldwin, 21 December 1988. (Baldwin was not a participant; he was remembering what Lye had told him.)
6 Interview with Ann Lye, 1985.
7 ibid.
8 Interview, 1980.
9 'After' Puerto Rico, 1967' (poem for Ann).
10 One of the academics sympathetic to his work who had organised guest lectures was Richard Heindel, president of Wagner College on Staten Island and a personal friend of the Lyes.
11 Interview, 1980.
12 Letter from Howard Conant, 12 August 1980.
13 Letter to Lye, 26 April 1966.
14 Letter, 5 December 1966.
15 Letter from Cecile Starr, 27 December 1980.
16 Lecture notes, 17 May 1967.
17 Interview with Philip Lye, 1981.
18 Interview with Paul Barnes, 1980.
19 ibid.
20 Interview with Erik Shiozaki, 1980.
21 Interview with Paul Barnes.
22 Interview with Erik Shiozaki.
23 ibid.
24 Robert Del Tredici, 'Len Lye Interview', *The Cinemanews* (San Francisco), Nos 2–4, 1979, p 6.
25 'Feedback: "Contemporary Voices In The Arts",' in *A Quick Graph: Collected Notes and Essays*, San Francisco, Four Seasons Foundation, 1970, p 356.
26 Grace Glueck, 'Single-Channeled You Mustn't Be', Art Notes, *New York Times*, 5 February 1967.
27 ibid.
28 Interview, 1995, and *A Quick Graph*, p 358.
29 Matthews interview with Lye, 1978.
30 John Perreault, review, *Village Voice*, Vol 12, No 21, 9 March 1967, p 13.
31 ibid.
32 Interview with Erik Shiozaki.
33 *A Quick Graph*, p 361.
34 Interview with Ann Lye, 1980.

fortyeight the snake god

1 Another example was a favourable review of 'Sound, Light and Silence' in *Artforum*,

January 1967, pp 51–52, by Robert Pincus-Witten: 'To my mind the major work of the exhibition is Len Lye's "Universe" ... easily one of the most powerful sculptures yet conceived by one of our pioneer abstractionists.'

2   Interview, 1985.

3   Interview, 1988.

4   Written and produced by Merrill Brockway, with research by Mary Gay Hackman and camerawork by Michael Livesey, the film was released in 1968. A sequence of Lye teaching a student group was not used.

5   Interview with Howard Wise, 1980. In a letter to Sam Hunter (24 June 1965), Lye said that Vera List saw only a 9-foot 'Snake God' and not the current 30-foot version, but Wise was sure that List had seen the larger one.

6   Interview with Allan Temko, 1981.

7   Letter from Lye to Temko, 22 March 1966. Other details are based on my 1981 interview with Temko.

8   ibid.

9   Letter to Philip Lye, 18 March 1967.

10   E.g. 'Hospitality for art', *The Telegram* (Toronto), 23 August 1967.

11   Richard Snell, 'A "sculpt-in" for High Park', *Toronto Daily Star*, 21 April 1967.

12   ibid.

13   Interview with Ann Lye, 1985.

14   Letter from Lye to Yusing Jung, 11 October 1967.

15   ibid.

16   ibid.

17   Don Delaplante, 'High Park sculpture lies in garbage pile; artist blames city', *The Globe & Mail*, 22 May 1968, p 1. Some sources say that the wand fell down of its own accord — that point remains unclear.

18   Interview with Ann Lye, 1985.

19   Letter from Lye to Yusing Jung, 11 October 1967.

fortynine genetics

1   *No Trouble* (published in 1930), quoted in *Figures of Motion*, p 99.

2   ibid., p 105.

3   'Song Time Stuff' (1938) — for example, pages 116, 118, 119.

4   Interview with Ann Lye, 1985.

5   There are many examples of his references to genetics in the early 1960s. For example, in an essay published in 1962 he wrote: 'Dr Van

R. Potter, at the 1960 American Chemical symposium, in summing up the "modulation of gene expression by chemical feedback" said, "An individual may have genetic potential to be a great musician, but unless this potential is developed by environment it will never emerge." Look at what does emerge, and tell me if there is not something rotten in the state of Value.' Discussing his proposed film 'Utopia Now' he added: 'Roll that for a title inside the helixes of your DNA.' And in a 1963 letter to Alastair Reid he wrote: 'Happiness in the blood cell as tight as the gene is an unbelievable pattern deviser for the peripheries and I'm putting some of the periphery back into the marrow with a bit of film I'm making now.'

6   'Identity is Value', unpublished ms.

7   Howard Schmeck, Jr., 'Bubbles Linked to Deep Sea Life', *New York Times*, October 5 1964.

8   See, for example, Lye's analysis of the painting in *Len Lye: A Personal Mythology*, pp 52–54.

9   This was circa 1976 (according to Lye). My account summarises a long period of research and speculation.

10   'Identity is Value', p 46.

11   2 June 1966.

12   *Len Lye: A Personal Mythology*, p 54 (an idea attributed by Lye to 'the great naturalist Luther Burbank').

13   *The Rand McNally Atlas of the Body and Mind*, New York, Rand McNally, 1976, p 116.

14   Cf. Robert Del Tredici, 'Len Lye Interview', *The Cinemanews* (San Francisco), Nos 2–4, 1979.

15   Soon after he formulated his ideas about genetics Lye acknowledged this parallel: 'It's something like the Jungian mass psychology theory,' he wrote in a 1966 manuscript, 'Sight Sound Consanguinity'. Anne Kirker's (unpublished) interview with Lye includes a detailed discussion of Jung.

16   Quoted by Aniela Jaffe in her 'Symbolism in the Visual Arts', in *Man and His Symbols*, ed. Carl G. Jung, New York, Dell Laurel, 1968, p 310.

17   See, for example, 'Identity is Value', unpublished ms.

18   Letter to Lye, 8 March 1967.

19   'Identity is Value'.

20   The Lyes went to Montreal on their way to

Toronto to see what was happening with the 'Wind Wand'.

21 Quoted in *McLaren*, Montreal, National Film Board of Canada, 1980, p 9.

22 Letter from McLaren to Tony Rimmer, 30 June 1972.

23 Letter from Elfriede Fischinger, September 1981.

24 'Gene-Deep Myth', in *Figures of Motion*, p 91.

25 Oswell Blakeston, 'Len Lye's Visuals', *Architectural Review*, Vol 72, July 1932, p 25.

26 'Phagocytosis', *McGraw Hill Encyclopedia of Science and Technology*, Vol 10, New York, McGraw Hill, 1977, p 105. See also 'Macro-phage' in Eleanor Lawrence, *Henderson's Dictionary of Biological Terms*, Harlow (Essex), Longman Scientific and Technical, 1989 (10th Edition), pp 296–97. In some of Lye's discussions I suspect he is confusing 'macrophage' with 'bacteriophage' with respect to one detail — the way the bacterio-phage (a virus that attacks invading bacteria) injects DNA through its tail, which sounds close to what happens in *Tusalava*.

27 'Identity is Value'.

28 Letter to Philip Lye, 18 June 1969.

29 'Did Einstein's Doodles Have A Genetic Source?' unpublished ms.

30 For example, the central character in the novel *Altered States* by Paddy Chayefsky (which Ken Russell made into a film in 1980) is Edward Jessup, a young physiologist who uses psychedelic mushrooms obtained from a tribe of Indians in Mexico. Their religion contains information about prehistoric times. The mushrooms cause Jessup not only to have visions of pre-history but to revert physically to 'a more primitive self'. In his words: 'We've got millions and millions of years stored away in that computer bank we call our minds! We've got trillions of dorm-ant genes in us, our whole evolutionary past. Perhaps I've tapped into that!' He suggests that what 'triggered some very old genes to work' was the release of 'free radicals'. Ultimately the big questions that *Altered States* wants to explore are not about science but about human nature. Those who simply can not *believe* Lye's theory might try thinking of it as science fiction, as a text like Chayefsky's that plays with the idea of 'What if . . . ?' in order to raise important issues. Another writer whom Lye did not know but would surely have found congenial is the

poet Robert Bly whose poetry of the late 1970s was directly influenced by *The Lives of a Cell*. To quote a typical passage from Bly's prose-poem 'The Origin of the Praise of God': 'My friend, this body is made of bone and excited protozoa . . . and it is with my body that I love the fields. How do I know what I feel but what the body tells me? . . . When we come near each other, we are drawn down into the sweetest pools of slowly circling energies, slowly circling smells. And the protozoa know there are odors the shape of oranges, of tornadoes, of octopuses. . . . The sound that pours from the fingertips awakens clouds of cells far inside the body, and beings unknown to us start out in a pilgrimage to their Saviour, to their holy place. Their holy place is a small black stone, that they remember from Protozoic times. . . .' Like Lye in his later years, Robert Bly is a disconcerting mix of an 'old brain' artist and a 'new brain' essayist, a private poet and a public prophet.

31 Lewis Thomas, *Lives of a Cell: Notes of a Biology Watcher*, New York, Viking Press, 1974.

32 'Len Lye in Mythology', unpublished ms.

33 The problem for many readers is that it falls between two stools — neither fully art nor fully logical exposition, neither an autobio-graphical account nor a general discussion, but a mix of the two. Compare his comment: 'my struggle is to write a new brain [essay] on my old brain ideas and, in turn, keep a bit of old brain's personal idiom into their telling' (1974 note for 'Old Brain's Eye Lock'). At best Lye's theory writing is a unique mix of philosophical phrasing with lively colloquialisms and whimsical humour.

fifty the absolute truth of the happiness acid

1 Interview, 1988.

2 Unpublished ms.

3 Letter from Lye to Philip Lye, 1 December 1967. The idea was to alternate summers at Sing Song with the Southern Hemisphere summers.

4 Letter from Lye to Philip Lye, 14 October 1966.

5 See Jim and Mary Barr, *When Art Hits the Headlines*, Wellington, National Art Gallery, 1987.

6 Letter from Lye to Philip Lye, 9 August 1967. Also see letter of 5 December 1966 from Lye to Philip Lye. (Tomory had left earlier.)

7 Letter from Lye to Philip Lye, 14 October 1966.

8 Interview with Hamish Keith, 1995.

9 Letter from Lye to Hamish Keith, 23 October 1968.

10 Interview, 2000.

11 David Rider, 'The Happiness Acid', *Films and Filming*, Vol 15, No 8, May 1969, p 72.

12 17 November 1968.

13 Interview with Ann Lye, 1985.

14 ibid.

15 Letter from Graves to Lye, 17 November 1971. Lye later wrote a memorial message for Graves: 'GOOD / GRAND / MYTH OLD / COMET / ROBERT / YOUR GRAVE / IS MY GRAVE / MYTH MEN / LOVE / LEN'. (Beryl Graves commented in a letter on 27 October 2000: 'I have [this] hanging up as it is so like Len'.)

16 Interview with Ann Lye, 1985.

17 Letter from Lye to Daniel Thomas, undated (1966?).

18 Interview with Ann Lye, 1980.

19 *Dominion*, 18 November 1967. Other early reports were Alan Smythe's 'Sculptural Image Maker in Unexplored Field', *New Zealand Herald*, 1 October 1966, and Hamish Keith's 'New Zealander Has Led Way in Kinetic Sculpture Field', *Auckland Star*, 7 November 1968.

20 Interview with Peter McLeavey, 1995.

21 Quoted by Lye in his letter to John Turner, 27 March 1969.

22 Letter, 23 May 1995.

23 See Michael Dunn's 'Gordon Walters: Some Drawings from the 1940s' in *Bulletin of New Zealand Art History*, Vol 8, 1980, and 'Walters and Primitivism in the 1940s' in *Gordon Walters: Order and Intuition*, ed. James Ross and Laurence Simmons, Auckland, Walters Publication, 1989.

24 'Walters and Primitivism in the 1940s', p 49.

25 Quoted in Lye's letter to John Turner, 27 March 1969. Some sources say 'National Film Library' but research notes for *Len Who?* support the idea that it was the National Film Unit.

26 See Roger Horrocks, 'Alternatives', in *Film in Aotearoa New Zealand*, ed. Jonathan Dennis and Jan Bieringa, Wellington, Victoria University Press, 1992.

27 Interview with Ann Lye, 1988.

28 Letter from Lye, 1 June 1969.

29 'Primitive Perceptions: Changing Attitudes Towards Pacific Art', *Art New Zealand*, No 69, Summer 1993–94, p 78.

30 According to Richard Wolfe: 'Few artefacts anywhere have experienced such museological extremes: from mysterious beginnings to banishment, controversy and international recognition'. Brought to the museum in 1878, the figure ended up in a small basement store room. It was rescued in 1962 for the exhibition 'Primitive Sculpture', and selected for the cover of the catalogue — evidence of a growing aesthetic appreciation of work of this kind. Unfortunately the figure was returned to storage when the exhibition ended, apparently because the wood was deteriorating. Kawe continued to have champions within the museum such as anthropologist Janet Davidson who had a strong interest in the culture of Nukuoro. In late 1967 or early 1968, after some conservation work, the figure was put on display in the alcove on the south side of the approach to the present Pacific Hall, which was 'an obscure and dark place, although a fully public one'. It was in this temporary location that the Lyes found her at the end of 1968. The museum already had plans for a new gallery.

31 See also the *New Zealand Herald* items 'Forgotten Statue Rare Lady' and 'Goddess Safely Back at Home' (25 October 1985).

32 Interview with Ann Lye, 1980. The Barry Lett Gallery session was on 28 December 1968.

33 Letter from Lye to Turner, 27 March 1969.

34 Comments from Ann Lye's Diary.

35 Including Peter McLeavey and Alan Smythe. (Smythe was working with Roger Donaldson's Aardvark film company.)

36 The complete title included the phrase 'Into an Unknown'. This was presumably a wordplay on the title of what was then a popular science fiction series on New Zealand television: 'Out of the Unknown'.

37 His comments are interesting both because of his huge influence and because he had known Lye on a personal basis. (He had lived round the corner from Lye in the late 1950s and used to visit him.) In interview footage filmed but not used in the documentary Greenberg remarked: 'I think that more kinetic sculpture will be made, [and] if it's

going to be any good, they'll have to look at Lye.' He also spoke enthusiastically about Lye's 1930s paintings such as 'The King of Plants Meets the First Man' and his film-making ('damn good films'). He added: 'Why Lye isn't better known, I can't say', though he suspected it was because the artist had not put enough effort into 'getting out there showing [his work]'. When the inter-viewer then asked: 'In what respect is it his own fault?', Greenberg argued that it was up to an artist to 'drive' the situation so that critics were confronted by the work in the galleries and 'had to write about it'. He also noted that Lye had 'dispersed himself' over three media. He added that it would been 'presumptuous' to tell Lye to drive harder, particularly as the artist himself seemed so relaxed: 'In terms of living he's a happier man than far more famous artists that I know. . . . Why? He's calm, he's fun to be with, you can see he's not eaten up with anxieties. There are unknown artists who pass for great, and some of them are very boring, and some just afflict you with their awful lives. You know about the suicides among American artists and writers. . . . Well, it's nice to see Len Lye isn't any part of that business. Not a tragic artist, not at all.' Lye thought highly of Greenberg — 'Clem is one of the best, but mighty rigorous on his own metaphysics', as he wrote to Hamish and Susan Keith — but when the director of the documentary explained he was going to Greenberg for an assessment of the artist's work, Lye was less polite: 'Whatever C. Greenberg says or thinks is unimportant to me!'

38 See Lye's letter to his brother, August 1973 ('a complete waste of time and energy').

39 'Close Look at Len Lye, Kinetic Artist', *The Press*, 26 June 1973, p 4. The *Christchurch Star* described *Len Who?* in similar terms as 'an intelligently compiled look at an expatriate kinetic artist who merits the attention of his countrymen'.

40 Interview with Hamish Keith, 1995. He explained the context: 'Contemporary artists in New Zealand had been beaten about for generations. We were constantly being told that the only artists of any worth were the ones that didn't live here. So we were determined to see what was happening here as important.'

fiftyone utopias

1 Press release, Howard Wise Gallery.
2 Interview, 1980.
3 'Considering a Temple' in *Figures of Motion*, p 90.
4 'Mecca Art', unpublished ms. Any Temple descriptions in this chapter not otherwise acknowledged are taken from some version or other of 'Mecca Art' or 'Considering a Temple.'
5 ibid.
6 Letter from Lye, 11 February 1963.
7 *Film Comment,* Vol 2, No 3, Summer 1964, p 14. See also p 11 and p 26.
8 ibid.
9 It was a method Stan Brakhage developed in his own way for the titles of his films. In relation to New Zealand art it is interesting to compare the use of words and numbers by Colin McCahon (a calligraphy that at first seems rough but is in fact highly skilful).
10 He screened it also as part of 'The Creative Imagination' lecture he gave at the Albright-Knox Gallery in Buffalo in February 1968.
11 'Art and the Genes, II' (slide-tape programme), circa 1971.
12 The news item appears on a slide of the 'Art & the Genes, II' programme.

fiftytwo homes

1 Undated note.
2 Interview with Ann Lye, 1980.
3 Lorelei Albanese, 'Ann's Wonderland of Color', *The San Juan Star*, 28 July 1983, p 29.
4 Lorraine Blasor, 'Ann's Garden of Eatin'', *Caribbean Business*, 14 April 1982, p M43.
5 Interview with Ann Lye, 1995.
6 Interview with Jean Matos, 1995.
7 Interview with Bob McCoy, 1995.
8 Interview with Jim Frye, 1995.
9 Interview with Lorraine Blasor, 1995.
10 Interview with Bob McCoy.
11 Penny Maldonado, 'Artist and Film Master Settles in San Juan', *The San Juan Star,* 8 February 1973, p 72.
12 Interview with Ann Lye, 1980.
13 Letter from Ray Thorburn, 10 August 1981.
14 John Matthews, 'The New Zealand Collection', *Art New Zealand,* No 17, 1980, p 32.
15 ibid., p 32.
16 Letter from Ray Thorburn, 10 August 1981.
17 'June the Merry Something 1974ish',

unpublished note.

18 Interview with Shirley Horrocks, December 1994.
19 Interview with John Matthews, 1994.
20 Interview with Shirley Horrocks, 1994.
21 *Art New Zealand,* No 17, p 32.
22 Interview with John Matthews, 1994.
23 See *The Press* (Christchurch), 31 March 1977. This was a one-twentieth of a horsepower motor.
24 Interview with John Matthews, 1994.
25 ibid.
26 *The Press*, 31 March 1977.

fiftythree new plymouth

1 Postcard from Lye to Philip Lye, 18 June 1975.
2 Interview with Ann Lye, 1980.
3 Interview with Judith Childs, 1980.
4 Unpublished note, 21 May 1978.
5 T. S. Matthews, *Jacks or Better*, New York, Harper and Row, 1977, p 329.
6 The note is dated 'March 1977'. Lye was quoting from memory from 'No Trouble' (*Figures of Motion*, pp 99–100). The text and punctuation have been adjusted to conform to the original.
7 Letter from Lye, 23 April 1978.
8 Interview with Ann Lye, 1980.
9 See Wystan Curnow, 'Len Lye at the Govett-Brewster', *Art New Zealand*, No 5, April–May 1977, pp 23–25.
10 Interview with Shirley Horrocks, December 1994.
11 'In Arcadia People are Talking About … Len Lye', *Spleen*, No 7, pp 4–7, 1977.
12 Letter from Lye, 23 April 1978.
13 Letter from Lye to 'Abby and Henry' [Abigail Child and Henry Hills], 20 January 1979, printed in *The Cinemanews*, 1978 No 6–1979 No 1, p 19. (*Mañana* means 'tomorrow' and implies procrastination.)
14 Interview with Ann Lye, 1985. She thinks the first painting was 'Land and Sea' but is not certain.
15 'Land and Sea' was an oil painting.
16 *The Cinemanews,* 1978 No 6–1979 No 1, p 19, p.19.
17 Letter from Len Lye to Philip Lye, 20 December 1978.
18 Interview with Jean Matos, 1995.
19 Wystan Curnow, note, May 1978.
20 When he re-made some paintings he gave

them new titles. 'Cagn Who Made Things' became the 'God of Light' or 'The Big Bang Man'. 'Martha's Vineyard' became 'Lagoon Pond', and a detail then became 'Ancestor'. A new painting was known first as 'Shark Killers' then as 'Rift Fish'. Even though Lye had learned that the protagonist of *Tusalava* could be seen as 'the spitting image' of a macrophage, he chose to call his new painting 'Witchetty Grub' rather than 'Macrophage' — as though trying to throw the new brain off the scent.

21 'Len Lye's Paintings' in *Len Lye: A Personal Mythology*, Auckland City Art Gallery, 1980, p 13.
22 Letter from Lye to Ernest Smith (Director, Auckland City Art Gallery), 16 February 1979.
23 Interview with Ann Lye, 1980.
24 Attachment to letter from Lye to Ernest Smith, 16 February 1979.
25 Letter from Lye to Barbara Ker-Seymer, 23 April 1978.
26 I discovered this when I started taking work there on Lye's behalf.
27 See, for example, Brauer's essay in *Len Lye: A Personal Mythology*, pp 21–24.

fiftyfour relationships

1 Letter from Lye, 28 December 1964. (Yancy is now Yancy McCaffrey.)
2 Letter from Len to Ann Lye, 6 March 1962.
3 Letter from Len to Ann Lye, 22 March 1959.
4 Interview with Ann Lye, 1980. Many others have spoken of how dynamic Lye was even in his final years. For example Anne Kirker, who visited the Lyes in 1979, records her impression: 'When I finally met Len I found he exuded sexual appeal and along with Ann Lye had a youthful demeanor which belied his actual age' (letter, 3 October 2000).
5 Interview with Margareta Akermark, 1980.
6 Letter, 18 November 1978. (Thanks to Simon Ryan for passing this on.)
7 'In the Presence', *Art New Zealand*, No 17, 1980, p 30.
8 13 May 1980.

fiftyfive direct film apprentices

1 Letter from Ann Lye, 25 March 1979.
2 Robert Del Tredici, 'Len Lye Interview', *The Cinemanews*, Nos 2–4, 1979, p 35.

3 Letter from Dr A. A. Cintron-Rivera, 2 April 1979.

4 Letter from Lye to Gerhard Brauer, '6 or 7 May' 1980.

5 Letter from Lye to Pam Riding, 20 August 1979.

6 Letter from Paul Barnes to Ann Lye, 9 July 1980.

7 NEA Grant Q1–3436–225, 1979 (Media Arts, general program grant). Arts Council grant of $7500. New Zealand Film Commission grant of $4500.

8 Interview with Paul Barnes, 1980. Compare Steve Jones: 'Len was taking out images that could be dispensed with, not because they were necessarily bad, but just because the body of the film would have been just as good without those parts — it would keep the film shorter and sweeter' (interview, 1980).

9 Interview with Steve Jones, 1980.

10 Interview with Paul Barnes, 1980.

11 Letter from Paul Barnes to Ann Lye, 9 July 1980.

12 Interview with Steve Jones, 1980.

13 A print was sent to the NEA on January 24 1980.

fiftysix quitting the lot

1 The exhibition consisted of 14 recent paintings, 9 earlier ones, 3 sculptures ('Fountain', 'Blade', and 'Universe'), and 10 films (including the premieres of the new versions of *Free Radicals* and *Particles in Space*). The exhibition also borrowed Rayner Hoff's marble 'Head of Len Lye' from the Art Gallery of New South Wales.

2 Andrew Bogle, 'Len Lye's Paintings' in *Len Lye: A Personal Mythology*, p 20.

3 See the review by Leonard Bell, 'Len Lye: A Personal Mythology', *Art New Zealand*, No 17, 1980, p 26.

4 Letter to Jane and Alexander Eliot, (December?) 1980.

5 *Len Lye: A Personal Mythology,* p 90.

6 April 1980.

7 Interview, 1980.

8 Interview with Hamish Keith, 1995.

9 Interview with Steve Jones, 1980.

10 Interview with Selina Trieff, 1980.

11 Interview with Ann Lye, 1980.

12 ibid.

13 Susan Maxwell, 'An Artist with a Whirring Mind', *New Zealand Herald*, 6 August 1980, Section 2, p 1.

14 This failed to find a publisher but a selection of the poems appeared in the New Zealand periodical *A Brief Description of the Whole World*, No 3, June 1996. The film-maker, Shirley Horrocks, later directed two documentaries on Lye: *Flip and Two Twisters* and *Len Lye: Two Studios*.

15 Interview with Ann Lye, 1980. Some details were later reported in Susan Maxwell, 'NZ Art Maverick Dies In His Adopted Home', *New Zealand Herald*, 16 May 1980.

16 Interview with Max Gimblett, 1999.

epilogue

1 *New York Times*, 16 May 1980, p D 15.

2 *Art New Zealand*, No 17, 1980, p 63.

3 Letter, 2 September 1980.

4 Letter, 8 August 1980.

5 *The Warwick Advertiser Photo News*, No 4971, 21 May 1980.

6 'Artist Memorial Plan Attacked — And Defended', *New Zealand Herald*, 12 June 1980, p 8.

7 *New Zealand Herald*, 12 June 1980. For more of the debate, see the *Herald*'s 'Letters to the Editor' column between June 21 and June 28. For documentation of a similar but less public debate about Lye's importance, see Dennis McEldowney, *Then and There: a 1970s Diary*, Auckland University Press, 1995, pp 189–90 and pp 195–96.

8 Susan Maxwell, 'An Artist with a Whirring Mind', *New Zealand Herald*, 6 August 1980, section 2, p 1.

9 Interview, 1980.

10 Letter from Judith Hoffberg, 21 July 1985.

11 Letter, 1 April 1981.

12 Letter, 20 October 1982.

13 Important artists who were less fortunate include John Banting and Kanty Cooper.

14 See for example 'Sights and Sounds', John Roberts's interview with Michael Smither, in the *Listener* (New Zealand), 7 March 1981, p 35. Meanwhile the Govett-Brewster continues to maintain its remarkable record as a provincial public gallery that is consistently dedicated to innovative contemporary art.

15 Interview for the documentary *Flip and Two Twisters*, 1995.

16 See J. K. Raine, J. J. Harrington, E. A. Webb

and Z. A. Meredith, 'Expanding "Universe": Design Study for Scaling Up a Kinetic Sculpture' in the *Journal of Engineering Design*, Vol 7, No 4, 1996, pp 397–410.

17 In England, Keith Griffiths made the remarkable Lye documentary *Doodlin'* in 1987 for Channel Four.

18 Pontus Hulten, Preface, *Territorium Artis*, Kunst- und Ausstellungshalle der Bundesrepublik Deutschland, Verlag Gerd Hatje, 1992, p 19.

19 The exhibition and the opening were documented in an item directed by Shirley Horrocks for the New Zealand television arts programme *Backch@t* (TV One, May 2000).

20 *Len Lye*, ed. Jean-Michel Bouhours and Roger Horrocks, Paris, Centre Pompidou (Cinema Quinze Vingt et Un series), 2000.

21 It should be noted that the New Zealand commercial gallery, Gow Langsford, has taken Lye sculptures to Art Cologne and other European art fairs. Some sponsorship for Lye activities in Europe has come from the popular music channel MTV Europe, which is headed by Brent Hansen, an expatriate New Zealander with a strong interest in art who has arranged for ongoing screenings of Lye's films among today's rock videos.

index

Artistic and literary works listed are by Len Lye unless otherwise indicated.